Communications
in Computer and Information Science 153

Gang Shen   Xiong Huang (Eds.)

Advanced Research on Computer Science and Information Engineering

International Conference, CSIE 2011
Zhengzhou, China, May 21-22, 2011
Proceedings, Part II

 Springer

Volume Editors

Gang Shen
International Science & Education Researcher Association
Wuhan Section, Wuhan, China
E-mail: 1073648534@qq.com

Xiong Huang
International Science & Education Researcher Association
Wuhan Section, Wuhan, China
E-mail: 499780828@qq.com

ISSN 1865-0929   e-ISSN 1865-0937
ISBN 978-3-642-21410-3   e-ISBN 978-3-642-21411-0
DOI 10.1007/978-3-642-21411-0
Springer Heidelberg Dordrecht London New York

Library of Congress Control Number: Applied for

CR Subject Classification (1998): C.2, I.2, H.4, H.3, D.2, I.4

Typesetting: Camera-ready by author, data conversion by Scientific Publishing Services, Chennai, India

Printed on acid-free paper

Springer is part of Springer Science+Business Media (www.springer.com)

Preface

The International Science & Education Researcher Association (ISER) puts its focus on the study and exchange of academic achievements of international researchers, and it also promotes educational reform in the world. In addition, it serves as academic discussion and communication platform, which is beneficial for education and for scientific research, aiming to stimulate researchers in their work.

The CSIE conference is an integrated event concentrating on computer science and information engineering. The goal of the conference is to provide researchers working in the field of computer science and information engineering based on modern information technology with a free forum to share new ideas, innovations, and solutions. CSIE 2011 was held during May 21-22, in Zhengzhou, China, and was co-sponsored by the ISER, Beijing Gireida Education Co. Ltd., the and Yellow River Conservancy Technical Institute, China. Renowned keynote speakers were invited to deliver talks, and all participants had the chance to discuss their work with the speakers face to face.

In these proceedings, you can learn more about the field of computer science and information engineering from the contributions of international researchers. The main role of the proceedings is to be used as a means of exchange of information for those working in this area. The Organizing Committee made great efforts to meet the high standard of Springer's *Communications in Computer and Information Science* series. Firstly, poor-quality papers were rejected after being reviewed by anonymous referees. Secondly, meetings were held periodically for reviewers to exchange opinions and suggestions. Finally, the organizing team held several preliminary sessions before the conference. Through the efforts of numerous individuals and departments, the conference was successful and fruitful.

During the organization, we received help from different people, departments, and institutions. Here, we would like to extend our sincere thanks to the publishers of CCIS, Springer, for their kind and enthusiastic assistance and support of our conference. Secondly, the authors should also be thanked for their submissions. Thirdly, the hard work of the Program Committee, the Program Chairs, and the reviewers is greatly appreciated.

In conclusion, it was the team effort of all these people that made our conference a success. We welcome any suggestions that may help improve the conference in the future and we look forward to seeing all of you at CSIE 2012.

March 2011   Gang Shen

Organization

Honorary Chairs

Chen Bin	Beijing Normal University, China
Hu Chen	Peking University, China
Chunhua Tan	Beijing Normal University, China
Helen Zhang	University of Munich, Germany

Program Committee Chairs

Xiong Huang	International Science & Education Researcher Association, China
Li Ding	International Science & Education Researcher Association, China
Zhihua Xu	International Science & Education Researcher Association, China

Organizing Chairs

ZongMing Tu	Beijing Gireida Education Co. Ltd., China
Jijun Wang	Beijing Spon Technology Research Institution, China
Quan Xiang	Beijing Prophet Science and Education Research Center, China

Publication Chair

Gang Shen	International Science & Education Researcher Association, China
Xiong Huang	International Science & Education Researcher Association, China

International Program Committee

Sally Wang	Beijing Normal University, China
Lin Chen	Yellow River Conservancy Technical Institute, China
Guangchao Du	Yellow River Conservancy Technical Institute, China
Jian Hu	Yellow River Conservancy Technical Institute, China
Kun Shang	Yellow River Conservancy Technical Institute, China
Xinfa Dong	Yellow River Conservancy Technical Institute, China
Jianhai Ye	Yellow River Conservancy Technical Institute, China
Aiping Ding	Yellow River Conservancy Technical Institute, China
Xiuchi Hu	Yellow River Conservancy Technical Institute, China

Jianling Tan	Yellow River Conservancy Technical Institute, China
Yongxia Tao	Yellow River Conservancy Technical Institute, China
Huili Yang	Yellow River Conservancy Technical Institute, China
Ge Wang	Yellow River Conservancy Technical Institute, China

Co-sponsored by

International Science & Education Researcher Association, China
Yellow River Conservancy Technical Institute, China
VIP Information Conference Center, China

Reviewers

Chunlin Xie	Wuhan University of Science and Technology, China
Lin Qi	Hubei University of Technology, China
Xiong Huang	International Science & Education Researcher Association, China
Gang Shen	International Science & Education Researcher Association, China
Xiangrong Jiang	Wuhan University of Technology, China
Li Hu	Linguistic and Linguistic Education Association, China
Moon Hyan	Sungkyunkwan University, Korea
Guangwen	South China University of Technology, China
Jack H. Li	George Mason University, USA
Marry Y. Feng	University of Technology Sydney, Australia
Feng Quan	Zhongnan University of Finance and Economics, China
Peng Ding	Hubei University, China
Song Lin	International Science & Education Researcher Association, China
XiaoLie Nan	International Science & Education Researcher Association, China
Zhi Yu	International Science & Education Researcher Association, China
Xue Jin	International Science & Education Researcher Association, China
Zhihua Xu	International Science & Education Researcher Association, China
Wu Yang	International Science & Education Researcher Association, China
Qin Xiao	International Science & Education Researcher Association, China

Weifeng Guo	International Science & Education Researcher Association, China
Li Hu	Wuhan University of Science and Technology, China
Zhong Yan	Wuhan University of Science and Technology, China
Haiquan Huang	Hubei University of Technology, China
Xiao Bing	Wuhan University, China
Brown Wu	Sun Yat-Sen University, China

Table of Contents – Part II

Table of Contents – Part I

An Improved Pathfinding Algorithm in RTS Games

Xiang Xu and Kun Zou

Department of Computer Engineering
University of Electronic Science and Technology of China Zhongshan Institute
Zhongshan, P.R. China
xushawn@sina.com

Abstract. Pathfinding is core component in many games especially RTS(real-time strategy) games, the paper proposed an improvement algorithm to solve the pathfinding problem between multi-entrances and multi-exports buildings. Firstly, the paper studied the A* algorithm, aiming at the buildings with multiple entry and exit characteristic in games, improved the algorithm and make it can find a shortest path by only one traverse between multiple start nodes and multiple stop nodes, avoided frequent call for the algorithm. Secondly the algorithm had given the solution to the actual terrain cost problem, and calculated actual path cost according to the different terrain influence factor. Finally, introduced collision detection to the dynamic path change state space, solved effectively the influence of dynamic path changes.

Keywords: pathfinding; RTS game; A* algorithm; terrain cost; collision detection.

1 Introduction

Traditionally the algorithm using in pathfinding is A* algorithm[1][2], used in performing fast search for the optimal path connecting two points on the map of a game. A* is more suited to an environment where there are multiple routes around the environment. In other words, it is a very time consuming and more complexity method in game's implementation. In order to better use A* algorithm in games, still need to solve a series of problem, such as data storage structure optimization and search strategy improvement, heuristic function selection, collision detection, obstruction avoiding collision and so on. The paper firstly studied A* algorithm in theory, and put forward some actual problems when using A* algorithm in RTS games, finally a set improvement strategy with application value is given.

2 Background

A* is a graph search algorithm that finds the least-cost path from a given start node to one goal node (out of one or more possible goals). It uses a distance-plus-cost heuristic function (usually denoted f(n)) to determine the order in which the search visits nodes in the tree. The distance-plus-cost heuristic is a sum of two functions: the path-cost

G. Shen and X. Huang (Eds.): CSIE 2011, Part II, CCIS 153, pp. 1–7, 2011.
© Springer-Verlag Berlin Heidelberg 2011

function (usually denoted g(n), which may or may not be a heuristic) and an admissible heuristic estimate of the distance to the goal. The path-cost function g(n) is the actual cost from start node to current node, and h(n) is the estimate cost from current node to the goal. Because g(n) is known, it can be calculated by reverse tracking from current node to start node in accordance with a pointer to its parent, then accumulate all costs in the path. So, heuristic function f(n)'s heuristic information relies mainly on h(n). According to a certain known conditions of state space, heuristic function will select one node with minimum cost to search, again from this node continue to search, until reach the goal or failure, but not expanded nodes need not search [3].

The quality of A* algorithm depends on the quality of the heuristic estimate h(n). If h(n) is very close to the true cost of the remaining path, its efficiency will be high; on the other hand, if it is too low, its efficiency gets very bad. In fact, breadth-first search is an A* search, with h(n) being trivially zero for all nodes -- this certainly underestimates the remaining path cost, and while it will find the optimum path, it will do so slowly. Here adopt the Manhattan heuristic function, namely obtain the minus of abscissa from current node to the goal, and also the minus of ordinate from current node to the goal, again both absolute value adding together. The Manhattan heuristic function is shown below:

$$h(n) = (abs(dest.x - current.x) + abs(dest.y - current.y)) \qquad (1)$$

In order to enhance the efficiency of the algorithm, may preprocess those unreachable nodes in the game map before starting search. And may adopt the binary heaps structure for the Open list.

There are situations where A* may not perform very well, for a variety of reasons. The more or less real-time requirements of games, plus the limitations of the available memory and processor time in some of them, may make it hard even for A* to work well. A large map may require thousands of entries in the Open and Closed list, and there may not be room enough for that. Even if there is enough memory for them, the algorithm used for manipulating them may be inefficient. On the other hand, in many RTS games, the start location and the goal does not have to be a single location but can consist of multiple locations. The estimate for a node would then be the minimum of the estimate for all possible nodes. Next, because A* algorithm is according to the grid map, although the path is the shortest, but often zigzag and not realistic, this is caused by the fact that the standard A* algorithm searches the eight neighbour nodes surrounding current node, and then proceeds to next node. It is fine in primitive games where units simply hop from node to node, but is unacceptable for the smooth movement required in most RTS games today.

3 Pathfinding between "Container Game Object"

3.1 Problem Statement

In many RTS games, some game objects (e.g. barracks), often stationed a number of units. By Specifying a destination, these units should go out from the game object and move to the destination. Usually called this kind of game object as a "container game object"[4]. In actual games, "container game object" usually demonstrated as buildings or all kinds of transporters, this kind of building usually has multiple entry or multiple exit. The game pathfinding problem will become searching a shortest path between multiple entry nodes and multiple exit nodes. The similar phenomenon might be found in other games. For example: a player need to dispatch some units to move to a target area, possibly has many contiguous barracks can be selected, how to choose one barracks which is recent to the target area, and guarantee units may fastest arrive, becoming game's inevitable problems.

Regarding multiple start nodes of situation, pathfinding's main work is to select the optimal node from all exit nodes surrounding the game object, and let these units start leaving from this node. The simplest and most rapid method is predefined a node order, then choose a walkable node, but this method does not consider position of the destination, before leaving, those units will usually forced to walk round and round in the game object. To avoid this problem, should choose the optimal exit node, and ensure the chosen exit node to the destination has a minimum path cost, meanwhile this path has already considered obstacles distributed situation between the start node and the destination. One effective method is calculating each path cost from each exit node to the destination, and chooses the lowest cost path. Such need call A* algorithm many times, and carries on the comparison many times, performance overhead is too high.

The same problem also appears in multiple entry nodes. In game development, the supposition dispatches some units to garrison a game object (e.g. barracks), namely, gives a combat task is to choose an optimal entry from all entry nodes surrounding the game object, let the units enter. If only simple choice an entry node has minimum straight distance, will face not considered the obstacles. General solution is to calculate each path cost between each entry node and start node, need continuously call A* algorithm, then found an optimal entry node through the comparison.

Above problems all boil down to multiple start nodes and multiple stop nodes pathfinding problem, among which, the first game object provides multiple start nodes in the exit location, and the second game object provides multiple stop nodes in the entry location.

3.2 Algorithm Improvement

Through examining the A* algorithm, can find that algorithm most of time is carrying on node traversal. Regarding need to call A* algorithm with sole start node and sole stop node many times, the traversal number of times will increase greatly, even many nodes are repeated traverse. Through revising standard A* algorithm, let it accepts multiple start nodes as function parameter, and before start searching, set these start nodes' G value(path cost value) equals 0, and H value(estimate cost value) calculated by the Manhattan heuristic function. After calculated each start node's F value, put them all into the Open list, and guarantee sorting. The rest of the treatment process is the same with the sole start node process. Because the Open list provides all start nodes sorting, it can help us choose an optimal start node, and treat it as a part of the final path. The same holds for multiple stop nodes, considering the goal node's main purpose is as traverse stop point, can use multiple stop nodes to replace one goal node. These stop nodes set on the way to the goal. In pathfinding process, once discovered a stop node, can think path has been found. The improved algorithm flow chart shown below:

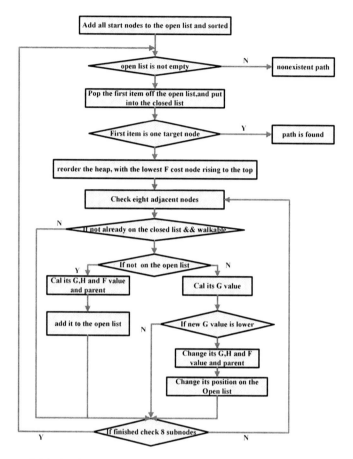

Fig. 1. Improved A* algorithm flow chart. Support multiple start nodes as function parameter, and once searched a stop node, the algorithm will think path has been found.

In Figure 2, the barracks is seen as a game object, it peripheral has 8 exit nodes. There have some obstacles in the map. The optimal exit node can guarantee a minimum cost path to the goal. The barracks' right bottom corner has an exit node, it has the shortest straight distance to the goal, but it is not an optimal exit node.

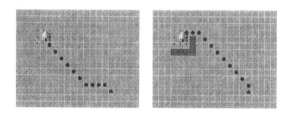

Fig. 2. Left Graph does not have any obstacles, the barracks' right bottom exit node is the optimal node; Right Graph has some obstacles nearby the barracks, caused the optimal node to turn the top right corner exit node

Figure 3 is given more than one entry node, to find the optimal entry node. The barracks is surrounded by 8 entry nodes. The optimal entry node can guarantee a minimum cost path from the start node. The barracks' left top entry node has the shortest straight distance from the start node, but it is not an optimal entry node.

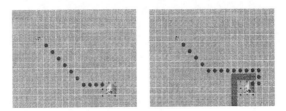

Fig. 3. Left Graph does not have any obstacles, the barracks' left top entry node is the optimal node; Right Graph has some obstacles nearby the barracks, caused the optimal node to turn the top right corner entry node

Figure 4 shows an example of two buildings -- barracks A and barracks B. Barracks A provides more than one exit node, barracks B provides more than one entry node. Assuming that the goal location is on the barracks' left bottom corner (marks with the flag image), this position is away from each entry node the distance is the same.

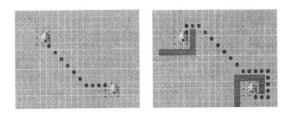

Fig. 4. Left Graph does not have any obstacles; the barracks A's right bottom exit node is the optimal node, and the barracks B's left top entry node is the optimal node. Right Graph has some obstacles nearby two barracks, caused the optimal node changed.

4 Introduction Terrain Influence Factor

The cost of going from one position to another can represent many things: the simple distance between the positions; the cost in time or movement points or fuel between them; penalties for traveling through undesirable places (such as points within range of enemy artillery); bonuses for traveling through desirable places (such as exploring new terrain or imposing control over uncontrolled locations); and aesthetic considerations-for example, if diagonal moves are just as cheap as orthogonal moves, you may still want to make them cost more, so that the routes chosen look more direct and natural.

Due to the path-cost function g(n) has taken terrain cost into account, just before assumes all terrain costs are same, so set each node cost is equal. But in the actual game, when calculates g(n), may for the different terrain node designation different cost, thus realizes the lowest path cost, rather than the shortest path.

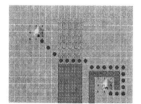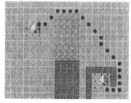

Fig. 5. Left Graph has not considered the terrain cost. Right Graph has considered the terrain cost, and set the lawn terrain influence factor equals 1, the mountain road terrain influence factor equals 2.

After introduced the terrain influence factor, searched path can judge different types of terrain cost, and choose a lowest cost, rather than the shortest path. Of course, the actual game will have more complex terrain, but can still by setting different terrain cost to realize. This method will make the game role walk the path of more and more intelligent and realistic.

5   Adapt to Dynamic Path Change State Space

In games, often encounter such a situation that may originally through the path now became cannot pass. For instance a node that has a bridge built on it suddenly blew up, either has built up a house suddenly, either other unit happen to moved this position [5]. This will block the path of moving, and now need pathfinding algorithm adapt to the dynamic changes of the state space.

In order to recognize this state changes in moving process, need to introduce collision detection subsystem. Because in the game, every character or obstacles is an independent entity, if can pass through mutually, will give the human one kind of false feeling, reduced game's authenticity and reality. A* algorithm in decision making realize character movement before must first get collision detection subsystem decision-making. Once discovered the next node become a blocked node, needed to re-run pathfinding. Usually can search a new path from blocking preceding node to the goal (the following chart shows), but this approach sometimes with a frequent search algorithm calls, search efficiency is quite low. Can only search a new path from the last walkable node before breaking to the first walkable node after breaking, then links this new path to the original path, replaces the breaking part. This can improve efficiency,

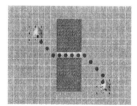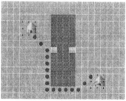

Fig. 6. Left Graph shows the path before the bridge blows up. Right Graph shows found path after the bridge blows up.

because many has obtained the paths can reuse, and search two not far away nodes is very fast, expand node less often. Also can be in certain steps before check the node status, not only check the next node, it increases the authenticity, but also will increase time consumption [6].

6 Conclusion

The paper studied the application of A* pathfinding algorithm in RTS games. According to the problem of pathfinding between "container game object", the algorithm is improved and optimized. Unified multiple start nodes together into the Open list for pathfinding, effectively avoid the frequent algorithm called. Meanwhile, in order to truly reflect different types of terrain influence, introduced terrain influence factor into the algorithm, and g(n) used for the calculation of different terrain cost, enables the path can find the good recognition terrain. After a series of improvement, generated by the search path can be reflected in the game actual path effect, and embodies the certain intelligence and humanization. Considering the RTS games of moving Units usually not one, but has a group, the next step will do further research on "Coordinated Unit Movement". Hope that the future games have more intelligent, more humanized characters, and hope there will be more better algorithm to solve problems in game pathfinding.

References

1. Dechter, R., Pearl, J.: Generalized best-first search strategies and the optimality of A*. Journal of the ACM 32, 505–536 (1985)
2. Bourg, D.M., Seemann, G.: AI for Game Developers, 1st edn., pp. 51–75. O'Reilly Media, Sebastopol (2004)
3. Khantanapoka, K., Chinnasarn, K.: Pathfinding of 2D & 3D Game Real-Time Strategy with Depth Direction A*Algorithm for Multi-Layer. In: 2009 Eighth International Symposium on Natural Language Processing (SNLP 2009), Bangkok, Thailand, pp. 185–186 (2009)
4. Higgins, D.: Generic Pathfinding. AI Game Programming Wisdom (2002)
5. Roth, U., Walker, M., Hilmann, A., et al.: Dynamic path planning with spiking neural networks, pp. 1355–1363 (1997)
6. Stentz, A.: Optimal and efficient path planning for partially-known environments. In: Proceedings of the IEEE International Conference on Robotics and Automation, San Diego, pp. 3310–3317 (1994)

Improved Particle Swarm Optimization Algorithm Based on Periodic Evolution Strategy

Congli Mei, Jing Zhang, Zhiling Liao, and Guohai Liu

School of Electrical and Information Engineering, Jiangsu University
Zhenjiang, China
clmei@ujs.edu.cn

Abstract. This paper proposed a novel improved PSO algorithm based on an periodic evolution strategy (PSO-PES). From experiments, we observe that the novel search strategy enables the improved PSO to make use of swarm's information on velocity more effectively to generate better quality solutions iteratively when compared to exiting PSO variants. And PSO-PES significantly improves the PSO's performance and gives the better performance than original PSO. Another attractive property of the improved PSO is that it does not introduce any complex operations to the original simple PSO framework. The only difference from the standard PSO is the best solution will update by a periodic evolution strategy. PSO-PES is also simple and easy to implement like the original PSO.

Keywords: Particle swarm optimization, Global optimization, Periodic evolution.

1 Introduction

The standard particle swarm optimizer (PSO) is a population based algorithm that was invented by Kennedy and Eberhart [1]. The standard PSO model is based on the following two factors [1]: The autobiographical memory, which remembers the best previous position of each individual (Pi) in the swarm; the publicized knowledge, which is the best solution (Pg) found currently by the population. Recently, several investigations have been undertaken to improve the performance of standard PSO. Kennedy and Mendes investigated the impacts of population structures to the search performance of PSO [2]. Shi and Eberhart introduced inertia weight into original PSO and they found the significant impact of the new parameter on the PSO [3]. Then, Shi and Eberhart have found a significant improvement in the performance of the PSO method with a linearly decreasing inertia weight over the generations [4]. A fuzzy system was designed to dynamically adjust the inertia weight to improve the performance of the PSO [5]. And experimental results illustrated that the fuzzy adaptive PSO is a promising optimization method. Since chaos mapping enjoys certainty, ergodicity and stochastic property, chaos mapping into the particle swarm optimization to dynamically adjust inertia weight [6].A novel improved PSO algorithm was proposed to solve the problem of premature of PSO with the idea of swarm energy conservation (SEC-PSO) [7].

G. Shen and X. Huang (Eds.): CSIE 2011, Part II, CCIS 153, pp. 8–13, 2011.
© Springer-Verlag Berlin Heidelberg 2011

An improved PSO based on periodic evaluation strategy (PSO-PES) is proposed in the paper based on the idea of controlling the energy of particles [7].A perturbation strategy is designed to construct a dissipative system of particles .And a size limit function based on particles' energy is proposed to control perturbations. Well-known test functions are used to test the PSO-PES algorithm. Experimental results show the significant performance of the global convergence properties.

2   Proposed New Developments

In the particle swarm algorithm, the new velocities and the positions of the particles for the next fitness evaluation are calculated using the following two equations:

$$v_{id} = v_{id} + c_1 rand1(\cdot)(p_{id} - x_{id}) + c_2 rand2(\cdot)(p_{gd} - x_{id}) \tag{1}$$

$$x_{id} = x_{id} + v_{id} \tag{2}$$

Where c_1 and c_2 are constants known as acceleration coefficients, and $rand1$ () and $Rand(2)$ are two separately generated uniformly distributed random numbers in the range [0,1]. Empirical results have shown that a constant inertia of $w = 0.7298$ and acceleration coefficients with $c_1 = c_2 = 1.49618$ provide good convergent behavior. Theoretical analysis provided sufficient conditions that particles converge to a stable point, which can be stated as [8].

$$0 < c_1 + c_2 < 2(w+1), 0 < w < 1 \tag{3}$$

Although PSO may outperform other evolutionary algorithms in the early iterations, it may convergence to local optimal solutions, called premature. To prevent premature, a strategy should be designed to make particles own enough energy. Because particles' behavior can be controlled by controlling swarm' energy[7], so perturbations can be introduced to update p_{gd} of PSO by designing a function on swarm' energy and the function can control the limit size of perturbations. In our view, the global optimal solution can be any point of the whole search space with little priori knowledge. So p_{gd} can be designed as defined as

$$p_{gd} = p_{gd} + \exp(-K) * (sign(rand(\cdot) - 0.5) * Limit - p_{gd}) \tag{4}$$

Where $Limit$ is determined by the upper and lower limits of the search space and the center of search space is set to zero. K is the value of particle' energy and can be designed as

$$K = v_i^T v_i \tag{5}$$

The procedure of the improved PSO can be described as Table1.

Table 1. The pseudo code for the improved PSO

---

begin
    initialize the population
    While(termination condition=false)

$$K = v_i^T v_i$$

$$P_{gd} = P_{gd} + \exp(-K) * (sign(rand(\cdot)) - 0.5) * Limit - p_{gd})$$

    do
    for(i =1 to number of particles)
    evaluate the fitness:= $f(x)$

      update p_{id} and P_{gd}

        for d=1 to number of dimensions
        calculate the new velocity

$$v_{id} = v_{id} + c_1 rand1(\cdot)(p_{id} - x_{id}) + c_2 rand2(\cdot)(p_{gd} - x_{id})$$

        calculate the new position

$$x_{id} = x_{id} + v_{id}$$

      increase d
      end for
      increase i
    end for
    end do
  end

---

3 Experimental Settings and Simulation Strategies for Benchmark Testing

Four well-known benchmark functions used in evolutionary optimization methods were used to evaluate the performance. These benchmarks are widely used in evaluating performance of PSO methods. The performance of PSO-PES method is compared with PSO and SEC-PSO. The first two functions are simple unimodal functions whereas the next two functions are multimodal functions designed with a considerable amount of local minima. All functions have the global minimum at the origin or very close to the origin. All benchmarks used are given in Table2. Table3 shows the dynamic range of the search for each function. In this paper, all empirical experiments were carried out with a population size of 20. All benchmarks were tested with dimensions 20. For each function, 20 trials were carried out and the average optimal value and the standard deviation (inside the brackets) are presented. The number of maximum generations (G_{max}) is set at 1000 for all the problems. Use the same stopping criteria for different benchmarks is reported in the literature. However, all benchmarks have the global optimum value of 0.00. [7]

Table 2. Benchmarks for simulations

Name of the function	Mathematical representation
sphere function	$f_1(x) = \sum_{i=1}^{n} x_i^2$
Rosenbrock function	$f_2(x) = \sum_{i=1}^{n} [100(x_{i+1} - x_i^2)^2 + (x_i - 1)^2]$
Rastrigrin function	$f_3(x) = \sum_{i=1}^{n} [x_i^2 - 10\cos(2\pi x_i) + 10]$
Griewank function	$f_4(x) = \dfrac{1}{4000} \sum_{i=1}^{n} x(i)^2 - \prod_{i=1}^{n} \cos(\dfrac{x_i}{\sqrt{i}}) + 1$

Table 3. Dynamic range of the search for benchmarks

Name of the function	Range of search
sphere function	$(-1, 1)^n$
Rosenbrock function	$(-30, 30)^n$
Rastrigrin function	$(-5.12, 5.12)^n$
Griewank function	$(-10, 10)^n$

4   Results from Benchmark Simulations

Table 4 presents the means and variances of the 20 trials of PSO-PES, SEC-PSO and PSO algorithms on the four test functions with 20 dimensions. The better results are shown in bold. PSO-PES achieves better results on f_1, f_2, f_3 and f_4 than SEC-PSO and PSO. Though PSO-PES performs better than PSO for all the functions, it does not converge to local optimum solutions and will achieve global optimum solutions with evaluation for every function. PSO converges to local optimum solutions for f_2 and f_3.

Table 4. Comparison results of the PSO-PES and PSO

Function	MBF(SD)		
	PSO-PES	SEC-PSO	PSO
f_1	**7.42e-006**	2.60e-001[*]	5.22e-001
	(1.94e-005)	(4.73e-002)[*]	(1.82e-001)
f_2	**4.56e-000**	4.86e+001[*]	6.61e+001
	(7.29e-000)	(4.09e-000)[*]	(2.12e+001)
f_3	**1.56e-002**	7.90e+001[*]	4.95e+001
	4.95e+001	(4.05e-000)[*]	(1.43e+001)
f_4	**2.52e-005**	5.80e-001[*]	2.71e-002
	(5.47e-005)	(3.73e-002)[*]	(1.43e-002)

[*]ref. [7].

Fig.1 and Fig.2 show that K value of PSO-PES changes periodically, but the K value of PSO converges to zero fast. So we can conclude that K value of PSO-PES could not converge to zero and PSO-PES has the performance of global convergence ability.

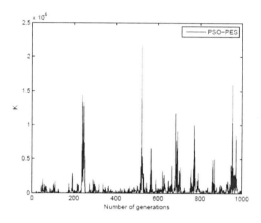

Fig. 1. Variation of PSO-PES K value for 20D f_3 with 20 trials

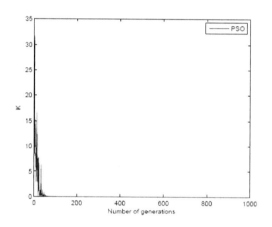

Fig. 2. Variation of PSO K value for 20D f_3 with 20 trials

5   Conclusions

This paper presents an improved PSO (PSO-PES) employing a novel periodic evaluation strategy. The new strategy makes the particles have the ability of searching the whole space. From experiments, we observe that this learning strategy enables PSO-PES to make use of the information in swarm energy more effectively to generate better quality solutions frequently when compared to SEC-PSO and PSO. Based on the results, we can conclude that PSO-PES significantly improves the PSO's performance and gives the better performance than original PSO.

Another attractive property of PSO-PES is that it does not introduce any complex operations to the original simple PSO framework. The only difference from the original PSO is the velocity update equation. The improved PSO is also simple and easy to implement like the original PSO.

Acknowledgment

The work is supported by the Natural Science Foundation of Jiangsu University of China Grant 08KJD510011, China's Post-doctoral Science Fund Grant 20090451171 and Natural Science Foundation for Qualified Personnel of Jiangsu University of China Grant 08JDG017.

References

1. Kennedy, J., Eberhart, R.: Particle swarm optimization. In: IEEE Int. Conf. on Nueral Networks, pp. 1942–1948. IEEE Service Center, Piscataway (1995)
2. Kennedy, J., Mendes, R.: Population structure and particle swarm performance. In: Proceedings of the 2002 Congress on Evolutionary Computation CEC 2002, pp. 1671–1676 (2002)
3. Shi, Y., Eberhart, R.: A modified particle swarm optimizer. In: IEEE World Congress on Computational Intelligence, pp. 69–73. IEEE Press, Piscataway (1998)
4. Shi, Y., Eberhart, R.: Empirical study of particle swarm optimization. In: Proceedings of the 1999 Congress on Evolutionary Computation, Washington, DC, USA, pp. 1945–1950 (1999)
5. Shi, Y., Eberhart, R.: Fuzzy adaptive particle swarm optimization. In: Proc. of IEEE Conf. on Evolutionary Computation, pp. 101–106. IEEE Press, Los Alamitos (2001)
6. Jiang, C.W., Etorre, B.: A hybrid method of chaotic particle swarm optimization and linear interior for reactive power optimization. Mathematics and Computers in Simulation 68(1), 57–65 (2005)
7. Wang, J.L., Xue, Y.Y., Yu, T., Ma, J.N.: Particle swarm optimization based on swarm energy conservation. Control and Decision 25(2), 269–277 (2010)
8. Trelea, I.C.: The particle swarm optimization algorithm: convergence analysis and parameter selection. Information Precessing Letters 85(6), 317–325 (2003)
9. Solis, F., Wets, R.: Minimization by Random Search Techniques. Mathematics of Operations Research 6(1), 19–30 (1981)

Multi-modal Genetic Algorithm Based on Excellent Sub-population Migrating Strategy

Huijuan Shi[*] and Kongyu Yang[**]

School of Information Management, Beijing Information Science & Technology University,
100192, BeiJing, China
helenjanet1986@sina.com, yangkongyu@tsinghua.org.cn

Abstract. The research status of multi-modal genetic algorithm is summarized. By analysis the mechanisms of Niche Genetic Algorithm (NGA) and Simple Sub-population Genetic Algorithm (SSGA), the faults of them are pointed out and a new Migrating-Based Genetic Algorithm (MBGA) with strategy of excellent sub-population migrating is proposed. The concept of complete convergence of multi-modal genetic algorithm is proposed. Using mathematical methods of Markov chains theory, it is proven that NGA is not complete convergence but MBGA is. The simulation experiments for NGA and MBGA are performed and the results show that complete convergence proven above is right, also testify that MBGA has availability on solving multi-modal optimization problems, completely convergence ability and wonderful stability of search results.

Keywords: Multi-modal optimization; Niche Genetic Algorithm; Complete convergence; Excellent sub-population migrating.

1 Introduction

In real world, many reality problems are multi-modal optimization problems, which mean that the problems have a lot of optimal solutions or one optimal solution and some partial optimal solutions. Similarly, there is Multi-peaked function which exists many extreme points in mathematics. MGA (Multi-modal Genetic Algorithm) is a special Genetic Algorithm, which is used to resolve above problems and search multi-peaked or partial optimal solutions of Multi-modal function.

SGA(Standard Genetic Algorithm) characterized by probability selection mechanism local search, it is likely to resolve the Multi-modal optimization problems. But, after the individuals which locate in the near of different peaks value crossing, both sides depart each peak, owning to the random matched-pair mechanism of the crossover operator; what is more, it is hard to search peaks at the same time, and always

---

[*] Huijuan Shi. Female, postgraduate student, research fields are logistics and supply chain management, genetic algorithm.

[**] Kongyu Yang. Male, professor of Beijing Information Science & Technology University, research fields are genetic algorithm, artificial intelligence etc.

G. Shen and X. Huang (Eds.): CSIE 2011, Part II, CCIS 153, pp. 14–20, 2011.
© Springer-Verlag Berlin Heidelberg 2011

only converge at a certain modal, because peak modal is constantly eliminated, which has small fitness in the progress of searching. So, some people put forward many improved Genetic Algorithm, while the NGA is proposed by the Doctor Holland and his students, who is the founder of Genetic Algorithm and put forward based on fitness share and restriction mechanism; on this condition[1-2], Spears put forward another Simple Sub-population Algorithm[3] based on share fitness. But, these two means have obvious defect: they cannot realize the complete convergence searching all the peaks. So, this paper put forward a new algorithm which based on excellent sub-population migrating strategy, and prove in theory that annual NGA cannot recognize complete convergence besides the new algorithm. At last, it verifies the right conclusion and the effectiveness of new algorithm through the simulation experiments compared the NGA with new algorithm this paper.

2   The Introduction of the Present Multi-modal Genetic Algorithm

2.1   Niche Genetic Algorithm (NGA)

The Doctor Holland put forward the niche technique[1] in 1975, then Goldberg and Richardson[2] firstly recognized this imagination in 1987,which is that based on SGA, taking the actions of fitness share and restricted mate, make the Genetic Algorithm conduct multi peaks search. Therefore, they put forward the Niche Genetic Algorithm (NGA).

It is the so-called fitness share that the single individual shares the fitness with its near individuals by a share function. So, the number of individuals nearby the peak can be controlled effectively, which makes that the individuals of the group cannot crowd in some peak totally. The purpose of restricted mate is restricting the individuals of different peaks crossover. By the way of randomly choosing two individuals, compute the distance of two them, and compare it with the restricted radius σ_{share}. If the distance is less than the restricted radius, the two individuals can cross, or they cannot.

Through, the NGA has multi-modal searching function, and there also exists many problems. For instance, it is necessary to know the distance of peaks in advance, and conduct a similar comparison by the way of computing the distance of different each other, then the operation is up to $O(n^2)$.

2.2   Simple Sub-population Genetic Algorithms (SSGA)

Aimed at the NFA shortages, the Simple Sub-population Genetic Algorithm [3] (SSGA) is proposed by William M. Spears in 1994, which main idea is that increasing a label for every chromosome, which indicates under the sub-population. The SSGA is easier than NGA, which doesn't need to assume that the peaks are equidistant and know the distance between peaks. The fitness share of individual is the primary fitness dividing the scale of sub-population, therefore avoiding to compute the distance between individuals, and the operation time is reduced, but the amount of sub-population must more than the number of peaks (it still need to be predicted). Restricted cross proceed in the internal of the same sub-population, but owning to it is possible that the individuals locating the same sub-population distributed in the different peaks, the result of two individuals located in different peaks conducting cross will make the sub-population become more distributed, which goes against that sub-position assemble to a peak. Spears posed the second implantation method on the limitation above mentioned, and the main improvement is that when cross not only is restricted in the internal of the same sub-population, but also need to consider the relationship of individuals' location. That means that only the nearby individuals locating the internal of same sub-population can conduct cross. So, adopting a circle topology, each individual has two neighbors at forward and backward, which only cross with its neighbors.

3 Algorithm Design Based on the Excellent Sub-population Migrating Strategy

3.1 Excellent Sub-population Migrating Strategy and Algorithm Description

SGA always reserves the elite to guarantee the convergence of algorithm [4]. Form this, in the process of MGA optimization, we can reserve the optimization which has been found to a solo sub-population to special nurture, so we can reserve the peaks which have been found in time, further find out all peaks. This solo sub-population is called 'excellent sub-population', and the excellent sub-population migrating strategy is proposed from here. The concrete method is as follows: designing a migration operator, when the fitness of excellent individual among the sub-population is more than a threshold (which is called migration threshold), the excellent individual will migrate to excellent sub-population; once the individual migrated to the excellent sub-population, deleting the same individual of the original population, then checking whether there are excellent individuals in the population again. If there are, continue migrating, or else stop the migration operation. After the migration operation stop, checking the number of individuals of population, if it is smaller than original population scale, fill in with new individuals which are randomly generated. At the same time, in the excellent population, once new excellent individual entered to the excellent sub-population, conduct gradient evolution to the individual promptly until it reach the peak which it belongs[5]. Then, we compare the individuals which have evolved one by one with other individuals which belong to the temporary sub-population, and delete the individuals (who are called near relatives) which similarity is above certain threshold.

3.2 Algorithm Description: Excellent Sub-population Migrating Genetic Algorithm

Step1. Take NGA every step till the end of all the genetic operation, recount the individual fitness, then call the migration operator (Step2-6);

Step2. Individuals in the population are ordered by fitness share, check the individual which has the greatest fitness share in the population, if its fitness share is more than migration threshold, then continue; or go to Step5;

Step3. The individual migrates to the excellent sup-population, comparing whether the excellent sup-population exist near relatives, if existing, delete the individuals which have small fitness share in the near relatives, then, conduct gradient evolution until they reach the belonging peak.

Step4. Judge the ending condition? If meet, output, or go on;

Step5. Delete all the individuals which are repeated with the migration individual in the population, make them extinct in the population. Go on Step2;

Step6. Checking the number of individuals in the population, if it is smaller than original population size, fill in with new individuals which are randomly generated;

Step7. Return to NGA, go on conducting every step of genetic cycle.

Migration operator is set up after the SGA genetic operation, which makes the excellent individuals of original population reserve and conduct specially nurture. But once individual migrates to excellent population, it will be cleaned out and fill up to new individual, therefore, the population diversity is greatly increased.

3.3 The Analysis on Running Mechanism of Excellent Sub-population Migrating

Setting a migration threshold and making all the fitness of peaks is bigger than it. Because the target function $f(x)$ is a multi-modal function, which has m peaks, $f_1, f_2, \ldots, f_m$ respectively, we can provide $f_1 \geq f_2 \geq \ldots \geq f_m$. According to GA theory, on account of genetic operator, the individuals gradually gather in some higher peaks. When the individual which has the biggest fitness meets the condition of migrating, given the number of operation generation is t_1, the individual which has biggest fitness is $C(t_1)$ which belongs to the peak f_k, $C(t_1) \in f_k$, $0 < k \leq m$. It is the time that the individual begins to migrate, delete it and its near relatives in the original population. When the individual enters the excellent sub-population, it can conduct gradient evolution and reach the belonging peak f_k in the end, thus it finishes a migration and find a peak. Then, check the surplus individuals of original population weather meet the migration condition or not, if they meet, they go on migrating, else fill up with new individuals and go on cycle. When operate to the generation t_2, the second migration happens, meanwhile, the migration individual is $C(t_2)$ belonging peak f_k', now, compare the similarity of f_k and f_k', if it is bigger than some threshold, this means that they are the same peak and substitute f_k' for f_k or we find the second peak and reserve in the excellent sub-population. Because the original population keeps on evolving, migrating and filling new individuals, adding the effect of mutation, these make it is possible that every peak exists the individual which meets the migration condition. Once the individual which belong to a peak has the chance to migrate, the peak which it belongs will be found and reserved in the excellent sub-population. The evolution continuing, all the peaks will be found. At the end of evolution, all the individuals in the excellent sub-population are the corresponding individuals of peaks, and it is no need to conduct other analysis.

4   The Convergence Simulation Experiments of MGA

4.1   Experiments Scheme

Here, we choose four functions[6] as experiment function. Using MBGA and NGA make the many searching tests at the same condition respectively, and compare the quantity of searched peaks and stability. The four functions which are used to test are as follows, and function graphic as shown in Figure 1.

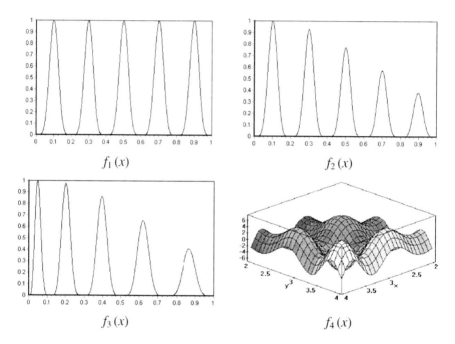

Fig. 1. Four graphics of test functions

$$f_1(x) = \sin^6(5\pi x) , \quad x \in [0,1] . \tag{1}$$

$$f_2(x) = f_1(x) \times e^{-2\ln 2 \times (x-0.0667)^2} . \tag{2}$$

$$f_3(x) = \sin^6(5\pi x^{0.75}) \times e^{-2\ln 2 \times (x-0.0667)^2} . \tag{3}$$

$$f_4(x) = x_1 \cdot \sin(x_1^2) + x_2 \cdot \sin(x_2^2) , \quad x_1, x_2 \in [2,4] . \tag{4}$$

Among the four functions, the first three are SISO one-dimensional functions, which have five peaks on their domains, including that the five peaks of f_1 are equal high and equal distance, the five peaks of f_2 are unequal high but equal distance, the five peaks of f_3 are unequal high and unequal distance. The forth function f_4 are two-dimensional function which have two input and one output and four unequal high peaks, but they are evenly distributed. In order to be easy to describe, we number the peaks of test functions, and the five peaks form function f_1 to f_3 are numbered in the order left-to-right one by one. For function f_4, the number of peaks as shown in Fig 1. The parameters setting for the experiment of GA are as shown in Table 1, and every function is tested fifty times.

Table 1. The parameters setting for the experiment of GA

Parameter/genetic operator	Parameter value	Operation method
Population size(n)/ coding method	20	Real coding
crossover probability/ crossover operator	0.3	Restricted crossover
mutation probability/ mutation operator	0.02	Random mutation
Mate share (σ_{share}) / selection operator	0.15	Proportion selection based on share
Maximum operation generation	200	t=200

4.2 The Test Result and Comparative Analysis

For the sake of comparison, the above experimental comparative results are listed in the Table 2.

Table 2. Simulation experiment results contrast

Test function	Algorithms	Peak number and the found number of fifty				
		1	2	3	4	5
$f_1(x)$	NGA	30	26	31	28	35
	MBGA	50	50	50	50	50
$f_2(x)$	NGA	44	35	16	3	2
	MBGA	50	50	50	50	50
$f_3(x)$	NGA	48	35	0	3	0
	MBGA	50	50	50	50	50
$f_4(x)$	NGA	32	41	26	30	n0
	MBGA	50	50	50	50	no

It can be seen from Table 2 that the search results of NGAcannot stability converge at all the peaks in the domain while the MBGA with excellent sub-population migration are very stable. They not only can search all the peaks in the domain, but the number of operation generation can further be decreased.

5 Conclusion

MGA is one of the hot spot on the research of Evolutionary Computation and has a widely applying prospect. The current MGA such as NGA and MGA, they need more prior knowledge and have some various defects in huge calculation, not recognizing complete convergence and unstable searching results etc. Based on the revelation of elitist preservation method, this paper provides excellent sub-population migrating strategy which overcomes the present algorithm shortcomings effectively. In this paper, the non complete convergence of present algorithms is proved in theory. Meanwhile, MGA with excellent sub-population migrating strategy can ensure complete convergence. In order to verify the efficiency, theory and conclusion of new algorithm, we carry out the simulation experiment to the test functions from different angles. The simulation results show that the proposed algorithm is better than present algorithm form some aspects such as, speed, accuracy, convergence and so on. At the same time, the searching speed and accuracy are greatly raised, and all peaks of the searching space can be ensured to be found. That means that the proposed algorithm has the complete convergence and stability, which also verified our theory and conclusion.

Acknowledgement

This paper is a project supported by Humanities and Social Sciences of the Ministry of Education project (07JA630063) and Beijing outstanding personnel training fund project (J0734006).

References

[1] Holland, J.H.: Adaptation in natural and artificial system: An Introduction Analysis with Applications to Biology, Control, and Artificial Intelligence. The University of Michigan Press, Michigan (1975)
[2] Goldberg, D.E., Richardson, J.: Genetic algorithms with sharing for multi-modal function optimization. In: Proceedings of the Second International Conference on Genetic Algorithms, pp. 41–49. The Massachusetts Institute of Technology, Cambridge (1987)
[3] Spears, W.M.: Simple Sub-population Schemes. In: Proceedings of the Third Annual Conference on Evolutionary Programming, San Diego, California, pp. 296–307 (1994)
[4] Weinin, Y., Yukang, X.: The Analysis of Global Convergence and Computational Efficiency for Genetic Algorithm. J. Control Theory & Applications 13(4), 455–460 (1996)
[5] Liu, H., Wang, X.: Adaptive genetic algorithm for multi-peak searching. J. Control Theory & Applications 21, 203–205 (2004)
[6] Liu, H.: Research of Genetic Algorithms and Its Application on Finance Forecast and Financial Decisions. D. Nankai University Master's degree paper, pp. 69–89, Tianjin (2002)

The Design and Realization of Fiber Bragg Grating Strain-Testing System Based on Virtual Instrument Technology

Xiaoping Wang and Hanbin Xiao

School of Logistics Engineering, Wuhan University of Technology, Wuhan, China
wxpwhut@yahoo.cn, xhb@whut.edu.cn

Abstract. The paper choose fiber Bragg grating(FBG) as an object of study, design the test system of FBG and apply it in the strain test of strength beam, obtain the conclusion and the condition of FBG stress system reliability and data validity. And then research the test system of FBG stress based on virtual instrument develop the platform of LabView.

Keywords: Fiber Bragg Grating strain sensor, strain-testing system, virtual instrument(VI), LabView.

1 Introduction

With the development of ample application of sensor technology, communications technology, diagnostic technology in industry, monitoring and diagnosis of structural stress has been provided a comprehensive and efficient platform. We have completed the design of fiber grating strain sensor VI system, constructed the test of fiber Bragg grating strain system, and researched on the theory of hardware and software design method of stress-monitoring and diagnosis of large mechanical structures in ports, which would lie a solid foundation on the developing of the structural stress online monitoring and diagnosis system based on Bragg grating based strain sensor and resistance strain electrical measurement technology.

2 Experiment of Fiber Bragg Grating Strain Sensor System

In the experiment, we took the static and dynamic loading and unloading experiments with the uniform strength beam as the object. Meanwhile the experiment with resistance strain electrical measurement technology was taken. After analysis and comparison, the result of the experiment on Fiber Bragg Grating strain sensor system could be given, and as well as the concrete conditions of effectiveness and reliability of the VI stress system.

G. Shen and X. Huang (Eds.): CSIE 2011, Part II, CCIS 153, pp. 21–26, 2011.
© Springer-Verlag Berlin Heidelberg 2011

2.1 Constructing of the Experiment

1）Experiment principle
In the constant temperature conditions, the experiment principle is given as shown in Fig.1.

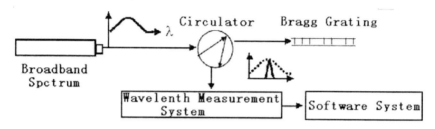

Fig. 1. Experiment principle

2）Experiment system structure
The strain experiment system takes uniform strength beam as the object of the study, which consists of fiber grating strain test system and electrical measurement strain system composition. By comparison, we inquired about that its general character and the difference. The two major installations include:

- Optical fiber modem, fiber grating strain sensor, VI test system, data acquisition communication and so on.
- In the electrical method the test installation includes: Resistance strain gauge, DH3819 static state strain gauge, DH5935 dynamic strain gauge;
- Computer, uniform strength beam and series of weights and experimental accessory connecting lead and so on.
- Major installation parameters are:
- The fiber grating modem parameter is shown in Table 1.

Table 1. Fiber grating modem parameter

Optical index	channel number	sensing unit	wave length scope	resolution	characteristic request	scanning, frequency
Parameter	1	1~10	1295 ~ 1315	1pm	R>90%, BW<0.25nm	<1hz

- The peak's central wave length of two diffraction gratings, in the FBG counter-spectrum's respectively is: 1297.35nm, 1297.45nm; the index of reflection is bigger than 90%; Physical length is the same 6mm; the FBG reflection band width approximately is 0.25nm.
- DH3819 static resistance strain reflector; DH5935 dynamic resistance strain reflector.

- The uniform strength beam is of Q235 steel, young's modulus (E) 2.0×105MPa, 120Ω resistance strain gauge as well as other auxiliary bodies.

2.2 Experiment of Fiber Grating Strain Sensor's Static Characteristic

The linear relations of two different central wave length's fiber grating wave length and the strain could be described by the fitted curve and the fitting formula obtained from the empirical datum, and the fiber grating strain sensitivity curve could then be got, as shown in Figure 2.

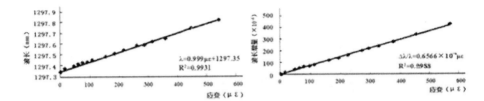

Fig. 2. Fitted curve and fiber grating strain sensitivity curve

By the above experimental result, the optical fiber Bragg diffraction grating's central wave length and the strain correlation coefficient reaches above 0.99, with no sluggish phenomenon, indicting a very good linear relationship[1][2].

2.3 Dynamic Strain Experiment

Connecting separately the fiber grating strain test system and the resistance strain test system, we carry on the dynamic strain test experiment, and the experimental method is as before increasing the force gradually. By computer recording experiment test procedure, optical fiber dynamic test strain time curve and electrical method dynamic test curve are obtained as shown in Fig.3. The fiber grating dynamic test has a smoother curve and a faster response than the resistance strains.

The fiber grating strain sensor's basic parameter obtained in the experiment are nearly the same of the compared sensor's basic parameter, which explains that it is feasible to replace the resistance strain gauge with the fiber grating strain sensor.

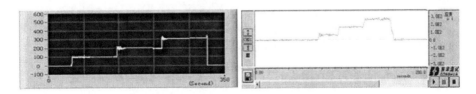

Fig. 3. Comparison of optical fiber dynamic test and electrical method strain time curve

3 Fiber Grating Strain Test System's Research and Development Based on VI Technology

3.1 Virtual Instrument VI Composition

Virtual instrument procedure based on Lab View platform includes three major components: Procedure front panel, diagram procedure and icon/coupling.

3.2 Constitution Project Design of Fiber Grating Strain VI Measurement System

1）System development environment
The system development environment is WinXP; the software development platform is LabView (above 6.1 edition); the hardware has PC, fiber grating strain sensor, modem device, the data acquisition card and so on[2].

2）Project design
The system's constitution plan is as shown in Figure 4.

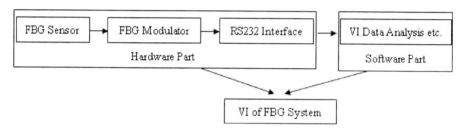

Fig. 4. Fiber grating strain VI system construction

3.3 Virtual Instrument System Hardware Design

The fiber grating strain VI system hardware design mainly includes: selection of fiber grating strain sensor; selection of the fiber grating modem device; VI system data acquisition card part; modem device and data acquisition card RS232 mechanics of communication and so on.

1）Selection of fiber grating strain sensor and the fiber grating modem device
    it is decided to select the fiber Bragg diffraction grating,at the same time select FSA-C type FBG modulator.
2）Selction of data acquisition card /assembly/ data acquisition card
    We choose the PCI8333 multi-purpose data acquisition card which is connected to the fiber grating modem device through RS232 serial port in the VI system.

3.4 VI System's Software Design

1）VI system's software demand analysis
The main purpose of VI fiber grating strain test system's software is to gather the data from data acquisition card, to demonstrate the data as well as essential analysis and

processing, complete functions of storage, warning and so on. The system must satisfy the following request: Sampling request; online monitor; Data management function; online analysis.

2) Function module's dividing and realizing

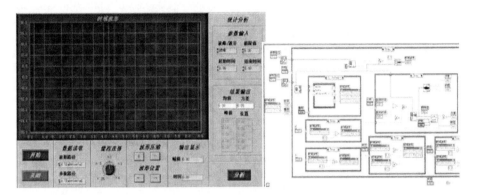

Fig. 5. Front panel of the data time domain analysis sub-module and diagram procedure code

In this VI system, mainly has the following several modules: Data acquisition parameter establishment module; Data online display module; Data online analysis module; Data and parameter establishment information storage module; Data frequency range analysis module; Data time domain analysis module; Data correlation analysis module; Report generation and printing module; Other auxiliary module such as users' information module and so on. Figure 5 shows the front panel of the data time domain analysis sub-module and diagram procedure code. Figure 6 shows Data frequency range analysis module's front panel and diagram procedure.

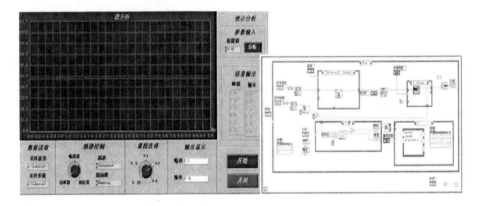

Fig. 6. Data frequency range analysis module's front panel and diagram procedure code

4 Conclusion

Applying FBG strain in uniform strength beam,the fiber grating strain test system definitely may be applied in the large-scale metal structure online monitor. From now on we would make further research on the harbor large-scale machinery's structure monitor and the diagnosis, and explore a highly effective examination and diagnosis integration technology which organic syntheses the technology of fiber grating sensing, embedded system, wireless data transmission and neural network expert system.

References

1. Li, B., He, L., Wang, L.: Based on the virtual instrument's sensor automated test system's design and realization. Micro Computer Application 5, 45–46, 49 (2010)
2. Hao, L., Zhao, W.: Two key questions on the signal imitation output based on LabVIEW. Electrical Electron Teaching Journal 3, 16–19 (2010)

A Method of Agent and Patient Relation Acquisition for Short-Text Classification

Xinghua Fan and Dingbang Wei[*]

College of Computer Science and Technology,
Chongqing University of Posts and Telecommunications,
Chongqing 40065, China
weifeng0207@126.com

Abstract. This paper presents an automatic method to extract the agent and patient relation of the short-texts. With the aid of the "HowNet", the real agent and patient relation in the real short-texts are determined via the common feature and the "sememe-tree" structure. Moreover, the strength of the relations can be calculated by using the length in the "sememe-tree". Furthermore, the extracted word pairs are used for the classification of short-texts. The experiments demonstrate the validity of the proposed approach in extracting the agent and patient relation from short-texts. And the relations are beneficial for improving the performance of short-text classification.

Keywords: Short-text, Classification, Agent relation, Patient relation, HowNet.

1 Introduction

The short-text classification is an automatic classification for short texts. (The text length is usually less than 160 characters), on which the filtering of short message sent by the mobile phone is based. As the length of the text is short and the signal it described is weak the classification is a challenging task.

One feasible way to assist the classified is using some additional information [1-3]. The purpose of the introduction of additional information is to tap the amount of information expressed by a short text and to remedy the inherent defects in natural short text. Wang Xiwei[4] proposed a method that based on association rule for short text classification, while Wang Sheng[5] using the hyponymic relation can also work. Attempts to find a new semantic relation are surely worthwhile. The patient and agent relation are important semantic relations. Using the relations to expand a short text is also an effective way.

An effective method of the automatic acquisition of the relation has not be developed yet. To obtain the agent and patient relation in the short text automatically and then apply them to the text classification, we must address the following issues: (1)How to determine whether there is agent or patient relation between the words. As the information contained in the short-text is very limited, this paper introduce an idea of using an external resources, "HowNet", for the relation word-pairs taking. (2)How

---

[*] Corresponding author.

G. Shen and X. Huang (Eds.): CSIE 2011, Part II, CCIS 153, pp. 27–33, 2011.
© Springer-Verlag Berlin Heidelberg 2011

to acquire a collection of relation word-pairs which could help the short-text classification. The word-pairs extracted directly by "HowNet" are limited. To solve this problem, this paper presents an improved extracting model. In order to ensure the precision, this paper also presents a standard for calculating the strength of the relations. (3)How can we use the agent and patient relation to affect short-text classification.Taking the characteristics of agent and patient relation in syntax into account, we modify the extending method of reference [4]. Then we classify the test text extended in order to test and verify the effect of the agent and patient relation.

2   The Method and Application

Definition: Agent relation is the relation between the agent of an event and this event, such as: "consumer" and "purchase". Patient relation is the relation between the patient of an event and this event, such as "product" and "purchase". Agent and patient usually act as the main role in an event, therefore, agent and patient relation reflect a kind of links between nouns and verbs.

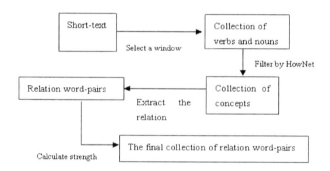

Fig. 1. The steps of extracting relation

This paper presents a model of extracting agent and patient relation (Fig.1).

(1) Select a suitable window to extract the verbs and nouns from the real text.

(2) Filter the words by "HowNet", in order to make the words into the concepts.

(3)Use the information provided by HowNet and the method of this paper to make sure whether the concept pairs have agent or patient relation.

(4)According to actual needs, calculate the strength of relation and filter the word-pairs which do not meet our requirements.

Step (3) is the most important step of this model. It will be described in detail in 2.1 and 2.2 of this section.

2.1   HowNet and a Conventional Method

HowNet[9] use the concepts of Chinese or English words as described objects, in order to reflect the relation between different concepts. The designer of HowNet uses a special kind of language to describe concepts. The word of this language is "Sememe". "Sememe" is the smallest unit to describe a concept.

The language of HowNet provide: When a concept and an event have the dynamic role-relation, the language will use a specific symbol to describe it."*", a symbol, is used to identify the agent relation, and "$" is used to identify patient relation.

This description by symbol of HowNet expresses agent or patient relation between an entity and a specific event. Usually, the first sememe is the main feature of this concept. Therefore, a conventional method believes: If the DEF of an entity have a Sememe "v" with * or $, and the first Sememe of an event's DEF is also "v", this entity and event have agent or patient relation.

2.2   An improved Method

Using the method mentioned in 2.1 to extract the agent and patient relation, the number and the coverage of the relations are limited. That is because of the HowNet's coverage and its language's characteristic.

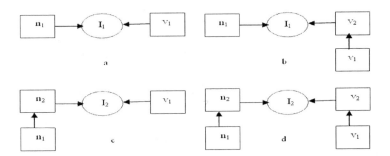

Fig. 2. Model 1 to 4

Sememes exist in the signature-file as a structure of tree. The trees do not only reflect the hyponymic relation but also mark the common features in []. The common features are the properties of a class of concepts which use this sememe as the first sememe. Moreover, the lower sememe could succeed its higher sememe's agent-feature or patient-feature. Because of these characteristics, an improved method based on the common features and the hyponymic structure can be described as:

Extract the features of each Sememe in the [] from signature-file to be a collection of agent-feature (or patient-feature).For a concept-pair record $(N_1:V_1)$. If the conventional method cannot determine it, get n_1, the first sememe of N_1 and v_1, the first sememe of V_1. n_2 is a higher sememe of n_1 and v_2 is a higher sememe of v_1. I_1 is the collection of n_1's agent-feature (or patient-feature) while I_2 is the collection of n_2's agent-feature (or patient-feature), there are 4 models:

Model 1 : If $v_1\epsilon I_1$ (fig.2.a)
Model 2 : If Model 1 cannot be met, $\ni v_2$, and $v_2\epsilon I_1$ (fig.2.b)
Model 3 : If both Model 1 and 2 cannot be met, $\ni n_2$, and $v_1\epsilon I_2$ (fig.2.c)
Model 4 : If all of Model 1 to 3 cannot be met, $\ni n2$ $v2$, and $v2\epsilon I2$ (fig.2.d)

If either of model 1 to 4 can be met, we will extract (N1:V1) and save it to the result.

2.3 Calculation of Relation Strength

The strength of the relation word-pairs extracted by method mentioned in 2.1 and 2.2 are different. If we use this collection of word-pairs in short-text classification, it will cause plenty of noises. Therefore, it is essential for us to calculate the relation strength and set up a threshold to filter the word-pairs which are not reliable. The following is the method for calculation of this paper:

1) The strength of the word-pairs extracted by the method in 2.1 is set to be 1.

2) Because we use the sememe-tree in the improved method, the length of sememe [10] is used to calculate the strength:

$$Degree(N_1, V_1) = \phi_1 \frac{\alpha}{Dis(n_1, n_2) + 1 + \alpha} + \phi_2 \frac{\beta}{Dis(v_1, v_2) + \beta} , \qquad (1)$$

$Dis(n_1, n_2)$ is the length between n_1 and n_2 in the sememe-tree, while $Dis(v_1, v_2)$ is the length between v_1 and v_2. α and β are adjustable parameters. Φ_1 and Φ_2 are adjustable weights($\Phi_1 + \Phi_2 = 1$).

2.4 Application in Short-Text

The algorithm of this paper to extend the short test text by agent and patient relation can be described in the following:

Input: short-text for test, collection of agent and patient relation
Output: Vector space of the short-text after be extended
Step1: For a word of short-text, select the collection of word-pairs. If there is only one word-pairs $t_i \rightarrow t_j$, go to step 3, else if the word-pairs is several, go to step 2, else go to step 6.
Step2: Extract the right words of all the word-pairs of t_i to be collection T_x, if $\exists t_j \in T_x$, and t_j can be found in the vector space of this short-text, go to step 5, else extract t_j, the right word of the word-pair with the highest strength, go to step 4.
Step3: Extract t_j ,the right word of this word-pair, t_j cannot be found in the vector space of this short-text, go to step 4, else go to step 5.
Step4: Insert t_j to the vector space of this short-text.
Step5: Raise the frequency of t_j in the vector space of this short-text for λ. ($0 < \lambda < 1$)
Step6: Don't extend this word, input and treat next word.

The main difference between this algorithm and reference[4] is Step 5.The purpose is to strengthen the weight of the original relation words of the short-text, because agent and patient relation are always exist in the real text for subject-predicate structure or verb-object structure, which are the major components of a sentence[6].

3 Experiment

2 groups of experiment are designed in this paper. The dataset used here is 4702052 Chinese short-text which composed of 12 categories, including finance, real estate, international news, national news, military, science and technology, women, cars, book reviews, sports, games, entertainment. All of short-texts are titles of the news

from Sina website and Netease website. We averagely divided texts of each category into four parts randomly, one part as testing data, the rest as training data.

3.1 Experiment for Relation Acquisition

Experiment introduction:Considering the characteristics of agent and patient relation in syntax, we take a sentence of the text as the window for extracting the word-pairs of verbs and nouns. Moreover, we use the method 2.1 and method 2.2 to determine whether the word-pairs have agent (or patient) relation separately, and then calculate the strength by the formula (1). 2 Evaluations are used in this experiment.

$$\textbf{Precision (P)} \; = \; \frac{\text{The number of right word pairs in the result}}{\text{The number of wordpairs in the result}}, \tag{2}$$

$$\textbf{Feature Coverage\_ rate (F)} = \frac{\text{The number of feature - words in the result}}{\text{The number of words in feature space}}, \tag{3}$$

The difference between this evaluation and the conventional one is that we do not use Recall. The reason is the relation word-pairs are used to help classification, so they can be available only if they are in the feature space. The size of the feature space used in this experiment is 4000. There is a group of result in Table 1.

Conclusions are summarized as follows: (1) Although the word-pairs extracted directly by the conventional method (method 2.1) are accurate, the number and the feature-coverage are too limited. (2)The number of word-pairs extracted by the improved method (method 2.2) is increased, but the precision is decreased. The reason may be that only the first sememe and some special symbol sememes are used in this method, but some information from other sememes is ignored. (3) The precision of threshold 0.7 and that of 0.5 is different obviously. It implies that the precision is decreased with the further of the length between the sememes. Therefore, the addition of calculating strength is essential.

Table 1. Result of extraction

	Number of word-pairs	Precision	Feature Coverage
Method 2.1	1863	89%	14.05%
Method 2.2 and threshold 0.7	6099	68%	26.825%
Method 2.2 and threshold 0.5	20514	43%	33.4%

3.2 Experiment for Short-Text Classification

Experiment introduction: This experiment use CHI to select feature, and take the Naïve Bayes as classifier. Then 8 groups of experiments for short-text classification are taken, and the sizes of the feature space are 500, 1000, 1500, 2000, 2500, 3000, 3500, 4000. Use these 4 methods.

Method 1: The test corpus is the original texts.

Method 2: The test corpus is extended by the method mentioned in 2.4, and the collection of relation is extracted by method 2.2.

Method 3: The test corpus is extended by the method mentioned in 2.4, and the collection of relation is extracted by method 2.2(threshold 0.7).

Method 4: The test corpus is extended by the method mentioned in 2.4, and the collection of relation is combined by the collection of method 2 and method 3.

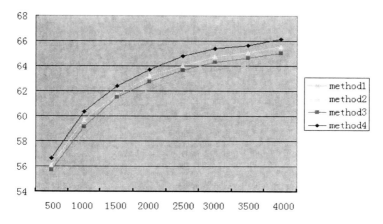

Fig. 3. Curve of Macro-F1

The Evaluation of Classification Performance: In this experiment, we use the following measures in the evaluation of classification: Precision (P), Recall (R), F1-measure,and Macro-F1= $\frac{1}{n} \sum_{i=1}^{n} F1_i$

From Fig.3, we can draw these conclusions as follows:1) Agent and patient relation can help enhance the performance of short text classification, but the effect is not very obviously. The reason may be that the degree of extending is not enough. 2) Though the collection of method 3 is larger than method 2, the effect to classification is worse. That may be because of the lower precision, which would cause more noises. 3) The effect of method 4 is the best, but the distance is not obviously compared with the other methods.

4   Conclusion

In view of the characteristics of short-text, this paper concludes with a method of extracting the agent and patient relation in the text by using the "HowNet", and then class the text by the extracted words. Conclusions are summarized as follows:1) Compared with the conventional use of "HowNet ", the method we present can improve the number of extracted words and the coverage of the characteristic. 2) The agent and patient relation can help enhance the performance of short text classification. 3) The lack of the precision of agent and patient relation may lead to the limited increase in improving the classification performance. Agent and patient are only part of the event, which can cover only part of the verbs and nouns, to extract and integrate more effective semantic relations will be the further research.

Acknowledgment

This research is supported both by the National Natural Science Foundation of China under grant number 60703010 and the Science and Technology Project of Chongqing Municipal Education Commission in China under grant number KJ070519.

References

1. Zelikocitz, S., Hirsh, H.: Improving short text classificaton using unlabeled background knowledge to assess document similarity. In: Proceedings of the 17th International Conference on Machine Learning, pp. 1183–1190. Morgan Kaufmann, San Francisco (2000)
2. Zelikocitz, S.: Transductive LSI for short text classification problems. In: Proceedings of the 17th International Florida Artificial Intelligence Research Society Conference. AAAI Press, Florida (2004)
3. Zelikocitz, S., Marquez, F.: Transductive learning for short text classificaton problems using latent semantic indexing. International Journal of Pattern Recognition and Artificial Intelligence 19(2), 143–151 (2005)
4. Wang, X., Fan, X.: Method for Chinese short text classification based on feature extension. Journal of Computer Applications 29(3), 843–845 (2009)
5. Wang, S., Fan, X.: Chinese short text classification based on hyponymy relation. Journal of Computer Applications 30(3), 603–606 (2010)
6. Hao, X., Yang, E.: HowNet Based Acquisition of Role & semanteme Features of Event Category. Journal of Chinese Information Processing 15(5), 26–32 (2001)
7. Zhou, Q., Feng, S.: Build a relation network representation for HowNet. Journal of Chinese Information Processing 14(6), 21–27 (2000)
8. Dong, Z., Dong, Q.: HowNet (1999), http://www.keenage.com
9. Fan, X., Sun, M.: A High Performance Two-Class Chinese Text Categorization Method. Chinese Journal of Computers 29(1), 124–131 (2006)
10. Li, F., Li, F.: An New Approach Measuring Semantic Similarity in Hownet 2000. Journal of Chinese Information Processing 21(3), 100–105 (2007)

Optimization Strategy for AODV Routing Protocol Based on Modified Ant Colony Algorithm

Weihua Hu and Yuanzhou Li

Hangzhou Dianzi University, Computer Science,
310018 Zhejiang Hangzhou, China
hwh@hdu.edu.cn, yuanzhou999@163.com

Abstract. The Ad hoc On-Demand Distance Vector (AODV) routing protocol doesn't consider the node itself condition in the route discovery. So it may cause some local nodes congestion, thus affects the whole transmission characteristic of the net; Meanwhile, in high-speed mobile network conditions, due to the dynamic change of topology structure, causes the communication link expire frequently, therefore increased the transmission latency greatly. This paper combines with ant colony algorithm, based on AODV routing protocol, proposed a modified routing protocol. The modified routing protocol considers the node routing load, remaining power, routing hop count, and so on. In the route discovery stage, the downward node in communication link makes the judgment to its own situation, avoids the node blindly processing route request; with the improved ant algorithm, the modified routing protocol makes the source node establish many ways to the destination node. Finally, the NS2 simulation shows that the modified protocol reduces the average delay, routing load and packet loss rate while increasing the data forwarding capacity of nodes.

Keywords: Ad hoc, AODV, ant colony algorithm.

1 Introduction

Ad hoc Network is a special kind of wireless network architecture, which emphasizes multi-hop, self-organization, no centers. It can be applied in many situations, particularly where needs for establishing a network for a limited period of time and where a wired infrastructure maybe nonexistent or is very difficult to be deployed. These applications include battlefields, search and rescue missions, industrial and academic purposes, where participants can share information dynamically through their mobile devices. However, Ad hoc's node moves frequently so the network architecture dynamic change. This causes the traditional routing protocol to be very difficult to obtain the ideal transmission. Therefore, it is the core issue of Ad hoc network that designs a good performance routing protocol.

Nowadays, the most common recognition of Ad hoc network routing protocols include DSDV, CGSR, WRP, AODV, DSR, TORA and so on. AODV[1] routing protocol is one of the routing protocols that is recommended by the IETF's MANET working group for its superior and simple but practical performance. AODV is

G. Shen and X. Huang (Eds.): CSIE 2011, Part II, CCIS 153, pp. 34–41, 2011.

designed for Ad hoc networks with populations of tens of thousands of mobile nodes. It is essentially combined with DSR and DSDV. It borrowed the DSR's route discovery and the foundation program of the route maintenance, and the DSDV's Hop-by-hop routing, the destination node serial number and the cycle of updated mechanism of route maintenance phase. Based on the DSDV protocol, it combined with the on-demand routing and improved the thoughts of DSR. But AODV also has some disadvantages:

1. AODV routing protocol relies on the hop count as the only routing measure. It does not consider the node current load. This would cause some nodes in the middle of the network be used by many links in many situations, but the nodes at network edge are never used. This does not only cause the network resource consumption inequality, moreover, seriously influence network latency and throughout once the congestion happens because the ability of single node is limited.
2. In a high speed situation, the network topology changes frequently. Therefore communication link expires could be very frequent. This would increase route discovery of the network greatly and the network latency.

Ant colony algorithm[2-6] is proposed by Italian scholar M. Dorigo, V. Maniezzo and A. Colorni in 1991. It uses for solving series combination optimization question. Because of its distributed features, ant colony algorithm is very suitable to solve the network routing problem. This paper proposed one kind of new on demand routing protocol DA_AODV. DA_AODV routing protocol based on AODV routing protocol. It makes the improvement to the route discovery stage and route maintenance stage with an optimized ant colony algorithm. DA_AODV considers the node routing load, remaining power, routing hop factors, thus equilibrium network power consumption.

2 Improved AODV (DA_AODV)

According to seek road in the ant colony algorithm, DA_AODV introduces two kinds of ants in Ad hoc: FANT and BANT. FANT expresses from the source node to the goal node ant. It carries the route request information to establish to the source node reverse pheromone pathway. BANT is the ant that from the destination node or the middle node which has a route to the destination node to the source node. It is to establish the source node to destination node pheromone path. The function of route request packet RREQ and route reply packet RREP in AODV is as the same as FANT and BANT in DA_AODV, so FANT and BANT is designed on the basis of RREQ and RREP. It can simplify the complexity of the algorithm design.

2.1 Pheromone Update Strategy in Route Discovery

FANT is local update the pheromone of the node. According to the idea of the max-min ant system, the next hop node pheromone of each node is initialized as $\tau_{ij} = C$, C is the max allowed pheromone value of the network. Pheromone update expression is formula 1:

$$\tau_{ij}(t+1) = (1-\rho) \cdot \tau_{ij}(t) + \rho \cdot \Delta \tau_j + \omega \tag{1}$$

$$\Delta \tau_j = \frac{\varepsilon \cdot q_{free} / q_{total}}{hop} \tag{2}$$

ρ is evaporation coefficient of pheromone, $\rho \in (0,1)$; $\Delta \tau_j$ is the adjusted value of pheromone of the node j; ε is the percentage of remaining power of current node; q_{free} is the total idle queue length of the current node's received queue. q_{total} is the total length of the received queue of the current node; hop is the routing hops from the source node to the current node; ω is the pressing factor of the previous hop, it is the ratio of send queue situation and the remaining power capacity;

BANT globally updates pheromone which is on the communication link. The update expression is formula 3

$$\tau_{ij}(t+1) = (1-\mu) \cdot \tau_{ij}(t) + \Delta \tau^* \tag{3}$$

$$\Delta \tau^* = \frac{\gamma}{L_{best}} \tag{4}$$

μ is the secondary evaporation coefficient of the pheromone, $\mu < \rho$; γ is the enhancement factor of the pheromone, it is proportional to the product of the remaining power of the previous hop node and the use of the received queue of the previous hop node; L_{best} is the total number of hops from source to destination in communication link.

2.2 Route Select

After establishment of the route, there may be multi-path in the route table whose destination nodes are the same. When needs to send data, the source node selects the routing which has the largest probability to the destination node. The probability is based on the pheromone which has the same destination node. The expression is formula 5:

$$p_{nd}^s(t) = \frac{\tau_{nd}^\alpha(t) \cdot \eta_{nd}^\beta(t)}{\sum_{k \in R_{sd}} \tau_{kd}^\alpha(t) \cdot \eta_{kd}^\beta(t)} \tag{5}$$

$p_{nd}^s(t)$ expresses, at time t, the routing probability with source node s, destination node d, and next hop n; $\tau_{nd}^\alpha(t)$ expresses, at time t, the pheromone with the destination node d, the next hop n; α is the important index of pheromone; $\eta_{nd}^\beta(t)$ is the path heuristic function, β is the important index of the function; R_{sd} is the set of all routes which reach the same destination node. The path heuristic function is formula 6:

$$\eta_{nd}(t) = \frac{1}{L_{nd}} \tag{6}$$

L_{nd} expresses the total hop with destination node is d, next hop is n.

2.3 Route Discovery

The main algorithm flow is as follows:

When the source node needs to send data:

```
If there is a route in the route table
  Send packet;
Else
  Store the packet which needs to send;
  /* FANT  carries  in  remaining  power  information,
     utilization of send queue, and a list of visited
     nodes.
  */
  Broadcast a FANT to its neighbors;
```

When the node receives a FANT packet:

```
If the node is destination node
  /* BANT  carries  in  remaining  power  information,
     utilization of received queue, pheromone of the
     node, and a list of visited nodes.
  */
  Send a BANT packet to the source node;
Else if  there  is  an  available  route  in  the  routing
          table
  If send queue length / queue length > 80% && remaining
     power < 20%
   Delay a period of time;
   Send a BANT packet;
  Else
   Calculate  the  pheromone  which  reaches  the  source
   node;
   Calculate the transition probability of the next hop;
   Establish the reverse route to reach the source node;
    Send a BANT packet to the source node;
    Send a FANT with G=1 to the destination node;
  Else
    If send queue length / queue length > 80% && remaining
       power < 20%
     Delay a period of time;
     Broadcast the FANT;
    Else
     Broadcast the FANT immediately;
```

2.4 Route Maintenance

In order not to add additional routing overhead, DA_AODV does not update the pheromone by sending addition control messages. The pheromone update expression is formula 7:

$$\tau(t+1) = (1-\lambda) \cdot \tau(t) + \Delta\tau \tag{7}$$

$$\Delta\tau = \frac{\varepsilon \cdot q_{free} / q_{len}}{L}$$

λ is the evaporation coefficient of pheromone; ε is the percentage of remaining power of the current node; q_{free} is the idle queue length of the receive queue; q_{total} is the total queue length of the current node's receive queue; L is the hop from the source node to the destination node.

Each node which is on communicating will establish a backup route, so that is able to switch to the backup route to send data when current communication link is failure. The active nodes broadcast FANTs with B=1 every BACKUP_ROUTE_ INTERVAL time. The un-allowed table has the full path of communication link. The node which receives this packet will drop it if the node is in the proper place in the un-allowed table. Otherwise, the node will forward it until reaching the destination node.

In order to prevent algorithm stagnating earlier, the source node sends unicast FANT to the destination follow the communication link every FIND_ROUTE_ IN-TERVAL time so that can update the pheromone on the communication link. The source node broadcasts a FANT every 2*FIND_ROUTE_INTERVAL time for discovering a new path.

3 NS2 Simulation and Analysis

We simulate AODV and DA_AODV using the NS2[7] simulator. The specific parameter settings are as follows: the maximum queue length of node is 50, there are 1000 mobile nodes in the network, range of motion topology is 1000m x 1000m, random start CBR flows are 5, 10, 15, 20, 25, 30, the node pause time is 10s, node sends 5 packets per second which is 512 Byte, the simulate time is 500s. The maximum speeds of mobile node are 10m/s, 20m/s, 30m/s, 40m/s, 50m/s. We analysis the result by packet delivery fraction, average end to end delay, routing load.

Experiment 1:

In the environment with CBR connections is 10, the maximum node moving speed is 10m/s, 20m/s, 30m/s, 40m/s, 50m/s. The simulated result is shown in Fig. 1 – 3:

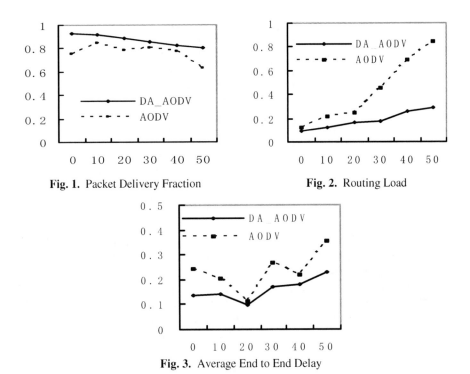

Fig. 1. Packet Delivery Fraction   **Fig. 2.** Routing Load

Fig. 3. Average End to End Delay

Fig. 1 - 3 are shown that the packet delivery fraction, average end to end delay, routing load in AODV and DA_AODV are marked by a downward trend with the maximum node moving speed increasing. But the performance of DA_AODV is apparently better than AODV when the speed increased to 30m/s. With the node moving speed increasing, the network topology changes quickly. It causes the communicating link fail frequently, but DA_AODV has multi-way reach the destination so that is able to use another path when the main path is failure.

Experiment 2:
In the environment with the maximum node moving speed 10m/s, CBR connections is 5, 10, 15, 20, 25, 30. The simulated result is shown in Fig. 4 – 6:

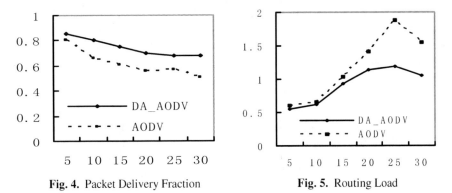

Fig. 4. Packet Delivery Fraction   **Fig. 5.** Routing Load

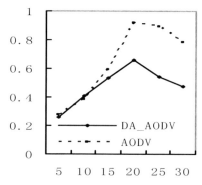

Fig. 6. Average End to End Delay

In the situations of different CBR connections, because AODV doesn't consider the node queue situation and remaining power, it will be seriously affected network traffic when the overload nodes do not work. DA_AODV can monitor the queue situation of the forwarding nodes, be selective response to routing requests. Through Fig. 4 - 6, we can infer that DA_AODV have a better performance than AODV at routing load and average end to end delay especially when CBR connections is larger than 20.

4   Conclusions

In this paper, we proposed an improved routing protocol, called DA_AODV. The communication latency is considered as the focus factor, it has a very good adaptation for dynamic topology changes, take into account routing load, remaining power, route hops and other factors. Through simulation and analysis Packet delivery ratio, average end to end delay, routing load, packet loss rate. The results show that DA_AODV enhances node's data forwarding capability while reducing the routing load and packet loss rate. The protocol is not perfect because of limit time, so this part of work will also be the next focus of the study.

Acknowledgments

We thank all people in the reference. In addition, the authors would like to thank the anonymous reviewers for their considerate comments and suggestions. This paper could not have been done without their research production. We also thank all people who read the paper.

References

1. Perkins, C., Belding-Royer, E., Das, S.: Ad Hoc On-Demand Distance Vector(AODV) Routing, RFC 3561 (2003)
2. Dorigo, M., Maniezzo, V., Colorni, A.: Positive feedback as a search strategy. Technical Report 91-106, Dipartimento di Elettronica, Politecnico di Milano, IT (1991)

3. Dorigo, M.: Optimization, Learning and Natural Algorithma(in Italian). Ph. D. thesis, Dipartimento di Elettronica, Politecnico di Milano, IT (1992)
4. Colorni, A., Dorigo, M., Maniezzo, V.: Distributed optimization by ant colonies. In: Proceedings of the First European Conference on Artificial Life, pp. 134–142. Elsevier, Amsterdam (1992)
5. Dorigo, M., Di Caro, G.: The Ant Colony Optimization meta-heuristic. In: Corne, D., Dorigo, M., Glover, F. (eds.) New Ideas in Optimization, pp. 11–32. Mcgraw Hill, London (1999)
6. Dorigo, M., Di Caro, G., Gambardella, L.M.: Ant algorithms for discrete optimization. Artificial Life 5(2), 137–172 (1999)
7. Fall, K., Varadhan, K.: The NS manual,
   http://www.isi.edu/nsnam/ns/doc/index.html

Analysis of Operating Vehicle Handling and Driving Stability Impact Elements

Xingdong Guo[1], Wenlong Guo[2], Hao Zhang[3], and Qibo Wang[3]

[1] No.8 Weixian Middle Road, Weifang City, Shandong Transport Vocational College Driver Training Center 261206
[2] No.69 Changnan Street, Weicheng City, Shandong Weifang Business School 261011
guowenlong@yahoo.cn
[3] College of Traffic, Jilin University 130022

Abstract. Based on characteristic and theories analysis of operating vehicle, there are some structures which impact on vehicle handling and driving stability mainly such as suspension, steering system and transmission system. And there are some factors which affect vehicle handling and driving stability for instance vehicle speed, lateral forces of vehicle, center of gravity position, tire cornering characteristics, steering system stiffness, steering transmission ratio and vertical axis of inertia moments and so on. Factors including steering system, alignment parameters of wheel, tires, suspension have a greater impact for operating passenger car on vehicle handling and driving stability. But factors including alignment parameters of wheel, centroid height and suspension have a greater impact for operating freight car on vehicle handling and driving stability. Finally, it should take driver and vehicle as a hole for vehicle handling and driving stability analysis.

Keywords: Operating vehicle, handling stability, driving stability, impact analysis.

1 Introduction

Operating vehicles can be divided into operating passenger car and operating freight car.

Integral body structure is usually used in operating passenger car which played the role as vehicle body and frame. All components are fixed to the vehicle body which bore all the power. There isn't any relative motion between vehicle body and frame. Integral body structure without frame can reduce the quality of vehicle and make the floor lower so that it can be got on and off easily Most of operating passenger car adopted independent suspension, as shown in Figure 1.

Side beam frame which is the most used in operating freight car is composed by two stringers and many beams. Besides, side beam frame is rigid structure which is connected with stringers and beams by riveting or welding. Beams are used to ensure torsion stiffness of vehicle frame and bear the longitudinal load, and also can

G. Shen and X. Huang (Eds.): CSIE 2011, Part II, CCIS 153, pp. 42–47, 2011.
© Springer-Verlag Berlin Heidelberg 2011

support main vehicle parts. In operating freight car, vehicle body and framework are connected by riveting, so there will be relative motion between them under a certain condition. Dependent suspension is used in front and rear suspension by majority, as shown in Figure 2.

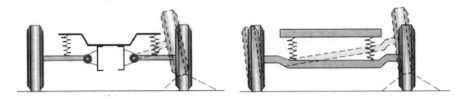

Fig. 1. Independent suspension   **Fig. 2.** Dependent suspension

Vehicle handling and driving stability is the driver does not feel too much tension or in fatigue conditions, vehicle can travel following the driver through the steering system and steering wheel for a given direction and when encountered outside interference, vehicle can resistant interference and maintain stable driving ability[1].

There are two different interrelated parts in vehicle handling and driving stability: handling stability and driving stability[2]. The main factors are different which impact on the vehicle handling and driving stability, since distributed load on front and rear axles and the structures of operating passenger car and operating freight car are different when they carry. The factors which including structure establishment of steering system, alignment parameters of wheel, tires, suspension have a greater impact for operating passenger car on vehicle handling and driving stability. The factors including alignment parameters of wheel, centroid height and suspension have a greater impact for operating freight car on vehicle handling and driving stability.

A detailed description about all factors will be described as follows.

2   Influence of Steering System

The steering system which controls driving direction is the most important system with vehicle handling and driving stability in vehicle chassis[2].

Vehicle wheel will become roll and interfere steering, if steering system is incompatible with the kinematics when carriage roll. It will cause front wheel rotation and damage vehicle handling and driving stability, if there is relative motion between carriage and vehicle-bridge when vehicle drives straightly. Vehicle steering system stiffness will cause deformed turning, when steering system stiffness lowers and the deformed steering angle become large that will increase the trend of under-steer. If steering system stiffness increases and the deformed angle becomes smaller, vehicle will trend to over-steer. Vehicle may instability when it breaks away, drifts or turns over. It can draw a conclusion that vehicle steering system stiffness should be too high to avoid danger.

3 Influence of Tire

The driving plane which is perpendicular to the wheels bears reaction force comes from ground in the driving, because of centrifugal force produced by lateral tilting, lateral driving or curve driving. The main tire parameters which influence vehicle handling and driving stability are depended on cornering properties of tire. Vehicle handling and driving stability will be well, if cornering stiffness is much high in tire. There is high cornering stiffness in large side tire. In wide tire, the flat ratio (the ratio of tire section high and section width is represented by percentage) is smaller, the cornering stiffness is higher. In addition, tire pressure also has significant impact on cornering stiffness. Cornering stiffness increases with the increase of pressure, but it will not change with too high pressure.

For freight car, it is common that flat ratio is lower and tire pressure is much higher, so tire hasn't great influence on vehicle handling and driving stability. Passenger car and minivan, opposite, in the full-size, the flat ratio is lower; tires have small influence on vehicle handling and driving stability.

4 Influence of Suspension

The distributed vertical load on front and rear axles is the main factor influences handling and driving stability, when there is side force[3].

Passenger car adopts independent suspension, the side of wheels produce vibration own to rough road or some reasons have smaller influence on the other side, the weight distribution is much uniform, the distributed vertical load in front and rear axles two wheels is small. Above all, we can get conclusion that suspension has small impact on handling and driving stability in passenger car. Freight car adopts non-independent suspension, there are some elastic elements which are made by leaf springs on non-independent suspension. Both side of wheels produce vibration own to rough road or some reasons have great influence on the other side, the weight distribution is much uniform, the axle weighing of front axle is significant greater than that of rear axle. The distributed vertical load in front and rear axle's two wheels is much large, when fright car is driving on the rough load. Suspension has a great impact on handling and driving stability in passenger car.

Suspension should be the most important in all the parameters impact handling and driving stability in passenger car.

5 Influence of Wheel Alignment Parameters

Alignment parameters of wheel includes camber angle of front wheel, kingpin castor angle, kingpin inclination, toe-in of front wheel and so on[3,4].

5.1 Camber Angle of Front Wheel

Front wheels are installed on vehicle-bridge, its plane of rotation has the characteristics of extraversion, and this is called as camber angle of front wheel, as shown in

Figure 3. The angle between wheel's plane of rotation and longitudinal symmetric plane is called camber angle of front wheel.

In order to make the tire wear uniform and reduce the load of hub pedestal bearing, wheels should have much camber angle before we install wheel. It could prevent wheel inclination. Camber angle can compatible with cambered load at the same time. Besides, it will increase the security of wheel and steering portability.

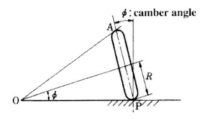
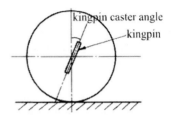

Fig. 3. Camber angle   **Fig. 4.** Kingpin caster angle

The camber angle of the lateral wheel will increase and vehicle inclination will decrease at the same time when negative camber angle vehicle turns. When car turns at a high speed, the centrifugal force will increase and lateral inclination of vehicle-bridge also increases, so the positive camber angle become larger, the distortion of lateral tire become more serious because of extra load on lateral suspension. For the difference of roll radius between outside and inside of tire, outside is smaller than inside, tire is worn out and the performance of steering is depressed. Camber angle of front wheel in modern car is smaller or negative which made roll radius between outside and inside of tire equally and improve vehicle handling and driving stability.

5.2 Kingpin Caster Angle

Kingpin is fixed at the former axis which top leans back; this phenomenon is known as kingpin caster. In longitudinal vertical plane, the angle between perpendicular line and kingpin axis is called the kingpin angle, as shown in Figure 4.

If caster angle is too larger that will cause heavy steering and driver will get fatigue. If caster angle is too small, when vehicle is driving straight, front wheels prone to shimmy, swing the steering wheel, capacity of steering wheel automatic return-to-center becomes weak. If caster angle becomes larger and vehicle speed is faster, stability of front wheels is better, if caster angle is too large that will cause heavy steering. So caster angle can close to zero and even negative.

5.3 Kingpin Inclination Angle

Viewing from vehicle front, angle between steering axis and ground plumb line is called kingpin inclination angle.

If kingpin inclination angle or front wheel angle is larger, vehicle front height will be lifted higher. In this situation, front wheel can return to center easily, but it's hard to move steering and wear of the steering wheel tire will be increased. Kingpin castor and kingpin inclination both have the task of returning to the steering wheel's straight-ahead position and maintaining the car drive at straight-ahead position. But the role of the return-to-center of kingpin castor is relevant to the vehicle speed, while to the kingpin inclination, it is irrelevant. Therefore, the role of the return-to-center of kingpin castor plays a leading position at high speed while at low speed. It major depends on the role of the return-to-center of kingpin inclination. In addition, when the front wheel is deflected by occasionally impaction, it depends on the role of the return-to-center of kingpin inclination.

5.4 Toe-In

When viewing from vehicle front, it is distance difference between front tires front and rear and can be measured at spindle height.

The role of toe-in is used eliminating the wheal's side slip caused by roll angle. It tilts outward at the top with positive side slip in front wheel. When vehicle is moving forward, wheels roll toward outside and lead to side slip which will cause tire wear. Therefore, the role of toe-in is to eliminate the external beam generated by side slip angle. When toe-in is larger, tire wear will be uneven which will affect the vehicle handling and driving stability.

6 Influence of Centroid Height

Vehicle centroid height cause great influence on vehicle handling and driving stability. Passenger car also has a relatively low centroid height and floor so that passenger can get conveniently. Lower centroid height makes passenger care has a relatively good handling and driving stability, when one side of wheels are lifted because the road surface is uneven or they encounter with a slope or sub grade. If vehicle centroid height is relatively low, the vehicle won't cause side tumbling and won't encounter with tail flick or shock rotating phenomenon when passenger car travel on the slippery road[5-7].

The centroid height of truck depends on the quality of the goods and height that loaded. Normally, truck always has a higher centroid height. Higher centroid height reduces the handling and driving stability. Truck will easily cause side tumbling when side wheels are raised for some reason; truck has more possibility to encounter tail flick or shock rotating when travelling on the slippery road. Therefore, it is important and necessary to reduce centroid height as low as possible.

7 Influence of Driver

Assuming that driver's task is merely to turn the steering wheel to a sharp angle and to maintain the same angle mechanically, he is not allowed to make any manipulation; any feedback from driver is not allowed. In this assumption, the handling stability depends entirely on the vehicle's structure and parameter the inherent characteristics of the vehicle.

The study of the vehicle's handling and driving stability should take driver and vehicle as a whole. It can be seen that in the system of driver and vehicle, it can feedback output to input control parameters by driver[8], as shown in Figure 5. Therefore, the system of driver and vehicle is a closed one. The influence of driver is very large in vehicle handling stability.

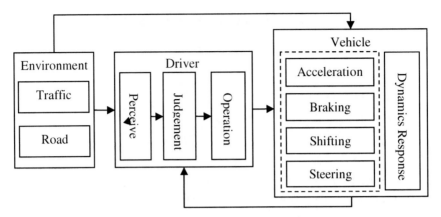

Fig. 5. Vehicle-Driver-Environment System

8 Conclusion

Because vehicle is a very complex system, its structures and components have influence on each other. Except the above six main affecting factors, there are other factors. The first five factors are objective factors, it can be used as objective evaluation index, and the sixth factor is subjective factor of drivers, it can be used as subjective evaluation index. For an experienced driver, accidents rate is usually smaller than the one who is not skillful. For different types of vehicles, factors are not the same about handling and driving stability.

References

1. Yu, Z.: Vehicle Theory, 3rd edn., vol. 10, p. 103. China Machine Press, Beijing (2002)
2. Wang, S.: Study on the Suspension K&C Characteristics of a Mini-car and Its Influence on the Vehicle. Handling Stability P6, P63–P67
3. Zhao, Q.: The Exploration of the Handling Stability. Simulation Research Based on ADAMS 6, P27–P31 (2006)
4. Qin, D.: Modeling. Simulation and Optimization Oriented to Handling and Stability of Sport Utility Vehicle, P28–P34
5. Yang, Y.: Research on Dynamics Models of Coach-bus. Maneuverability and Stability 6, P62–P71 (2002)
6. Liu, X.: Study of Maneuverability and Stability of Coach-bus via Modeling. Verification and Simulation 5, P48–P53 (2003)
7. Lei, B.: Simulated Analysis for Maneuverability and Stability of Coach-bus, 6, P68–P70 (2000)
8. Zhang, H.: Research on the Driver Shift Quality Based on Fuel Economy, vol. 6, p. P9 (2009)

Multi-core CPU Based Parallel Cube Algorithms

Guoliang Zhou and Han Zhang

Information of Department, Baoding Electric Power Voc. & Tech. College
071051 Baoding, Hebei
yu_bing_2000@163.com

Abstract. In recent years, computer hardware technology has greatly developed especially large memory and multi-core, but algorithm efficiency is not beneficial from the development of hardware. The fundamental reason is that there is insufficient utilizing CPU cache, as well as the limitations of single-thread programming. In the field of data warehousing and OLAP, data cube computing is an important and time-consuming operation, how to improve efficiency of data cube calculation is continuing to pursue goals. Based on the characteristics of modern CPU, we have proposed two parallel algorithms TASK_PMW and DATA_SSMW, TASK_PMW is task-based division of the parallel algorithm, each CPU core is responsible for one *Cuboid*; DATA_SSMW is data partition, and scanned sharing raw data, ensure load balancing, has good scalability and high efficient. Through experiments on dual-core CPU, TASK_PMW improve 1/3, DATA_SSMW 2/3 than the original algorithm.

Keywords: multi-core, parallel algorithm, Cube algorithm, cache conscious.

1 Introduction

The traditional cube algorithm is limited by disk I/O and main cost is reading data from disk [1]. The researchers design a lot of technologies to reduce the consumption of the disk I/O, which include fast data cube algorithm [2-5], materialized view technology [6,7], parallel cube algorithms [8-10], etc. As the development of computer hardware, computer configures larger memory. In theory, 64-bit computer can configure 23^2*4GB memory. So in most case we can store all of base data into the memory instead of disk I/O. The preview algorithms were not considering the new situations and cube algorithm is limited by the capability of CPU instead of disk I/O.

Recently computer hardware technology has greatly developed especially large memory and multi-core. The CPU is not faster limited by Power Wall, Memory Wall and Frequency Wall, but wider. Manufactures improve computing capacity using multi-core. As development of multi-core, the designing of parallel algorithm is one of the hot spots using parallel computing resources in the field of database [11]. On the other hand, the speed of CPU and memory develop in an unbalanced state. The CPU develops in the speed of Moore's Law; it is faster than the speed of memory. Designing data structure and algorithm with Cache Conscious is one of researching spot in data managing field.

G. Shen and X. Huang (Eds.): CSIE 2011, Part II, CCIS 153, pp. 48–53, 2011.
© Springer-Verlag Berlin Heidelberg 2011

The original cube algorithm based one-thread is not adapted to modern CPU. The reason is not fully use CPU cache and limited by the one-thread programs. For these two reasons, we design parallel cube algorithm with Cache Conscious and parallel. An intuitive parallel algorithm is based on the task. Every core is responsible for the computing of a *Cuboid*. But every core need scan all of data, which cannot be shared and bandwidth competition. We propose a parallel cube algorithm based on partition data with multi-thread which can be sharing scan. The algorithm use the order from top to bottom, ensure the balance of loading by partitioning the data when computing aggregated units. Multi threads can scan different partitions of data in the same time, and then compute synchronously all of the Cuboids in the next level.

The first section will explain the basic concepts and related work. We will introduce the basic parallel algorithm based on task—TASK_PMW in second section. The third section will describe the method of computing based on classified data which can be scanned and shared—DATA_SSMW. The forth section is detailed experimental study. At last we summarize the meaning of the article and purpose the works in the future.

2 Basic Concepts

In this section, we will introduce the basic concept of data cube. In order to understand the algorithm optimization, we will introduce the architecture of modern computer, and briefly introduce Multi-Way algorithm which is the base of our parallel algorithm.

2.1 Data Cube

Data cube is composed of multidimensional dataset. An n-dimensional data collection can be expressed as $R(D_1,...,D_n,M_1,...,M_m)$, D_i is dimension, M_j is measure. Multi-dimensional dataset can be stored in multi-dimension array. All of multi-dimensional arrays can compose a cube grid [2]. The n-dimensions of multi-dimensional array are named base *Cuboid*, and any multi-dimensional array is named *Cuboid*. Multi-dimensional Array is a logical structure for storing data. Data will be stored in the hard disk or memory in the form of one-dimensional array.

2.2 Architecture of Multi-core CPU

In the structure of modern computer, CPU has multi-core. The CPU cache (multi-level)—memory forms a leveled storing structure.

Two CPU cores are integrated into one chip. Every core is an independent computing unit which can perform computing tasks and have independent registers, L1 Cache. Two cores share L2 Cache. L1 and L2 are named CPU Cache which uses small capacity cache with faster speed to storing data and instructions in memory. L1 and L2 compose two-level cache in the modern computer which has smaller capacity and faster speed as gradually attending the CPU cache. Cache is composed of many cache line which is the transmit unit between Cache and memory.

When the data needed by CPU are in the L1 Cache, program will rapidly run, otherwise it will cause Cache Miss. Data need to be fetched from the lower-level Cache

(L2). If not in L2, data are fetched from the memory. L1 can run in the speed of CPU. Visiting L2 can cause the delay of dozens of clock cycles, but visiting memory can cause the delay of hundreds of clock cycles. As the speed of CPU and memory have inconsistent development, the relative consumption of the delay becomes bigger and bigger. We must reduce Cache Miss, especially the lack of L2.

3 The Parallel Algorithm Based on Task

Analyzing the Multi-Way algorithm, every thread is responsible for the computing of a lower-level *Cuboid* when computing from Base *Cuboid* to lower-level *Cuboid*. The algorithm is simply named TASK_PMW(Parallel Multi-Way). The algorithm is simply described into: Firstly, threads are created according to the numbers of lower-level *Cuboid*, and then every thread is responsible for the computing of a lower-level *Cuboid*. When the computing of a level has finished, a new computing of the next level *Cuboid* begins based on the input of this *Cuboid*. For instance, in figure 1 three threads are firstly created, which are responsible for computing AB, AC and BC. Then A and B are computed based on the input of two threads named as AB, C is based on the input of a thread named as AC, all is based on the input of a thread named as A.

The input of the algorithm is a linear stored one-dimensional array, as output every *Cuboid* also is linearized into one-dimensional array. One-dimensional array can easily be compressed in order to make algorithm to adapt sparse data set, and data are stored in form of one-dimensional array in disk finally.

The capacity of memory (M) which is required by the algorithm must be satisfied with the following conditions:

$$\prod_{j=1}^{m}|D_j| + \sum_{i=1}^{m}\left(\prod_{j=1,j\neq i}^{m}|D_j|\right) \leq M \tag{1}$$

Where $|D_j|$ is the cardinality of j dimension.

The above algorithm has the following problems. If the *Cuboid* which needs computing and the number of CPU cores is greater than the number of Cuboids, it will cause exist free CPU cores which cannot be used fully. Every thread need fetch data from memory into Cache when computing every *Cuboid*, which means the basic data are not shared by threads. Although the parallel performance of algorithm will be improved by conveyor belt phenomenon, and can share data partly. That is, the core of computing the first *Cuboid* will cause Cache Miss to fetch data from memory into Cache when multi-cores compute different Cuboids, but other cores can gain the first fetched data from the shared L2 Cache. The capacity of different Cuboids is not same, which can cause the loading in different cores is not in balance. In order to solve the problems, we propose data parallel algorithm scan sharing.

4 The Data Parallel Algorithm

In order to solve the problems in TASK_PMW algorithm, we design the data parallel algorithm shared scanning DATA_SSMW(Scan Sharing Multi-Way). The main idea of algorithm is dividing the original data firstly which is divided into equivalent chunks, and creating threads according to the number of CPU cores. Every thread scans different chunk, and compute all of Cuboids in the lower-level and so on until all of the computing of Cuboids are finished.

The data fetched by different thread can be written into the same position because of the partition. The synchronous objects such as mutex or critical region will be needed, that can guarantee the only element in *Cuboid* can be written by one thread. The method affects largely the performance of algorithm. So we open up some temporary space to store the temporary computing result according to the numbers of threads in order to reduce thread conflict when computing temporary result. When the process of the whole data partition is finished, data in the temporary partition will be stored synchronously into the corresponding *Cuboid*. Although the temporary spaces increase, the costs needed synchronization will decrease largely, and the higher algorithm throughput will be gained.

Algorithm 1. DATA_SSMW(*data, m, n*).

input: linear multi-dimensional array in blocks named as data, the number of dimension is m, the CPU cores numbers is n.

output: the whole cube

01 data are divided into *xn chunks, x is an integer*
02 create n threads $(T_1, T_2, ..., T_n)$
03 every thread$(T_i)$is performed parallel
04 **for each** *chunk, subscript chunk_pos*
05　**if** *chunk_pos % n==i*
06　　The chunk is processed by thread T_i
07　　$(p_1, p_2, ..., p_m) = R\text{-}LINEAR\ (chunk\_pos)$
　　　　/* gain the coordinate of chunk, inverse linear */
08　**for each** *element in chunk, subscript pos_in_chunk*
09　　$(d_1, d_2, ..., d_m) = R\text{-}LINEAR\ (pos\_in\_chunk)$
　　　/* gain the relative coordinate of element in the block */
10　　**for each** dimension *j (0,...,m-1)*
11　　　$pos\ += LINEAR(d_1, d_2, ..., d_{j-1}, d_{j+1}, ..., d_m)$
12　　　*tempcuboid_j [pos] += element*
13　　**for each** dimension *j (0,...,m-1)*
14　　$pos = LINEAR\ (p_1, p_2, ..., p_{j-1}, p_{j+1}, ..., p_m)$
15**for each** *element in tempcuboid_j, subscript pos_in_temp_cuboid*
16　**Enter_Critical_Section**　　　//synchronously
17　*cuboid_j [pos + pos_in_temp_cuboid] += tempcuboid_j [pos_in_temp_cuboid]*
18　**Leave_Critical_Section**

If the temporary space is larger than the capacity of L2 Cache, Cache threshing will happen. That is, the temporary space will be in and out frequently. The efficiency of algorithm will decrease. In order to avoid it, it meets the need of the capacity of temporary space and chunks.

$$n\left(\left(\sum_{i=1}^{m}\left(\prod_{j=1, j\neq i}^{m}|C_j|\right)\right)+\left(\prod_{j=1}^{m}|C_j|\right)\right) \approx L2 \tag{2}$$

Which *n* is the numbers of CPU cores, *m* is the numbers of dimension, and $|C_j|$ is the cardinality of *j* dimension.

5   Experiment Results

In order to verify the effectiveness of parallel cube computing method based on modern CPU, we make detailed experimental research. We compare the methods of
TASK_PMW, DATA_SSMW and Multi-Way. It is shown in experiment that the efficiency of TASK_PMW can increase by 1/3 than the original algorithm based on
two-cores CPU, and the efficiency of DATA_SSMW can increase by 2/3. We only
compare the computing time because the output results are completely same.

The algorithm is designed using Visual Studio 2005, and the thread is created and
managed by windows API. The experiment is respectively made in the machine with
two-cores CPU and four-cores CPU.

We will respectively test the performance of algorithm in the case of two-core CPU
and four-core CPU, the result of experiment is shown in Figure 1, 2:

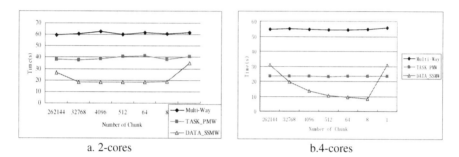

a. 2-cores   b.4-cores

Fig. 1. The comparisons of different algorithms of 3-dimension

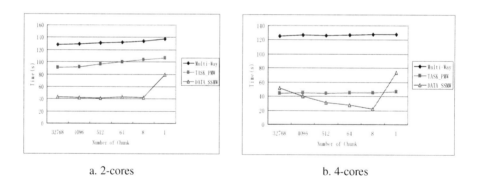

a. 2-cores   b. 4-cores

Fig. 2. The comparisons of different algorithms of 4-dimension

We compare respectively the efficiency of three algorithms in the case of 3-
dimensions, 4-dimensions, 10-dimensions, and the efficiency of the algorithm is higher
as the sensitivity for Cache and the using for multi-cores resource. The algorithm has
better extension. The computing time of 4-cores CPU is similarly 4 times than ones of
2-cores CPU using DATA_SSMW.

6 Summarize

This article has proposed two parallel algorithms TASK_PMW and DATA_SSMW, one is based on task-division, and another is based on data-divided shared parallel scanning. Designing and improving new cube algorithms to adapt modern CPU is our next work. Whether designing uniform optimization principle in order to optimize the cube algorithm in the higher level, it is our researching work in the future.

References

1. Gray, J., Chaudhuri, S., Bosworth, A., Layman, A., Reichart, D., Venkatrao, M., Pellow, F., Pirahesh, H.: Data cube: a relational aggregation operator generalizing group-by, cross-tab, and sub-totals. Data Mining and Knowledge Discovery 1(1), 29–53 (1997)
2. Zhao, Y., Deshpande, P.M., Naughton, J.F.: An array-based algorithm for simultaneous multidimensional aggregates. In: Proceedings of ACM SIGMOD International Conference on Management of Data, pp. 159–170. ACM Press, New York (1997)
3. Beyer, K., Ramakrishnan, R.: Bottom-up computation of sparse and iceberg CUBEs. In: Proceedings of ACM SIGMOD International Conference on Management of Data, pp. 359–370. ACM Press, New York (1999)
4. Xin, D., Han, J.W., Li, X.L., Wah, B.W.: Star-Cubing: computing iceberg cubes by top-down and bottom-up integration. In: Proceedings of the 29th International Conference on Very Large Data Bases, pp. 476–487. Morgan Kaufmann Publishers, San Francisco (2003)
5. Shao, Z., Han, J.W., Xin, D.: MM-Cubing: computing iceberg cubes by factorizing the lattice space. In: Proceedings of the 16th International Conference on Scientific and Statistical Database Management, pp. 213–222. IEEE Computer Society, Washington (2004)
6. Hurtado, C.A., Mendelzon, A.O., Vaisman, A.A.: Maintaining Data cubes under dimension updates. In: Proceedings of the 15th International Conference on Data Engineering, pp. 346–355. IEEE Computer Society, Washington (1999)
7. Lee, K.Y., Kim, M.H.: Efficient incremental maintenance of data cubes. In: Proceedings of the 32nd International Conference on Very Large Data Bases, pp. 823–833. ACM Press, New York (2006)
8. Dehne, F., Eavis, T., Hambrusch, S., Rau-Chaplin, A.: Parallelizing the data CUBE. Distributed and Parallel Databases 11(2), 181–201 (2002)
9. Dehne, F., Eavis, T., Rau-Chaplin, A.: Cluster architecture for parallel data warehousing. In: Proc. IEEE International Conference on Cluster Computing and the Grid (CCGrid 2001), Brisbane, Australia (2001)
10. Ng, R., Wagner, A., Yin, Y.: Iceberg-cube computation with PC clusters. In: Proceedings of SIGMOD Conference on Management of Data, Santa Barbara, California, pp. 25–36 (2001)
11. Han, W., Kwak, W., Lee, J., Lohman, G.M., Markl, V.: Parallelizing query optimization. In: Proceeding of 2008 VLDB, Auckland, New Zealand, pp. 188–200 (2008)

The Reflections on the Application of Modern Information Technology into Mathematic Teaching

Ai-Ling Wang

Department of Mathematics, Heze University, Heze, 274000, China
fly123406@163.com

Abstract. The current application of modern information technology to mathematic teaching and its status quo of the related research have mixed with expectations and worries. With those two investigations, we finally come to know that it not automatic to convert the information technology into mathematic educational technology, but it makes out only with the mutual integration of the technology itself and its user, which helps us to put forward a series of research subjects of great concern for later studies on this topic.

Keywords: modern information technology, mathematic education, courseware.

1 Introduction

With the development of the social economy in the 21st century, the condition of the schools has been bettered, which means that the multi-media classrooms have been built in many schools in which there are large screen, projector and computer. Being equipped by all those devices, the teaching courseware can be made and put into use. The operation on multi-media devices is a new technical ability for teachers in the tendency, which inspires great interests in the field. From this point, we get some reflections on the reality of the application of the modern information technology into mathematic teaching and the prospect of the study.

2 Investigation on the Application of Modern Information Technology

The investigation on the application of modern information technology in mathematic teaching. We choose the southwest of Shandong Province as the target district to do research for it is a relatively moderate developed place and a typical representative for most regions. In the investigation, 481 copies of questionnaires are provided, of which 467 are effective, with the percentage of 97.1%. The questionnaire includes 28 questions of 15 one-choice ones, 9 multiple-Choice ones, 2 sequencing ones and 2 open-ended questions. All of the questions lie in the integration of the information technology and mathematic teaching from different perspectives and at different frequency. The questionnaire-answering also reveals the difficulties mathematic teachers encounter and we herewith come up with related suggestions. The result of the questionnaire-answering are presented as the following fig and table:

G. Shen and X. Huang (Eds.): CSIE 2011, Part II, CCIS 153, pp. 54–60, 2011.
© Springer-Verlag Berlin Heidelberg 2011

Table 1. The basic factors influencing teachers' application of multimedia technology

Influencing factors	Lack of equipments	Lack of funds	Not valued by leaders
Scale (%)	20.8	35.9	36.3

Difficulty in making courseware	Lack of cooperation and communication among teachers	Lack of time for the complexities of the technology
46.7	59.6	78.2

This table tells us that the last three factors of the difficulty in making courseware, the lack of cooperation and communication among teachers and the lack of time for the complexities of the technology occupy the whole situation, and especially the last reason seems to be reasonable in real life to some extent. The phenomenon presented here is in accordance with the result we get from lots of symposiums, interviewing and visiting to schools. Hence they reflect the basic situation of the modern information technology applied in the mathematics teaching of elementary and secondary schools. But the validity of the information technology in mathematic teaching has been up in the air for there is no strict experiment or admissive data to confirm the truth.

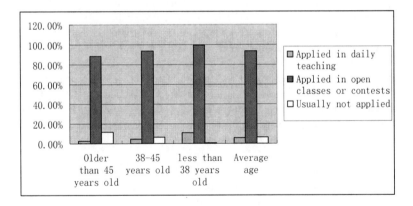

Fig. 1. The application of modern information technology

This fig presents that the older teachers use less than the younger teachers. It is definitely used in open classes and teaching competitions, while seldom used daily with only the percentage of 6%. We try to analyze the reasons implied: firstly, the devices are exclusively equipped in the multi-function classroom. And secondly, the use of the information technology as the prerequisite for the appraising system is only in teaching competition. Then we therefore explore the factors affecting the use of the multi-media technology as table 1 presents:

The investigation on the survey of the application of modern information technology to mathematic teaching. To investigate and analyze the status quo of the domestic studies, we choose the related articles from Peking University's core journal of *Journal of Mathematics Education*, which is an authoritative journal on the mathematics education of elementary and secondary schools in China. We summarize the articles from 2007 to 2008, among which there are 12 articles talking about this topic, among which 3 published in the year of 2007 and 9 in 2008. Here we classify these essays into 5 categories.

The study on the efficiency and the application levels. Three articles have talked about this topic. The first one (to see the Reference) written by Sun Mingfu and Fang Qinhua state that the effectiveness of the information technology in application is still at a lower level. Teachers mainly apply the made-up courseware to present the teaching content which weakens the efficiency of the teaching activities. The traditional blackboard-writing, teachers' inspecting and affective interactions between teacher and students have been neglected, and the teaching effect is wanting. In the essay, the writers thought that there is no appraising standard for the effective use of the information technology, no reasonable methods nor a clear target. Then Wen Jianhong and Tu Rongbao in their essay on thinking of the application of technology in mathematic teaching thought that the efficiency lives in the liveliness of the class and the training of students' thinking. As for the great impropriety in the design of the courseware, the author advised to make dynamic pictures and highlight the features of mathematic teaching by weakening the background. Shang Xiaochun in his essay divides the role of information technology into 4 kinds: ruler, supporter, cooperator and impellor. The conversion of the technology into teaching is not accomplished in an action, but involved in the understanding of the basic knowledge, the teaching methods and the mastering of the skills step by step. So he concluded that the information technology is still the supporter and cooperator for most Chinese mathematic teachers.

The comparative analysis and research on this topic. Qian Yun made a comparative analysis between the traditional teaching method and the multi-media teaching method, which defines the meaning of the teaching method as the ways by which the teacher and the students make interactions on knowledge and emotions. He stressed the accordance between the teaching method and teaching content. Both of these two ways shares merits and demerits. So new views of mathematics and teachings have to be established, and the teaching method should be in necessity and efficiency. In addition to this, the vagueness of the complex mathematic teaching activities makes teachers to think about the effective design of the courseware to put the mathematical spirit into practice. Yuan Zhiqiang made a comparative study on the 6 different teaching textbooks with *Mathematics 1* as the case.

The study on the factors and problems of the application of information technology. In Wen Yuchan and Zhou Ying's essay, the inner factors and the external factors combine to affect the application. The former consists of the teacher's intellectual skill, life and learning experience and his/her motivation. The later means the teaching devices and the management of the class. These two establishes a theoretical model and they have made questionnaire survey to get the conclusion that the external factors affect the expressing of the inner factors. Then Wang Lidong made a deep analysis of the reasons. He thought that the overstatement of the CAI weakens the teaching methods. CAI actually is found in open classes. The extreme for the formal beauty, the skilled operation, and the demonstration deteriorates the pursuit for the internal beauty, the affective interaction, and above all the pursuit for the process and the thinking ability. So finally he gets a principle of appropriateness, suitability, timeliness and moderateness for the deficiency in the computer-assisted instruction of mathematics.

The strategic study on specific teaching methods and subjects. Wu Hua and Ma Dongyan make a study from the perspective of "situation-question", talking about 4 types of situations. They are cooperative experimental situation, dynamic changing situation, spatial imaginative situation, and game-playing situation, all of which can be created to optimize the presence of mathematics knowledge. Liu Xiumei in her first essay states how to optimize mathematics teaching by applying network. Then in her second essay she studies eight strategies of geometry sketchpad applied in mathematics analysis.

The study on the strategy of modern information technology application. Zhang Guifang states that computers make mathematics teaching process easier to bring about than the past, which needs to think of class teaching as a whole process of exploring and discovering. The process is a chain stringed by many micro-activities and micro-processes, through which the composing chain should follow two orders: the logical order of the related teaching activities and the cognize order of the learning process. Zhu Guoquan and Wang Hui regard the application of information technology as the fundamental way to change teaching patterns, teaching structures, and learning methods. However, the fast calculation and presentation of the computer would influence the development of students' brains, their operating ability and thinking ability, as well as the interaction between students and teachers. They move deeper to reveal the inextricable objective contradiction between the information technology and teaching methods and the implied reason for the contradiction is of the traditional teaching method with information technology.

3 Relative Analysis and Studies

The unborn "Modern Educational Technology". The multi-media technology or called as the modern educational technology is seldom applied in daily teaching activities as the survey tells us. The exclusive application on special occasions is of no use in reality. The main reason not to apply the computer is that the making of courseware is much time-consuming, and the teachers have no enough time for this. To analyze the problem in detail, here we suggest two meanings: the problems of teachers' time and the problem of the skills. It is known that there is no shortcut for the making of courseware therefore the teacher has to spend more than 5 times of the time than the traditional in preparing lessons. But the efficiency of applying modern technology is not yet proved, except of popularized areas where teachers frequently use the multi-media room in daily teaching activities. So from this phenomenon, we can see that it not feasible to apply the modern technology into mathematic education due to the lack of simple and convenient techniques to assist teachers. It is certainly of significance to use electronic blackboard, projector, calculator, graphing calculator and the Internet. And the multi-media devices also can be used on the special occasions such as competition and contests.

Besides, many problems in the application have been read in the related essays. The modern technology propagates a most invalid teaching method in a way for which the conversion of the technology is actually the movement of the teaching plan into the screen so the cramming education system is never changed. We still not convert our ideas on mathematics-teaching, so the fuse of modern technique is only a matter of the reproduction of spoon-feeding education. So it does not make out for the feasibility of modern technology in mathematic teaching. The day for the modern educational technology does not arrive until the new technique is conveniently and availably applied in teaching, the reform of the education method in math teaching is put into practice and teachers' ideas have been changed.

The advantages of traditional teaching methods. From the above, we can find that there are many advantages for the traditional teaching methods in the related study. Though demerits they have, they are very effective and feasible in mathematic teaching. The traditional devices such as paper, chalk, book, and the blackboard never fades away. Some of the disadvantages can be made up, and some can be changed into advantages in cultivating students' thinking and working ability for the effective interaction between students and teachers. Qian Yun thinks that the traditional teaching method and the new views of mathematics and teaching derive a new teaching method, which is easily integrated with the traditional devices. They are cheap and handy, though the handwriting needs to take pains. Qian says that mathematics has double logic structures in which the teaching activity involves presuming and testifying on one hand, and on the other hand, teaching has been involved in the constructing of intellectual skills and the processing of growth. For the above reason, the traditional teaching method will not fade away for a long time, and will be bettered by the modern technology gradually.

4 The Need for Further Studies

Through the deep consideration and investigation on the application of modern information technology and its survey in practical mathematic teaching, we find a series of related issues and problems which are put forward for the further study.

The need for a experimental study on the effectiveness. From the materials on these two investigations, we get to know the situation that most of the mathematic teachers are not enthusiastic for information technology, and the essential reason, as what we have analyzed, is that they do not realize the effectiveness. The so-called "effective application" is an idea from the aspects of dialectical studies and conjectures, but not from the physical aspect. The domestic study on investigation and statistical analysis is of no significance because we seldom put information technology into daily mathematic-teaching activities. So a strict and scientific experimental study is in great need so that we can get believable conclusions which are based on the application of teaching means and modern information technology, the time and energy that teachers devote in the teaching process, and the evaluation of the quality and quantity of mathematic teaching. Therefore, it would weave into a valuable subject.

The need for a flexible way to make courseware. A chaotic state runs with the teachers-guiding but students-centered classes, and with their joint participation in constructing lessons. Both of the practical mathematic teaching and investigating indicate the existing of the state of being chaotic in mathematic classes. As a result, teachers should adapt themselves quickly to the changing in class. None pre-designed courseware can be completely presented in the classes though they often appear in the traditional teaching activities and interrupt the routine of the teaching procedure. Thus, the great need for a flexible courseware is in great use. And besides that, a related devising and programming system is also in need. So we can set about on developing courseware about the teaching content in the classes and outside the classes for students according to the accumulated experiences.

In fact, the academic reports for different subjects and the teaching in distance education is a representation of the traditional but old-fashioned spoon-feeding education system though they apply the skills of modern technology, because they do not break through the veil of the limitation on flexibility of the modern information technology.

The employing and investigating of these principles inspires deeper exploration for the future research. They pave way for more rewarding.

5 Conclusion

The application of modern information technology to mathematic teaching has matched for a long time, and there are still problems we have to face in the long match in the future. The high development of the information technology stimulates a more effective teaching idea in mathematic education, but the reflections on the application favors our betterment of the infusion of the information technology. The topic we have made is with extensive future on how modern educational technology is effectively applied in the mathematics teaching courses of elementary and secondary schools. This paper directs the ways for the future studies with the instructive reflections.

References

1. Sun, M., Fang, Q.: Enhancing the Effectiveness of Mathematical Classroom Teaching with Information Technology by Assessment. Journal of Mathematics Education 16(1), 89–92 (2007)
2. Qian, Y.: Mathematics Teaching Effect Comparison between Traditional Teaching Instrument and Multimedia Teaching. Journal of Mathematics Education 16(2), 81–89 (2007)
3. Wen, Y., Zhou, Y.: Analysis of Factors Affecting Teachers' Integration of ICT in Mathematics Instruction. Journal of Mathematics Education 16(3), 44–48 (2007)
4. Wu, H., Ma, D.: Multi-media Technique and the "Situated Problem Based Instruction" Teaching. Journal of Mathematics Education 17(1), 87–90 (2008)
5. Wen, J., Tu, R.: Thoughts about Applying Information Technology Effectively in Mathematics Teaching. Journal of Mathematics Education 17(1), 91–94 (2008)
6. Zhang, G.: Process of Computer-based Mathematics Teaching and its Sequences. Journal of Mathematics Education 17(2), 93–96 (2008)
7. Wang, L., et al.: Problems of Computer-aided Instruction Mathematics. Journal of Mathematics Education 17(2), 97–99 (2008)
8. Liu, X.: Organizing and Implement Tactics of Mathematics Teaching Content of Teachers' College under Network Environment. Journal of Mathematics Education 17(2), 100–102 (2008)

9. Liu, X.: Research on the Strategy of Geometers Sketchpad to Helping Teaching of Mathematical Analysis. Journal of Mathematics Education 17(4), 97–101 (2008)
10. Yuan, Z.: Comparative Study on Integrating Information Technology into Mathematics Textbooks Based on Standards for Senior High School Mathematics Curriculum of China. Journal of Mathematics Education 17(3), 88–90 (2008)
11. Shang, X.: Level-analysis on the Implement of Information Technology in Mathematics Classroom Teaching. Journal of Mathematics Education 17(4), 93–96 (2008)
12. Zhu, G., Wanghui: Analysis and suggestions on the application of information technology in the mathematics teaching of high schools. Journal of Mathematics Education 17(6), 96–98 (2008)

Theory Explanation and Policy Recommendation on Inverted Socialized Support

Mei Wang, Sheng Zhou, and Fei Mao

Department of Military Finance, Military Economics Academy,
Luojiadun.122, Wuhan 430035, China
icymayybx@126.com

Abstract. The concept of inverted socialized support summarizes the all-round urgent supporting actions implemented by the army for rescue and relief to the stricken people and areas in the serious natural calamities. In this article, we discussed the origin of this phenomenon in the way of institutional analysis. At the micro level, we draw a conclusion that the army's ideology and non-symmetry information urge armyman to pursue his own self-value. At the macro level, we find that the bureaucratic institution and scale economy of the army reduce the transaction costs of the urgent support of rescue and relief which guarantee the effective implementation of urgent support by the army.

Keywords: Inverted socialized support, Production of public goods, Institutional analysis, Incentive mechanism, System of bureaucracy.

1 Definition of Inverted Socialized Support

In recent years, a phenomenon which causes people's great attention is that the army's duties have already turned from single traditional task of combat into diversified tasks of support, due to the various non-traditional threats to the national security. Civilian people are usually involved in such supporting actions, especially under the paroxysmal circumstance such as the serious natural calamities. Such repeated military behavior must be built and constructed in the steady incentive mechanism and organizational system. This text analyzes from the institutional point of view and provides a rational theoretic explanation to these military operations.

Our theoretic analysis is based on the observation that under the system of market economy, with the market as its fundamental method of resource distribution, the organizational behavior mentioned above is in contravention of the recent theoretic mainstream that the production of pubic goods must be built upon the market. According to the principle of Ostrom that the production of public goods should be separated from their offering, when serious natural calamities occur, the government only needs to be responsible for the provision and doesn't need to get involved into the production. This indicates that the rescue and relief in the natural calamities can be produced by the private organizations in way of signing contracts with the government. However, carefully observing the serious natural calamities took place in the past few years, we can easily find that in course of the rescue and relief operations,

G. Shen and X. Huang (Eds.): CSIE 2011, Part II, CCIS 153, pp. 61–66, 2011.
© Springer-Verlag Berlin Heidelberg 2011

especially at their initial stage, military organizations undoubtedly serve as the pioneer to meet the urgent need of rescue. In other words, while the serious natural calamities happen suddenly, it is the army who provides the all-round urgent support to the disaster-stricken people and areas. These military operations other than war present completely opposite mechanism to those of socialized support, so that we can call this kind of organizational behavior as the inverted socialized support.

2   Institutional Analysis of Inverted Socialized Support

There are various reasons for the formation of inverted socialized support, and this text only analyzes from the institutional angle and proposes an explanatory framework. The logical starting point of institutional analysis is the motive of people's behavior, so we begin the cognition for the phenomenon of inverted socialized support with the behavior of public department (army) at the micro level. We can't help thinking that, at the micro level why army or armyman has the motive to reuse the stricken people in disregard of gain and loss, and at the macro level what kind of organizational system and arrangement can create opportunities to change the altruistic motive into the real altruistic behavior.

2.1   Incentive Mechanism and Micro Behavior

Our analysis starts from such a prerequisite: the army is composed of the officers and soldiers who are willing to serve the people. Under this assumed condition, we put forward such a proposition that the officers and soldiers pay close attention to the embodiment of the armyman's value. We can say that the armyman's value is the core content of the army's ideology, and the pursuit of the armyman's value is the incentive element for officers and soldiers to benefit the other people without hesitation when in face of the dangerous disasters. Next, we will further the discussion to this proposition and explore the incentive mechanism behind it, especially its relationship with the developing ideology in recent years. Our basic trains of thought are that, (1) the army's mission of new period encourages the officers and soldiers to realize their own value; and (2) the information asymmetry makes the rescue and relief tasks in time of peace send out the signal to the realization of the officers and soldiers' own value. These two factors interact mutually, and offer the steady and lasting micro foundation to the army's implementation of urgent support during the natural calamities.

Our analysis starts with such an observing point that, in time of peace, the embodiment of armyman's value needs a concrete and tangible material carrier, and there are also some other difficulties in the value realization. Because in time of war, the threat to the national security mainly comes from the war, thus leads to the fact that the army's function is relatively single, the armyman's value can be reflected directly and concretely during the war. While in time of peace, people often think the war is far away from them, thus underestimate their demand for security, and mistakenly think armyman's importance is declining. The basic reason for this is the information asymmetry. Thereupon, officers and soldiers eagerly hope to send out the signal showing their own value to the civilian people through other methods. Thus the urgent support of rescue and relief can serve as an effective signal to reflect the officers and soldiers' value in the time of peace. It can be analyzed from the following two respects. First, the effective signal indicates the fundamental difference between the armyman and the main body of market economy. It cannot be denied that in front of serious natural calamities, some bodies of market economy are willing to donate money or materials, but their philanthropy is limited to the extent not causing any harm to their lives and property. Whereas rescuing people from the danger is the armyman's bounden duty, which means people's interests are the most important things. Second, the rescue and relief actions of urgent support can reflect the value of armyman in the time of peace more directly. Armyman's brave behavior in front of the serious natural calamities such as earthquake, flood and snowstorm is more noticeable, and it can immediately win the respect of civilian people. As a positive and effective signal, it will become a strong incentive leading the armyman to convert the pursuit of one's own value into the effective implementation of urgent support during the serious natural calamities.

2.2 Macro Arrangement of Institutional System

As for the institutional selection about the production of urgent support in rescue and relief tasks, it is not enough to explain the producing behavior of the army with the motive of altruism. We also need to compare the cost and benefit between the two producing behaviors of the army and of the market.

The urgent support during the serious natural calamities has the strict time limit and the character of scale. So, the urgent support for the natural calamities must race with time. Obviously, in front of the large-scale natural calamity, the individual effort of small social organizations seems feeble and weak. Therefore on the premise of large-scale economy, our research can be nailed down to the comparison of the producing efficiency between the army and the large-scale organizations in the market. To solve this problem, we need to transfer the studying angle from the micro aspect to the macro aspect. Observing form the angle of institutional system, the difference between the army and large-scale organizations in the market is that, the army has a bureaucratic institutional framework of typical style, adopting the mechanism of centralized decision and administrational coordination, while the large-scale organizations in the market are composed of a plurality of economic subjects with the flat institutional framework, usually adopting the mechanism of dispersed decision and marketing coordination.

It is obvious in reality that in the rescue and relief operations of serious natural calamities, the greatest challenge is not the deficiency of material supply, but the demand for fast, high-efficient and accurate accomplishment of the various sophisticated tasks with the comprehensive targets. To realize this, the information transmission, organization and coordination must be the key factors. Whether the information transmission is unobstructed and whether the organization and coordination is flexible have close connections with the institutional framework. Here we use the Theory of Transaction Cost from Coase for the analysis. Coase held that the transaction cost cannot be zero in the real world [1]. Likewise, during the rescue and relief operations in the natural calamity, there exist high costs for finding out the situation of stricken place, rescuing the wounded and so on. Because the serious natural calamities always inflict heavy losses on the public infrastructure in many fields such as the railway, highway, electricity and communication, all of this cause the failure of market. Even if some functions of the market run effective, the high cost of would make the transmission of information and the coordination of system unpractical. By contrast, the army is a composite unit possessing multifunction of communication, transportation, military supplies, medical treatment, etc. Under the abominable condition, the army can still rely on one's own strength to realize the collection and analysis of information, and the bureaucratic structure of the army can guarantee the fast transmission of information and the high-efficient coordination among various supporting strengths. Accordingly, the bureaucratic framework of the army can greatly reduce the transaction costs of dispersive decision and execution.

3 Applicable Border of Inverted Socialized Support

The relief and rescue tasks in the natural calamity are implemented stage by stage, and the inverted socialized support is only applicable to the stage of urgent support. It is determined by the strict time limit of urgent support. When the factor of time is not the constraint condition any more, the inverted socialized support will withdraw from the supporting field, and the socialized support will resume its basic position. We still use the Theory of Transaction Cost to explain this argument.

Suppose that we do not consider the constraint condition of time, as described in the traditional new classical model, producer produces goods according to the consumer's preference and adjust the output according to the market price. The output is determined when the marginal cost equals to the marginal benefit, thus the maximization of profit is realized. From this view point, adopting the market mechanism to produce the public goods (rescue) is undoubtedly the most efficient method. However, considering the time-constrain, this conclusion is no longer correct, because the influence of the transaction cost emerges constantly. At this moment, the normal running condition of the market is destroyed, and the price mechanism fails. In order to conclude the transaction, producers have to pay more transaction costs in searching demand information, looking for trading target than those in the sound market; he also pays a large amount of extra costs for the negative effect on the dealing activities because of the destruction of market mechanism. And with the increasing effect of time-constraint, transaction costs will become the hindrance to concluding the transaction even more. So in this case, the rescue and relief offered by the market mechanism may not have the optimum efficiency. Consequently the socialized support is only applicable to the later stage of rescue and relief tasks, and is not suitable for the stage of urgent support.

In the same way, if the time-constraint is not considered, the efficiency of the army producing the support after calamities is much lower than the latter under the condition of mature labor division and market operation. However, if the factor of time joins in, the conclusion also needs revising in the real world. The bureaucratic institutional structure make the resource distribution and production process inside of the army be arranged according to the administrative decrees and plans, thus greatly reducing the transaction costs of rescue and relief operations. So we can say that, the inverted socialized support is applicable to the stage of urgent support in the rescue and relief tasks, and not suitable to the later stage thereof.

In sum, in the condition of strong time-constraint, transaction cost is the key factor to determine the producing efficiency, and then the method of inverted socialized support should be chose. When the condition of time-constraint is loosening gradually, the factor of the transaction cost becomes weak, whereas the factor of management cost and production cost becomes strong little by little, and then we should choose the method of socialized support. But what is the border for the supporting method converting from inverted socialized support into socialized support? Now, we will illuminate it with a simple model.

If the time is expressed with Δt; the transaction cost is expressed with AC, and at the same time AC is supposed to be a definite value with the purpose to conclude a transaction; the management cost and production cost in unit time are expressed with $(MC+PC)_i$, among which $i=1$ denotes the organization of army, $i=2$ denotes the organization of enterprise, the analysis is as follows according to the above text.

$$(MC + PC)_1 > (MC + PC)_2 \tag{1}$$

The total cost of inverted socialized support for the rescue and relief tasks of urgent support, i.e. TC_1 is above.

$$TC_1 = \Delta t \times (MC + PC)_1 \tag{2}$$

The total cost of socialized support in the same period, i.e. TC_2 is above.

$$TC_2 = \frac{AC}{\Delta t} + \Delta t \times (MC + PC)_2 \tag{3}$$

When

$$\Delta t < \sqrt{\frac{AC}{[(MC + PC)_1 - (MC + PC)_2]}}, \tag{4}$$

$TC_1 < TC_2$, we adopt the inverted socialized support. And when

$$\Delta t > \sqrt{\frac{AC}{[(MC + PC)_1 - (MC + PC)_2]}}, \tag{5}$$

$TC_2 < TC_1$, we adopt the socialized support.

As a result, $\Delta t^* = \sqrt{\dfrac{AC}{[(MC + PC)_1 - (MC + PC)_2]}}$ is the transition point between the inverted socialized support and socialized support.

4 Conclusion

This text analyzes from the institutional angle of view and puts forward that the phenomenon of inverted socialized support is the product chosen by the production system of public goods. According to the principle of Ostrom that the production of public goods should be separated from their offering, the rescue and relief in the urgent calamities can be produced by either the public department or the private department. The final selection of the production system is determined by the comparison of producing efficiency between two systems. Our research indicates the reason of choosing the inverted socialized support at the stage of urgent support is that, at the micro level the army's ideology and non-symmetry information urge armyman to pursue his own self-value, and at the macro level the bureaucratic institution and scale economy of the army reduce the transaction costs of the urgent support of rescue and relief, and consequently guarantee the immediate and effective implementation of urgent support by the army. This study has important significance both in theory and in practice.

First, the great natural calamities took place frequently all over the world in recent years. In face of the diversified threats and challenges of natural calamities, most western countries take the militarized rescue (public production) as a tendency, and the inverted socialized support of the PLA is also a measure tanken to tackle the above circumstance. The practice of snow disaster and earthquake calamity of 2008 in China fully indicates that the immediate and effective arrangement and coordination are the key elements for the urgent rescue and relief in the natural calamities.

Second, the inverted socialized support and the socialized support are applicable to the different circumstances, and the selection of supporting method depends on the comparison between the saving transaction cost and the extra management cost and production cost of the inverted socialized support. When the saving transaction cost is higher than the extra management cost and production cost, we can adopt the inverted socialized support, and when the saving transaction cost is lower than the extra management cost and production cost, it is uneconomical to implement the inverted socialized support.

Third, because the normal order of operation is upset or destroyed in wartime, the transaction expense in the market rises sharply. At this moment, the war finance can only implement the mode of the inverted socialized support.

Fourth, responding to various security threats and accomplishing diverse military tasks becomes an important part of military missions in the new period, so the research on how to further the urgent support of army is of top priority. We should roundly summarize the successful experience and flaws in the previous rescue and relief operations. According to the demand of urgent support, we should establish the urgent mechanism of quick reaction and the united mechanism of army-and-civilian operation. Besides, we should improve the institutional arrangement of military finance in as to enhance the ablity of urgent support.

Reference

1. Coase, R.H.: The New Institutional Economics. Journal of Institutional and Theoretical Economics, 229–231 (March 1984)

The Biorthogonality Traits of Vector-Valued Multivariant Small-Wave Wraps with Poly-Scale Dilation Factor

Yongmei Niu and Xuejian Sun

School of Education, Nanyang Institute of Technology, Nanyang 473000, China
hjk123zas@126.com

Abstract. In this paper, we introduce a class of vector-valued wavelet wraps with poly-scale dilation factor for vector multivariant function space. A procedure for designing a class of biorthogonal vector multivariant wavelet wraps according to a pair of biorthogonal vector scaling functions, is presented and their biorthogonality traits are characterized by virtue of matrix theory, time-frequency analysis method, and operator theory. Three biorthogonality formulas concerning these wavelet wraps are derived. Moreover, it is shown how to gain new Riesz bases of space $L^2(R^s, R^v)$ from these small-wave wraps.

Keywords: Poly-scale dilation factor, operator theory, iteration method, Riesz bases, biorthogonality traits, small-wave wraps.

1 Introduction

The last two decades or so have witnessed the development of wavelet theory. The main advantage of wavelets is their time-frequency localization property. Already they have led to exciting applications in signal analysis [1], fractals [2] and image processing [3], and so on. Wavelet wraps, owing to their nice characteristics, have been widely applied to signal processing [4], code theory, image compression, solving integral equation and so on. Coifman and Meyer firstly introduced the notion of univariate orthogonal wavelet packets. The introduction for biorthogonal wavelet packets attributes to Cohen and Daubechies. Vector-valued wavelets are a class of special multiwavelets. Chen [6] introduced the notion of orthogonal vector-valued wavelets and investigated the properties orthogonal vector-valued wavelet packets [7], However, vector-valued wavelets and multiwavelets are different in the following sense. For example, prefiltering is usually required for discrete multiwavelet trans-forms [8] but not necessary for discrete vector-valued transforms. Examples of vector-valued signals are video images. Therefore, it is useful for us to study vector-valued wavelets in representations of signals. It is known that the majority of infor-mation is multidimensional information. Shen [9] introduced multivariate orthogonal wavelets which may be used in a wider field. Thus, it is necessary to generalize the concept of multivariate wavelet wraps to the case of multivariate vector-valued wavelets. The goal of this paper is to give the definition and the construction of biorh -ogonal vector-valued mall-wave wraps and construct several new Riesz bases of space $L^2(R^s, R^v)$.

G. Shen and X. Huang (Eds.): CSIE 2011, Part II, CCIS 153, pp. 67–72, 2011.
© Springer-Verlag Berlin Heidelberg 2011

2 Preliminaries on Vector-Valued Function Space

Let us introduce several notations. R and C stand for all real and all complex numbers, respectively. Z and N denote the set of integers and positive integers, respectively. Set

$Z_+ = \{0\} \cup N, s, u \in N$ and $m, s \geq 2$, $Z^s = \{(v_1, v_2, \cdots, v_s) : v_r \in Z, r = 1, 2, \cdots, s\}$, $Z_+^s = \{(n_1, n_2, \cdots, n_s) : n_r \in Z_+, r = 1, 2, \cdots, s\}$. For any $X, X_1, X_2 \subset R^s, mX = \{mx : x \in X\}$, $X_1 + X_2 = \{x_1 + x_2 : x \in X_1, x \in X_2\}$, $X_1 - X_2 = \{x_1 - x_2 : x_1 \in X_1, x_2 \in X_2\}$. There exist m^s elements $\mu_0, \mu_1, \ldots, \mu_{m^s-1}$ in Z_+^s by the finite group theory such that

$$Z^s = \bigcup_{\mu \in \Gamma_0} (\mu + mZ^s) ; \quad (\mu_1 + mZ^s) \cap (\mu_2 + mZ^s) = \phi,$$

where $\Gamma_0 = \{v_0, v_1, \ldots, v_{m^s-1}\}$ denotes the set of all different representative elements in the quotient qroup $Z^s / (mZ^s)$ and μ_1, μ_2 denote two arbitrary distinct elements in Γ_0 .Set $v_0 = \underline{0}$,where $\underline{0}$ is the null of Z_+^s. Let $\Gamma = \Gamma_0 - \{\underline{0}\}$ and Γ, Γ_0 be two index sets. By $L^2(R^s, C^u)$,we denote the aggregate of all vector-valued functions $\hbar(x)$, i.e., $L^2(R^s, R^u) := \{\hbar(x) = (h_1(x), h_2(x), \cdots, h_u(x))^T : h_l(x) \in L^2(R^s), l = 1, 2, \ldots, u\}$, where T means the transpose of a vector. Video images and digital films are examples of vector valued functions where $h_l(x)$ in the above $\hbar(x)$ denotes the pixel on the l column at the point x . For arbitrary $\hbar(x) \in L^2(R^s, R^u)$, Define $\|\hbar\| := (\sum_{l=1}^u \int_{R^s} |h_l(x)|^2 dx)^{1/2}$, its integration is defined to be $\int_{R^s} \hbar(x) dx = (\int_{R^s} h_1(x) dx, \int_{R^s} h_2(x) dx \cdots, \int_{R^s} h_u(x) dx)^T$. The fourier transform of $\hbar(x)$ is defined as $\hat{\hbar}(\gamma) := \int_{R^s} \hbar(x) e^{-ix \cdot \gamma} dx$,where $x \cdot \gamma$ denotes the inner product of real vectors x and γ . For $F, G \in L^2(R^s, R^u)$, their symbol inner product is defined by

$$[F(\cdot), G(\cdot)] := \int_{R^s} F(x) G(x)^* dx , \tag{1}$$

Definition 1. We say that a pair of vector-valued multivariant functions $\hbar(x), \tilde{\hbar}(x) \in L^2(R^s, R^u)$ are biorthogonal ones, if their translations satisfy

$$[\hbar(\cdot), \tilde{\hbar}(\cdot - k)] = \delta_{0,k} I_u, \quad k \in Z^s , \tag{2}$$

where I_u is the $u \times u$ identity matrix and $\delta_{0,k}$ is the general Kronecker symbol.

A vector-valued multiresolution analysis of the space $L^2(R^s, R^u)$ is a nested sequence of closed subspaces $\{Y_l\}_{l \in Z}$ such that (i) $Y_l \in Y_{l+1}, \forall l \in Z$; (ii) $\bigcap_{l \in Z} Y_l = \{0\}$ and $\bigcup_{l \in Z} Y_l$ is dense in $L^2(R^s, R^u)$,where 0 denotes an zero vector of space C^u ; (iii) $H(x) \in Y_l \Leftrightarrow H(mx) \in Y_{l+1}, \forall l \in Z$: (iv) there exists

$F(x) \in Y_0$,called a vector-valued scaling function, such that its translates $\{F_k(x) := F(x-k), k \in Z^s\}$ constitutes a Riesz basis of subspace Y_0 .

Since $F(x) \in Y_0 \subset Y_1$ by the above definition, there exists a finitely supported sequence of constant $u \times u$ matrice $\{P_k\}_{k \in Z^s} \in \ell^2(Z^s)^{u \times u}$ such that

$$F(x) = \sum_{k \in Z^s} P_k F(mx - k). \tag{3}$$

$$m^s P(\gamma) = \sum_{k \in Z^s} P_k \cdot \exp\{-ik \cdot \gamma\}, \quad \gamma \in R^s . \tag{4}$$

where $P(\gamma)$, which is a $2\pi Z^s$ periodic function, is called a symbol of $F(x)$. Thus, equation (4) becomes

$$\hat{F}(m\gamma) = P(\gamma)\hat{F}(\gamma), \quad \lambda \in R^s . \tag{5}$$

Let $X_j, j \in Z$ be the direct complementary subspace of Y_j in Y_{j+1} . Assume that there exist $m^s - 1$ vectorvallued functions $\Psi_\mu(x) \in L^2(R^s, C^u), \mu \in \Gamma$ such that their translations and dilations form a Riesz basis of X_j ,i.e.,

$$X_j = \overline{(Span\{\Psi_\mu(m^j \cdot -k): k \in Z^s, \mu \in \Gamma\})}, \quad j \in Z . \tag{6}$$

Since $\Psi_v(x) \in X_0 \subset Y_1, v \in \Gamma$,there exist $m^s - 1$ finite supported sequences of constant $u \times u$ matrice $\{B_k^{(v)}\}_{k \in Z^s}$ such that

$$\Psi_\mu(x) = \sum_{k \in Z^s} B_k^{(\mu)} F(mx - k), \quad \mu \in \Gamma . \tag{7}$$

Taking the Fourier transform for the both sides of (9) gives

$$\hat{\Psi}_\mu(\gamma) = B^{(\mu)}(\gamma/m)\hat{\Phi}(\gamma/m), \quad \gamma \in R^s, \quad \mu \in \Gamma . \tag{8}$$

$$B^{(\mu)}(\gamma) = \frac{1}{m^s} \sum_{k \in Z^s} B_k^{(\mu)} \cdot \exp(-ik \cdot \gamma), \quad \mu \in \Gamma . \tag{9}$$

We say that $\Psi_\mu(x), \tilde{\Psi}_\mu(x) \in L^2(R^s, R^u), \mu \in \Gamma$ are pairs of biorthogonal vector-valued small-waves associated with a pair of biorthogonal vector-valued scaling functions $F(x)$ and $\tilde{F}(x)$,if the family $\{\Psi_\mu(x-k), k \in Z^s, \mu \in \Gamma\}$ is a Riesz basis of subspace X_0, and

$$\langle F(\cdot), \tilde{\Psi}_\mu(\cdot - k)\rangle = 0, \quad \mu \in \Gamma, \quad k \in Z^s . \tag{10}$$

$$\langle \tilde{F}(\cdot), \Psi_\mu(\cdot - k)\rangle = 0, \quad \mu \in \Gamma, \quad k \in Z^s . \tag{11}$$

$$\langle \Psi_\rho(\cdot), \tilde{\Psi}(\cdot - k)\rangle = \delta_{\rho,\mu}\delta_{0,k}I_u, \quad \rho, \mu \in \Gamma . \tag{12}$$

Similar to (5) and (9) , there exist m^s finite supported sequences of $u \times u$ constant matrice $\{P_k\}_{k \in Z^s}$ and $\{B_k\}_{k \in Z^s}$, $\mu \in \Gamma$ such that $\tilde{F}(x)$ and $\tilde{\Psi}_\mu(x)$ satisfy the following refinement equations:

$$\tilde{F}(x) = \sum_{k \in Z^s} \tilde{P}_k \tilde{F}(mx - k), \tag{13}$$

$$\tilde{\Psi}_\mu(x) = \sum_{k \in Z^s} \tilde{B}_k^{(\mu)} \tilde{F}(mx - k), \ \mu \in \Gamma. \tag{14}$$

3 The Biorthogonality Traits of Multivariant Small-Wave Wraps

To introduce vector-valued small-wave wraps, we set

$$G_0(x) = F(x), \ G_\mu(x) = \Psi_\mu(x) \ , \ \tilde{G}_0(x) = \tilde{F}(x) \ , \ \tilde{G}_\mu(x) = \tilde{\Psi}_\mu(x) \ ,$$
$$Q_k^{(0)} = P_k, \ Q_k^{(\mu)} = B_k^{(\mu)}, \tilde{Q}_k^{(\mu)} = \tilde{P}_k, \tilde{Q}_k = \tilde{B}_k \ , \ \mu \in \Gamma, k \in Z^s. \text{ For any }$$

$\alpha \in Z_+^s$ and the given vector-valued biorthogonal scaling functions $G_{(0)}(x)$ and $\tilde{G}_{(0)}(x)$, iteratively define, respectively,

$$G_\alpha(x) = G_{m\sigma + \mu}(x) = \sum_{k \in Z^s} Q_k^{(\mu)} G_\sigma(mx - k) , \tag{15}$$

$$\tilde{G}_\alpha(x) = \tilde{G}_{m\sigma + \mu}(x) = \sum_{k \in Z^s} \tilde{Q}_k^{(\mu)} \tilde{G}_\sigma(mx - k) \tag{16}$$

where $\mu \in \Gamma_0, \sigma \in Z_+^s$ is the unique element s.t. $\alpha = m\sigma + \mu, \mu \in \Gamma_0$ holds.

Definition 2. We say that $\{G_{m\sigma + \mu}(x), \sigma \in Z_+^s, \mu \in \Gamma_0\}$ and $\{\tilde{G}_{m\sigma + \mu}(x), \sigma \in Z_+^s, \mu \in \Gamma_0\}$ are vector-valued small-wave wraps with respect to a pair of biorthogonal vector-valued scaling functions $G_0(x)$ and $\tilde{G}_0(x)$, respective-ly, where $G_{m\sigma + \mu}(x)$ and $\tilde{G}_{m\sigma + \mu}(x)$ are given by (15) and (16),respectively.

Taking the Fourier transform for the both sides of (15) and (16) yields, respectively,

$$\hat{G}_{m\sigma + \mu}(\gamma) = Q^{(\mu)}(\gamma / m) \hat{G}_\sigma(\gamma / m), \ \mu \in \Gamma_0, \tag{17}$$

$$\tilde{G}_{\sigma + \mu}(\gamma / m) = Q^{(\mu)}(\gamma / m) \tilde{G}_\sigma(\gamma / m), \ \mu \in \Gamma_0 \tag{18}$$

$$Q^{(\mu)}(\gamma) = \frac{1}{m^s} \sum_{k \in Z^s} Q_k^{(\mu)} \ \exp\{-ik \cdot \gamma\}, \ \mu \in \Gamma_0, \tag{19}$$

$$\tilde{Q}^{(\mu)}(\gamma) = \frac{1}{m^s} \sum_{k \in Z^s} \tilde{Q}_k^{(\mu)} \ \exp\{-ik \cdot \gamma\}, \ \mu \in \Gamma_0. \tag{20}$$

Lemma 1[18]. Let $F(x), \tilde{F}(x) \in L^2(R^s, R^u)$. Then they are biorthogonal ones if and only if $\sum_{k \in Z^s} \hat{F}(\gamma + 2k\pi) \tilde{F}(\gamma + 2k\pi)^* = I_u$.

Lemma 2[8]. Assume that $G_\mu(x), \bar{G}_\mu(x) \in L^2(R^s, R^u)$, $\mu \in \Gamma$ are pairs of biorthogonal vector-valued small-wave wraps associated with a pair of biorthogonal scaling functions $G_0(x)$ and $\tilde{G}_0(x)$. Then, for $\mu, v \in \Gamma_0$, we have

$$\sum_{\rho \in \Gamma_0} Q^{(\mu)}((\gamma + 2\rho\pi)/m)\tilde{Q}^{(v)}((\gamma + 2\rho\pi)/m)^* = \delta_{\mu,v} I_u. \tag{21}$$

Lemma 3[8]. Suppose $\{G_\beta(x), \beta \in Z_+^s\}$ and are vector-valued small-wave wraps with respect to a pair of biorthogonal vector-valued functions $G_0(x)$ and $\tilde{G}_0(x)$, respectively. Then, for $\beta \in Z_+^s$, $\mu, v \in \Gamma_0$, we have

$$< G_{m\beta+\mu}(\cdot), \tilde{G}_{m\beta+v}(\cdot - k) >= \delta_{0,k}\delta_{\mu,v}I_u, \quad k \in Z^s. \tag{22}$$

Theorem 1. If $\{G_\alpha(x), \alpha \in Z_+^s\}$ and $\{\tilde{G}_\alpha(x), \alpha \in Z_+^s\}$ are vector-valued small-wave wraps with respect to a pair of biorthogonal vector-valued scaling functions $G_0(x)$ and $\tilde{G}_0(x)$, then for any $\alpha, \sigma \in Z_+^s$, we have

$$\left\langle G_\alpha(\cdot), \tilde{G}_\sigma(\cdot - k) \right\rangle = \delta_{\alpha,\sigma}\delta_{0,k}I_u, \quad k \in Z^s. \tag{23}$$

Proof. When $\alpha = \sigma$, (23) follow by Lemma 3 as $\alpha \neq \sigma$ and $\alpha, \sigma \in \Gamma_0$, it follows from Lemma 3 that (23) holds, too. Assuming that α is not equal to β, as well as at least one of $\{\alpha, \sigma\}$ doesn't belong to Γ_0, we rewrite α, σ as $\alpha = m\alpha_1$, $+\rho_1, \sigma = m\sigma_1 + \mu_1$, where $\rho_1, \mu_1 \in \Gamma_0$. **Case 1.** If $\alpha_1 = \sigma_1$, then $\rho_1 \neq \mu_1$, (23) follows by virtue of (17), (18) as well as Lemma 1 and Lemma 2, i.e.,

$$\left\langle G_\alpha(\cdot), \tilde{G}_\sigma(\cdot - k) \right\rangle = \frac{1}{(2\pi)^s} \int_{R^s} \hat{G}_{m\alpha_1+\rho_1}(\gamma)\hat{\tilde{G}}_{m\sigma_1+\mu_1}(\gamma)^* \cdot \exp\{ik \cdot \gamma\}d\gamma$$

$$= \frac{1}{(2\pi)^s} \int_{[0,2\pi]^s} \sum_{\sigma \in \Gamma_0} Q^{(\rho_1)}[(\gamma + 2\pi u)/m] \cdot \tilde{Q}^{(\mu_1)}[(\gamma + 2\pi u)/m]^* \cdot \exp\{ik \cdot \gamma\}d\gamma$$

$$= \frac{1}{(2\pi)^s} \int_{[0,2\pi]^s} \delta_{\rho_1,\mu_1}I_u \cdot \exp\{ik \cdot \gamma\}d\gamma = O.$$

Case 2. If $\alpha_1 \neq \sigma_1$, order $\alpha_1 = m\alpha_2 + \rho_2$, $\sigma_1 = m\sigma_2 + \mu_2$, where $\alpha_2, \sigma_2 \in Z_+^s$, and ρ_2, $\sigma_2 \in \Gamma_0$. Provided that $\alpha_2 = \sigma_2$, then $\rho_2 = \sigma_2$. Similar to Case 1, (23) can be established. When $\alpha_2 \neq \sigma_2$ we order $\alpha_2 = m\alpha_3 + \mu_3$, $\sigma_2 = m\sigma_3 + \mu_3$, where $\alpha_3, \sigma_3 \in Z_+^s, \rho_3, \sigma_3 \in \Gamma_0$. Thus, after taking finite steps (denoted by k), we obtain $\alpha_k, \sigma_k \in \Gamma_0$, and $\beta_k, \mu_k \in \Gamma_0$. If $\alpha_k = \sigma_k$, then $\beta_k \neq \mu_k$ Similar to the Case 1, (23) follows. If $\alpha_k \neq \sigma_k$, then it gets from (10)-(12):

$$(2\pi)^s \left\langle G_\alpha(\cdot), \tilde{G}_\sigma(\cdot - k) \right\rangle = \int_{R^s} \hat{G}_{\alpha_1}(\gamma)\hat{\tilde{G}}_{\sigma_1}(\gamma)^* \cdot e^{ik \cdot \gamma}d\gamma = \int_{R^s} \hat{G}_{m\sigma_1 - k_1}(\gamma)\hat{\tilde{G}}_{m\beta_1+\mu_1}(\gamma)^* \cdot \exp\{ik \cdot \gamma\}d\gamma$$

$$= \int_{R'} Q^{(\rho_1)}(\gamma/m)\hat{G}_{a_1}(\gamma/m)\bar{\hat{G}}_{\sigma_1}(\gamma/m)^* \cdot \tilde{Q}^{(u_1)}(\gamma/m)^* \cdot \exp\{ik \cdot \gamma\}d\omega = \cdots\cdots$$

$$= \int_{[0,2\cdot4^k\pi]^s} \{\prod_{t=1}^{k}Q^{(\rho_1)}(\frac{\gamma}{m^l})\}\{\sum_{u\in Z^s}\hat{G}_{\alpha_k}(\frac{\gamma}{m^l}+2u\pi)\}\cdot\bar{\hat{G}}_{\sigma_k}(\frac{\gamma}{m^l}+2u\pi)^*\}\cdot\{\prod_{l=1}^{k}\tilde{Q}(\mu_l)(\frac{\gamma}{m^l})\}\cdot e^{ik\cdot\lambda}d\gamma$$

$$= \int_{[0,2\cdot m^k\pi]^s} \{\prod_{l=1}^{k}Q^{(\rho_1)}(\frac{\gamma}{m^l})\}\cdot\{\prod_{l=1}^{k}\tilde{Q}^{(u_1)}(\frac{\gamma}{m^l})\}^* \cdot \exp\{-ik\cdot\gamma\}d\gamma = O \ .$$

Therefore, for any $a,\sigma\in Z_+^s$, result (23) is established.

Theorem 2. The family of vector-valued functions $\{G_\alpha(\cdot-k),\ k\in Z^s,\ \alpha\in\Lambda_m\}$ forms a Riesz basis of $D^m X_0$. In particular, $\{G_\alpha(\cdot-k),\ k\in Z^s,\ \alpha\in Z_+^s\}$ consitutes Riesz basis of space $L^2(R^s,R^u)$.

4 Conclusion

The notion of biorthogonal vector-valued higherdimensional wavelet packets is introduced. Their biorthogonality property is characterized by virtue of timefrequency analysis method, matrix theory and operator theory, and three biorthogonality formulas regarding these small-wave wraps are obtained.

References

1. He, H., Cheng, S.: Home network power-line communication signal processing based on wavelet packet analysis. IEEE Trans. Power Delivery 20(3), 1879–1885 (2005)
2. Iovane, G., Giordano, P.: Wavelet and multiresolution analysis: Nature of ε^∞ Cantorian space-time. Chaos, Solitons & Fractals 32(3), 896–910 (2007)
3. Zhang, N., Wu, X.: Lossless Compression of Color Mosaic Images. IEEE Trans. Image Processing 15(16), 1379–1388 (2006)
4. Philippe, P., Saint-martin, F., Lever, M.: Wavelet packet filterbanks for low time delay audio coding. IEEE Trans. Speech and Audio Processing 7(3), 310–322 (1999)
5. Yang, S., Cheng, Z.: A-scale multiple orthogonal wavelet packets. Mathematica Applicata 13(1), 61–65 (2000) (in chinese)
6. Chen, Q., Cheng, Z.: A study on compactly supported orthogonal vector-valued wavelets and wavelet packets. Chaos, Solitons & Fractals 31(4), 1024–1034 (2007)
7. Chen, Q., Cheng, Z., Feng, X.: Multivariate Biorthogonal Multiwavelet packets. Math-Ematica Applicata (in Chinese) 18(3), 358–364 (2005)
8. Xia, X.G., Geronimo, J.S., Hardin, D.P., Suter, B.W.: Design of prefilters for discrete multiwavelet transforms. IEEE Trans. Signal Processing 44(1), 25–35 (1996)
9. Shen, Z.: Nontensor product wavelet packets L_2 (R^s). SIAM Math. Anal., 26(4), 1061-1074 (1995)

Combined Contract of Buyback and Pricing Flexibility to Coordinating Supply Chain Under Price Updating

LinaYin and Qi Xu

Glorious Sun School of Business and Management, Donghua University,
200051, Shanghai, China
lnyin@mail.dhu.edu.cn, xuqi@dhu.edu.cn

Abstract. The supply chain contracts are an essential methodology to the coordination of supply chain. This paper focuses on the jointly contracts of buyback and quantity flexibility to study coordination mechanisms in a supply chain. In the fix price case, buy back contracts play an important role to collaborate supply chain system's profit. In the price setting case, however, it is difficult to realize perfect coordination. In this paper, we investigate the model of jointly contracts by the analysis partier's expected profits of three scenarios. The first is none of supply contracts is adopted. The second is under the adoption of buyback contracts. The third is under the adoption of jointly contract of buyback and quantity flexible. In doing so, we illustrated the benefit of the joint adoption contracts to the coordination of supply chain and flexible the arrangement of profits between suppliers and retailers.

Keywords: Buyback contract, Pricing flexibility contract, Demand-related price, Supply chain coordination.

1 Introduction

Enterprises in a supply chain need to coordinate and cooperate with others to achieve the system's optimization and the overall competitiveness of the supply chain since the complex and volatile external environment in the increasingly competitive global market. Supply chain contract, which is able to improve the performance of the supply chain, is one of the coordinating mechanisms. Supply chain contract is defined in [1] as a coordination mechanism that provides incentives to all of its members so that the decentralized supply chain behaves nearly or exactly the same as the integrated one. Under the incentives and constraints of the contract, both the suppliers and buyers could achieve coordination in order quantities or price at different levels. Supply chain contracts like Revenue-Sharing, Buy-Back, Quantity-Discounts, Pricing-Flexible and Backup-Agreement are quite common in the literature. The framework of the contracts is usually different because of the impact of the product feature, game power of both sides in the profit distribution, demand change and other factors.

Tsay [2] and Cachon [3] discussed coordination of supply chain in the case of unchanged sales price according to the above contracts. Bellantuono [4] considered a joint

G. Shen and X. Huang (Eds.): CSIE 2011, Part II, CCIS 153, pp. 73–79, 2011.
© Springer-Verlag Berlin Heidelberg 2011

adoption of revenue sharing and advanced booking discount program. Moutaz [5] studied a supply chain problem under the condition that the demand is price-independent and the multiple discounts can be used to sell excess inventory. Pasternack [6] proposed pricing and return policy could achieve channel coordination for the products with short shelf or demand life. These studies has produced a very important academic influence on the researches of supply coordination using supply contracts, however, a certain type of supply contract clearly has its limitations in the case of changing market.

In this paper, we consider a combined contract of buyback and pricing flexibility with changing price which is demand-related. The contract achieved coordination through: (1) the suppliers buy-back the unsold products at an agreed price in the end of the sale season; (2) the flexible customization of the retail price. In this paper, we consider a two-stage supply contract between a supplier (S) and a retailer (R), and discuss the supply chain coordination in the following three cases: without any contract, with a single buy-back contract and with the combined contract.

2   The General Case

The general case refers to the supplier and retailer develop their strategies respectively to maximize their own profits without any supply contract. The supplier determines the wholesale price w first, and then the retailer determines his optimal order quantity Q. Suppose x as the random demand, $f(\cdot)$ as the probability density function of the demand and $F(\cdot)$ as the probability distribution function. c is the production cost incurred by the supplier, p is the retail price and s is the salvage value of product not sold in the retail market, and it is constrained by $s < c < w < p$.

If the order is greater than the demand ($Q \geq x$), the retailer's expected profit is:

$$E_1 Z_R(Q) = \int_0^Q [(p-w)x - (w-s)(Q-x)] f(x) dx . \tag{1}$$

If the order is less than the demand ($Q < x$), the retailer's expected profit is:

$$E_1 Z_R(Q) = \int_Q^\infty (p-w) \cdot Q \cdot f(x) dx . \tag{2}$$

Simultaneous Eq. 1 and Eq. 2, we can get the retailer's expected profit as:

$$E_1 Z_R(Q) = \int_0^Q [(p-w)x - (w-s)(Q-x)] f(x) dx + \int_Q^\infty (p-w) \cdot Q \cdot f(x) dx$$

$$= (p-w)Q + (p-s) \int_0^Q x f(x) dx - (p-s) \int_0^Q Q f(x) dx \tag{3}$$

To get the order quantity Q which leads to maximum expected profit, we try to find the derivative of Eq.3 using the derivation formula of the parametric variable's integral equation, there is:

$$\frac{dE_1 Z_R(Q)}{dQ} = (p-w) + (p-s)Q f(Q) - (p-s)[\int_0^Q f(x) dx + Q f(Q)]$$

$$= (p-w) - (p-s) \int_0^Q f(x) dx \tag{4}$$

Of which $E_1Z_R(Q)$ is concave on Q, so that $\dfrac{dE_1Z_R(Q)}{dQ} = 0$, and we can get the optimal order quantity as:

$$Q^* = F^{-1}(\frac{p-w}{p-s}) \tag{5}$$

For $\dfrac{d^2E_1Z_R(Q)}{dQ^2} = -(p-s)f(Q) < 0$, the retailer achieves the maximum expected profit while the order quantity equals to Q^*. Then the supplier's profit is determined by the retailer's optimal order quantity Q^*, and his maximum expected profit is:

$$E_1Z_S(Q^*) = (w-c)Q^* \tag{6}$$

The expected profit of the supply chain system is the addition of both the supplier and the retailer's, that is:

$$E_1Z(Q^*) = E_1Z_R(Q^*) + E_1Z_S(Q^*). \tag{7}$$

Obviously, the supplier is in a passive situation in the case of non-contract to coordinate, his profitability depends on the retailer's order quantity. Then we would compare the retailer's optimal order quantity of decentralized decision-making without coordination with the one of the centralized supply chain system. In the centralized control system, the retailer and the supplier is a community of interests, they are willing to have unified decision-making and operation, so the expected profit of the supply chain could up to the optimal, while the retailer's order quantity gets optimal. Pity to know that this model is quite rare in the actual operation, however, it is usually used as a standard of perfect coordination in the theoretical study and management practice to explain the effectiveness of the coordination among the members in the given supply chain.

Suppose $\phi(x)$ is the expect sales in the centralize-controlled supply chain, that is:

$$\varphi(x) = \int_0^Q xf(x)dx + \int_Q^\infty Qf(x)dx = [1 - F(Q)]Q + \int_0^Q xf(x)dx. \tag{8}$$

We can get the total expected profit of the supply chain system similarly, it is:

$$EZ(Q) = (p-c)Q - (p-s)\int_0^Q F(x)dx. \tag{9}$$

Set $\dfrac{p-c}{p-s} = F(Q)$, then the optimal order quantity under the centralized system is:

$$Q^0 = F^{-1}(\frac{p-c}{p-s}). \tag{10}$$

Compare Eq.10 with Eq.5, it is reasonable that $p > w > c > s$ is always established, so there is always $Q^* < Q^0$. That is, the retailer's optimal order quantity in the case of decentralized and non-contract is always less than the one in a centralized system, and leads to "Double Marginalization" as a result. So we can conclude that the retailer's optimal decision is unable to make the whole supply chain to achieve optimal, the system has not been coordinated.

3   The Case with Buy-Back Contract

When there is a buy-back contract between them, the supplier would determine the wholesale price w himself and agreed upon the buy-back price b with the retailer. He would buy back part of the unsold goods at a price b from the retailer at the end of the sale season and the unit salvage value is s. The retailer would determine his order quantity to achieve the largest profit based on the buy-back price. In this case, the supplier could determine the production planning, the wholesale price and the buy-back price to the maximum profit according to the retailer's information like ordering cost, selling price and demand distribution. Assume c as the marginal cost of the supplier, there are $s \le b$ and $c \le w \le p$ to ensure the effectiveness of buy-back contract, then:

The retailer's expected profit with buy-back contract in the decentralized supply chain system is:

$$E_2 Z_R(Q) = \int_0^Q [(p-w)x - (w-b)(Q-x)]f(x)dx + \int_Q^\infty (p-w) \cdot Q \cdot f(x)dx$$
$$= (p-w)Q - (p-b)\int_0^Q F(x)dx. \tag{11}$$

The retailer's order quantity Q^{**} which leads his maximum expected profit with buy-back contract can be obtained similarly by:

$$Q^{**} = F^{-1}(\frac{p-w}{p-b}). \tag{12}$$

Then the supplier's maximum expected profit is:

$$E_2 Z_S(Q^{**}) = (w-c)Q^{**} - b\int_0^Q F(x)dx. \tag{13}$$

And the expected profit of the system with buy-back contract is:

$$E_2 Z(Q^{**}) = E_2 Z_R(Q^{**}) + E_2 Z_S(Q^{**}). \tag{14}$$

Obviously, in order to make the total profit of the decentralized supply chain system under buy-back contract achieve the profit of the centralize-controlled one, i.e. $E_2 Z(Q^{**}) = EZ(Q)$, then $Q^0 = Q^{**}$ is necessary, that is:

$$F^{-1}(\frac{p-c}{p-s}) = F^{-1}(\frac{p-w}{p-b}). \tag{15}$$

By the strictly monotonic of $F^{-1}(\cdot)$, there is $\dfrac{p-c}{p-s} = \dfrac{p-w}{p-b}$, so we can obtain the equation as:

$$b = \frac{s(p-w) + p(w-c)}{p-c}. \tag{16}$$

The expected profit of both sides, the system's expected profit and the optimal order quantity can be obtained by substitute Eq.16 into Eq.11 to Eq.13. From Eq.16, we discover that the supplier's buy-back price is related to the wholesale price. Then we will analyze the relationship between the wholesale and buy-back prices by a numerical example.

Assuming an apparel product which has a normal distributional demand, with the average demand $\mu = 249$, the standard deviation $\sigma = 125$, $p = 115$, $s = 25$, $c = 35$, then we can obtain the optimal order quantity is 403. Furthermore, substitute the above parameters into the corresponding formula for the expected profit, and the profits of both sides can be obtained by using the Normdist function (as shown in Table 1).

Table 1. The expected profit under different combinations of the wholesale and buy-back prices

w	b	Q^*	The retailer's Expected profit	The supplier's Expected profit	The system Expected profit
75	0	233	5580	9360	14940
35	25	403	17830	0	17830
45	36.25	403	15600	2230	17830
55	47.5	403	13373	4458	17830
65	58.75	403	11144	6686	17830
75	70	403	8915	8915	17830
85	81.25	403	6686	11144	17830
95	92.5	403	4458	13373	17830

From analysis of Table 1, the system could be coordinated with the buy-back contract when the retail price is fixed, for the expected profit of decentralized system is equal to the expectations of the centralized system. However, the expected profits of both the retailer and the supplier have different changes because of the different combinations of the wholesale and buy-back prices. Under the condition which ensures the coordinated system, the supplier have to raise the wholesale prices according to the increasing buy-back price, otherwise his expected profit would reduced. And the increase in the wholesale price would make the retailer's expected profit decreases. When the wholesale price is consistent with the buyback price in a certain combination (as $w = 75$, $s = 70$ in Table1), the supplier's expected profit is equal to the retailer's. But the retailer's expected profit now is less than before the contract (without the buyback contract, i.e. $b = 0$, the retailer's maximum order quantity is 234 and the supplier's expected profit is 9360), so the supplier may not be willing to sign the contract. The above analysis which shows that a single buyback contract could coordinate the supply chain, but it could not guarantee the equal increase in profit of both participates. Especially when the retail prices changing, it is more difficult to reflect the supply chain's spirit of mutually beneficial with the single buy-back contract.

4 The Case with Combined Contract of Buy-Back and Pricing Flexibility under Price-Related Demand

In section 2, we have analyzed the buy-back contract, in which the retail price was treated as a fixed constant. But in reality, retailers always adjust the retail price dynamically since the changing demand, to maximize his profits by optimization of order quantity and retail price. Then we will discuss a combined contract in this section. Assuming that the retail price is dynamically adjusted, it is p_0 before adjustment and p later, and the demand $D(p)$ is retail-price-related; w is a linear function of flexible price (i.e. $w = w(p)$), α is a constant coefficient which is called change-rate of the wholesale price with the retail price, and $0 < \alpha < 1$; δ is the difference between the wholesale and retail prices; $E[\cdot]$ is the expectation of the function, other parameters have the same meaning with the section above. Then there is $\Delta w = \alpha \Delta p$ and $b = w - \delta$, in which, $\Delta p = p_0 - p$, $\Delta w = w_0 - w$. Set $w^0 = \alpha p_0 + (1-\alpha)c$, then we will get $\delta = (1-\alpha)(c-s)$. Similar to Eq.11, the retailer's expected profit in this case is:

$$
\begin{aligned}
E_3 Z_R(Q, p) &= (p-w)Q - (p-b)E[Q - D(p)]^+ \\
&= [p - w_0 + \alpha(p_0 - p)]Q - [p - w_0 - \alpha(p-p_0) + (1-\alpha)(c-s)]E[Q - D(p)]^+ \quad (17) \\
&= (1-\alpha)((p-c)Q - (p-s)E[Q - D(p)]^+).
\end{aligned}
$$

And the supplier's expected profit in this case is:

$$
\begin{aligned}
E_3 Z_S(Q, p) &= (w-c)Q - (b-s)E[Q - D(p)]^+ \\
&= \alpha((p-c)Q - (p-s)E[Q - D(p)]^+).
\end{aligned}
\quad (18)
$$

So we can get the expected profit of the whole supply chain system, it is:

$$
E_3 Z(Q, p) = E_3 Z_R(Q, p) + E_3 Z_S(Q, p) = (p-c)Q - (p-s)E[Q - D(p)]^+. \quad (19)
$$

In addition, we can get the follow equations from the assumptions:

$$
w = c + \alpha(p-c); \quad b = s + \alpha(p-s). \quad (20)
$$

From Eq.20, and compare Eq.17 and Eq.19 with Eq.9 in the concentrated manner, we can obtain the following conclusions:

1 For any given initial retail price p_0, the supply chain with the combination of buy-back and pricing flexibility contracts could achieve coordination, when the wholesale price changes with the retail price and with $0 < \alpha < 1$.

2 The value of α depends on the game ability of both sides, and the larger its value, the higher the wholesale price, while the higher buy-back price. Therefore, the supplier is more willing to use an appropriate combined contract. Similarly to the retailer, the wholesale price is for each product he bought and the buy-back price only for the unsold ones. So the value of α is not the larger the better

The above analysis only considered the situation that the wholesale and buyback prices are related to the retail price, if the wholesale price is not only relevant with the retail price but also associated with the order quantity, then the conditions of coordination is:

$$w = \alpha p + (1-\alpha)c - \alpha(p_0 - p)E[Q-D(p)]^+; \quad b = s + \alpha(p-s). \tag{21}$$

From Eq.21, we can see that when $p < p_0$ (the price declines) the supplier's wholesale price considered order quantity is lower than without, which shows that for the impact of order quantity the supplier would consider the retailer's loss of revenue when the price reduced, and he would like to reduce the wholesale price. The wholesale price would reduce when the order quantity increases, that is, the supplier's whole price would be lower while the retailer orders more products. When $p > p_0$ (the price increases) the wholesale price is higher than the one without considering the order quantity. If the price increases, the wholesale price would increase and along with the order quantity as the retailer could obtain more profit. In summary, in the process of increasing price, the supplier's profit increases with the retailer's, the supply chain system achieves the perfect coordination.

5 Conclusion

Supply contract is an important method to achieve coordination of supply chain. In this paper, we established a model of combined contract of buy-back and price flexibility when the wholesale price changed with the retail price. The result shows that with a given changing rate α ($0 < \alpha < 1$) and there's a certain relationship between the wholesale and the retail prices, the supply chain system could be perfect coordinated, and the flexibility in the profit allocation between the supplier and the retailer could be obtained with the proposed combined contract.

Acknowledgments

This work is supported by the National Natural Science Foundation of China (Grant No. 70772073), and the Doctorate Foundation of Donghua University.

References

1. Wang, C.X.: A general framework of supply chain contract models. Supply Chain Management: An International Journal 7(5), 302–310 (2002)
2. Tsay, A.A.: Managing retail channel overstock: markdown money and return policies. Journal of Retailing 77(4), 457–492 (2001)
3. Cachon, G.P., Lariviere, M.A.: Supply chain coordination with Revenue-sharing contracts: strengths and Limitations. Management Science 51(1), 30–44 (2005)
4. Bellantuonoa, N., Giannoccaro, I., et al.: The implications of joint adoption of revenue sharing and advance booking discount programs. International Journal of Production Economics 121(2), 383–394 (2009)
5. Khouja, M.J.: Optimal ordering, discounting, and pricing in the single-period problem. International Journal of Production Economics 65(2), 201–216 (2000)
6. Pasternack, B.A.: Optimal pricing and return policies for perishable commodities. Marketing Science 4(2), 166–176 (1985)

Research for Pharmacodynamic Effect Transitive Relation Based on Regression Method

Bin Nie[1], JianQiang Du[1], RiYue Yu[1,2,3], YuHui Liu[2], GuoLiang Xu[1,2,3,*],
YueSheng Wang[4], and LiPing Huang[2]

[1] School of Computer Science, Jiangxi University of Traditional Chinese Medicine,
330006, Nanchang, China
[2] College of Pharmacy, Jiangxi University of Traditional Chinese Medicine,
330006, Nanchang, China
[3] Key Laboratory of Modern Preparation, Ministry of Education, Jiangxi University of
Traditional Chinese Medicine,
330006, Nanchang, China
[4] National Pharmaceutical Engineering Centre for Solid Preparation in Chinese Herbal
Medicine, 330006, Nanchang, China
xuguoliang6606@126.com, ncunb@163.com

Abstract. Research for pharmacodynamic effect is the only way to find new drug of traditional Chinese medicine, and is beneficial to finding the drug new acts.Traditional Chinese Medicine prescription may include some active substance group ,generate pharmacodynamic effect indexs.Whether or no some relationship among the pharmacodynamic effect indexs,is our focus of attention in the paper.Statistical methods is a important tool for research medicine and pharmacy. Explore and analyze the relationship among the pharmacodynamic effect indexs be of great signifiance,the paper put forward research for pharmacodynamic effect transitive relation based on regression method. It was proved to be feasible and effective after tested.

Keywords: Traditional Chinese Medicine, transitive relationship, pharmacodynamic effect, Regression.

1 Introduction

Uniform designs, proposed by Fang [1], Wang [2] and et al. The experiments based on uniform designs have the number of runs less than 50, and the level of each factor could more than 10 for five factor. The traditional optimized method or orthogonal experimental design is hard to realize.

The theory make great progress in recent years such as the paper[3-7].The uniform design-regression(UD-R) analysis method can reduce the number of experimental runs, analyze the relationship between the independent variable and dependent variable, for example[8-11].

---

* Corresponding author.

G. Shen and X. Huang (Eds.): CSIE 2011, Part II, CCIS 153, pp. 80–86, 2011.
© Springer-Verlag Berlin Heidelberg 2011

Regression may be classified into linear regression, curve estimation regression, binary logistic regression, multimomial logistic regression, nonlinear regression, etc. Regression also may be classified into Simple Regression, multiple regression, partial regression, and etc.

In the paper, TCM prescription Gegen Qinlian Decoction treat diabetes mellitus, reseach the relationship of dosage and pharmacodynamic effect,and among the pharmacodynamic effects may be have some relations.This work focus on pharmacodynamic effect transitive relation based on regression method.

2 Data Sources

In the paper, the data sources of National Basic Research Program of China (973 Program), the experiment using uniform design method, its includes 4 factors Gegen (Radix Puerariae), Huangqin (Radix Scutellariae), Huanglian (Rhizoma Coptidis), Gancao (Glycyrrhiza uralensis), and 16 levels, the total dosage is 120g, experimental subject is mouse, experiment purpose is to analyze the relationship between TCM prescription' dosage and pharmacodynamic effect of treat diabetes mellitus. The pharmacodynamic effect indexs consists of HbA1c,CHOL,TGL,XHDL, LDL, insulinum, fasting blood glucose(FBG).

3 The Basic Theory of Multiple Linear Regression

Before discuss the releation, introduction the basic theory of multiple linear regression[12]. If the Independent variable $X_1, X_2, \cdots, X_m$,and the dependent variable Y . β_0 as constant, $\beta_1, \beta_2, \cdots, \beta_m$ denote partial regression coefficient, ε denote residual, than the multiple linear regression model show as fellows:

$$Y = \beta_0 + \beta_1 X_1 + \beta_2 X_2 + \cdots + \beta_m X_m + \varepsilon \tag{1}$$

Compute the estimated value $b_0, b_1, b_2, \cdots, b_m$ of the sample data $\beta_0, \beta_1, \beta_2, \cdots \beta_m$, if let the $\hat{Y}$ is estimated value of Y ,the multiple regression equation to describe as fellows:

$$\hat{Y} = b_0 + b_1 X_1 + b_2 X_2 + \cdots + b_m X_m \tag{2}$$

The multiple linear regression model may be meet the conditions, must hypothesis testing for the multiple regression equation and each Independent variable, evaluate the fit result and the effect of each Independent variable. Apart from this, it is important that select independent variable.

There are many ways for independent variable entering the equation of regression, such as backward stepwise method, forward stepwise method, bidirectional stepwise regression method, and etc. The basic thoughts carry the independent variable of regression result was obvious into the equation of regression, otherwise, exclude it.

In the backward stepwise method selection program, independent variables are sequentially removed from a full (all regression items included) method. In contrast, forward stepwise program start with an empty iterm method, and proceed by adding items.

First round of backward stepwise iterations, the regression items are each removed from the "full" starting equation, and the regression calculation is acted to search the improvement in the residual sum of squares for each of these resulting equations relative to the starting equation. For each new equation, F-test methods used in the independent variables have the maximum of sum of spuares, this variable while have statistical significance will be entering the equation. This provides a new starting equation for the next round, then the backward stepwise program will stop.

First round of forward stepwise iterations, the regression items are each added to the starting equation, and the regression calculation is acted to search the improvement in the residual sum of squares for each of these resulting equations relative to the intercept only equation. When all of the one-item equations have been created, the forward stepwise program selects the variable have the minimum of sum of spuares, this variable while have no statistical significance will be excluding the equation. This provides a new starting equation for the next round, then the forward stepwise program will stop.

bidirectional stepwise regression method is integrate backward stepwise method and forward stepwise method, its more better in theory.

4   Research for the Traditional Chinese Medical Pharmacodynamic Effect Transitive Relation

The pharmacodynamic effect indexs consists of HbA1c, CHOL, TGL, XHDL, LDL, insulinum(yd), fasting blood glucose(FBG). Research the relation, first to make scatter diagram and correlational analysis, second to decide the regression method,third to hypothesis testing and analyze the result. Because the experiments model mouse easy to die, Under the condition of data not obeying normal distribution, Exploratory data analysis for the relationship in the procedure using median of the experiments data.

This work, analyze the relationship using spss 16.0, the result of fasting blood glucose(FBG)(2010-07-16 Collected data) and other pharmacodynamic effect indexs (HbA1c, CHOL, TGL, XHDL, LDL, insulinum) describe as fellows:

The same result of bidirectional stepwise regression method and the forward stepwise method:

Variables Entered/Removed^a

Model	Variables Entered	Variables Removed	Method
1	LDL		Stepwise (Criteria: Probability-of-F-to-enter <= .050, Probability-of-F-to-remove >= .150).

a. Dependent Variable: 0716-xt

Fig. 1. Variables Entered/Removed of pharmacodynamic effect indexs

Model Summary^b

Model	R	R Square	Adjusted R Square	Std. Error of the Estimate	Durbin-Watson
1	.735^a	.540	.507	3.09498	1.232

a. Predictors: (Constant), LDL

b. Dependent Variable: 0716-xt

Fig. 2. Model Summary of pharmacodynamic effect indexs

ANOVA^b

Model		Sum of Squares	df	Mean Square	F	Sig.
1	Regression	157.624	1	157.624	16.455	.001^a
	Residual	134.105	14	9.579		
	Total	291.729	15			

a. Predictors: (Constant), LDL

b. Dependent Variable: 0716-xt

Fig. 3. ANOVA of pharmacodynamic effect indexs

Coefficients^a

Model		Unstandardized Coefficients		Standardized Coefficients		
		B	Std. Error	Beta	t	Sig.
1	(Constant)	91.646	20.253		4.525	.000
	LDL	-34.403	8.481	-.735	-4.057	.001

a. Dependent Variable: 0716-xt

Fig. 4. Coefficients of pharmacodynamic effect indexs

Criteria such as figure 1: Probability-of-F-to-enter $<= 0.050$, Probability-of-F-to-remove $>= 0.150$, only LDL enter the equation.

Figure 2 indicate Model Summary of 0716-xt (insulinum) and LDL, R is equal to 0.735 and R Square is equal to 0.540 indicate the dependent variable have 54 percent to Interpret the independent variable.

Figure 3 indicate ANOVA of 0716-xt (insulinum) and LDL, hypothesis testing F is equal to 16.455, significance test value 0. 001 less than 0.05 level indicate statistical significance.

Figure 4 indicate Coefficients of 0716-xt (insulinum) and LDL, Constant Unstandardized Coefficients is 91.646, t is 4.525, significance test value 0 less than 0.05 level indicate statistical significance. LDL Unstandardized Coefficients is -34.403, t is -4.057, significance test value 0.001 less than 0.05 level indicate statistical significance.

The multiple regression equation of 0716-xt(insulinum) and LDL as fellows:

$$Y = 91.646 + (-34.403 * LDL) \tag{3}$$

The result of bidirectional backward stepwise method:

Criteria: Probability-of-F-to-enter $<= 0.050$, Probability-of-F-to-remove $>= 0.150$, yd, XHDL, HbA1c, TG, LDL, CHOL enter the equation, then TG, CHOL, LDL, yd Removed.

Model Summary of 0716-xt (insulinum) and XHDL, HbA1c, R is equal to 0.788 and R Square is equal to 0.620 indicate the dependent variable have 62 percent to Interpret the independent variable.

ANOVA of 0716-xt (insulinum) and XHDL, HbA1c, hypothesis testing F is equal to 10.616, significance test value 0.002 less than 0.05 level indicate statistical significance.

Coefficients of 0716-xt (insulinum) and XHDL, HbA1c, Constant Unstandardized Coefficients is -13.316, t is -0.971, significance test value 0.349 more than 0.05 level indicate no statistical significance. HbA1c Unstandardized Coefficients is 16.258, t is 3.160, significance test value 0.008 less than 0.05 level indicate statistical significance. XHDL Unstandardized Coefficients is -23.173, t is -3.460, level of significance test value 0.004 less than 0.05 level indicate statistical significance.

The multiple regression equation of 0716-xt (insulinum) and XHDL, HbA1c as follows:

$$Y = -13.316 + 16.258 * HBAlC$$
$$+(-23.173 * XHDL)$$

(4)

5 Conclusion

Explore and analyze the relationship among the pharmacodynamic effect indexs effect be of great signifiance, the paper do some work using Uniform Design and regression method for it, and to obtain some significative result.The further work will try to make better the experiments model and the data, and along the thinking of Uniform Design and regression method.

Acknowledgments. The authors wish to express their gratitude to the anonymous reviewers for their valuable comments and suggestions, which have improved the quality of this paper. The team members also include JianJiang Fu, WenHong Li,Bo Liu,Fei Qu, YingFang Chen, QiYun Zhang, BingTao Li.This work is supported by National Basic Research Program of China(973 Program:2010CB530603).This work also supported by National Science and Technology Major Project and Grand New Drug Development Program (2009ZX09310), and Supported by Jiangxi province Natural Science Foundation (2009GZS0058), Supported by Technology project of Educational Committee of Jiangxi Province (GJJ11541).

References

1. Fang, K.T.: The uniform design: application of number-theoretic methods in experimental design. Acta Math. Appl. Sinica 3, 363–372 (1980)
2. Fang, K.T., Wang, Y.: Number-Theoretic Methods in Statistics. Chapman and Hall, London (1994)
3. Yang, Z.-H., Fang, K.-T., Liang, J.-J.: A characterization of multivariate normal distribution and its applicationl. Statistics & Probability Letters 30, 347–352 (1996)
4. Chan, L.-Y., Fang, K.-T., Mukerjee, R.: A characterization for orthogonal arrays of strength two via a regression model. Statistics & Probability Letters 54, 189–192 (2001)
5. Fang, K.-T., Li, R.-Z., Liang, J.-J.: A multivariate version of Ghosh's T3-plot to detect non-multinormality. Computational Statistics & Data Analysis Computational Statistics 28, 371–386 (1998)
6. Fang, K.-T., Qin, H.: A note on construction of nearly uniform designs with large number of runs. Statistics & Probability Letters 61, 215–224 (2003)
7. Fang, K.-T., Tang, Y., Yin, J.: Lower bounds of various criteria in experimental designs. Journal of Statistical Planning and Inference 138, 184–195 (2008)
8. Leung, S.-Y.L., Chan, W.-H., Leung, C.-H., et al.: Screening the fabrication conditions of ultrafiltration membranes by using the uniform design and regression analysis methods. Chemometrics and Intelligent Laboratory Systems 40, 203–213 (1998)

9. Leung, S.-Y.L., Chan, W.-H., Luk, C.-H.: Optimization of fabrication conditions of high-efficiency ultrafiltration membranes using methods of uniform design and regression analysis. Chemometrics and Intelligent Laboratory Systems 53, 21–35 (2000)
10. Chan, W.-H., Tsao, S.-C.: Fabrication of nanofiltration membranes with tunable separation characteristics using methods of uniform design and regression analysis. Chemometrics and Intelligent Laboratory Systems 65, 241–256 (2003)
11. Liu, Y., Zhang, L., Cheng, L., et al.: Regression analysis Uniform design and regression analysis of LPCVD boron carbide from BCl3–CH4–H2 system. Applied Surface Science 255, 5729–5735 (2009)
12. Sun, Z., Xu, Y.: Medical statistics. People's Medical Publishing House, Beijing (2002)

Analyze the Relationship between TCM Prescription' Dosage and Pharmacodynamic Effect Based on UD-OPLS/O2PLS

Bin Nie[1], JianQiang Du[1], RiYue Yu[1,2,3], YuHui Liu[2], GuoLiang Xu[1,2,3,*],
YueSheng Wang[4], and LiPing Huang[2]

[1] School of Computer Science, Jiangxi University of Traditional Chinese Medicine,
330006, Nanchang, China
[2] College of Pharmacy, Jiangxi University of Traditional Chinese Medicine,
330006, Nanchang, China
[3] Key Laboratory of Modern Preparation, Ministry of Education,
Jiangxi University of Traditional Chinese Medicine, 330006, Nanchang, China
[4] National Pharmaceutical Engineering Centre for Solid Preparation in Chinese Herbal
Medicine, 330006, Nanchang, China
xuguoliang6606@126.com, ncunb@163.com

Abstract. Traditional Chinese Medicine have the secret is dosage, the Traditional Chinese Medical clinical therapeutic effect key is prescription' dosage. The paper aim to explore and analyze the relationship between TCM prescription' dosage and pharmacodynamic effect. The methods: the rats were done into diabetic model,and taken Gegen Qinlian Decoction(Radix Puerariae, Radix Scutellariae, Rhizoma Coptidis, Glycyrrhiza uralensis) which have been design using Uniform Design(UD) method, extract pharmacodynamic effect indexs from the rats, analyze the relationship between TCM prescription' dosage and pharmacodynamic based on Orthogonal Partial Least Square Analysis(OPLS) /O2PLS.The result indicate the order of Variable importance is Radix Puerariae, Rhizoma Coptidis, Glycyrrhiza uralensis, Radix Scutellariae,and the Coefficients of TCM relative to the pharmacodynamic effect indexs.

Keywords: Traditional Chinese Medicine, dosage, pharmacodynamic effect, Uniform Design, OPLS/O2PLS.

1 Introduction

Traditional Chinese Medicine have the secret is dosage, the Traditional Chinese Medical clinical therapeutic effect key is prescription' dosage. the Traditional Chinese Medical dosage affected by the follwing factors:properties of medicinal herbs, compatibility and formulation, the condition of illness, the patients' physique and age, methods of decocting chinese medicinal herbs, methods of taking chinese medicinal, and etc. As the dosage of a medicinal herb has direct relationship with its therapeutic effect.

---

* Corresponding author.

G. Shen and X. Huang (Eds.): CSIE 2011, Part II, CCIS 153, pp. 87–92, 2011.
© Springer-Verlag Berlin Heidelberg 2011

Uniform designs, proposed by Fang [1], Wang [2] and et al. The experiments based on uniform designs have the number of runs less than 50, and the level of each factor could more than 10 for five factor. The traditional optimized method or orthogonal experimental design is hard to realize.

The theory make great progress in recent years such as the paper[3-7].The uniform design-regression(UD-R) analysis method can reduce the number of experimental runs, analyze the relationship between the independent variable and dependent variable, for example[8-10].

2 Data Sources

In the paper, the data sources of National Basic Research Program of China (973 Program), the experiment using uniform design method, its includes 4 factors Gegen (Radix Puerariae), Huangqin (Radix Scutellariae), Huanglian (Rhizoma Coptidis), Gancao (Glycyrrhiza uralensis), and 16 levels, the total dosage is 120g. experimental subject is mouse, experiment purpose is to analyze the relationship between TCM prescription' dosage and pharmacodynamic effect of treat diabetes mellitus. the pharmacodynamic effect indexs consists of HbA1c, CHOL, TGL, XHDL, LDL, yd (insulinum).

3 The Basic Theory of Orthogonal Partial Least Square Analysis

Principal components analysis (PCA) (http://www.umetrics.com/) extract a small orthogonal set of principal components from the original variables of the data X, the principal components represent for most of the variance. The components are obtained on order of decreasing importance, the aim being to reduce the dimensionally of the data.

Definition 1: PC modeling shows the correlation structure of data matrix X, approximating it by a matrix product of lower dimension (TP'), principal components plus a matrix of residuals (E).

$$X = Xbar + TP' + E \qquad (1)$$

Where Xbar contains X average, T is a matrix of scores that summarizes the X-variables, P' is a matrix of loading showing the influence of the variables, E is a matrix of residuals, the deviations between the original values and the projections.

Partial Least Squares (PLS) (http://www.umetrics.com/), as in multiple linear regressions, the main purpose of partial least squares regression is to build a linear model 1.

The PLS model 1 accomplishing these objectives can be expressed as:

$$X = Xbar + TP' + E \qquad (2)$$

$$Y = Ybar + UP' + F \qquad (3)$$

$$U = T + H \qquad (4)$$

Where Xbar contain X average, Ybar contains Y average, T is a matrix of scores that summarizes the X-variables, U is a matrix of scores that summarizes the Y-variables, P' is a matrix of loading showing the influence of the Y-variables, F is a matrix of residuals, the deviations between the original values and the projections is the inner relation.

Orthogonal Partial Least Square Analysis (http://www.umetrics.com/) (OPLS) [11-13] developed a modification of PLS, which is designed to handle variation in X that is orthogonal to Y. O2PLS is a generalization of OPLS [14-15].O2PLS is bidirectional to Y and Y to X, in other words, X and Y can be used to predict each other. The O2PLS model 1 can be written as, for model 1 of X:

$$X = T_P P'_P + T_O P'_0 + E \qquad (5)$$

For model 1 of Y:

$$Y = U_P Q'_P + U_O Q'_O + F \qquad (6)$$

Where a linear relationship exists between T_P and U_P. the score vectors in T_P and T_O are mutually orthogonal. T_O :matrix of scores that summarizes the X variation orthogonal to Y, U_O :matrix of scores that summarizes the Y variation orthogonal to X, P_0 expresses the importance of the variables in approximating X variation orthogonal to Y, in the selected component, Q_O expresses the importance of the variables in approximating Y variation orthogonal to X, in the selected component.

In the model, the influence on Y variation of every X-variables called variable importance in the projection(VIP).The sum of squares of all VIP'S is equal to 1, so the more VIP values larger, the more relevant for explainint Y. If the VIP values larger than 1, shows the most relevant for explaining Y.

Regression coefficients as a parameter is used to express correlation of the Y variables and the X variables in the multiple regression models. The coefficients absolute values more lager, the relevant more better. The coefficients is positive value representative positive correlation, else, negative correlation.

4 Analyze the Relationship between TCM Prescription' Dosage and Pharmacodynamic Effect Based on OPLS/O2PLS

Analyze the relationship, first to exploratory analysis the raw data, second to decide the regression method. Because the experiments model mouse easy to die, Under the condition of data not obeying normal distribution, Exploratory data analysis for the relationship in the procedure using median of the experiments data.

This work, analyze the relationship using simca-p+12,the Prescription' Dosage indexs:Radix Puerariae(X1), Radix Scutellariae(X2), Rhizoma Coptidis(X3), Glycyrrhiza uralensis(X4), the pharmacodynamic effect indexs consists of HbA1c, CHOL, TGL, XHDL, LDL, yd(insulinum).The relationship indicate such as figure 1-4.

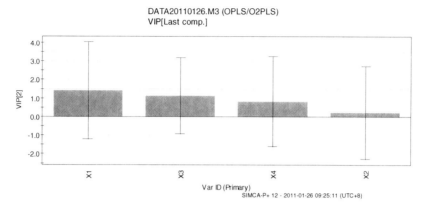

Fig. 1. VIP of no interaction prescription's dosage to pharmacodynamic effect indexs

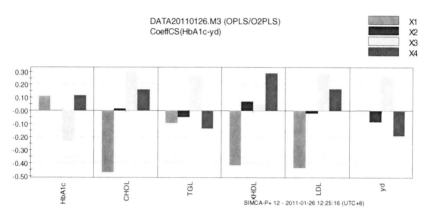

Fig. 2. coefficients of no interaction prescription's dosage to pharmacodynamic effect indexs

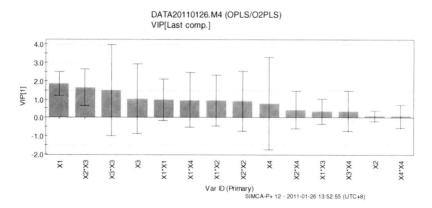

Fig. 3. VIP of interaction prescription's dosage to pharmacodynamic effect indexs

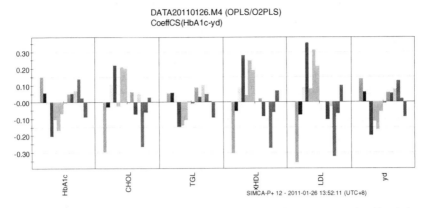

Fig. 4. coefficients of interaction prescription's dosage to pharmacodynamic effect indexs

Note: each pharmacodynamic effect indexs corresponding prescription's dosage sequence is: X1,X2,X3,X4,X1*X1,X2*X2,X3*X3,X4*X4,X1*X2,X1*X3,X1*X4, X2*X3,X2*X4,X3*X4.

In figure 1, consider the prescription's dosage no interaction to pharmacodynamic effect indexs, its indicate the order of Variable importance is Radix Puerariae, Rhizoma Coptidis, Glycyrrhiza uralensis, Radix Scutellariae. In figure 2, consider the prescription's dosage no interaction to pharmacodynamic effect indexs, its indicate the Coefficients of TCM prescription's dosage relative to the pharmacodynamic effect indexs.

In figure 3, consider the prescription's dosage have quadric interaction to pharmacodynamic effect indexs, its indicate the order of Variable importance is X1,X2*X3,X3*X3,X3,X1*X1,X2*X2,X1*X4,X1*X2,X4,X3*X4,X2*X4,X1*X3,X2 ,X4*X4.

In figure 4, consider the prescription's dosage have quadric interaction to pharmacodynamic effect indexs, its indicate the Coefficients of TCM prescription's dosage relative to the pharmacodynamic effect indexs.

5   Conclusion

Explore and analyze the relationship between TCM prescription' dosage and pharmacodynamic effect be of great signifiance, the paper do some work using Uniform Design and OPLS/O2PLS method for it, and to obtain some significative result. The further work will try to make better the experiments model and the data, and along the thinking of Uniform Design and regression method.

Acknowledgments. The authors wish to express their gratitude to the anonymous reviewers for their valuable comments and suggestions, which have improved the quality of this paper. The team members also include JianJiang Fu, WenHong Li, Bo Liu,Fei Qu, YingFang Chen, QiYun Zhang, BingTao Li. This work is supported by National Basic Research Program of China(973 Program:2010CB530603).This work also supported by National Science and Technology Major Project and Grand New

Drug Development Program (2009ZX09310),and Supported by Jiangxi province Natural Science Foundation (2009GZS0058),Supported by Technology project of Educational Committee of Jiangxi Province (GJJ11541).

References

1. Fang, K.T.: The uniform design: application of number-theoretic methods in experimental design. Acta Math. Appl. Sinica 3, 363–372 (1980)
2. Fang, K.T., Wang, Y.: Number-Theoretic Methods in Statistics. Chapman and Hall, London (1994)
3. Yang, Z.-H., Fang, K.-T., Liang, J.-J.: A characterization of multivariate normal distribution and its applicationl. Statistics & Probability Letters 30, 347–352 (1996)
4. Chan, L.-Y., Fang, K.-T., Mukerjee, R.: A characterization for orthogonal arrays of strength two via a regression model. Statistics & Probability Letters 54, 189–192 (2001)
5. Fang, K.-T., Li, R.-Z., Liang, J.-J.: A multivariate version of Ghosh's T3-plot to detect non-multinormality. Computational Statistics & Data Analysis Computational Statistics 28, 371–386 (1998)
6. Fang, K.-T., Qin, H.: A note on construction of nearly uniform designs with large number of runs. Statistics & Probability Letters 61, 215–224 (2003)
7. Fang, K.-T., Tang, Y., Yin, J.: Lower bounds of various criteria in experimental designs. Journal of Statistical Planning and Inference 138, 184–195 (2008)
8. Leung, S.-Y.L., Chan, W.-H., Luk, C.-H.: Optimization of fabrication conditions of high-efficiency ultrafiltration membranes using methods of uniform design and regression analysis. Chemometrics and Intelligent Laboratory Systems 53, 21–35 (2000)
9. Chan, W.-H., Tsao, S.-C.: Fabrication of nanofiltration membranes with tunable separation characteristics using methods of uniform design and regression analysis. Chemometrics and Intelligent Laboratory Systems 65, 241–256 (2003)
10. Liu, Y., Zhang, L., Cheng, L., et al.: Regression analysis Uniform design and regression analysis of LPCVD boron carbide from BCl3–CH4–H2 system. Applied Surface Science 255, 5729–5735 (2009)
11. Trygg, J., Wold, S.: J.O2-PLS, a Two-Block(X-Y) Laten variable regression(LVR) Method with an integral OSC Filter. Journal of Chemometrics 17, 53–64 (2003)
12. Holmes, E., Tsang, T.M., Jeffrey, T., Huang, J., et al.: Metabolec profiling of CSF:Evidence that early intervention may impact on disease progression and outcome in schizophrenia. Pls Medicine 3, 1420–1428 (2006)
13. Wold, S., Antti, H., Lindgren, F., Ohman, J.: Orthogonal signal correction of near-infrared spectra. Chemometrics Intelligent Lab Systems 44, 175–185 (1998)
14. Brindle, J.T., Antti, H., Holmes, E., Tranter, G., Nicholson, J.K., et al.: Rapid and noninvasive diagnosis of the presence and severity of coronary heart disease using 1H-NMR-based metabonomics. Nat. Med. 8, 1439–1444; Clerk Maxwell, J.: A Treatise on Electricity and Magnetism, 3rd ed., vol. 2. Clarendon, Oxford, pp. 68–73 (1892)
15. Trygg, J., Wold, S.: J. O2-PLS, a Two-Block(X-Y) Laten variable regression(LVR) Method with an integral OSC Filter. Journal of Chemometrics 17, 53–64 (2003)

Design of Sample Integrator and Data Correlations Process for High Accuracy Ultraviolet Photometer

Ping Chuan Zhang[1,2,*], Hai Liang Xie[2], and Hang Sen Zhang[2]

[1] Huazhong University of Science and Technology, Wuahn, China, 430074
[2] Dept. of Machine and Electronic Engineering
Luohe Vocational Technology College, Henan Province, China, 462002
goldensword@126.com

Abstract. The sample integrators is a key circuit in it and the data processing algorithm play an important role on its precision and processing speed. This paper designed a novel sample integrator and data correlation processing algorithm for improving ultraviolet spectrum photometer. Compared with the tradition spectral analysis method, the designed device is very practical with the characteristics of simple operation, quick analysis speed; high sensitivity and accuracy, good selectivity.

Keywords: Data process, Correlation algorithm, Ultraviolet spectrum photometer, sample Integrator.

1 Introduction

The ultraviolet photometer [1] is a widely used instrument for the spectrum analysis, such as the chemical experiment, materials science research, food industry and so on many domains. The ordinary ultraviolet obvious spectroscope is mainly composed of six parts [2, 3]: the photo source, the monochromatic, the sample pond (extinction pond), the detector, the recording equipment. Because of the traditional ultraviolet photometer using the ordinary sample integrator and simple data processing [4], the data processing method and sample integrator affected the precision and the speed. Therefore, this article used the advanced sample integrator and the correlation data algorithm to constructe high performances ultraviolet photometer in processing speed and accuracy.

2 Principles of Sampling Gates and Integrator

The sample is one kind of frequency compressing technique, it through sampling point by point a high recurrence rate's signal, time variation simulation quantity transformation doubling time separate changing quantity, this type and quantity namely for signal low frequency duplication, thus achieves to this low-frequency signal peak-to-peak

---

* Corresponding author.

G. Shen and X. Huang (Eds.): CSIE 2011, Part II, CCIS 153, pp. 93–97, 2011.
© Springer-Verlag Berlin Heidelberg 2011

value, the phase and the profile survey. The key issue is the sampling process integral. Figure 1 is the stationary position sample and the synchronous storage principle schematic.

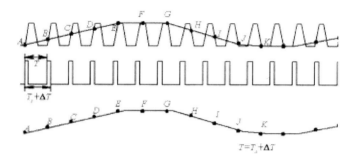

Fig. 1. The stationary position sample and the synchronous storage principle

T is the sampling period ΔT for sampling interval TS is signal period

$$SNR_O = \frac{S_o}{n_o} = \sqrt{N_s} \cdot \frac{S_i}{n_i} = \sqrt{N_s} SNR_i \tag{1}$$

The Signal-to-Noise Ratio was improved through the Ns sample averaging. The sample integrator principle diagram is shown as figure 2.

$$SNIR = \frac{SNR_O}{SNR_i} = \sqrt{N_s} \tag{2}$$

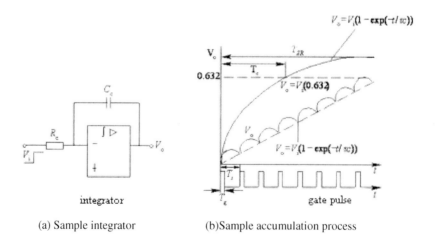

(a) Sample integrator   (b)Sample accumulation process

Fig. 2. Sample integrator's principle

2.1 Fixed-Point Type Sample Integrator

The fixed-point sample integrator principle block diagram is shown in Figure3.

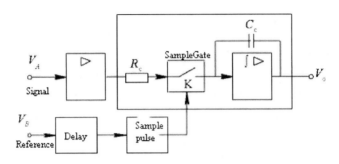

Fig. 3. Fixed-point type sample integrator principle block diagram

In fig.3, Trigger signal V_B keeps synchronization with input testing signal V_A. The trigger signal is delayed t_d through delay circuit, sampled by the signal V_A fixed point pulse sample circuit, and produces the adjustable sampling pulse (pulse width is T_g) to control the sampling gate.

2.2 Signal-to-Noise Ratio Improves

If the sampling pulse gate width is T_g, and by δ_t, then in testing waveform at any point, in the gate extends to T_g scope, the sample number is

$$N_s = \frac{T_s}{\Delta T} \qquad (3)$$

$$SNIR = \sqrt{\frac{T_g}{\Delta T}} \qquad (4)$$

$$N_i = \frac{T_{SR}}{T_s} \qquad (5)$$

$$\Delta T = \frac{T_B}{N_i} \qquad (6)$$

$$SNIR = \sqrt{\frac{T_g T_{SR}}{T_B T_s}}$$
(7)

2.3 Signal Resolution

The signal sample interval is decided by the gate width Tg, the narrower Tg is, the smaller sample interval is, then the signal restored resolution to be higher. Know from Eq.(4), Tg is smaller, SNIR will be smaller. If maintain SNIR constant, only to reduce δt. Therefore the resolution cannot be enhanced unlimitedly, only compromise consideration according to the survey request.

Supposing the input testing signal is a sine wave with expression $V_s(t) = V_m \cdot \sin(\omega_c t)$, the gate width is the T_g at t_1, sampling pulse is $V_s(t)$, after the RC integral the output is

$$V_O(t) = \frac{V_m K_v}{C_c} \int_{t_1}^{t_1 + \frac{T_g}{2}} \sin \omega_c t dt$$
(8)

$$V_O(t) = \frac{2V_m K_v}{\omega_s C_c} \sin \frac{\omega_s T_g}{2} \sin \omega_c t_1$$
(9)

$$[V_O(t)]_{LF} = \frac{2V_m K_v}{\omega_s C_c} \cdot \frac{\omega_s T_g}{2} \sin \omega_c t_1$$
(10)

Eq.(8) and Eq.(9) extracts by the type restores the signal high frequency and ratio of the low frequency component is

$$\frac{[V_O(t)]_{HF}}{[V_O(t)]_{LF}} = \sin \frac{\omega_s T_g}{2} / (\frac{\omega_s T_g}{2})$$
(11)

$$f_{s\max} T_g \leq 0.42$$

$$T_g \leq 0.42 T_{SH}$$
(12)

In order to achieve the level of the resolution required in T_g situation, integrator's response time T_C should be shorter than sample storage time T_g , namely $T_C \prec N_S T_g$, or

$$AT_C = N_S T_g \tag{13}$$

In the formula, A is a constant, usually chooses A=5. Then

$$T_c = 0.2 N_s T_g \tag{14}$$

When the ray radiation arrives weakly separates the photon pulse which appears, with the digital correlation instrument may realize the correlation reception. Figure 7 (b) is for digital correlation schematic diagram.

3 Conclusion

The designed sample integrator and data correlation processing algorithm for ultra-violet photometer. The performance compared with the tradition have been enhanced greatly, mainly manifests in: the resolution enhanced, and the precision improved. This would have provided a good instrument sample for scientific research and the practical production.

Acknowledgment

Thanks to the support of the Natural Science Fundamentation of Henan Province education(NO.2011C510009).

References

1. Wu, W.-m.: Application of UV-VIS Recording Spectra Photometer. Life Science Instrument 7, 60–62 (2009)
2. Li, C.h.: Ultraviolet obvious spectrophotometer book. Chemical industry publishing house, Beijing (2005)
3. Lin, M.: Principle and troubleshooting of 751-type spectra photometer. Medical Equipment Information 20(2), 71–73 (2005)
4. Davis, J.A., Day, T., Lilly, R.A., et al.: Multi-channel optical correlator/convolver utilizing the magneto-optics spatial light modulator. Appl. Opt. 26, 2479–2483 (1987)

Dust Explosion Test System Based on Ethernet and OPC Technology

Nan Miao, Shengjun Zhong, and Qian Zhang

School of Materials and Metallurgy Engineering, Northeastern University,
Liaoning Shenyang 10004

Abstract. Dust explosion characteristics such as maximum explosion pressure, maximum rate of pressure rise, minimum explosible concentration and limiting oxygen concentration are important characteristics to reflect severity and sensitivity of specified combustible dust. A 20L spherical dust explosion test system was developed for dust explosion risk assessment, and the key technologies were described. The test apparatus was developed according to related international standards, and electrostatic ignition was added as alternative ignition source other than pyrotechnical ignition. The control and data acquisition system include programmable logic controller (PLC), personal computer and data acquisition card. The communication between PLC and computer is based on Ethernet and OPC technology. The software working as a virtual instrument was developed using C#. It supports functions of remote control, data acquisition, data analysis and database management.

Keywords: Dust explosion, Measurement, Virtual Instrument, OPC.

1 Introduction

Combustible dusts, such as dusts and powders processed in grain, coal, chemical, textile, metal, pharmacy and other industries, can bring dust explosion hazards in certain conditions [1]. Explosion characteristics include maximum explosion pressure p_{max}, maximum rate of pressure rise (explosion index) K_{st}, minimum explosible concentration MEC and limiting oxygen concentration LOC. These explosion characteristics are important for explosion prevention and mitigation design.

The basic principles for determination of p_{max}, K_{st} were described in ASTM and EN standards [2-4]. A dust cloud is formed in a closed combustion chamber by introduction of dust sample with air. Ignition of the dust-air mixture is then attempted after a specified delay by a pyrotechnical ignition source located at the center of the chamber. The pressure change inside the chamber is transmitted into an electrical signal by the pressure sensor mounted at the chamber wall, recorded by a high-speed data acquisition system. By analyzing the pressure time curve, the p_{max} and K_{st} can be obtained. The determination methods of MEC and LOC are similar with those of p_{max} and K_{st}, which were described in the following standards: ASTM E1515-2007, EN 14034-3-2006 and EN 14034-4-2004.

Traditional explosion test apparatus didn't have communication between control box and computer, or the communication protocols didn't support connection of

G. Shen and X. Huang (Eds.): CSIE 2011, Part II, CCIS 153, pp. 98–103, 2011.

several computers. Normally virtual instrument technology was not applied. High speed data acquisition was carried out by data acquisition systems for general purpose. Sometimes, oscillograph was used for data acquisition, which is not convenient for data analysis and database management.

Tradition ignition source for explosion test is pyrotechnical igniter. Pyrotechnical igniters are not safe during production and transportation, and they are not easy to be obtained because of terrorism control. Furthermore, pyrotechnical igniters are not environmental friendly.

A dust explosion test system was developed according to the international standards. One advantage of the developed test system is that it supports electrostatic ignition up to 10kJ. The other advantage is the advanced design of automation, data analysis and database management. The developed system has good extendibility, maintainability and portability. The concept used in this paper is very good for large scale explosion test which need remote control to prevent from possible hurt in case of unexpected accident during the explosion test.

2 Main Architecture

The explosion test system (Fig. 1) consists of 20L spherical explosion chamber, control and data acquisition system and accessories.

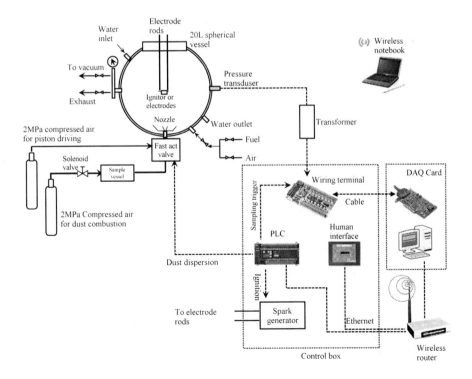

Fig. 1. Schematic of the 20L spherical explosion test system

The explosion chamber is a double-layered stainless steel spherical vessel, and the volume is 20L. Water or other substances can be filled into the double layered jacket to maintain constant temperature inside the chamber. The chamber has inlet/outlet connections for vacuum, exhaust, introduction of flammable gas and compressed air. A fast act valve is mounted at the bottom of the vessel, which is used to disperse dust from sample vessel into the test chamber by compressed air.

A programmable logic controller (PLC), a spark generator, a pressure acquisition board, and a human interface are equipped in the control box.

The spark generator can generate electrostatic energy up to 10kJ, which can be used as an alternative ignition source. The schematic of the spark generator is shown as Fig. 2. The right part of the electrodes is arc-sustaining circuit (main discharge circuit). The voltage of the arc-sustaining power U2 is around 1kV, and the main capacity is 22000 μF. The left part of the electrodes is trigger circuit. The voltage of trigger power U1 is 10kV, and the capacity of trigger capacitance is very small. The principle is to store energy in capacitor with big capacity and relative low voltage, and to break down the gap of electrodes by a capacitor with small capacity and high voltage. After the gap was break down by C1, energy stored in C2 is release in the form of arc-sustaining discharge.

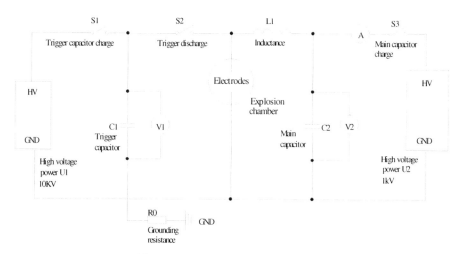

Fig. 2. Schematic of the spark generator

The PLC used for experimental process control is connected with computers by Ethernet cables. Ethernet communication has advantages of faster data transmission, higher reliability and more convenience of system integration.

A data acquisition card installed in a computer working as test server was used for high speed data acquisition. Remote control, data analysis, database management can be done by any computer connected in the local network.

3 Software

The software for process control and data acquisition was developed using C#. Any computer equipment with the test software can be used as a virtual instrument to monitor and control the devices of the test system. The structure of the software is shown as Fig. 3. The main modules of the software are virtual instrument panel and data analysis and management module.

The virtual instrument panel controls the PLC by "OPC DA.Net wrapper", which is a .Net component to support access of OPC server. "OPC DA.Net wrapper" communicates with PLC hardware by lower level device drivers provided by the PLC manufacturer. Currently, the PLC is made by Omron, and "SYSMAC OPC Server" is used as OPC server.

"ActiveDAQ Pro" is an ActiveX library used for data acquisition (DAQ) of Advantech DAQ devices. It is used for fast data acquisition of pressure signal. To use "ActiveDAQ Pro" is much convenient than to use Advantech device driver directly because "ActiveDAQ Pro" is highly encapsulated.

The database platform is Microsoft SQL Server, and it supports network access of different client computers. The data analysis and management module accesses the database by ADO.Net, which is included in Visual Studio. Net development platform.

Test data file is in Microsoft Excel format, and test report is in Microsoft Word format. Office API is used to write and read Excel and word files.

Other computers in the network can monitor and control the test devices by OPC DA.Net wrapper, and they can access the database by ADO.Net. Exactly, they can use the same software as used in the test server. However, fast DAQ function can't be provided in client computers.

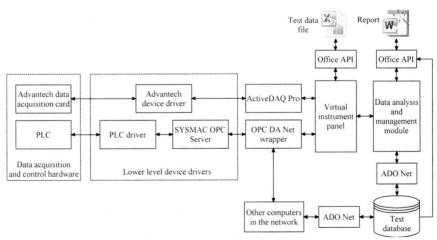

Fig. 3. Structure of the software

4   Key Technologies of the Development Scheme

4.1   Net Platform

Virtual instrument technology is widely used in the field of automation. Typical developed platform of virtual instrument is LabVIEW developed by National Instruments [5]. The advantage of LabVIEW is its easiness to integrate and re-configure a complex automation system. However, for a system that doesn't need frequent reconfiguration, .Net platform is another good solution for virtual instrument development.

Visual Studio .Net was used as the main development platform, and the software was developed using C#. The advantage of .Net platform is that it provides a very good "container" for many third party software components. For example, the curve drawing was powered by ZedGraph, a free component with C# source code.

4.2   OPC Technology

The OPC (OLE for Process Control) standard, proposed in the second half of the 1990s, is a novel process control architecture. OPC consists of a set of standard interfaces, properties and methods that can be used for device communication in process control and manufacturing applications.

OPC is managed by the OPC Foundation, supported by the majority of the companies that operate in the field of process control. OPC was developed as an industrial standard using Microsoft's Object Linking and Embedding (OLE) technology. It defines an industry interface standard, so that access of applications to different hardware can follow the same interface standard, and enables different control devices to communicate with each other by exchanging data[6]. Thus, OPC-based local control systems located in different places can communicate with each other on the LAN without using bus architecture.

5   Conclusion

Through development of the dust explosion test system, we got the following conclusions:

(1) By using OPC technology, the communication with devices of automation becomes very simple.
(2) By using Ethernet communication, test data can be shared by different computers. Ethernet also provides fast and reliable data transfer between control devices and computers.
(3) Microsoft .Net is a good platform for virtual instruments development.

The developed explosion test system has the following advantages:

    (1) electrostatic ignition support;
    (2) high integration, easiness to extend and reconfigure;
    (3) advanced data management and report generation.

References

1. Eckhoff, R.K.: Dust Explosions in the Process Industries, 3rd edn. Gulf Professional Publishing/Elsevier, Boston (2003)
2. ASTM E1226-2005. Standard test method for pressure and rate of pressure rise for combustible dusts
3. EN 14034-1-2004. Determination of the maximum explosion pressure p_{max} of dust clouds
4. EN 14034-2-2006. Determination of the maximum rate of explosion pressure rise $(dp/dt)_{max}$ of dust clouds (2006)
5. Jimeenez, F.J., De Frutos, J.: Virtual instrument for measurement, processing data, and visualization of vibration patterns of piezoelectric devices. Computer Standards & Interfaces 27, 653–663 (2005)
6. Sahin, C., Bolat, E.D.: Development of remote control and monitoring of web-based distributed OPC system. Computer Standards & Interfaces 31, 984–993 (2009)

Optimizing Amplifier for Improving Ultraviolet Photometer Accuracy

Ping Chuan Zhang[1,2,*] and Bo Zhang[2]

[1] Huazhong University of Science and Technology, Wuahn, China, 430074
[2] Dept. of Machine and Electronic Engineering
Luohe vocational Technology College, Henan Province, China, 462002
goldensword@126.com

Abstract. The ultraviolet spectrum photometer is a widely used instrument in science research field and industry applications. Current spectrum photometer uses ordinary circuit structure and data processing algorithm, so its measurement precision and speed needes to be improved. This article improved the ultraviolet spectrum photometer using the lock-in amplifier. Compared with the tradition spectral analysis method, the performance characteristics of the designed systemd are: easy operation, high sensitivity, better selectivity, high accuracy.

Keywords: Lock-in amplifier; Ultraviolet spectrum photometer; band width; Data acquisition.

1 Introduction

Ultraviolet photometer [1] is a widely used instrument for analyzing materials spectrum, suh as the chemical experiment, materials research in food and so on. The traditional ultraviolet spectroscope is mainly composed of six parts [2, 3]: photo source, monochromatic, sample pond, detector, recording devices. There exists an impedance matching problem [4] because the traditional ultraviolet photometer using the ordinary amplifier. Therefore, this article designed an advanced lock-in amplifier to improve its performances.

2 Spectrophotometer Data Acquisition Principle

The basic principle of spectrophotometer [5] is a court attendant Bert birr (Larnbert Beer)law, namely solution extinction Abs, absorption coefficient A, density C, liquid film thickness L is proportional. Namely:

$$Abs = -\lg;T = \lg;I_O / I_t = aCL \quad . \tag{1}$$

---

* Corresponding author.

G. Shen and X. Huang (Eds.): CSIE 2011, Part II, CCIS 153, pp. 104–108, 2011.
© Springer-Verlag Berlin Heidelberg 2011

Where, T is the transmissibility, Io is the incident luminous intensity, It is penetrates the luminous intensity. Each material has specific absorption spectrum, its absorption curve is drawn through the measuring material's extinction or the transmissibility, then distinguishes this material through comparing with the known spectral or determines this material density. Spectrophotometer basic structure commonly used as shown in Figure 1.

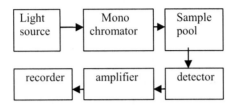

Fig. 1. Spectrophotometer basic structure diagram

Double light beam spectrophotometer signal path [5] as shown in Figure 2. Provide the visible light and the ultraviolet ray continual photo source separately by the tungsten lamp and the atmosphere lamp. After monochromator is splitted into light beam and monochromatic light by a fast rotation's fan-shaped pivoting mirror. The two light beam pass into in the sample pond and the reference pond separately, eliminates the error caused by the photo source change, (therefore is called double light beam type spectrophotometer), (multiplier phototube PMT) receives the luminous intensity signal which alternately with the identical detector penetrates.

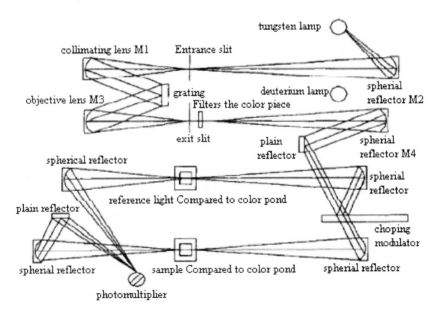

Fig. 2. Double light beam spectrophotometer structures

3 Lock-In Amplifier Design

3.1 Lock-In Amplifier

The lock-in amplifier has two signal channels, one is for testing signal, another is synchronization reference signal, simultaneously is sent to sensitive detector PSD. The lock-in amplifier principle block diagram is shown as Figure 3. It is mainly composed of three parts: the signal channel, the reference channel and the sensitive detector.

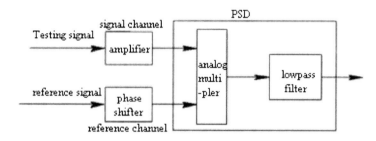

Fig. 3. Lock-in amplifier principle block diagram

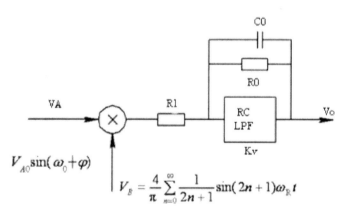

Fig. 4. Sensitive detector principle block diagram

Supposing the testing signal and the reference signal respectively is

$$V_A = V_{A0} \sin(\omega_0 t + \varphi) \qquad (2)$$

$$V_B = \frac{4}{\pi} \sum_{n=0}^{\infty} \frac{1}{2n+1} \sin(2n+\varphi)\omega_R t \qquad (3)$$

Where, reference square-wave signal V_B with the frequency ω_R, phase continuously adjustable range $0°\sim360°$. Through simulates the multiplier (shown as Figure 4) to be possible to obtain output voltage V_o and the phase θ_{2n+1} first-level approximate expression:

$$V_o = \frac{2R_0V_{A0}}{\pi R_1} \sum_{n=0}^{\infty} \frac{1}{2n+1} \frac{\cos\left\{\left[\omega_0-(2n+1)\omega_R\right]t+\varphi+\theta_{2n+1}\right\}}{\sqrt{1-\left\{\left[\omega_0-(2n+1)\omega_R\right]R_0C_0\right\}^2}}$$

(4)

$$\theta_{2n+1} = \arctan\left[\omega_0-(2n+1)\omega_R\right]R_0C_0$$

(5)

Usually let that sensitive detector PSD take the reference signal frequency ω_R as the central frequency of square-wave matched filter. Its fundamental wave ($n=0$) response may be expressed as

$$V_{o1} = \frac{2R_0V_{A0}}{\pi R_1} \frac{\cos\left[(\omega_0-\omega_R)t+\varphi+\theta_1\right]}{\sqrt{1+\left[(\omega_0-\omega_R)R_0C_0\right]^2}}$$

(6)

When signal frequency $\omega_0 = \omega_R$, and supposing the fundamental wave initial phase

$\theta = 0$, correlation instrument output voltage V_0 is

$$V_o = \frac{2R_0V_{A0}}{\pi R_1}\cos\varphi$$

(7)

3.2 Lock-In Amplifier's Main Parameter

Since the PSD integrator is RC filter, its equivalent noise band width definition is

$$\Delta f_n = \frac{1}{4R_0C_0}$$

(8)

Known from (7), the lock-in amplifier output signal V_0 is proportional to the testing signal's peak-to-peak value and ($\omega_0 - \omega_R$) is related to the testing signal and reference signal's frequency difference. Therefore, the equivalent band pass filter band width may be very much narrow, also may use RC filter to reduce the band width. The equivalent signal band width of PSD RC low pass filter

$$\Delta f_s = \frac{1}{2\pi R_0 C_0}.$$

(9)

Δf_s may also regard as the equivalent band pass filter's band width. If $R_0 C_0 = 300s$, then $\Delta f_s = 5.3 \times 10^{-4} Hz$.

4 Conclusion

This paper have improved ultraviolet photometer by designing the lock-in amplifier. The main performance compared with that of the traditional have been enhanced greatly, mainly includes: The resolution is enhanced, the precision and the wave number precision is improved, the wave number scope is increased. This would provide an advanced instrument for scientific research and industry production.

Acknowledgment

Thanks to the support of the Natural Science Fundamentation of Henan Province education(NO.2011C510009).

References

1. Wu, W.-m.: Application of UV-VIS Recording Spectra Photometer. Life Science Instrument 7, 60–62 (2009)
2. Li, C.h.: Ultraviolet obvious spectrophotometer book. Chemical industry publishing house, Beijing (2005)
3. Lin, M.: Principle and troubleshooting of 751-type spectra photometer. Medical Equipment Information 20(2), 71–73 (2005)
4. Royer, H.: Interferometry beyond the coherence length of the light source: the use of channeled spectral lines. J. Opt. 12(4), 229–232 (1981)
5. Davis, J.A., Day, T., Lilly, R.A., et al.: Multi-channel optical correlator/ convolver utilizing the magneto-optics spatial light modulator. Appl. Opt. 26, 2479–2483 (1987)

Game Analysis on Innovative Dynamic Factors and Strategies of Corporations in the Industrial Cluster

Cai Shao-Hong[1,2]

[1] Economy Development Study Center, Guizhou College of Finance and Economics,
Guiyang, 550004, China
[2] Guizhou Key Laboratory of Economics System Simulation, Guiyang, 550004, China
caish@mail.gzife.edu.cn

Abstract. Situated in game theory, this article studies and analyzes the innovative dynamic factors of corporations and their choices of innovative strategies influenced by the factors. It draws the conclusion: the innovative impetus of corporations correlates to the factors about their innovative environments such as the innovative abilities, the capacities of the corporations, innovative cost, expected payoffs, and overflow effect of the cluster. Only can the industrial cluster retains the long-term vitality, the competitive advantage, and sustainable development if it has a good innovative environment, an effective innovative incentive mechanism, and inspired endlessly self-innovation. The crucial reason why some of small/medium-sized corporations in the industrial clusters decay is that they lack of innovative abilities and sufficient innovative impetus.

Keywords: Industrial cluster, corporation innovation, dynamic factors, innovative strategy, game analysis.

1 Introduction

Nowadays, the outstanding performance of the industrial clusters catches the eyes of the world economy. Studies and practices have proved that the industrial clusters take leading role and unique competitive advantages in the regional economy. Generally, the development and evolution of the industrial cluster experiences three stages: regional corporation community, regional industrial cluster, and regional innovation network. Cai (2007) pointed out that the key impetus of the cluster to a higher stage is synergic competition and sustainable innovation. However, the results he (2006) obtained show that many economical systems of regional agglomeration in real society pause their pace of development and evolution when arriving at a certain stage, decaying, shrinking, and even disappearing. One important reason is that the industrial clusters have not had their high effective and ordinal self-organized structures, and the corporations are in the state of insufficient innovative impetus and less innovative capability, which forces the clusters to wander at the lower stage or even to go into "lemon market" because of being in a low-price malignant competition cycle. Therefore, it takes a significant role for the industrial clusters to keep competitive

G. Shen and X. Huang (Eds.): CSIE 2011, Part II, CCIS 153, pp. 109–119, 2011.
© Springer-Verlag Berlin Heidelberg 2011

advantages and sustainable development via observing and analyzing the innovative incentive mechanism of the corporations; finding out the primary reasons which result in the decay of their innovative impetus; taking the measures to improve and optimize their innovative environments; inspiring their innovative impetus; and maintaining their sustainable innovative vitality.

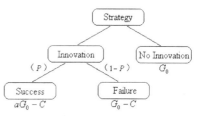

Chart (1) Game Tree of Innovation

2 Game Analysis of Innovative Impetus within Corporation Itself

The innovative activities are important ways to the growth of a corporation. A corporation is in a brutal competitive environment and faces stiff competition for survival from other corporations, thus it would have to keep searching and reforming in pursuit of profit. Innovation is the key point of the searching and reforming. It combines the elements of the corporation resources effectively to improve their inherent utility and to help the corporation get more competitive advantages.

Suppose the innovation of a corporation has only two cases: success and loss, the probability of success is P; the cost of innovation is C; the gain of succeeded innovation is G_S; the gain of failed innovation is G_L; the original gain of no innovation is G_0; we get the following patterns:

$$0 < P < 1 , \quad C = \beta G_0 , \quad G_S = aG_0 - C , \quad G_L = G_0 - C \tag{1}$$

in which $\beta > 0$ means cost coefficient of innovation, $a > 1$ means the coefficient of income growth after innovation has succeeded. The game model is showed in Chart (1). The expected profit of corporation innovation is:

$$\pi_I = (aG_0 - C)P + (G_0 - C)(1 - P) = (a - 1)G_0 P + G_0 - C \tag{2}$$

while the corporation without innovation is:

$$\pi_N = G_0 \tag{3}$$

and when $\pi_I > \pi_N$, the rational corporation has a desire to innovate, meaning there is a critical probability P_C which makes $\pi_I = \pi_N$:

$$P_C = C / (a - 1)G_0 \tag{4}$$

it is only when the probability P of innovation has succeeded in being larger than P_C, that is:

$$P > P_C \tag{5}$$

that the corporation has the impetus for innovation.

With the equation (4), we can conclude that the critical probability P_C relates to expected income growing multiple a, innovative cost C and original gain G_0. In the same condition, the bigger a is, the smaller P is; the bigger C is, the bigger P_C is; and the bigger G_0 is, the smaller P_C is. That is to say: the corporation will get a great profit if innovation succeeds and get a tremendous loss if it fails. The probability P reflects the research and exploited ability of the corporation innovation in association with its researchers, key technology, technological information, and knowledge level. When the research and exploited ability remain unchanged, the larger the cost of the innovation is, and the bigger the successful possibility is. In addition, the bigger the original gain the corporation gets, the smaller the innovative impetus is.

3 Game Analysis of Innovative Impetus without Side Effect of Overflow

In real situation, it is true that there are several homogenous corporations competing mutually as well as facing the situation of overflow effect of knowledge, information and technology. For simple analysis, we first discuss the innovative impetus of the corporations without side effect of overflow (namely, independent intellectual property protected fully). Suppose there are two corporations, A and B, which produce the same products and which do not consider the probability of the innovative success (namely, it can succeed with innovation). Without having innovation, the gains of both corporations will be G_{A0} and G_{B0}; with having innovation succeeded, the gains of both corporations will be G_{AS} and G_{BS}; corporation A having innovation while B not having any, the gains of them will be G_{AH} and G_{BL}; corporation A without having innovation while B does, the gains of them will be G_{AL} and G_{BH}. The income matrix of innovative game of A and B is showed in Table (1) gains of both corporations will be G_{A0} and G_{B0}; with having innovation succeeded, the gains of both corporations will be G_{AS} and G_{BS}; corporation A having innovation while B not having any, the gains of them will be G_{AH} and G_{BL}; corporation A without having innovation while B does, the gains of them will be G_{AL} and G_{BH}. The income matrix of innovative game of A and B is showed in Table (1).

Table 1. Matrix of innovative game income

Corporation A / Corporation B	Innovation	No Innovation
Innovation	(G_{AS}, G_{BS})	(G_{AL}, G_{BH})
No Innovation	(G_{AH}, G_{BL})	(G_{A0}, G_{B0})

We assume that all the profits obtained by the corporation without having innovation are used for innovation, and the original market proportions of A and B are r_A and r_B. We also assume that there are only two corporations in the cluster and the market capacity is limited, then we get:

$$r_A + r_B = 1 \qquad (6)$$

If the corporations both have innovation, then their market proportions are invariant, that is r_A and r_B ; but the gains of A and B will be a times of the original ones because the new products have stronger function, better quality and higher price than the old ones. If corporation A has innovation and succeeds, while B doesn't, corporation A will take part in B's market proportion because of its higher quality products, then their market proportion will be $(r_A + r_{A/B})$ and $(r_B - r_{A/B})$ respectively. On the contrary, their market proportion will be $(r_A - r_{B/A})$ and $(r_B + r_{B/A})$. (Among them, r_A, r_B, $r_{A/B}$ and $r_{B/A}$ are positive numbers, $r_{A/B} < r_B$, $r_{B/A} < r_A$). According to the aforementioned, we can get equations as follows:

$$G_{A0} = r_A G_0 \quad , \quad G_{B0} = r_B G_0 \tag{7}$$

$$G_{AS} = r_A a G_0 \quad , \quad G_{BS} = r_B a G_0 \tag{8}$$

$$G_{AH} = (r_A + r_{A/B}) a G_0 \quad , \quad G_{BL} = (r_B - r_{A/B}) G_0 \tag{9}$$

$$G_{AL} = (r_A - r_{B/A}) G_0 \quad , \quad G_{BH} = (r_B + r_{B/A}) G_0 \tag{10}$$

in which $a > 1$, in accordance with (7) to (10) , we get the game matrix which is showed in Table (2). We can thus conclude:

$$G_{AH} > G_{AS} > G_{A0} > G_{AL} \quad , \quad G_{BH} > G_{BS} > G_{B0} > G_{BL} \tag{11}$$

This manifests that all the corporations will have innovative impetus when without side effect of overflow. However, Chen (2002) claimed that there is a very strong overflow effect of information in the industrial cluster. The innovative motivation and behaviors are more complicated in the real industrial cluster.

Table 2. Matrix of innovative game income without overflow effect

Corporation A / Corporation B	Innovation	No Innovation
Innovation	$r_A a G_0$, $r_B a G_0$	$(r_A - r_{B/A}) G_0$, $(r_B + r_{B/A}) a G_0$
No Innovation	$(r_A + r_{A/B}) a G_0$, $(r_B - r_{A/B}) G_0$	$r_A G_0$, $r_B G_0$

4 Impetus Conditions of Independent Innovation with Overflow Effect

The aforementioned analysis shows that the corporation will be kicked out of the industrial cluster if it has no innovative and upgraded products. However, because of a very strong overflow effect of the technological information in the cluster, it is possible for many corporations to choose either "independent innovation" (the technological breakthrough or the prototype innovation) or "imitative innovation" (imitating competitors' technology). We will analyze the impetus conditions of the independent innovation chosen by the corporation later.

We assume that there are two corporations, A and B, in the cluster which have had independent innovation in the same way and both succeeded. Then their gains will be G_{AS} and G_{BS}; if both A and B imitate the opponent's technology, their gains will be G_{A0} and G_{B0}; if A has independent innovation while B imitates, their gains will be G_{AZ} and G_{BM}; if A imitates while B has independent innovation, their gains will be G_{AM} and G_{BZ}. The game matrix is showed in Table (3).

Table 3. Matrix of innovative game income

Corporation A / Corporation B	Independent innovation	Imitative innovation
Independent innovation	(G_{AS}, G_{BS})	(G_{AM}, G_{BZ})
Imitative innovation	(G_{AZ}, G_{BM})	(G_{A0}, G_{B0})

Suppose the cost of the independent innovation is C_Z, and the cost of the imitative innovation is C_M, then we get:

$$C_Z = \beta_Z G_0 , \quad C_M = \beta_M G_0 , \quad \beta_Z \gg \beta_M \geq 0 \qquad (12)$$

in which β_Z and β_M are cost coefficients of innovative, if the original market proportions of A and B are r_A and r_B, then we get:

$$G_{A0} = r_A G_0 , \qquad G_{B0} = r_B G_0 \qquad (13)$$

and if the gain after successful independent innovation is a times of the original one, then we get:

$$G_{AS} = r_A a G_0 - C_Z = r_A a G_0 - \beta_Z G_0 = (r_A a - \beta_Z) G_0 \qquad (14)$$

$$G_{BS} = r_B a G_0 - C_Z = r_B a G_0 - \beta_Z G_0 = (r_B a - \beta_Z) G_0 \qquad (15)$$

whereas of corporation A has independent innovation while B imitates, due to the overflow effect, corporation B will get extra gain $G_{B/A} = \gamma_{B/A} G_0$ by imitating A's new technology. And corporation A will be forced to lose the equal gain; here we refer $\gamma_{B/A}$ to the overflow coefficient of innovative gain $(\gamma_{B/A} > 0)$. It relates to the original market proportion of A and B. From (13) to (15), we get:

$$G_{AZ} = G_{AS} - G_{B/A} = G_{AS} - \gamma_{B/A} G_0 = (r_A a - \beta_Z - \gamma_{B/A}) G_0 \qquad (16)$$

$$G_{BM} = G_{B0} + G_{B/A} - C_M = (r_B - \beta_M + \gamma_{B/A}) G_0 \qquad (17)$$

and similarly, when corporation B has independent innovation while A imitates, suppose A's extra gain by imitation is $G_{A/B} = \gamma_{A/B} G_0$ ($\gamma_{A/B} > 0$), then we get:

$$G_{BZ} = G_{BS} - G_{A/B} = G_{BS} - \gamma_{A/B} G_0 = (r_B a - \beta_Z - \gamma_{A/B}) G_0 \qquad (18)$$

$$G_{AM} = G_{A0} + G_{A/B} - C_M = (r_A - \beta_M + \gamma_{A/B})G_0 \qquad (19)$$

and put (13) to (19) into table (3), and we get the game matrix showed in Table (4).

To A, if B takes the strategy of independent innovation, and only when $G_{AS} > G_{AM}$, A will have the impetus of independent innovation. From (14) and (19), we can infer the impetus conditions of A's innovation:

Table 4. Matrix of innovative game income with overflow effect

Corporation A / Corporation B	Independent innovation		Imitative innovation	
Independent innovation	$(r_A a - \beta_z)G_0$	$(r_B a - \beta_z)G_0$	$(r_B a - \beta_z - \gamma_{A/B})G_0$	$(r_A - \beta_M + \gamma_{A/B})G_0$
Imitative innovation	$(r_A a - \beta_z - \gamma_{B/A})G_0$	$(r_B - \beta_M + \gamma_{B/A})G_0$	$r_A G_0$	$r_B G_0$

$$\gamma_{A/B} < (a-1)r_A - (\beta_z - \beta_M) \qquad (20)$$

If B takes the strategy of imitation, and only when $G_{AZ} > G_{A0}$, A will have the impetus of independent innovation. From (13) and (16), we can infer the following:

$$\gamma_{B/A} < (a-1)r_A - \beta_z \qquad (21)$$

Similarly, to B, if A takes the strategy of independent innovation, and only when $G_{BS} > G_{BM}$, B will have the impetus of independent innovation. From (15) and (17), we can infer:

$$\gamma_{B/A} < (a-1)r_B - (\beta_z - \beta_M) \qquad (22)$$

If A takes the strategy of imitation, and only when $G_{BZ} > G_{B0}$, B will have the impetus of independent innovation. From (13) and (18), we can infer:

$$\gamma_{A/B} < (a-1)r_B - \beta_z \qquad (23)$$

Thus we can get the impetus condition of independent innovation as shown in Table (5).

The analysis above shows that the independent innovative impetus of the corporation has relation to certain factors such as profit rate,

Table 5. The impetus condition of independent innovation of the corporations

Independent innovation impetus Prerequisites		Corporation A	Corporation B
Opponent behavior	Independent innovation	$\gamma_{A/B} < (a-1)r_A - (\beta_z - \beta_M)$	$\gamma_{B/A} < (a-1)r_B - (\beta_z - \beta_M)$
	Imitative innovation	$\gamma_{B/A} < (a-1)r_A - \beta_z$	$\gamma_{A/B} < (a-1)r_B - \beta_z$

cost, overflow rate, corporation scale (market proportion), and etc. These factors are the innovative environmental parameters of the corporation. Generally speaking, when the cost of independent innovation is not too much ($\beta_z < (a-1)r_i$, i =A,B) and the overflow effect is small enough, the corporation has the impetus of independent innovation.

However, in real environment, due to the stronger overflow effect, higher cost of innovation, and the larger difference between the capacities of corporations, the corporation could not satisfy the conditions of pattern (20) to (23) simultaneously or totally. We will discuss the situation above later among corporations which have bigger difference of capacities and among those which have no difference of capacities.

5 Game Analysis of Innovation When the Difference of Capacity Is Large

In the industrial cluster, there is great difference in scale and capacity between large corporations and small ones. It mainly refers to the difference of the corporation in the market proportion. Suppose there are two corporations, A and B, in the cluster, and A>>B (meaning the capacity of A is much stronger than that of B), namely, $r_A >> r_B$.

Then we get $\gamma_{B/A} >> \gamma_{A/B}$, $\beta_Z >> \beta_M$ generally. To analyze simply and generally, we propose a hypothesis: $r_A = 0.8$, $r_B = 0.2$, $a = 5$. With it, we make computation on the cost of innovation and overflow effect to get three different kinds of innovative environmental parameters of the corporations, as presented in Table (6).

Table 6. Innovation environmental parameters when A>>B

Type	r_A	r_B	a	β_Z	β_M	$\gamma_{B/A}$	$\gamma_{A/B}$	Input rate Overflow rate
I	0.8	0.2	5	0.4	0.04	0.2	0.02	Low
II	0.8	0.2	5	0.6	0.06	0.4	0.04	Medium
III	0.8	0.2	5	0.8	0.08	0.6	0.06	High

Put values in Table (6) into Table 4 respectively, we get three types of innovative income matrix shown in Table (7). Table (7) tells us that, to the lager corporation A, its optimal game strategy is independent innovation no matter what strategies the corporation B chooses: independent or imitative innovation. However, when A chooses independent innovation, there are three kinds of possibility to B: when the independent innovative cost is lower and so is the probability of the overflow effect, B's optimal option is independent innovation; when the independent innovative cost and the probability of the overflow effect are neither high nor low, B's optimal option is imitative innovation; when both the independent innovative cost and probability of overflow effect are higher, B's optimal option is still imitative innovation.

Table 7. Matrix of innovative game income when A>>B(Unit: G_0)

Type		I		II		III	
Corporation A / Corporation B		Independent innovation	Imitative innovation	Independent innovation	Imitative innovation	Independent innovation	Imitative innovation
Independent innovation		3.60, 0.60	0.78, 0.56	3.40, 0.40	0.78, 0.36	3.20, 0.20	0.78, 0.14
Imitative innovation		3.40, 0.36	0.80, 0.20	3.00, 0.80	0.80, 0.20	2.60, 0.52	0.80, 0.20

6 Game Analysis of Innovation If There Is No Difference of Scale and Capacity

There is a little difference of scale and capacity among medium and small corporations in a cluster. To make it simple, we suppose there are two corporations, A and B, in the cluster, with their scale and capacity nearly in the same stage (namely, A≈B). Then we get $r_A = r_B = 1/2$, $\gamma_{B/A} = \gamma_{A/B}$. To keep it general, we make $r_A = r_B = 1/2$, $\gamma_{B/A} = \gamma_{A/B}$. To make the analysis simpler and clearer, we manipulate as we did for Table (6) to get innovative environmental parameters shown in Table (8).

Table 8. Innovative environmental parameters when A≈B

Type	r_A	r_B	a	β_z	β_M	$\gamma_{B/A}$	$\gamma_{A/B}$	Input rate Spillover rate
I	0.5	0.5	4	1	0.1	0.30	0.30	Low
II	0.5	0.5	4	1	0.1	0.55	0.55	Medium
III	0.5	0.5	4	1	0.1	0.80	0.80	High

Put the parameters in Table (8) into Table (4) respectively to get three types of innovative income matrix shown in Table (9). We can infer from Table (9) that there are three possible options of innovative game for the corporations to choose, based on the innovative environmental parameters, when there is no difference of scale and capacity between the two corporations. When the probability of overflow effect is lower, the optimal game strategies of both are independent innovation; when the probability of overflow effect is neither high nor low, their optimal game strategies will be changed depending on the opponent's option; when the probability of overflow effect is higher, their optimal game strategies are both imitative innovation.

Table 9. Matrix of innovative game income when A≈B(Unit: G_0)

Type		I		II		III
Corporation A / Corporation B	Independent innovation	Imitative innovation	Independent innovation	Imitative innovation	Independent innovation	Imitative innovation
Independent innovation	1.00, 1.00	0.70, 0.70	1.00, 1.00	0.95, 0.45	1.00, 1.00	1.20, 0.20
Imitative innovation	0.70, 0.70	0.50, 0.50	0.45, 0.95	0.50, 0.50	0.20, 1.20	0.50, 0.50

In the real medium/small corporation cluster, which innovative model is chosen is depended mainly on the innovative environmental parameters and on the consideration of the corporation in balancing those aspects such as innovative risks, cost, gains, and etc. If the intellectual property cannot be protected well and the side effect of overflow cannot be prevented effectively, the related corporations would choose "imitative" strategy and share freely the technological overflow of the innovative corporations due to the probability of overflow effect; this would restrain the innovative impetus of the independent innovative corporations. Then, "independent innovation" is not good strategy for both the game players. If all the corporations choose the "optimal" rational strategy which is waiting and imitation, the industrial cluster will be in the situation of "the Prisoner's Dilemma" as presented in type III of Table (9), which leads to the technology of the whole cluster to be stagnant. Furthermore, some malignant behaviors, such as copying, plagiarizing, faking, lower pricing, and etc., would be worse and worse, driving the industrial cluster into the "lemon market" which means "the bad driving out the good". The malignant repeated competition would at last bring the whole corporation agglomeration to be destroyed functionally or even disappear. The similar situations happened in the history of the economic development in countries or regions such as Taiwan, Italy, and Japan. This happens very often especially in those regions with many small corporation communities.

7 Strategies to Push the Independent Innovation of the Corporations

7.1 Establish Approximate Perfect Incentive Mechanism of Innovation and Inspire Innovative Impetus of the Corporations

The innovative impetus of the corporation is derived from its pursuit of maximized economic benefit. To do so, first, establish approximate perfect market incentive mechanism to protect the technological innovative impetus of the corporations. Second, make the reasonable policies to push the innovation of the corporations; form suitable innovative incentive system for the corporations to participate in the innovative activities actively; give policy supports to the corporations in finance, taxation, banking, research and exploiting, and governmental purchase; compensate those corporations which participate in independent innovation to make them earn.

7.2 Build Moral Innovative Atmosphere to Protect Innovative Enthusiasm by Enhancing the Protection of Intellectual Property

It is important to strengthen consciousness of protecting intellectual property and to form moral atmosphere of respecting others' intellectual property in the society of the industrial cluster. The owner of the technology innovation should enhance the consciousness of self-protection, apply for patent right and trademark immediately, and ensure the intellectual property to be used with payment. The owner should learn to protect self-legal right with law. The corporations with intellectual property are encouraged to set up trade associations or organizations, alliances for protecting intellectual property, and industrial associations for protecting intellectual property. The government should build the mechanism of arbitration and coordination to deal with the cases of infringing intellectual property severely for protecting the innovative enthusiasm of the corporations.

7.3 Build Public Service Platform of Technology Innovation to Enhance Innovative Ability in the Cluster

It is important to encourage the research and introduction of the crucial general technology and key technology in/into the industrial cluster, engendering a integrated technological innovative chain, which is from theory research to applied research, to exploited research, and finally to technology industrialization. To improve the innovative ability and efficiency of the corporations in the clusters and to provide the support of the leading information and technology, and to offer human resources for the corporations, it is necessary to employ fully the research advantages of the universities and research institutions. To achieve this goal, it is also important to set up the innovative resources center, corporation hatch base, technological service institution, the platform for attracting capital and entrepreneurs, and network for communication and cooperation.

7.4 Establish Approximate Perfect and Efficient Innovative Mechanism of Collaboration and Cooperation of the Corporations to Restrain Overflow Loss

It is necessary to establish a high efficient and ordinal cooperative innovative mechanism, in which the corporations in the clusters should take risks and share benefits together. To make the mechanism work, we can make a system of responsibility in which the corporations should take risks and share benefits brought by the cooperative innovation. The ways of cooperation may be innovative models and organizational forms, such as technological contract, project cooperation, base cooperation, fund cooperation, research cooperation, etc. The extent of responsibility for each corporation should be based on its investment, obligation, benefit, risk, etc, with the form of cooperation. In detail, the risk responsibility should be divided into different levels and stages, which means whoever invests more will get more; who makes decision will take charge of the project; who takes charge of the project will be responsible for it; and who takes great risk will get great benefit. To do so, the innovative overflow-loss will be restrained effectively and greatly.

7.5 Build Effective Investment and Financing System to Reduce Innovation Risk in the Cluster

Because the traditional way of loan and financing from the bank is not suitable to high-risk feature of corporation innovation, it is necessary to reform the system of investment and financing, to take use of financial instruments such as risk investment, industrial fund, etc., and to build a risk-decentralized mechanism of corporation innovation. It is also necessary to encourage private capital to be used in hi-tech risk investment and in establishing risk investment fund. All these done are satisfying the various demands of investing and financing of the corporation innovation in different stages, enhancing the confidence of the corporation innovation, and reducing the risks of corporation innovation.

Acknowledgments

This work was sponsored by the National Social Science Foundation of China under Grant No. 10XJY0022, governor's specified fund of Guizhou Province, and Guizhou specified fund for senior scholars.

References

1. Gordon, I., McCann, P.: Industrial Clusters: Complexes, Agglomeration and/or Social Networks. Urban Studies 37(3), 513–532 (2000)
2. Morgan, K.: The Exaggerated Death of Geography Learning, Proximity and Territorial Innovation Systems. Journal of Economic Geography 4(1), 3–21 (2004)

3. Feldman, F., Bercovitz, J.: Bercovitz Creating a Cluster While Building a Firm: Entrepreneurs and the Formation of Industrial Clusters. Regional Studies 39(1), 129–141 (2005)
4. Cai, S.-h., Wang, J.-s.: Self-organized Cooperative Mechanism of Evolution from Regional Enterprise Community to Industrial Cluster. Inquiry Into Economic Problems (3), 69–73 (2007) (in Chinese)
5. Cai, S.-h.: Cyclic Industrial Cluster — The New Model of Industrial Organization for Ecologic Development of Western Regions. The People's Publishing Press, Beijing (2010) (in Chinese)
6. Zhang, W.-y.: Game Theory and Information Economics. Shanghai San Lian Press, Shanghai (2004) (in Chinese)
7. Hua, Y.-j.: Game Analysis of Research and Development Dilemma in Medium and Small Enterprises. Economy and Management 19(12), 59–61 (2005) (in Chinese)
8. Liu, Z.-b., Chen, X.-h.: Game Analysis of Investment Strategy Evolution for Corporation Innovation. Engineering Management 19(1), 56–59 (2005) (in Chinese)

Learning Frequent Episodes Based Hierarchical Hidden Markov Models in Sequence Data

Li Wan

Chongqing University, Computer Science and Technology College, China
wanli@cqu.edu.cn

Abstract. We present a non-overlapping serial Episodes Based Hierarchical Hidden Markov Model (EBHHMM). Each EBHHMM is associated with two types of temporal frequent patterns, i.e. non-overlapping serial episodes and the presented SEI (Serial Episode Interactions). Serial episode interaction is a set of non-overlapping serial episodes which are correlated and occurs frequently in sequence. As the key advantage of our approach, we do not need any prior-knowledge to learn the structure of EBHHMM. Extensive experiments perform on real world data demonstrate that EBHHMM gets larger maximum log likelihood (has better quality) than existing models.

Keywords: Serial Episode, Hierarchical Hidden Markov Model, Sequence Data.

1 Introduction

Domains such as bioinformatics, sensor network, WWW, finance generate massive amounts of sequence data [1,2,3]. A sequence can be considered as a set of ordered tokens, where a token is a categorized symbol in a finite alphabet. Each token is associated with a timestamp or index. In real world applications, we observe that temporal frequent patterns occur in sequence in a hierarchical way. Therefore, we can get more information from a hierarchy of frequent patterns than frequent patterns in a single scale. Non-overlapping serial episode is a type of frequent pattern of tokens. A **serial episode** is a subsequence that appears in a single sequence with frequency no less than a user-specified threshold. A **NOSE (Non-Overlapping Serial Episode)** is a serial episode, such that any two of its occurrences which contribute to its frequency do not intersect with each other. In real world sequence data, some non-overlapping serial episodes usually occur correlated. Therefore, these correlated non-overlapping serial episodes are not only frequent pattern their selves, but also form frequent temporal patterns in larger scale. We define a set of correlated non-overlapping serial episodes with frequency exceeds a user-specified threshold as **SEI (Serial Episode Interaction)**.

However, temporal frequent pattern, such as NOSE and SEI, can only represent local feature (knowledge) of sequence. Learning generative model is an approach to discover global feature in sequence. S. Laxman etc. [4] presented an Episode Generated Hidden Markov model (EGH) as generative model of sequence. Since each EGH is associated with only one episode, one EGH cannot generate the whole observed

G. Shen and X. Huang (Eds.): CSIE 2011, Part II, CCIS 153, pp. 120–124, 2011.

sequence accurately. Therefore, mixture EGH model is presented in Ref.[5]. Each EGH in mixture EGH associates with a weight which indicates the probability the symbol generated by this EGH really occurs in the observed sequence. However, mixture EGH cannot describe the transition relation and probability among EGHs. To model gaps between tokens, M. Zaki et al. [6] present VOGUE, a variable order hidden Markov model with state durations. However, all the three models cannot incorporate the complex hierarchical structure of subsequences and tokens. Hierarchical Hidden Markov Model (HHMM) [7] is a type of generative model which is motivated by the complex multi-scale structure of tokens which appears in many natural sequences, such as DNA. To represent a sequence by its local features (frequent patterns) and global feature (generative model) complementarily, we propose a hierarchical generative model **EBHHMM (serial Episode Based Hierarchical Hidden Markov Model)** which associate with two types of hierarchical frequent patterns, i.e. NOSE and SEI.

Contributions:

- We design a specialized class of HHMM, namely Episodes Based HHMM (EBHHMM). An EBHHMM has a four level state hierarchy which is decided by a set of NOSE and SEI discovered from the observed sequences.
- We propose a greedy algorithm to learn EBHHMM and measure quality of estimated models by maximum log-likelihood (larger maximum log likelihood indicates better quality).
- Extensive experiments on real world dataset demonstrate that EBHHMM has better quality than HMM and mixture Episode Generated HMM (mixture EGH).

The remainder of the paper is organized as follows. Section 2 gives the details of EBHHMM and presents algorithms to discover SEI and learn EBHHMM. Section 3 presents the experimental evaluation. Section 4 concludes the paper.

2   Frequent Episodes Based HHMM

We utilize existing algorithm NOE [4] to discover non-overlapping episode. Then we define the concept of serial episode interactions.

2.1   Serial Episode Interactions Discovery

Intuitively, serial episode interaction (SEI) is a type of frequent pattern of correlated serial episodes. Since "Overlap" is the most popular correlated relation between correlated serial episodes, we concern on overlapping relation of NOSEs.

Definition 1 (Overlapping relation [8]): Serial episode α overlaps β, if and only if $\alpha.begin < \beta.begin < \alpha.end < \beta.end$, where $e.begin$ and $e.end$ denotes the begin time and end time of episode e respectively. The overlapping relationship of α and β is donated as $\alpha \_ overlap \_ \beta$.

To study overlapping relations among a set of NOSEs, we present episode graph to organize all the discovered NOSE occurrences. Each occurrence of NOSE corresponds to a vertex in episode graph. If two NOSE occurrences are overlapping, there exists an edge between their corresponding vertices in the episode graph. Episode graph is a weighted graph with weights on vertices. The weight on a vertex is the name (or index) of the NOSE represented by the vertex. As illustrated in Fig.1, the NOSEs in (a) are organized in an episode graph in (b).

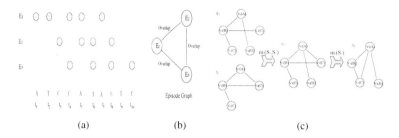

| (a) | (b) | (c) |

Fig. 1. An example of episode graph: (a) occurrences of NOSE: E_1, E_2, E_3. (b) an episode graph constructed from occurrences of NOSEs in (a). (c)An example of merging sub-graphs into SEI.

Since frequent sub-graphs in episode graph represent stable overlapping relations among NOSEs, we reduce serial episode interaction discovery into frequent sub-graph discovery and aggregation in an episode graph.

Definition 5 (Serial *episode interaction*)**:** Given a set of frequent sub-graphs in episode graph, a set of SEIs is discovered by aggregating the sub-graphs. A serial episode interaction is denoted as $I = (V, R)$, where $V = \{\alpha_1, \alpha_2, ..., \alpha_n\}$ is a set of NOSEs, R is an overlapping relation on set V. If $rel(\alpha_i, \alpha_j)$, then $(\alpha_i, \alpha_j) \in R$.

As illustrated in Fig. 1(c), S_1 and S_2 merge into a maximal sub-graph S_3 which represents a SEI. We utilize vSIGRAM algorithm [9] to find frequent sub-graphs in episode graph. For limited space, we do not list details of this function here.

2.2   Model Description

An EBHHMM has a four level state hierarchy associated with a set of NOSEs and SEIs. Therefore, the states of an EBHHMM emit sequences contain frequent patterns rather than a single symbol or sequences without the embedding frequent patterns. An EBHHMM generates sequences by a recursive activation of one of the sub-states of a state. This process of recursive activations ends when we reach a special state which we term a production state. The production states are the only states which actually emit observable symbols through the usual HMM state output mechanism. Hidden states that do not emit observable symbols directly are called internal states. We term the activation of a sub-state by an internal state a vertical transition. Upon the completion of a vertical transition, control returns to the state which originated the recursive activation chain. Then, a state transition within the same level, which we call a horizontal transition, is performed. Only the states in the second level (sub-states of root) can associate with a SEI and the state in the third level (sub-states of the state associate with a SEI) can associate with a NOSE.

Figure 2 gives an example of EBHHMM. We note that there are some constraints on *pattern* state and *noise* state. A pattern state associated with serial episode interaction, $q_i^2(SEI_j)$, can only have one noise sub-state and each of its pattern sub-states must associate with a serial episode which is included in the associated serial episode interaction SEI_j. A *pattern* state $q_i^3(Epi_k)$ associates with a NOSE Epi_k, such that $\left|\Gamma(q_i^3(Epi_k))\right| = 2N+1$, where $N = \left|Epi_k\right|$. As illustrated in the dash box in Fig.2, a token state $q_j^4(o_i)$ can only transit to a noise state $q_{j+1}^4(noise)$ or the token state $q_{j+2}^4(o_{i+1})$, where o_{i+1} occurs right after o_i in Epi_k, where $o_i, o_{i+1} \in \Sigma$. The noise state $q_{j+1}^4(noise)$ can transit to itself or $q_{j+2}^4(o_{i+1})$. Under these constraints, EBHHMM can generate sequence in which NOSEs and SEIs embed in noise.

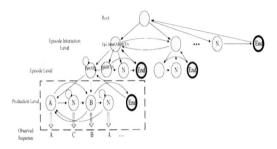

Fig. 2. An example of EBHHMM

3 Experimental Evaluation

The experiments were run on a PC with Intel Celeron at 2.50GHz and 2GB RAM. We implemented the model learning algorithms using Matlab, pattern discovery algorithms using Java. The quality of generative model is measured by log likelihood: $LH = \log P(X \mid \Lambda)$, where $P(X \mid \Lambda)$ is the probability of model Λ generates observed sequence X. The model gets higher log likelihood is better. Gene Database [10] is used to evaluate our model and it has 3190 records of splice junctions and each record has 60 symbols. Splice junctions are points on a DNA sequence at which 'superfluous' DNA is removed during the process of protein creation in higher organisms.

We compare EBHHMM with mixture EGHMM on Gene Database. We split this database into 10 datasets with the same size and estimate models on these datasets respectively.

As illustrated in Fig. 3(a), in almost all of the experiments, log maximum likelihood of EBHHMM is around 10% larger than that of mixture EGH. In Fig. 3 (b), we give the log maximum likelihood of EBHHMM with different number of episode states. For space limitation, we only list results on dataset 1 to 5 sampled from Gene Database. The results in Fig. 3(b) show that selecting proper episode and episode interactions to form EBHHMM structure is important for learning EBHHMM. EBHHMM associated with proper frequent patterns can improve LH up 25%.

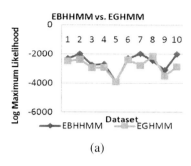
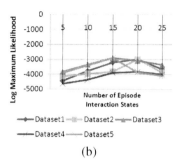

(a)   (b)

Fig. 3. (a) Log maximum likelihood comparison between EBHHMM and EGHMM. **(b)** Selecting different structure to estimate EBHHMM.

4 Conclusions

We present a generative model, EBHHMM, which formulate multi-scale structures in sequence formed by token, non-overlapping serial episode and serial episode interaction. Our experimental evaluations show that EBHHMM can model observed sequences better than mixture EGHs.

References

1. Durbin, R., Eddy, S., Krogh, A., et al.: Biological Sequence Analysis. Cambridge University Press, Cambridge (1998)
2. Jensen, K., Styczynski, M., Rigoutsos, I., et al.: A generic motif discovery algorithm for sequential data. Bioinform. 22, 21–28 (2006)
3. Nanopolulos, A., Katsaros, D., Manolopoulos, Y.: A data mining algorithm for generalized Web prefetching. IEEE Trans. Knowl. Data Engin. 15(5), 1155–1169 (2003)
4. Laxman, S., Sastry, P.S., Unnikrishnan, K.P.: Discovering frequent episodes and learning Hidden Markov Models: A formal connection. IEEE Transactions on Knowledge and Data Engineering 17(11), 1505–1517 (2005)
5. Laxman, S.: Stream Prediction Using A Generative Model Based On Frequent Episode. In: Event Sequences Proceeding of KDD (2008)
6. Zaki, M.J., Carothers, C.C., Szymanski, B.K.: VOGUE: A Variable Order Hidden Markov Model with Duration based on Frequent Sequence Mining. ACM Transactions on Knowledge Discovery From Data 4(1) (2010) Article 5
7. Fine, S., Singer, Y., Tishby, N.: The Hierarchical Hidden Markov Model: Analysis and Applications. Machine Learning 32, 41–62 (1998)
8. Carl, H.M., John, F.R.: Mining relationships between interacting episodes. SIAM, Philadelphia
9. Kuramochi, M., Karypis, G.: Finding frequent patterns in a large sparse graph. Data Mining and Knowledge Discovery (2005)
10. Molecular Biology (Splice-junction Gene Sequences) Data Set,
    http://archive.ics.uci.edu/ml/datasets/

Discovering Probabilistic Sequential Pattern in Uncertain Sequence Database

Li Wan

Chongqing University China
wanli@cqu.edu.cn

Abstract. Sequence data are subject to uncertainties in many applications due to incompleteness and imprecision of data. We propose a novel formulation of probabilistic sequential pattern discovering problem and an algorithm UCMiner to discover probabilistic sequential pattern in uncertain sequence database. Extensive experiments evaluate the factors impact our techniques and shows that our approach is significantly faster than a naïve approach.

Keywords: sequential pattern; uncertain sequence; temporal frequent pattern.

1 Introduction

Domains such as bioinformatics, sensor network, WWW, finance generate massive amounts of sequence data. But existing studies [1,2,3,4] on frequent pattern mining in sequence data only considered deterministic sequences which are precise and complete. However, sequence data are generally subject to uncertainties caused by noise, incompleteness and inaccuracy in practice.

We deal with **uncertain sequence** data. This uncertain sequence data is a series of tokens in which each token is a categorized symbol in a finite alphabet and associated with a timestamp and an existence probability. The existence probability of a token indicates the possibility of the token occurring in the sequence. We are interested in knowledge in the form of sequential pattern in uncertain sequence database. Such a pattern can look like "the price of Sun stock goes up then Microsoft stock's price goes down and finally IBM stock keep going up for two days, the expectation value of this pattern is 0.75". This **probabilistic sequential pattern** is associated with an expectation value computed from uncertainties and this value indicates the chance of the pattern existing in reality. Existing studies on mining uncertain data focus on frequent itemset mining [5], sub-graph mining [6], clustering [7], classification [8], and so on. However, all the approaches do not investigate problem of discovering probabilistic sequential pattern in uncertain sequence data.

Contributions

- We present an algorithm, UCMiner, using two proposed optimal strategies to improve the efficiency of discovering probabilistic sequential patterns.
- Extensive experiments were carried out to evaluate factors impact the efficiency of UCMiner.

G. Shen and X. Huang (Eds.): CSIE 2011, Part II, CCIS 153, pp. 125–131, 2011.

The remainder of this paper is organized as follows: Section 2 formulates the problem of discovering probabilistic sequential pattern. Section 3 presents UCMiner algorithm. Section 4 gives experimental results and Section 5 concludes this paper.

2 Problem Statement

Definition 1 (*Uncertain Sequence*): An uncertain sequence is a system $S = (O, \Sigma, P)$, where Σ is a set of token types, $P : O \rightarrow (0,1]$ is a function assigning existence possibility values to tokens, and $O = \{(o_1, t_1, p_1), (o_2, t_2, p_2), ..., (o_n, t_n, p_n)\}$ is an ordered sequence of tokens. A token appears in uncertain sequence is a tuple (o_i, t_i, p_i) such that $o_i \in \Sigma$ occurs at time point t_i with probability $p_i = P(o_i)$.

Definition 2 (*Complete Implicated Sequence*): An implicated sequence $I_c^S = (O', \Sigma')$ of $S = (O, \Sigma, P)$ is a complete implicated sequence of S such that all the tokens can occur in S occur in I_c^S, i.e. $o_i' = o_i$ for $\forall o_i' \in O', o_i \in O$, $\Sigma' = \Sigma$. Thus, an uncertain sequence S can only implicate one complete implicated sequence.

Definition 3 (*occurrence*): A subsequence $\alpha = \{o_1 \rightarrow o_2 \rightarrow ... \rightarrow o_k\}$ occurs in an implicated sequence $I = (O', \Sigma')$ if there exists at least one ordered sequence of tokens $s' = \{(o_1, t_1), (o_2, t_2), ..., (o_k, t_k)\}$ such that $s' \subseteq O$ and $\forall i \in \{1, ..., k-1\}$, $0 < t_{i+1} - t_i \leq \max Gap$. $\max Gap$ is a user-defined threshold that represents the maximum time gap allowed between two consecutive tokens. The interval $[t_i, t_k]$ is called an occurrence of α in I. $occ(\alpha, I)$ denoted the set of all the occurrences of α in I.

Definition 4 (*minimal occurrence*): Let $[t_s, t_e]$ be an occurrence of a subsequence α in the implicated sequence $I = (O', \Sigma')$. If there is no other occurrence $[t_s', t_e']$ such that $(t_s < t_s' \wedge t_e' \leq t_e) \vee (t_s \leq t_s' \wedge t_e' < t_e)$ i.e. $[t_s', t_e'] \subset [t_s, t_e]$, then the interval $[t_s, t_e]$ is called a minimal occurrence of α. $mo(\alpha, I)$ denotes the set of all minimal occurrences of α in I.

The significance of the subsequence α can be measured by the expected value of the support of α in uncertain sequence database, D, called *expected support*, i.e.

$$e\sup_D(\alpha) = \sum_{i=1}^{m} \alpha_i P(\alpha_i) = \sum_{d \in I(D)} \sup_d(\alpha) P(D \Rightarrow d) \tag{1}$$

Definition 5 (*Probabilistic Sequential Pattern*): A subsequence α is probabilistic sequential pattern in uncertain sequence database D, if the expected support of α in D exceeds a user-specified threshold $\min \sup \in [0,1]$.

3 Discovering Probabilistic Sequential Pattern

If subsequence α occurs in an uncertain sequence $S \in D$ is denoted by $\alpha \subseteq_U S$, the probability of α occurring in S is

$$P(\alpha \subseteq_U S) = \sum_{I \in I(S)} P(S \Rightarrow I) \psi(I, \alpha)$$

where $I(S)$ is the set of all implicated sequence of S, $\psi(I, \alpha) = 1$ if $occ(\alpha, I) \cap mo(\alpha, I_c^S) \neq \phi$ and $\psi(I, \alpha) = 0$ otherwise. Thus, Eq. (1) can be rewritten as follows.

$$e \sup_D(\alpha) = \sum_{d \in I(D)} \sup_d(\alpha) P(D \Rightarrow d) = \sum_{d=\{I_1, I_2, \dots, I_{|D|}\} \in I(D)} (\frac{P(D \Rightarrow d)}{|D|} \sum_{i=1}^{|D|} \psi(I_i, \alpha)) \quad (2)$$

$$= \frac{1}{|D|} \sum_{i=1}^{|D|} \sum_{I \in I(S_i)} \psi(I, \alpha) P(S_i \Rightarrow I) = \frac{1}{|D|} \sum_{i=1}^{|D|} P(\alpha \subseteq_U S_i)$$

Consequently, the essential problem of computing expected support of a subsequence in the uncertain sequence database is to compute the existence probability of it in each uncertain sequence in database, i.e. $P(\alpha \subseteq_U S_i)$. However, it is difficult to calculate this probability directly according to its definition. Therefore, we transform the problem of computing $P(\alpha \subseteq_U S_i)$ to the *Disjunctive Normal Form (DNF)* counting problem. To compute $P(\alpha \subseteq_U S)$, we first discover all minimal occurrences of α in the complete implicated sequence $I_c^S \in I(S)$. Then we construct a DNF formula $F_\alpha = C_1 \vee C_2 \vee \dots \vee C_n$ with $mo(\alpha, I_c^S)$ using the method given previously. By the Inclusive-Exclusive Principle [9], we have

$$P(\alpha \subseteq_U S) = \sum_{1 \le i \le n} P(S \Rightarrow \alpha_i) - \sum_{1 \le i < j \le n} P(S \Rightarrow \alpha_i \wedge \alpha_j) + \dots + (-1)^{n-1} \sum_{1 \le i_1 < i_2 < \dots < i_n \le n} P(S \Rightarrow \alpha_{i_1} \wedge \alpha_{i_2} \wedge \dots \wedge \alpha_{i_n}) \quad (3)$$

where $P(S \Rightarrow \alpha_{i_1} \wedge \alpha_{i_2} \wedge \dots \wedge \alpha_{i_n})$ denotes the probability of all the minimal occurrences $\alpha_{i_1}, \alpha_{i_2}, \dots, \alpha_{i_n}$ synchronously occur in an implicated sequence of S. Supposing tokens independently occur in sequence, we have

$$P(S \Rightarrow \alpha_{i_1} \wedge \alpha_{i_2} \wedge \dots \wedge \alpha_{i_n}) = \prod_{o_i \in \alpha_{i_1} \cup \alpha_{i_2} \cup \dots \cup \alpha_{i_n}} Pr(o_i) \quad (4)$$

Above all, to solve the problem of discovering probabilistic sequential patterns in uncertain sequence database, we have to solve three sub-problems: (1) discover all the minimal occurrences of a subsequence in the complete implicated sequence of each uncertain sequence; (2) calculating its existence probability defined by Eq. (3); (3) calculate its expected support defined by Eq. (2). We use algorithm proposed by N. Meger et al [1] to solve sub-problem (1).

3.1 Computing Existence Probability of Subsequence

We propose an efficient algorithm to calculate the existence probability based on the following theorem.

Theorem 1: Suppose $\alpha_1, \alpha_2, ..., \alpha_n$ are n minimal occurrences of subsequence α in implicated sequences of uncertain sequence S. If α_p and α_q $(1 \le p < q \le n)$ do not share tokens occur at the same time points in implicated sequences.

$$P(S \Rightarrow \alpha_{i_1} \wedge \alpha_{i_2} \wedge ... \wedge \alpha_{i_n}) = P_1 \cdot P_2 / P_3 \tag{5}$$

where $P_1 = P(S \Rightarrow \alpha_1 \wedge \alpha_2 \wedge ... \wedge \alpha_{p-1} \wedge \alpha_{p+1} \wedge ... \wedge \alpha_n)$, $P_2 = P(S \Rightarrow \alpha_1 \wedge \alpha_2 \wedge ... \wedge \alpha_{q-1} \wedge \alpha_{q+1} \wedge ... \wedge \alpha_n)$
$P_3 = P(S \Rightarrow \alpha_1 \wedge \alpha_2 \wedge \alpha_{p-1} \wedge \alpha_{p+1} \wedge ... \wedge \alpha_{q-1} \wedge \alpha_{q+1} \wedge ... \wedge \alpha_n)$

To get the minimal occurrences do not share tokens efficiently, we use a matrix $M_{mo(\alpha, I_c^S)}$ to represent relations between minimal occurrences in $mo(\alpha, I_c^S)$. $M_{mo(\alpha, I_c^S)}$ is a $\left| mo(\alpha, I_c^S) \right| \times \left| mo(\alpha, I_c^S) \right|$ matrix, its element $m_{ij} = 1$ if minimal occurrence $\alpha_i, \alpha_j \in mo(\alpha, I_c^S)$ share tokens at the same time points and $m_{ij} = 0$ otherwise.

3.2 Computing Expected Support of Subsequence

Although we can prune a candidate of probabilistic sequential pattern whose prefix is infrequent, the calculation of $P(\alpha \subseteq_U S_i)$ to get $e \, sup_D (\alpha)$ is computationally expensive. We present a prune strategy which prune infrequent candidate subsequences without calculating all the $P(\alpha \subseteq_U S_i)$ ($i = 1, 2, ..., k$).

Theorem 2: Given an uncertain sequence database D. $prefix(\alpha)$ is the prefix of subsequence α, for $k = 0, 1, ..., |D|$,

$$e \sup_D (\alpha) \le \frac{1}{|D|} (\sum_{i=1}^{k} P(\alpha \subseteq_U S_i) + \sum_{i=k+1}^{|D|} P(prefix(\alpha) \subseteq_U S_i)) \tag{6}$$

The right side of inequation (6) is the upper bound of expected support of α. If the value of the right side of inequation (6) is less than the user-defined mini-mum expected support $\min Sup$, then α is infrequent. Since all the $P(prefix(\alpha) \subseteq_U S_i)$ have been calculated before visiting α, we only need to calculate $P(\alpha \subseteq_U S_i)$ ($i = 1, 2, ..., k$) to calculate the value of right side of inequation (6).

4 Experiments

In this section, three real data sets downloaded from the UCI[1] repository were used in the experiments, i.e. *Promoter* [10], *Splice* [11] and *Unix-user* [12]. We note that these real datasets are deterministic datasets. In order to obtain uncertain datasets, we introduced the uncertainty to each token in these datasets. We assume that the uncertainty of those tokens follows different distributions, i.e. uniform distribution and normal distribution $N(\mu, \sigma^2)$ with different value of parameters.

We compare UCMiner with a NAIVE algorithm which calculates expected support and prune candidate subsequences, but not utilize the proposed prune strategies presented in subsection 3.1 and 3.2. We ran these two algorithms under different minimum support and maximum gap constraint to compare their efficiency on datasets with different sizes and existence probability distributions. The experiments were conducted on a machine with 2.66GHz CPU and 2G main memory installed. The operating system is Windows7. We implemented the algorithms in Java. In all experiments, the runtime was measured in milliseconds (ms).

4.1 Time Efficiency of UCMiner

We report results for different values of $\min Sup$ and $\max Gap$ in Figure 1 and Figure 2. Figure 1 illustrates results get from experiments on *Splice* dataset. The results reported in Figure 2(a) base on *Promoter dataset* with existence probability following uniform distribution, and the results in Figure 2(b) base on *Promoter dataset* with existence probability following normal distribution $N(0.6, 1/21)$. UCMiner beats NAÏVE at almost all the settings of $\min Sup$ and $\max Gap$ .The speed up due to the presented prune strategies is significant and increases with $\min Sup$. Figure 3 illustrates results get from experiments on *Unix-user* dataset. The UCMiner works faster

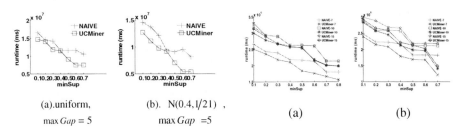

(a).uniform,   (b). N(0.4,1/21) ,

$\max Gap = 5$ $\max Gap =5$ (a)   (b)

Fig. 1. *Splice* dataset   **Fig. 2.** *Promoter* dataset

---

[1] http://archive.ics.uci.edu/ml/

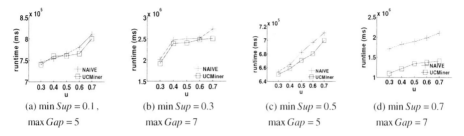

(a) min $Sup = 0.1$,
max $Gap = 5$

(b) min $Sup = 0.3$
max $Gap = 7$

(c) min $Sup = 0.5$
max $Gap = 5$

(d) min $Sup = 0.7$
max $Gap = 7$

Fig. 3. *Unix-user* dataset with existence probability following normal distribution $N(u, 1/2l)$, u is the mean value of normal distribution

than NAÏVE for databases in which most of the tokens have high existence probabilities. The reason is straightforward, the higher the existence probability of tokens, the higher the probability that a given subsequence is probabilistic sequential pattern, thus the number of computations that can be pruned decreases.

5   Conclusion

This paper investigates the problem of mining probabilistic sequential patterns in uncertain sequence database. In context of uncertainty, the probabilistic sequential pattern mining problem is formalized by introducing the expected support. A discovering algorithm, UCMiner, is presented to discover probabilistic sequential patterns in uncertain sequence database. Experimental results show that UCMiner has high efficiency.

References

1. Meger, N., Rigotti, C.: Constraint-based mining of episode rules and optimal window sizes. In: Boulicaut, J.-F., Esposito, F., Giannotti, F., Pedreschi, D. (eds.) PKDD 2004. LNCS (LNAI), vol. 3202, pp. 313–324. Springer, Heidelberg (2004)
2. Mannila, H., Toivonen, H.: Discovering generalized episodes using minimal occurrences. In: Proceedings of SIGKDD (1996)
3. Agrawal, R., Srikant, R.: Mining sequential patterns. In: Proceeding of the 1995 International Conference on Data Engineering (ICDE 1995), pp. 3–14. IEEE Computer Society Press, Washington, USA (1995)
4. Gong, C., Xindong, W.: Mining sequential patterns across time sequences. New Generatoin Computing 26, 75–96 (2008)
5. Aggarwal, C.C., Li, Y., Wang, J., Wang, J.: Frequent pattern mining with uncertain data. In: KDD, pp. 29–38 (2009)
6. Zhaonian, Z., Li, J., Hong, G., Shuo, Z.: Frequent subgraph pattern mining on uncertian graph data. In: Proceedings of CIKM (2009)
7. Cormode, G., McGregor, A.: Approximation algorithms for clustering uncertain data. In: PODS, pp. 191–200 (2008)

8. Tsang, S., Kao, B., Yip, K.Y., Ho, W.-S., Lee, S.D.: Decision trees for uncertain data. In: ICDE, pp. 441–444 (2009)

9. Mitzenmacher, M., Upfal, E.: Probability and Computing: Randomized algorithms and probabilistic analysis. Cambridge University Press, Cambridge (2005)

10. http://archive.ics.uci.edu/ml/datasets/Molecular+Biology+%28 Promoter+Gene+Sequences%29

11. http://archive.ics.uci.edu/ml/datasets/Molecular+Biology+%28 Splice-unction+Gene+Sequences%29

12. http://archive.ics.uci.edu/ml/datasets/UNIX+User+Data

A Context-Aware Semantic-Based Access Control Model for Mobile Web Services

HaiBo Shen and Yu Cheng

School of Computer, Hubei University of Technology, Wuhan 430068, China
jkxshb@163.com, chengyu125@126.com

Abstract. The emergence of ubiquitous mobile devices, such as mobile phones, PDAs, and laptops, has sparked the growth of mobile web services. Unlike traditional identity/role based approaches for access control, access decisions for mobile web services will depend on the combination of the required attributes of user and the contextual information. As well as, it is crucial that the policy system can understand and interpret semantics of the context. This paper proposes a context-aware semantic-based access control model (called CASBAC) to be applied in mobile web services environment by combining semantic web technologies with context-aware policy mechanism. The proposed model adopts a context-centric policy method, and grants permissions to users according to current context information and allows high-level description and reasoning about contexts and policies. The model-theoretic semantics of CASBAC is an extension of the model-theoretic semantics defined in the OWL standard and SWRL.

Keywords: Mobile Web Services, Context-Aware, Semantic-Based Access Control, OWL, Ontology, SWRL.

1 Introduction

With the recent developments of 3G and 4G mobile telecommunications technologies, the high-end mobile phones and PDAs are becoming pervasive and are being used in different application domain. Integration of the web services and mobile telecommunication domains leads to the new application domain, mobile web services [1]. Mobile web services are the application of web services technology to the mobile environment. Mobile web services are defined as web services that are deployed on mobile devices and are published over the Internet, wireless network or within the operators' network. The goal of mobile web services is to offer new personalized services to consumers on their mobile devices such as telephones, wireless-LAN-enabled PDAs and laptop computers.

In mobile web services environment, users are mobile and typically access resources using mobile devices. The context of a user (i.e. location, time, system resources, network state, user's activity, devices, etc.) is highly dynamic, and granting a user access without taking the user's current context into account can compromise security as the user's access privileges not only depend on "who the user is" but also on "where the user is" and "what is the user's state and the state of the user's

G. Shen and X. Huang (Eds.): CSIE 2011, Part II, CCIS 153, pp. 132–139, 2011.

environment". As well as, even an authorized user can damage the system as the system may have different security requirement within different contexts. Therefore, it is crucial to have a policy system that understands and interprets semantics of the context correctly. This type of access control is called semantic access control [2] or semantic-based access control [3]. Traditional access control mechanisms based on the identity or role of access requester break down in such an environments and a context-aware semantic-based access control mechanism that based on semantic information of a user and context information is required [4].

Therefore, this paper proposes a context-aware semantic-based access control model (called CASBAC) for mobile web services by combining semantic-based access control with context-aware policy mechanism. In CASBAC, this paper uses OWL (Web Ontology Language [5])-based semantic representations to formally represent knowledge of the domain, context information and policy. Furthermore, this paper specifies access control policies as rules over ontologies representing the concepts introduced in the CASBAC model, and uses semantic web rule language (SWRL [6]) to form policy rule and infer those rules by inference engine.

The paper is organized as follows: Second 2 briefly surveys the related works. Section 3 presents CASBAC model for mobile web services. In the last section, the conclusion is given.

2 Related Work

Yuan et al. [7] and Shen et al. [8] proposed respectively an attribute-based access control (ABAC) model for web services. Michael et al. [9] presented a contextual attribute-based access control model for mobile computing. They used environment attributes to capture relevant context information for restricting and regulating user privileges. But they didn't use semantic web technologies for access control.

Toninelli et al. [10] suggested a semantic context-aware access control framework for secure collaboration in pervasive computing environments. They proposed a simple OWL-based context model and based on this model, they proposed a context-aware policy model and express policy statements using description logic.

Naumenko et al. [11] proposed to use semantics-based access control (SBAC) model for mobile web services. SBAC model is a result of introducing vocabularies and interpretations of specific security-related concepts inheriting all features of OWL and SWRL due to the compatibility with their direct model-theoretic semantics.

Liu et al. [12] presented semantic access control for web services. They set up access control policy ontology for web services, and specify access control policies in OWL-S by using it and SWRL. He et al. [13] showed how semantic web technologies can be used to build a flexible access control system for web service. Their access control model was represented by an OWL-DL ontology, and specific semantic rules are constructed to implement dynamic roles assignment.

Chen et al. [14] concentrated on representing contexts in a formal way. This work serves as a very first approach in using semantic technologies for context representation.

3 Context-Aware Semantic-Based Access Control Model

In this section, we will introduce CASBAC model and its access control implementation architecture.

3.1 CASBAC Model

The model-theoretic semantics of CASBAC model is an extension of the direct model-theoretic semantics defined in the OWL standard and SWRL. The CASBAC model is a result of introducing vocabularies and interpretations of specific security-related concepts inheriting all features of OWL and SWRL due to the compatibility with their direct model-theoretic semantics. Figures 1 shows the core part of the CASBAC model. The CASBAC model defines the following concepts and relations.

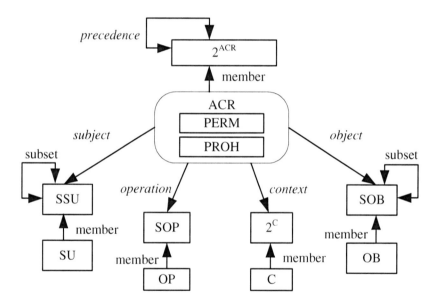

Fig. 1. The core part of CASBAC model

--A subject of access is a service requestor (a person or agent) who invokes the protected web services by the service provider using a mobile phone or regular computer through Internet and mobile networks.

--An object of access represents a protected web service.

--An operation of access is an event that a subject seeks to perform on objects.

-- A context is any information that can be used to characterize the situation of an entity, which is relevant for access control decisions and enforcement.

--C is a set of contexts

--SU is a set of subjects, and SSU is a set of subsets of subjects, that is $SSU \subseteq 2^{SU}$

--OB is a set of objects, and SOB is a set of subsets of objects, that is $SOB \subseteq 2^{OB}$

--OP is a set of operations that could be actions, transactions, access modes, etc. SOP is a set of subsets of operations, that is $SOP \subseteq 2^{OP}$.

--SSU, SOB and SOP sets can be partially ordered by the transitive subset relation.

--ACR is a set of access control rules that denotes a many-to-many abstract relation between subject, operation, object and context of access using the four binary relations described below. Binary relations *subject, operation, object* and *context* are defined between ACS and the corresponding sets of subsets of subjects, operations, objects, and contexts respectively, that is *subject*:ACR→SSU, *operation*:ACR→SOP, *object*:ACR→SOB, and *context*:ACR→2^C.

--PERM is a set of permission rules, which is a subset of ACR, that is $PERM \subseteq 2^{ACR}$. A permission is a positive authorization of subjects to access objects using some operations within some contexts.

--PROH is a set of prohibition rules, which is a subset of ACR, that is $PROH \subseteq 2^{ACR}$. A prohibition is a negative authorization subjects to access objects using some operations within some contexts. Introducing means for the specification of prohibitions into CASBAC model enhances expressivity of the policy language to make negative authorization explicit.

--*precedence* is a binary relation between sets of access control rules, that is *precedence*: $2^{ACR} \rightarrow 2^{ACR}$. Because the policies with permissions and prohibitions are not free from conflicts in an arbitrary case, those policies require mechanisms to resolve conflicts and ambiguity for the guarantied decidability.

--Authorization rules formally define the decision making functions for policies with only permissions or prohibitions or both with different precedence. In the most general form, a policy rule that decides on whether a subject *su* can have the permission, or prohibition to perform a operation *op* on an object *ob* in a given context *c*, is a Boolean function of *su, ob, op* and *c*, that is *access*: $SU \times OP \times OB \times C \rightarrow Boolean$. In CASBAC model, a policy rule *access* can be expressed as blow:

   access(su,op,ob,c)=($\exists$ perm∈ PERM, su∈ *subject*(perm), op∈ *operation*(perm), ob ∈ *object*(perm), c ∈ *context*(perm), ((*precedence*(PERM, PROH) $\vee$ (*precedence*(PROH,PERM), ¬ ($\exists$ proh∈ PROH, su∈ *subject*(proh), op∈ *operation*(proh), ob∈ *object*(proh), c∈ *context*(proh))))

--The CASBAC model is expressed in the form of ontologies (including subject ontology, object ontology, operation ontology and context ontology), and the related ontologies define the CASBAC policy language. We can specify the ontology-based access control policies (policy ontology) according to the related ontologies in CAS-BAC model.

3.2 CASBAC Access Control Architecture

The CASBAC access control architecture is illustrated in Figure 2 below.

The diagram reflects the following logical actors involved in CASBAC model:

1. The Knowledge Base (KB) is a data repository of domain ontology. KB is composed of the set of security policy rules in SPR, subject attributes (SA), object attributes (OA), subsumption relations between concepts (SUB) and context information (CI). Inference of implicit authorization rules is based the facts and rules in the KB.

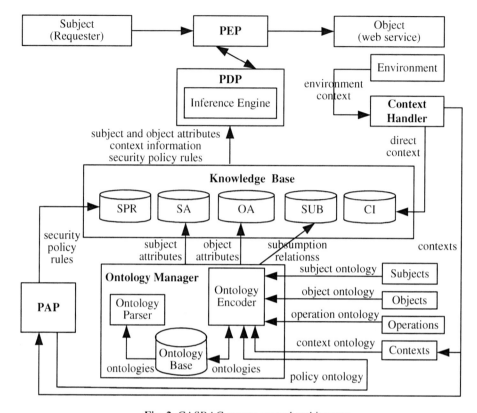

Fig. 2. CASBAC access control architecture

2. The Ontology Manager is responsible for gathering and updating ontologies in domains of subjects, objects, operations, contexts and policies and also reducing the semantic relations to the subsumption relation.

3. The Context Handler is responsible for getting the contextual information from external environment, and performing assertion to the KB database according to the model of the domain knowledge as well as maintaining the consistency of the KB since the KB has to accurately reflect the dynamic changes of the environment.

4. The Policy Enforcement Point (PEP) is responsible for requesting authorization decisions and enforcing them. In essence, it is the point of presence for access control and must be able to intercept service requests between service requester and providers. Although the diagram depicts the PEP as a single point, it may be physically distributed throughout the network. The most important security engineering consideration for the implementation of a PEP is that the system must be designed such that the PEP cannot be bypassed in order to invoke a protected web service.

5. The Policy Decision Point (PDP) is responsible for evaluating the applicable policies and making the authorization decision (permit or deny) by making use of an inference engine, based on facts, attributes, contexts and rules in the KB. The PDP is

in essence a policy execution engine. When a policy references a subject attributes, object attributes, or context that is not present in the request, inference engine (for example, JESS rule engine) in PDP contacts the KB to retrieve the attribute value(s) and contextual information.

6. The Policy Administration Point (PAP) is responsible for creating a policy or policy set.

3.3 Context-Aware Access Control Policy

Access control policies specify the actions that subjects are allowed to perform on resources depending on various types of conditions, e.g., resource state and context aspects. Policies are usually written in the form of restricted rules in that the action component of the rule returns a "Deny" or "Allow" decision. Moreover, to make easier the task of policy evaluation, policies are enforced through a set of authorizations, stating for each subject the rights she has on the protected resources. Thus, we can encode each policy as a rule, that is, a rule whose antecedent represents the conditions stated in the policy subject and object specifications, and the consequent represents the entailed authorizations. In addition, a policy must be able to use the contexts of the situation in order to perform access control in mobile web services environment. Therefore, this paper develops a policy ontology (called CASBACPloicy, shown in Figure 3.) to integrate it with other ontologies in CASBAC model.

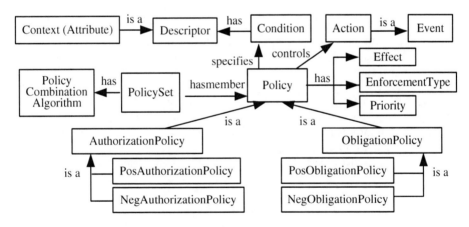

Fig. 3. CASBACPolicy ontology

In CASBACPolicy, a policy defines a set of conditions, which are evaluated to determine whether a set of actions may be performed on a resource. So access control policy can be described as condition-action rules. A condition determines whether or not an action should be performed. In other words, conditions specify the environment (i.e. the descriptor) for an action to be executed. Descriptors, such as time, location or other contexts, express the condition of a policy. Context is a subclass of Descriptor. Thus, every policy is context-aware.

In CASBAC model, context-aware access control policy is introduced. Context-aware access control policy is an access control policy but written in a form of rules to be able to capture the situational context. If the policy requires defined contexts, it will be written with a set of rules which identify which contexts are under consideration. In other words, these rules provide the parameters to reason over the KB in order to obtain the accurate information of the context. The context ontology provides contexts and their semantics to the policy in order to construct policy rules. The context-aware access control policy can always look up the meanings of the contexts from the context ontology. Context ontology and handling framework can be found in our previous work [15].

SWRL has been introduced to extent the axioms provided by OWL to also support rules. In SWRL, the antecedent (called the body) and the consequent (called the head) are defined in terms of OWL classes, properties and individuals. This paper adopts SWRL to encode policy rules where the antecedent encodes the conditions specified in the policy, whereas the consequent encodes the implied authorizations or prohibitions. As consequence, the access control policies can be enforced by simply querying the authorizations, that is, the KB. The query can be easily directly implemented by the ontology reasoner by means of instance checking operations, or can be performed by a SPARQL [16] query, if the ontology is serialized in RDF.

4   Conclusion

This paper proposes a context-aware semantic-based access control model (CASBAC) to be applied in mobile web services environment by combining ontology technologies with context-aware access control policy mechanism. CASBAC uses OWL-based semantic representations to formally represent knowledge of the domain, context information and access control policy, and SWRL to form context-aware access policy. OWL+SWRL can be used to define ontologies, using which one can declaratively define facts, policies, and rules in terms of what needs to be true or false for a policy to hold. As a future work, we are now concentrating on the design of a deployment model that includes different components in charge of monitoring contexts, installing policies into the system, performing policy refinement and evaluation, and enforcing policies.

Acknowledgment. This work is supported by National Natural Science Foundation of China under grant No. 60873024.

References

1. Farley, P., Capp, M.: Mobile web Services. BT Technology Journal 23(2), 202–213 (2005)
2. Ercan, T., Yıldız, M.: Semantic Access Control for Corporate Mobile Devices. In: Hsu, C.-H., Yang, L.T., Park, J.H., Yeo, S.-S. (eds.) ICA3PP 2010. LNCS, vol. 6082, pp. 198–207. Springer, Heidelberg (2010)
3. Javanmardi, S., Amini, M., Jalili, R., Ganjisaffari, Y.: SBAC: semantic based access control. In: The 11th Nordic Workshop on Secure IT-Systems, pp. 157–168. IEEE Press, New York (2006)

4. Satish, N.S., Matthias, J., Wolfgang, P.: Security analysis of mobile web service provisioning. International Journal of Internet Technology and Secured Transactions 1(1), 151–171 (2007)
5. McGuinness, D.L., van Harmelen, F.: OWL web ontology language semantics and abstract syntax (2004), http://www.w3.org/TR/owl-semantics/
6. Horrocks, I., Patel-Schneider, P.F., Boley, H.: SWRL: A Semantic Web Rule Language Combining OWL and ReleML (2004), http://www.w3.org/Submission/SWRL/
7. Yuan, E., Tong, J.: Attributed Based Access Control (ABAC) for Web Services. In: The 2005 IEEE International Conference on Web Services (ICWS 2005), pp. 561–569. IEEE Press, New York (2005)
8. Shen, H.B., Hong, F.: An attribute-based access control model for web services. In: The Seventh International Conference on Parallel and Distributed Computing, Applications and Technologies (PDCAT 2006), pp. 74–79. IEEE Press, New York (2006)
9. Michael, J.C., Manoj, R.S.: A contextual attribute-based access control model. In: Meersman, R., Tari, Z., Herrero, P. (eds.) OTM 2006 Workshops. LNCS, vol. 4278, pp. 1996–2006. Springer, Heidelberg (2006)
10. Toninelli, A., Montanari, R., Kagal, L., Lassila, O.: A semantic context-aware access control framework for secure collaborations in pervasive computing environments. In: The 5th International Semantic Web Conference on Collaborations in Pervasive Computing Environments, pp. 5–9. ACM Press, New York (2006)
11. Naumenko, A., Srirama, S., Terziyan, V.: Semantic authorization of mobile web services. Journal of Theoretical and Applied Electronic Commerce Research 1(1), 1–15 (2006)
12. Liu, M., Xie, D.Q., Li, P.: Semantic access control for web services. In: the International Conference on Networks Security, Wireless Communications and Trusted Computing (NSWCTC 2009), pp. 55–58. IEEE Press, New York (2009)
13. He, Z.Q., Huang, K.Y., Wu, L.F.: Using semantic Web techniques to implement access control for web service. In: The International Conference on Information Computing and Applications (ICICA 2010) 2010, pp. 258–266. IEEE Press, New York (2010)
14. Chen, H., Finin, T., Joshi, A.: An ontology for context-aware pervasive computing environments. Special Issue on Ontologies for Distributed Systems, Knowledge Engineering Review 18(3), 197–207 (2004)
15. Shen, H.B., Cheng, Y.: A semantic-aware context-based access control framework for mobile web services. In: The 3rd International Conference on Networks Security, Wireless Communications and Trusted Computing, NSWCTC 2011 (2011) (in press)
16. SPARQL Query Language for RDF (2008), http://www.w3.org/TR/rdf-sparql-query/

Investigation of the Information Security in Mobile Internet

Pengwei Zhang, Xiaojing Jiao, and Ruijin Zhou

Henan Institute of Science and Technology
Xinxiang, Henan, China
zhangpw7611@163.com

Abstract. Mobile Internet brings great convenience to our works with the rapid development of mobile Internet. This paper analyzed the concept of mobile internet, indicated the problems of the information security in mobile internet and the technical reasons of these problems, and put forward some feasible suggestions from the following three aspects such as mobile terminal, mobile networking and business application, respectively.

Keywords: Mobile internet, Information security, Terminal, network.

1 Mobile Internet Concept

With the changes of the times, the Internet has been taken from PC (Personal Computer) to the mobile terminal, and mobile terminal is more and more intelligent. Mobile Internet is compared with the traditional fixed Internet character, and it is the combination of mobile communication and mobile Internet, emphasizing the access to the Internet and use business. It is to use mobile phones, PDA (PDA, Personal Digital Assistant), portable computer, special mobile Internet terminals as terminals, mobile communication network or wireless LAN as access method, directly or through the WAP protocol access to the Internet and use the Internet business.

2 The Information Security of Mobile Internet

Mobile Internet brings positive side to people's life and work, also brings a lot of security problems, such as indiscriminate garbage information, stealing privacy information of threats to Internet security cases. By the end of 2009, the viruses that can run on smartphone platform have nearly 800. Mobile Internet has inherited the vulnerability of the traditional technology of the Internet and mobile communication network, and faced two risk threats of many Internet and are YiDongWang double IP mineralization security, can be expected, mobile Internet security issues in the near future will be highlighted, the worst-hit areas safety problems can be summarized as terminals, network, business three aspects.

G. Shen and X. Huang (Eds.): CSIE 2011, Part II, CCIS 153, pp. 140–144, 2011.
© Springer-Verlag Berlin Heidelberg 2011

2.1   Terminal Security Problems

As gradually strengthened communication technology progress, the popularity of intelligent terminals and processing ability of memory and chip, a potential threat of intelligent terminal appeared such as unauthorized tampering information, unauthorized access, modifying the information in the terminal through the operating system, damaging data using viruses and malicious code, viruses, trojans, worms, phishing prevailed, etc. We can analyze security problems of mobile internet information from characteristics of mobile intelligent terminals.

(1) User individuation of mobile terminal. Generally, smartphone, PDA, and so on belong to mobile Internet terminals. It has more personalized characteristics than ordinary personal computer. The storage contents may include some personal data such as location information, communication of information and consumer preferences, user contacts information, ordering relationship information of business application, internet trajectory information of users, communication recording, schedule, family information, private photos, etc. it will bring big damage to users if the information was illegally gained, and even worse if these personal information was malicious forged and became more deceptive.

(2) Limited defense capabilities. There was no safety protective measures for most smatphones and PDA terminals such as firewall, anti-virus software etc before using the mobile internet business in relative close application environments. Due to the particularity of mobile internet terminals, the traditional anti-virus software and other measures cannot copy them directly to the limited bandwidth of mobile internet. Besides, mobile internet uses wireless access, however, because of the frequency resource constraints, access rate generally lower than traditional way of cable access. So, the bandwidth resource of mobile internet terminals is easily exhausted if there was an attack from the traditional internet.

2.2   Problem of Network Security

Network security threats include illegal access networks, the destruction to the confidentiality and integrity of data, conducting the denial-of-service attack, leading to the network overload by using various means to produce data packets, attacking by using sniffer tools, systematic vulnerabilities and program vulnerabilities. Currently trojans, eavesdropping software, rogue software, etc have become increasingly rampant. It had been discovered more than 600 kinds of malicious software around the world and the numbers are increasing. Usually, these malicious softwares were automatically installed to mobile phone users without knowing and bring various kinds of harm to the user such as order services, mass texting and malicious pay without informing users; cluster spam messages or forwarding virus and damaging user credit according to the communication recoding list of users mobile; even causing mobile phone run slowly, crash by damaging cell phone software and hardware. Typical problems can be summarized as follows:

(1) Malicious harassment

Because the users usually carry cell phone, malicious harassment in the phone has great effect on users, such as spam messages, harassing phone calls and spam, etc. 3G networks of high bandwidth to malicious harassment provides more convenience conditions to users, such as poping up advertisement in the desktop of mobile phone, joining a bookmark into the mobile phone favorites folder, adding specific recording phone number in mobile communication, etc.

(2) Illegal eavesdropping

The current massive mobile network does not use encryption mechanism, and some parts used the lower strength encryption mechanism to access network. So it can be cracked in a comparatively short time, the user information content can be easily accessed by unauthorized users. Although agreements about encryption were defined in mobile communication network, there was no application due to cost in most countries.

(3) User identity counterfeit

Deceiving internet for service by disguised as a legitimate terminal. In the current mobile network, there are a lot of no authentication situations. Although using authentication agreements, it still easily is to be cracked. Even using MAC address for access control, it is still difficult to prevent MAC address fake. In mobile communication network, 2G network provides a one-way authentication, and the authentication algorithm intensity is weak and may be forced to be cracked. In 3G networks, this situation was improved and the possibility of user identity counterfeit is reduced greatly.

(4) Damaging data and signal integrity

Damaging the data integrity by modifying, inserting, and deleting user data or signaling data. The current wireless means lack the protection to signaling and data integrity. Malicious users affect the normal online users by inserting, replaying, etc means, such as forcing users off-line.

3   Business Security Problems

Business security include unauthorized access business, unauthorized access data, flooding garbage information, adverse dissemination of information, disclosure of personal privacy and sensitive information, content copyright theft, etc. For example, the users of mobile internet may suffer from various channels of garbage information such as SMS, WAP, interference E-mail, etc. All kinds of information of users generally will be saved in core network of the mobile network and business database such as location information, communication information and consumer preferences, customer contact information, billing dialog information, business application order relations information, users online trajectory information, users pay information, users right information, etc. The lawbreakers can accurately extract this information by using of mobile network technology, and in extreme cases, they will conduct illegal and criminal activities.

4 The Strategies to Solve the Problem of Information Security in Mobile Internet

4.1 The Strategies of Terminal Security

Aiming at the malicious harassment phenomenon in terminal, setting a firewall resisted configuration; Aiming at the phenomenon that users to find their own personal privacy was leaked, through setting passwords, smart way and entity differential mechanism personal privacy ,we make the security protection, and can use anti-theft products protect privacy. If the user found the malicious programs on a terminal, we can use monitor system and terminal software to intercept and delete the virus. For safety protection and access control to data information, we can set access control policy to ensure safety; for the stored internal data in a terminal, we can set the test of the integrity of the data for hierarchical and isolation storage to ensure security.

4.2 Network Security Policy

At present, in the mobile Internet access, we have a set of intact security mechanism for 2G or 3G. The current mobile Internet content most the WAP websites and the number of WAP website is small, we can reduce adverse information, guarantee the network security under the supervision for the WAP site.

(1) Security system construction
First, based on the operating system of Window, we can increase firewall software against the virus in terminal network. Secondly, we can configure intrusion detection products to monitor host in the network segment; finally, we can configure mobile security testing machine that loading scan and anti-virus software to complete of other devices of scanning loophole and checking virus.

(2) Construction of safety system in network
First, the terminal need to be equipped with anti-virus software, that be able to control for all nodes anti-virus software for centralized control, including centralized issued, centralized updates, centralized configuration management, remote installation, remote antivirus, remote alarm function; Secondly, the terminal need to be equipped with firewall centralized management software, that can be centralized configured and managed on all nodes firewall equipment; In addition, the terminal need to be equipped with centralized analysis software that can analyze the firewall log on the all node; Finally, the terminal need to be equipped with intrusion detection control software to centralized control the all node intrusion detection software.

Since March, 2009, International communication office, Ministry of Industry and Information Technology of the P.R.C., Ministry of Public Security of the P.R.C., Ministry of Culture of the P.R.C., State Administration for Industry and commerce, State Administration of Radio film and television, General Administration of Press and Publication and China Baking Regulatory Commission jointly launch the special action which focused on regulating the vulgar use of mobile phone, purifying mobile internet network environment from the source. Specific as follows:

a. Operators should take social responsibility and taking the technical measures for the WAP gateway, to ensure teenagers have clean internet without suffering yellow etc. bad violations by filtering vulgar website and bad information

b. Software vendors should speed up the development of green internet software which is suitable for different operating systems, computational power and limited memory cell phone. The government should advocate mobile phone manufacturer who should preinstall related green internet software.

In order to thoroughly solve security problems in mobile internet network, it should start from the whole industry chain, installing the relevant filtering software and firewall in the client-side (mobile) to prevent from receiving garbage information. For service provider (SP), it should strengthen management, strict control, optimize and adjust the Content Provider (CP). Meanwhile, government should carry out the corresponding supervision and establish the reasonable policy regulation system.

4.3 Business Security Strategy

Mobile internet business security needs the help from whole industry chain, not only the efforts from equipment provider, the software provider, etc such value chain parties to achieve a network security, but also the corresponding regulation from government departments which establish reasonable policy regulation system for it. First, in order to track and reprimand all kinds of mobile internet crime and intensify law enforcement, the government should coordinate the benefit of different supervision department, establish and perfect the safety supervision mechanism of mobile internet, establish complete information service permission, filing system and information release system for mobile internet, establish a complete news publication business rules for examination and approval for mobile internet and establish and perfect relevant laws and regulations. Second, equipment manufacturers must strengthen the safety performance study of equipment, enhance the safety performance of the developed product and at the same time install safe protection software to ensure equipment safety by using integrated firewall, antivirus software or other technology and protect business safety from hardware. Third, software providers provide integral safety technology products and improve the development level of software technology according to the needs change of customers, transiting from the single functional products protection type to the centralized and unified management products type, continuously improving cooperation with safety operators and providing encryption business to users.

References

1. Liang, W.: Green internet of mobile internet. Modern Telecommunication Technology 5, 37–39 (2009)
2. Jianfeng, Y.: Security threats exploration to mobile internet. Telecommunication Network Technology 13, 29–32 (2009)
3. He, L.: Development situation and problem analysis of domestic and foreign mobile internet. Modern Telecommunication Technology 25, 60–61 (2009)
4. Jun, M., Hui, M.: Problem analysis and suggestions for mobile internet security. Modern Telecommunication Technology 97, 33–36 (2009)
5. Liang, W.: Mobile internet security framework. ZhongXing Communications Technology 26, 29–30 (2009)

Network Security Technology in P2P

Pengwei Zhang, Xiaojing Jiao, and Ruijin Zhou

Henan Institute of Science and Technology
Xinxiang, Henan, China
zhangpw7611@163.com

Abstract. The current main threat that P2P networks are facing to is network virus, routing attack, access attack, malicious attacks and Sybil attack, etc. This paper summarized the P2P network security technology including anonymous technology, cryptography technology, security routing technology, etc and pointed out that solving the crux of the problem of the P2P network security is the application of trust model.

Keywords: Peer-to-peer network; Network security; Trust model.

1 Introduction

P2P network is widely used on file sharing, peer-to-peer computing, instant messaging, information retrieval, etc and brings convenience and shortcut to users. However, many P2P network layer technologies are not mature enough and there are many problems need to be solved. This paper reviewed the existing security threats of P2P network, common safety technology, safety trust model and other circumstances and expected to provide theoretical basis for the future development of networks.

2 The Main Security Threats

2.1 Network Virus

In P2P environment, convenient sharing and rapid choosing way mechanism provides better invasion opportunity for certain network virus. As long as there is one node infection virus, it can spread to nearby neighbor node by passing an internal shared and communication mechanism. In a short time, it can lead to network congestion even paralysis, confidential information stolen, and then completely control the P2P networks through the network virus.

2.2 Routing Attack

The attacker which as the participants of P2P systems, sending incorrect routing information to other nodes, destroy the routing table of other node, causing the system nodes carry out incorrect routing operation. Specific routing attacks contain wrong routing inquiry, wrong routing updates, etc.

G. Shen and X. Huang (Eds.): CSIE 2011, Part II, CCIS 153, pp. 145–149, 2011.

Wrong routing inquiry. In P2P network, routing inquiry is through the ordinary node of network. So, it was difficult to ensure that those nodes that participating to the routing inquires are normal users. If malicious node involved in the process of routing inquiry, it can bring inquiry to an incorrect even non-existent node. Furthermore, once malicious node involved in P2P network, and then participating to the process of routing inquires, it will remain online without invalidation. In this way, redirected inquiry could be rearranged and referred to another malicious node.

Wrong routing updates. Because routing information which is maintained by every node in the P2P network is obtained through other nodes inquiries, false renewal request of routing information which is sent to other nodes by a malicious node can destroy the routing table of each node. The effect of such attacks may cause some innocent node will also send inquiry to the vicious or nonexistent node by mistake.

2.3 Access Attacks

The attackers correctly perform inquiry agreement, but refuse to provide the saved data by their own nodes, causing other nodes cannot get data. Appearance of such kind of circumstance can cause increase of hitchhiker in P2P network and damage the trust mechanism as well as the existing incentive mechanism that has been already established in system network. These malicious attacks will finally damage the overall interests of network.

2.4 Malicious Attacks

Attackers can attack mid-range distant nodes in network, however, show all normal illusion to the nodes close to it. Then, the distant node can easily find this as an attacker, but the neighbor nodes think this as a normal node. The method that dealing with this attack is distance nodes send a message to the neighbor node of the attacker and tell it the information of attacker. However, if there is no support of public key and digital signature mechanism, this message sending mechanism cannot be established.

This is a kind of common attacking method to network, for the purpose of occupying resources such as memory, CPU and network bandwidth of the target host, making them unable to provide the normal service to outside or unable to be normal operation. The main methods are sending junk data to the goal and then make it too late to response, or elaborately constructing abnormal data packets by using the vulnerabilities of target host that causing the collapse of the target system. At the beginning of the design of P2P network, failure problem of a single point and equality status of each node in network is considered, and then P2P networks will not collapse because of a node collapse.

2.5 Sybil Attack

Many large-scale P2P networks are facing the security threats from remote malicious node or nodes failure. In order to solve these problems, many P2P systems introduced redundancy copy mechanism. P2P systems must ensure that each node ID only labeled one node in network. Otherwise, if a node is corresponding to multiple nodes ID, such things probably appear: when a node is in redundancy copies, on the surface it chose a group of different ID nodes in network, but in fact it is likely to be cheated by malicious node, causing the same node was chosen. Thus effectiveness of redundancy copy was destroyed.

3   Application of Network Security Technology in P2P

3.1   Cryptography Technology

P2P application contains a lot of cryptography technology including: symmetrical cipher technology, public-key cipher technology and one-way hash function etc. Symmetrical cipher technology is mainly used for data encryption. When communicating parties are sharing keys, symmetric cryptosystem can guarantee confidentiality of communication data. In Skype system, the AES symmetric algorithm for data encryption was used in the communication process of end-to-end encryption. Public-key was mostly used in the key of consultation session. When communicating parties have public key of each other, conversation key agreement can use public-key algorithm, and then the safety of session keys was ensured. In P2P systems one-way hash function is frequently used. Especially in DHT network, most of the DHT networks are using one-way hash function mapped to 128 b ID space through client IP address, documents of keywords and the content of the document, constructing virtual address of DHT network. The mono-direction of one-way hash function guaranteed these ID can not be forged.

3.2   The Identity Authentication Technology

The identity authentication technology is a technology that can verify the authenticity and efficacy of the identity of users through the validation and verification of authentication system in the information network. The purpose is to distinguish legitimate users and illegal users. Thus illegal user access to system was prevented. The identity authentication problem in P2P networks can be regarded as an issue that how to choose reliable resources in a free center environment, that is how to authenticate nodes and build reputation among the nodes. P2P network greatly weakens the role of the server in the network, making there is lack of an authoritative entity in network, thus authentication problem becomes more difficult.

3.3   Anonymous Technology

Anonymous problem mainly involves two aspects, one is communication concealment and the other is privacy protection. In many occasions, people hopes that hide their true identities from other participant or possible eavesdropper, or prevent the other unauthorized people from finding their own identity through the traffic flow analysis and other means. In P2P system, each anonymous user provides anonymous service to other users as a server at the same time. This means the information that passes through a node may be originated from the same node or other nodes. So, it is difficult to distinguish these two cases. Any node in P2P network can become a node in anonymous communication network. Anonymous communications system can receive the same scale node resources from P2P network, and nodes that initiating anonymous communication and receiving anonymous communication are hiding in anonymous channels. P2P network is not managed by any specific organization, and thus any users that using P2P software can join the P2P network and become a node in this network. It is impossible that a organization can control all the nodes in the whole P2P network.

3.4 Safety Technology

At present, security routing technology mainly applied in P2P network based on the structural DHT. In structured P2P network, it only needs a few routing to locate the query node. The local routing table of each node only store limited routing information of several nodes. Because of these characteristics of structured P2P network, a fraction of malicious nodes may block normal news forwarding. The realization of the security routing can be divided into three parts: distribution safety of node ID, safe preservation of the routing table and the safety of news forwarding.

4 P2P Security Trust Model

4.1 Trust Model Establishment

Introducing trust value of node to the P2P environment reflects the interactive history between this node and other nodes in network, and to a certain extent, reflects service ability and quality of this node. Therefore, it is necessary that constructing a good distribution trust model and effective management mechanism. Trust model means the base and scope of nodes trust value. Trust management mechanism includes solving agreement, trust value placement and related safety problems.

4.2 Trust Model Classification

Trust models based on PKI. In this kind of system, the minorities of central node is in charge of the supervision of whole network and regularly announce the illegal node. The legality of central nodes is guaranteed by CA certificate. This type of system is often relied on by center with the problems of scalability and single-point failure. This kind of examples of actual system has Onsale Ex-change, eBay, eDonkey etc.

Trust models based on local recommendation. In this kind of system, the nodes gain the trust value from some node by inquiring limited other nodes. Generally it adopts a simple means of partial broadcast, thus the trust value obtained from nodes is often partial and one-sided. For example, this method was adopted for the improvement suggestions of Cornelli to Gnutella.

Data signature. This method doesn't follow the credibility of nodes, but emphasizes the credibility of the data. With the application of file sharing as an example, the user judge the authenticity of the data after each download was completed. If the authenticity of the data was approved, the user will sign this data. More signatures were obtained, more higher the authenticity was. However, this method is only for data sharing application and is unable to prevent collective fraud, namely collective signature of an untrue data by a malicious group. Currently Kazaa, a popular file sharing application adopted this method.

Entire reliability model. In order to acquire the node trust value of the whole, this model mutually iterated through mutual satisfaction between adjacent nodes, and then obtained the entire trust value of this node. At present, the eigenRep of Stanford is a known typical and entire trust model. The core thought of eigenRep is: when node i need to know the entire trust value of node k, firstly node i obtained trust value of node k from interacted nodes of node k. Then node i summarizes the trust value of node k according to the partial trust value of these interactive nodes.

5 Conclusion

Currently, P2P network is facing the quite serious security threats. Safety is the focus of future research of P2P network. The thorough research of safety problems provides protection for further improvement and development of P2P network.

References

1. Yajian, Z., Yixian, Y.: The problem of information security related to P2P technology. Telecom Engineering Technics and Standardization 5, 1–2 (2006)
2. Shaojing, L., Rongtian, L.: Information security in peer-to-peer network. Information Technology 7, 94–96 (2006)
3. Ooi, B.C., Chu, Y.L.: Managing trust in peer-to-peer systems using reputation-based techniques. In: The 4th Interna-tional Conference on Web Age Information Management, pp. 159–162. WAIM, Chengdu (2003)
4. Yuanyuan, X., Xiangguang, H.: Review of trust model research in P2P network. Military Communications Technology 6, 38–41 (2009)

The Research and Implementation of Distributed SOA Architecture

Shujun Pei and Deyun Chen

Computer Science and Technology Harbin University of Science and Technology
150080 Harbin, China
peisj@hrbust.edu.cn, chendy@hrbust.edu.cn

Abstract. This article outlined the basic principle, feature and core technology of distributed SOA, analyzing the distributed object technology and the Web technology integration, describing the differences between distributed SOA and centralized SOA. On this basis, it discussed the function and concrete implementation of SOA in distributed architecture, proposing a SOA based distributed multi-layer architecture and the application integration framework for achieving J2EE. It can connect the distributed application program without constraint and realize the share of data and function among application programs. It not only eases the realization of functional layers, but also provides better maintainability and scalability.

Keywords: Distributed System, Distributed Architecture, SOA, Multi-layer Application.

1 Introduction

The Distributed SOA Architecture is the trend of SOA development in future. The distributed SOA Architecture best support the incremental deployment opinion that generally accepted by the industry. At the same time, it endows the system with more flexibility, adaptability and maintainability when being deployed. The Distributed SOA Architecture aims at achieving long-distance telecommunication with another service, especially the mutual share of data and function among the application programs. This Architecture fundamentally changed the construction methods of IT system, from the proprietary sole application to more advanced and integral application. This kind of service characterizes itself by making full use of the existed, sharable and reusable service function.

2 The SOA-Based Distributed Architecture

2.1 SOA Summary

SOA is a service-oriented architecture and also a distributed system. This system is to integrate the different functional parts (called service) of applicative programs on the heterogeneous platform through the interfaces and specifications among the service

G. Shen and X. Huang (Eds.): CSIE 2011, Part II, CCIS 153, pp. 150–156, 2011.

by loosely coupled manner, it means to integrate several existed application programs into a new system via network[1] .The SOA basis must support all the relevant standards and container when needs running. Fig1. is a typical SOA foundation structure.

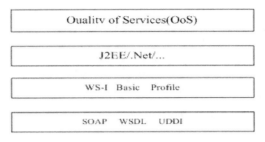

Fig. 1. Typical SOA Architecture

SOA supplies a new method that enables applicative programs function as a service to the end-user applications or other services when construct Distributed system [2]. The whole Distributed System is constructed by various objects by dynamic formation. The objects can exist in any network and host. The developers not only need to develop each program component, but also need to assemble the premium network service according to the client's requirement. The process of development and distribution is completely separated in a Distributed System. And in the process of developing object, there is no need considering the system-level.

2.2 Principle, Characteristics and Core Technology of Distributed SOA

The Distributed SOA is to build an intermediate platform that is highly flexible and based on standard IT environment, so that it can be more adjustable to the constant changes of the technical and business environment. The Distributed SOA is a way that is light-weighted and non-invasive, it hardly occupy special resource. Therefore, the Distributed SOA can better satisfy the requirement of application program which is based on SOA Architecture to various technology and cost. In addition, the Distributed SOA permits clients to deploy services progressively in accordance to their own plans, such as to deploy one or two services at one time, to add service orchestration, management, storage and other advanced functions according to business needs in future. It is challenging to search for information resource and the service it supplies, while the semantic web technologies like SOA offer effective solutions [3].

In Distributed SOA system, we need to define the functions of different objects. The distribution of these objects is available. Information of a variety of content (message body) is needed to be defined by these objects. Generally speaking, it contains three basic elements of the object --functional objects, service objects, task objects. Coordination, information transmission and other complex operation are encapsulated in the system kernel, different application systems are evolved through a simple interface. Information such as system configuration, object allocation, and object publishing are defined in configuration files of each individual body system. A distributed network system can be dynamically built by these configuration files, to complete the specific application. Through configuration, the object can be dynamically loaded and unloaded [4]. The whole distributed system is always in the state of dynamic adjustment.

The Distributed SOA Architecture make the service-enabled application automatically find other services through intelligent application endpoint. What's more, the intelligent endpoints are high of availability and security which are the features of enterprise services. Thus, it can ensure the required performance of the critical applications of the present enterprises.

2.3 Distributed Object Technology and Web Technology

The Distributed SOA considers the various software resources that distributed on the Internet as services with no connection to the state. It keeps a static state until the arrival of the next requirement [5]. With the mature of Distributed SOA in Web Technology, service-oriented architecture is becoming an inevitable choice for solving integrated application, increasing the reuse of the software and expediting the implementation of application. We can rapidly construct the flexible and strong application which is based on service-oriented system.

In the distributed environment, a robust distributed framework will bring about significant benefits for achieving mutual share of information and software resources. The distributed object technology is of incomparable significance for improving the computing competency of Web. By using the Web technology, users can directly interact with the Web server, even the back-end database via CGI, JDBC or other means. This greatly enhances the customer's operational. The bottleneck of CGI can be eliminated after combining the distributed object technology and Web technology, so that clients can directly call for the methods on the server. The clients can use the pre-compiled stub to deliver the parameters. The server directly accepts the calling through a pre-compiled program and the expenditure of the server is rather small.

The Internet is the largest-scaled distributed application so far and the SOA Architecture should have the distributed properties of the Internet. When the users click the URL links by browser, their request is not routed by the central control program which is installed on the server or the Hub, but is directly delivered to the network server on the request page by browser. The method is suitable for the Internet and also for the enterprise SOA Architecture. The request need not through the central server, so free Internet can update for each endpoint without affecting the client and other point, and also there is no need updating the Hub or central server.

The Distributed SOA should first interconnect the unconnected component and package it by using scalable enterprise product no matter it is based on .NET or on Java. This kind of packaging is just like the different original network protocols being encapsulated by TCP/IP. If using low-cost SOA solution, we can begin with small-scaled SOA and enlarge its scale as the growth of the business, and enhance the service quality and other functions according to the requirement. At mean time, we should use point to point communication to avoid extra expensive server and Hub.

2.4 Comparison between Distributed SOA and Centralized SOA

The Centralized SOA Architecture such as bus architecture has the weakness of traditional EAI product. It will increase the cost, limit the reuse of the resources, reduce the flexibility of the system and is likely to form high cost system bottlenecks. In addition, it is the first reason that the user cancels the SOA project since it is probably to deviate from the principal of technological neutrality to bind the user to the proprietary technology of the supplier [6].

The main purpose of distributed computing system is to connect the users and resources in a transparent, open and scalable manner. We can use the Distributed SOA Architecture to solve the integrated problem, to conduct SOA package to the old system. It means to deploy a small intelligible terminal on every application, to use the light-weighted plug-ins rather than a centralized control platform to complete the communication with SOA network. The advantages of this approach are small investment, supporting the gradual deployment, technology neutrality and without bottlenecks. More importantly, this approach is consistent with the open and distributed SOA nature. A good SOA architecture is not only able to complete what the EAI system or J2EE application server can, it also include a centralized system and add them into the reusable service system [7].

The current SOA is a largely a kind of tightly coupled SOA that is tied together with enterprise databases, operating systems and servers. But it lacks of interoperability with other systems and difficult to maintain neutrality and compatibility in technology. Only by turning a tightly coupled system into a distributed network system, turning a system tied together with integrators and developer into an independent one, can service be timely provided. Since customers dominate the system. This is the nature of distributed SOA.

3   SOA-Based Distributed Multi-tier Architecture

The Distributed SOA is presented in a way of service interfaces and service implementations. Service is usually a coarse-grained and free-packaged software entity which is contractual and meaningful. It is reusable, interoperable, can be assembled, released and dynamically discovered. Its interaction is based on information, external applications or other service. From the perspective of technology, distributed SOA is a component model based on XML technology. It describes interface by using XML-based web services description language in WSDL protocol. SOAP, WSDL and UDDI and a series of standards composed of the Web services. SOA is not just a software development framework, but also a business development framework. It can combine services of different types and on different platforms and able to update and maintain a cross-regional multifunctional application entity dynamically and timely.

The key features of n-tier architecture are: loose coupling, coarse-grained, heterogeneity and temporal characteristics. A typical architecture of J2EE system can be divided into 5 tiers. In order to meet the complex business process in practice, a business transport layer can be added up between the Web presentation layer and business process layer depending on the circumstances. Then, it evolves into the 6-tier architecture of J2EE the Web presentation layer, business transport layer, business process layer, business logic layer, data access layer and data layer. Each layer provides the upper layer for interfaces with the implementation of the next layer. Their relation of interaction is shown as follows: Web presentation layer、business transport layer、business process layer、business logic layer、data access layer、data layer. The structure is shown in Fig 2:

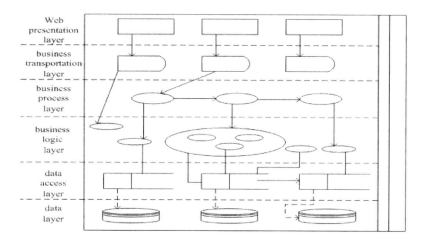

Fig. 2. SOA-based Distributed Multi-tier Architecture

Web presentation layer: For human-computer interaction, mainly dealing with user's requests and displaying the system information;

Business transport layer: The data adaptation layer used for transporting data to Web presentation layer by business process on the background;

The business process layer: In charge of the program process;

The business logic layer: Processing complicated systematic business logic and the business logic which consists of many business processes;

Data access layer: Completing the data manipulation functions, providing a unified interface;

Data layer: Handling the database, storing the enterprise data;

4   Distributed SOA Run-Time Framework for J2EE

J2EE is the first enterprise-oriented, distributed, multi-level software specification that is based on Java technology. It has a complete set of services, applications interfaces and protocols and it is the total solution to Java technology. J2EE platform greatly simplifies the development process through the component-based application model. It also supports any distributed system and multi-level application development. J2EE has been widely used to develop enterprise application software, middleware technologies and component software. The framework uses a stateless session EJB as the realization component of Web service. As the service provider, Web service implements a unified management by using the service bus. Through the coarse-grained division to the service and the use of bus service, loosely coupled system and the transparency of the service can be achieved. This context adopts the J2EE. Its running framework is shown as Fig 3. as follows:

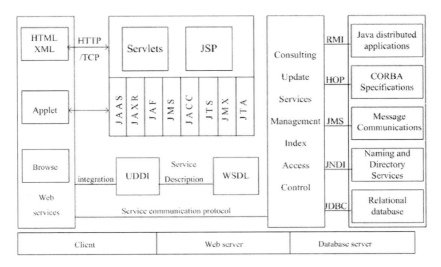

Fig. 3. SOA-based Run-time J2EE Framework

Web presentation layer is achieved by Applet, Jsp and Html; business process layer is achieved by Struts or the Action in Servlet. Business logic layer is achieved by Session Bean; data access layer is achieved by Hibernate and JDBC, and so on.

5 Conclusion

Distributed SOA architecture is the simplest means in the aspect of share and reuse. This paper describes the basic principle and related technology of distributed SOA, giving SOA-based distributed multi-tier application system and its J2EE realization. Its characteristics are independent layer relation and each layer offers specific service, this kind of SOA-based distributed architecture also characterized by low cost and high-return. Apart from the function of schedule, governance, security, data conversion, transaction processing, etc, it can also eliminate the isolated island phenomenon by packaging present system to realize integration of heterogeneous application environment.

References

1. Bocchi, L., Ciancarini, P.: On the Impact of Formal Methods in the SOA. Electronic Notes in Theoretical Computer Science 160, 113–126 (2008)
2. Ouyang, C., Li, Y.: SOA-based Collaborative Service Model and Optimal Design. Micro-Computer Information 04-3, 175–177 (2009)
3. Ma, Z., Chen, H.: A Service-oriented Architecture Reference Model. Computers 29(7), 1011–1019 (2009)
4. Votis, K., Alexakos, C., Vassiliadis, B., Likothanassis, S.: An Ontologically Principled Service- Oriented Architecture for Managing Distributed E-government Nodes. Network and Computer Applications 31, 131–148 (2009)

5. Ding, Z., Dong, C.: SOA-based Distributed Application Integration. Computer Engineering 33(10), 246–248 (2008)
6. Xiaogang, D.: Design and Implementation of J2EE Web Application development framework. Master thesis of University of Defense Technology
7. Li, Y.: The Design, implementation, application of SOA architecture. Master Thesis of Jilin University

Analysis on Problems and Countermeasures in EHR Construction of Chinese Enterprises

Jianlin Qiu

Guangxi University of Finance and Economics, Nanning, P.R. China, 530001

Abstract. In recent years, with the establishing of ERP, SAP and other application platform of computer aided management in Chinese enterprises, the construction of EHR also rapidly developed, but there are still many problems and difficulties in the process of development. In accordance with the experience in the teaching human resources management in university and experience in the consulting services for enterprises in human resource management, the author has studied and explored the status of EHR construction and the existing problems. In the paper, the author put forward some suggestions on the construction of EHR, hoping to help the construction of EHR in Chinese enterprises.

Keywords: human resources management, electronization, enterprise, system.

1 Concept of EHR

"EHR" means electronic human resource, which is the development trend of human resources management at this stage based on computer technology and network technology, it is also a human resources management system that takes the emergence and development of ERP, ASP and other management platforms as the specific implementation environment, puts the advanced software platform into the human resources management network. The EHR system of enterprises includes the following three aspects.

1.1 Network-Based Human Resource Management Process

EHR implements analysis on the decentralized information and even the electronization and centralization of paper-based information management which are related to human resources management, achieves the comprehensive network of human resource management through process reengineering, as well as information exchange and match with other systems such as financial system inside the enterprises.

1.2 Achieve Self-management Inside the Enterprises

Establish a human resource management platform which has the participation of employees, open up new communication channels to fully achieve the interaction and people management, and establish self-management platform for employees.

G. Shen and X. Huang (Eds.): CSIE 2011, Part II, CCIS 153, pp. 157–161, 2011.
© Springer-Verlag Berlin Heidelberg 2011

1.3 Establishment External Communication Channels for Human Resource Management

The external resources can be effectively used in EHR system to communicate with them, such as information provided by personnel websites and human resources service providers etc. Enterprises can also sent the human resource management information such as personnel demand to the outside world to achieve communication with them.

2 The Functions of EHR

EHR is bound to bring a series of changes in the management of organizations, the application of computer network technology in human resource management will not only replace human labor for tedious and repetitive affairs, it is more significant that a series of changes to the management will improve management and efficiency.

2.1 Improve the Level of Human Resource Management

The large amount of data, reports and records in human resources management takes the management staff a lot of energy in data collection, statistics, updates, copying, calculations and other work. Implementation of electronic human resource can also complete the work that human can not do so that they can focus on research, analysis, management activities, as well as modeling and forecasting work, and better fulfill the functions of modern human resources management.

2.2 Promote the Quantification of Human Resources Management

Application of computer network technology can simplify many modern human resource management practices, such as capacity assessment, job analysis, value engineering, decision theory and network technology and other high-level mathematical models, thus contributing to the quantification of human resource management, as well as changes of the traditional qualitative analysis.

2.3 Change the Structure of Human Resources Management Information

EHR has changed the irrational structure without coordination of horizontal linkages in the past, and changed the vertical structure to network structure, realize centralized storage and while using the database to store and information sharing, so that labor and personnel data can be more effectively treated and transferred, expand the applications of labor and personnel data management, and then ensure the uniqueness accuracy and timeliness of the data,.

3 The Main Problems in the EHR Construction of Chinese Enterprises

The development history of EHR construction in China is not long, there are still many outstanding problems in the implementation of corporate EHR.

3.1 The Enterprises Lack Professional Personnel in Human Resources Management

It has just been more than a decade since the modern concept of human resources management was introduced into China. So the human resource management in enterprises is still in relatively early stage, the lack of human resources management education in universities, as well as the laggard concept of the corporate executives have led to the lack of human resources management personnel with professional education, many human resource managers do not master the content and business processes of modern human resources management system, failed to recognize the importance and urgency of information technology, and do not commit to the promotion of HER.

3.2 The Enterprises Lack of Sufficient Funds for EHR Construction

It requires a large number of funding in the implementation of EHR, either self-development or software purchase will need a great investment. Some small enterprises with poor efficiency may not consider to put the huge sums of money for investment in software development of EHR, at the same time, funding problems also exists in the purchase of human resources management system products, in addition to the expensive purchase fees, the costs of personnel training, system maintenance and upgrade are also very high.

3.3 EHR Software Is Not Well Developed

EHR construction is based on the development of human resources management software, a lot of EHR software does not consider the process reengineering, services, product upgrades and other issues that companies are concerned, some software products are still centered on the traditional "personnel management", but can not meet the needs of modern human resource management. Most of corporate EHR construction just follows the establishment of ERP, SAP and other management software platforms, which led to the unsmooth exchange between EHR software module and other modules on the management platform. The enterprise infrastructure is relatively weak, they do not fully consider the level of human resource management, lack enough analysis on EHR requirements,   pursue the latest, most comprehensive and best software, affecting the EHR process.

3.4 The Lack of Human Resources Management Capacity of Computer Network Technology

Implementation of human resource management information, human resources management capacity of computer network technology has put forward higher requirements. More than a thousand in our country, human resource manager of the survey, more than 50% of respondents in the general level of computer network technology. Among them, human resources management has been implemented in the information technology enterprise human resource managers, computer network technology with moderate or close to 50%. The implementation of human resource management without the enterprise information technology personnel in human resources management, computer network technology in the "general" and "basic" level of 68%. Shows that the corporate human resource managers of computer network technology also can not meet the human resources management information requirements.

3.5 The Information Content Is Not Suitable for the Functional Requirements of Modern Human Resource Management

The corporate human resources management information software module function mainly in the human resources information, payroll, recruitment, appraisal and other transaction management, very few relate to human resource planning, job analysis, self-management and so on. According to the survey found no human resources management of information technology companies more than 70%. In human resources management information has been the construction of the enterprise, 18% of the enterprise information system can not meet the requirements of modern human resources management, its causes, including system functions are too simple; human resources management business processes unreasonable; system stability is poor, the speed and slow.

4 Human Resource Management Information Measures Construction

Construction of human resource management information system project is the overall planning, information technology success or failure depends on close cooperation of all parties within the enterprise, depending on the needs analysis is in place, the underlying data is perfect, whether they have such a variety of hardware and software environment.

4.1 Enhanced Awareness of All Staff

Human resource management organizations in all sectors of information covering all employees have the interests of an organization closely linked, therefore, enhance employee awareness of information is necessary for organizations, which contribute to human resource management information and provide good atmosphere; for individual employees, the information will stimulate the awareness of staff awareness and improve individual skills competition.

4.2 The Detailed and Comprehensive Needs Analysis

Human resource management information is a strategic human resource management extension with the business concept of human resource management integration can not be divorced from the human resource development and human resources development stage of development independently. Meanwhile, the enterprise also has to consider the future strategic development, e-HR system upgrade to leave room for improvement to enhance the follow-up to prepare.

4.3 Adequate Preparatory Work

Channels of information flow on the network requirements increase, you must have a good network environment and computer hardware. Must have sufficient basic data preparation, data integrity and accuracy and specifications. Optimization of management processes with corporate strategy, transformation processes and lack of coordination at the waste of human resources, optimize the management process and reduce internal transaction costs and management costs, integration of human resource management functions to form a stable management.

4.4 Training for Human Resources Management Information System Personnel

Human resource management information is the use of information technology systems for human resources management business bearing, optimizing the process of recycling and even,, e-HR systems require a higher quality of the staff, the implementation of e-HR on all employees before the different levels of technology training and human resource management training to enable them to more fully understand the human resource management information of the essence.

4.5 Select the Appropriate Application Software Platform for Its Own Characteristics

According to its own characteristics, select the appropriate human resources management software. Management software the option of following types of software and business needs of the principle of the decision, do not choose the best, choose the most suitable. Second, the software selection process is that the enterprises of the modern concept of human resource management process of cognition.

5 Conclusion

The construction of electronic human resource is a revolution in human resource management, although the process is tortuous, the human resources management will be developed to a high level as long as the corporate managers have courage to explore.

References

1. Dan, Y.: EHR Construction in Enterprises. Hubei Electric Power (6) (2005)
2. Jun, X.: Problems and Solutions of China's Electronic Human Resource. Science and Management (3) (2005)
3. Wanghong: Self-service of Human Resource Management Information System. Nonferrous Metals Industry (9) (2005)
4. Rongguo, S.: Analysis on the Reform of Human Resource Management in New Economic Era. Modern Management Science (10) (2005)

The Security and Prevention of E-Commerce in China

Jianlin Qiu

Guangxi University of Finance and Ecomomics, Nanning, P.R. China, 530001

Abstract. The security of e-commerce is a complex and systematic project which should be safeguarded from technical and legislative perspective as well as other aspects so that various types of problems regarding e-commerce will be regulated. This paper discussed the security issues existing in the applications of e-commerce, and carried out analysis on the security techniques of e-commerce.

Keywords: e-commerce; security issues; security of network protocol; information security.

Today's world is a digital information society, and high-tech technologies especially electronic information technology has given great impact to all walks of life. E-commerce was generated in such an information age and is developing rapidly, it has gradually become a new model for business activities. In recent years, China's e-commerce is also booming, such as Alibaba, E-BAY, Taobao etc., have achieved considerable success and brought great changes to people's ideas and ways of life. However, the supporting technology and management can not keep up with the rapid development of e-commerce, so securities become impediments in the development process.

1 Security Issues of E-Commerce

1.1 Security of Network Protocol

TCP / IP itself is open, enterprises and users send data through data packets in the process of electronic transaction, the malicious attacker can easily intercept the packets of e-commerce sites, and even modify and counterfeit the data packets.

1.2 Security of User Information

At present, the major mode of e-commerce is based on e-commerce site in B / S (Browser / Server) structure, users log on for transaction by using the browser, as users may use a public compute, then if there are malicious Trojan program or virus in the computer, the user's login information including user name, password may be lost.

G. Shen and X. Huang (Eds.): CSIE 2011, Part II, CCIS 153, pp. 162–165, 2011.

1.3 Security of E-Commerce Sites

Some e-commerce sites built by companies may exist some security risks in design, the server operating system itself also have loopholes, if unscrupulous attackers enter the e-commerce site, a large number of user information and transaction information will be stolen.

1.4 The Lack of Credit

The lack of credit in today's business trade has become an increasingly serious problem. Web-based e-commerce connects the seller and the buyer who are separated by time and space, thus credit issue appears much more prominent. Many buyers may worry about the quality of goods and if the goods truly meet their requirements before the payment since they can not see the real objects; and also worried about whether the seller can really keep their promise to deliver goods. Similarly, the seller doubts about whether the buyer will pay in due course. The credit problems have brought a lot of worries to people, and e-commerce is difficult to be generally accepted by the public. China has joined the WTO and will carry out more cross-border trades, the credit issue is not only related to whether the orderly operation of domestic e-commerce, but also to the smooth proceeding of Internet trade home and abroad.

1.5 Legal System Is Imperfect

With the deepening of electronic commerce into our lives, it becomes more and more eager to create a special set of perfect laws and regulations to address these issues. The main characteristics of e-commerce is that it exists in the virtual world, and it is easy to produce online transaction disputes such as arbitration, electronic contracts, the validity of online contracts, tax, privacy or protection of property rights and other issues, in addition, the international e-commerce involves the political system, social status, economic level, current laws and regulations, cultural issues, social traditions and other problems in different countries, so it is very complicated to propose legislation to these issues.

2 Technical Safety Measures of E-Commerce

The safety policy of e-commerce can be divided into two parts: one is computer network security, the second is business transaction security. The security technologies of e-commerce mainly include the following:

2.1 Data Encryption Technology

The data encryption is the most basic e-commerce security measure of information system. It uses encryption algorithms to convert the information to ciphertext according to encryption rules, ensuring the confidentiality of the data. The use of data encryption technology can meet the confidentiality requirements of the information itself. Data encryption can be divided into symmetric key encryption and asymmetric key encryption.

2.2 Digital Signature Technology

A series of symbols and codes will be generated through specific cryptography, and then form the electronic signature password to realize the digital signature instead of writing signature or seal, such electronic signatures can also be verified, the accuracy of verification is incomparable by the verification of handwritten signature and seal. Digital signature technology can guarantee the integrity and non-repudiation of information transfer.

2.3 The Certification Body and Digital Certificates

The so-called CA certification authority uses PKI (Public Key Infrastructure) technology, digital certificates, asymmetric and symmetric encryption algorithms, digital signatures, digital envelopes and other encryption technologies to establish a high level of security system with functions of encryption and decryption, as well as authentication to ensure safe and effective operation of electronic transactions, and other parties can not be aware of the information except the sender and receiver(confidentiality); guarantee the information not to be tampered with during transmission (integrity and consistency); ensure the sender that the receiver is not counterfeit; sender can not deny his sending behavior (non-repudiation). Solutions of e-commerce security have greatly promoted the development of electronic commerce. In electronic transactions, no matter digital time stamp service or digital certificate issuance can not be completed by two parties, but should be completed by an authoritative and impartial third party. As an authoritative, reliable and impartial third party, CA certification authority provide network authentication services, responsible for issuing and management of all digital certificates required by entities involved in online trading.

2.4 Security Authentication Protocol

Currently there are two frequently used security authentication protocols in e-commerce, including SSL (Secure Sockets Layer) protocol and SET (Secure Electronic Transaction) protocol.

2.5 Other Security Technologies

There are some common methods used in e-commerce security, such as network firewall, virtual private network (VPN) technology, anti-virus protection. A single e-commerce security technology is not enough, and it must be integrated with other security measures so as to provide users with a more reliable security base of e-commerce.

3 Solution to the Credit Problem

The United States has the world's most sophisticated consumer credit in the world, we can learn from the practices of a set of comprehensive personal credit system to establish a credit system suitable for China. First, China can set up a special credit agency - credit bureau which is run by the Government, and has social credibility like banks;

second, establish an accurate and fair personal credit file. Information on credit files should include commercial, taxation, public security, judicial, banking, security, insurance, trade and many other aspects. In addition, a comprehensive and dynamic management should be implemented to the credit files in order to achieve full and effective credit supervision for everyone; third, design a scientific and transparent credit score model. The best is to invite bid by the state to design a scientific and transparent credit score model, and give it to the community for free use, the property right is owned by the state; fourth, improve the external environment of personal credit.

5 Conclusion

E-commerce security is a complex and systematic project, in addition to technical prevention, we must also improve the e-commerce legislation so as to regulate various problems existing in rapid development of e-commerce, guide and promote the rapid and healthy development of e-commerce in China.

References

1. Qinzheng, L.S.: Electronic Commerce Overview, vol. (6). Higher Education Press, Beijing (2006)
2. Xiaobing, Y.: On the Security of E-commerce. Technology Advisory Review (2) (2007)
3. Fengsheng, Z.: Security Requirements and Protection Strategies of E-commerce. Database and Information Management (6) (2007)
4. Weixin, W.: Technical Analysis of E-commerce Security. Journal of Xi'an University of Arts and Science (3) (2006)

Improved Nonlinear Filter for Target Tracking in Radar Network

Lu Jie

Chongqing University of Science and Technology,
Chongqing, 401331
Lj116758@163.com

Abstract. Radar network composes many types of radar. This system can out-perform each single radar. In this paper, the principle of radar network based on transmitting diversity is described and then the nonlinear filter technique for radar network is presented. In this method, the detection result of each detector of radar network is integrated in data nonlinear filter, a final detection result is get which includes all the information of each detector result.

Keywords: Signal processing, radar network, target tracking.

1 Introduction

It has been recently shown that radar network system has the potential to dramatically improve the performance of the communication systems over single antenna system [1],[2]. Unlike the traditional beam-forming approach, Which employ highly correlated signals of transmitting or receiving antenna arrays to steer a beam towards a certain direction in space, radar network makes use of the independence between signals from different transmitters and receivers to improve the more information received from the target and the robustness of the transmit-receive link.

The probing signal design problem for the narrowband radar network radar has been addressed. Our approach to this design problem is similar to the mathematical approach and is different from the more pragmatically approach. Our main contributions are the following: i) we address the question of determining a desirable transmit beam pattern, and show how to obtain such a beam pattern; ii) we modify the beam pattern matching criterion in several ways; and iii) we outline an efficient Semi-definite.

Quadratic Programming (SQP) algorithm for solving the signal design problem in polynomial time (the recent full version also considers a convex optimization algorithm for solving the design problem, yet one that is less efficient than the SQP algorithm proposed herein). In addition, we consider a new minimum side-lobe beam pattern design which is not considered. Finally, we demonstrate the advantages of these radar network transmit beam pattern designs over their phased-array counterparts.

Motivated by the radar network technique in communication systems, the two new concepts of radar network radar are introduced. One is transmitting diversity radar network radar [3], the other one is receiving and transmitting diversity radar network

G. Shen and X. Huang (Eds.): CSIE 2011, Part II, CCIS 153, pp. 166–171, 2011.
© Springer-Verlag Berlin Heidelberg 2011

radar [4]. The proposed radar network radar enjoys the same benefits that radar net-work communication systems have. Specifically, the transmitting diversity radar network radar can greatly improve the radar's performance over traditional radar on anti-intercept of radar signal, weak target detection, etc.[3]

The remainder of the paper is organized as followed. First, the principle of radar network radar based on transmitting diversity was introduced. Then receiving signal processing method of radar network radar based on transmitting diversity was pre-sented. And then, the data fusion for radar network radar is presented. At last, some conclusions are drawn.

2   The Principle of Radar Network Based on Transmitting Diversity

To detect small RCS targets, such as cruise missile or stealth fighter, surface-based or ship-based phased radars are usually designed for high peak power levels and large power-aperture-gain (PAG) products. Unfortunately, this will bring some problems. First of all, these radars must operate in the presence of strong clutter, resulting in challenging requirements on system dynamic range fundamentally limited by the "state of the art'" Secondly, strong clutters also result in challenging requirements on phase noise, stability, isolation, spurs, and other hardware-related specification. Third-ly, due to high peak power levels, radar signals will suffer more easily from harmful electromagnetic interference (EMI) and enemy Electronic Intercept (ELINT) system.

To partially address these problems, radar arrays are being designed to use Digital Beam Formation (DBF) on receives [5]. [6].In a DBF system, analog-to-digitization (AID) conversion is performed at each of the receive elements in the array, so can reduce A/D dynamic range by N times (N is the number of receive sub-arrays) and facilitate the formation of multiple simultaneous receive beams (which enables faster search rates).Through such arrays offer many benefits, they still operate much like earlier phased array radar mode and can not resolve the signals anti-intercept problem. Radar network radar based on transmitting diversity can solve well the problems described above. On surface-based or ship-based phased array, on transmitting, the array aperture would be subdivided into low-gain elements group (or sub-arrays) in elevation, each radiates a unique, orthogonally coded waveform (note that the various emitted signals will not be combined to form a single focused beam, instead, the ra-diated energy will cover a broad angular sector) shown in Fig. 1. Because the array is subdivided into M subarrays, the transmit gain and the transmitted power per channel are reduced by M times.

On receiving the signal at each individual receiver is processed through a bank of M matched filters. Each filter is matched to one of the transmitted waveforms, there-by recovering the returns due to a single transmit signal. This produces a total of MN matched filter outputs. Since the locations of each transmit and receive element are known, these MN signals can be phased and combined (analogous to normal transmit and receive bean-forming) to form high gain receive beams in one or more directions. By digital time-delay or DBF technique, the beams will cover the volume

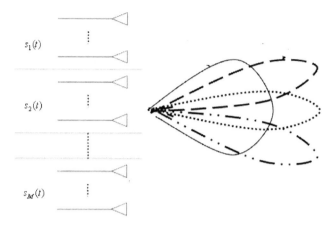

Fig. 1. The principle of radar network radar based on transmitting diversity

of space illuminated by the wide transmit beam. Further integration (i.e., Doppler processing) is used to maintain sensitivity, and to achieve the same range, as desired.

System above can be in either the MIIMO or the conventional transmit modes (all subarrays transmit the same signal), as needed, a great deal of flexibility is provided.

3   Radar Network Signal Processing

According to the principle described above, the configuration of radar network radar based on transmitting diversity is depicted. Now consider an radar network system with transmit   elements (or sub-arrays) and M receiving elements (or subarrays), transmitting orthogonal waveforms $S_1(t), S_2(t), \cdots, S_M(t)$.

Assuming narrow signals (this is not a necessary requirement, but simplifies the discussion) and isotropic elemental radiators, the aggregate waveform incidents upon any target can be represented as

$$p(t) = \alpha_1 \sum_{m=1}^{M} S_m(t - \tau_m) \qquad (1)$$

Where, $\tau_m = \dfrac{(m-1)d \sin \theta}{c}$, d is the delay time from the transmit to the target. α_1 is the attenuate factor, which is same for all transmitter. Then, the summation of all waveform is

$$p(t) = \alpha_1 \sum_{m=1}^{M} S_m(t)\alpha_m(\theta) \qquad (2)$$

Where, θ is the target direction of arrival, $\alpha_m(\theta)$ is the transmit response vector   of mth element. The wave is reflected back to antenna. The n-th subarray received waveform is then

$$x_n(t) = \alpha_2 \cdot p(t - \tau_n) = \alpha_2 \cdot p(t)e^{-j\phi_n} \qquad (3)$$

Where, $\phi_n = \dfrac{2\pi d \sin\theta}{\lambda}(n-1)$. α_2 is the sum of the propagation attenuation and scatter coefficient, the received signal vector is then:

$$\mathbf{X}(t) = \alpha_2 \cdot b(\theta) \cdot p(t) + \mathbf{V}(t) \tag{4}$$

Where,

$\mathbf{X}(t) = [x_1(t), x_2(t), \cdots, x_N(t)]^T$

$b(\theta) = [1, e^{-j\phi}, \cdots, e^{-j(N-1)\phi}]^T$

$\mathbf{V(t)} = [v_1(t), v_2(t), \cdots, v_N(t)]^T$

Substitute (3) into (4), we get

$$\mathbf{X}(t) = \alpha \cdot b(\theta) \sum_{m=1}^{M} S_m(t)\alpha_m(\theta) + \mathbf{V(t)} \tag{5}$$

Where α is a complex scalar, $b(\theta)$ is the usual $N \times 1$ "receive array vector," and $\mathbf{V(t)}$ is an $N \times 1$ vector of noise at time t. For simplicity, (5) makes implicitly an assumption of mono-static or pseudo mono-static aperture configuration; this is not strictly required.

4   Nonlinear Filter for Radar Network

The problem of radar target tracking, especially with mono-pulse techniques, can be divided into two categories: viz. active tracking and passive tracking. Active radar target tracking uses both range and bearings measurements. This is the most common type of tracking in real applications. Traditionally, the Kalman filter and its variations have been used for active tracking. However, when the target under track can perform maneuvers, multiple dynamic models will be adopted to describe the target. These models usually involve strong nonlinearities. In these cases, Kalman filter based methods will not provide accurate estimations. Passive tracking is different from active tracking, where only the bearings measurement, i.e. the direction of arrival (DOA), is available. Because of this reason, bearings-only tracking is also called DOA tracking. The problem of bearings-only tracking arises in a variety of important practical applications in surveillance, guidance or positioning systems. Typical examples are aircraft surveillance (using a radar in a passive mode or an electronic warfare device), underwater target tracking using passive sonar. The purpose of bearings-only tracking is to estimate the kinematics (the positions and velocities) of a target using its noise-corrupted bearings measurements.

Due to the inherent nonlinearities in the observation model, bearings-only target tracking has become a standard nonlinear filtering problem that receives intensive investigations. Target tracking using sensor networks is an emerging new tracking application. Sensor networks are typically composed of one or more central information processing units with a large number of sensor nodes, which have limited communication and computation capabilities and limited power supply. During recent years, the continuing miniaturization of computing and (wireless) communication circuitry as well as sensor devices has enabled mass production of intelligent wireless micro-sensors at a low cost. Tracking targets with geographically dispersed and cooperating sensors is attractive for several reasons.

First, it can improve the robustness of tracking algorithms; sensors deployed close to targets would result in more reliable signal readings. Also, it can be more cost effective. The challenge is to design a tracking method which ingeniously reconciles the two defining characteristics, abundance in quantity and inferiority in quality, to realize the desired robustness. One important application of wireless sensor networks is target tracking, where the target of interest ranges from moving objects in civil and military surveillance applications, to changes in light, temperature, pressure, and acoustics in environmental monitoring. The type of signals to be sensed is determined based on the types of objects to be tracked. In this dissertation, a multiple sensor fusion and tracking algorithm based on particle filtering was developed for ground vehicle tracking using acoustic sensor networks.

Visual target tracking is also an important issue in many applications, such as intelligent video surveillance systems, human computer interfacing, smart room and teleconferencing, and others. The objective of visual target tracking is to estimate the target's position and the velocity in the image plane or develop its trajectory over time by using a combination of the objects appearance and movement characteristics. Visual target tracking remains a challenging research topic not only because of the target dynamics can be highly nonlinear and its distribution can be non-Gaussian, but also the target may have changes in scale (zooming), illumination, pose, and possible occlusion. In this dissertation, several particle filter based visual tracking algorithms were developed by exploring the method of multiple target dynamic models and multiple measurement cues to achieve reliable and accurate estimations, as published in the works of the dissertation's author.

In a tracking problem, a target is usually described by a state space model, which contains a state process model and an observation model (or measurement model). The state space approach to time series modeling focuses the attention to the state vector of a system. The state vector contains all relevant information required to describe the system. For example, in tracking problems, the system state could be the kinematic characteristics of the target (i.e. position, velocity, etc.). In the current literature, the target tracking problem is always formulated as a state estimation problem, which is also known as filtering. In state estimation, the Kalman filter is widely used when the model is linear and the additive noise is Gaussian. But the real world dynamic systems are often more complex, typically involving nonlinear and non-Gaussian elements.

5 Conclusion

In this paper, we firstly investigated the radar network signal model and its signal processing steps. The each subarray of MIMO radar performs detection respectively, and then the result is processed by the nonlinear filter. The final detection result is get.

References

[1] He, z.-s., et al.: MIMO radar and its technical characteristic analysis. ACTA Electronic Sinica 33(12)A, 2441 (2005)

[2] Foschini, C.J.: Layered space-time architecture for wireless communication in a fading environment when using multiple antennas. Bell Labs Technical Journal 1, 41 (1996)

[3] Foschini, G.J., Gans, M.J.: On the limits of wireless communications in a fading environment when using multiple antennas. Wireless Press Communication 6, 311 (1998)

[4] Doucet, A., de Freitas, N., Gordon, N.: Sequential Monte Carlo Methods in Practice. Springer, New York (2001)

[5] Rabideau, D.J., Parker, P.: Ubiquitous MIMO digital array radar. In: The 37th Asilomar Conference on Signals, Systems and Computers, p. 1057 (2003)

[6] Ristic, B., Arulampalam, S., Gordon, N.: Beyond the Kalman Filter: Particle Filters for Tracking Applications. Artech House Publishers, Boston (February 2004)

[7] Fishler, E., Haimowich, A., Blum, R., Cimini, L., Chizhik, D., Valenzuela, R.: Statistical MIMO radar. In: 12th Conf. on Adaptive Sensor Array Processing (2004)

[8] Rabideatu, D.J., Howard, L.C.: Mitigation of digital array nonlinearities. In: Proc. IEEE Radar Conf., p. 175 (2001)

[9] Nardone, S., Lindgren, A., Gong, K.: Fundamental properties and performance of conventional bearings-only target motion analysis. IEEE Transactions on Automatic Control 29(9), 775–787 (1984)

[10] Teneketzis, D.: The decentralized quickest detection problem. IEEE International Large-Scale Systems Symposium (1982)

[11] Kovattana, T. Theoretical analysis of intrusion alarm using two complementary sensors.Final Technical Report, Stanford Research Institute, MenloPark,

[12] Fefjar, A.: Combining techniques to improve security in automated entry control. In: Proceedings of the Carnahan Conference on Crime Countermeasures (1978)

[13] Stearns, S.D.: Optimal detection using multiple sensors. In: Proceedings of the Carnahan Conference on CrimeCountermeasures (1982)

[14] Chair, Z.: Ph.D. dissertation in progress, Syracuse University, N.Y.

Space-Time Signal Processing for MIMO Radar Target Detection

Lu Jie

Chongqing University of Science and Technology,
Chongqing, 401331
Lj116758@163.com

Abstract. MIMO radar (Multiple input multiple output radar) is a hot topic recently. It can achieve better detection performance than conventional phased radar. In this paper, the MIMO radar signal model is studied, and then the signal processing flow of the MIMO radar is researched. An then, the space time signal processing technique is applied into target detection in MIMO radar. At last, conclusion is drawn. Some item for future research in presented.

Keywords: signal processing, target detection, space-time processing.

1 Introduction

MIMO radar is a novel radar technique developed recently [1] which is divided into two kinds. One kind of MIMO radar is refer to as collated antenna MIMO radar[2], the other kind of MIMO radar is widely separated antenna MIMO radar[3] which is also called multi-static MIMO radar. For the first kind of MIMO radar, Fishler[4] aimed at building the multi-static MIMO radar to counter target's RCS-fluctuating and improve the detection performance; Berkerman[5] proposed MIMO radar can forming narrow beam; Fishler[6] verify that the CRB of MIMO radar is better than conventional phased radar.

While coding and signal processing are key elements to successful implementation of a MIMO system, the communication channel represents a major component that determines system performance. A considerable volume of work has been performed to characterize communication channels for general wireless applications. However, because MIMO systems operate at an unprecedented level of complexity to exploit the channel space-time resources, a new level of understanding of the channel space-time characteristics is required to assess the potential performance of practical multi-antenna links.

The second kind of MIMO radar is widely research [7,8,9]. In this kind of MIMO radar, antennas transmit orthogonal signals. But the antennas are not separated widely as in first kind MIMO radar. Usually, the distance between antennas is half of the wavelength. As it has been researched, the kind of MIMO radar has many advantages such as high resolution, low intercept probability etc. In this paper, we investigate the signal model and signal processing of the collated antenna MIMO radar (in this paper, it is refer to as MIMO radar). Then a simulation platform is founded to testify the advantage of MIMO radar and some simulation result is presented.

G. Shen and X. Huang (Eds.): CSIE 2011, Part II, CCIS 153, pp. 172–176, 2011.

The remainder of this paper is organized as followed. First, signal model and signal processing of MIMO radar is introduced. Then the space time signal processing for MIMO radar is described. Finally, some conclusions are drawn.

2 Signal Model

It is assume that the radar transmit array is composed of $L_1 \times L_2$ antennas. In MIMO radar model, the array is divided into L_2 sub-arrays. Each sub-array has L_1 antennas which transmits signal with p_t power. The array is shown in figure 1. Contrarily, in conventional phased radar, each antenna send the same signal.

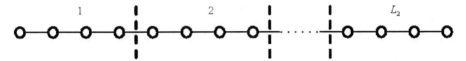

Fig. 1. The configuration of radar array

The T-MIMO radar signal processing is shown in figure 2. At each receiver, the signal is firstly separated by a bank of band filter. The filter frequencies are different and are same with the frequency of each send signal. The target echo is sum of all transmitting signal. So, it includes all the send signal components. Processed by the match filters, each signal component is separated. Each transmit signal is obtained now. Those separated signals are multiply by a coefficient and then sum up. This is equivalent to DBF at both transmitter and receiver.

And then, the moving target detection (MTD) is employed to find the velocity of the target. At last, the constant false alarm is used to detect the target. This flow is demonstrated in figure 2.

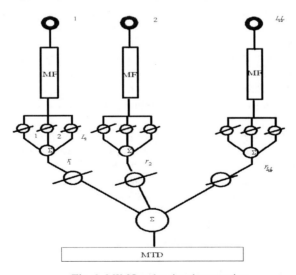

Fig. 2. MIMO radar signal processing

3 Space-Time Signal Processing

Driven by the desire to boost the quality of service of wireless systems closer to that afforded by wire line systems, space-time processing for multiple-input multiple-output(MIMO) wireless communications research has drawn remarkable interest in recent years. Exciting theoretical advances, complemented by rapid transition of research results to industry products and services, have created a vibrant and growing area that is already established by all counts.

This offers a good opportunity to reflect on key developments in the area during the past decade and also outline emerging trends. Space-time processing for MIMO communications is a broad area, owing in part to the underlying convergence of information theory, communications, and signal processing research that brought it to fruition. Among its constituent topics, space-time coding has played a prominent role, and is well summarized in recent graduate texts.

Several other topics however, are also important in order to grasp the bigger picture in space-time processing. These include MIMO wireless channel characterization, modeling, and validation; model-based performance analysis; spatial multiplexing; and joint transceiver design using channel state information (CSI).Our aim in embarking on this edited book project was twofold:(i) present a concise, balanced, and timely introduction to the broad area of space-time processing for MIMO communications;(ii)outline emerging trends, particularly in terms of spatial multiplexing and joint transceiver optimization. In this regard, we were fortunate to be able to solicit excellent contributions from some of the world's leading experts in the respective subjects.

The channel sounding process is then described for a specific narrowband MIMO system operating at 2.45 GHz and three representative indoor propagation scenarios. Useful plots of channel magnitude, phase, and capacity distributions are provided. This part will be especially useful for practicing engineers interested in channel sounding. We then discusses common simplified random matrix models of the MIMO wireless channel and their statistical properties. Going beyond the commonly assumed Rayleigh model, the chapter also explores geometric discrete scattering models and statistical cluster models, including an extension of the well-known Saleh–Valenzuela model. Parsimonious MIMO channel models facilitate system design,for they enable preliminary performance assessment via simulation. A comparison of capacity distributions obtained from measured versus model-based synthesized channels is included, and the impact of angle, polarization, and mutual coupling on channel capacity is illustrated.

Among the many types of space-time codes, the class of orthogonal space-time block codes (OSTBCs)is special in many ways. It includes the celebrated 2×1 Alamouti code, which was instrumental in the development of the area, and quickly made it all the way to standards and actual systems. Orthogonal space-time block codes have numerous desirable properties, not the least of which is simple linear optimal decoding. By Gharavi-Alkhansari, Gershman, and Shahbazpanahi ,covers both basic and advanced aspects of OSTBCs, with notable breadth and timeliness. The exposition is built around certain key properties of OSTBCs. For example, the fact that OSTBCs yield an orthogonal equivalent mixing matrix irrespective of the MIMO channel matrix (so long as the latter is not identically zero) enables a remarkably general performance analysis, even for non separable constellations. The chapter also covers important recent developments in the area, such as blind channel estimation for OSTBC-coded systems, and multiuser interference mitigation in the same context. OSTBCs have numerous desirable features, but other linear space-time block codes may be preferable if the goal is to maximize the information rate. Early designs of the latter kind were based on maximizing ergodic capacity. Since diversity was not explicitly accounted for in those designs, the resulting codes could not guarantee full diversity.

4   Space-Time Signal Processing for MIMO Radar

More recently, specific examples of full-rate, full-diversity designs appeared in the literature, based on number theory. Still, a general systematic design methodology was missing. By Zhang,Liu,and Wong, makes important steps in this direction, using cyclotomic field theory. The development is based on exploring the structural properties of good codes, leading to the identification of trace orthogonality as the central structure. Trace-orthogonal linear block codes are proven to be optimal from a linear MMSE receiver viewpoint, and several examples of specific trace-orthogonal code designs are provided and compared to the pertinent state of the art.

Spatial multiplexing for the multiuser MIMO downlink: Multiple antennas can also be used for spatial multiplexing: that is, the simultaneous transmission of multiple streams, separated via transmit or receive 'beams'. The uplink scenario, wherein a base station employs multiple receives antennas and beamforming to separate transmissions from the different mobiles has been thoroughly studied in the array processing literature. More recently, transmit beamforming/precoding for multiuser downlink transmission is drawing increasing attention. This scenario corresponds to a non degraded Gaussian broadcast channel, and, until very recently, this was unchartered territory for information theorists.

Interestingly, the aforementioned multiuser multi-antenna downlink scenario is quite different, and, at the same time, closely tied, via duality, to the corresponding uplink scenario.

Peel, Spencer, Swindlehurst, Haardt, and Hochwald deliver a concise overview of recent developments in this exciting area. The authors present linear and nonlinear pre-coding approaches. Simple regularized channel inversion pre-coding is shown to perform well in many cases. Attaining sum capacity turns out to require so-called Dirty-Paper coding, also known as Costa coding, which is nonlinear and often complex to implement. As an interesting alternative, the authors propose Sphere Precoding, an interesting application of the Sphere Decoding algorithm on the transmitter's end instead of the receiver's end, as is usual. Generalizations to multiple-antenna receivers are also considered, including joint transmit–receive beam forming.

While multiple antennas help in improving performance, there are situations wherein it pays to work with a properly selected subset of the available antennas. Each 'live' antenna requires a separate down-conversion chain, and it often makes better sense to employ a few down-conversion chains along with a cross-bar switch to choose from the available elements.

5 Conclusion

MIMO radar (Multiple input multiple output radar) is a hot topic recently. It can achieve better detection performance than conventional phased radar. In this paper, the technique of space-time signal processing is employed into MIMO radar target detection.

References

[1] He, z.-s.: MIMO radar and its technical characteristic analysis. ACTA Electronic Sinica 33(12A), 2441 (2005)

[2] Li, J., Stoica, P.: MIMO Radar with Colocated Antennas. IEEE Signal Processing Magazine 24, 106 (2007)

[3] Haimovich, A.M., Blum, R.S., Cimini, L.J.: MIMO radar with widely separated antennas. IEEE Signal Processing Magazine 25, 116 (2008)

[4] Fishler, E., et al.: Spatial Diversity in Radars —Models and Detection Performance. IEEE Trans. On Signal Processing 54, 823–838 (2006)

[5] Bekkerman, Tabrikian: Target detection and localization using MIMO radars and sonars. IEEE Trans. On Signal Processing 54, 3873–3883 (2006)

[6] Fishler, E., et al.: MIMO radar: An idea whose time has come. In: Proceeding of the IEEE Radar Conference, p. 71. Philadelphia, PA (2004)

[7] Rabideau, D.J., Parker, P.: Ubiquitous MIMO multifunction digital array radar. In: The Thirty-Seventh Asilomar Conference on Signals,Systems and Computers, p. 1057 (2003)

[8] Forsythe, K.W., Bliss, D.W., Fawcett, G.S.: Multiple-output Multiple-input(MIMO) radar. In: The Thirty-Seventh Asilomar Conference on Signals, Systems and Computers, p. 54 (2003)

[9] khan, H.A., et al.: Ultra wideband Multiple-output Multiple-input radar. In: 2005 IEEE international Radar Conference, p. 900. Arlington, Virgrinia (2005)

Research on Hybrid Genetic Algorithm for Min-Max Vehicle Routing Problem

Chunyu Ren

School of Information Science and Technology, Heilongjiang University,
15080 Harbin, China
rency2004@163.com

Abstract. The present study is focused on the Min-Max Vehicle Routing Problem. According to the characteristics of model, hybrid genetic algorithm is used to get the optimization solution. First of all, use natural number coding so as to simplify the problem; apply insertion method so as to improve the feasibility of the solution; retain the best selection so as to guard the diversity of group. The study adopts 2- exchange mutation operator, combine hill-climbing algorithm to strengthen the partial searching ability of chromosome. At last, it uses simulated experiments to prove the effectiveness and feasibility of this algorithm, and provides clues for massively solving practical problems.

Keywords: MMVRP; insertion method; improved ordinal crossover; hill-climbing algorithm; hybrid genetic algorithm.

1 Introduction

Vehicle Routing Problem is a typical NP problem. The research method of VRP mainly includes exactness algorithm, heuristic algorithm and intelligent optimized algorithm. When getting the solution of problem with big scale and multi-restricted-condition, intelligent algorithm is more widely applied. Ali applied genetic algorithm to study dynamic VRP with the different capacities [1]. Bent used simulated annealing algorithm to solve VRP with time windows [2]. Fermin applied TS algorithm to solve VRPB [3]. In practice, there exists a type of problems, whose aim is not to demand the shortest distance of the whole route, but to demand the shortest distance of the longest sub route throughout the whole route, for which is called Min-Max Vehicle Routing Problem, MMVRP.

Michael firstly solved the minimum boundary value of the objective function in MMVRP, and then used taboo search algorithm to get the solution [4]. Carlsson studied MMMDVRP, and used heuristic algorithm based on region division to solve the problem [5]. Esther proposed an approximate algorithm to solve MMVRP. This algorithm consists of two parts: (1) seek the shortest route in each route's distance constraints. (2) reduce the longest distance as possible as it can [6]. David applied improved branch and bound algorithm to solve MMVRP [7].

Considering the complexity of MMVRP, the essay proposed to apply hybrid genetic algorithm.

G. Shen and X. Huang (Eds.): CSIE 2011, Part II, CCIS 153, pp. 177–182, 2011.
© Springer-Verlag Berlin Heidelberg 2011

2   Mathematical Model

$$Z = Min\left\{Max\sum_{i\in S}\sum_{j\in S}\sum_{k\in V} X_{ijk} d_{ij}\right\} \tag{1}$$

Constraints:

$$\sum_{i\in H}\sum_{j\in S} q_i X_{ijk} \le W_k, \quad k\in V \tag{2}$$

$$\sum_{i\in S} X_{ijk} = Y_{ik}, \quad j\in S, \quad k\in V \tag{3}$$

$$\sum_{j\in S} X_{ijk} = Y_{ik}, \quad i\in S, \quad k\in V \tag{4}$$

$$\sum_{i\in S}\sum_{j\in S} x_{ijk} \le |m| - 1, \quad \forall m \subseteq \{2,3...,n\}, \quad k\in V \tag{5}$$

$$\sum_{k\in V}\sum_{i\in S} X_{ijk} d_{ij} \le D_k, \quad j\in H \tag{6}$$

In the formula: $G\{g_r|r=1,...R\}$ is a series of aggregations of distribution centre in the place R ; $H\{h_i|i=R+1,..R+N\}$ is a series of clients' aggregations in the place N ; $S\{G\}\cup\{H\}$ is the combination of all distribution centres and clients. $V\{v_k|k=1,..K\}$ is travel vehicle k 's aggregation; q_i is the demand amount of client $i(i\in H)$; W_k is travel vehicle k 's loading capacity; d_{ij} is the linear distance from client i to client j ; D_k is the travel vehicle k 's maximum travel mileage.

3   Parameter Design for Hybrid Genetic Algorithm

3.1   The Formation of Initial Solution

Given h_k as the total number of client nodes served by vehicle k , aggregation $R_k = \{y_{ik}|0\le i\le h_k\}$ to correspond the client nodes served by the number k vehicle. The procedures as such:

Step1:   Order   vehicles'   initial   remaining   load   capacity: $w_k^1 = w_k$, $k=0$, $h_k=0$, $R_k=\Phi$;

Step2: The demand amount corresponding to the i client node in a route q_i , order $k=1$;

Step3: if $q_i \le w_k^1$, then order $w_k^1 = Min\{(w_k^1 - q_i), w_k\}$, if not turn to Step6;

Step4: if $w_k^1 - q_i \le w_k$, and $D_{i-1} + D_i \le D_k$; then $R_k = R_k \bigcup \{i\}$, $h_k = h_k + 1$ if not turn to Step6;

Step5: if $k > K$, then $k = K$, otherwise, $k = k$;

Step6: $k = k + 1$, turn to Step3;

Step7: $i = i + 1$, turn to Step2;

Step8: repeat Step2-7, K recorded the total used vehicles, R_k and recorded a group of feasible routes.

3.2 Crossover Operator

The crossover operation is improved, and concrete operating process is as followings.

Step1: Randomly select one segment as crossover segment in two generation father chromosomes.

Step2: If two genes on chromosome crossover point are all equal to zero, directly take ordinal crossover operation.

Step3: If the genes on chromosome crossover point are not all equal to zero, crossover point move to the left (right), and then take ordinal crossover operation.

3.3 Mutation Operator

The mutation strategy of this study is adopted 2- commutation mutation strategy, namely, randomly selecting mutated individual chromosome according to some mutation probability and two gene locations in this chromosome, exchanging gene in two places and form into new gene clusters. If it is continuously appeared with zero code in gene clusters, exchange zero code and non-zero code in random place.

3.4 Mountain Climbing Operation

Supposed routing line before exchanging is $s = \{...,x_i,x_{i+1},...x_j,x_{j+1},...\}$, it can get the routing line $s' = \{...,x_j,x_{i+1},...x_i,x_{j+1},...\}$ after exchanging location of two points. If the distance is equal to $\{d(x_{i+1},x_j)+d(x_i,x_{j+1})\}<\{d(x_{i+1},x_i)+d(x_j,x_{j+1})\}$, exchanging is successful and keeps exchanging result. The concrete steps are as followings.

Step1: Initial recycling time variable t=1, when the most optimal solution at present $s^* = s$ and its length is $l(s^*)$.

Step2: Randomly selecting two top points x_i, x_j in the most optimal route and $i < j$. x_i is not close to x_j .

Step3: Calculate saving distance $\Delta c = \{d(x_{i+1},x_j)+d(x_i,x_{j+1})\}<\{d(x_{i+1},x_i)+d(x_j,x_{j+1})\}$. If $\Delta c > 0$, it isn't exchanged. If $t = t + 1$, it shifts into step4. Otherwise, execute exchanging. And the corresponding solution is s'. And the optimal solution is $s^* = s'$. If $t = 1$, it shifts into step2.

Step4: If $l(s^*)$ isn't reduced in the last x a circulation, this algorithm is over. Otherwise, it shifts into step2.

Step5: Repeat step 1 to step 4 till reaching certain exchanging times.

4   Experimental Calculation and Result Analysis

Example One: The data originates from Document [8]. There are one depot and 20 client nodes, six vehicles of the same type, and the vehicle's load capacity is 8.

4.1   Solution of Hybrid Genetic Algorithm

The main parameters: population size of 60, the maximum number of iterations is 500; crossover 0.90, mutation operator is 0.2. Randomly solve ten times.

Here, the longest line is 205.767 km, the corresponding optimal total length of 1088.167 km. The concrete route can be seen in table 1 and figure 1.

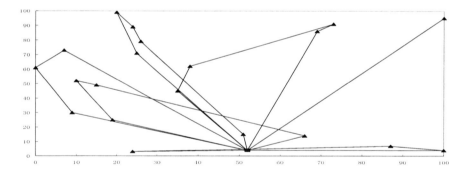

Fig. 1. Optimization route of MMVRP using hybrid genetic algorithm

Table 1. Optimal results by hybrid genetic algorithm

Line No.	Running Path	Mileage
1	0-16-2-20-0	178.799
2	0-3-9-11-13-4-0	201.402
3	0-18-10-7-0	152.486
4	0-6-5-14-17-0	197.247
5	0-15-0	205.767
6	0-12-8-1-19-0	152.466

4.2 Solutions by Genetic Algorithm

Reference [8] is adopted genetic algorithm to get the solution.

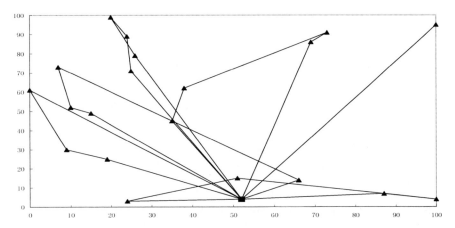

Fig. 2. Optimization route of MMVRP using genetic algorithm

Table 2. Optimal results by genetic algorithm

Line No.	Running Path	Mileage
1	0-1-8-16-19-0	185.945
2	0-9-13-11-4-0	201.293
3	0-18-3-7-10-0	156.254
4	0-6-5-14-17-0	197.247
5	0-15-0	205.767
6	0-12-20-2-0	159.731

4.3 Analysis on Two Algorithms

The proposed hybrid genetic algorithm has a strong search capability, high computational efficiency and high quality on algorithm solving.

Table 3. Comparison among GA and Algorithm of this study

	Genetic Algorithm	This Study
The Total Mileage	1106.237	1088.167
Average Mileage	184.373	181.3612
The longest line	205.767	205.767

5 Conclusions

In general, the proposed hybrid genetic algorithm has strong searching ability, rapid convergence rate, strong ability to overcome the fall into local optimum and high solving high quality. Therefore, it is more practical significance and value so as to reduce operating cost and improve economic benefit.

References

1. Haghania, A., Jung, S.: A dynamic vehicle routing problem with time dependent travel times. Computers & Operations Research 32, 2959–2986 (2005)
2. Bent, R., Van Hentenryck, P.: A two-stage hybrid local search for the vehicle routing problem with time windows. Transportation Science 38, 515–530 (2004)
3. Alfredo, F., Dieguez, R.: A tabu search algorithm for the vehicle routing problem with pick up and delivery service. Computers & Operations Research 33, 595–619 (2006)
4. Molloy, M., Reed, B.: A Bound on the Strong Chromatic Index of a Graph. Journal of Combinatorial Theory, Series B 69, 103–109 (1997)
5. Carlsson, J., Ge, D., Subramaniam, A., Wu, A., Ye, Y.: Solving min-max multi-depot vehicle routing problem. Report (2007)
6. Arkin, E.M., Hassin, R., Levin, A.: Approximations for Minimum and Min-max Vehicle Routing Problems. Journal of Algorithms, 1–16 (2005)
7. Applegate, D., Cook, W., Dash, S., Rohe, A.: Solution of a min-max vehicle routing problem. INFORMS Journal on Computing 14, 132–143 (2002)
8. Xia, L.: Research on Vehicle Routing Problem. PhD thesis of Huazhong University of Science and Technology, pp.24-44 (2007)

A Study of Key Techniques of Subject Information Gateway Service

Lanjing Wang

Institute of Documentation and Information, Henan University, Minglun Street 85,
475001 Kaifeng, China
lanjing@henu.edu.cn

Abstract. The purpose of this article is to draw the attention of all sectors of the society to subject information gateway construction and guide the experts in computer science and library and information science to attach importance to utilization and exploitation of key information techniques of subject information gateway service. The Internet survey and literature investigation are research methods of this article. The conclusion shows that people don't concern about utilization of subject information gateway because of the lack of in-depth exploitation. This paper expounds 4 key techniques of subject gateway service: information organization technology, meta-searching technique, XML technique and computer security technique.

Keywords: subject information gateway, information service, information organization, information technology.

1 Introduction

As a kind of retrieval tool of excellent information resources, subject gateway meets the needs of professional users, selects, describes and organises some valuable web information and establishes standard navigation system of authoritative professional information resources in certain subjects or disciplines. Subject information gateway integrates information resources, retrieval tools and information service into an entity and provides users with a convenient information retrieval, browsing and service entrance. Subject gateway service must rely on some important modern information techniques. Therefore the author mainly discusses the key techniques required by subject information gateway from information organization technology field, computer technology field, computer security technology field and so on.

2 Information Organization Technology

Information organization is a hot issue at home and abroad recently [1], [2]. Foreign research on information organization focuses on the following fields such as bibliographic objectives, bibliographic entities, bibliographic languages, principles of description,subject languages and subject-languages syntax and so on. Subject language research accounts for merely fraction of foreign research on information organization

G. Shen and X. Huang (Eds.): CSIE 2011, Part II, CCIS 153, pp. 183–187, 2011.

and foreign research on information organization focuses on metadata. Whereas information organization research in China centers on subject cataloguing content of information resources. Information organization should not only absorb subject cataloging achievements but also pay more attention to the information organization problems of digital library and subject information gateway.

In 1996, *Subject Cataloging Manual* compiled by the Cataloging Policy and Support Bureau of Library of Congress determined the subject indexing principles clearly [3]. The catalogists need to apply these principles to indexing and description of subject gateway information resources. People choose corresponding metadata standards according to types of information resources, which plays a great role in promoting information resources integration and normalizing subject gateway construction.

Metadata describe information resources or data objects. Their purpose is to enable users to discover, identify and assess, select, position and invoke the related information resources, track the changes of resources in use process and realize integration, effective management and preservation of information resources [4]. People usually classify metadata in accordance with their functions. Metadata can be divided into management type metadata (its main purpose is to help SIG staff maintain resources, mainly including resources maintainer, the date of resources addition, recording the latest update date and the expiration date of resources, resources submission, resource cataloguists, source of resources and ownership declaration), descriptive type metadata (used to describe and identify information resources content,and their relationship with other resources), preservation type metadata (preservation and management of relevant information resources, specially attributes related to long-term preservation of resources objects), use type metadata (about information resource use types and levels) and technological metadata (recording how to operate the information resources) [5]. Metadata are composed of all the aspects of attributes of a group of relevant resources and each attribute includes one or more attribute values of a attribute type. There are a variety of metadata standards, such as MARC (MAchine-Readable Cataloging), DC (Dublin Core), PICS (Platform for Internet Content Selection), RDF (Resources Description Frame), EAD (Encoding Archival Description), TEI (Text Encoding Initiative), etc. MARC was developed originally by the American Library of Congress in America. MARC metadata set up corresponding access points according to search functions of the traditional entry and set the related fields and sub-fields based on the description requirements of the traditional entry. Meanwhile, MARC21 sets record heading section, address section, control field and variable data section considering the characteristics of machine-readable catalogue. MARC metadata leave plenty of leeway for setting new field in data field area. In order to be able to handle the network information resources, MARC metadata set up "856 electronic document address and search" field. MARC metadata refer to and use the relevant international standards in the establishing process. The machine-readable catalogue Established on the basis of MARC metadata can provide users with multiple search means. DC metadata focus on information resources description, integration and control and pay special attention to faith to the original resources and normal forms and glossary adoption in indexing process. Metadata syntax structure defines description method and description format of the elements and modifiers. Metadata can be realized through specific description framework and language. The priority of resources description of subject gateways should be given to the internationally universal metadata format. Adopted metadata need accommodate any type of data in subject gateway, including distinctive object resources (such as teaching plans, syllabus and so on collected by GEM), traditional content object (books, periodicals, documents, etc.), content object combination (e.g. courseware, composed of some text, images and video), content object resources collection (library, website, database, etc.) and resources collection knowledge organization mechanism (such as the classification, thesaurus, semantic networks) [6]. With the development of RDF framework and XML language, skipping semantic content and directly realizing metadata interoperability from the syntactic structure become possible.

3 Meta-searching Technique

As the amount of information available on the Internet increases, no one search engine can cover the entire network. In order to obtain the needed information, people sometimes have to use multiple search engines. As a kind of search engine, metasearch engine is used to perform network search through multiple independent search engines. Metasearch engine is a network resources retrieval tool which mainly adopts meta-searching technique. Metasearch engine helps users select and use appropriate search engine to realize retrieval operation in multiple search engines through a unified user interface. The technique of Calling, controlling and integrating the independent search engines is called meta-searching technique which is the core of metasearch engine.

Metasearch engine is composed of retrieval request submission module, retrieval interface agent module and retrieval results fusion module. Users firstly put forward retrieval request for metasearch engine; metasearch engine issues retrieval request submission to multiple source search engines via search interface according to the request again; source search engines transmit retrieval results to metasearch engines after they execute the retrieval request of metasearch engine via retrieval interface in response; metasearch engine integrates retrieval results from multiple source search engines and then transmits them to users in response again [7].

Metasearch, Metacrawler, Profusion, Inquirus and Mamma are some representative metasearch engines. Metasearch engine has neither Web searching mechanism nor their own Web document index databases. Metasearch engine has its own key techniques in retrieval request submission, retrieval interface agent and the retrieval results fusion.

4 XML Technique

In computer technology field, XML technique should be one of the most important techniques. The technique not only refers to the XML standard itself, but also a serie of related XML-based languages, such as XHTML, XSLT, XSL, XML Schema, SOAP and so on. XML is a text file similar to HTML tag which defines a tree structure to describe stored data. XML, an international information processing standard, is used to define a markup language with special purpose. XML allows a file to contain text, voice, images, symbols and other data types and defines an infinite identifier set, each

of them with different semantics. Expressive form of XML syntax is as follows: <
markup attribute = value > information content </> markup. The front "<>" refers to
the start tag of information content and the behind "</>" means the closing tag of
information content. Both the tags come in pair. The "properties"in the start tag is used
to prompt computer reference information. This form is clear and distinct.

5 Computer Security Technique

Computer security is safety measures of technology and management adopted to protect data processing system. Its purpose is to protect computer hardware, software and
data from damage, alteration and leak because of occasion or intention. With expanding
and popularization of computer network, people require higher computer security and
wider application and pay more attention to computer network security. Current network security faces many attacks, such as denial of service attack, E-mail attack,
network monitoring attack and virus attack which will cause a serious threat to network
security. Therefore the security of network systems requires virus prevention and improvement of ability of system to resist illegal foreign hackers and confidentiality of
remote data transmission to protect remote data from illegal appropriation in the
transmission way. The author thinks how to guarantee safe and effective operation
technically is an indispensable problem in subject gateway construction.

Firewall has become an emerging technical measure in protecting computer network
security recently. It is an isolating control technology which sets barriers between an
institution network and unsafe network and prevents the unauthorized access to information resources. An effective firewall should be able to ensure all the Internet
information to go through the firewall and all the information going through firewall to
be inspected.

Subject gateway can use firewall to set "card" between inside and the Internet and
monitor all the access information and formulate network security policy according to
network security personnel to decide which information is able to pass. Technical
solutions of firewall configuration include packet filtering. Currently most routers and
switches have embedded packet filtering functions. The administrator can set access
list to realize the packet filtering function. The administrator installs a router containing
packet filtering functions in the Internet gateway to realize packet filtrating firewall.
The packet filtering technology is a security technology completely based on the network layer, judges only by sources of data packets, goals and port and other network
information and is unable to identify the malicious invasion based on the application
layer such as malicious Java program and virus attached to E-mail. Experienced
hackers forge IP address easily and cheat packets filtrating firewall. Theoretically, the
firewall is at the bottom of network security and is responsible for security certification
and transmission between networks. With the overall development of the network
security technique and constant changes of network application, modern firewall
technique has gradually moved towards the other security level besides network layer
which not only needs to complete filtering tasks of the traditional firewalls, but also can
provide various network application with corresponding security service.

Windows server is one of many server operating systems, but the system has more
security vulnerabilities than any other one. Therefore the system needs to use safety

configuration. At the beginning of gateway planning and construction, it is necessary to clear security needs, formulate security policy, establish firewall systems conforming to security policy in the border, devide internal security policies domain, use reasonable discernment mechanism and security system of access control strategy, establish an effective monitoring system, consider adopting appropriate operating system, application system, security system to ensure network center safety and implement strict foreign personnel management system.

6   Conclusion

Subject gateway conforms to digital, networking, integrated and knowledgeable trends of information needs and becomes an effective measure of web information resources organization and exploitation. The conclusion shows that we need to explore and use network information resources effectively and deeply and further study how to broaden the scope of subject gateway service and develop and utilize the key techniques. The author elaborates the key techniques of subject gateway service so as to draw the attention of computer science and library and information experts and further promote subject gateway construction.

References

1. Lin, H.M., Lou, C.Q.: Domestic research status of information organization in the Past Ten Years. Library and Information 6, 35–38 (2004)
2. Gao, D.: Study summary on Internet information organization. New Technology of Library and Information Service 9, 54–57 (2004)
3. Cataloging Policy and Support Office of Library of Congress: Subject Cataloging Manual: Subject Headings. Cataloging Distribution Service of Library of Congress, Washington (1996)
4. Wu, K.H., Xing, C.X., Luo, D.Y.: A study of metadata for digital library. The Journal of the Library Science in China 28, 43–46 (2002)
5. Li, G.J.: Library Network Information System in Digital Era. Beijing Library Press, Beijing (2006)
6. Zhang, X.L.: Open metadata mechanism: ideas and principles. The Journal of the Library Science in China 29, 9–14 (2003)
7. Qu, C.Q., Li, Y.F.: Study on metadata engine. Modern Computer 187, 17–20 (2004)

Software Process Integration Based on Design Structure Matrix

Weimin Zhang and Shangang Jia

Beijing Aerospace Control Center, BACC
Beijing, China
zwm1962@sina.com

Abstract. A software lifecycle is composed of many software processes which are not independent. In order to improve a process, the process should be integrated into a larger process context environment and the synchronization between processes should be insured. This paper introduces the concept of process modeling and the design structure matrix (DSM) describing complex process systems. By using software process integration as an example, the method of integrating software processes based on DSM is discussed. By analyzing and rearranging the DSM of the integrated process purposely, the process could be improved to reduce the iterative rework in the process and the whole process completion time could be shortened.

Keywords: Process model, Design structure matrix, Process integration, Process improvement.

1 Introduction

The standard of ISO/IEC 12207 defined 17 software lifecycle processes [1]. CMMI for development reduced the best practices in the product development to 22 process areas [2]. The software lifecycle processes in ISO/IEC 12207 and the process areas in CMMI are all composed of a group of activities or practices. The purpose of a process is implemented by executing the activities or practices in the process.

Both ISO/IEC 12207 and CMMI only defined the purpose of the process and the activities in the process. The connecting patterns, the sequential relationships and the interactions among the activities were not defined. In order to manage the processes effectively in the aspect of schedule, resources and quality, we should establish process models to describe the relationships and interactions among activities.

On the other hand, some of the activities of the processes in ISO/IEC 12207 and CMMI need to be decomposed. For example, the activity of perform verification in the verification process may be decomposed to sub-activities as verify requirements, verify design, verify code, verify documents and verify processes. These sub-activities may be executed in different phases in the software development process by different persons. Therefore, in order to manage the activities and processes effectively, we should decompose this kind of activities. And, the relationships and interactions among these sub-activities should be defined.

G. Shen and X. Huang (Eds.): CSIE 2011, Part II, CCIS 153, pp. 188–193, 2011.

Furthermore, the processes in ISO/IEC 12207 or CMMI are not independent. Sequential restriction and information flow exist among the processes. In order to manage the whole software engineering project, the interactions among the processes must be managed and harmonized effectively. Therefore, we should integrate these processes to specify the relationships and interactions among processes.

The basic concept of process modeling is introduced in section 2. Design structure matrix and its application are presented in section 3. By applying the process integration method described in [3] to software processes, the method of software process integration based on DSM is discussed in section 4.

2 Process Modeling

Generally speaking, a process can be modeled based on two kinds of objects, i.e. activity and deliverable [4]. An activity is an element of the process and consists of a package of work that must be done to produce the expected results. Deliverables denote the information, data, results and materials needed or produced by activities.

In a software process, an activity needs information and perhaps other inputs to accomplish its task and create satisfied results. An activity produces preliminary results, status report and validations or refusals proposed to other activities. Therefore, in order to establish the dependences of the activities, we must find out what the activities need to work and what information and deliverables they produce.

Theoretically speaking, a process can be accomplished by executing every activity once according to a specific order. Practically, very few processes can be done in this way. Typically, before all requirements are satisfied, some of the activities may need to be reworked. The iterative reworks are generally caused by incomplete input information and defects produced in an upstream activity and detected by the following activities. Therefore, according to the results of an activity, the process may go back to an earlier activity to rework some of its task.

In most cases, overlapping activities may save time but cost more than executing activities sequentially. Suppose two nominal sequential activities are overlapped partly. The downstream activity will start to work according to the preliminary information from the upstream activity. Along with the advance of the upstream activity, its output information will evolve to its final form and will be delivered to the downstream activity. In this case, the downstream activity may need some rework to accommodate the new information.

3 Design Structure Matrix

A design structure matrix (DSM) is a square matrix [3,5,6]. The elements on the main diagonal denote the activities of the design process. These activities are ordered from upper left to the bottom right according to their rough executing sequence. An element above or under the diagonal denotes the dependence of an activity on another activity, e.g. the flow of the deliverables. Reading along a column, we can get the inputs origination of an activity. Reading along a row, we can see the output pool of an activity. For example, in the DSM in Fig.1, activity Act_1 provides one or more deliverables for Act_2 and Act_5. Activity Act_2 relies on the deliverables from Act_1 and Act_6 and provides deliverables for Act_3 and Act_4.

In the DSM in Fig.1, Act_2 depends on the deliverables from Act_1 and Act_2 do not depend on the deliverables from Act_1. These two activities should be executed sequentially. Act_3 and Act_4 do not depend on each other and they could be executed in parallel. Act_5 and Act_6 depend on deliverables from the other. They are interdependent or called coupling.

	Act_1	Act_2	Act_3	Act_4	Act_5	Act_6
Act_1	Act_1	X			X	
Act_2		Act_2	X	X		
Act_3			Act_3		X	
Act_4				Act_4	X	
Act_5					Act_5	X
Act_6		X			X	Act_6

Fig. 1. Example of design structure matrix

DSM is not the only tool to model process. But, it could be noticed that the DSM expression is more concise and clear than the traditional flow diagram expression. Furthermore, DSM emphasizes an important aspect of the process structure, i.e. the marks below the diagonal have special importance. These marks denote the dependences of the upstream activities on the downstream activities. If the activities in Fig.1 are executed according to the specific order, a supposition about the outputs of Act_6 must be made before Act_2 are executed. After Act_6 finishes, Act_2 may need some rework if the supposition is not totally correct. DSM may emphasize this kind of iteration and rework conveniently.

Some usefully process analysis can be made by using DSM [3]. For example, a mark below the diagonal denotes that the execution of the process may go back to the upstream part of the process. This kind of feedback rework may impact the cost and schedule of the process greatly. Rearranging the order of the activities in the process may move a mark in the lower triangle to the upper triangle or nearer to the diagonal sometimes. It will reduce the impact on the process cost and schedule. Some simple algorithms could be used to this kind of rearranging.

4   Software Process Integration Based on DSM

The software processes are not independent to each other. An activity of a process may require deliverables produced by activities inside the process and outside the process. When we want to improve a process, we must look into inside and outside the process. We should integrate the process into a larger process context circumstance and assure obtain the required input at correct time, i.e. keep the related activities synchronized.

In order to synchronize and coordinate the activities of software processes, the process should be integrated with the other related processes. Then, the process will become a part of a larger integrated process. Therefore, process integration is a pre-mise to synchronizing processes.

To integrate software processes by using DSM, the DSM describing processes should be extended [3]. An area is added to the top and right of the DSM. The upper area describes the inputs of the process from outside the process and the right area denotes the outputs of the process to outside the process. Observing a column of the main matrix of the DSM shows from where an activity obtains its input deliverables. Looking up to the upper area of the extended DSM along with the column, we can find the input of the activity from outside the process. Similarly, looking to the right extended area along with a row, we could find the outputs of the activity to the out-side of the process.

In order to simplify the depiction, we will discuss the method of software process integration using DSM by taking the integration of the development process, the veri-fication process and the validation process of the software processes as an example.

There are interfaces between the development process and the verification process and between the development process and the validation process. The development process provides developed products to the verification and validation process to verify and validate and receives the results of the verification and validation. The development process may need some rework according to the results of the verifica-tion and validation.

Apart from the interfaces among the three processes, there may be interfaces be-tween any of them and another outside processes. We use A, B and C to denote the development, the verification and the validation processes. Then, we can express the integration of the three processes by the extended DSM as showed in Fig.2.

In Fig.2, an "X" in the main matrix denotes an interface between two of the three processes. An "X" in the upper area expresses an input interface to the three processes from other outside processes. An "X" in the right area expresses an output interface to other outside processes from one of the three processes. In spite of there is no inter-face between verification process and validation process, there is time order restric-tion relationship between them. The validation process must be executed after the verification process. Symbol "*" describes this kind of sequential restriction in the DSM in Fig.2.

		X	X	X	
process A	**A**	X	X		X
process B	X	**B**	*		X
process C	X		**C**		X

Fig. 2. The integrated process described by a DSM

In order to manage the integrated process of the three processes effectively, we need to know what activities each of them includes and what input and output delive-rables these activities need and produce. And we also need to know the interfaces among these activities. For this purpose, we establish a DSM process model for each of the three processes. For the purpose of simplification, in these process models, only parts of the practical activities of the three processes are considered and the interfaces between one of them and outside activities are not considered.

Suppose the development process can be decomposed into four activities, i.e. requirements analysis, design, code and unit test and assemble test. We use A_1, A_2, A_3 and A_4 to denote these activities. An upstream activity of the four activities provides phase products to its next downstream activity and to verification process. The verified assembled products are delivered to the validation process. The development process can be described by a DSM as showed in Fig.3 (a).

We decompose the verification process into four activities, i.e. requirements verification, design verification, code verification and assemble verification. We use B_1, B_2, B_3 and B_4 to denote these activities. An activity of the four activities gets verification objects from the development process and provides verification results to the development process. The activities in the development process may need to rework according to the results. The verification process can be described by a DSM as showed in Fig.3 (b).

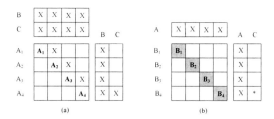

Fig. 3. Software development process and verification process

Suppose the validation process only has one activity. We use C_1 to denote the activity. The validation activity feeds back validation results to the development process. If some defects are found by the validation activity, some activities of the development process may need to rework.

According to the structure of the DSM in Fig.3, the decomposed three processes can be integrated into a lower level integrated software process as depicted in Fig.4.

	A_1	A_2	A_3	A_4	B_1	B_2	B_3	B_4	C_1
A_1	A_1	X			X				
A_2		A_2	X			X			
A_3			A_3	X			X		
A_4				A_4				X	X
B_1	X				B_1				
B_2		X				B_2			
B_3			X				B_3		
B_4				X				B_4	*
C_1	X	X	X	X					C_1

Fig. 4. DSM of a lower level integrated software process

By rearranging the order of the activities in the integrated process DSM in Fig.4, some of the feed back rework may be reduced. Because the validation activity validates the products being developed and verified, the position of it can not be changed. Activity C_1 must be behind all the other activities. Rearranging the activities of the

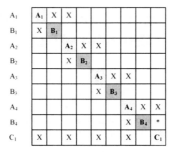

Fig. 5. The integrated software process after rearranging

development process and the verification process can produce a new integrated process as showed in Fig.5.

By decomposing, modeling and integrating processes, we can understand the activities of these processes and their relationships better. Furthermore, we can manage, control, coordinate and synchronize the activities of different processes more effectively by doing so. And it is helpful to manage and improve the whole integrated process.

5 Conclusion

Every software process is a constituting part of a larger system environment. A software process must be coordinated with other software processes to provide the expected results. In order to execute software processes collaboratively and effectively, the software processes should not be piled up simply. The software processes should be integrated properly. DSM is an effective modeling tool that could be used to model, decompose, integrate and synchronize complicated processes. By analyzing the DSM of the integrated process purposely, the process could be improved to reduce the iterative rework in the process and the whole process completion time could be shortened.

References

1. IEEE/EIA: Industry Implementation of International Standard ISO/IEC 12207:1995. IEEE, New York (1998)
2. CMMI Product Team: CMMI for Development Version 1.2. Pittsburgh, PA (2006)
3. Tyson, R.: Browning: Process Integration Using the Design Structure Matrix. System Engineering 5(3), 180–193 (2002)
4. Tyson, R.: Browning, Ernst Fricke, and Herbert Negele: Key Concepts in Modeling Product Development Processes. System Engineering 9(2), 104–128 (2006)
5. Steward, D.V.: The Design Structure System: A Method for Managing the Design of Complex Systems. IEEE Trans. on Engineering Management. 28(3), 71–74 (1981)
6. Weimin Zhang, Bosheng Zhou and Wenjie Luo: Modeling and Simulating Sequential Iterative Development Processes (in Chinese). Computer integrated manufacturing system. 14(9), 1696–1703(2008)

3D-SSM Based Segmentation of Proximal Femur from Hip Joint CT Data

Weiwei Song, Shukun Cao, Hui Zhang, Wenming Wang, and Kaifeng Song

School of Mechanical Engineering, University of Jinan,
Jinan, P.R. China
me_songww@ujn.edu.cn

Abstract. A new method based on 3D SSM (statistical shape model) is presented for segmentation of proximal femur from hip joint CT images consisting of the collapsing femoral head caused by ANFH. The main idea of the method is to take the biological variability of anatomical shape as the prior knowledge model to guide the process of segmentation. The processing scheme consisted of the following four steps. First, constructing 3D shape model by statistical analysis from a training set. Next, fitting a 3D model to the object. Then, estimating the location of the landmarks by neighborhood points gray information. Finally, model deformation by an iterative process of searching and registration. Experimental results show that the proposed method is efficient to predict and rehabilitate the morphological shape of the collapsing femoral head from the incomplete information in the hip joint CT data.

Keywords: statistical shape model; segmentation; hip joint; CT data.

1 Introduction

Image segmentation is a principal problem in image analysis and visualization. In the area of clinical surgery planning and implant design applications require accurate and compact representations of the patient's bone. Therefore, the bone must be parted from the soft tissues first and then be separated from each other. However, the normal structure of the femur consists of an interior of more loosely organized trabecular bone and a superficial shell of compact cortical bone. The image intensity of the cortical bone is not very different from that of the trabecular bone. Likewise, it is possible to find interior bone structures which exhibit the same intensity as the cortical bone. An even worse case is that the low intensity values on the cortical bone and the weakly defined joint space between femoral head and acetabulum especially in the images of patients of avascular necrosis of femoral head (ANFH) in which the gap between the acetabulum and femoral head can hardly be seen. Under such circumstances, model based segmentation can become more helpful than traditional methods. Based on statistical knowledge acquired from training sets, they can successfully predict the shape of organs even in regions where no corresponding image evidence is present.

Recent work has shown that prior knowledge being applied into medical image segmentation is essential for robust performance. Model-based segmentation methods have been studied as one of the most successful approaches for image analysis for

G. Shen and X. Huang (Eds.): CSIE 2011, Part II, CCIS 153, pp. 194–199, 2011.

nearly two decades. Because of the prior information, this approach is more stable than conventional algorithm to against local image artifacts and perturbations. Probably the best-known methods in the area are the active shape models (ASMs) [1] and active appearance models (AAMs) [2] by Cootes et al.. ASMs have found widespread application in 2D. The satisfied effects [1,2,3,4] have been achieved in X ray image, CT, MRI, or ultrasound images segmentation and contour extraction. Nowadays, many 3D SSMs have been explored [5,6,7,8], they are used in face recognition and various medical image processing areas. According to the survey of [8], 3D segmentation is the major application of statistical shape models. 3D SSMs have been used for the segmentation of a variety of structures in the human body. However, the study focusing on separating bones at a joint in CT images is sparse. Recovery of the shape of collapsing femoral head using a SSM based on a dense mesh has not been reported yet.

In this paper we presented a SSM based method, which can segment robustly the pelvic bone and the femur from CT images even for highly pathological cases.

This paper is organized as follows: Section 1 discusses the introduction and related work. Section 2 describes the construction of the 3D statistical shape model of the proximal femur. Section 3 gives the frame of segmentation based on SSM. The last section makes a conclusion and talks about future work.

2   Construction of a 3D Statistical Shape Model of the Proximal Femur

The statistical shape models used in this work were created from 50 hip joint CT datasets comprise proximal femurs of healthy volunteers of various age groups and sex. Each data set was automatically segmented by the method we proposed previously [4]. After getting a series of contours of proximal femur, the surface model of proximal femur can be constructed by implicit function algorithm following the method of field function definition introduced in [9], defined field function as a distance function with symbol. Based on significant anatomical and geometrical features, a consistent sub-division into patches, i.e. regions of the mesh with the topology of a disc, was performed over all training shapes. These patches can make point to point correspondences be established for all training shapes.

In order to save the calculating time and raise the efficiency, all surfaces are simplified using the edge-collapsing algorithm proposed in [10]. Being reduced the number of triangles, the mesh model obtaining meshes with about 2136 triangles (see Fig.1), which is about 10 percent of original model.

Before any meaningful statistical analysis of the mesh vertices could be performed, instances of the study population had to be transformed into a common coordinate system. As shown in Fig.2, the coordinate system was defined by three anatomical landmarks: the femoral head center, the lesser trochanter and the greater trochanter. In all anatomical structure points, the femoral head center is more important and easy to acquire than any other. So the center of the coordinate system was defined on the femoral head center instead of other points.

After all shapes properly aligned in the coordinate system and landmark points are determined, the statistics of their variation can be captured. As a result of this process, all training shapes can be represented in a common vector space.

Fig. 1. Mean shape model of simplification based on edge-collapse

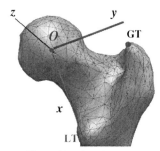

O – the center of femoral head   GT–Greater Trochanter
LT-Lesser Trochanter

Fig. 2. Anatomical landmarks for definition of the coordinate system

Here the principal component analysis (PCA) is applied on training set to obtain the shape model

$$S(b,F) = F\left(\bar{v} + \sum_k b_k P_k\right) \tag{1}$$

where $\bar{v}$ represents the mean shape, P_k is the modes of shape variation, b_k is the shape weights. Any instance of a consistent surface mesh of the proximal femur comprised in the statistical analysis, i.e. any training shape may now be represented by such a linear combination. Fig.3 shows some results of training.

3   3D SSM Based Segmentation of Proximal Femur

Having constructed the statistical model of shape, the segmentation method following a global to local approach is divided into three steps: pose initialization to estimate position, image gradient analysis and model deformation. The segmentation process can be formulated as the problem of finding those shape parameters, and using the transformation from the model coordinate frame to the image coordinate frame. A detailed description of each step is given in the following sections.

3.1   Fitting a Model to the Object in Volume Data

In order to ensure convergence in the subsequent iteration process, the average model used for initialization should be placed near target and aligned to the actual volume data

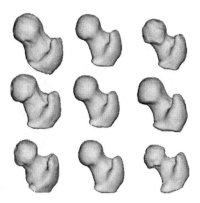

Fig. 3. The first three modes of variation ($\pm\sqrt{\lambda_m}$) of the proximal femur

by rotating, scaling and translating as precisely as possible. This is a matching process between the average shape model in training set and the target, i.e., finding the optimal mapping relationship between corresponding points of the models. Generally, it usually achieved through the geometric transformation in formula (2), (3). The corresponding anatomical landmarks as used for its definition have to be marked interactively on the actual model, and the optimal positioning can be reached by relying on the standardized anatomical coordinate system.

$$E = |T(x_2) - x_1|^T w |T(x_2) - x_1| \qquad (2)$$

$$T(x_2) = \begin{bmatrix} s\cos\theta & -s\sin\theta \\ s\sin\theta & s\cos\theta \end{bmatrix} \begin{pmatrix} x_{2k} \\ y_{2k} \end{pmatrix} + \begin{bmatrix} t_x \\ t_y \end{bmatrix} \qquad (3)$$

3.2   Estimating the Location of the Landmarks by Gray Information

After initialization, a corresponding 3D model was fitted to the target segmentation region. But in matching process, the pose adjustment of average shape model must by means of gray statistical model of label point neighborhood. In each step of the iteration the image grayscale values are extracted along the normal to the surface at each vertex of the mesh. Points with sufficiently high derivative magnitude are selected as boundary point candidates. Those points which belong to the true external bone surface with a high level of certainty should be selected. Accordingly, only those points which fulfill the selection conditions will be identified as target edges.

3.3   Model Deformation and Matching

After reliable boundary patches are extracted, the model is fitted to these points as closely as possible. At first, the affine transformation is determined, which minimizes the sum of squared distances between the selected boundary points and their corresponding mesh vertices using homogeneous coordinate representation. Then applying this affine adjustment in each step significantly reduces the number of necessary iteration steps. The local image gradient information suggests a better position for each landmark point by examining the region of the image around each current point to find the best nearby match. Then, the shape model attempts to deform itself to fit to these new suggested positions within the constraints imposed by its plausible variation. This process is repeated until convergence. The shape similar to those observed in the training set will be located in the volume data. Finally, we get the segmented or rehabilitated model.

3.4 Results and Discussion

The automatic segmentation algorithms were implemented on different data sets, one for healthy hip joint CT data set and the other for ANFH patients' CT data set. Fig.4 (a) is the hip joint volume data of a healthy volunteer. The region of femoral head and acetabulum is highly confusing. Applying our method, the model of femoral head can be segmented from the hip joint data completely (see Fig.4(b)(c)). In case of severe arthritis, the femoral head has lesion or even collapsing, as shown in Fig. 5(a), the head will be predicted solely based on the prior statistical shape models and information about remnant parts of the femur. As Fig.5(b)(c)(d)demonstrates, the satisfying segmentation and reconstruction results have confirmed the validity of the proposed method in the patient CT data with incomplete information.

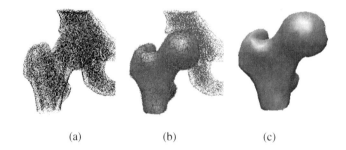

(a)   (b)   (c)

Fig. 4. Segmentation result of proximal femur from hip join

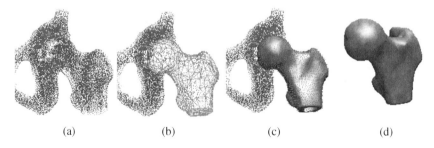

(a)   (b)   (c)   (d)

Fig. 5. Segmentation result of a patient

4 Conclusions

Computer assisted biomedical modeling, surgery planning, and image-guided surgery of joints require the separation of bones at the joints. This paper offers a practical solution via a SSM based strategy that can be readily used. This algorithm reveals some of the general properties of surface estimation and restoration, so it is efficient and has a wide range of practical applications. It can also be further used to construct rehabilitative model of any collapsing joint bone.

Sensitivity to initial model placement and model matching precision are two key problems in the segmentation algorithm. Further work will be focused in solving these problems as well as improving the searching efficiency in model matching process.

Acknowledgment. This work is supported by the Ph.D. Program Foundation of University of Jinan (XBS0909).

References

1. Cootes, T.F., Cooper, D., Taylor, C.J., Graham, J.: Active Shape Models—Their Training and Application. Computer Vision and Image Understanding 61(1), 38–59 (1995)
2. Cootes, T.F., Edwards, G.J., Taylor, C.J.: Active Appearance Models. IEEE Trans. Pattern Analysis and Machine Intelligence 23, 681–685 (2001)
3. Davies, R.H., Twining, C.J., Daniel, P.D., Cootes, T.F., Taylor, C.J.: Building Optimal 2D Statistical Shape Models. Image and Vision Computing 21, 1171–1182 (2003)
4. Song, W.W., Li, G.H., Ou, Z.Y.: Model-based Segmentation of Femoral Head and Acetabulum from CT Images. In: 2007 IEEE/ICME International Conference on Complex Medical Engineering, vol. 1, pp. 581–585. IEEE Press, Beijing (2007)
5. Van Assen, H.C., Danilouchkine, M.G., Behloul, F., Lamb, H.J., van der Geest, R.J., Reiber, J.H.C., Lelieveldt, B.P.F., Cardiac, L.V.: Segmentation Using a 3D Active Shape Model Driven by Fuzzy Inference. In: Ellis, R., Peters, T. (eds.) MICCAI 2003. LNCS, vol. 2878, pp. 533–540. Springer, Heidelberg (2003)
6. Mitchell, S.C., Bosch, J.G., Lelieveldt, B.P.F., van der Geest, R.J., Reiber, J.H.C., Sonka, M.: 3D Active AppearanceModels: Segmentation of Cardiac MR and Ultrasound Images. IEEE Trans. Med. Imaging. 21(9), 1167–1178 (2002)
7. Park, U., Jain, A.K.: 3D Model-Based Face Recognition in Video. In: Lee, S.-W., Li, S.Z. (eds.) ICB 2007. LNCS, vol. 4642, pp. 1085–1094. Springer, Heidelberg (2007)
8. Heimann, T., Meinzer, H.P.: Statistical Shape Models for 3D Medical Image Segmentation: A Review. Medical Image Analysis 13, 543–563 (2009)
9. Jones, M.W., Chen, M.: A New Approach to the Construction of Surfaces from Contour Data. Technical report, Computer Graphics Forum (1994)
10. Hoppe: Progressive Meshes. In: Proceedings of the 23rd Annual Conference on Computer Graphics and Interactive Techniques, SIGGRAPH 1996, New Orleans, pp. 99–108 (1996)

Research on the Real-Time Image Edge Detection Algorithm Based on FPGA

Xuefeng Hou[1,2], Yuanyuan Shang[1,2,*], Hui Liu[1,2], and Qian Song[3]

[1] College of Information Engineering, Capital Normal University
[2] Beijing Engineering Research Center of High Reliable Embedded System,
Capital Normal University, Beijing, China
syy@bao.ac.cn
[3] National Astronomical Observatories, Chinese Academy of Sciences
snowsummit@126.com

Abstract. Real-time and effective is the bottleneck of edge detection algorithm. In this paper, six different kinds of classical edge detection algorithm is studied and compared by simulating in MATLAB. The result reveals that three operators, such as Roberts, Sobel and Kirsch are better than the others through the comparison of the edge detection accurateness. In order to improve this performance, the real-rime image edge detection system based on FPGA is designed, which contains image buffer module, operator calculation module and threshold processing module. The testing consequence shows that Sobel edge detection operator is more superior in the limit resources hardware platform.

Keywords: FPGA, Roberts, Sobel, Kirsch, Prewitt, Edge detection.

1 Introduction

The image edge detection is one of the key works of image processing. It removes a lot of unimportant information, significantly reduces the amount of data and retains important structural features of the original image for saving a lot of calculations of follow-up of the image processing. It has been a long time on studying edge detection algorithm. Now classical edge detection operator such as Roberts, Sobel, Prewitt has been formed, and as emerging technologies and related development of the theory, new edge detection algorithm is still emerging [1].

Nowadays, software programming based on PC cannot satisfy people's need. More and more people pay attention to the hardware to realize edge detection algorithm and application to daily life. For the widely use and the rapid increasing of integration of FPGA, its features like flexibility, high speed, easy transplantation and real time provide a powerful platform for hardware design on real-time image edge detection [2].

---

[*] Yuanyuan Shang(1977-), Female, Ph.D., Professor
Engaged in high-performance imaging technology and high reliability embedded systems research.

G. Shen and X. Huang (Eds.): CSIE 2011, Part II, CCIS 153, pp. 200–206, 2011.
© Springer-Verlag Berlin Heidelberg 2011

To provide a good pretreatment image for image segmentation, it is essential to find an effective edge detection algorithm to realize real-time image edge detection using the FPGA technology. The algorithm requires an easier hardware implementation. Due to the limited resource of the platform, the edge detection algorithm which occupies fewer logic resources is the key point [3]. For the whole image the algorithm can detect most details of the edge, without increasing the cost of noise, the more the better of edge details. The algorithm should have a better inhibitory effect on noise.

2   Research and Comparison of Edge Detection Algorithm

2.1   Principle of Edge Detection Algorithm

Roberts operator is based on first-order differential and using difference of vertical and horizontal of image to approximate the gradient operator. Such as formula (1)

$$E(i, j) = \sqrt{(f(i, j) - f(i+1, j+1))^2 + (f(i, j+1) - f(i+1, j))^2} \tag{1}$$

So get a 2 x 2 template respectively expressed in vertical and horizontal directions

$$\begin{bmatrix} 1. & 0 \\ 0 & -1 \end{bmatrix} \begin{bmatrix} 0. & 1 \\ -1 & 0 \end{bmatrix} \tag{2}$$

With this template, image respectively convolution, square, add, square root, and then application threshold processing to judge image edge.

Sobel operator is first-order differential edge detection operator too, it is the weighted average of different neighbor as different weights for up and down, left and right, diagonal of each pixel of the image, close to the pixel with large weights, such as formula(3)

$$E(i, j) = \sqrt{\begin{array}{l}(f(i-1, j+1) + 2f(i, j+1) + f(i+1, j+1) - f(i-1, j-1) - 2f(i, j-1) - f(i+1, j-1))^2 \\ + (f(i-1, j-1) + 2f(i-1, j) + f(i-1, j+1) - f(i+1, j-1) - 2f(i+1, j) - f(i+1, j+1))^2\end{array}} \tag{3}$$

So get Sobel operator template as formula (4)

$$\begin{bmatrix} -1 & 0 & 1 \\ -2 & 0. & 2 \\ -1 & 0 & 1 \end{bmatrix} \begin{bmatrix} 1 & 2 & 1 \\ 0 & 0. & 0 \\ -1 & -2 & -1 \end{bmatrix} \tag{4}$$

Image with this template respectively convolution, square, add, square root, and then application threshold processing to judge image edge.

Prewitt is similar to Sobel. The difference is the template. In the process of the weighted average, the points nearly the pixel is the same weights as the others, templates as formula (5)

$$\begin{bmatrix} -1 & 0 & 1 \\ -1 & 0. & 1 \\ -1 & 0 & 1 \end{bmatrix} \begin{bmatrix} 1 & 1 & 1 \\ 0 & 0. & 0 \\ -1 & -1 & -1 \end{bmatrix} \tag{5}$$

Kirsch operator has different eight 3×3 template to convolution respectively with image and output the maximum. It can detect the edge of all directions, reduce the lost details for average, but also increase the calculation. Eight 3×3 template as formula (6)

$$\begin{bmatrix} 5 & 5 & 5 \\ -3 & 0 & -3 \\ -3 & -3 & -3 \end{bmatrix} \begin{bmatrix} -3 & 5 & 5 \\ -3 & 0 & 5 \\ -3 & -3 & -3 \end{bmatrix} \begin{bmatrix} -3 & -3 & 5 \\ -3 & 0 & 5 \\ -3 & -3 & 5 \end{bmatrix} \begin{bmatrix} -3 & -3 & -3 \\ -3 & 0 & 5 \\ -3 & 5 & 5 \end{bmatrix} \begin{bmatrix} -3 & -3 & -3 \\ -3 & 0 & -3 \\ 5 & 5 & 5 \end{bmatrix} \begin{bmatrix} -3 & -3 & -3 \\ 5 & 0 & -3 \\ 5 & 5 & -3 \end{bmatrix} \begin{bmatrix} 5 & -3 & -3 \\ 5 & 0 & -3 \\ 5 & 5 & -3 \end{bmatrix} \begin{bmatrix} 5 & 5 & -3 \\ 5 & 0 & -3 \\ -3 & -3 & -3 \end{bmatrix}. \tag{6}$$

Frei-Chen operator is jointly proposed by Frei and Chen, the operator has nine 3×3 template.

$$\begin{bmatrix} 1 & \sqrt{2} & 1 \\ 0 & 0 & 0 \\ -1 & -\sqrt{2} & -1 \end{bmatrix} \begin{bmatrix} 1 & 0 & -1 \\ \sqrt{2} & 0 & -\sqrt{2} \\ 1 & 0 & -1 \end{bmatrix} \begin{bmatrix} 0 & -1 & \sqrt{2} \\ 1 & 0 & -1 \\ -\sqrt{2} & 1 & 0 \end{bmatrix} \begin{bmatrix} \sqrt{2} & -1 & 0 \\ -1 & 0 & 1 \\ 0 & 1 & -\sqrt{2} \end{bmatrix} \begin{bmatrix} 0 & 1 & 0 \\ -1 & 0 & -1 \\ 0 & 1 & 0 \end{bmatrix} \begin{bmatrix} -1 & 0 & 1 \\ 0 & 0 & 0 \\ 1 & 0 & -1 \end{bmatrix} \begin{bmatrix} 1 & -2 & 1 \\ -2 & 4 & -2 \\ 1 & -2 & 1 \end{bmatrix} \begin{bmatrix} -2 & 1 & -2 \\ 1 & 4 & 1 \\ -2 & 1 & -2 \end{bmatrix} \begin{bmatrix} 1 & 1 & 1 \\ 1 & 1 & 1 \\ 1 & 1 & 1 \end{bmatrix}. \tag{7}$$

$$\quad V1 \qquad\quad V2 \qquad\quad V3 \qquad\quad V4 \qquad\quad V5 \qquad\quad V6 \qquad\quad V7 \qquad\quad V8 \qquad\quad V9$$

among

$$\theta e = \cos^{-1} \sqrt{\frac{\sum_{i=1}^{4}(V_i, b)^2}{\sum_{i=1}^{9}(V_i, b)^2}} \quad . \tag{8}$$

is the result of Frei-Chen, $(\cdot, \cdot)$ is

$$(b, c) = \sum_{i=0}^{8} b_i c_i. \tag{9}$$

Images convolute respectively with V1~V4 which is edge of space-based. $\sum_{i=1}^{4}(V_i \bullet b)^2$ is the sum of the first four convolution. Then convolution respectively with all space-based as V1~V9, the result is $\sum_{i=1}^{9}(V_i \bullet b)^2$. Taking arccosine after divided between the edge of space-based and all space-based, getting θe of the pixel. For every pixel has its θe, giving a threshold T, if θe >T, then it is the edge point, else it is not.

Wallis operator is using geometric mean first and then difference calculation, for details, if the pixel's logarithm subtraction the average of the four adjacent pixels' logarithm is T, and there is a T_0 which is the threshold, if T>T_0 then the pixel is the edge,

such as formula(10).

$$b(i, j) = \log_b(f(i, j)) - \frac{1}{4}(\log_b(f(i-1, j)) + \log_b(f(i, j+1)) + \log_b(f(i+1, j)) + \log_b(f(i, j-1))). \tag{10}$$

2.2 MATLAB Simulation and Comparison

Debugging environment: Windows XP system, E2160 dual-core, 1.8GHz, 2GB memory, HP desktop computer, MATLAB7. 1 version.

Depending on the definition of the edge detection operator to write and realize different operators, and using MATLAB own timing function tic and toc to get the complete edge detection time of different operator. If Lena image as the test image, then get the best images of different operator, shown in Fig.1.

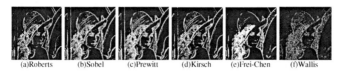

(a)Roberts   (b)Sobel   (c)Prewitt   (d)Kirsch   (e)Frei-Chen   (f)Wallis

Fig. 1. The best images of different operators

By lowering the threshold it is to test the noise immunity and edge detection improvable of different operator. It is shown in Fig.2.

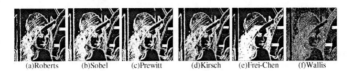

(a)Roberts   (b)Sobel   (c)Prewitt   (d)Kirsch   (e)Frei-Chen   (f)Wallis

Fig. 2. Noise immunity of different operators

Some comparison and summary are shows below in Fig.1 and Fig.2.

Table 1. Six operator characteristic summary table

	Time	Edge details	Edge thickness	Noise suppression	Easily implemented in hardware
Roberts	0.171	++	Thin	+	Yes
Sobel	0.218	++	Thick	++	Yes
Prewitt	0.219	++	Thick	++	Yes
Kirsch	0.625	++	Thin	++	Yes
Frei-Chen	0.641	+	Thick	+++	No
Wallis	1.61	+++	Thin	+	No

The six kinds of operators have their own advantages and disadvantages, however, the operator needs to find faster, better effect image, easily implemented in hardware, inhibitory effects of noise, edge more thin, and the speed is a significant factor in the decision. In order to obtain the optimal operator, Roberts, Sobel, Kirsch are selected for further comparison in hardware platform. As Prewitt is similar as Sobel and inferior Sobel, so select Sobel only to the next step for comparison.

3 System Design

CMOS sensor is used to collect real-time image. And FPGA is for real-time image processing. LCD displays real-time treatment image. Framework shown in Fig.3:

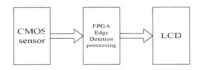

Fig. 3. System framework

CMOS sensor is terasic TRDB-D5M, LCD is TRDB-LTM touch screen, FPGA is Altera CycloneII EP2C70 on DE2-70.

4   Hardware Implementation of Edge Detection Algorithm

The realization of edge detection algorithm modules under the premise of conversion effectively of RAW to RGB, G component is the gray component. By using Megafunctions which is provided by Quartus II software and Verilog HDL to achieve edge detection algorithm. Further description of image buffer module and operator calculation module is shown below.

4.1   Image Buffer Module

SDRAM is caching, processing the real-time image and display to the LCD. However, SDRAM is just image buffer, no address concept to access the image value of each pixel. In order to obtain 2×2 and 3×3 template, altshift_taps shift register which is using Megafunction is data storage.

Take Sobel operator as an example. As the operator is 3×3 template, it is need to define three shift register. If the image size is 5×4, then the three lines requires every five pixels to take, and specific buffering effect is as shown in Fig.4(a). Simulation results are shown in Fig.4(b).

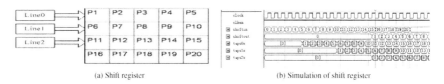

(a) Shift register   (b) Simulation of shift register

Fig. 4. Simulation of image buffer module

In the processing of data transmission, Line0, Line1 and Line2 are respectively data storage for every five pixel. Then in the beginning of the third line storage, we can get the P6 of the second line and P11 of the third line. And with the clock in turn be P2, P7, P12 values, and so on.

4.2   Operator Calculation Module

In operator calculation module, convolution is using the Megafunction altmult_add as multiply-and-accumulate, and according to the different operator, defined different number of adders. Square root operation used altsqrt. Taking absolute value is lpm_abs, and other calculations using Verilog HDL code to achieve.

Sobel operator as an example, calculation is required convolution, square operation, addition operation, square root operation. Finally, the edge is judged by threshold processing module, and the output is 0, else 1023.

Roberts operator is similar to Sobel in calculation. But the definition of the process needs to define 2×2 template parameters. Kirsch operator in the calculation process does not require square root, however, after taking absolute value needs to judge the maximum value of eight results. Roberts and Kirsch is the same thresholds processing module as Sobel.

5   System Test and Analysis

CMOS sensor of 500 mega-pixel is real-time acquisition the plant, and through different combinations of keys to complete the adjustment of the thresholds.

As shown in Fig.5, component G is the gray component and the best effect image of different edge detection operator in the hardware platform.

(a) G component gray image   (b) Roberts   (c) Sobel   (d) Kirsch

Fig. 5. Best effect in the hardware platform

Lower threshold tested the noise immunity and improvement situation of the edge detection of different operators, shown in Fig.6.

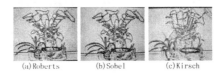

(a) Roberts   (b) Sobel   (c) Kirsch

Fig. 6. Noise immunity of different operators in the hardware platform

Through the best effect image of each algorithm by comparing, the three edge detection operators have their own adaptation and disadvantages. Roberts operator is especially sensitive with step edge obvious point, and also have a very good recognition result, but also very sensitive to noise points. Increase the threshold value can suppress some noise, but the detected edge points are greatly reduced, the details lost more serious, the cost is relatively large. Sobel operator is using the weighted average and then differential, not strong sensitivity to noise as Roberts. It can be more accurate detection the image edge, fairly good grasp on image details, less noise points, relatively clean. The disadvantage is the recognition edge is thick. Kirsch operator can detect all directions variations, it has eight different templates to detect variation of point in any direction, and find the maximum as calculated, detection edge line is thin, good effect, however, the number of resources used in the algorithm is quite more, computation large, can not effectively prevent noise interference. The price is relatively large for platform with limited resources. Summarize the advantages and disadvantages of three operators as TABLE2.

Based on the demand, it is need to find one kind of edge detection operator. As limited resources, the operator is required using few resources, and can detect the most details of edge. The image after edge detected need clear, and has a better inhibitory effect on the noise. As Sobel operator is more superior than the other two operators in these areas, using fewer resources, detecting the most of edge details, relatively insensitive to noise. Although the edge is thick, it does not affect the overall recognition performance. Therefore, research and comparison on the different operators in

Table 2. Performance comparison of three kinds of operators

	Resource(Les)	Edge details	Edge thickness	Noise suppression
Roberts	405	++	Thin	+
Sobel	470	++	Thick	++
Kirsch	1780	+++	Thin	+

hardware platform, the conclusion is that Sobel edge detection operator is superior for limited resources.

6 Conclusions

Six kinds of classic edge detection algorithm of Roberts, Sobel, Prewitt, Kirsch, Frei_Chen, Wallis are studied and compared by MATLAB. Three operators of Roberts, Sobel, Kirsch are better than the others through the comparison of the best images. Image buffer module, operator calculation module and threshold processing module is designed to achieve the real-time image edge detection system. They are all based on FPGA which is Cyclone II EP2C70. And the real-time edge detection image is displayed on LCD. According to real-time edge detection results, the conclusions is that Sobel operator has more superior in the hardware platform with limited resources.

References

1. Ye, R.: Study of Edge Detection and Image Restoration and its FPGA realization, Master's thesis, Fuzhou University, 5 (2006)
2. Shang, Y., Guan, Y., Zhang, W., et al.: A high dynamic range complementary metal oxide semiconductor camera using multi-slope response and an image reconstruction algorithm. Measurement Science and Technology 20(10), 104005 (2009)
3. Ye, M., Zhou, W., Gu, W.: FPGA Based Real-Time Image Filtering and Edge Detection. Chinese Journal of Sensors And Actuators 3 (2007)

Design and Research on a Digital Ultrasonic Test System

Beitao Guo

Beitao Guo, Shenyang University of Chemical Technology, Shenyang,
Liaoning, China
guobabt@qq.com

Abstract. A Digital ultrasonic test system which could achieve high speed data acquisition is presented in this paper. The principle of ultrasonic testing is introduced firstly. Base on this principle the structure of ultrasonic test system composed by hardware modules is illustrated in Fig.2. In sequence, each function of main hardware modules and circuits are discussed in detail. In this ultrasonic test system MCU and CPLD played a role of control core to fulfill data acquisition, analyzing and displaying for ultrasonic echo signal of defects in work pieces.

Keywords: Ultrasonic; Test system; Circuit; MCU.

1 Introduction

With the rapid development of modern industry nondestructive testing technique are playing an important role in inspecting normal running state of equipments and proving product quality. As a main branch of nondestructive testing technique ultrasonic testing is used widely in many fields such as petrochemical industry, medicine industry and other industry, for its advantages as nondestructive to work pieces, low cost and safety.

Modern ultrasonic testing is a technique based physic, electronic, mechanic and material science. At the same time many high technologies, for example, signal processing, pattern recognition, and artificial intelligence are applied in testing procedure. This paper introduces a digital ultrasonic testing system. It can achieve data acquisition, analyzing and displaying for ultrasonic echo signal of defects in work pieces.

2 The Principle of Ultrasonic Testing

To test macroscopic defects in materials is based on some characteristics of ultrasonic propagation such as energy loss during ultrasonic wave pass, or reflections occur between interfaces. Pulse reflection method shown as Fig.1 is often used in ultrasonic testing.

When there are no defects in specimen wave emission pulse T and echo signal B of bottom surface are only shown in Fig.1(a). But when some defects exist echo

G. Shen and X. Huang (Eds.): CSIE 2011, Part II, CCIS 153, pp. 207–211, 2011.

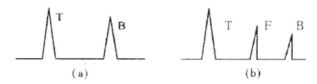

Fig. 1. The back wave of defects method

signal F of defects could appear between T and B in Fig.1(b). Evaluating the size of defects is according to the height of F, and the depth of defects is calculated from the time difference between emission pulse T and echo signal B.

3   The Structure of Ultrasonic Test System

Ultrasonic test system for material detecting was composed of transmitting circuit, amplifying and filtering circuit, data acquisition, microcomputer (MCU) controller, Complex Programmable Logic Device(CPLD), storage and display modules, etc. The structure diagram is shown in Fig.2

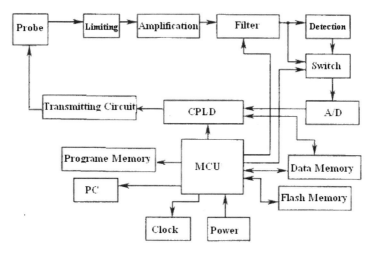

Fig. 2. The structure diagram of ultrasonic testing system

MCU and CPLD are the kernel control chips which control ultrasonic a serials operation include pulse transmitting, signal receive, amplifying and filtering and data acquisition, etc. At first a transmitting circuit droved probe to emit ultrasonic wave which would passed through work piece. If there were some defects the echo signal of defects would appear and were sent to data acquisition circuit, then it would be storied and displayed, furthermore, some research about discriminating and analyzing could be carried on later in PC

4   Main Function Modules of Ultrasonic Testing System

4.1   Transmitting Circuit

Transmitting circuit could send out 400V narrow pulse which could drive probes to emit ultrasonic wave. The control signal of transmitting circuit was provided by MCU. The work frequency demanded was between 1MHz and 10MHz and different probes had its own resonant frequency, so the width of excitation signals could be adjusted which was provided by CPLD. The diagram of transmitting circuit is shown as Fig.3.

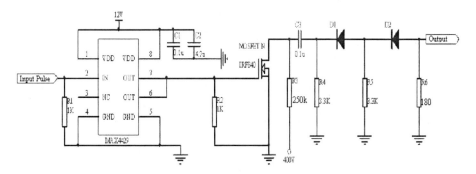

Fig. 3. The diagram of transmitting circuit

4.2   Signal Process Circuit

Because the echo signal was weak and mixed with different frequency clutter signal, amplifier circuit and band-pass filter circuit were used. High frequency amplifier circuit was applied to amplify echo signal ranging from -10db to 110db. For the thickness of work pieces are not same, the echo signals were also different. Therefore a variable gain amplifier circuit controlled by MCU was designed on the basis of high frequency amplifier circuit. The band-pass filter circuit is used to filter noise before analog-digital conversion. For the emission frequency range of ultrasonic probe was from 400KHz to 10MHz, there were always two or three groups filter circuits consisting of different second-order RLC.

4.3   Analog-Digital (A/D) Conversion

Only when analog was converted to digital quantity ultrasonic echo could be treated, analyzed and displayed well. In order to improve discrimination accuracy the sample rate of analog-digital conversion should be increased greatly. AD9283 of which actual sample rate is up to 200MSP was used in this ultrasonic testing system. Analogs with clock signal were sampled at the same time on 100M sample rate. The timing diagram of this ultrasonic test system is shown in Fig.4.

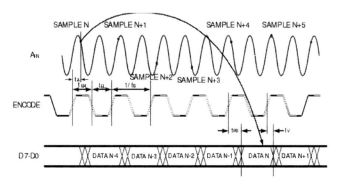

Fig. 4. The timing diagram of AD9283

5 Software Designing

According to the functional requirements the software designing of ultrasonic testing system concluded two parts: one was CPLD programming which achieved system logic, timing control and data buff; the other was MCU programming which achieved the whole system control.

Single-chip microcomputer (MCU) C8052 acted as a core controller in this test system. It could achieve functions as follow: to control display module and keyboard module to finish human-computer interaction, and to providing reliable data transmission; realizing manage power module, etc.

CPLD can become an expand ports of MCU instead of decoder, latch and buffer to simply hardware. So CPLD can realize counting, frequency division and other basic logic functions in this ultrasonic test system.

6 Conclusion

This paper introduces a digital ultrasonic test system which could test many kinds of material work pieces in different size. Utilizing MCU and CPLD in this ultrasonic test system it can realize high speed data acquisition. The digital ultrasonic testing system overcomes shortages of traditional ultrasonic testing and improve liable and efficiency. As a high speed and real time data acquisition and processing it has wide applicational prospects in ultrasonic nondestructive test field.

References

1. Yu, H.-S., Aho, B.-G.: A Study on Ultrasonic Test for Evaluation of Spot Weldability in Automotive Materials. KSME Interantional Journal 13, 775–782 (1999)
2. Honarvar, F., Sheikhzadeh, H., Moles, M.: Improving the time-resolution and signal-to-noise ratio of ultrasonic NDE signals. Ultrasonics 41, 755–763 (2004)
3. Altera Corporation. MAX II Device Handbook (2004)

4. Phang, A.P.Y., Challis, R.E., Ivchenko, V.G., Kalashnikov, A.N.: An intergrated ultegratied ultrasonic correlation spectrometer. Review of Quantitative Nondestructive Evaluion 27, 1575–1582 (2008)
5. Shoa, A., Shirant, S.: Run-Time Reconfigurable Systems for Digital Signal Processing Applications: A Survey. Journal of VLSI Signal Processing 39, 213–235 (2005)
6. Bellows, P.: High-Visibility Debug-By-Design for FPGA Platforms. The Journal of Supercomputing 32, 105–118 (2005)

Data Mining and Ergonomic Evaluation of Firefighter's Motion Based on Decision Tree Classification Model

Lifang Yang and Tianjiao Zhao

Harbin Institute of Technology, Harbin, China, 150001
yanglifang@hit.edu.cn, ztj22@163.com

Abstract. It is effective means to promote firefighter's clothing design through research of firefighters' motion. In this paper, substantive data and picture information are obtained by investigation methods. Based on the survey, the motion is systematically classified according to both intrinsic factors and extrinsic factors. The decision tree classification model for firefighters' motion is obtained by pattern recognition technique. The key features that affect the motion classification are selected by feature evaluation methods. The research lays foundation for research of firefighter's clothing design.

Keywords: Firefighter's motion analysis, decision tree, motion classification, feature extraction.

1 Introduction

Firefighters' job as a special work with fatalness and difficulty has its own character and motion discipline. Before ergonomics analysis, we should extract the typical motion according to some standard.

Motion classification means that the motion should be assembled and classified according to some rules and the development regulation of the motion. Only in this way the principle and characters of the motion can be obtained. There are two methods for motion classification nowadays[1]. (1) According to the body movement character (including direction and speed) and relative movement of various parts of the body, the motion can be classified. (2)The technical character of the motion can also be as a classification principle.

Traditional methods for motion classification are limited to semantic techniques that depend on summarization. In this paper, we propose a decision tree classification model for firefighters' motion based on pattern recognition techniques. Decision tree learning is a method to approximate the discrete objective function and has been widely used in medical diagnosis, credit evaluation and other fields. This model for motion classification is simple and easy to understand[2-3].

The movement of different parts of the body may have different impact on the motion classification. Hence, feature selection methods are used to evaluate the importance of the movement of different parts. Since there are many factors that affect the motion of firefighters, the complexity for motion classification and analysis would be very high. The important movements are selected for motion analysis.

G. Shen and X. Huang (Eds.): CSIE 2011, Part II, CCIS 153, pp. 212–217, 2011.

2   Investigation Plan

The whole process is divided into three parts including data input, motion classification and data output.

In the paper, the classification method is based on comprehensive consideration of internal and external causes. The external causes include the environment factor and tool factor and the internal factor means the internal motion which is generated by people themselves.

Survey data are the base of classification. At first, the survey method is identified. During the survey, according to different point of emphasis four methods are adopted: the interviewing method, the observational method, the questionnaire method and the data collection method. The investigation methods are showed in Fig.1.

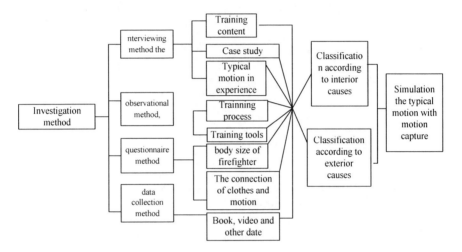

Fig. 1. Investigation methods for firefighters' motion

3   Motion Collection

Firefighting is a high antagonism job that requires the firefighters have good physical fitness and technology. Though the above investigation, the basic work of the fire-fighters is listed as the following categories: Queue training, physical training, the professional fire services training, psychological training, the theoretical study and other trainings. Among all of these trainings, the professional fire service training is most important for firefighter's motion analysis.

(1) Classification by extrinsic factors. During the classification, the tools are defined as the exterior factors. Different tools lead to different motions, so the motions are classified according to the tools.

(2) Classification by intrinsic factors. The human body can be divided into the trunk and four limbs. The Hanavan human body model [4] is adopted to simplify the skeleton and the human body is broken into the following parts: trunk, legs, left arm, right arm and hand.

4 Decision Tree Model

In this section, the decision tree model is established. To establish the classification model, the process of data acquisition and feature extraction should be finished. Then proper classifiers should be chosen to establish the model.

The process of data acquisition is to collect the motion information of the fire-fighters. Then effective features should be extracted to construct the decision table. From Tab.1 we can see that six features are extracted, including the movement of upper limbs, lower limbs, trunk and hands. After data acquisition, the semantic information in the decision table should be translated into numeric information.

Table 1. Extracted features and their semantic information

Sequence number	Legs	Left Arm	Right Arm	Head	Trunk	Hand	Motion
1(A)	Running	Swinging	Swinging	Looking up	Leaning forward	Grip ladder	Ladder training
2(B)	Erection	Elevation	Erection	Looking down		stretch	Ground hose connection
3(C)	Rising alternative	Holding	Holding	Foresight	Curling		Aloft hose connection
4(D)	Crouch	Nipping	Lift	Look horizon			Rescue people

With the data quantized, a dataset with fourteen samples, six condition attribute and one decision attribute is gotten as shown in Tab.2.

Table 2. Quantized dataset

Sample	Legs	Left Arm	Right Arm	Trunk	Head	Hand	Training
1	1	1	1	1	4	1	A
2	2	2	2	1	1	1	A
3	3	2	2	3	1	1	A
4	4	3	3	3	2	2	B
5	1	3	4	1	3	2	B
6	1	3	3	1	4	1	B
7	1	1	4	1	3	1	B
8	1	4	3	1	3	1	B
9	4	3	3	3	2	2	C
10	1	4	3	1	3	2	C
11	3	1	4	1	4	1	C
12	2	3	3	1	2	1	C
13	4	3	3	1	4	1	D
14	2	3	3	1	4	2	D

After data acquisition and feature extraction, the decision tree model of the fire-fighters' motion is established. In these tree structures, leaves represent classifications and branches represent conjunctions of features that lead to those classifications [5]. In this paper, C4.5 is used to get the decision tree model.

C4.5 builds decision trees from a set of training data in the same way as ID3, using the concept of information entropy. At each node of the tree, C4.5 chooses one attribute of the data that most effectively splits its set of samples into subsets enriched in one class or the other. Its criterion is the normalized information gain (difference in entropy) that results from choosing an attribute for splitting the data. The attribute with the highest normalized information gain is chosen to make the decision. The C4.5 algorithm then recurs on the smaller sublists.

In this paper the weka software is used to get the decision tree model of the fire-fighters' motion. The classification tree of firefighters' motion is shown in Fig. 2. Four decision rules can be obtained from the decision tree:

```
(1) if Right Arm <= 2, then A
(2) if Right Arm > 2 and Head <= 3 and Right Arm <= 3, then C
(3) if Right Arm > 2 and Head <= 3 and Right Arm > 3, then B
(4) if Right Arm > 2 and Head > 3, then D
```

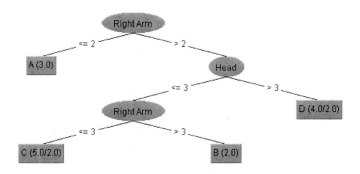

Fig. 2. Classification tree model of the firefighters' motion

When the numeric information in the rule is replaced by the sematic information, the rules could be translated into:

(1) If the movement of the firefighters' Right Arm is elevation or swinging, then they have ladder training.

(2) If the movement of the firefighters' Right Arm is holding and the head is not looking horizontally, then they have Ground water hose connection training.

(3) If the movement of the firefighters' Right Arm is nipping and the head is not looking horizontally, then they have aloft water hose connection training.

(4) If the movement of the firefighters' Right Arm is nipping and the head is look horizontally, then they have exert life heal training.

By the decision rules, the motion of the firefighters can be easily classified when the movement of the head and right arm is known. This is the advantage that establishes the classification model of the firefighters' motion.

5 Feature Evaluation

By decision tree technique, the classification model of the firefighters' motion is gotten. There are six features to decide the motion of the firefighters. In this part, feature evaluation technique is used to rank the features and SVM-RFE and RELIEF are used to evaluate weight of the features.

SVM is a large margin classifier based on structure risk minimization. SVM try to find an optimal hyper plane to separate the samples into different classes.

Given a set of training samples $\{x_i, y_i\}, i = 1,...,l, y_i \in \{-1,1\}, x_i \in \Re^n$ (where x_i is a n dimensional feature vector, y_i is the corresponding label) .SVM can be seen as a constrained optimization problem

$$\text{minimize } \frac{1}{2}\|w\|^2 \text{ subject to } y_i(wx_i + b) \geq 1 \tag{1}$$

The discrimination function can be written as:

$$f(x) = sign(\sum_{i=1}^{SV} a_i y_i(x_i x) + b), w = \sum_{i=1}^{SV} a_i y_i x_i \tag{2}$$

w is a weight vector, $w = \{w_1, w_2, ..., w_n\}$. The less $|w_i|$ is, the corresponding feature is more important. Hence, w can be used to evaluate features. For SVM-RFE, the most significant feature is selected from the attribute subset by greedy algorithm.

RELIEF also is a large margin feature selection technique and is very effective in feature evaluation. The weight vector is updated by gradient decent technique.

In weka software, SVM-RFE and RELIEF are used to rank the features. The evaluation result is shown in Tab. 3. From the table we can see that the movement of Right Arm, head and Left Arm is the first three important features, which means that they are more significant for the motion classification. Hence, we would only need to analyze the movement of these three parts in the force analysis.

Table 3. Feature evaluation results

Feature	Legs	Left Arm	Right Arm	Head	Trunk	Hand
RELIEF	4	3	1	6	2	5
SVM	4	3	1	5	2	6

6 Conclusion

As an important and dangerous job, the design of firefighting clothes should be paid more attention to. In this paper, the firefighter's motion analysis is utilized as means of promoting clothes fitness. Through data mining and ergonomics analysis of firefighter's motion, we get the following conclusions.

1. Through data mining of firefighter's motion, the key factors of firefighter's motion is collected and the foundation of further analysis is laid.

2. During the classification, data are quantized and visualization according to the classification method which is divided into interior and outside reason.

3. It is the first time to connected the Decision Tree with the classification of the motion of fireman. By this way, the complex work are simplified.

4. Feature evaluation technique is used to rank the features and SVM-RFE and RELIEF are used to evaluate weight of the features lay foundation for further research of the motion capture , the motion simulation and motion analysis.

References

[1] Jisheng, W.: Research about the classification of gymnastic performances. Guangzhou Sports institute journal 01, 68–74 (1981)

[2] Baihua, J., Wenbiao, W., Xiugan, Y.: Simulation of Astronauts rolling body technology, vol. (6), pp. 43–48 (1998)

[3] Rui, L., Xianmei, W.: An improved decision-making learning Algorithm. Science and Technology Engineering 9(20), 6039–6041 (2009)

[4] Meng, C., Liping, C.: Modeling and Simulation of the Body Based on the Ergonomic Engineering. Mechanical Science and Technology 20(4), 21–25 (2001)

[5] Rokach, L.M.: Top-down Induction of Decision Trees Classifiers – a survey. IEEE Transactions on Systems, Man, and Cybernetics, Part C: Applications and Reviews 4(35), 476–487 (2005)

Optimization of the Expected Utility Portfolio Selection Model with Box Constraints*

Peng Zhang and Lang Yu

School of Management, Wuhan University of Science and Technology,
Wuhan Ps.R. China, 430081

Abstract. A new expected utility (EU) portfolio selection model is proposed under the assumption that the trading volume has the box constraints. In the model, the expected utility function is quadratic. The model is solved by a pivoting algorithm which needn't be added any slack, surplus and artificial variable, and is easy to operate and works efficiently. A numerical example of a portfolio selection problem is given to compare the new model and the EU portfolio selection model not considering upper bounds. The comparison shows that when the risk preference coefficient is greater than a critical value, the risk and expected return don't increase as the coefficient increases; The relationship between the risk preference coefficient and the expected return (or risk) is non-linear while that is linear in the case when short sales are allowed; the efficient portfolio selection considering the box constraints is subset of that not considering the constraints.

Keywords: Portfolio selection; Utility; Pivoting algorithm; The box constraints.

1 Introduction

The mean–variance methodology for the portfolio selection problem, posed originally by Markowitz [1], has played an important role in the development of modern portfolio selection theory.It combines probability and optimization techniques to model the behavior investment under uncertainty. The return is measured by mean, and the risk is measured by variance, of a portfolio of assets. The Markowitz's mean–variance model for portfolio selection can be formulated mathematically in two ways: minimizing risk when a level return is given, maximizing return when a level risk is given. Numerous models have been developed based on mean–variance such as models proposed in [2,3]. Though mean–variance has been a rather popular in portfolio selection, it has limitations [4]. One distinguished limitation is that analysis based on mean–variance considers high returns as equally undesirable as low returns because high returns will also contribute to the extreme of variance. Then, many scholars proposed a variety of EU (expected utility) portfolio selection models to determine the optimal investing strategy. For example, Baron. D. P. and Steinbach. M.C proposed an EU portfolio selection model with a risk preference coefficient and analyzed the efficient frontier

---

* The work was supported by a research grant of Education Ministry, No. 08JC630062.

G. Shen and X. Huang (Eds.): CSIE 2011, Part II, CCIS 153, pp. 218–225, 2011.
© Springer-Verlag Berlin Heidelberg 2011

[5,6]. Jose Twagilimana proved that the efficient frontier of the EU portfolio selection model is a kind of parabola and there is a linear relationship between the risk preference coefficient and the expected return of a portfolio [7]. Zhang Peng etc proposed an EU portfolio selection without short sales and solve it by a pivoting algorithm [8]. But they didn't study the EU portfolio selection model with the box constraints. However it is very significant to study the model concerning the box constraints especially in an underdeveloped security market.

This paper is organized as follows. We propose a new EU portfolio selection model with the box constraints and introduce a pivoting algorithm for this model in section 2. In section 3, we compare the new model and an EU portfolio selection model without considering box constraints by an example. Finally, we give the concluding remarks in section 4.

2 The Portfolio Selection Model with the Upper and Lower Bounds

Let us consider a capital market with n risk assets. An investor allocates his or her wealth among the n risk assets. We assume that no taxes and no costs are associated with the transaction, all assets are infinitely divisible and the total value of the assets remains constant during the transaction.

The following notations will be employed. R_i is the rate of return on asset i whose expected rate is $r_i = E(R_i), i = 1, 2, \cdots, n$; the covariance matrix is $G = (\delta_{ij})_{n \times n}$ where $\delta = COV(R_i, R_j)$ is the covariance between $R_j and R_j, i, j = 1, 2, \cdots, n$; x_i is the rate of wealth invested in the ith asset to the total wealth; $R_p = R^T x$ is the rate of return of the portfolio, $r_p and x^T Gx$ are respectively the expected rate and the variance of $R^T x$, where $R = (R_1, R_2, \cdots, R_n)^T, r = (r_1, r_2, \cdots, r_n)^T, x = (x_1, x_2, \cdots, x_n)^T$; e is an n-dimensional vector of all 1s. μ_i is the upper bound on asset i. l_i is the lower bound on asset i satisfying $l_1 + l_2 + \cdots + l_n \leq 1$. The utility function which was proposed by Jose Twagilimana is $U(R^T x) = \theta R^T x - \frac{R^T x^2}{2}$, where the risk preference coefficient θ characterizes the preference of an investor for the return and risk[5]. Since the expected utility function

$$U(r_p) = E[U(R^T x)] = \theta E[R^T x] - \frac{E[(R^T x)^2]}{2} = \theta r^T x - \frac{x^T Gx + (r^T x)^2}{2}$$

which is an increasing function of $r^T x$, it implies that $\theta \geq r^T x$.

In order to find the EU-efficient portfolios with the upper and lower bounds, we have to solve the following optimization problem: $max \theta r^T x - \frac{x^T Gx + (r^T x)^2}{2}$

$$\text{s.t.} \begin{cases} e^T = 1 \\ l_i \leq x_i \leq u_i & i = 1, 2, \cdots, n \end{cases} \tag{1}$$

Which is equivalent to $min \frac{x^T Gx + (r^T x)^2}{2} - \theta r^T x$

$$\text{s.t.} \begin{cases} e^T x = 1 \\ l_i \leq x_i \leq u_i & i = 1, 2, \cdots, n \end{cases} \tag{2}$$

The Kuhn-Tucker's conditions for (2) are as follows.

$$\begin{cases} \delta_{i1}x_1 + \delta_{i2}x_2 + \wedge + \delta_{in}x_n + (r_1x_1 + r_2x_2 + \cdots + r_nx_n)r_i - \theta r_i + \mu_1 - \lambda_i + k_i = 0 \\ x_1 + x_2 + \cdots + x_n = 1 \\ \lambda_i \geq 0, k_i \geq 0, \quad i = 1.2, \cdots, n \\ \lambda_i(x_i - l_i) = 0, k_i(-x_i + u_i) = 0, \quad i = 1, 2, \cdots, n \\ x - i \geq l_i, -x_i \geq -u_i, \quad i = 1, 2. \cdots, n \end{cases} \quad (3)$$

whereµ $\mu_q, \lambda_i, k_i, i = 1, 2, \cdots, n$ are Lagrange multipliers.

There are $5n + 1$ linear equalities and inequalities and $3n + 1$ variables in (2). If we only delete $\lambda_i, i = 1, 2, \cdots, n$ associated with the n nonnegative inequalities, there are still $4n + 1$ linear equalities and inequalities and $2n + 1$ variables remained. We shall show how to delete all the λ_i and $k_i, i = 1, 2, \cdots, n$ so that it becomes a small problem. Note that for a given $\bar{x} = (\bar{x}_1, \bar{x}_2, \cdots, \bar{x}_n)^T$, both $x_i = l_i$ and $-x_i = -\mu_i, i = 1, 2, \cdots, n$ can not be satisfied simultaneously, therefore at least one of λ_i and $k_i, i = 1, 2, \cdots, n$ would be zero. Let $g_i(x, \mu_1) = \delta_{i1} + \cdots + \delta_{in}x_n + (r_1x_1 + \cdots + r_nx_n)r_i - \theta r_i + \mu_1$.

If $\bar{x}_i = l_i$, k_i will be zero, so that $\lambda_i = g_i(x, \mu_1) \geq 0$; If $\bar{x}_i = \mu_i$, λ_i will be zero, so that $k_i = -g_i(x, \mu_1) \geq 0$; If $\bar{x}_i$ isn't equal to either of l_i and $|mu_i$, both λ_i and k_i would be zero, so that $g_i(x, \mu_1) = 0$. Therefore we can just use one of $g_i(x, \mu_1) \geq 0$ and $-g_i(x, \mu_1) \geq 0$during the computational process. It can be verified that if we obtain a solution to the following system:

$$\begin{cases} g_i(x, \mu_1) \geq, x_i \geq l_i, g_i(x, \mu_1)(x_i - l_i) = 0, i \in I_1 \\ -g_i(x, \mu_1) \geq 0, -xi \geq -u_i, -g_i(x, \mu_1)(x_i - \mu_i) - 0, i \in I_2 \\ x_1 + x_2 + \cdots + x_n = 1 \end{cases} \quad (4)$$

which satisfies $-x_i \geq -\mu_i, i \in I_1$ and $x_i \geq l_i, i \in I_2$also, this solution would be a solution to system (3) where$I_1$and $I_2$is a partition of $\{1, 2, L, n\}$.

In (4), $g_i(x, \mu_1) \geq 0$ and $x_i \geq l_i$ are called complementary inequalities and their coefficient vectors are called complementary vectors. Similarly,$-g_i(x, \mu_1) \geq 0$ and $-x_i \geq -\mu_i$ are called complementary inequalities and their coefficient vectors are called complementary vectors. Introduce artificial inequality $\mu_1 \geq -M$ (M is a number large enough) into (4). Also, $x_1 + x_2 + \cdots + x_n = 1$ and $\mu_1 \geq -M$ and their coefficient vectors are called complementary. We shall solve the linear part of system (4) by the pivoting algorithm [9-12] while maintaining complementarity's conditions. The coefficient vector of $g_i(x, \mu_q) \geq 0$ is denoted by g_i, i.e., $g_i = (\sigma_{i1} + r_i r1 \cdots, \sigma_{i1} + r_i r_n, 1), i = 1, 2, \cdots, n$. The coefficient vector of $-g_i(x, \mu_1) \geq 0$ is $-g_i$. The coefficient vector of the equality is denoted by g_{n+1}, i.e., $g_{n+1} = (1, \cdots, 1, 0)$. The coefficient vectors of $x_i \geq l_i$ and $\mu_1 \geq -M$are denoted by $e_i(i = 1, \cdots, n + 1)$ that is the ith row of the identity matrix of order $n + 1$. The coefficient vectors of $-x_i \geq -\mu_i$ is$-e_i(i = 1, \cdots, n + 1)$. According to the definition of basic solution, if exactly one of the complementary vectors g_i and e_i, $-g_i$and $-e_i$is basic, the complementarity's conditions would be satisfied. For convenience, we shall take $M = 0$ in our algorithm.

We shall first solve (4) for $I_1 = \{1, \cdots, n\}$ and $I_2 = \emptyset$. For this, let $x_1 \geq l_q, \cdots, x_n \geq l_n, \mu_1 \geq 0$ be the initial basic inequalities, i.e., $e_1, \cdots, e_n, e_{n+1}$are the initial basic vectors and $y^{(0)} = (l_1, \cdots, l_n, 0)^T$ is the initial basic solution. The deviation of nonbasic vector g_i is $\delta_i = g_i y^{(0)} - \theta r_i, i = 1, \cdots, n$ and $\delta_{(n+1)} = g_{(n+1)} y^{(0)} - 1$. The initial table is as following:

Table 1. Initial Table for Model (4)

	e_1	...	e_n	e_{n+1}	σ_i
g_1	$\sigma_{11}+r_1 r_1$	...	$\sigma_{1n}+r_1 r_n$	1	$g_1 y(0) - \theta r_1$
...	...	...	...	...	...
g_n	$\sigma_{n1}+r_n r_1$	...	$\sigma_{nn}+r_n r_n$	1	$g_n y(0) - \theta r_n$
g_{n+1}	1	...	1	0	$g_{n+1} y(0) - 1$

Then, let g_1 enter and e_{n+1} leave, $g_{(n+1)}$ enter and e_1 leave the basis. In the following, we shall perform pivoting operations to interchange non-basic inequalities and basic ones until all the deviations of nonbasic inequalities are nonnegative.

Up till now, we haven't considered inequalities $-g_i(x, \mu_1) \geq 0$ and $-x_i \geq -\mu_i$. They are needed when the value of x_i of the basic solution is greater than l_i and $-x_i \geq -\mu_i$ is chosen to enter the basis. We deal this case as follows. Replace e_i by $-e_i$, replay the deviation δ_i of e_i by $\mu_i - l_i - \delta_i$, reverse signs of other elements in the row of e_i, correspondingly replace g_i by $-g_i$, and reverse signs of elements in the column of $-g_i$. We refer to such operations as a vector substitution which interchanges $x_i \geq l_i$ and $-x_i \geq -\mu_i$, $g_i(x, \mu_1) \geq 0$ and $-g_i(x, \mu_1) \geq 0$ respectively. Similarly, if the value of x_i of the basic solution is less than l_i and $x_i \geq l_i$ is chosen to enter the basis, we carry out a vector substitution to interchange $-x_i \geq -\mu_i$ and $x_i \geq l_i$, then $-g_i(x, \mu_1) \geq 0$ and $g_i(x, u_i) \geq 0$.

The computational steps for system (4) are as follows.

Algorithm 1 The procedure for solving system (4)[9-12].

Step 1. Initial step. Let $I_1 = \{1, \cdots, n\}$, $I_2 = \varnothing$, let $x_1 \geq l_1, \cdots, x_n \geq l_n, \mu_1 \geq 0$ be the initial basic system of inequalities and construct the initial table as shown by table 1.

Step2. Preprocessing. Let g_1 enter and e_{n+1} leave, and then g_{n+1} enter and e_1 leave the basis. Delete the row of e_{n+1} and delete the column of g_{n+1}.

Step 3. Main iterations (by the smallest deviation rule):

(i) If all the deviations of nonbasic vectors are nonnegative, the current basic solution is optimal for model (2).Otherwise

(ii) choose a nonbasic vector with the most negative deviation to enter the basis. If this vector is not listed in the table, perform a vector substitution. If the diagonal entry in the pivoting row is positive, perform a pivoting on that entry; return (i); otherwise perform two pivoting operations first on the largest entry in the same row and then on the symmetrical entry return (i).

3 An Example

In this section, we give a numerical example to illustrate the new model proposed in this chapter. Comparisons between this new model and the model not considering the upper bound are also presented.

Consider the following portfolio selection problem. The return of six stocks from time 1 to 8 are given in following table [13]:

Table 2. Security returns

Period	1	2	3	4	5	6	7	8
Stock1	0.04	0.07	0.09	0.13	0.14	0.17	0.21	0.24
Stock	0.14	0.06	0.08	0.15	0.11	0.13	0.10	0.11
Stock3	0.13	0.13	0.11	0.15	0.10	0.07	0.14	0.11
Stock	0.12	0.04	0.18	0.13	0.19	0.16	0.14	0.11
Stock5	0.18	0.06	0.22	0.15	0.14	0.06	0.08	0.09
Stock	0.15	0.04	0.08	0.06	0.13	0.05	0.10	0.09

The utility function is $U(r_p) = \theta r^T x - \frac{x^T G x + (r^T x)^2}{2}$. The upper and lower bounds are respectively 0.6 and 0. Solve the optimal portfolios for risk preference coefficients $\theta = 0.12, 0.13, 0.14, 0.15, 0.2, 0.3, 0.35, 1$ and 2 respectively.

We can formulate the portfolio selection problem considering the upper bound $x_i \leq 0.6$. We use the algorithm 1 to solve this problem. We summarize the numerical results in the following table.

Table 4. The optimal result considering the upper bounds

θ	Optimal solution						r_p	σ_p
	x1	x2	x3	x4	x5	x6		
0.12	0.0762	0.1689	0.5508	0.1790	0.0000	0.0251	0.1198	0.0164
0.13	0.0951	0.0515	0.5932	0.2603	0.0000	0.0000	0.1231	0.0169
0.14	0.1150	0.0000	0.5782	0.3068	0.0000	0.0000	0.1246	0.0177
0.15	0.1328	0.0000	0.5321	0.3351	0.0000	0.0000	0.1254	0.0186
0.2	0.2217	0.0000	0.3015	0.4768	0.0000	0.0000	0.1294	0.0269
0.3	0.3978	0.0000	0.0000	0.6000	0.0022	0.0000	0.1347	0.0427
0.35	0.4000	0.0000	0.0000	0.6000	0.0000	0.0000	0.1347	0.0428
1	0.4000	0.0000	0.0000	0.6000	0.0000	0.0000	0.1347	0.0428
2	0.4000	0.0000	0.0000	0.6000	0.0000	0.0000	0.1347	0.0428

When the risk coefficient is greater than the critical value ($ie, \theta = 0.3$), it has no effect on the optimal solution of table 4 and the expected rate and the risk (standard deviation) don't increase with the increasing of the coefficient. When risk coefficient is less than some value ($ie, \theta = 0.12$), it can't satisfy that $\theta \geq r^T x$.

From the table 4, we can get the optimal investment strategy. For example, if risk preference is 0.12, the optimal investment rate of stock 1 to 6 are respectively 7.62%,16.89%,55.08%,17.90%,0% and 2.51%.

We also can formulate the portfolio selection problem not considering the upper bounds We use the algorithm in the paper [9] to solve this problem. We summarize the numerical results in the following table.

Table 5. The optimal result not considering the upper bounds

θ	Optimal solution						rp	σp
	x1	x2	x3	x4	x5	x6		
0.1200	0.0762	0.1689	0.5508	0.1790	0.0000	0.0251	0.1198	0.0164
0.1300	0.0951	0.0515	0.5932	0.2603	0.0000	0.0000	0.1231	0.0169
0.1400	0.1150	0.0000	0.5782	0.3068	0.0000	0.0000	0.1246	0.0177
0.1500	0.1328	0.0000	0.5321	0.3351	0.0000	0.0000	0.1254	0.0186
0.2	0.2217	0.0000	0.3015	0.4768	0.0000	0.0000	0.1294	0.0269
0.3000	0.3532	0.0000	0.0000	0.6468	0.0000	0.0000	0.1346	0.0422
0.3500	0.3751	0.0000	0.0000	0.6249	0.0000	0.0000	0.1347	0.0424
1.0000	0.6599	0.0000	0.0000	0.3401	0.0000	0.0000	0.1354	0.0507
2.0000	1.0000	0.0000	0.0000	0.0000	0.0000	0.0000	0.1363	0.0686

From the table 5, we can get the optimal investment strategy. For example, if risk preference is 1, the optimal investment rate of stock 1 to 6 are respectively 65.99%,0%,0%,34.01%,0%,0%.

From the table 4 and table 5, we can get the figure 1.

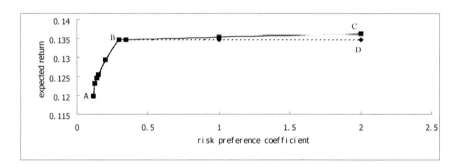

Fig. 1. The relationship betweenθand rp

The curve AB+BC and AB+BD respectively show the relationship between θ and r_p on the portfolio selection not considering and considering the upper bound.

From the figure 1, we can see that the relationship between the risk preference coefficient and the expected return is not linear but more complex, which is different from the result of Jose Twagilimana's[5]. When the risk preference coefficient is greater than the critical value, it has no effect on the expected return. So the risk preference coefficient can just reflect investors' preference within some intervals. when the risk coefficient is greater than the some value(ie, $\theta = 0.35$), the expected return from the model with upper bound is smaller than the model without the upper bound.From the table 4 and table 5, we can get the figure 2.

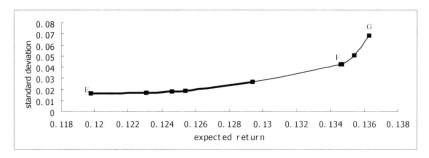

Fig. 2. The efficient portfolio selection

The curve EG and EF respectively show the efficient portfolio selection not considering and considering the upper bound.

From figure 2, we can get the result that the efficient portfolio selection considering the upper and lower bounds is subset of that not considering the upper bounds. With the increasing of the expected return, the standard deviation also increases.

4 Concluding Remarks

In this paper, we propose a new EU portfolio selection model. In the model, the trading volume has the upper and lower bounds.

A pivoting algorithm is designed to solve the correponding optimization problems because investment rate has the upper and lower bounds and it can't be efficiently solved by the exsiting traditional optimization methods. This algorithm needn't add any slack, surplus and artificial variables[9]. It is easy to operate and works efficiently.

A numerical example is given to illustrate the new portfolio selection model and an EU portfolio selection model not considering the upper bouns. The comparison shows that when the model with the upper and lower bounds, the risk preference coefficient can only be efficient within a certain interval. If the risk preference coefficient is greater than the critical value, the risk and expected return don't increase as the coefficient increases. It is useful for investors to select portfolios according to their risk preference coefficients. We sincerely wish the model and the algorithm are used in practice.

References

[1] Markowitz, H.: Portfolio selection. The Journal of Finance 7, 77–91 (1952)
[2] Hirschberger, M., Qi, Y., Steuer, R.E.: Randomly generating portfolio-selection covariance matrices with specified distributional characteristics. European Journal of Operational Research 177, 1610–1625 (2007)
[3] Leung, M.T., Daouk, H., Chen, A.S.: Using investment portfolio return to combine forecasts: a multiobjective approach. European Journal of Operational Research 134, 84–102 (2001)
[4] Grootveld, H., Hallerbach, W.: Variance vs downside risk: is there really that much difference? European Journal of Operational Research 114, 304–319 (1999)

[5] Baron, D.P.: On the utility theoretical foundations of mean-variance analysis. The Journal of Finance 32, 1683–1697 (1977)

[6] Steinbach, M.C.: Markowitz revisited: mean-variance models in financial portfolio analysis. Siam Review 43, 31–85 (2001)

[7] Twagilimana, J.: Mean-variance model in portfolio analysis. M. A thesis, University of Louisville (2002)

[8] Zhang, P., Zhang, Z.-z., Yue, C.-y.: The Pivoting Algorithm for the Portfolio Selection Model Maximizing the Utility. Journal of Finance and Economics 31, 116–125 (2005) (in Chinese)

[9] Zhang, P., Zhang, Z.-z., Zeng, Y.-q.: The Optimization of The Portfolio Selection with The Restricted Short Sales. Application of Statistics and Management 27, 124–129 (2008) (in Chinese)

[10] Zhang, P., Zhang, Z.-z., Yue, C.-y.: Optimization of The Mean Semi-absolute Deviation Portfolio Selection Model With The Restricted Short Selling Based on The Pivoting Algorithm. Chinese Journal of Management Science 14, 7–11 (2006) (in Chinese)

[11] Zhang, P.: The Comparison Between Mean-variance and Mean-VaR Portfolio Models Without Short Sales. Chinese Journal of Management Science 16, 30–35 (2008) (in Chinese)

[12] Zhang, Z.-z.: Convex programming: Pivoting Algorithms for Portfolio and Net Network Optimization. Wuhan University Press, Wuhan (2004) (in Chinese)

[13] Wang, S.-Y., Xia, Y.-S.: Portfolio Selection and Asset Price. Springer, Heidelberg (2002)

Optimal Operation of Hydropower Station Based on Improved Particle Swarm Optimization Algorithm

Xin Ma

School of Management and Economics, North China University of Water
Conservancy and Electric Power, Zhengzhou, Henan Province, 450011 China
maxin72@163.com

Abstract. Hydropower station optimal operation is a complex nonlinear combinatorial optimization problem. An improved particle swarm optimization (IPSO) algorithm is suggested. The culture algorithm is introduced and local random search operator to achieve knowledge structure in belief space and enhance the population diversity and increase the capacity of global search with the introduction of culture algorithm, The simulation results of new algorithm compares with particle swarm optimization (PSO) algorithm and shows that this new algorithm can overcome the shortcomings of the traditional PSO and to gain better convergence speed and computational accuracy.

Keywords: Hydropower station, optimal operation, nonlinear problem, improved particle swarm algorithm.

1 Introduction

Hydropower station optimal operation is a complex and dynamic constraint nonlinear programming problem and its solving process is very complicated. Dynamic programming method [1], network flow model [2] and genetic algorithms [3] and the other methods have been studied by many scholars. Dynamic programming approach has the curse of dimensionality and takes too long tome to solve the problem; successive optimization method easy to fall into local optimum, so the calculation speed greatly reduced; genetic algorithm is not easy to convergence when there is close to the global optimum and it is also not easy to deal with complex constraints [4]. Particle swarm optimization (PSO) algorithm is a kind of random heuristic search evolutionary algorithms [5]. But there are also some disadvantages [6]. This paper attempts to introduce particle swarm optimization with cultural algorithm model and the optimal result indicates that improved particle swarm optimization can provide a new way for solving the optimal operation of hydropower stations.

2 Problem Formulation

Object function:

$$MaxF = \sum_{t=1}^{T} AQ_t H_t M_t \qquad (1)$$

G. Shen and X. Huang (Eds.): CSIE 2011, Part II, CCIS 153, pp. 226–231, 2011.
© Springer-Verlag Berlin Heidelberg 2011

Water balance constraints:

$$V_{t+1} = V_t + q_t - Q_t - S_t \tag{2}$$

Reservoir storage capacity constraints::

$$V_{t\,min} \le V_t \le V_{t\,max} \tag{3}$$

Reservoir discharged flow constraints:

$$\begin{cases} Q_{t\,min} \le Q_t \le Q_{t\,max} \\ S_t \ge 0 \end{cases} \tag{4}$$

Power output constraints:

$$N_{t\,min} \le A Q_t H_t \le N_{t\,max} \tag{5}$$

Where, A is output coefficient of hydropower station; Q_t is the generating flow of hydropower station in the time t, unit is m^3/s; Q_{tmax} and Q_{tmin} are the maximum /minimum permitted discharge flow in the time t, unit is m^3/s; H_t is the average water head of hydropower generation in time t, unit is m; T is the total calculating period during the year (calculation period for months, $T = 12$); M_t is the number of hours in time t; V_{t+1} is the storage capacity of reservoir in time $t+1$; V_t is the storage capacity of reservoir in time t; V_{tmax} and V_{tmin} are the maximum/minimum permitted storage capacity of reservoir in time t; q_t is the average inlet flow of reservoir in time t; S_t is the split flow of reservoir in time t; N_{tmax} and N_{tmin} are the maximum/ minimum output limit constraint, unit is kW.

3 Improved Particle Swarm Algorithm

The population space (lower space) and belief space (upper space) of particles swarm in built to form the improved particle swarm optimization (IPSO) algorithm based on culture algorithm model.

3.1 Particle Swarm Optimization Algorithm

If the dimension of solution space is D, There will first initial a swarm of random particles in solution space as: $\Xi = \{p_1, p_2, \cdots, p_g, \cdots, p_w\}$. Each particle p_g represents a possible solution of this optimal problem, and the state of each particle is described by its location x_i and velocity v_i: $x_i = \{x_{i,1}, x_{i,2}, \cdots, x_{i,D}\}$, $v_i = \{v_{l,1}, v_{l,2}, \cdots, v_{l,D}\}$. All the particles will trace the optimal solution of this particle in order to seek the best solution:

$$v_{i,j}^{t+1} = w v_{i,j}^t + \gamma_1 \beta_1 (pbest_{i,j}^t - x_{i,j}^t) + \gamma_2 \beta_2 (gbest_{i,j}^t - x_{i,j}^t) \tag{6}$$

$$x_{i,l}^{t+1} = x_{i,l}^t + v_{i,l}^{t+1} \tag{7}$$

γ_1, γ_2 are celebration factor; w is particle acceleration constants; t is the number of evaluation; β_1, β_2 are uniformly distributed random number between [0,1].

3.2 Culture Algorithm

Procedure of culture algorithm.

```
Begin
    t=0;
    initialize population space PS(t);
    initialize belief space BS(t);
    repeat
        evaluate population space PS(t);
        Update(BS(t),Accept(PS(t)));
        Generate(PS(t),Influence(BS(t)));
        t=t+1;
        Select PS(t) from PS(t-1);
    Until termination condition achieved
End
```

3.3 Framework of Improved Swarm Optimization Algorithm

For the constraint optimal problem:

$$MinF(\vec{x})$$

$$\text{s.t.} \begin{cases} C_b(\vec{x}) \leq 0, & u = 1,2,\cdots,B \\ C_e(\vec{x}) = 0, & e = 1,2,\cdots,E \\ x_a^q \leq x_a \leq x_a^p, & a = 1,2,\cdots,A \end{cases} \tag{8}$$

$$\Theta(\vec{x}) = F(\vec{x}) + \psi[\sum_{u=1}^{U} \max(0, C_b(\vec{x})) + \sum_{e}^{E} |C_e(\vec{x})|] \tag{9}$$

Where, $F(\vec{x})$ is the fitness function; $C_b(\vec{x})$ is un-equation constraint; $C_e(\vec{x})$ is equation constraint; $\vec{x} = (x_1, x_2, \cdots, x_A)$ is A-dimensional real vector; Ψ is a punishment factor. The fitness function is constructed following.

If a particle x_a beyond the constraint, then revise it according following equation:

$$\begin{cases} x_a = x_a + \lambda(x_a^p - x_a^q) & x_a < x_a^q \\ x_a = x_a - \lambda(x_a^p - x_a^q) & x_a > x_a^p \end{cases} \tag{10}$$

If the excellent individual set is: $Excllence = \{ y_1, y_2, \ldots, y_m \}$. Then the fitness value satisfied the following condition: $F(y_1) \geq F(y_2) \geq \ldots \geq F(y_m)$ only r best individuals are taken into the excellent individual set when the situation knowledge is initialized.

$$r = \theta\% POP_{size} \tag{11}$$

The renewable situation knowledge decided by the best individual x_{best}^t in each iteration. If x_{best}^t better than the worst individual in excellent individual set, then worst is replaced by x_{best}^t [5]. The data structure is shown as Table 1.

Table 1. Data structure of standardization knowledge

l_1	u_1	l_2	u_2	...	l_n	u_n
$F(l_1)$	$F(u_1)$	$F(l_2)$	$F(u_2)$	...	$F(l_n)$	$F(u_n)$

l_i, u_i are the lower and upper limit of decision variable number i; $F(l_i), F(u_i)$ are the corresponding fitness value for decision variable number i. The situation knowledge in belief space is renewed through the following function.

$$l_j^{t+1} = \begin{cases} x_{i,j}^t & if \quad x_{i,j}^t \le l_j' or F(x_i^t) < F(l_j') \\ l_j' & otherwise \end{cases} \tag{12}$$

$$F(l_j^{t+1}) = \begin{cases} obj(x_i) & if \quad x_{i,j}^t \le l_j' or F(x_i^t) < F(l_j') \\ F(l_j') & otherwise \end{cases} \tag{13}$$

$$u_j^{t+1} = \begin{cases} x_{k,j}^t & if \quad x_{k,j}^t \ge u_j' or F(x_k^t) < F(u_j') \\ u_j' & otherwise \end{cases} \tag{14}$$

$$F(u_j^{t+1}) = \begin{cases} obj(x_i) & if \quad x_{i,j}^t \ge l_j' or F(x_i^t) < F(u_j') \\ F(u_j') & otherwise \end{cases} \tag{15}$$

The next velocities of particles are calculated as follows:

$$v_{i,j}^{t+1} = \begin{cases} v_{i,j}^{t+1} = w v_{i,j}^t + \gamma_1 \beta_1 (pbest_{i,j}^t - x_{i,j}^t) + \gamma_2 \beta_2 (gbest_{i,j}^t - x_{i,j}^t) \\ \quad if \quad x_{i,j}^t < l_j' and x_{i,j}^t < gbest_{i,j}^t \\ v_{i,j}^{t+1} = w v_{i,j}^t + \gamma_1 \beta_1 (pbest_{i,j}^t - x_{i,j}^t) + \gamma_2 \beta_2 (gbest_{i,j}^t - x_{i,j}^t) \\ \quad f \quad x_{i,j}^t > u_j' and x_{i,j}^t > gbest_{i,j}^t \\ v_{i,j}^{t+1} = w v_{i,j}^t \pm \gamma_1 \beta_1 (pbest_{i,j}^t - x_{i,j}^t) \pm \gamma_2 \beta_2 (gbest_{i,j}^t - x_{i,j}^t) \\ \quad otherwise \end{cases} \tag{16}$$

4 Simulation and Analysis

The normal reservoir water level is 877m, dead water level is 817 m, contributing factor is 8.5, installed capacity is 760,000 kW, guaranteed contribution is 160,000 kW, the largest machine flow is 1000m³ • s⁻¹. The water level required does not exceed flood limit water level 850m in flood period (6~9 months), reservoir optimal operation will be divided into 12 time periods on a monthly basis. The parameters of IPSO are: population size $POP_{size} = 100$; maximum number of iterations $IT_{max} = 100$; celebration factor $\gamma_1 = \gamma_2 = 2$; punishment factor $\Psi = 15000$; particle acceleration constant w linear decreases from 0.9 to 0.4; initial selection ratio $\theta \% = 15\%$; benchmark electric price of 0.25 $ / kW.

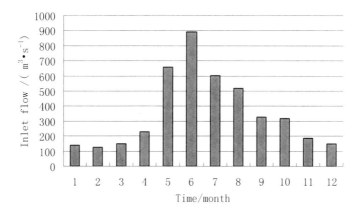

Fig. 1. Inlet flow of reservoir during 12 months

Table 2. Result of optimal operation of hydropower station based on IPSO and PSO

Time/month		1	2	3	4	5	6	7	8	9	10	11	12
IPSO	Generating flow/($m^3 \cdot s^{-1}$)	166	162	159	229	810	890	616	524	326	160	185	150
	Power output/MW	183	179	173	244	770	788	535	463	290	163	208	169
PSO	Generating flow/($m^3 \cdot s^{-1}$)	152	156	159	229	790	878	602	521	326	160	185	150
	Power output/MW	171	173	173	244	759	769	531	461	290	163	208	169

The result of optimal operation of hydropower station based on PSO and IPSO algorithm shown in Table 2 and Table3. The annual power output of IPSO increases 0.395×10^6 MWh than PSO, The total revenue of IPSO increases 0.099×10^9\$, the economic benefits are significant. IPSO has a fast convergence than PSO and enhances global convergence ability to avoid a fall into local optimum situation.

Table 3. Comparison between IPSO and PSO

Algorithm	Annual energy production(MWh)	Total revenue($\$$)	Calculation time(s)
PSO	30.088×10^6	7.522×10^9	27
IPSO	30.483×10^6	7.621×10^9	22

5   Conclusion

In this paper, the IPSO algorithm is a better way to overcome the shortcomings of the precocity of basic PSO and easy to fall into local optimum, and IPSO algorithm also obtain a good convergence speed and calculation accuracy. Simulation shows that the

IPSO algorithm can effectively solve strong constraint combinatorial optimization problem such as a non-linear optimal operation of hydropower station, and IPSO algorithm also has a good performance than the basic PSO. IPSO algorithm is simple and convenience, it takes up less memory and easy to program while enhances the global convergence ability and accuracy, and provides a new and effective method to solve the optimal operation problem of hydropower station.

References

1. Yang, J.S., Chen, N.: Short-term hydrothermal coordination using multi-pass dynamic pro- gramming. IEEE Trans. on Power System 4, 1050–1056 (1989)
2. Franco, P.E.C.: A network flow model for short-term hydro-dominated hydro thermal sche- duling problems. IEEE Trans. on Power Systems 9, 1016–1022 (1994)
3. Wardlaw, R.: Evaluation of genetic algorithms for optimal reservoir system operation. Water Resource Planning and Management 125, 25–33 (1999)
4. Zhang, X.P.: Adaptive swarm algorithm with dynamically changing inertia weight. Journal of Xi'an Jiaotong University 39, 1039–1042 (2005)
5. Saleem, S.: Cultural algorithms in dynamic environments. In: Proceedings of Congress on Evolutationary Computation, Piscataway, vol. 2, pp. 1513–1520. IEEE Service Center, New Jersey (2000)
6. Gao, L.L.: Particle swarm based on cultural algorithm for solving constrained optimization problems. Computer Engineering 34, 179–181 (2008)

Exploration and Analysis of Copyright Infringement Liability in P2P System

Jianhong Zhou

College of Humanities and Law, Hebei Normal University of Science and Technology,
Qinhuangdao Hebei 066004, China
zhjhong163@163.com

Abstract. The application of P2P system makes the spread of the works faster and more convenient, which also makes the infringement possible. To seek a balance between the spread of cultural and artistic works and the protection of the benefits of the copyright holders, this issue is studied from the perspective of combining Network technology with legal method. It is believed that the principle of fault liability can be applied to copyright infringement in P2P system. According to this principle, as long as the content provided by ICP infringes, it should be responsible for that, the software provider should bear tort liability in case he continues to provide services while knowing or should know the software piracy, the "notice and take down "rules applies to software operators, when evidences shows that someone utilizes P2P system to infringe copyright, software operators shall stop the corresponding service or will be exposed to tort liability. While for the P2P users, they can be asked to take the responsibility for the works in their shared folders.

Keywords: software provider, software operator, fault liability, consistency of interests and risks.

P2P is a popular and controversial network technology in recent years, it is welcomed by the market because it broke up the limit of special file storage server, shared computer resources and services through the direct exchange, and it has many characteristics like: decentralized network resources, self-adaptive to network links, no-time-bound information and multi-link downloading, all these make the spread of the works easier and faster.

Especially with the improvement of personal computer performance, P2P technology is also increasingly popular because of its superiority on transmission and spread of information. On the other hand, P2P makes copyright infringement easier and more frequent, which has been fully manifested in recent year's dispute. In the United States, the "Napster" case and the "Grokster" case are very typical, in Canada, France, Netherlands and other countries P2P copyright lawsuits have also emerged. In Hong Kong, China, three major record companies sued Tianhu network's P2P litigation in 2003; Naiming Chen was sentenced to imprisonment for 3 months for illegal distribution of films by using BT in 2006, which is the most widely used P2P free software in Asia; in the mainland, there were copyright disputes between Shanghai Busheng Music Culture Media Co. Ltd. and Beijing Flight Network Music

G. Shen and X. Huang (Eds.): CSIE 2011, Part II, CCIS 153, pp. 232–238, 2011.
© Springer-Verlag Berlin Heidelberg 2011

Software Development Co. Ltd. and other concerned cases. These are highlights of P2P. In addition, the most important thing is confirmation of copyright infringement in P2P system. This issue is studied from the perspective of combining Network technology with legal method.

1 The Subjects of Copyright Infringement in P2P System

In P2P systems, the subject of copyright infringement is very complex, the identification of its tort liability is also more difficult, on the other hand, in P2P system, the behavior of the subjects are closely tied together, for example, a common P2P user's downloading is bound to involve content providers, network service providers, all these can make it difficult to determinate the liability.

In addition to P2P users, the subjects of the network behavior includes many categories, different scholars have different views, some scholars believe that the subjects of network behavior includes ISP, ICP, IAP, OSP, IPP, ASP, and IEP[1][31-32]; and some scholars believe that all of the network service provider can be interpreted as network service providers, different from the network user.

In fact, the variety of subjects is directly related to the classification and division of the definition of their rights and obligations, and infringing accountability based on various natures of the subject acts, we believe that all the main categories can be divided as follows:

1.1 Internet Content Provider (ICP)

ICP is the abbreviation for Internet Content Provider, referring to the provision of various information service providers, in general, the content of ICP may be available from its own, may be from web users or web sites. But in overall, ICP is responsible for the content by itself, thus easily become the subject of copyright infringement.

1.2 Internet Service Provider

In addition to ICP, another subject is ISP in P2P system, ISP is also known as network service providers, in fact, different Internet service providers offer different services, Professor Xinbao Zhang believes that the ISP includes access service providers and many types of intermediaries like transport host, information host, exchange services and transaction services, but he also introduces IAP and ISP as a parallel concept, [1] [31-32] Professor Lixin Yang believes that the network service provider (ISP) includes online information service provider network (ICP), the Internet access providers (IAP) and the network platform provider (IPP). IAP and IPP are collectively known as online service providers (OSP) [2][221]; some scholars believe that Internet service provider includes ICP and ISP, and the ISP includes network access provider (IAP) and host service provider. [3] I think that in P2P system ISP includes software provider, software operator and network access software provider (IAP). IAP is generally not easy to become the subjects of infringement; IAP does not bear tort liability, unless there is evidence that IAP is still providing services for the tort-feasor.

1.3 P2P Users

P2P users are the most controversial subjects, as the common software users, they are directly involved in copyright infringement, but on the other hand, P2P users are the most massive and hidden group, it is difficult to find P2P software users, it is particularly difficult to find that a P2P user is a violation of their copyright works. Therefore in practice it is also quite difficult to investigate copyright infringement liability of P2P users.

2   The Responsibility Principle of Copyright Infringement in P2P System

The responsibility principle of Copyright infringement is another hot topic among scholars in recent years.

National scholars have paid much attention to responsibility principle of network infringement but little to that of infringement in P2P system. Some scholars think that fault-liability should be applied, [4] some believe that no-fault liability should be adopted. [2][303-304] some others divide network service providers into active type and passive type, thinking that faulty-liability should be applied to the passive type and no-fault liability applies to the active type. [5]

In U.S, strict liability was adopted in the case of playboy Enterprise Inc. V. Frena, which was accepted by the White Paper "IPNII"[6] The "Digital Copyright and Technical Education Act" emphasized that the intermediary service provider should not bear the liability when they received the copyright notice and had reasonable opportunity to restrict the alleged violations and they did not edit or modify the power.

In EU, Germany developed the "Multimedia Law", it stipulates that the information providers should take full responsibility for editorial content, while the intermediate service providers do not take responsibility for the information of the third parties, unless the information was used intentionally. And the "E-Commerce Directive "made reference to the German" Multimedia Law "and the United States" Digital Millennium Copyright Act ". [1][57-58]

Accordingly, I think that the principle of fault liability should apply to this issue. The reasons are as follows:

2.1 Balance the Interests of All the Parties

The development of Internet technology and applications make the works spread more quickly, efficient and timely, it not only broke the constraints of time and space, but also abandoned the ethnic, racial barriers, greatly contributed to the spread of scientific, cultural and artistic works; it can not be replaced. On the other hand, the rights of copyright holders on the Internet are increasingly violated. It is obvious not good to reduce the protection of the rights of the copyright holders in order to promote the spread of works, either to suppress the application of network technology and development in order to protect the rights of the copyright holders, Our copyright law should be search for a new balance between the promotion of network technology and the protection of rights of the copyright holders.

According to Non-fault Liability, so long as the actor has causality with the damage result, he should take responsibility, no matter what his intentions are. The victims do not have to find evidence to prove the actor's fault. Neither the actor can defend for that. [7] This approach will undoubtedly increase the burden of online service providers, may even limit the development of this new industry, and the operating costs of network service providers will arise, which will ultimately increase the consumer price, or even worse that a lot of people can not enjoy this new service, in turn will limit the development of the Internet industry. On the contrary, the fault liability takes fault as a criterion to determine whether they will take the responsibility for the damage caused by the perpetrator. In the general tort damages cases the party who had subjective fault should be responsible for the damages. Subjective fault liability is one of the elements, if this element was lacked, the perpetrator will not take the responsibility even if he did have something to do with the damage result. Compared to fault liability, no-fault liability is more conducive to social and productive forces.

Mr. Zejian Wang believes that the moral concept of fault liability is the requirement of justice to recognize he who made the damage results should take the responsibility and it can reconcile the conflict between the two basic values the "personal freedom" and "social security". Moreover, this principle recognizes personal power to make choices, and the ability to tell what is right from wrong, and it can also reflects the respect for the dignity of individuals. [8] Fault liability takes the perpetrator's fault for one of the constituent elements; the size of the fault of the perpetrator has a decisive role on the responsibility. This principle of tort liabilities can not only promote the dissemination of the works, but also well protect the interests of copyright holders; it is natural selection to the imputation of Internet copyright infringement.

2.2 Cost and Benefit Analysis

According to cost and benefit analysis, when the responsibility principle of the Internet copyright infringement has been determined the costs and benefits of enterprises should be considered. The purpose of business is to pursue the maximization of benefits, which will reach the top when the marginal cost of output is equal to its marginal revenue. If the marginal revenue is greater than marginal cost, the enterprise should reduce the production because the loss of reduced production will be less than the cost savings. [9] According to non-fault liability the Internet service providers (ISP) must bear the duty to monitor all content for the network users, which means that Internet service providers, in addition to the original obligation, will take the same obligations as network content providers, which will greatly increase the marginal cost of ISP, and its marginal revenue does not increase, which will greatly affected the enthusiasm of ISP even will do harm to the entire Internet industry. Therefore, non-fault liability should be excluded in our country and the liability should apply to instead.

3 The Confirmation of Copyright Infringement in the P2P System

According to the principle of fault liability of Internet copyright infringement, copyright infringement liability on the Internet should include four elements: the act of copyright infringement, the result of violations, the link between the act and results, the subjective fault. In theory and practice, identifying the fault is the most difficult problem. On the Internet, a variety of subjects take the corresponding obligations according to their different status and roles, once the obligation is violated the subjective fault will be found and they shall bear tort liability. Here I will analyze it from the subjects of ICP, P2P software providers, P2P operators and users.

3.1 The Tort Liability of ICP

ICP is designed to provide Internet content, which includes operational information and non-operational information. The implementation of licensing system is for the former, and the registration system for the latter, the Internet information services can not be engaged without them. The content provided by ICP may be from its own or from Internet users or from other sites. In either case, as long as the ICP provides a source of infringing works to download for other P2P users it should bear tort liability. Since the ICP provides content services it has the obligation to review the contents, once the content they provide is against the rights of others, then it can be considered fault, thus shall bear tort liability.

3.2 The Tort Liability of P2P Software Providers

P2P software providers include developer of software and software disseminator who are representatives of new technology and are not necessarily involved in copyright infringement. In fact, just from the perspective of communication works, P2P software providers do has a very important significance for the dissemination of the works. So the law need to balance many relationships, on the one hand, over-protection for emerging technologies may infringe the interests of copyright owners, which may interfere with the spread of the works, on the other hand, excessive protection of the interests of copyright owners may also restrict the development of science and technology, which is also very dangerous for a country. In my opinion, P2P software providers` tort liability can be identified by their knowing degree of violation. if it knows or should have known P2P software is used for infringement, and still provide P2P software, the software providers have fault and should take responsibility; If the software providers do not know or should not know the infringement of others, and the software itself has substantial no infringing use, then the software providers do not have fault and should not bear tort liability.

3.3 P2P Software Operators

The operators of P2P software refer to the beneficiaries who take P2P software as a profit-making tool, it should be noted that P2P software operators do not necessarily need to control the P2P users. In the Napster case, using a concentration of file-sharing technology, users need a user name and password to log in Napster's servers,

Napster companies are able to control the P2P users, therefore, although the defendant can not be well aware of each of the specific violations, it did know that violations occurred in their system and it had ability to control the behavior of users yet turned a blind eye, thus it need to bear tort liability. [10]

Operators of P2P software is also directly benefit from the business activities, but P2P software operators do not directly interfere with infringing content, therefore they can not be identified fault as ICP. According to cost-benefit theory, the costs and benefits of enterprises should be considered in determining the principle of Internet copyright infringement. The purpose of business is to pursue the maximization of benefits, when the marginal cost of output of a business is equal to its marginal revenue, the profits get the top. If the marginal revenue is greater than marginal cost, the enterprise should reduce its production because the loss of income will be less than the cost savings. [9] [241-242] giving too many obligations to P2P software providers will affect the development of China's Internet industry. I think that our country can also introduce the "notice and take down " rule, that is, the software operators are not responsible for the violations of others, but once there is evidence that anyone is using the P2P system to infringe, P2P software operators are obliged to remove infringing work or control the transmission of copyright works, of course, evidence of the infringement should be submitted or the software operator can refuse the request.

3.4 The Confirmation of Copyright Infringement Liability of Internet Users in the P2P System

In P2P systems every user's shared directory replaced the storage server; users can access or download information through their P2P shared directory. That is, each P2P user's software utilizing behavior includes uploading and downloading, and most of these works are unauthorized, even if they are, the authorized work can not infringe the copyright holders' legitimate rights. Thus, on the Internet, every P2P users has become the most direct tortfeasor of copyright. P2P users have known they are not authorized, and still downloading works, and providing them to other P2P users, the fault is self-evident.

In fact, the behavior of P2P users have indeed caused a great loss to the copyright owners According to a survey of international recording industry alliance, till June 2003, P2P users are sharing 1 billion MP3 music, over the past 3 years, the worldwide record sales decreased by 14%, among which by 30% in Canada and Germany, and the loss were 800 million and 425 million Euros respectively, nearly by 50% in Denmark ,the major record companies lay off 10%, the main reason were the exchange of MP3 music by P2P software, Therefore, the copyright owners are paying more and more attention to the P2P user's infringement. In May 2006 International Federation of Phonographic Industry (IFPI) announced that 3500 German E-Donkey users will be sued with criminal prosecution, saying that it was "the largest single action against illegal file-sharing around the world." The Association of American music is also (RIAA) also sued P2P users who shared music online by a total number of 18,000 using P2P system till May 2006.

Because P2P users can control the content in their shared folders, according to social control theory, it is appropriate that the users take the tort liability of infringement, and it is more in line with the requirements of law and economics.

4 Concluding Remarks

The principle of attribution of copyright infringement and the confirmation of responsibility in P2P system is related to the promotion of dissemination of cultural, science and technology works, and to the protection of the rights of the copyright owners, it is difficult to tell which one is better, a new balance between them should be found, scholars of the world who hold different views are still working on it. For example, the United States, in the Grokster case and in the Napster case, emphasized the protection of copyright. In the December 2005, the French House of Commons approved the legalization of P2P software [11], which had paid more attention to the promotion of new technologies. I think that a collective management system on copyright should be created and perfected, the copyright collective organization, not the copyright owner, will exercise the rights of copyright, which will not only reduce the cost of P2P system provider's and P2P users` using the author's the work, but also protect the interests of copyright holders and will promote the development of science and culture of our country while protecting the interests of copyright owners.

References

[1] Zhang, X.: Research on Infringement in internet. China Renmin University Press, Beijing (2003)
[2] Yang, L.: E-Commerce Tort Law. Intellectual Property Press, Beijing (2005)
[3] Zhang, C.: E-Commerce Law Materials, p. 32. China Renmin University Press, Beijing (2007)
[4] Pei, H.: Analysis on Responsibility Principle of Copyright Infringement, vol. 6, pp. 76–77. China Law Press, Beijing (2002)
[5] Ma, H.: Discuss on Tort Liability of Internet Service Provider. Zhejiang: Journal of Wuxi Institute of Commerce 3, 86–89 (2004)
[6] United States Patent and Trademark Office; Intellectual Property and the National Information Infrastructure, the Report of the Working Group on Intellectual Property Rights[EB/OL].[2010-6-15],
     http://www.uspto.gov/web/offices/com/doc/ipnii/
[7] Zhang, X.: China Tort Law, p. 69. China Social Science Press, Beijing (1998)
[8] Yang, L.: Discuss on Tort Law, p. 122. The People's Court Press, Beijing (2004)
[9] Qian, H.: Jurisprudence of Economic Analysis, pp. 241–242. Law Press China, Beijing (2003)
[10] Xue, H.: Intellectual Property and E-Commerce, p. 364. Law Press China, Beijing (2003)
[11] http://www.techweb.com.cn/news/2005-12-24/33507.shtml
      [2010-6-15]

Active Synchronization of Different Autonomous Systems

Xiao-Jun Liu and Li-Xin Yang

School of Mathematics and Statistics, Tianshui Normal University,
Tianshui Gansu 741001, China
flybett3952@126.com

Abstract. Based on Lyapunov stability theory, a novel active synchronization method is proposed for a class of parametrically excited chaotic systems. The method is predominant in theoretical deduction and engineering realization, the systemic designing of controller is simple, and can be applied to synchronize a class of parametrically excited chaotic systems. The active synchronization of the nonlinear gyros system and the Mathieu function is achieved by the proposed method. The effectiveness and the robustness of the proposed schemes are demonstrated by numerical simulations.

Keywords: Autonomous system; Chaos; Active synchronization; Error dynamical system.

1 Introduction

Since synchronization of chaotic systems was first introduced by Fujisaka and Yamada [1] and Pecora and Carroll [2], chaos synchronization has been an active research topic in nonlinear science. During the last two decades, synchronization in chaotic dynamical system has received a great deal of interest among scientists from various research fields [3-10], and a variety of approaches have been proposed for the synchronization of chaotic systems. Active synchronization is one of the most important methods for chaotic systems, in this paper, a novel active synchronization method is proposed for a class of parametrically excited chaotic systems. The method is predominant in theoretical deduction and engineering realization, the systemic designing of controller is simple, and can be applied to synchronize a class of parametrically excited chaotic systems.

2 Active Synchronization

For a class of non-automatic chaotic systems, suppose the drive system in the form of

$$\dot{x}(t) = Ax(t) + f(x(t)) , \tag{1}$$

where $x(t) \in R^n$ is an n-dimensional state vector of the system, $A \in R^n$ is a parameters matrix, and $f(x(t))$ is the nonlinear part of the system (1).While, the response system is taken as

$$\dot{y}(t) = By(t) + g(y(t)) + U(t) , \tag{2}$$

G. Shen and X. Huang (Eds.): CSIE 2011, Part II, CCIS 153, pp. 239–243, 2011.
© Springer-Verlag Berlin Heidelberg 2011

where $\mathbf{y(t)} \in R^n$ is an n-dimensional state vector of the system, $\mathbf{B} \in R^n$ is a parameters matrix, $\mathbf{g(y(t))}$ is the nonlinear part of the system , and $\mathbf{U(t)}$ is the active controller.

Let $\mathbf{e} = (e_1, e_2, \cdots, e_n)^T$ is the synchronization error vector. The goal is to design an appropriate controller $\mathbf{U(t)}$ such that the trajectory of the response system (2) with initial conditions $\mathbf{y_0}$ can approaches asymptotically the drive system (1) with initial conditions $\mathbf{x_0}$, in this sense, we have $\lim_{t \to \infty} \|\mathbf{e}\| = 0$, where $\|\bullet\|$ is the Euclidean norm. At this point, it means that the drive system (1) and the response system (2) are synchronized under the controller $\mathbf{U(t)}$ as time t tends to infinity.

The error dynamical system is

$$\begin{aligned} \dot{\mathbf{e}}(t) &= \mathbf{By(t)} + \mathbf{g(y)} - \mathbf{Ax(t)} - \mathbf{f(x)} + \mathbf{U(t)} \\ &= \mathbf{Be(t)} + (\mathbf{B} - \mathbf{A})\mathbf{x(t)} + \mathbf{g(y)} - \mathbf{f(x)} + \mathbf{U(t)} \end{aligned} \quad (3)$$

Let $\mathbf{C} = \mathbf{B} - \mathbf{A}$, then the dynamical system can be rewriter as

$$\begin{aligned} \dot{\mathbf{e}}(t) &= \mathbf{By(t)} + \mathbf{g(y)} - \mathbf{Ax(t)} - \mathbf{f(x)} + \mathbf{U(t)} \\ &= \mathbf{Be(t)} + \mathbf{Cx(t)} + \mathbf{g(y)} - \mathbf{f(x)} + \mathbf{U(t)} \end{aligned} \quad (4)$$

The active controller is taken as

$$\mathbf{U(t)} = -\mathbf{De(t)} - \mathbf{g(y)} + \mathbf{f(x)} - \mathbf{Cx(t)} , \quad (5)$$

Where $\mathbf{D} \in R^n$ is the feedback gain matrix. The controller $\mathbf{U(t)}$ is substituted to the system (4), we can get

$$\dot{\mathbf{e}}(t) = (\mathbf{B} - \mathbf{D})\mathbf{e(t)} . \quad (6)$$

Then the error dynamical system (4) can be rewritten as

$$\dot{\mathbf{e}}(t) = \mathbf{Me(t)} , \quad (7)$$

where $\mathbf{M} = (\mathbf{B} - \mathbf{D})$. The synchronization between the drive and response systems is transform to realize the unanimous asymptotic stability of the system (7) at the origin.

2.1 Active Synchronization of the Nonlinear Gyro System

The nonlinear gyro system is taken as the drive system. The dynamical behavior of the symmetric gyroscope mounted on a vibrating base can be described by the following differential equations [11]:

$$\begin{cases} \dot{x}_1 = x_2 \\ \dot{x}_2 = -\alpha^2 \dfrac{(1 - \cos x_1)^2}{\sin^3 x_1} - c_1 x_2 - c_2 x_2^3 + (\beta + f \sin \omega_1 t) \sin x_1 \end{cases}, \quad (8)$$

where $f \sin \omega_1 t$ represents a parametric excitation, $c_1 x_2, c_2 x_2^3$ is linear and nonlinear damping terms respectively, and $\alpha^2 \dfrac{(1 - \cos x_1)^2}{\sin^3 x_1} - \beta \sin x_1$ is a nonlinear resilience force. There exists a chaotic attractor when the parameters of system (8) are taken as $\alpha^2 = 100, \beta = 1, c_1 = 0.5, c_2 = 0.05, \omega_1 = 2, f = 35.5$ which is shown in Fig.1(a).

The Mathieu function is taken as the response system, which is defined as follows [12,13]:

$$\begin{cases} \dot{y}_1 = y_2 + u_1(t) \\ \dot{y}_2 = -y_1 - \delta(y_2 + n_1 y_1^2 y_2) - \mu y_1 - \beta_1 y_1^3 - \beta_2 y_1^5 \\ \quad + \beta_3 y_2^2 y_1(1 - y_1^2/6) + \beta_4 y_2^2 y_1^3(1 - y_1^2/6) \\ \quad -2\varepsilon \cos(\omega_2 t)(-y_1 + \alpha_1 y_1^3 + \alpha_2 y_1^5) + u_2(t) \end{cases}, \tag{9}$$

when the parameters are set $\delta = 0.5, n_1 = 3, \mu = 3, \beta_1 = 5, \beta_2 = 0.7, \alpha_1 = 1, \alpha_2 = 1, \beta_3 = 0.5,$ $\beta_4 = 0.5, \varepsilon = 10.5, \omega_2 = 2$, system (9) has a typical chaotic attractor which is shown in Fig.1(b).

Let the synchronization error variables between the drive system (8) and response system (9) are $e_1 = y_1 - x_1, e_2 = y_2 - x_2$, Subtracting system (8) from (9), the following error dynamical system between them is obtained:

$$\begin{cases} \dot{e}_1(t) = e_2 + u_1(t) \\ \dot{e}_2(t) = -y_1 - \delta(y_2 + n_1 y_1^2 y_2) - \mu y_1 - \beta_1 y_1^3 - \beta_2 y_1^5 \\ \quad + \beta_3 y_2^2 y_1(1 - y_1^2/6) + \beta_4 y_2^2 y_1^3(1 - y_1^2/6) \\ \quad -2\varepsilon \cos(\omega_2 t)(-y_1 + \alpha_1 y_1^3 + \alpha_2 y_1^5) + \alpha^2 \dfrac{(1 - \cos x_1)^2}{\sin^3 x_1} \\ \quad + c_1 x_2 + c_2 x_2^3 - (\beta + f \sin \omega_1 t)\sin x_1 + u_2(t) \end{cases}. \tag{10}$$

The aim of the section is to determine the active controller **u**, for the synchronization of drive and response systems. For this purpose, the controller is selected as follows:

$$\begin{cases} u_1(t) = V_1(t) \\ u_2(t) = y_1 + \delta(y_2 + n_1 y_1^2 y_2) + \mu y_1 + \beta_1 y_1^3 + \beta_2 y_1^5 \\ \quad - \beta_3 y_2^2 y_1(1 - y_1^2/6) - \beta_4 y_2^2 y_1^3(1 - y_1^2/6) \\ \quad + 2\varepsilon \cos(\omega_2 t)(-y_1 + \alpha_1 y_1^3 + \alpha_2 y_1^5) \\ \quad -\alpha^2 \dfrac{(1 - \cos x_1)^2}{\sin^3 x_1} - c_1 x_2 - c_2 x_2^3 + (\beta + f \sin \omega_1 t)\sin x_1 \\ \quad + V_2(t) \end{cases}. \tag{11}$$

where $\begin{pmatrix} V_1(t) \\ V_2(t) \end{pmatrix} = \mathbf{D}\begin{pmatrix} e_1(t) \\ e_2(t) \end{pmatrix}$, and $\mathbf{D} = \begin{pmatrix} d_1 & d_2 \\ d_3 & d_4 \end{pmatrix}$ is a constants matrix, then the error dynamical system can be rewritten in the matrix form as follows:

$$\begin{pmatrix} \dot{e}_1(t) \\ \dot{e}_2(t) \end{pmatrix} = \mathbf{M}\begin{pmatrix} e_1(t) \\ e_2(t) \end{pmatrix}, \tag{12}$$

where $\mathbf{M} = \begin{pmatrix} d_1 & 1 + d_2 \\ d_3 & d_4 \end{pmatrix}$. The eigenvalues of the matrix **M** are negative real when the parameters $d_1 = -1, d_2 = -1, d_3 = 1, d_4 = -3$.

For this numerical simulation, the system parameters are chosen as before such that the drive system (1) and the response system (2) display chaotic behavior. The initial conditions of the drive and response systems are taken as $\mathbf{x_0} = (1,-1)$ and $\mathbf{y_0} = (-0.3, 0.15)$ respectively. The state error signals e_1 and e_2 between systems (1) and (2), converge asymptotically to zeros as time t evolving in a short time interval $[0, 20]$, as shown in Fig.2.

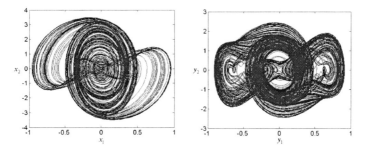

Fig. 1. (a) The chaotic attractor of system (8); (b) The chaotic attractor of system (9)

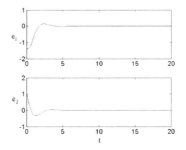

Fig. 2. Synchronization errors between drive and response systems with evolving time t

3   Conlusions

In this paper, the active synchronization of different autonomous systems is investigated. Based on Lyapunov stability theory, a novel active synchronization method is proposed for a class of parametrically excited chaotic systems. The method is predominant in theoretical deduction and engineering realization, the systemic designing of controller is simple, and can be applied to synchronize a class of parametrically excited chaotic systems. The active synchronization of the nonlinear gyros system and the Mathieu function is achieved by the proposed method.

Acknowledgements

This research is supported by Gansu Province Government of China (096RJZE106) and Scientific Research Foundations of Tianshui Normal University of China (TSA1012).

References

1. Fujisaka, H., Yamada, T.: Stability theory of synchronized motion in coupled-oscillator systems. Prog. Theor. Phys. 69, 32–71 (1983)
2. Pecora, L.M., Carroll, T.L.: Synchronization in chaotic systems. Phys. Rev. Lett. 64, 821–824 (1990)
3. Ott, E., Grebogi, C., Yorke, J.A.: Controlling chaos. Phys. Rev. Lett. 64, 1196–1199 (1990)
4. Park, J.H., Kwon, O.M.: A Novel criterion for delayed feedback control of time-delay chaotic systems. Chaos, Solitions Fractals 17, 709–716 (2003)
5. Lü, J.H., Chen, G.R., Cheng, D.Z., Celikovsky, S.: Bridge the gap between the Lorenz system and the Chen system. Int. J. Bifurcat and Chaos 12, 2917–2926 (2002)
6. Park, J.H.: Adaptive synchronization of a unified chaotic system with an uncertain parameter. Int. J. Nonlin. Sci. Numer. Simulat. 6, 201–206 (2005)
7. Chen, H.K.: Global chaos synchronization of a new chaotic system via nonlinear Control. Chaos Solitions & Fractals 23, 1245–1251 (2005)
8. Li, R.H., Xu, I., Li, S.: Anti-synchronization on autonomous and non-autonomous chaotic systems via adaptive feedback control. Chaos, Solitions & Fractals 11, 2215–2223 (2010)
9. Song, Q.K., Cao, J.D.: Synchronization and anti-synchronization for chaotic systems. Chaos Solitions & Fractals 33, 929–939 (2007)
10. Li, G.H., Zhou, S.P.: Anti-synchronization in different chaotic systems. Chaos, Solitions & Fractal 32, 516–520 (2007)
11. Yau, H.T.: Chaos synchronization of two uncertain chaotic nonlinear gyros using fuzzy sliding mode control. Mechanical Systems and Signal Processing 22, 408–418 (2008)
12. Li, X.F., Chu, Y.D., Liu, X.: Chaos control analysis for Mathieu equation by three methods. Journal of Vibration and Shock 26, 35–37 (2007)
13. Samuel, B.: Adaptive synchronization between two different chaotic dynamical systems. Comm. Nonlin. Science Numer. Simu. 12, 976–985 (2007)

An Execution Tracing Tool for Multi-tier Web Applications

Jian Xu, Hong Zhang, and QianMu Li

Institute of Computer Science and Technology, Nanjing University of Science
and Technology, 200 Xiao Ling Wei Nanjing,
210094 Jiangsu, China
{dolphin.xu,qianmu,zhhong}@mail.njust.edu.cn

Abstract. A precise request tracing tool is essential to help both developers and administrators debug performance problems of multi-tier web applications. This paper introduces a non-intrusive end-to-end runtime path tracing tool named ExeTracer, which does not require instrumentation of middleware or application source code, but is limited to co-located web/application server environments. We present the design and implementation in detail. Further, we evaluate the performance overhead associated with the tool. The results show that the low performance overhead makes it a promising tracing tool for using on multi-tier web applications.

Keywords: web application; execution trace; runtime path.

1 Introduction

Many commercially-important systems, especially web-based applications, are composed of a number of communicating components. These are often structured as multi-tiered systems, which might start with requests from Web clients that flow through a Web-server front-end and then to a web "application server," which in turn makes calls to a database server. In such environments, each of the different servers that make up the system generally produces multiple logs used for system monitoring. Although this information can be useful for assessing the performance of individual servers, it can prove difficult to piece the different logs together to form a coherent picture of the entire application. Thus, tools to understand complex system behavior are essential for many performance analysis and debugging tasks. Our aim is to develop a tracing tool to help developers and administrators to precisely trace each request and correlate activities of components into causal paths (runtime path).

A runtime path [1] contains the control flow (i.e. the ordered sequence of methods called that are required to service a user request), resources and performance characteristics associated with servicing a request. There are currently a number of end-to-end monitoring tools that have the ability to trace runtime paths through a system [2,3]. However, a major draw-back of the current tools is that they are intrusive, that is they require changes to the application source code or the server implementation. In many situations, however, it may not be possible to make such changes. Similar to our non-

G. Shen and X. Huang (Eds.): CSIE 2011, Part II, CCIS 153, pp. 244–250, 2011.

intrusive approach with no application modification is required, several systems [4, 5] use explicit identifiers to trace requests through multi-tier systems for performance profiling. Some also implement the tracing in the platform so that no application modification is required. Although their approach is less invasive than ours, it is more difficult to associate specific observations with specific request paths for failure management tasks.

In this paper, we introduce a non-intrusive end-to-end runtime path tracing tool, ExeTracer, which monitors the paths that the user requests take when traversing through the different tiers in the system. It also provides the ability to capture the control path and resource demands of application requests as they are serviced across components.

2 Problem Statement

Java Platform, Enterprise Edition (JEE) defines a standard for developing multi-tier web applications. It provides an architectural framework on four tiers that developers can use to build their systems. Servers in different tiers can be located at different nodes. In this situation, modules of an application are deployed at different nodes according to their functions. We refer to this case as a distributed environment. On the other hand, Web servers in web tier and business servers in business tier can be co-located in one node. Servers that are co-located run on the same JVM. In this situation, all modules of an application are deployed at one node. We refer to this case as a non-distributed environment. We focus on the later.

When an external request is serviced, a series of activities with causal relations are caused. We define a sequence of activities with causal relations caused by an external request as a causal path. The formal definitions are as follows.

Definition 1 (Causal Path). Given a request, a causal path is the control flow associated with servicing the request, which is denoted as $c\text{-}path = \langle reqType, pathtree \rangle$, where *pathtree* is a tree representing the invocation relationships among the active components servicing the request. Causal paths can be recorded during runtime by tracing each request through a live system, spanning the system's layers to access the direct component. Each path then provides a vertical slice of the system from a request's perspective. Fig. 1 shows an example of a typical multi-tier JEE application, with one possible causal path. This causal path shows how a user request is serviced, giving the ordered sequence of invocations and related performance. Note that we assume that this application is RPC-based and both calls and returns cause node operations. Though not all multi-tier JEE applications fall within the scope of our target applications, fortunately many popular JEE applications satisfy these assumptions.

By analyzing causal path, we can help greatly with system comprehension and can be applied to a number of different purposes in this area, such as fault detection, fault diagnosis, autonomic monitoring and so on. Therefore, our aim is to develop a tracing tool to help developers and administrators to precisely trace each request and correlate activities of components into causal paths.

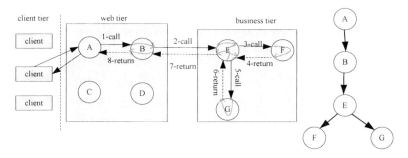

Fig. 1. An example multi-tier application showing a causal path

3   Design of the Tracing Framework

The applications based on JEE technology are generally required to handle high loads of concurrent users. Causal path tracing in such systems involves tracing each of these user requests as they pass through the different tiers that make up the whole application. To achieve this, external requests must be identifiable and the specific information of the invocations that make up the requests at different tiers also needs to be logged.

A tracing framework consists of three major parts, as shown in Fig. 2. The first part is an interceptor, which intercepts all incoming requests and outgoing responses, identifies the request URI, assigns a unique identifier to each request, and logs the beginning and ending of user requests. The second one is a tracer installed on each component, which intercepts all method invocations made to this component and logs the request specific information (RSI), along with component details. The component details describe the component that is called, giving information such as what component method was invoked, what arguments were passed and so on. The last one is an aggregator, which uses the logged information to construct the causal paths offline. The reconstruction process makes use of the RSI data to order the invocations and to determine what invocations make up each causal path.

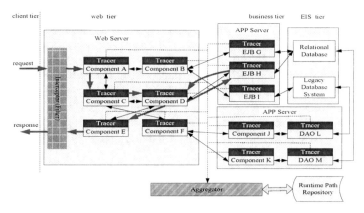

Fig. 2. The tracing Framework

3.1 Interceptor

The interceptor is an important function entity in the above tracing framework. On a new user request enters the system, the interceptor intercepts it, assigns a unique Id, and inserts the unique Id and the beginning time of this request into the local thread object *ThreadLocal*, which has been introduced in version JDK 1.2 and can be used to hold a particular value (or object) for the lifetime of the thread. On the corresponding response leaves the system, the interceptor also intercepts it and inserts the ending time of this request into the local thread object.

The interceptor can be implemented using intercepting filter pattern [6], which allows the creation of pluggable filters to process common services in a standard manner without requiring changes to core request processing code. The servlet 2.3 specification and a later specification also include a standard mechanism for building filter chains based on the intercepting filter pattern. Consequently, web applications running on servlet specification compliant web servers can be augmented with filters for pre- and post-processing in the web tier without the need to modify source code. The interceptor can be added declaratively through XML deployment descriptors.

3.2 Tracer

The tracer is another important function entity, which logs RSIs at different software tiers. For web tier example, there are two web components: servlets and JSP pages. For servlets, on every invocation of a component method, information is logged. The logged information contains the following data: user request identifier (a unique id), the beginning time and ending time of component method invocation, component details (i.e. component name and method name). We referred to such RSIs as local observations.

Definition 2 (Local Observation). Given a component in causal path, each local observation contains information about this active component, such as its name, location, timestamp, latency, and arguments, which is denoted as l-$obs = \langle reqID, C_{info}, st, et \rangle$, where st and et are the beginning time and ending time for method invocation respectively, $C_{info} = \langle c,l,m \rangle$, where c is the active component name, l is the location of the component c and m is the called method name.

The tracer is conceptually a proxy element with a one-to-one relationship with its target component (TC). In J2EE, the TCs are JSPs, Servlets and EJBs deployed in a target application. The tracer is implemented as a proxy layer surrounding the TC with the purpose of intercepting all method invocations and lifecycle events. The process of augmenting a TC with the proxy layer is referred to as probe insertion (PI). ExeTracer provides a trace code template (TCT), modifiable by the user, which consists of extensible logic for initiating event-handling operations and placeholders for component-specific information. Using the TCT and the extracted metadata from deployment descriptors, the PI process generates one tracer for each target application component. The placeholders in the template are replaced with the values extracted from the metadata. The proxy layer is an instantiation of the TCT, using the TC metadata values. A modified component (MC) results after the PI process has been applied to a TC, and this will enclose the original TC. In order to ensure a seamless transition from the TC to the MC, the PI transfers the TC metadata to the MC. The MC metadata will be updated to ensure the proper functionality of the proxy layer.

3.3 Aggregator

The aggregator is responsible for constructing causal paths by correlating local observations. In non-distributed situation, web servers and application servers are co-located at one node. They run on the same JVM. Thus, for a particular user request the same thread is used across the web server, EJB server and database driver. We can easily construct causal paths from local observations. Due to simplicity and space limit, we describe the correlation algorithm in detail no longer.

4   Experimental Evaluation

In this section, we evaluate our tool prototype ExeTracer by applying to two JEE applications: (1) a sample online banking application, called Duke's Bank and (2) a sample e-commerce application, called Pet Store. To assess the performance overhead incurred by ExeTracer, firstly we describe our experimental setup. Subsequently, we instrument the web and business tiers of these two applications. Lastly, we present results by running a number of performance tests, which show the overhead of the approaches.

The test environment was made up of three machines (Intel Core 2 Duo CPU P8600 @2.40 GHz, 2 GB RAM) running Windows XP, connected through a 100Mb switch. The first machine was used for load generation. Apache JMeter was used as a load generation tool. Duke's Bank and PetStore were installed on the second machine running JBoss 4.0 GA. Finally, the third machine was a database server running Mysql 5.5.1, which was employed to save the data produced by ExeTracer remotely such that the performance overhead on the second machine could be kept to a minimum. This is common practice for production environments.

In the following experiments, all experiments were done offline. We emulated a read/write mixed workload, which was created such that 20% of users purchased products while the remaining 80% browsed. We ran a number of test cases for two versions of each sample application (i.e. one version instrumented and the other version not). Before each test, the second machine was restarted and the JVM was warmed up as suggested in the literature [7]. During the different test cases, we observed the average response time and throughput of the application for the following loads: 10 users, 50 users, 100 users, 150 users, 200 users, 300 users, 400 users, 500 users, 600 users, 700 users, 800 users, 900 users, 1000 users. Users entered the system at a rate of one user per second with a random delay of between 1-2 sec. Each measurement period lasted for 30 min.

The tests carried out were on two versions of each sample application. We analyzed the average response time and throughput of the instrumented application against the average response time and throughput of the non-instrumented one for the same user load respectively. The results are shown in Fig. 3 and Fig. 4.

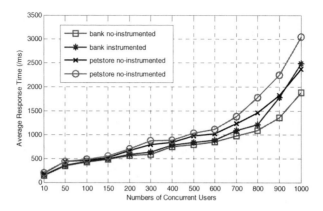

Fig. 3. The effect on the average response time

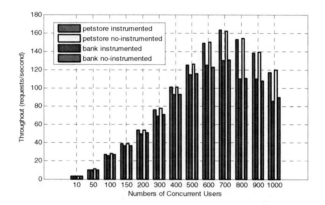

Fig. 4. The effect on throughput

From them, we observed that when the numbers of concurrent users were less than 200, ExeTracer had little effect on the throughput and average response time for either the instrumented or non-instrumented version of two applications. As the number of concurrent clients increased from 200 to 500, it had small effect on both of them. According to our statistics, the max overhead in terms of the decrease of throughput was 9.2%, and the max overhead in terms of the increase of average response time was less than 10.1%. Further, when the number of concurrent clients increased from 500 to 1000, the system was close to its saturation point and response time increased significantly. For the non-instrumented application, at 700 and 1000 users there was a maximal 23.4% and 151.2% increase in average response time compared with 500 users respectively, while there was a maximal 28.9% and 195.4% increase in average response time for the instrumented version compared with 500 users respectively. Moreover, we also observed that when the number of concurrent users increased from 700 to 800, the throughput decreased, while the average response time increased. This is an interesting question, which could be explained by the fact that at this point, the system seemed to be close to its saturation point. Any further increase in load at this point added to the bottleneck and increased response time significantly.

5 Conclusion

We introduce a non-intrusive end-to-end runtime path tracing tool named ExeTracer, which provides the ability to capture the control path of application requests as they are serviced across components. The monitoring framework used by ExeTracer takes advantage of a number of J2EE standard mechanisms to meet the monitoring requirements for J2EE systems in a non-intrusive and portable manner. However, J2EE does not provide a mechanism for piggy backing information with a remote request such that request specific information can be passed over a remote invocation in a distributed environment. Thus, an effort is currently being undertaken to enhance our approach such that it can be applied to J2EE applications that are distributed across multiple JVMs.

Acknowledgments. This work is funded in part by a grant from Research Fund for the Doctoral Program of Higher Education of China under grant No.20093219120024, and by a grant from NUST Research Funding under Grant No. 2010GJPY056.

References

1. Chen, M., Kiciman, E., Accardi, A., et al.: Using runtime paths for macro analysis. In: 9th Workshop on Hot Topics in Operating Systems. IEEE Press, New York (2003)
2. Chen, M., Kiciman, E., Fratkin, E., et al.: Pinpoint: problem determination in large, dynamic, internet services. In: Int. Conf. on Dependable Systems and Networks, Washington, DC (2002)
3. Gschwind, T., Eshghi, K., Garg, P.K., et al.: WebMon: a performance profiler for web transactions. In: 4th IEEE Int. Workshop on Advanced Issues of E-Commerce and Web-Based Information Systems. IEEE Press, New York (2002)
4. Barham, P., Donnelly, A., Isaacs, R., et al.: Using Magpie for Request Extraction and Workload Modeling. In: 6th OSDI, p. 18 (2004)
5. Agarwala, S., Alegre, F., Schwan, K., Mehalingham, J.: E2EProf: Automated End-to-End Performance Management for Enterprise Systems. In: 37th DSN, pp. 749–758 (2007)
6. Alur, D., Crupi, J., Malks, D.: Core J2EE Patterns: best practices and design strategies. Prentice Hall, Sun Microsystems Press (2001)
7. Buble, L.B.A., Tuma, P.: Corba benchmarking: A course with hidden obstacles. In: IPDPS Workshop on Performance Modeling, Evaluation and Optimization of Parallel and Distributed Systems (2003)

Uplink Capacity Analysis in TD-SCDMA System*

Hong He[1], Hong Dong[1,2], Tong Yang[3], and Lin He[3]

[1] Tianjin Key Laboratory for Control Theory and Application in Complicated Systems,
Tianjin University of Technology (China)
heho604300@126.com
[2] Scholl of Computer and Communication Engineering,
Tianjin University of Technology (China)
[3] Tianjin Mobile Communications Co., Ltd

Abstract. System capacity is one of important parameters in network planning. It is necessary to analyze it so that capacity gets a trade-off between the desired quality and overall cost. In this paper, TD-SCDMA system uplink capacity is analyzed. In the process of analysis, intra-cell and inter-cell interference are considered. What is more, the interference of other systems is considered. Furthermore it also considers the TD-SCDMA multi-user detection for the impact of the TD-SCDMA system capacity.

Keywords: capacity; uplink; interference; TD-SCDMA.

1 Introduction

TD-SCDMA is one of the third generation communication standards. It has distinct technological advantages with respect to other standards. The prospects of the TD-SCDMA technology are very attractive. It has time division duplexing properties. It is possible to change the switching point between uplink and downlink, depending on the capacity requirement between uplink and downlink. TD-SCDMA is equally adept at handling both symmetric and asymmetric traffic. It has great significance for quite different density distribution of mobile users in the region. The demand for data applications is high in urban areas with high user density while the demand for data applications is low in areas with low user density. Data applications have asymmetric traffic features, which the requirement of number of uplink and downlink time slots is quite different. At this time it can meet the requirements by changing the switching point between uplink and downlink. TD-SCDMA system is the Code Division Multiple Access system. It has multiple access interference (MAI). However, TD-SCDMA system uses a multi-user detection technology, reduces the multiple access interference within the system so that the system capacity can be increased.

System capacity is one of important parameters in network planning. It is necessary to analyze it so that capacity gets a trade-off between the desired quality and overall cost. The capacity of the system is analyzed in many papers. In [1]-[7], only a

---

* Hong He, School of Electrical Engineering, Tianjin University of Technology (China), 300384.

single system capacity is analyzed. The impact on the capacity of the interference for the presence of other systems did not consider. In [8] and [9], multi-user detection system is not considered.

This paper not only considers the impact of interference of TD-SCDMA system on the capacity, but also takes into account the presence of other systems for the impact on system capacity. In addition, it also considers multi-user detection technology for the impact on system capacity.

2   System Model

The TD-SCDMA system is two-tier cellular architecture which has 19 cells. Mobile users are uniformly distributed within each cell. It is assumed that TD-SCDMA system uses the frequency band is 1880MHz ~ 1920MHz.

Assume that the interference system WCDMA system with the TD-SCDMA system adjacent band, using of frequency bands 1755MHz ~ 1785MHz for uplink and 1850MHz ~ 1880MHz for downlink, respectively. WCDMA system is also two-tier cellular architecture. WCDMA base station location is randomly generated in the TD-SCDMA system. Fig.1 illustrates a two-tier cellular configuration.

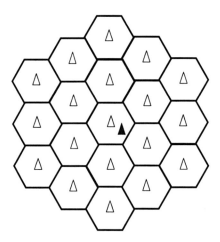

Fig. 1. System cell structure diagram

The hollow triangle represents the TD-SCDMA base station and solid triangle represents the WCDMA base station in Fig.1. To make clearly to indicate it, here only gives a WCDMA base station.

3   Interference Analysis

The interference of TD-SCDMA system is mainly the interference within the TD-SCDMA system and the interference of other systems. Interference within the system is mainly within the intra-cell interference and inter-cell interference. Because the code word is not completely orthogonal, CDMA system has multiple access interference. The user signals of multiple access interference have certain relevance. As the number of users and transmit power increases, MAI will rapidly increase. This analysis of the interference system is the WCDMA system which is adjacent with the TD-SCDMA system. WCDMA system uses of frequency bands 1755MHz ~ 1785MHz for uplink and 1850MHz ~ 1880MHz for downlink, respectively. As the WCDMA uplink band is far from the TD-SCDMA frequency bands, so this paper only considers the downlink frequency band on the impact of TD-SCDMA system. This means that only needs to assess WCDMA base stations on the impact of TD-SCDMA system. Therefore, interference of the TD-SCDMA base station in the uplink is:

$$I_{total} = (1-a)bI_{intra} + I_{inter} + I_{other} + N_0 \qquad (1)$$

Where I_{total} is interference experienced by the base station. I_{intra} is intra-cell interference which is generated by the mobile stations in the serving cell. I_{inter} is inter-cell interference which is due to the mobile stations in the neighbouring cells. I_{other} is the interference of TD-SCDMA system from the WCDMA system. N_0 is thermal noise.

$$I_{intra} = \sum_{j=1, j \neq i}^{N} P_{rj} \qquad (2)$$

I_{intra} can be calculated by the formula (2). P_{rj} is the base station received power from user j in the serving cell. N is the number of users in the serving cell.

$$I_{inter} = \sum_{m=1}^{M-1} \sum_{k=1}^{N} P_{rmk} \qquad (3)$$

$$P_{rmk} = P_{tmk} + G - L_{mk\_inter} \qquad (4)$$

$$P_{tmk} = P_{mk} - G + L_{mk} \qquad (5)$$

P_{rmk} is the interference power from the user k in cell m cell to the base station 0. P_{tmk} is the uplink transmit power of user k in cell m. P_{mk} is the received power of the base station m from user k in cell m. G is the Antenna gain. L_{mk_inter} is the path loss between the user k in cell m and base station 0. L_{mk} is the path loss between the user k in cell m and base station m.

$$I_{other} = \sum_{m=1}^{M} P_{rm} \qquad (6)$$

$$P_{rm} = P_{tm} + G_{WCDMA} + G_{TD-SCDMA} - L_m - ACIR \qquad (7)$$

P_{rm} is the received interference power from the WCDMA base station m to the TD-SCDMA base station 0. P_{tm} is the transmit power of the WCDMA base station m. G_{WCDMA} and $G_{TD-SCDMA}$ are the WCDMA TD-SCDMA base station antenna gains, respectively. Lm stands for the path loss between the WCDMA base station m and the TD-SCDMA base stations 0. ACIR is adjacent channel interference power ratio.

4 Propagation Model

In this paper, the propagation model between the base station and mobile station is applicable for simulation in urban and suburban areas outside the high rise core where the buildings are of nearly uniform height. Path loss can be obtained by the formula (8).

$$L = 40(1-4\times10^{-3}\text{Dhb})\lg(d)-18\lg(\text{Dhb})+21\lg(f)+80 \text{ dB} \qquad (8)$$

Where f is carrier frequency and d is the distance between transmitter and receiver. Dhb is the base station antenna height.

The propagation model between base stations uses the two slope line-of-sight propagation model. Path loss can be calculated by the formula (9).

$$L = \begin{cases} -27.56+20\lg(f)+20\lg(d) & 1<d<d_r \\ -27.56+20\lg(f)-20\lg(d_r)+40\lg(d) & d>d_r \end{cases} \qquad (9)$$

where L is the path loss. f is the carrier frequency. d is the distance between the base stations antennas. d_r is the first Fresnel radius, where $d_r = 4\times d_1 \times d_2 / \lambda$. d_1 and d_2 are the two base station antenna heights respectively.

5 Capacity Analysis

System capacity is one of important parameters in network planning. It is necessary to analyze it so that capacity gets a trade-off between the desired quality and overall cost. Because the CDMA system is an interference-limited system, it is necessary to analyze TD-SCDMA system capacity.

Mobile users can get the services provided by the base station only when the signal to noise ratio to reach the threshold E_b / I_{target}.

$$\frac{E_b}{I} = \frac{W}{R} \bullet \frac{P_{ri}}{(1-a)bI_{intra} + I_{inter} + I_{other} + N_0} \qquad (10)$$

Where P_{ri} is the received power from the user i to the base station 0. W is chip rate. R is the data rate. a is the orthogonality factor. b is the MUD factor. Need to meet the formula (11), the user i can get the services provided by the base station.

$$\frac{E_b}{I} \geq \frac{E_b}{I_{target}} \qquad (11)$$

Assume the TD-SCDMA system has the perfect power control. The TD-SCDMA base station can get the same power P from each user.

$$\frac{E_b}{I} = \frac{W}{R} \bullet \frac{P}{(1-a)b(N-1)P + \sum_{m=1}^{M-1}\sum_{k=1}^{N}P_{rmk} + \sum_{m=1}^{M}P_{rm} + N_0} \qquad (12)$$

The noise rise is defined as the ratio of the total received wideband power to the noise power. It is shown as the formula (13).

$$\eta = \frac{(1-a)b(N-1)P + \sum_{m=1}^{M-1}\sum_{k=1}^{N}P_{rmk} + \sum_{m=1}^{M}P_{rm} + N_0}{N_0} \qquad (13)$$

By increasing the number of users to satisfy the E_b / I_{target} and the noise rise, the number of users N can be obtained from the formula (12) and (13).

6 Simulation Results

In the simulation process, the mobile user location is randomly generated with uniform distribution in the TD-SCDMA system. Increase the number of users to satisfy the E_b / I_{target} and the noise rise. Table 1 shows the lists of parameters used in the simulation.

Table 1. Simulation Parameters

Parameter	Value
MUD factor	0.6
Orthogonality factor	0.5
Noise power	-103dBm
E_b/I_{target}	6dB
Chip rate	1.28Mchip/s
Data rate	12.2kbps
Antenna gain	11dBi

In this paper, the noise rise is assumed to be 6dB. N1 is the number of users without the interference of the WCDMA system in TD-SCDMA system, i.e. $I_{other} = 0$. N2 is the number of users with the interference of the WCDMA system in TD-SCDMA system. The relative capacity loss can be obtained from N1 and N2. Fig.2 it shows the

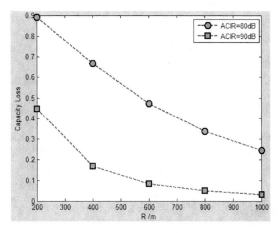

Fig. 2. The capacity loss with different cell radius

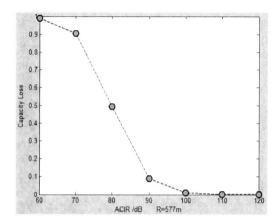

Fig. 3. The relationship between the ACIR and the capacity loss

relationship between the cell radius and the number of users supported in the cell 0 with different ACIR.

In Fig.3, it reflects the relationship between the ACIR and the number of users supported in the cell 0.

As the ACIR increases, the capacity loss reduces. When the ACIR is large, the impact of cell radius on the capacity is small. In order to obtain a larger system capacity, there should be a large ACIR. ACIR is an important factor to the affect the system capacity when two systems are in the same area. It reflects characteristics of the transmitter and receiver.

7 Conclusions

System capacity is one of important parameters in network planning. It is necessary to analyze it so that capacity gets a trade-off between the desired quality and overall cost. When two communication systems coexist, it is necessary to estimate the impact of interference between them. In this paper, TD-SCDMA system uplink capacity is analyzed when it is coexistence of WCDMA system. The multi-user detection features in the TD-SCDMA system must be also considered. To ensure the capacity of the system, there must be a suitable ACIR.

Acknowledgment

The title selection is mainly originated from Tianjin science and technology innovation special funds project(10FDZDGX00400) and Tianjin Key Laboratory for Control Theory and Application in Complicated Systems, Tianjin University of Technology, Tianjin 300384, China. The name of the project is "the research and development, demonstration and application of new generation mobile communication network coverage key technology".

References

1. Viveros-Talavera, J.G., Lara-Rodriguez, D.: Analytic Evaluation of the Uplink Erlang Capacity of CDMA Macrocells With Hotspot Microcells. In: Devices, Circuits and Systems, pp. 1–7 (2008)
2. Kim, D.K., Hwang, S.-H.: Capacity Analysis of an Uplink Synchronized Multicarrier DS-CDMA System. IEEE Communications Letters 6, 99–101 (2002)
3. Catrein, D., Imhof, L.A., Mathar, R.: Power Control, Capacity, and Duality of Uplink and Downlink in Cellular CDMA Systems. IEEE Transactions on Communications 52, 1777–1785 (2004)
4. Yang, M., Chong, P.H.J.: Uplink Capacity Analysis for Multihop TDD-CDMA Cellular System. IEEE Transactions on Communications 57, 509–519 (2009)
5. Chandrasekhar, V., Andrews, J.G.: Uplink Capacity and Interference Avoidance for Two-Tier Femtocell Networks. IEEE Transactions on Wireless Communications 8, 3498–3509 (2009)
6. Kishore, S., Greenstein, L.J., Poor, H.V., Schwartz, S.C.: Uplink User Capacity in a Multi-cell CDMA System with Hotspot Microcells. IEEE Transactions on Wireless Communications 5, 1333–1342 (2006)
7. Datta, S., Imran, M.A.: Constantinos Tzaras: Uplink Coverage-Capacity Estimation Using Analysis and Simulation. Telecommunications, 151–156 (2008)
8. Kim, J.G., Shin, S.-M.: Analysis of Uplink Capacity and Coverage in TD-SCDMA Systems. Advanced Communication Technology 1, 493–497 (2009)
9. Wu, X., Yang, L.-L., Hanzo, L.: Uplink Capacity Investigations of TDD/CDMA. Vehicular Technology Conference 2, 997–1001 (2002)

Inhibit Cross Time Slot Interference Research in TD-SCDMA System

Hong He[1,*], CongCong Wu[1], Tong Yang[2], and Lin He[2]

[1] Tianjin Key Laboratory for Control Theory and Application in Complicated Systems,
Tianjin University of Technology (China)
[2] Tianjin Mobile Communications Co., Ltd
heho604300@126.com

Abstract. Dynamic channel allocation in TD-SCDMA system belong to wireless resource management category, its main function is responsible for will channel allocation to the community, channel priority sequence, channel selection, channel adjustment and resources integration, thus better able to avoid interference and suit high-speed downlink asymmetric data business and multimedia services. Dynamic channel allocation (DCA) points slow DCA and rapid DCA. Slow DCA will be responsible to the community and wireless resource allocation downlink time buttress switch points adjust, be used to inhibit cross time buttress interference. Each district is divided into two parts, and only the cross time buttress channel resources to located inside, outside the mobile station residential area of mobile station can only use the cross time buttress channel resources.

Keywords: TD-SCDMA, Crossed Time Slot Interference, Dynamic Channel Allocation, DCA.

1 Introduction

TD-SCDMA system physical structure, each time a child frame in niche for 7 business time buttress (TS0 ~ TS6) and three special time buttress -- downlink guidance time buttress (DwPTS), up guiding time buttress (UpPTS) and protect time buttress (GP). Each business time buttress can support 1 ~ 16 mutually orthogonal different type code sudden business pulse simultaneous transmission[1].

Cross time buttress interference is TD-SCDMA system within the influence interference, because of TD-SCDMA system business time buttress is dynamically allocated, when appeared in neighboring cells or between residential frequency with between the normal moveout downlink do not agree, or when basestation synchronization between frames signal, it will appear this kind of interference..

TD-SCDMA system business time buttress is dynamically allocated, when this way appeared in neighboring cells or between residential frequency with between the normal moveout downlink abhorrent when may generate interference. For example,

---

* Hong He, School of Electrical Engineering, Tianjin University of Technology (China), 300384.

G. Shen and X. Huang (Eds.): CSIE 2011, Part II, CCIS 153, pp. 258–264, 2011.
© Springer-Verlag Berlin Heidelberg 2011

when the first residential use a time buttress transmission uplink information, while the second neighboring cells using this time buttress transmission downlink link information, then these two area exists between the interference. Basestation synchronization between frames signal, also will appear this kind of interference.

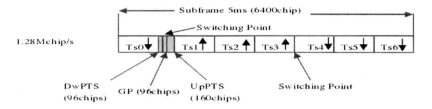

Fig. 1. System physical structure

Based on the analysis, by moving platform of assistance in the district switch, interference mobile users can avoid the interference of time and can avoid wireless carrier interference. Through a merger of time domain and frequency domain and airspace dynamic channel allocation technology, TD-SCDMA automatically will minimize interference system itself.

2 Dynamic Channels for Slow DCA

In the use of priority sorting order for slow DCA, when a certain area to create new channel demand, network will follow from high to low priority level this village channel testing: if a channel has been occupied, then skip the channel, if the channel to the current interference is free, and the measured value measurement values and threshold I_{th} comparison.

When K^{th} channel request, when the first produced i^{th} channel is to have the highest priority idle channel, then system to calculate the quality evaluation variables $s_i(k)$:

$$S_i(k) = \begin{cases} 1, I_i < I_{th} \\ 0, I_i > I_{th} \end{cases} \tag{1}$$

Then the ith channel priority could be calculated as follows:.

$$T_i(k) = T_i(k-1) + 1 \tag{2}$$

$$S_i(k) = S_i(k-1) + s_i(k) \tag{3}$$

$$p_i(k) = \frac{S_i(k)}{T_i(k)} \tag{4}$$

If using iterative calculation equations can be expressed as:

$$T_i(k) = T_i(k-1) + 1 \tag{5}$$

$$p_i(k) = \frac{T_i(k)-1}{T_i(k)} p_i(k-1) + \frac{s_i(k)}{T_i(k)} \tag{6}$$

Type (6) is in essence a kind of without weighted priority update process, and its updates are based on the channel in the past time preferences and the present moment channel interference values. From type (6) also can see, with the passage of time, the priority level adjustment for channel interference less sensitive, namely the priority tends to be fixed value. In order to overcome the limitations, using such as type (4) (6) is assignment-compatible priority weighting adjustment method.

$$p_i(k) = \frac{\sum_{h=0}^{\infty} \lambda^h s_i(k-h)}{\sum_{h=0}^{\infty} \lambda^h} \tag{7}$$

$$p_i(k) = \lambda p_i(k-1) + (1-\lambda)s_i(k) \tag{8}$$

Type (8) the iterative way also made full use of the regulating object current interference information and priority historical information. Parameter represents the system of the past when iteration record of the memory, so it is also called forgetting factor.

3   TD-SCDMA System Cross Time Buttress Disturbance Characteristics

According to neighboring cells downlink time buttress whether divided consistent, TD-SCDMA system disturbance characteristics mainly for cent two kinds of. When the neighboring cells downlink time buttress division consistent, main show is base station, the terminal, terminal - base station of interference, the interference and FDD mode is same, less influence, In neighboring cells downlink time buttress partition are abhorrent, main show is base station - base station, terminal, the terminal interference, this is TDD mode peculiar interference, called the cross time buttress interference, cross time buttress interference is stronger, serious will affect system performance.[2]

3.1 Neighboring Cells Downlink Time Buttress Division Agreement

Within the system of time buttress downlink adjacent area differentiate consistent, neighboring cells interference among performance for terminals, base station of interference and stations, terminal interference, as shown in figure 2 and figure 3 shown:

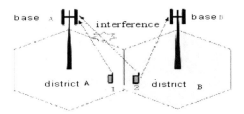

Fig. 2. Base station of interference

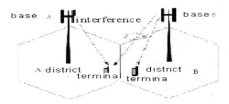

Fig. 3. The terminal interference

In fig.2, A village inside uplink channel by B village uplink signal interference. B area of terminal 2 what send A village of power interference uplink channel, but due to the terminal 2 power small and terminal 2 and base station between A path loss bigger, so interference ability is limited.

In fig.3, A village inside for downlink channel by B village downlink signal interference. B inside the village base station B has signal interference A community for downlink channel, although the power base station B launch larger, but for downlink channel better quality, strong anti-jamming capability, and the base station B and the terminal 1 between path loss bigger, so interference is not serious.[3]

3.2 Downlink Adjacent Area Differentiate Time Buttress Inconsistency

Within the system of time buttress downlink adjacent area differentiate abhorrent when, cross time buttress inside the village interference between performance for the base station and stations and terminal and terminal of interference, as shown in fig. 4 below.

Base station and base station of interference, in cross time buttress, A launch base for the terminal of received signal will 1 terminal 2 signal base B cause interference, the interference of the base stations incentive is negotiable. Because of the base station transmission power, big, antenna gain higher, and the path loss is small, so will seriously interfere with base station B receiving terminal 2 emission signal. Terminal and terminal disturbances, in the cross time buttress, terminal 2 launch to base station of B signal will receive A disturbance terminal 1 base of the signal, this is terminal and terminal of interference. Generally speaking terminal transmit power small and terminal between path loss is big, interference is not serious. But when terminal 1 and terminal 2 distance is close, terminal 2 would seriously interfere with terminal receiving A launch base station 1 of signal.

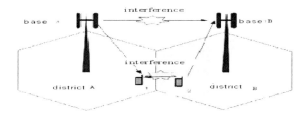

Fig. 4. Downlink adjacent area differentiate time buttress inconsistency

Research shows that cross time buttress within the interference very serious, especially with the interference of base stations serious influence the quality of traffic makes cross time buttress in bear uplink business district can hardly work. In the village, undertake downlink business cross time buttress can generally normal work, but in residential edge may be strong interference, make its not stable job, if not done special processing, cross time buttress within the strong interference can lead to large capacity loss.[4][5]

4 Slow DCA Channel Allocation

Due to the channel in the choice of sorting allocation strategies good compromise the DCA performance and computational complexity, so it has been widely used. To obtain DCA channel allocation cost function definition, first three collections[6][7]:

(1) $I(x)$ according to the specific criterion to the village said x exist interference of interference village set; (2) $\Lambda(x)$ for village x available channel set; (3) $F_D(x)$ for village x according to the channel reoccupy principle fixed allocation obtain S a channel collections, which if system channel for a total of M, multiplexing factor for K, then $S = M / K$; On the hexagonal village assumptions, $K = D^2 / 3R^2$, D for reuse distances, R for village radius.

Then for $i \in \Lambda(x)$, $y \in I(x)$ contribution by interference district and value $C_x(y, i)$ can be expressed as:

$$C_x(y, i) = v_y(i) + 2(1 - q_y(i)) , \quad \forall y \in I(x) \tag{9}$$

Here

$$v_y(i) = \begin{cases} 1, i \in \Lambda(x) \\ 0, \text{other} \end{cases} \tag{10}$$

$$q_y(i) = \begin{cases} 1, i \in F_D(y) \\ 0, \text{other} \end{cases} \tag{11}$$

In fact $C_x(y, i)$ only four value, namely

$$C_x(y, i) = \begin{cases} 0, & i \notin \Lambda(y) \cap i \notin F_D(y) \\ 1, & i \in \Lambda(y) \cap i \notin F_D(y) \\ 2, & i \notin \Lambda(y) \cap i \in F_D(y) \\ 3, & i \in \Lambda(y) \cap i \in F_D(y) \end{cases} \tag{11}$$

To sum up, for each $i \in \Lambda(x)$ channel, its cost function for

$$C_x(i) = q_x(i) + \sum_{y \in I(x)} \{C_x(y, i)\}, \forall i \in \Lambda(x) \tag{12}$$

Then the channel allocation principles for: if the $\Lambda(x) \neq \varnothing$, $i^* (\in \Lambda(x))$ is distribution channel should satisfy the:

$$C_x(i^*) = \min_{i \in \Lambda(x)} \{C_x(i)\} \tag{13}$$

If define a particular channel release event occurs, the village x is occupied channel set for A (x). For channel $j \in A(x)$, by interference village $y \in I(x)$ contributors to release cost function:

$$R_x(y, j) = b_x(y, j) + 2q_x(j), \quad \forall y \in I(x) \tag{14}$$

Here,

$$b_x(y, j) = \begin{cases} 0, \text{If j assigned to x in y locked} \\ 1, \text{other} \end{cases} \tag{15}$$

So $R_x(y, j)$ consists of four values:

$$R_x(y, j) = \begin{cases} 0, & j \in \Lambda_x(y, j) \cap j \in F_D(y) \\ 1, & j \notin \Lambda_x(y, j) \cap j \in F_D(y) \\ 2, & j \in \Lambda_x(y, j) \cap j \notin F_D(y) \\ 3, & j \notin \Lambda_x(y, j) \cap j \notin F_D(y) \end{cases} \tag{16}$$

Type(16), $\Lambda_x(y, j)$ said that if j in x, y village after release available channel collection. To sum up, the channel $j \in A(x)$ total cost function for release

$$R_x(J) = 1 - q_x(j) + \sum_{y \in I(x)} \{R_x(y, j)\}, \forall j \in \Lambda(x) \tag{17}$$

Type(17), $1 - q_x(j)$ the meaning of priority to release, the principle of distribution according to FCA does not belong to x village channel. Chooses is to put the principle of channel for $j^* \in A(x)$, makes

$$R_x(j^*) = \min_{j^* \in A(x)} \{ R_x(j) \} \tag{18}$$

If the actual release channel $j^\wedge$ is different from j^* channel, the case shall then be the business switch to the $j^\wedge$, j^* and then release channel resources.

5 Conclusion

Slow DCA completed tasks mainly in each district allocate time between the village, in order to achieve maximum capacity, so TD-SCDMA system use the slow DCA algorithm of orders for each district is reasonably according to its business arrange their village inside downlink time distribution, and considering the cross time buttress interference effects makes the system to achieve a maximum.

Acknowledgment

The title selection is mainly originated from Tianjin science and technology innovation special funds project(10FDZDGX00400) and Tianjin Key Laboratory for Control Theory and Application in Complicated Systems, Tianjin University of Technology, Tianjin 300384, China.The name of the project is "the research and development, demonstration and application of new generation mobile communication network coverage key technology".

References

1. Huan, J., Liu, J.: International Conference on Fuzzy Systems and Knowledge Discovery (2010)
2. Liu, Y.: Researeh of Adaptive Algorithm for Smart Anterma in TD-SCDMA System. Harbin Engineering University (2009)
3. Peng, M., Wang, W.: A framework for investing radio resource management algorithms in TD-SCDMA systems. IEEE Communications Magazine 43(6), 12–18 (2005)
4. Peng, M., Wang, W.: TDD-CDMA Capacity Loss due to Adjacent Channel Interference in the Macro Environment Employing Smart Antenna Techniques. AP-RASC 2004, 753–756 (2004)
5. Calin, D., Areny, M.: Impact of Radio Resource Allocation Policies on the TD-CDMA System Performance:Evaluation of Major Critical Parameters. IEEE Journal on Selected Areas in Communications 19(10), 1847–1859 (2001)
6. Zhang, Q., Xing, X.: Instrumentation Analysis Monitoring, vol.1, p. 22 (2010)
7. Information on http://bbs.cnttr.com/index.php

The Tightest Geometry for Lowest GDOP in Range-Based 2-D Wireless Location Systems

Qingyi Quan

Wireless Signal Processing and Network Lab
Key Laboratory of Universal Wireless Communication, Ministry of Education
School of Information and Communication Engineering
Beijing University of Posts and Telecommunications
Beijing, P.R. China
qyquan@bupt.edu.cn

Abstract. In wireless location systems the geometry between target and measuring points influences the positioning accuracy of the target. It is usually quantified by the geometric dilution of precision (GDOP). The GDOP depends on the geometry between target and measuring points. In this paper, firstly, a close form for the GDOP is derived as a function of both the number of measuring points and their bearing angle relative to the target. Then, such geometries that produce the lowest GDOP are reviewed with the close form expression of GDOP. Finally, a new geometry is proposed for absolute-range based 2-dimension (2-D) wireless location systems. The proposed geometry not only has the lowest GDOP but also forms the narrowest sector. In the proposed geometry all measuring points are distributed within a sector of $\pi/2$, relative to the target.

Keywords: GDOP, Absolute-range, Geometry, 2-D wireless location system.

1 Introduction

In the last decade, various wireless location systems have been studied for different applications [1][2]. Most of them are based on measurements of physical quantities related to the radio signal traveling between the target and a given set of measuring points whose location is known. These physical quantities generally provide information about the ranges between the target and measuring points, and/or the bearings of the target relative to the measuring points.

The positioning performance of these systems depends on both the measurement accuracy for physical quantities and the geometry between target and measuring points in the system. The influence of the geometry between target and measuring points on the positioning accuracy is usually quantified by GDOP. GDOP describes the effect of the geometry on the relationship between measurement error and position determination error.

It is shown in [3] that the lowest GDOP in range-based 2-D wireless location system is achieved when the measuring points surround the target uniformly. For the convenience of presentation, this geometric relationship between the target and

G. Shen and X. Huang (Eds.): CSIE 2011, Part II, CCIS 153, pp. 265–270, 2011.
© Springer-Verlag Berlin Heidelberg 2011

measuring points is denoted by GEO1. It is also shown in [3] that the GDOP is reduced with increasing the number of measuring points.

In [4] the geometry between target and measuring points is investigated in terms of the determinant of Fisher information matrix, instead of GDOP. Two geometries producing the maximum determinant of Fisher information matrix are presented for rang-based 2-D location system. One of them is GEO1. The other geometry is that in which all measuring points are uniformly distributed on one side of the target, i.e. all measuring points are distributed relative to the target within a sector having an angle of approximately 180 degrees. This geometry is denoted by GEO2.

This paper proposes a tighter geometry than the GEO2. In the proposed geometry, all measuring points are distributed within a sector of $\pi/2$, relative to the target. This geometry is denoted by GEO3.

2 Problem Formulation

There is a single stationary target located at $\mathbf{p}_T = [x_T, y_T]^T$. A set of N ($N \geq 2$) measuring points are placed at locations $\mathbf{p}_i = [x_i, y_i]^T$, $i = 1,2,...,N$. The i-th measuring point is a distance d_i away from the target, where $d_i = \sqrt{(x_i - x_T)^2 + (y_i - y_T)^2}$. In range-based wireless location system the measured range at the i-th measuring point obeys the following model

$$z_i = d_i + w_i, \ i = 1,2,...,N,$$

where w_i represents the noise caused by the receiver at $\mathbf{p}_i$. The measurement noises w_i, $i = 1,2,...,N$, are assumed to be mutually independent and Gaussian distributed with zero mean and the same variance σ^2, i.e. $w_i \sim N(0, \sigma^2)$. The range measurements from N measuring points can be stacked as follows

$$\mathbf{z} = \mathbf{d} + \mathbf{w} \tag{1}$$

such that $\mathbf{z} \sim N(\mathbf{d}, \mathbf{R})$, where $\mathbf{z} = [z_1, z_2,...,z_N]^T$, $\mathbf{d} = [d_1, d_2,...,d_N]^T$, and $\mathbf{R} = \sigma^2 \mathbf{I}_N$. Note that $\mathbf{I}_N$ is $N \times N$ identity matrix.

The range-based wireless location system produces an estimation $\hat{\mathbf{p}}_T$ of the target location $\mathbf{p}_T$ using the observable set of random range measurements $\mathbf{z}$. It is a nonrandom parameter estimation problem under white Gaussian noise. The variances of the minimum variance unbiased (MVU) estimator for the target location $\mathbf{p}_T$ is described by Cramer-Rao Lower Bound (CRLB) which is derived by the inverse of the Fisher information matrix [5].

According to the measurement model (1), the likelihood function of $\mathbf{p}_T$, given the measurement vector $\mathbf{z}$, is represented by

$$f(\mathbf{z}; \mathbf{p}_T) = \frac{1}{(2\pi\sigma^2)^{N/2}} \exp[-\frac{1}{2\sigma^2}(\mathbf{z} - \mathbf{d})^T(\mathbf{z} - \mathbf{d})].$$

Thus, the Fisher information matrix is as follows

$$\mathbf{I}(\mathbf{p}_T) = \frac{1}{\sigma^2}\mathbf{J}^T\mathbf{J} \tag{2}$$

where $\mathbf{J}$ is the Jacobian of the distance vector $\mathbf{d}$ with respect to the parameter $\mathbf{p}_T$. It follows from the definition of $\mathbf{d}$ that

$$\mathbf{J} = \begin{bmatrix} \dfrac{x_T - x_1}{d_1} & \dfrac{y_T - y_1}{d_1} \\ \dfrac{x_T - x_2}{d_2} & \dfrac{y_T - y_2}{d_2} \\ \cdots & \cdots \\ \dfrac{x_T - x_N}{d_N} & \dfrac{y_T - y_N}{d_N} \end{bmatrix} = \begin{bmatrix} -\cos\alpha_1 & -\sin\alpha_1 \\ -\cos\alpha_2 & -\sin\alpha_2 \\ \cdots & \cdots \\ -\cos\alpha_N & -\sin\alpha_N \end{bmatrix} \tag{3}$$

where α_i ($i = 1,2,...,N$) is the angle of the line linking points $\mathbf{p}_T$ and $\mathbf{p}_i$, relative to the baseline. It is illustrated in Figure 1. Without loss of generality we restrict the measuring point indexing such that $\alpha_j \geq \alpha_i$ when $j > i$ for $\forall i, j \in \{1,2,...,N\}$.

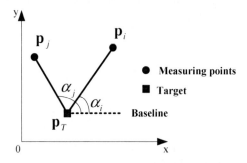

Fig. 1. The geometry between target and measuring points

Therefore, the variances of the MVU estimator for $\mathbf{p}_T$ are as follows

$$\mathrm{var}(\hat{x}_T) = [\mathbf{I}^{-1}(\mathbf{p}_T)]_{1,1} \tag{4}$$

$$\mathrm{var}(\hat{y}_T) = [\mathbf{I}^{-1}(\mathbf{p}_T)]_{2,2} \tag{5}$$

where $[\bullet]_{i,j}$ denotes the (i, j)-th element of a matrix.

In 2-D cases the GDOP is defined as [3]

$$GDOP = \frac{\sqrt{\mathrm{var}(\hat{x}_T) + \mathrm{var}(\hat{y}_T)}}{\sigma} \tag{6}$$

By using (2), (4) and (5), the GDOP in (6) can be represented as

$$GDOP = \sqrt{tr[(\mathbf{J}^T\mathbf{J})^{-1}]} \tag{7}$$

where $tr[\bullet]$ denotes the trace of a square matrix.

Substituting (3) into (7), The GDOP can be rewritten as

$$GDOP = \sqrt{2N / [\sum_{i=1}^{N}\sum_{j=1}^{N}\sin^2(\alpha_i - \alpha_j)]} \tag{8}$$

Note that $|\mathbf{J}^T\mathbf{J}| = \frac{1}{2}\sum_{i=1}^{N}\sum_{j=1}^{N}\sin^2(\alpha_i - \alpha_j)$

It is shown from (8) that the GDOP depends on the number of measuring points and their bearing angle relative to the target. The change in the distances between the target and measuring points does not influence the GDOP.

Therefore, the problem is formulated as finding the α_i ($i = 1,2,...,N$) that minimize the GDOP in (8), under a given number of measuring points N.

3   The Tightest Geometry for Lowest GDOP

The initial research on the lowest GDOP of range-based 2-D location system is addressed in [3]. It is shown in [3] that the lowest GDOP is $2/\sqrt{N}$ which is achieved when all measuring points are uniformly distributed around the target. It is briefly reviewed by the following Proposition 1 and Corollary 1.

Proposition   1.   Let $\alpha_{i+1} - \alpha_i = 2\pi / N$, $i = 1,2,...,N-1$,   and $N \geq 3$.   Then

$$\sum_{i=1}^{N}\sum_{j=1}^{N}\sin^2(\alpha_i - \alpha_j) = N^2 / 2 .$$

Corollary 1. If $\sum_{i=1}^{N}\sum_{j=1}^{N}\sin^2(\alpha_i - \alpha_j) = N^2 / 2$, then $GDOP = 2/\sqrt{N}$.

The corollary 1 is derived from the expression of GDOP in (8).

Recently, a new geometry GEO2 is addressed in [4] in addition to the above mentioned geometry GEO1. In the GEO2 all measuring points are uniformly distributed on a sector of approximately 180 degrees, relative to the target. Note that the GEO2 produces the lowest GDOP. It is concisely described by the following Proposition 2 and the above mentioned Corollary 1.

Proposition   2.   Let $\alpha_{i+1} - \alpha_i = \pi / N$, $i = 1,2,...,N-1$,   and $N \geq 2$.   Then

$$\sum_{i=1}^{N}\sum_{j=1}^{N}\sin^2(\alpha_i - \alpha_j) = N^2 / 2$$

In some applications, the measuring points are only possible to be distributed in a limited geometric space, relative to the target. They are, for instance, restricted to be distributed on only one side of the target, or within a sector of few degrees. Therefore, it is significant to study the tight geometries that produce the lowest GDOP.

The following Proposition 3 shows a tight geometry GEO3 which produces the lowest GDOP. In the geometry GEO3, all measuring points are distributed within a sector of $\pi / 2$.

Proposition 3. The number of measuring points N ($N \geq 2$) is even. Let $\alpha_i = 0$, $\alpha_{i+N/2} = \pi/2$, $i = 1,2,...,N/2$. Then $\sum\limits_{i=1}^{N}\sum\limits_{j=1}^{N}\sin^2(\alpha_i - \alpha_j) = N^2/2$

Here all measuring points are grouped into two groups. The measuring points in each group are distributed in a line. The case of odd N is described in the following corollary 2.

Corollary 2. The number of measuring points N ($N \geq 3$) is odd. Let $\alpha_i = 0$, $\alpha_{i+1+\lfloor N/2 \rfloor} = \pi/2$, $i = 1,2,...,\lfloor N/2 \rfloor$, and $\alpha_{1+\lfloor N/2 \rfloor} \in [0,\pi/2]$, where $\lfloor x \rfloor$ denotes the largest integer less than or equal to x. Then $\sum\limits_{i=1}^{N}\sum\limits_{j=1}^{N}\sin^2(\alpha_i - \alpha_j) = N^2/2 - 1/2$

The corollary 2 shows that the GDOP approaches the lowest value $2/\sqrt{N}$ with the increase of N.

Although GEO1, GEO2 and GEO3 produce the same lowest GDOP, the geometric spaces where the measuring points are distributed are different for GEO1, GEO2 and GEO3. It is summarized in the following Table 1. Here the geometric spaces are measured by the value of $(\alpha_N - \alpha_1)$. With the increase of the number of measuring points N, geometric spaces for GEO1 and GEO2 approach 2π and π, respectively. On the contrary, in GEO3 all measuring points are distributed within a sector of $\pi/2$, regardless of the number of measuring points N.

Table 1. The comparison of the geometric space among GEO1, GEO2 and GEO3

	GEO1	GEO2	GEO3
Geometric Space	$2\pi - 2\pi/N$	$\pi - \pi/N$	$\pi/2$

Proposition 4. If $\alpha_N - \alpha_1 < \pi/2$, then $\sum\limits_{i=1}^{N}\sum\limits_{j=1}^{N}\sin^2(\alpha_i - \alpha_j) < N^2/2$

The proposition 4 shows that the GEO3 is the tightest geometry with the lowest GDOP.

4 Conclusion

The close form for the GDOP in absolute-range based 2-D wireless location systems is derived based on the non-random parameter estimation theory. Then two existing geometries GEO1 and GEO2 are reviewed in terms of GDOP. The GEO2 is shown to produce the lowest GDOP. Finally a tight geometry denoted by GEO3 is proposed. The GEO3 is shown to produce the lowest GDOP. In the tight geometry GEO3, all measuring points are distributed within a sector of $\pi/2$, relative to the target. Also, it is shown that the GEO3 is the tightest one among the geometries that produce the lowest GDOP.

References

1. Porretta, M., Nepa, P., Manara, G., Giannetti, F.: Location, Location, Location. IEEE Vehicle Tech. Magazine 3(2), 20–29 (2008)
2. Mao, G., Fidan, B.: Localization Algorithms and Strategies for Wireless Sensor Networks. Information Science Reference (2009)
3. Levanon, C.: Lowest GDOP in 2-D Scenarios. In: IEEE Proc. Radar, Sonar Navig., vol. 147(3), pp. 149–155 (2000)
4. Bishop, A.N., Fidan, B., Anderson, B.D., Dogancay, K., Pathirana, P.N.: Optimality Analysis of Sensor-Target Localization Geometries. Automatica 46(3), 479–492 (2010)
5. Kay, S.M.: Fundamentals of Statistical Signal Processing. Estimation Theory, vol. 1. Prentice Hall, New Jersey (1993)

The Control of an IPM Synchronous Motor Drive Based on Using the Double-Regulation Control Mechanism

Wei Wang

Information School, Renmin University of China,
No.59, Zhongguancun, Beijing 100872, P.R. China
wwei@ruc.edu.cn

Abstract. In this paper, based on using a double-regulation control mechanism, we consider the control of an interior permanent-magnet (IPM) synchronous motor drive which may be interfaced by uncertainty and/or disturbance. The method can be summarized as follows: First, for the system which contains uncertainties and disturbances, we design the integral feedback by introducing a dynamic mechanism to adjust its gain so that the disturbances and uncertainties can be eliminated. Second, for the remaining part of the system, we choose the proper state feedback mechanism to ensure the required performance. Lyapunov analysis is provided to guarantee the stability of the relevant control system. Simulation results indicate the effectiveness of the method.

Keywords: synchronous motor; speed control; double regulation control mechanism.

1 Introduction

The control of a synchronous motor drive or a synchronous compensator has received increased attention in recent years ([1]-[6]). The uncertainties and/or disturbances of loading conditions are the main trouble in the control system synthesis. There have been many control methods proposed for dealing with uncertainties, for example, sliding-mode control, fuzzy-PI control, tuning of PI based on using particle swarm optimization, etc. ([1]-[9]).

If we can find an effective way to reject disturbances and uncertainties, the design for the remaining part will be easier. It is well known that the sliding mode (SM) method has played an important role for disturbance or uncertainty rejection ([1], [4], [5]). But the associated control switching will lead to chattering. Although PID-type control has strong ability to reject the uncertainty or disturbance, the tuning of its parameters will need more skills ([7]-[9]).

In order to solve the problem stated above, inspired by the idea of SM, we intend to find a systematic method so that disturbance compensation and high accuracy regulation can be implemented by using two kinds of feedback mechanism. That is the double-regulation control mechanism (DRCM) we will consider.

G. Shen and X. Huang (Eds.): CSIE 2011, Part II, CCIS 153, pp. 271–277, 2011.
© Springer-Verlag Berlin Heidelberg 2011

The paper is organized as follows: In section 2, the problem on the control of the synchronous motor is introduced. In section 3 the idea of DRCM is described, and the Lyapunov analysis is provided to guarantee the stability of the whole control system. In section 4, simulation results are shown to indicate the efficiency of the method, followed by some conclusions.

2   The Statement of the IPMSM Problem

For an interior permanent-magnet synchronous motor (IPMSM), the model can be described by the following differential equation

$$\frac{dx}{dy} = f(x) + g(x)u \tag{1}$$

where $x = (i_d \ i_q \ \omega_r)^\tau$, $u = (v_d \ v_q)^\tau$, $g(x) = \begin{pmatrix} 1/L_d & 0 \\ 0 & 1/L_q \\ 0 & 0 \end{pmatrix}$, and

$$f(x) = \begin{pmatrix} f_1(x) \\ f_2(x) \\ f_3(x) \end{pmatrix} = \begin{pmatrix} -\dfrac{R}{L_d} i_d + P \dfrac{L_q}{L_d} i_q \omega_r \\ -\dfrac{R}{L_q} i_q - P \dfrac{L_d}{L_q} i_d \omega_r - P \dfrac{\lambda_f}{L_d} \omega_r \\ \dfrac{3}{2} P \dfrac{L_d - L_q}{J} i_d i_q + \dfrac{3}{2} P \dfrac{\lambda_f}{J} i_q - \dfrac{B}{J} - \dfrac{T_L}{J} \end{pmatrix} \tag{2}$$

and the meanings and their values of the parameters in (1) and (2) can be found in [1] or [10]. We hope that the outputs i_d and ω_r can track the reference values $i_d^* = \frac{L_d - L_q}{\lambda_f} i_q^2$, ω_r^* respectively.

3   The Method of the Double Regulation Control Mechanism

For the sake of simplicity, we take, for an example, the second-order system in state-space form

$$\begin{cases} \dot{x}_1 = x_2 \\ \dot{x}_2 = f(x_1, x_2) + d(t) + bu \end{cases} \quad t \geq t_0 \tag{3}$$

where $f(x_1, x_2)$ be the definite function of x_1, x_2, and $d(t)$ be the representative of un-certainties and disturbances. We hope that the states x_1 and x_2 can track the set outputs respectively. In order to solve the synthesis problem, we hope to eliminate or reject the disturbances and uncertainties first, and then we force the system (3) to change in the following way

$$\begin{cases} \dot{x}_1 = x_2 \\ \dot{x}_2 = f(x_1, x_2) + bu_{II} \end{cases} \tag{4}$$

where u_{II} is the proper state feedback which is only for the remaining part.

Here we use u_I as the integral feedback with a variable gain. Therefore the control system synthesis can be divided into two parts: u_I and u_{II}, in which u_I is used for uncertainties and disturbances rejection, and u_{II} for the output regulation of the remaining part. That is the feature of the DRCM method.

To implement the idea proposed above, the key problem is the choice of a proper dynamic mechanism used for adjusting the gain of the integral feedback u_I. Here, based on the results considered in [11], we choose the dynamic mechanism $\mu(t)$ as follows, which is described by the following differential equation

$$\dot{\mu}(t) = \begin{cases} -\gamma \operatorname{sgn}(\sigma(x)), & as \, |\mu(t)| \le 1 \\ -\omega\mu, & as \, |\mu(t)| > 1, \quad \mu(t_0) = \operatorname{sgn}(\sigma(x(t_0))) \end{cases} \tag{5}$$

where $\sigma(x)$ should be the part which will be left after the rejection of uncertainties and disturbances, and $\omega \, (> 0)$ is a given positive constant.

As for the adjustment of $\mu(t)$ to the gain of the integral feedback, we will choose the form in the following way

$$u_I(t) = a_0 \mu(t) \int_{t_0}^t |x_1(\tau)| d\tau \tag{6}$$

where a_0 is also a design parameter.

As to the possibility of choosing the design parameters γ and a_0 to reject the disturbance, we have some theoretical results for second-order systems ([12]).

Theorem 1. Consider the following interconnected system

$$\begin{cases} \dot{x}_{i1} = x_{i2} \\ \dot{x}_{i2} = f_i(x_{i1}, x_{i2}) + g_i(x_1, \cdots, x_m) + d_i(t) + u_{Ii}(t) + u_{IIi}(t) \end{cases} \tag{7}$$

where $i=1,\ldots, m$, in which, $g_i(x_1,\ldots,x_m)$ are the interconnected parts, $x_i=(x_{i1},x_{i2})$. Suppose that $u_{Ii}(t)=a_{i0}\mu_i(t) \int_{t_0}^t \sum_{i=1}^m |x_{i1}| d\tau$, and $\mu_i(t)$ is also given by (5).

Let

$$\sigma_i(e) = d_i(t) + g_i(x_1, \cdots, x_m) + u_{Ii}(t) , \quad i=1,\ldots,m \tag{8}$$

Then as

$$a_{i0} > \sup_{t > t_0} \left| \frac{d_i(t) + g_i(x_1, \cdots, x_m)}{\int_{t_0}^t \sum_{i=1}^m |x_{i1}| d\tau} \right| , \quad i=1,\ldots, m \tag{9}$$

and

$$\gamma_i > \sup_{t > t_0} \left| \frac{a_{i0}(\sum_{i=1}^m |x_{i1}|) + \frac{d}{dt}[d_i(t) + g_i(x_1, \cdots, x_m)]}{a_{i0} \int_{t_0}^t \sum_{i=1}^m |x_{i1}| d\tau} \right| , \quad i=1,\ldots,m \tag{10}$$

hold, there is a finite time t', as $t \geq t'$, the following equalities hold

$$d_i(t) + g_i(x_1, \cdots, x_m) + u_{Ii}(t) = 0 \quad i=1,\ldots,m \tag{11}$$

From Theorem 1 we know that, instead of using an estimator or observer for disturbances and/or uncertainties, we can reject or compensate those factors by using $u_I(t)$. And, in contrast to other methods, the method on disturbance rejection has nothing to do with the interconnected terms of systems. Therefore the method has less requirements for systems' structure. That will greatly reduce the complexity for choosing the design parameters.

After the rejection of disturbances or uncertainties, and the interconnected terms, we need to choose the second state feedback mechanism.

In order to improve the efficiency of output regulations, based on the idea of nonlinear PID controllers ([13]), the control $u_{II}(t)$ can be chosen as

$$u_{II}(t) = -a_1|x_1(t)|^\alpha \text{sgn}(x_1(t)) - a_2|x_2(t)|^\alpha \text{sgn}(x_2(t)) \tag{12}$$

where $0 < \alpha < 1$.

The parameters such as a_1, a_2 in (12) can be chosen by using placement of poles. Especially, for linear error systems, we can choose the parameters based on the Hurwitz rules.

In such a case, we can choose the Lyapunov function as follows:

$$V = \frac{a_1}{\alpha+1}|x_1|^\alpha + \frac{1}{2}x_2^2 \tag{13}$$

From the Krasovskii Theorem, we know the remaining part is stable. So with the Lyapunov functions of (13), we can prove the stability of the whole system.

Based on the analysis above, we can give an explanation about the essential of control strategy. It uses VSC with continuous switch mechanism to reject the disturbance, and it chooses another sliding mode according to the given control requirements for the system. The combination of the two kinds of mechanism will strengthen the efficiency of any one of the other control.

4 Some Simulation Results

Now, we will present some simulation results on the output regulation for the IPMSM to indicate the effectiveness of the method based on DRCM.

According to the explanation of Theorem 1, we need the higher-order derivatives of errors. Therefore we should do some signal processing first by using TDs ([13]). For avoiding chattering or getting better filtering effects, we process $y(t)$ by using the discrete form of TDs ([14]). We denote that the signals obtained from the TDs are x_{11} and x_{12}, the signals from the second of the cascaded TDs are denoted as x_{13} and x_{14} respectively, we can regard x_{14} as the second-order derivative of $y(t)$.

Similarly, we can process the reference input $y_r(t)$ by choosing proper TDs. If we denote the relevant results as x_{21}, x_{22}, x_{23} and x_{24}, we can obtain the error of $y(t)$ and $y_r(t)$, and its related variables as follows:

$$\begin{cases} e_0 = \int_0^t (x_{11} - x_{21})d\tau \\ e_1 = x_{11} - x_{21} \\ e_2 = x_{12} - x_{22} \\ e_3 = x_{14} - x_{24} \end{cases} \tag{14}$$

where e_1, e_2, e_0, and e_3 are the error, the error's derivative, the error's integration, and second-order derivative, respectively.

Then, for a second-order system, let $\mu(t)$ be the one determined by the following differential equation

$$\dot{\mu} = \begin{cases} -\gamma \mathrm{sgn}(\dot{e}_3 + a_1|e_1|^\alpha \mathrm{sgn}(e_1) + a_2|e_2|^\alpha \mathrm{sgn}(e_2)), & as \; |\mu(t)| \leq 1 \\ -\omega\mu, & as \; |\mu(t)| > 1, \quad \mu(t_0) = \mathrm{sgn}(\sigma(e(t_0))) \end{cases} \tag{15}$$

And based on the DRCM, the total control input is the following one

$$u(t) = a_0\mu|e_0(t)|^\alpha - a_1|e_1(t)|^\alpha \mathrm{sgn}(e_1(t)) - a_2|e_2(t)|^\alpha \mathrm{sgn}(e_2(t)) \tag{16}$$

where a_0 can be determined by the ranges of disturbance and disturbance's derivative, and the parameters a_1, a_2 can be obtained by assigning, which should maintain the stability of the state $(0, 0)$ of the remaining error system.

So we can choose a_0 and γ according to (9) and (10) respectively, and then we assign a_1, a_2 properly. As for the other types of error systems, we can deal with them in a similar way.

Generally, the parameters r_0, h, h_0 of TD are chosen based on the rules given in [13] and [14].

It is evident that the model of synchronous motor drive is a MIMO interconnected system. By introducing the error variables $e_1 = i_d - i_d^*$, $e_2 = \omega_r - \omega_r^*$, we obtain the following error system

$$\begin{pmatrix} \dot{e}_1 \\ \ddot{e}_2 \end{pmatrix} = \begin{pmatrix} \tilde{f}_1 \\ \tilde{f}_2 \end{pmatrix} + \tilde{G}u \tag{17}$$

where $\tilde{f}_1 = f_1(x) - 2i_q \frac{L_d - L_q}{\lambda_f} f_2(x)$, $\tilde{f}_2 = \frac{3}{2}P\frac{L_d - L_q}{J} f_1(x)i_q + \frac{3}{2}P\frac{L_d - L_q}{J} f_2(x)i_d - \frac{B}{J}f_3(x)$

$+ \frac{3}{2}P\frac{\lambda_f}{J} f_2(x)$, and $\tilde{G} = \begin{pmatrix} \frac{1}{L_d} & -\frac{2(L_d - L_q)}{L_q\lambda_f}i_q \\ \frac{3}{2}\frac{P}{J}\frac{L_d - L_q}{L_d}i_q & \frac{3}{2}\frac{P}{J}\frac{|\lambda_f + (L_d - L_q)i_d|}{L_q} \end{pmatrix}$, in which f_1, f_2 and the parame-

ters are all the same as (1).

Then let $u = \tilde{G}^{-1}v$, this can realize the decoupling to the error system (17). Then we can choose v_1, v_2 respectively. From the structure of this error system, for the control of i_d, we use PI control, and for the control of ω_r, we use PID-type control. Owing to the complexity of the interconnected system, we choose the parameters as follows. In (15), $\gamma = 10$, $\omega = 0.5$. In (16), $\alpha = 0.6$, $a_1 = 100$, $a_2 = 20$. The parameters in TD are $r_0 = 2200$, $h = 0.001$, $h_0 = 0.01$. The tracking results of the outputs i_d, ω_r in (1) are shown in Fig. 1

and Fig. 2, respectively. Compared with the method used in [1], without the help of other control such as artificial intelligence (AI), we can still get satisfactory results. So the structure of the control system here is also a simple one.

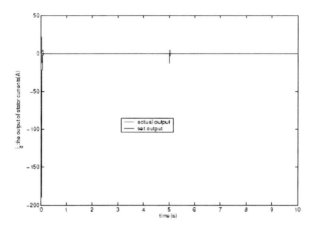

Fig. 1. The results of the output i_d in (1) tracking a given reference input

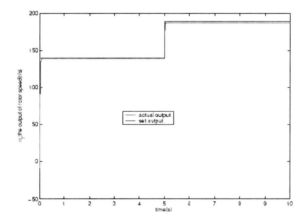

Fig. 2. The results of the output ω_r in (1) tracking a given reference input

It should be emphasized that, if we change the form of the model or the design parameters in certain ranges, the results on the output regulation may have almost no change at all. It indicates the robustness and adaptability of the method.

5 Conclusions

In this paper we consider the control of an interior permanent-magnet (IPM) synchronous motor drive by using a DRCM strategy. It is the DRCM that, by introducing a dynamic mechanism to adjust the gain of the integral feedback, we can reject disturbances or uncertainties. And then we can choose the gain or form of the state feedback (u_{II}) without concerning about disturbances or uncertainties. The idea and theoretical results are given. We also present some simulation results for certain parameters to indicate the effectiveness of the method.

It is the method proposed in this paper that we may use less design parameters in the controller. We need a small amount of information about the system. The method also has strong robustness and adaptability.

References

1. Foo, G., Rahman, M.F.: Sensorless Sliding-mode MTPA Control of an IPM Synchronous Motor Drive Using a Sliding-mode Observer and HF Signal Injection. IEEE Trans. on Ind. Electron. 57, 1270–1278 (2010)
2. Liu, C.-H., Hsu, Y.-Y.: Design of a Self-tuning PI Controller for a STATCOM Using Particle Swarm Optimization. IEEE Trans. on Ind. Electron. 57, 702–715 (2010)
3. Huang, W.-S., Liu, C.-W., Hsu, P.-L., Yeh, S.-S.: Precision Control and Compensation of Servomotors and Machine Tools via the Disturbance Observer. IEEE Trans. Ind. Electron. 57, 420–429 (2010)
4. Kim, B.K., Chung, W.K., Ohba, K.: Design and Performance Tuning of Sliding-mode Controller for High-speed and High-accuracy Positioning Systems in Disturbance Observer Framework. IEEE Trans. Ind. Electron. 56, 3798–3809 (2009)
5. Li, Y., Xu, Q.: Adaptive Sliding Mode Control with Perturbation Estimation and PID Sliding Surface for Motion Tracking of a Piezo-driven Micromanipulator. IEEE Trans. Control Syst. Technol. 18, 798–810 (2010)
6. Luo, A., Tang, C., Shuai, Z., et al.: Fuzzy-PI-based Direct-output-voltage Control Strategy for the STATCOM Used in Utility Distribution Systems. IEEE Trans. Ind. Electron. 56, 2401–2411 (2009)
7. Hernandez-Gomez, M., Ortega, R., Lamnabhi-Lagarrigue, F., Escobar, G.: Adaptive PI Stabilization of Switched Power Converters. IEEE Trans. Control Syst. Technol. 18, 688–698 (2010)
8. Hwu, K.I., Yau, Y.T.: Performance Enhancement of Boost Converter Based on PID Controller Plus Linear-to-nonlinear Translator. IEEE Trans. Power Electron. 25, 1351–1361 (2010)
9. Khodabakhshian, A., Hooshmand, R.: A new PID Controller Design for Automatic Generation Control of Hydro Power Systems. Int. J. Electrical Power & Energy Systems 32, 375–382 (2010)
10. Nasir Uddin, M., Abido, M.A., Azizur Rahman, M.: Development and Implementation of a Hybrid Intelligent Controller for Interior Permanent-magnet Synchronous Motor Drives. IEEE Trans. Ind. Appl. 40, 68–76 (2004)
11. Emelyanov, S.V., Korovin, S.K.: Control of Complex and Uncertain Systems: New Types of Feedback. Springer, Berlin (2000)
12. Wang, W.: The Stability Control for a Kind of Uncertain Networked Systems by Using a new Separation Principle. In: The 8th IEEE International Conference on Control and Automation, pp. 790–795. IEEE Press, New York (2010)
13. Han, J.Q., Wang, W.: Nonlinear Tracking-Differentiators. J. Syst. Sci. Math. Sci. 14, 177–183 (1994) (in Chinese)
14. Han, J.Q., Yuan, L.: The Discrete Form of Tracking-Differentiators. J. Syst. Sci. Math. Sci. 19, 268–273 (1999) (in Chinese)

A Hebbian-Based Quantum Learning Rule

Guang-Jun Xie and Hong-Jun Lv

School of Electronic Science & Applied Physics
Hefei University of Technology
Hefei, 230009, China
gjxie8005@hfut.edu.cn

Abstract. Because of the powerful and fantastic performance of quantum computation, some researchers have begun considering the implications of quantum computation on the field of artificial neural networks (ANNs). The purpose of this paper is to explore a universal Hebbian-based quantum learning rule for quantum neural networks (QNNs), at the same time, we concisely testify the converging performance of this new algorithm.

Keywords: Quantum computation; Quantum neural networks; Quantum learning.

1 Introduction

There are two main reasons to discuss quantum neural networks [1-3]. One has its origin in arguments for the essential role which quantum processes play in the living brain, and the second motivation is the possibility that the field of classical artificial neural networks can be generalized to the quantum domain by eclectic combination of that field with the promising new field of quantum computing. Both considerations suggest new understanding of mind and brain function as well as new unprecedented abilities in information processing. In this paper, we discuss a universal learning algorithm for quantum system, which act as one side of the discussion on quantum neural networks [4].

2 Quantum Hebbian-Based Learning Algorithm

Hebb's rule is assumed to be closely associated with biological learning, we think that Hebb's rule implemented in a quantum system leads to learning algorithm converging much faster because we observe that a Hebbian algorithm of learning framed as a quantum algorithm, leads to a much faster converging algorithm than it does as a non-quantum or classical algorithm [5]. Seen from the perspective of quantum computing this is not a surprising result.

Quantum systems are described by a wave function that exists in a Hilbert space. In the Dirac notation, we suppose that $|x\rangle = \alpha|0\rangle + \beta|1\rangle$, where $|0\rangle$ and $|1\rangle$ are quantum states, i.e. vectors in Hilbert spaces or qubits, they can be denoted by the different polarizations of photon or by the different spin directions of electron.

G. Shen and X. Huang (Eds.): CSIE 2011, Part II, CCIS 153, pp. 278–281, 2011.
© Springer-Verlag Berlin Heidelberg 2011

Consider, for example, a discrete physical variable called spin. The simplest spin system is a two-state system, called a spin-1/2 system, whose basis states are usually represented as $\uparrow$ (spin up) and $\downarrow$ (spin down).

Let us consider a perceptron, i.e. the system with n input channels $x_1, ..., x_n$, and one output channel y. The output of a classical perceptron is

$$y = f\left(\sum_{j=1}^{n} \omega_j x_j\right) \tag{1}$$

where $f(\cdot)$ is the perceptron activation function and ω_j are the weights tuning during learning process.

The Hebbian learning rule can be expressed as follows

$$\omega_j(t+1) = \omega_j(t) + \eta(d - y)x_j \tag{2}$$

where η is the learning rate and d is the desired output provided for teaching.

In the quantum system, we rewrite the perceptron using quantum mechanics symbols as

$$|y_i\rangle = \hat{F}\sum_{j=1}^{n} \omega_i^j |x_j\rangle \tag{3}$$

where $\hat{F}$ is an unknown operator that can be implemented by the network of quantum gates.

Now, the learning algorithm in that case is a quantum process, which makes original output state evolve into the desired output state. The learning process can be translated an evolutional process from the original quantum state to the ultimate quantum state, i.e. $|y\rangle_n \Rightarrow |d\rangle_m$. And then, the process of weights accommodation can also be interpreted as to find an appropriate set $\{\tilde{\omega}_i^j\}$, so, as Hamiltonian, it can be assumed as a quantum operator,

$$H = H_d + H_y = E\left\{\sum_{j=1}^{m} |d_j\rangle\langle d^j| + \sum_{j=1}^{m} |y_j\rangle\langle y^j|\right\} \tag{4}$$

where E is a constant, for the time being arbitrary. It is the eigenvalue of the Hamiltonian, i.e. it is in general the energy of the system. The unitary of the operator guarantees that there is conservation of probability.

Defining that $|d_i\rangle = (U_{H_d+H_y})_i^k |y_k\rangle$, we can get that $\tilde{\omega}_i^j = \sum_{k=1}^{m} (U_{H_d+H_y})_i^k \omega_k^i$.

We assume that the quantum states $|d_i\rangle$ and $|y_i\rangle$ are ortho-normal basis, then the weight matrix is changed to $\omega_i^j = |y_i\rangle\langle x^j|$ and $\tilde{\omega}_i^j = |d_i\rangle\langle x^j|$, the Hebbian learning rule can be expressed as follows

$$\delta\omega_i^j = \eta(|d_i\rangle - |y_i\rangle)|x^j\rangle$$

$$= -iE\sum_k \frac{\{(H_d + H_y)_i^k\}y_k\langle x^j|}{= -iE(|d_i\rangle\langle d|y\rangle + |y_i\rangle)\langle x^j|} \tag{5}$$

Specially, we used $\langle d|d\rangle = 1$, then $\langle d|y\rangle = a$, we yield

$$\delta\omega_i^j = -iE(|d_i\rangle a + |y_i\rangle)\langle x^j| \tag{6}$$

In succession, we simply testify the converge performance of the algorithm above-mentioned. Let us consider the simplistic case with $\hat{F} = 1$ being the identity operator. The output of the quantum perceptron at the time t will be

$$|y(t)\rangle = \sum_{j=1}^{n} \omega_j(t)|x_j\rangle \tag{7}$$

In analogy with the classical case, let us provide a learning rule

$$\omega_j(t+1) = \omega_j(t) + \eta(|d\rangle - |y(t)\rangle)|x_j\rangle \tag{8}$$

Then we yield

$$\left\| |d\rangle - |y(t+1)\rangle \right\|^2 = \left\| |d\rangle - \sum_{j=1}^{n} \omega_j(t+1)|x_j\rangle \right\|^2 \tag{9}$$

$$= (1 - n\eta)^2 \left\| |d\rangle - |y(t)\rangle \right\|^2$$

It is easy to show now, for small η ($0 < \eta < \frac{1}{n}$) and normalized input states $\langle x_j|x_j\rangle = 1$ the result of iteration converges to the desired state $|d\rangle$. This has been shown to correspond to a much shorter convergence time than the corresponding classical algorithm.

3 Discussion

Quantum computing owes its efficiency to quantum entanglement, a quantum learning algorithm for QNNs would correspond to an algorithm where the changes on the weights would be entangled, it may be useful to develop such algorithms because they could help study the relationship between information entanglement and Hebbian learning.

Acknowledgments. This work was supported by the Developing Talented People Foundation of Anhui province (No. 2007Z028) and the Natural Science Foundation of Anhui province (No. 090412038).

References

1. Kak, S.C.: On Quantum Neural Computing. Information Sciences 83, 143–160 (1995)
2. Ventura, D., Martinez, T.R.: Quantum Associative Memory. Information Sciences 124, 273–296 (2000)
3. Menneer, T., Narayanan, A.: Quantum-inspired Neural Networks, Technical Report R329, Department of Computer Science, University of Exeter, UK (1995)
4. Ezhov, A.A., Ventura, D.: Quantum Neural Networks. In: Kasabov, N. (ed.) Future Directions for Intelligent Information Systems and Information Sciences, pp. 213–235. Physica-Verlag, Heidelberg (2000)
5. Morel, B.: Biologically Plausible Learning Rules for Neural Networks and Quantum Computing. Neurocomputing 32-33, 921–926 (2000)

Design of Electrostatic Elimination System Based on PIC Microprocessor

JingZhong Wang, Jian Wang, and Fang Yang

Information Engineer College, North China University of Technology, BeiJing, China

Abstract. This paper introduces a kind of electrostatic elimination system based on PIC18LF6520 MCU. The equipment with PIC18LF6520 as control core generates high-voltage by Pulse AC Discharge to ionize the air to positive or negative ions that can neutralise the static in object surface. We can adjust the discharge frequency of stand-alone equipment so that it can have a good ions balance. Furthermore, the equipment can connect with others and transform data to the computer, which can monitor many sets of equipments status through the device's interface. So the system can eliminate the static electricity of work environment overall and efficiently.

Keywords: Electrostatic elimination; microcontroller; pulse AC.

1 Introduction

As the development of semiconductor manufacturing techniques, the importance of electrostatic control in production is increasing constantly. Electrostatic can cause device and light masking damage; equipment damage caused by electromagnetic interference reduced the equipment total usage, which is getting more frequent as control equipment microprocessor speed's improvement.

People have developed a variety of electrostatic processing methods. In Semiconductor manufacturing environment, conductors and electrostatic dissipative material grounding is used widely, but this can not eliminate static for charged insulators material. In this case, Static-eliminator can effectively eliminate static.

2 Static Eliminator Structure

As figure 1 shows, Static Eliminator uses PIC18LF6520 as CPU. As the high-grad MCU of PIC series, PIC18L6520 has high operation up to 10 MIPS, 10-bit and 12-channel A/D converter, lots of I/O interface up to 52, which fully meets our real-time data transmission, status display, data acquisition [4].

2.1 Input Module

Static-eliminator input module includes three parts, which is frequency adjustment, address setting and remote control receiving, respectively.

G. Shen and X. Huang (Eds.): CSIE 2011, Part II, CCIS 153, pp. 282–287, 2011.

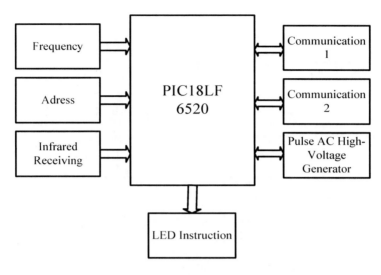

Fig. 1. Static Eliminator Whole Diagram

Frequency regulating module adjusts output voltage frequency, and through knob adjustment we can adjust eight different frequencies that are displayed by corresponding LED. Address setting provides 16 different addresses indicated by hex 0~9 and A~F, we can set the only identified address for running static-eliminator currently so that we can identify different equipments and show their working states respectively on PC. Infrared receiving modules offers long-distance manipulation for static-eliminator mainly used in the manipulation scope that static-eliminators are far away from people.

2.2 Communication Module

Each static-eliminator owes two communication interface, which can be used for data transmission among multiple static-eliminator series, also between the equipment and computer.

In many schemes of micro controller long-distance communication, RS485 bus has powerful anti-jamming capability. It's maximum transmission distance can be up to 1.2km and it's maximum transmission rate can reach 10Mbit/s. So communication between static-eliminator and PC uses RS485 communication mode [2].

This design communicates with external device by MAX485 chips. MAX485's connection is indicated as figure 2.

2.3 Pulse AC High-Voltage Generator

Voltage processing modules has two functions:

(1) Receiving square-wave signal from PIC microcontroller as voltage module inputs voltage.

The timer/counter TMR0/TMR1 module of PIC18F6520 can produce different frequencies of square wave by port pins RC0/RC1 as hardware timer controls. Because

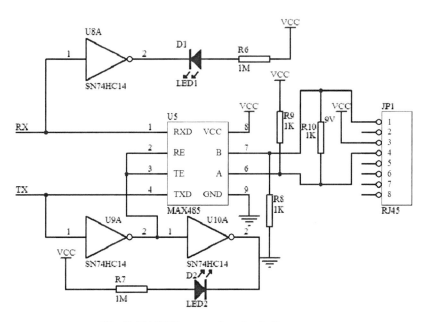

Fig. 2. MAX485 connection circuit diagram

TMR0/TMR1 is 8 bits wide, and has an optional prescaler, it can generate eight kinds of square wave signal with different frequencies.

This design's initial value is 2048. The instruction cycle will overflow after counting 2048. It can generate different frequencies by changing the divided frequency ratio. The output level of pins RC0 / RC1 will reverse when TMR0/TMR1 overflows, and a square wave signal cycles need two reversals.

When the divided frequency ratio is 1:256, the corresponding square wave signal frequency is 0.95 Hz. When the divided frequency ratio is 1:2, the corresponding square wave signal frequency is 122 Hz. It can generate 0.95 Hz, 1.9 Hz, 3.8 Hz, 7.6 Hz, 15.3 Hz, 30.5 Hz, 61, 122Hz respectively by changing TMR0 / TMR1's initial value.

(2) Check the output voltage value and return this value to microcontroller.

By figure 4 (a)indicating, we can see that the air only can be ionized into + or - ions in +3KV~+7KV and −3KV~−7KV, so the real-time monitoring for output voltage is necessary. Microcontroller judges the static-eliminator working condition through returned signal, and indicates different working condition through LED.

2.4   High-Voltage Discharge

It can ionize the air into positive or negative ions by high-voltage point discharge, which can neutralize the object surface static.

As is shown in figure 4, the pulse AC discharge generates + or-voltage at needle electrodes alternately, and it can generate more ions, which eliminates static quickly. Because the + or – ions are generated alternately at the same needle electrodes,

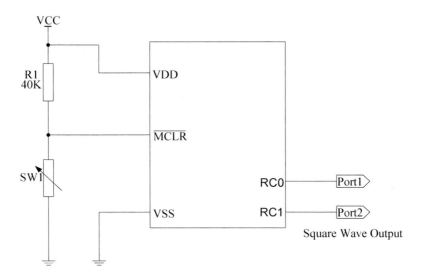

Fig. 3. Square wave signal generate circuit

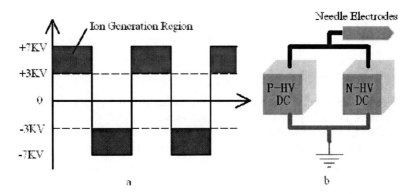

Fig. 4. Discharge port and waveform schemes

it has the excellent ion balance, especially it solves the disadvantage that pulse DC has terrible ions balance in both longer directions.

3 Software Design

Static-eliminator software control program mainly include the following modules: initialization module, data processing modules, data communication module, display module, interrupt module [1].

3.1 Initialization Module

The following is the initial PIC18F6520 procedures, which configure the A/D converter module and related registers.

```
void init()

{

ADCON0=0x81;

ADCON1=0x00;

ADIE=1;

PEIE=1;

TRISA=0xff;

TRISE0=1;

TRISE1=1;

TRISE2=1;

PORTA=0x00;

PORTE=0x00;

}
```

3.2 Data Processing Module

There are four special function registers related with timer/counter TMR0 in PIC18F6520, including accumulation count registers TMR0, interruption control register INTCON, control register CTL_REG and direction control of port RA register TRISA, in which the bit message of control register CTL_REG is:

D7	D6	D5	D4	D3	D2	D1	D0
TMR0ON	T08BIT	T0CS	T0SE	PSA	T0PS2	T0PS1	T0PS0

When the forth bit(PSA) is set to zero, TMR0 module is set to counter pattern, its frequency dividing ratio is decided by D2: DO (PS2 ~ PS0) of CTL_REG, and is 1:2, 1:4, 1:8, 1:16, 1:32, 1:64, 1:128, 1:256, which can generate eight kinds of separate frequency signal.

3.3 Data Communication

The system adopts master-slave response way, in which static-eliminator is in standby state usually, and is called by PC in time-sharing. System utilizes data-packet communication [3]. Communication data is transmitted in frames or in package, in which include guide code, length code, address code, command code, content, check code. Guide code is used for synchronization of per packet data's guide head, length code is total length of this package of data, command code is control command from host to static-eliminator(or static-eliminator answering machine),address code is static-eliminator local address, "Content" is various kinds of information of this package of data, check code is calibration mark.

4 Conclusion

This paper expounds a solution of electrostatic eliminating system, which makes PIC18LF6520 as control core of each piece of equipment, and transmits data to PC so that we can monitor the real-time system work condition. Also we can detect all equipment work condition only through one computer in large work space. And it achieves excellent ions balance by pulse AC alternating discharging way.

References

1. Lv, W., Zhang, K.: Design of Modern Greenhouse Control System Based on PIC18F6585. Mechatronics (8), 41–43 (2009)
2. Pan, Z.-r., Du, B.-q., Wang, S.-d., Xu, M.: The development of an industrial data acquisition card based on the PIC microcontroller. Industrial Instrumention & Automation (2), 71–74 (2007)
3. Chen, X.-x., Hu, Z.-r.: Design of PIC Based Central Air Conditioner Controller with Function of Network Communication. Instrument Technology (9), 34–36 (2010)
4. Microcchip Technology Inc., MicroChip PIC18LF6520 Datasheet, 131–135 (2004)

10 Series Battery Protection System Design Based on S-8261

ChangNian Zhang, Fang Yang, and Jian Wang

Information Engineering College, North China University of Technology,
Beijing, 100144, China
yf111221@163.com

Abstract. Single lithium battery protection circuit is easy to implement, but it is not widely used at present. This paper introduces a method of realizing power management for a lithium ion battery pack of multi-cell in series. A chip named S-8261 is the main component of the circuit system. The chip was designed for single-cell application. But we use it in 10 series battery protection system. The circuit system can provide over charge, over discharge, over current and short circuit protection for lithium battery. Circuit uses a simple and effective measure for energy balance which can improve the discharge efficiency of lithium batteries. At the same time there is a way to solve the heating phenomenon occurred during using. The system is simple to implement, low cost, and also efficient.

Keywords: Lithium cell, S-8261, Balance-protect.

1 Introduction

Lithium batteries have been widely used in consumer electronic device, electric vehicles and electric bicycle. There is little problem about single lithium battery's using. However, when multiple batteries connect in series tend to come out with a more serious problem. In the lithium group, every cell's normal operating voltage is maintained between two thresholds. If one of a battery voltage exceeds the maximum threshold (over voltage), or less than the minimum threshold (voltage) will damage the battery and reduce battery life. Therefore, batteries performance depends on the single worst performance cell of the batteries.

At present many literature only describes a single cell or 3-4 cells charge and discharge protection. There is little literature introduce more than 10 knots lithium batteries in series and no good balance measures. This paper introduces a protection system, which not only can achieve the basic functions of 10 series lithium battery power protection, but also can achieve power balance between the batteries and temperature protection. At the same time it is also relatively simple to implement and the performance is good. This system is mainly used in electric bicycles.

G. Shen and X. Huang (Eds.): CSIE 2011, Part II, CCIS 153, pp. 288–293, 2011.
© Springer-Verlag Berlin Heidelberg 2011

2 Single Lithium Battery Protection Systems

In order to improve efficiency and meet safety requirements, we need to provide a battery protection system for Battery pack. The system must meet the following requirements: over charge, over discharge, over-Current and short circuit, the protection of the battery temperature in the application process and power balance protection between the batteries. The system block diagram is shown in Fig. 1;

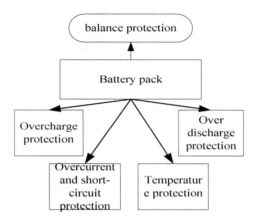

Fig. 1. Battery protection system block diagram

S-8261 is a chip which can meet the requirement of power management. The use of the chip is shown in Fig. 2. The chip detected battery voltage and controlled the circuit.

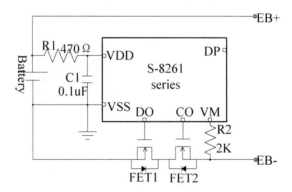

Fig. 2. Battery protection IC connection examples

When the battery voltage up to 4.2V and lasts longer than 1.2s, overcharge protection tube FET1 shut down. Then circuit stops charging. When the battery is discharging, the battery voltage is below 2.8V, and last more than 144ms, over discharge protection tube FET2 deadline stop provide power to the load. When the load current flows is greater, control FET1 stop provide power to the load discharge. This is Over-current protection. The purpose is to protect the battery and FET. Over-current detection is using of MOSFET on-resistance as a sense resistor to monitor its voltage drop, when the voltage drop exceeds a set value, to stop the discharge. EB+ and EB- positive and negative terminals respectively connected to the charger. In practice, the DP is not connected.

3   10 Series Lithium Battery Protection Circuit Subsystem

With the understanding of single lithium batteries protection circuit, we can expand a single lithium battery protection circuit so that it has more lithium batteries protection.

The first step is connecting the VM of each chip the positive terminal of the battery of the next cell and the last section of the VM connection way unchanged. As ten cells in series the discharge current is large, the system uses the same three FET1 parallel to control discharge in order to reducing the current flowing through each FET. Connection shown in Fig. 3:

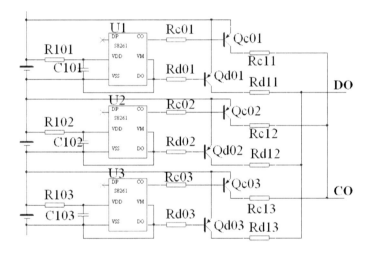

Fig. 3. 10 Lithium battery protection circuit connection string examples

3.1   Overcharge Protection

In the charging process, if the battery voltage exceeds the overcharge detection voltage (Vcu), and maintained at Overcharge detection delay time (Tcu by the chip set) or more, the chip is in the overcharge state. Then the chip will Output a low level in the CO pin, which will result in the PNP transistor connected to it on. The transistor emitter connected to the positive terminal of each battery. Then as long as the voltage of R1 above 0.7V, Q5 will turn on. Then gate voltage of Q4 is pulled down to low, and Q4 shut down. The charging path is disconnecting. The power in the circuit comes from the battery cell voltage 1-4 in Fig. 4.,

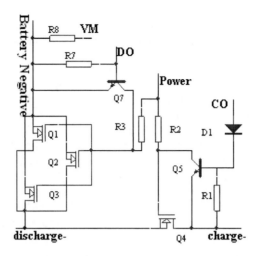

Fig. 4. Control circuit

3.2 Over-Discharge Protection

In the discharge process, if the battery voltage is lower than the over discharge detection voltage (VDL), and maintained at Overcharge detection delay time (TDL by the chip set) or more, the chip is over discharge state. Then the chip will outputs a low level in the DO Pin, the low will result in the PNP transistor connected to it on. The transistor emitter connected to the positive terminal of each battery, then as long as the voltage of R7 above 0.7V, Q7 will turn on. Then gate voltage of Q1, Q2, and Q3 is pulled down to low, and shut down. The discharging path is disconnecting.

Because discharging current is large, in case of safety reasons, we use three FET parallel to achieve the diversion effect. Use the switch's model is STP75NS04Z. Its internal resistance is relatively small and has good switching characteristics [2].

3.3 Over-Current and Short Circuit Protection

As shown in Fig. 4, a resistor connecting to VM pin of the last or the first protection chip in the main loop is used to measure the main circuit current. When the discharge current above the rated value, VM pin voltage is above the over-current detection voltage and the state to maintain a certain time (this time the decision by the circuitry inside the chip), the system will turn off the discharging FET, which is in over-current condition. In the over-current condition, the chip will make an internal short-circuit resistance to VM-VSS according to the voltage between VM and VSS. In the case of a load, VM pin voltage as determined by the load, and become the VDD voltage. After cutting off the load VM pin voltage change back to the VSS potential.

The load short-circuits protection, over current protection and over-current 1, 2 is the same protection principle, the difference is the circuit delay action.

3.4 Power Balance

In the battery pack application process maintaining power balance between the battery pack is a very important task. Generally Balancing circuits are divided into two categories: charge transfer and power consumption. Charge-transfer technology is difficult and costly. Therefore, the method we used is to balance the power consumption of electricity. Circuit shown in Fig. 5.:

As shown in Fig. 5, the circuit mainly use voltage difference between point a and b to balance the power. The value of R10 and R11 is equal. So the voltage of point a is the average of two lithium battery voltage, and the voltage of point b is the voltage value of CELL N. If the voltage of the two batteries is not equal, the input voltages of operation amplifier 741 are different. No matter positive or negative difference is, it always makes Q5 or Q6 conduction. The conduction transistor starts to adjust one of the lithium battery power until the two almost equal, then the difference between the op amp's input signal is becoming zero gradually. Then the transistor automatically turns off to achieve a balanced effect. For example, if the voltage of cell N +1 is larger than the voltage of cell N, then the voltage of point a is larger than the voltage of b. So the op amp's output is positive, which leads to Q5 conduction and Q6 closed. At this point the Q5, D1, D2, R13, CELL N +1 component a discharge circuit [3]. At the same time circuit use a set of back to back Zener diodes to protect the lithium battery from excessive self-discharge and damage.

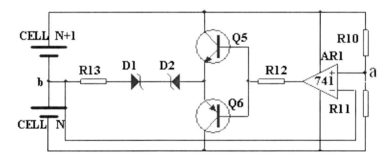

Fig. 5. Energy balance modules

Under normal circumstances, when the voltage of point a is equal to the voltage of point b, balance circuit will close and stop discharging. In the absence of the two Zener diodes, once one of the battery connections is not connected well, it could result in the voltage of a battery has been discharged to zero, and makes serious damage to the lithium battery.

3.5 Temperature Protection

Although the circuit consumes little power, in order to ensure their safety performance, we deposit a large area copper at drain at the FET switch when designing the PCB board. And put on a heating panel connected to the drain of FET to achieve better heat dissipation. It also plays a role in protecting circuit board.

4 Results

The circuit connects to the battery pack, and discharges through the bike and continued charging on and on. Lithium battery protection board can make electric bicycles work well. The results as shows in Table 1:

With the parameters, the battery protection board not only can ensure the provision of energy efficiency, but also to ensure the safe operation of electric vehicles.

Table 1. 10 string protection board parameters (Battery 36V/10Ah)

Battery voltage range	28V – 42V
Maximum charge current	8A
Maximum discharge current	20A
Monomer overcharge protection voltage	4.18V – 4.25V
Single over-discharge protection voltage	2.75V – 3.05V
Normal operating current	15A
Over Current	35A
Overcharge delay	1.4S
Over-discharge delay	0.15S

5 Summary

Lithium has been widely used in all walks of life, but there is not enough research in the protection of lithium batteries. This circuit is a simple way to achieve the effective power management, but this protection system without a interaction communication process with user. User can not get the condition of the battery at any time. Of course, in the future we can get a much Smarter, more efficient and more human power management system.

References

1. Tang, C., Ying, J., Jiang, C., et al.: Lithium iron phosphate cathode material to improve Research. Chemical Materials (9), 22–25 (2005)
2. S-8261 Data Sheet. Seiko instruments
3. Toth, A.: Method and system for monitoring and balancing cells in battery packs. World Intellectual Property Organization, 11-1 (2008)

An Improved Particle Swarm Optimization for the Vehicle Routing Problem with Simultaneous Deliveries and Pick-Ups

Chunhua Tang and Taosheng Wang

Business College of Hunan International Economics University, Changsha 410205, China
tangchunhua-2006@163.com

Abstract. The vehicle routing problem with simultaneous deliveries and pick-ups (VRPSDP) is an extension for the classical vehicle routing problem (VRP) where customers require simultaneous deliveries and pick-ups. In this paper, an integer programming model of VRPSDP was presented in detail from the point of bidirectional logistics (including the logistics and reverse logistics). Moreover, an improved particle swarm optimization (IPSO) was proposed to solve the model of VRPSDP. In the algorithm, an ordinal number coding method was adopted based on customers and an auxiliary operator based on integer order criterion (IOR) was adopted, and the evolution equation was improved such that search process was self-adapting with iteration. Finally, some numerical examples were presented to illustrate the efficiency of the proposed models and algorithms.

Keywords: Reverse Logistics; Vehicle Routing Problem; Particle Swarm Optimization; Numerical Simulation.

1 Introduction

The vehicle routing problem with simultaneous deliveries and pick-ups (VRPSDP) is an extension for the classical vehicle routing problem (VRP) where customers require simultaneous delivery and pick-up. Deliveries are supplied from a single depot at the beginning of the vehicle's service, while pick-up loads are taken to the same depot at the end of the service. One important characteristic of this problem is that a vehicle's load in any given route is a mix of delivery and pick-up loads [1]. Reverse logistics as the process of planning, implementing, and controlling the efficient, cost effective flow of raw materials, in-process inventory, finished goods and related information from the point of consumption to the point of origin for the purpose of recapturing value or proper disposal [2]. Reverse logistics can be defined as the reverse process of logistics, it including many planning problem, and the vehicle routing problem (VRP) is a famous one. In our work, the vehicle routing problem with simultaneous deliveries and pickups (VRPSDP) is a complex combinational optimization problem, and is a well-know non-polynomial hard (NP-hard) problem. VRPSDP often encountered in fact, and has broad prospects in theory and practice, for example in the soft drink industry, where empty bottles must be returned, and in the deliveries to grocery stores, where

G. Shen and X. Huang (Eds.): CSIE 2011, Part II, CCIS 153, pp. 294–300, 2011.
© Springer-Verlag Berlin Heidelberg 2011

reusable pallets/containers are used for the transportation of merchandise [3]. Reverse logistics is an important area in which the planning of vehicle routes takes the form of a VRPSDP problem, as companies become interested in gaining control over the whole lifecycle of their products. For example, in some countries legislation forces companies to take responsibility for their products during lifetime, especially when environmental issue are involved [5]. Moreover, returned goods are another example where the definition of vehicle routes may take the form of a VRPSDP problem. Owing to difficulty of the problem itself and deficiency of attention, even now little work can be found [1-3].

Most of the algorithms of solving the VRPSDP are based on those of the VRP. In recent years, most published research for the VRPSDP has focused on developing heuristics algorithm. Although the developments of modern heuristics and metaheuristics have led to considerable progress, the quest for improved performance continues. Dethloff [1] presented a mathematical model for VRPSDP and developed insertion-based heuristics that use four different criteria to solve the model. Tang and Galvao proposed a local search heuristics [4] and a tabu search algorithm [5] for solving VRPSDP. Particle swarm optimization [6-7] has drawn great attention from researchers due to its robustness and flexibility and has been used to tackle many combinatorial problems, including certain types of vehicle routing problem. In this paper, we adopted an improved particle swarm optimization (IPSO) to solve the VRPSDP.

We developed an integer programming mathematical model for VRPSDP in detail. Then an improved particle swarm optimization was constructed. In the IPSO, an ordinal number coding method was adopted based on customers order, and the evolution equation was improved such that search process was self-adapting with iteration. Last, some numerical experiments were used to verify the performance of IPSO.

2   Formulation for VRPSDP

The VRPSPD can be described as the following problem. There are $\bar{k}$ vehicles in the depot 0 and n customers need serve. The location of depot and customers are known. Each customer i requires both a delivery and a pickup operation of a certain amount of goods (d_i) and returning materials (p_i) and must be visited once for both operations. The customers has to be serviced with a given fleet of vehicles of limited capacities(Q)which are usually assumed to be identical; each vehicle leaves the depot carrying an amount of goods equal to the total amount it must deliver and returns to the depot carrying an amount of returning materials equal to the total amount it pick-ups. The total route distance should not exceed the maximum route distance of the vehicle. In each point along its tour each vehicle can not carry a total load greater than its capacity. The goal is to minimize the overall length of the tours. $V_0 = V \cup \{0\}$ is the set of clients plus depot (client 0), and V stands for the customers set, where n=$|V|$ is the number of customers. c_{ij} is the distance between customer i and customer j. If arc (i, j) belongs to the route operated by vehicle k, then the decision variable $x_{ijk} = 1$, otherwise is 0 ; y_{ij} is the demand picked-up in clients routed up to node

i and transported in arc (i, j); z_{ij} is the demand to be delivered to clients routed after node i and transported in arc (i, j).

The corresponding integer programming mathematical modes of VRPSDP is given as follows:

$$\text{minimize} \sum_{k=1}^{\bar{k}} \sum_{i=0}^{n} \sum_{j=0}^{n} c_{ij} x_{ijk} \tag{1}$$

$$\text{s. t.} \sum_{i=0}^{n} \sum_{k=1}^{\bar{k}} x_{ijk} = 1, \, j = 1, \cdots, n; \tag{2}$$

$$\sum_{i=0}^{n} x_{ijk} - \sum_{i=0}^{n} x_{jik} = 0, \, j = 0,1,\cdots,n; \, k = 1,\cdots,\bar{k}; \tag{3}$$

$$\sum_{j=1}^{n} x_{0jk} \leq 1, \, k = 1,\cdots,\bar{k}; \tag{4}$$

$$\sum_{i=0}^{n} z_{ij} - \sum_{i=0}^{n} z_{ji} = d_j, \, \forall j \neq 0; \tag{5}$$

$$\sum_{i=0}^{n} y_{ji} - \sum_{i=0}^{n} y_{ij} = p_j, \, \forall j \neq 0; \tag{6}$$

$$y_{ij} + z_{ij} \leq Q \sum_{k=1}^{\bar{k}} x_{ijk}, \, i, j = 0,1,\cdots,n; \tag{7}$$

$$\sum_{i=0}^{n} \sum_{j=0}^{n} d_{ij} x_{ijk} \leq L, \, k = 0,1,2,...,\bar{k} \tag{8}$$

$$x_{ijk} \in \{0,1\}, \, y_{ij} \geq 0, z_{ij} \geq 0 \tag{9}$$

The objective function aim at minimizing total traveled distance. Constraints (2) guarantee that each customer is visited by exactly one vehicle. Constraints (3) ensure that the same vehicle arrives and departs from each customer it serves. Restrictions (4) define that at most $\bar{k}$ vehicles are used. Restriction (5) and (6) are flow equations for deliveries and pick-ups loads, respectively. Constraints (7) establish that deliveries and pick-ups demands will only be transported using arcs included in the solution. Restrictions (8) are the maximum distance constraints, L is the upper limit on the total load transported by a vehicle in any given section of the route. Constraints(9) defines the range of the decision variables.

3   The Proposed IPSO for VRPSDP

Particle swarm optimization (PSO) is first proposed by Kennedy and Eberhart [7]. In this paper, we presented an improved particle swarm optimization (IPSO) to solve VRPSDP. VRPSDP is an NP-hard combinational optimization problem. In our IPSO, we suppose the search space is D dimensions and population size is NP, $X_i = (x_{i1}, x_{i2}, ..., x_{iD})$ is the location of individual i, $V_i = (v_{i1}, v_{i2}, ..., v_{iD})$ is the current flight velocity of individual i, $P_i = (p_{i1}, p_{i2}, ..., p_{iD})$ represents the best position of individual i, called as the best individual $pbest$, and $l_i = (l_{i1}, l_{i2}, ..., l_{iD})$ is the best neighborhood position of individual i, noted as $lbest$, $P_g = (p_{g1}, p_{g2}, ..., p_{gD})$ is the best globe position, noted as $gbest$. Then the evolution equation of composite particle swarm optimization can be described as :

$$
\begin{aligned}
v_{id}(t+1) = {} & w \cdot v_{id}(t) + c_1 \cdot rand\ () \cdot [p_{id}(t) - x_{id}(t)] \\
& + rand\ () \cdot [c_2(l_{id}(t) - x_{id}(t)) + c_3(p_{gd}(t) - x_{id}(t))
\end{aligned} \tag{10}
$$

$$
x_{id}(t+1) = x_{id}(t) + v_{id}(t+1), 1 \le i \le NP, 1 \le d \le D \tag{11}
$$

Where equations (10) represent the velocity and equations (11) is the position update formula. Especially, in equations (11), the first part is the current velocity, it provide the necessary momentum in the search space; and the second part represents the ccognitive part of the individual, it promote the individual flight to the best position $pbest$; the third part is the social part, it represents mutual cooperation and influence between the particles and prompt the individual flight to the best globe position $gbest$. $w = w_{max} - \dfrac{w_{max} - w_{min}}{T} \cdot t$ is iinertial weight, indicating that the velocity of the original particles are retained to the extent, and the larger w, the stronger capacity of local convergence, the smaller w indicated the stronger capacity of globe convergence. t, T is the current iteration times and the maximum times respectively, and let w updated dynamically from larger to smaller with iteration times. And set

$c_1 = 2$, $c_2 + c_3 = 2$, $c_2 = 2 \cdot (1 - t/T)$ and $c_3 = 2 \cdot t/T$, it illustrated that c_2 become smaller with iterations and c_3 changes larger with iterations, which indicated that the effect of $lbest$ decreasing and the role of $gbest$ enhanced with the evolution, $rand()$ generate the random number in interval $[0,1]$.

PSO is a novel parallel direct search method which works with a population of solutions, not with a single solution for the optimization problem. Like conventional GA for the VRP [8], we adopt an ordinal encoding scheme, and the position and velocity of each particle was formulated by a vector that is a permutation of the customers. When the elements of vector exceed their allowed ranges after performing formulation (10-11), we must consider an auxiliary operator based on integer order criterion (IOR) just like the largest-order-value (LOV) rules that Cao, et al [9] proposed. For the largest element of vector gives the largest customer ordinal number n, the second evaluated as $n-1$, the rest may be deduced by analogy. For example, the vector after evolution is [-7.1, 1.3, -5.6, 2.5, -3.7, 0, 3.3, 5.4], the number of the customers is 8, we obtain the final vector is [1, 5, 2, 6, 3, 4, 7, 8] by using IOR.

We check the capacity constraint(7) and maximum distance constraint(8) at the same time from the first element of particle, if do not violate the constraints, considering the next element; if it violate the constraints in someone element, we consider to use other vehicle from this element starting, and repeat the above process, till all of customers were serviced. For instance, there are 10 customers, a randomly generated particle position is 1 3 6 8 9 5 4 10 2 7, it can be interpreted as r =3 feasible routes: 0-1-3-6-0, 0-8-9-5-0, and 0-4-10-2-7-0. If $\overline{k}$ >= r, then this particle is legal; otherwise, it is illegal.

In order to prevent an illegal particle entering the next generation in great probability, a penalty function is designed. R is the total distance vehicles traveled of the corresponding particle, and let $m = r - \overline{k}$. If $r > \overline{k}$, then $m > 0$, and $R = R + Z \times m$, where Z is a very large integer. If $r < \overline{k}$, then $m = 0$. The fitness function can be expressed as $f = 1/(R + Z \times m)$. For convenience, capacity of the vehicles is the sameness, and the maximum distance that each vehicle can travel is equal, they can be denoted respectively as Q and L.

4   Numerical Experiments

The improved particle swarm optimization described in the previous sections is applied to solve the 8-customers vehicle routing problem with simultaneous deliveries and pickups. There are three vehicles in the depot, capacity(Q)of each vehicle is 8 tons, deliveries and pick-ups demands of the 8 customers are listed in Table 1, the distances between customers and depot is listed in Table 2. The parameters for the proposed IPSO are included as follows: $NP = 40$, $T = 300$, $w_{max} = 0.9$, $w_{min} = 0.4$, c_1 =2, $c_2 + c_3 = 2$, and the maximum distance L is 400 kilometers. There are 10 independent trials are carried out to evaluate the average performance. The results of simulations are presented in Table 3, and the best solution obtained is showed in Figure 1.

Table 1. The Deliveries and Pick-ups Demands of Customers

Customer i	1	2	3	4	5	6	7	8
Deliveries demands	2	1.5	4.5	3	1.5	4	2.5	3
Pick-ups demands	3	1	2	2	3	4	1.5	3

Table 2. The Distance Matrix of Customers and Distribution Center

i／j	0	1	2	3	4	5	6	7	8
0	0	40	60	75	90	200	100	160	80
1	40	0	65	40	100	50	75	110	100
2	60	65	0	75	100	100	75	75	75
3	75	40	75	0	100	50	90	90	150
4	90	100	100	100	0	100	75	75	100
5	200	50	100	50	100	0	70	90	75
6	100	75	75	90	75	70	0	70	100
7	160	110	75	90	75	90	70	0	100
8	80	100	75	150	100	75	100	100	0

Table 3. The Average Computational Results of Iterating 300

Vehicles	Distances (km)	Percentage of reaching optimal solution	Routes	Computational time(second)
3	790	100%	0-6-7-2-0;0-8-4-0; 0-3-5-1-0	1.4370

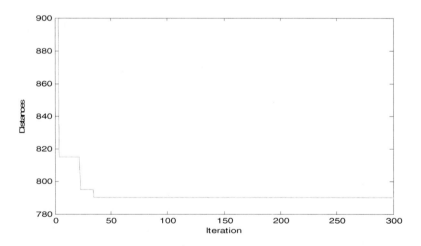

Fig. 1. The Results of Iterating 300 Times

5 Conclusions

This paper contributed to vehicle routing problem with simultaneous deliveries and pickups in the following respects: (a) an integer programming mathematic model of VRPSDP was proposed for describing the characters of the problem in details; (b) an improved particle swarm optimization was proposed to solve VRPSDP, aiming at the total traveled distance minimization; (c) the effectiveness of the model and the improved particle swarm optimization were shown by some numerical experiments.

References

1. Dethloff, J.: Vehicle routing and reverse logistics: the vehicle routing problem with simultaneous delivery and pick-up. OR Spektrum 23(1), 79–96 (2001)
2. Biabchessi, N., Righini, G.: Heuristic algorithms for the vehicle routing problem with simultaneous pick-up and delivery. Computers & Operations Research 34(2), 578–594 (2007)
3. Min, H.: The multiple vehicle routing problems with simultaneous delivery and pickup points. Transportation Research A 23(5), 377–386 (1989)
4. Tang, F.A., Galvao, R.D.: Vehicle routing problems with simultaneous pick-up and delivery service. Journal of the Operational Research Society of India (OPSEARCH) 39(1), 19–33 (2002)
5. Alfredo, F., Montane, T.: A tabu search algorithm for the vehicle routing problem with simultaneous pick-up and delivery service. Computer & Operations Research 33(3), 595–619 (2006)
6. Kennedy, J., Eberhart, R.: Particle swarm optimization. In: Proc. IEEE Int. Conf. on Neural Networks, Perth, Australia, pp. 1942–1948 (1995)
7. Mendes, R., Kennedy, J., Neves, J.: Watch thy neighbor or how the swarm can learn from its environment. In: Proc. IEEE Int. Conf on Evolutionary Computation, Indianapolis, pp. 88–94 (2003)
8. Gen, M., Cheng, R.: Genetic Algorithms &Engineering Optimization. Wiley, New York (2000)
9. Cao, E., Lai, M.: The open vehicle routing problem with fuzzy demands. Expert Systems with Applications 37(3), 2405–2411 (2010)

Research on Coordination Mechanism of Decentralized Assembly Furniture Supply Chain

Zhongwei Wang and Yixiong Kang

College of Logistics, Central South University of Forestry and Technology,
Changsha 410004, China
kyx@mail.gofront.com

Abstract. The coordination problem of a supply chain with n different furniture suppliers in upstream and one furniture retailer in downstream was analyzed. An optimal decision model was proposed under centralized decision setting. In decentralized decision setting, the conventional wholesale price contract can not reach the optimal profit of this furniture supply chain system, then a revenue sharing contract was presented in order to coordinate this supply chain system, specifically, we study and compare the wholesale price and revenue sharing contracts, and obtain optimal decisions and results respectively. Finally, we verify the contract models by adopting a numerical analysis.

Keywords: supply chain management; game analysis; coordination mechanism; wholesale price; revenue sharing.

1 Introduction

Recently many companies of furniture industries have shifted their manufacturing strategies from doing most everything internally to operating in a decentralized assembly fashion wherein the assembler of a final product out sources components manufacturing to independent suppliers. This is a typical decentralized assembly supply chain system. Obviously, the decentralized assembly system can reduce cost due to their professional division of work and mass production. However, in making their decisions suppliers and the assembler all behave strategically, each to maximize its own profit rather than the total supply chain profit. Such strategic decisions of independent firms in general induce inefficiency in the supply chain. Some researchers consider the channel structure and performance of decentralized assembly supply chain.

Wang [1] consider a joint pricing-production decision in supply chains of complementary products with uncertain demand by employing a consignment-sales contract with revenue sharing. Gerchak and Wang [2] adopt a revenue sharing to determine the production quantity, and then apply whole-sales contract to determine whole-sale price, and did not consider the joint price and quantity decision-making. Liu Jian and Ma Shihua [3] address advantages of interest sharing contract by comparing revenue

G. Shen and X. Huang (Eds.): CSIE 2011, Part II, CCIS 153, pp. 301–307, 2011.

sharing contract and traditional whole-sale contract, and introduces influential factors and methods of contracting.

Generally believed that the furniture retailer closest to the consumer, and has an advantage over furniture suppliers in the market demand information. So the furniture retailer determine the amount of purchased products based on market demand information, and the retail price of final product is higher than the sum of the wholesale price of outsourcing components productions. And the suppliers determine their wholesale price according to their costs individually. Thus there are vertical and horizontal price and quantity game problems. It is a key issue how to determine the outsourcing components quantities and pricing from the viewpoint of supply chain.

2 Centralized Decisions

Consider n suppliers each produce one of a set of n components that are needed by an assembler to assemble a final product. The assembler buys the components from individual suppliers, assembles them into final products and sells them to the market. The suppliers each contract with the assembler by charging a wholesale price for their individual products. Without loss of generality, we assume furniture suppliers and furniture retailers are risk neutral, the furniture suppliers have different production cost $c_i > 0, i = 1, 2...n$,and the production cost of furniture retailers is $c_0 > 0$,the channel total cost is $C = \sum_{i=0}^{n} c_i$ .The retail price of final furniture is $p_0 = a_0 - b_0 Q$, the price elasticity of demand is increasing with $\frac{1}{b_0}$,obviously, $a_0 > p_0 > C > 0$ must meet.

The individual have the complete information, and the furniture retailer first determine the number of purchased products Q according to market demand; then furniture suppliers provide products to furniture retailers while determining the wholesale price $w_i, i = 1, 2...n$ according to their production costs. The furniture retailer charged the total wholesale price $W = \sum_{i=1}^{n} w_i$ .Since a final product consists of one unit of each of the n components, it would obviously be suboptimal for the assembler to order different quantities from different suppliers. To simplify the problem, we assume the furniture suppliers do not take into account the impact of other furniture suppliers when they make decisions, that is to say, the simultaneous decision of suppliers. The furniture retailer's profit is $\Pi_R = (p_0 - W - c_0)Q$, and the profit of furniture supplier i is

$\Pi_i = (w_i - c_i)Q$, the channel profit is $\Pi_T = \Pi_R + \sum_{i=1}^{n} \Pi_i = (p_0 - C)Q$.

For obtain a benchmark, we consider the centralized decisions case. A centralized supply chain system is viewed as one entity that aims to optimize channel performance. There   are   only   one   decision-maker,   and   the   channel   total   profit   is

$\Pi_T = (a_0 - b_0 Q - C)Q$, from the first order condition, we have the optimal the optimal production quantity $Q^c = \dfrac{a_0 - C}{2b_0}$, and obtain retail price $p_0^c = \dfrac{a_0 + C}{2}$, the

channel total profit is $\Pi_T^c = \dfrac{(a_0 - C)^2}{4b_0}$.

3 Decentralized Decision under Wholesale Price Contract

A decentralized supply chain differs from a centralized system in that $n+1$ members act independently to optimize their individual preference. The problem is analyzed as a Stackelberg game in which the retailer acts as the leader by announcing the quantities of outsourcing in advance, and the suppliers acts as the follower by determining wholesale price. Under wholesale price contract, the profit of furniture retailer is $\Pi_R^w = (p_0 - W - c_0) \cdot Q$, and the optimal quantities are $Q^w = \dfrac{a_0 - W - c_0}{2b_0}$, then

the optimal retail price is $p_0^w = \dfrac{a_0 + W + c_0}{2}$. From the profit function of supplier

i $\Pi_i^w = (w_i - c_i) \cdot Q = (w_i - c_i) \cdot \dfrac{a_0 - c_0 - \sum\limits_{i=1}^{n} w_i}{2b_0}$, we know the optimal wholesale price

of supplier i is $w_i^w = \dfrac{a_0 + c_i - c_0 - \sum\limits_{j \neq i}^{n} w_j}{2}$, $i = 1, 2, \ldots n$. Solving the above n

equations simultaneously, we obtain the optimal furniture wholesale price $w_i^w = \dfrac{a_0 - C}{n+1} + c_i$, then the total wholesale is $W^w = \dfrac{na_0 + C}{n+1} - c_0$.

So the profit of furniture retailer is

$\Pi_R^w = (p_0^w - W^w - c_0) \cdot Q^w = \dfrac{(a_0 - c_0 - W^w)^2}{4b_0} = \dfrac{(a_0 - C)^2}{4b_0(n+1)^2} = \dfrac{1}{(n+1)^2} \cdot \Pi_T^c$,

and the profit of furniture supplier is

$\Pi_i^w = (w_i^w - c_i) \cdot Q^w = \dfrac{(a_0 - c_0 - W^w)(a_0 - C)}{2(n+1)b_0} = \dfrac{(a_0 - C)^2}{2b_0(n+1)^2} = \dfrac{2}{(n+1)^2} \cdot \Pi_T^c$. The

total profit of all furniture suppliers is $\sum\limits_{i=1}^{n} \Pi_i^w = \dfrac{n(a_0 - C)^2}{2b_0(n+1)^2}$, and the channel total

profit is $\Pi_T^w = \Pi_R^w + \sum\limits_{i=1}^{n} \Pi_i^w = \dfrac{(2n+1)(a_0 - C)^2}{4b_0(n+1)^2} = \dfrac{2n+1}{(n+1)^2} \Pi_T^c$.

Obviously the assembly supply chain does not reach the channel optimal profit under wholesale price contract, and the wholesale price contract can not coordinate the assembly furniture supply chain system. It is consistent to the supply chain comprise of the one supplier and one retailer. We obtain the following results by analyzing.

Proposition 1. Under a wholesale-price contract, when furniture suppliers set their individual wholesale prices simultaneously, the profit of furniture members and the total channel profit is decreasing with the channel total cost increasing, however, the allocation of channel total cost among different members does not affects the profit of individual member and channel total profit.

Proposition 2. Under a wholesale-price contract, when furniture suppliers set their individual wholesale prices simultaneously, the retail price higher than that of centralized decision, and the production quantity is lower than that of centralized decision, the channel total profit is lower that of the centralized decision, the ratio of channel profit $\frac{2n+1}{(n+1)^2}$ decreases as the number of furniture suppliers n increases.

3   Decentralized Decision under Revenue Sharing Contract

The revenue sharing contract can be described by the two parameters (w_i, ϕ), the supplier i charges the retailer a unit wholesale price w_i lower than the unit marginal cost c_i, in exchange for a percentage ϕ $(0 < \phi < 1)$ of the retailer's revenue. To simplify the problem, we assume that the share of all furniture suppliers extracted is $1 - \phi$, then each individual furniture supplier obtain same revenue share $\frac{1-\phi}{n}$. Under the revenue sharing contract, the profit of furniture retailer is $\Pi_R^r = \phi \cdot p_0 Q - (\sum_{i=1}^{n} w_i + c_0) \cdot Q$, then the optimal production is $Q^r = \frac{\phi \cdot a_0 - W - c_0}{2 b_0 \phi}$. So considering the channel total profit

$$\Pi_T = \Pi_R + \sum_{i=1}^{n} \Pi_i = (p_0 - C)Q = (a_0 - b_0 Q - C)Q, \Pi_T \text{ reach the maximum}$$

value when $Q^c = \frac{a_0 - C}{2b_0}$, the channel total profit does not reach maximum when $Q = Q^r = \frac{\phi a_0 - W - c_0}{2 b_0 \phi}$. When $Q \in [Q^r, Q^c]$, Π_T increases as Q increases.

So the channel total profit reach maximum if and only if $Q^r = Q^c$, then we have $\phi C = \sum_{i=1}^{n} w_i + c_0$, that is to say $W = \phi C - c_0$. Conditions $W = \phi C - c_0 > 0$ must be meet, then $\frac{c_0}{C} < \phi < 1$, and $w_i < c_i$.

Proposition 3. When $W = \phi C - c_0$ (or $\phi = \dfrac{\sum\limits_{i=1}^{n} w_i + c_0}{C}$), the supplier i charges the

retailer a unit wholesale price w_i lower than the unit marginal cost c_i, and the revenue

sharing contract can reach the channel optimal profit $\Pi_T^r = \Pi_T^c = \dfrac{(a_0 - C)^2}{4b_0}$.

In fact, under the revenue sharing contract, the furniture retailer's profit

is $\Pi_R^r = \phi \cdot p_0 Q - (\sum\limits_{i=1}^{n} w_i + c_0) \cdot Q = \dfrac{\phi - \phi^2}{\phi + 1} \cdot \Pi_T^c$, and the profit of furniture sup-

plier i is $\Pi_i^r = \dfrac{1-\phi}{n} p_0 Q + (w_i - c_i) \cdot Q = \dfrac{1-\phi}{n}(\dfrac{a_0 + C}{2}) \cdot \dfrac{a_0 - C}{2b_0} + (w_i^r - c_i) \cdot \dfrac{a_0 - C}{2b_0} =$

$\dfrac{a_0 - C}{2b_0}[\dfrac{(1-\phi) \cdot (a_0 + C)}{2n} + w_i^r - c_i] = \dfrac{a_0 - C}{2b_0}[\dfrac{(1-\phi) \cdot (a_0 + C)}{2n} + \dfrac{a_0 \phi^2 - C)}{n(\phi + 1)}] = \dfrac{\phi^2 + 1}{n(\phi + 1)} \cdot \Pi_T^c$.

Obviously, the channel total profit is $\Pi_T^r = \Pi_R^r + \sum\limits_{i=1}^{n} \Pi_i^r = (\dfrac{\phi - \phi^2}{\phi + 1} + \dfrac{\phi^2 + 1}{n(\phi + 1)} \cdot n) \cdot \Pi_T^c = \Pi_T^c$.

Moreover, when $n = 1$, the Proposition 5. is consistent with the result of reference[4].

Although the supply chain channel profit can reach maximum under revenue sharing contract and higher than that of the wholesale price contract, however, an effective coordination mechanism must satisfy the following incentive compatibility conditions: $\Pi_i^r > \Pi_i^w$ and $\Pi_R^r > \Pi_R^w$ must simultaneously meet.

So $\dfrac{\phi^2 + 1}{n(\phi + 1)} \cdot \Pi_T^c > \dfrac{2}{(n+1)^2} \cdot \Pi_T^c$ and $\dfrac{\phi - \phi^2}{\phi + 1} \cdot \Pi_T^c > \dfrac{1}{(n+1)^2} \cdot \Pi_T^c$ simultaneously meet,

When $\phi \in (\dfrac{n^2 + 2n - \sqrt{n^4 + 4n^3 - 8n - 4}}{2(n+1)^2}, \dfrac{n^2 + 2n + \sqrt{n^4 + 4n^3 - 8n - 4}}{2(n+1)^2})$, the

furniture supplier i charges the retailer a unit wholesale price w_i lower than the unit

marginal cost c_i, and all suppliers obtain the same profit $\dfrac{1 + \phi^2}{n(\phi + 1)} \Pi_T^c$, and the fur-

niture retailer obtain the profit $\dfrac{\phi - \phi^2}{\phi + 1} \Pi_T^c$. Each and every individual's profit is larger

than that of the wholesale price contract. Combination the Proposition 5., and

set $A = \max\{\dfrac{c_0}{C}, \dfrac{n^2 + 2n - \sqrt{n^4 + 4n^3 - 8n - 4}}{2(n+1)^2}\}$, we have the following result.

Proposition 4. When $\phi \in (A, \dfrac{n^2 + 2n + \sqrt{n^4 + 4n^3 - 8n - 4}}{2(n+1)^2})$, each and every

individual's profit increases than wholesale price contract.

Moreover, when $n \geq 5$, considering the profit between all furniture suppliers and retailer, when $\phi \in (\dfrac{n - \sqrt{n^2 - 4(n+1)}}{2(n+1)}, \dfrac{n + \sqrt{n^2 - 4(n+1)}}{2(n+1)})$, the profit of retailer is higher than the profit of furniture individual supplier, and when $\phi = \dfrac{n - \sqrt{n^2 - 4(n+1)}}{2(n+1)}$ or $\phi = \dfrac{n + \sqrt{n^2 - 4(n+1)}}{2(n+1)}$, all of the supply chain member have the same profit, when $\phi \in (\dfrac{n^2 + 2n - \sqrt{n^4 + 4n^3 - 8n - 4}}{2(n+1)^2}, \dfrac{n - \sqrt{n^2 - 4(n+1)}}{2(n+1)})$ or $\phi \in (\dfrac{n + \sqrt{n^2 - 4(n+1)}}{2(n+1)}, 1)$, the profit of furniture supplier obtained higher than that of the retailer. And the length of the feasible interval ϕ increases as the number of supplier n increases, and it represent the perfect competition when $n \to \infty$, and ϕ can take the all value of interval $(0,1)$, n larger, the more favorable of this coordination mechanism.

5 Numerical Experiment

We performed numerical studies of channel performance, production quantity, retail price under centralized decisions and decentralized decisions based on wholesale price contract and revenue sharing contract, and revealed the performance of proposed coordination mechanisms. We assume there are an assembly furniture supply chain comprise of five furniture suppliers and one retailer.

The production cost of each supplier as follows $c_1 = 1$, $c_2 = 2$, $c_3 = 3$, $c_4 = 4$, $c_5 = 5$, the production cost of retailer is $c_0 = 5$, and the retail price is determined by $p_0 = a_0 - b_0 Q = 100 - 0.5Q$. From the calculation of the previous analysis, we know the optimal revenue share of retailers is $\phi \in (0.25, 0.9428)$, and the furniture retailer and furniture suppliers determine

Table 1. Numerical experiment results of different model

Parameters / Models	Retailer's revenue share ϕ	Total whole-sale price W	Retail price p_0	Production quantity Q	Supplier's profit	Retailer's profit	Channel total profit Π_T
Centralized decisions	5/7	\	60	80	\	\	3200
Wholesale price contract	1/36	81.67	93.33	13.33	177.7	88.89	977.67
Revenue sharing contract	0.6	7	60	80	544	480	3200

the proportion of their revenue derived based on their bargaining power within this range[4], when retailer and suppliers obtain revenue share by forty-six into all the proceeds, the numerical results obtained as shown in the table 1.

Table 1 indicates that the channel total profit is lower than centralized decision under a wholesale-price contract due to retail price increases and production quantity decreases. And the revenue sharing contract can coordinate the assembly supply chain and have obvious advantage compared to wholesale price contract. Moreover, the allocation of channel total cost among different members does not affect the profit of individual member and channel total profit. When $\phi = 1/3$ or $\phi = 1/2$, each and every member have the same profit $3200/6$.

6 Conclusion

In this paper, we considered an assembly furniture supply chain comprised of n suppliers and one retailer, and proposed two contracts that tried to coordinate this supply chain. In particular, this paper contributed to assembly supply chain management in the following respects:(1) under wholesale contract, the retail price higher than that of centralized decision, and the production quantity is lower than that of centralized decision, the channel total profit is lower that of the centralized decision, and the member's profit has a very interesting relationship with the channel number of suppliers and cost's allocation(Proposition 1-2);(2) the revenue sharing contract can coordinate the assembly supply chain, and each and every individual's profit increases than wholesale price contract.

References

1. Wang, Y.: Joint Pricing-Production Decisions in Supply Chains of Complementary Products with Uncertain Demand. Operations Research 54(6), 1110–1127 (2006)
2. Gerchak, Y., Wang, Y.: Revenue-Sharing vs. Whole-Price Contracts in Assembly Systems with Random Demand. Production and Operations Management 13(1), 23–33 (2006)
3. Liu, J., Ma, S.: Research on Supply Chain Partnering and Contract. Journal of Industrial Engineering/Engineering Management 18(1), 85–87 (2004)
4. Cachon, G.P., Lariviere, M.A.: Supply Chain Coordination with Revenue-Sharing Contracts: Strength and Limitations. Management Science 51(1), 30–44 (2005)
5. Carr, S.M., Karmarkar, U.S.: Competition in Multiechelon Assembly Supply Chains. Management Science 51(1), 45–59 (2005)
6. Carr, S.M., Karmarkar, U.S.: Competition and Structure in Serial Supply Chains with Deterministic Demand. Management Science 47(7), 966–978 (2001)

Modeling and Stability Investigation of Single-Ended Forward DC/DC Converter

YingWu Wang, JunFeng Wang, LiuJun Di, YouBao Liu, Yang Wang, and Kai Wang

Xi'an Microelectronic Technology Institute, Xi'an,
710054 Xi'an China
kkww19@sina.com

Abstract. This paper present small signal model and compensation network for the analysis and design of single-ended forward DC/DC converter in the average current mode, in order to design and simulate amplitude-frequency characteristic and phase-frequency characteristic of the control loop, the state equation of single-ended forward converter is derived. the stability and dynamic response of switch-mode power supplies is elevated by optimizing its compensation network. The results of the analysis are simulated and verified experimentally.

Keywords: Small-signal modeling Compensation network Transient response.

1 Introduction

Modeling is analysis and design theoretical basisa of DC/DC converter, it is significant to establish small signal modeling and large modeling for the study of its stability and dynamic performance. The small signal modeling utilizes mathematical approach to characterize operating state of DC/DC converter, this mothod averages variables of DC/DC converter in a ON-OFF period,and decompose average variables to the summation of DC and AC small signal, distill and linearize AC component, a linearization system will be received.

This paper present and analysis ON and OFF operating states of DC/DC converter,the state equation of single-ended forward converter is established to analysis its small signal model and to design and simulate amplitude-frequency characteristic and phase-frequency characteristic in continuous conduction mode. the stability and dynamic response of switch-mode power supplies is improved by optimizing its compensation network.

2 Single-Ended Forward Converter Small Signal Switch Modeling

2.1 Establish the State Equation

a. The power transistor ON state t_{on}

The principle of equivalence circuit is shown in fig.1(a).during the switch Q ON for a time t_{on},the primary current i_i of power transformer increase step by step, diode

G. Shen and X. Huang (Eds.): CSIE 2011, Part II, CCIS 153, pp. 308–313, 2011.

rectifier turns on and free-wheeling diode turns off, the output filters LC averages the modulated rectangular maveforms at rectifier cathodes,out voltage V_o maintains a operating level. The average value of the state variables $V_L(t)$ and $i_c(t)$ is respectively[1].

$$V_L(t)_{on} = L\frac{di_L(t)}{dt} = nV_i(t) - V_c(t) \approx n < V_i(t) >_{T_s} - < V_c(t) >_{T_s} \tag{1}$$

$$i_c(t)_{on} = C\frac{dV_c(t)}{dt} = i_L(t) - \frac{V_c(t)}{R} \approx < i_L(t) >_{T_s} - \frac{< V_c(t) >_{T_s}}{R} \tag{2}$$

b.the power transistor OFF state t_{off}

The principle of equivalence circuit is shown in fig.1(b).when the switch Q turns OFF,the current in the magnetizing inductance forces a reversal of polariries on second winding, the diode rectifier turns off and free-wheeling diode turns on, the average value of state variebles $V_L(t)$ and $i_c(t)$ is respectively.

$$V_L(t)_{off} = -L\frac{di_L(t)}{dt} = -V_c(t) \approx - < V_c(t) >_{T_s} \tag{4}$$

$$i_c(t)_{off} = C\frac{dV_c(t)}{dt} = i_L(t) - \frac{V_c(t)}{R} \approx < i_L(t) >_{T_s} - \frac{< V_c(t) >_{T_s}}{R} \tag{5}$$

The inductance voltage and capacitance current are averaged over the full period, the non-linear AC small signal state equation is gained after importing in disturbance and separating AC small signal.

$$L\frac{di_L^{\wedge}(t)}{dt} = nDv_g^{\wedge}(t) + nd^{\wedge}(t)V_g + nd^{\wedge}(t)v_g^{\wedge}(t) - v_o^{\wedge}(t) \tag{6}$$

$$C\frac{dv_c^{\wedge}(t)}{dt} = i_L^{\wedge}(t) - \frac{v_c^{\wedge}(t)}{R} \tag{7}$$

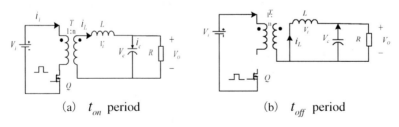

(a) t_{on} period   (b) t_{off} period

Fig. 1. The principle of equivalence circuit of switch Q operating process.the single-ended forward converter topology is widely used topology.(a) when the power transistor Q is turn on, the secondary current flows the output filter LC,the free-wheeling diode reverse.(b)when the power transistor Q is turn off, the free-wheeling diode curren flows the out filter LC,the current wave is at ramp-on-a step waveform.

2.2 Linearization the State Equation

After igonring $nd^\wedge(t)v_g^\wedge(t)$, the input-output transfer function $G_{vg}(s)$ and the duty ratio-output transfer function of the single ended forward converter is gained respectively [2]:

$$G_{vg}(s)=\frac{v_o^\wedge(s)}{v_g^\wedge(s)}\bigg|_{d(s)=0}=\frac{nD}{s^2LC+\dfrac{sL}{R}+1} \tag{9}$$

$$G_{vd}(s)=\frac{v_o^\wedge(s)}{d^\wedge(s)}\bigg|_{v_g^\wedge(s)=0}=\frac{nV_g}{s^2LC+\dfrac{sL}{R}+1} \tag{10}$$

3 Compensation Network Analysis and Design

3.1 Unit Negative Feedback Compensation

Figure 2 shows the DC/DC converter closed loop model, $G_{vd}(s)$ is the duty ratio-output transfer function, $H(s)$ is voltage sample network transfer function, $PI(s)$ is error amplifier transfer function, $G_{pwm}(s)$ is PWM transfer function. The open loop transfer function is :

$$\Psi(s)=G_{vd}(s)H(s)PI(s)G_{pwm}(s) \tag{11}$$

Suppose single ended forward converter operates in a continuous state and is a unit compensation system.simulation parameters are respectively: $V_i=28\text{V}$, $H(s)=\dfrac{1}{3}$, $PI(s)=-1$, $V_{P-P}=1.2V$, $f_s=500kHz$, L=25uH, C=10 0uF, $R_{esr}=0.45\Omega$。Figure 3 shows gain frequency and phase frequency characteristic of DC/DC converter unit negative feedback open loop transfer function. This control loop is a critical stable system because there are extremely little gain margin and phase margin.lower frequency gain is 24.5dB,crossover frequency and phase margin are 84.1 kHz and $\varphi_m=1°$ respectively.

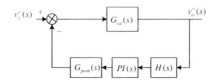

Fig. 2. DC/DC converter colsed loop transfer function model

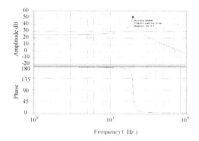

Fig. 3. The amplitude-frequency characteristic and the phase-frenquency characteristic of unit negative feedback single-ended converter

3.2 Compensation Network $PI(s)$ Design

In order to stabilize this control loop, the phase margin must be improved, zero-pole compensation network Figure 4 is shown that the crossover frequency is lower than unit negative feedback compensation and higher frequency gain attenuation slope is -40dB/dec[3].

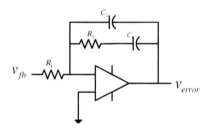

Fig. 4. PI voltage-error amplifier compensation schematic

Where the transfer function of compensation network for average current control scheme can be derived as:

$$PI(s) = \frac{1 + R_2 C_1 s}{R_1 s(C_1 + C_2)(1 + sR_2 \frac{C_1 C_2}{C_1 + C_2})} \qquad (12)$$

Let crossover frequency $f_c \approx \frac{1}{5} f_s = 100kHz$, K factor parameter $\frac{f_c}{f_z} = \frac{f_p}{f_c} = K$ (here K=6), the phase of compensation network $\theta_{ea} = 136°$, first zero $f_z = 16.67kHz$,second pole $f_p = 600kHz$. Let $R_1 = 10k\Omega$, then $R_2 = 11.2k\Omega$, $C_1 = 820pF$, $C_2 = 22pF$, the phase margin of crossover frequency f_c is 153°, the feedback control loop system is a stable system.compensation network bode figure 5 is shown and open loop transfer function of compensated system is:

$$\Psi(s) = \frac{nV_g}{s^2LC + \dfrac{sL}{R} + 1} \frac{1 + R_2C_1s}{R_1s(C_1 + C_2)(1 + sR_2\dfrac{C_1C_2}{C_1 + C_2})} H(s)G_{pwm}(s) \tag{13}$$

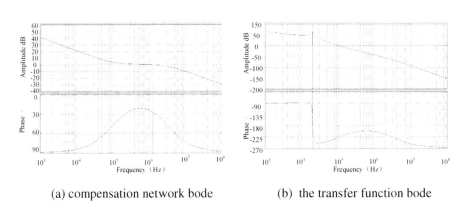

(a) compensation network bode   (b) the transfer function bode

Figure 5 is the amplitude-frequency characteristic and the phase-frenquency characteristic, Figure (a) is pole-zero compensation network bode, figure (b) is the transfer function bode of compensed system, Which is a stable and a outstanding transient response.

4 Experimental Verifacation

To validate the proposed model, a prototype single-ended forward converter in average current control mode was constructed. The circuit is reset by the resonance of parasitic capacitances of switching modes of the circuit in one switching period are analyzed. In order to improved dynamics state the topological feedforward control structure was designed, the crossover frequency and phase margin were optimized,the circuit parameters for both the model simulation and the prototype are listed. Input voltage $V_i = 28V \pm 12V$, output load current $I_o = 5A$, switch frequency $f = 500kHz$, filter inductance $L = 25\mu H$,output capacitance $C = 100\mu F$. Figure 6 shows the output voltage transient response when the load current is changed from 2.5A to 5A or from 5A to 2.5A. Figure7 shows the output voltage transient response when the input voltage is changed from16V to 40V or from 40V to 16V.

As illustrated in Figure6, when the load is changed from full load to half load(2.5A~5A),the output voltage generates the voltage overshoot, which is 280mV and need 70µs to restore to 1% the steady state value. When the load becomes to light,the filtering inductor will store energy and release o the load which arouse the output voltage will overshoot.the ouput capacitor with a lower ESR will reduce the output voltage overshoot, you can parallel capacitor to reduce the ESR actually. optimized phase margin φ_m and critical bandwidth will reduce the voltage restoration

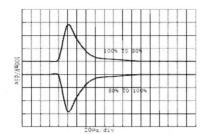   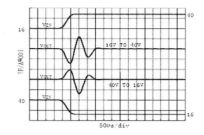

Fig. 6. The measured load transient reponse   **Fig. 7.** The measured input voltage transient reponse

time[4], the change from half load to full load vice versa. Figure 7 shows, when the input voltage jumps from 16v to 40v,the voltage undershoot will be generated, the output voltage will restore to the stable state value because of the damping attenuation of the control feedback system, it takes 150μs to restore to 1% the stable value. The feedforward control system in power circuit will restrain the voltage changes in advance, and improve the input voltage response, excessive compensation of the feedforward control system will aroused the output voltage undershoot.

5   Conclusions

In this paper, the continuous operation mode small signal model for single-ended forward DC/DC converter is proposed. The measured results of prototype are given in Figure6 and Figure7,the load response and input voltage transient response are improved by analyzing and designing the phase-frequency characteristic and amplitude-frequency characteristic. the small signal model derived from equivalent circuits can be easily used to facilitate the control-loop design optimization and predict the system's dynamic response which will aid engineers in the control loop design.

References

1. Zhang, W.: Modeling and control of switch converter publishing house of china electric power (2005)
2. Iannello, C., Luo, S., Batarseh, I.: Small-Signal and Transient Analysis of a Full-Bridge Zero-Current-Switched PWM Converter Using an Average Model. IEEE Transactions on Power Electronics 18(3), 793–801 (2003)
3. Zhang, Z., Cai, X.: The theory and design of switching power supply(revision). Publishing House of Electronics Industry (2004)
4. Yao, K., Ren, Y., Lee, F.C.: Critical Bandwidth for the Load Transient Response of Voltage Regulator Modules. IEEE Transactions on Power Electronics 19(6), 1454 -1461 (2004)

A Workflow Instance Migration Algorithm for Improving Time Complexity

HaiLan Pan, JiaQi Wu, and CuiHong Wu

School of Computer and Information,
Shanghai Second Polytechnic University,
Shanghai 201209 China
hlpan@it.sspu.cn, jqwu@it.sspu.cn, chwu@it.sspu.cn

Abstract. The current rapid economic development leads to extremely unstable of the enterprise business flow, so workflow model needs accommodate the dynamic change to better serve for enterprises. The problem of how to make the current workflow instance move to a new workflow model timely and accurately will be solved by the algorithm proposed in this paper. The article firstly illustrates the necessity of using the original workflow instance in new model, and analyzes the errors of the workflow instance migration process, then proposes a new workflow instance migration algorithm for improving time complexity based on Petri nets.

Keywords: workflow instance; Petri net; migration; polynomial; reachability.

1 Introduction

Along with the application of the workflow technology in enterprise, the dynamic change of supporting business requirements becomes the key in current research area. However, many problems need to be solved to improve the adaptability of workflow system [1], and which includes workflow instance migration which refers that current instance of the workflow model can be accurately rerun in new workflow model after dynamic changes. The article [2] points out that using method of workflow version control can only use the new workflow instance for the changed model, and so after realizing the dynamic change the instance operating cannot be promptly migrated, but this method is also the most commonly method in current workflow system. Of course the related research has been proposed, the article [3-4] puts forward solution for workflow instance migration strategy, and they all can achieve the goal of moving operational instance to new model in real-time, but they do not realize the generality, and cannot be used in all workflow changes, and time complexity is factorial level.

This paper puts forward the workflow instance migration algorithm based on Petri net, and it describes workflow model using WF-net, and expresses tasks with Transformation, and shows condition with Place, and verifies the usability of migrating workflow instance to new model by analyzing whether each state can reach after migrating, also avoids mistakes produced in the process of the dynamic change. The migration algorithm also improves the time complexity, and achieves time complexity

G. Shen and X. Huang (Eds.): CSIE 2011, Part II, CCIS 153, pp. 314–320, 2011.
© Springer-Verlag Berlin Heidelberg 2011

according with polynomial, and it realizes generality of the dynamic change through describing by WF-net, not only limited to a few workflow models.

2 The WF-Net Model Based on Petri Net

Petri net is expressed with formula PN= (P, T, F), and the letter P stands for Place, and the letter T stands for Transition, and $F(P \times T) \cup (T \times P)$ stands for collection of Connections. If the letter M stands for the state of Petri net, and the state M shows by $|P|$ dimension vector composed of Tokens in each Place ($|P|$ means the total Place in Petri nets). $M(p)$ stands for Token quantity containing by Place. (PN, M_0) shows Petri net whose initial state has given, and $[M]$ stands for the collection of reachable state starting from state M .

Definition 1: WF-net [5]

If Petri net (PN, M_0) can be defined as WF-net, it must satisfy the following three conditions:

   ① Existing a source Place i and it satisfies $\bullet i = \phi$;
   ② Existing a output Place o and it satisfies $o \bullet = \phi$;
   ③ Adding a new Place $t \bullet$ to PN, and it is used to connect Place i and Place o , and satisfies $\bullet t^* = \{o\}$, $t^* \bullet = \{i\}$, then this PN is strongly connected.

   PN added the new Place $t \bullet$ is named extended net ($\overline{PN}, M_0$) of WF-net (PN, M_0), and they satisfy $\overline{PN} = (\overline{P}, \overline{T}, \overline{F})$; $\overline{P} = P$; $\overline{T} = T \cup \{t^*\}$; $\overline{F} = F \cup \{< o, t^* >, < t^*, i >\}$.

Definition 2: Rationality of WF-net [5]

The original state M_0 of workflow is defined as follow: source Place i has one Token, and the Token quantity in the other Place is zero. A WF-net (PN, M_0) is rational when it satisfies the following three conditions:

   ① For state M which can be reached from each original state M_0 , there are an implemented sequence realizing from state M to end state M_e ;
   ② State M_e is the only end state that can be reached from state M_0 , and this state contains a Token only in output Place o ;
   ③ There is no endless Transition in (PN, M_0).

In an ordinary way workflow must verify its rationality when modeling, and the rational validation of WF-net can be solved in polynomial time [6-7], and this paper assumes WF-nets involved context are reasonable.

3 The Related Definitions of Workflow Instance Migration

If the original model W is changed to the new model W' by Workflow dynamic change and the state M is the current state some instance carrying out. Workflow instance migration refers to the process of the current state M of Workflow instance migrated from original model to new model, and this instance can be run in new model. If the state M migrated to new model is called the state M', then the definition of the state M' is that the quantities of Tokens of increased Place are all zero in the new model, and the quantities of Tokens in original Place are equals with the quantities of Tokens of each Place described by the state M.

3.1 Dynamic Change Error

The rationality definition of WF-net can validate that if WF-net is reasonable, then the instances will inevitably correctly run from start state to terminate state. However, after Workflow dynamic change, it is possible that instances migrated to new model can not correctly operate until terminate stat. This situation is called dynamic change error shown in Fig 1.

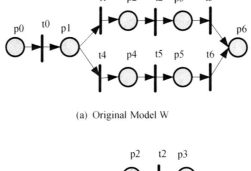

(a) Original Model W

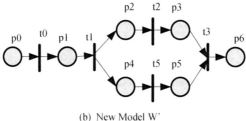

(b) New Model W'

Fig. 1. The original model and the new model in Workflow dynamic change

When the state $M =(0,0,0,0,0,1,0)T$ is the current state one instance running in original model, and if this model is changed, then the state $M'=(0,0,0,0,0,1,0)T$ is defined as the current state M migrated to new model. In new model, after M' fires Transition t_5, there is one Token in Place p_5, and the quantities of Tokens in other Place are all zero, then this instance will remain in this state forever, and no change can be fired, so this instance occurred Dynamic Change Error when migrated.

3.2 The Correctness Standards of Workflow Instance Migration

In order to avoid dynamic change error occurs, the correctness standards of migration should be abided by when instance is migrating.

Definition 3: The correctness of the instance migration

Instance migration is correct when and only when state M ' migrated from the current state M is reachable in new model.

The rationality definition of WF-net refers that if state after migrated is reachable in new model then this state must arrive end state correctly, and so dynamic change error can be avoided.

Usually, the validation of state reachability of WF-net is the problem of NP, but if this WF-net is Free-Choice net, its state reachability can be verified in polynomial time.

Definition 4: Free-Choice net

Petri net is Free-Choice net when and only when it satisfies $\forall t_1, t_2 \in T \Rightarrow (\bullet t_1 \cap \bullet t_2 = \phi) \vee (\bullet t_1 = \bullet t_2)$.

The parallel structure, sequence structure, condition selecting and loop structure of workflow can model without prejudice to the attribute of free-choice, and net model of process is usually free-choice, so the model of WF-net can be described by Free-Choice net. Many problems of Free-Choice net can be determined in polynomial time, and which is another reason that adopts Free-Choice net in this paper.

4 The Realization of the Algorithm of Workflow Instance Migration

According to the correctness of workflow instance migration, if workflow instance migration is correct then state after migrated must ensure reachability in the new model. Normally state reachability of Petri net can be verified through the method of constructing reachable graph, but the algorithm of constructing reachable graph is only exponential level. In this session some properties of Petri net and Free-Choice net is analysis and verified firstly, and then a new algorithm of workflow instance migration is put forward, and which can ensure state after migrated is reachable, and the time complexity of the algorithm is polynomial.

4.1 The Validation of According with Polynomial Time Complexity

Definition 5: Circular Petri net

(PN, M_0) is a circular Petri net when and only when it satisfies $\forall M \in [M_0] \Rightarrow M_0[M]$.

Theorem 1: The extended net $(\overline{PN}, M_0)$ is alive, bounded and circular Petri nets corresponded to the reasonable WF-net (PN, M_0).

The proof of Theorem 1 is as follows that the extended net $(\overline{PN}, M_0)$ is alive and bounded has been proved in article [5], so if $(\overline{PN}, M_0)$ is circular can be verified then Theorem 1 is correct. Because (PN, M_0) is a reasonable WF-net, there is formula $\forall M \in [M_0] \Rightarrow M \xrightarrow{\bullet} M_e \xrightarrow{t\bullet} M_0$ in (PN, M_0), that is $M_0 \in [M]$, and these above accord with definition 5, then Theorem 1 is correct.

Theorem 2: State M is reachable in reasonable WF-net (PN, M_0) when only when State M is reachable in its extended net $(\overline{PN}, M_0)$.

The proof of Theorem 2 is from two aspects, the first aspect is that state M is reachable in (PN, M_0) $\Rightarrow M$ is reachable in $(\overline{PN}, M_0)$, and which is obviously established; the second aspect is that the deduction of state M is reachable in (PN, M_0) $\Rightarrow M$ is reachable in $(\overline{PN}, M_0)$ will divided into two circumstances: ① in $(\overline{PN}, M_0)$, if when state M_0 migrates to state M it does not fires Transition $t*$ then there will be $\exists \sigma = t_1 t_2 ... t_n \Rightarrow M_0 \xrightarrow{\sigma} M$, so obviously state M is also reachable in (PN, M_0); ② in $(\overline{PN}, M_0)$, if when state M_0 migrates to state M it fires Transition $t*$ and (PN, M_0) is reasonable WF-net, then the implementation of $t*$ must change from termination state to original state, therefore there will be $\exists \sigma = t_1 t_2 ... t_n \Rightarrow M_0 \xrightarrow{\cdot} M_e \xrightarrow{t*} M_0 \xrightarrow{\sigma} M$, and obviously $M_0 \xrightarrow{\sigma} M$ is established, that is state M is reachable in (PN, M_0). If $t*$ is fired many times then $M_0 \xrightarrow{\sigma} M$ is also established. Through demonstrating the above two aspects Theorem 2 is correct.

According with Theorem 2, the reachability of state M in WF-net (PN, M_0) can be transferred to the reachability of state M in its extended net (PN, M_0). Theorem 1 has proved that extended net of rational WF-net is an alive, bounded and loop Petri nets, and the state reachability of Free-Choice net having alive, bounded and circular can be judged in polynomial time, so the problem of state reachability of free-choice WF-net (PN, M_0) can also be judged in polynomial time.

4.2 The Evolution of Migration Algorithm

Definition 6: The states M_1 and M_2 are assumed as two states of (PN, M_0), and I is assumed as an invariant (S_-). If $I \cdot M_1 = I \cdot M_2$, then M_1 and M_2 are the same to I; if M_1 and M_2 are the same to all invariants (S_-) in (PN, M_0), then $M_1 \sim M_2$.

Definition 7: Trap

If $P' \subseteq P$ and $(P') \cdot \subseteq \cdot (P')$ then P' is called a trap. If $\forall p \in P'$ and $M(p) = 0$ then trap P' is not labeled by state M, otherwise trap P' is not labeled by state M. If no trap in P contains P' then P' is the biggest trap in P.

Theorem 3: If (PN, M_0) is an alive, bounded and circular Free-Choice Petri net then $M \in [M_0]$ when and only when it satisfies the following two conditions:

① $M \sim M_0$;
② All traps in (PN, M_0) are labeled by state M [7].

Theorem 4: If M is a state in (PN, M_0) and C is incidence matrix of (PN, M_0) then $M \sim M_0$ when and only when $\exists X \in R^{|T|} \Rightarrow M = M_0 + CX$ [7].

According with the correctness standard of instance migration in definition 3, if state migrated to new model is reachable then instance can be migrated to new model and run successfully, otherwise instance can not be migrated to new model and run successfully, so the key of instance migration algorithm to verify whether state migrated to new model can reach. To state M, whose reachability in Free-Choice WF-net (PN, M_0) can be proved only when state M of extended net $(\overline{PN}, M_0)$ whether satisfies two conditions of Theorem 3 at the same time. Condition① of Theorem 3 proves whether $M \sim M_0$ is correct in extended net $(\overline{PN}, M_0)$, and this can be verified by proving whether equation $M = M_0 + CX$ has solution of real number. However whether Linear equation has solution can judge by rank of matrix, so if Rank(C)=Rank($[C \mid (M - M_0)]$) then equation has solution of real number, and Condition① is established, otherwise Condition① is not established. Condition② of Theorem 3 proves whether all traps in $(\overline{PN}, M_0)$ has labeled by state M, and which can be transformed as follow: if there is not exist a not null biggest trap in set Q of Place whose quantity of current Token is zero (the algorithm of biggest trap can be seen the algorithm 5.6 of the article[8]), and which explains that all traps in $(\overline{PN}, M_0)$ are all labeled by state M, then Condition② is established, otherwise Condition② is not established.

43 The Algorithm of Workflow Instance Migration

Based on the analysis of section above, the specific of workflow instance migration algorithm is put forward.

Algorithm 1: Workflow instance migration algorithm

The algorithm supposes that (PN, M_0) is the new model, and the state M refers to current state of running instance migrated to new model, and (PN, M_0) and state M is input of algorithm, and output is success migration or failure migration. The step of algorithm as follows:

Step1: Calculate rank of incidence matrix C of extended net $(\overline{PN}, M_0)$, and that is Rank(C);

Step2: Calculate rank of augmented matrix $[C \mid (M - M_0)]$ of the equation $M = M_0 + CX$, and that is Rank($[C \mid (M - M_0)]$);

Step3: Compare Rank(C) with Rank($[C \mid (M - M_0)]$), and if Rank(C)$\neq$Rank($[C \mid (M - M_0)]$), then return failure migration;

Step4: Calculate the set Q of Place whose quantity of current Token is zero;

Step5: Calculate the biggest trap of the set Q of Place in $(\overline{PN}, M_0)$, and if trap is null then return success migration, otherwise return failure migration

The analysis of algorithm above: in step 1, incidence matrix C of $(\overline{PN}, M_0)$ is a $|P| \times |T|$ matrix, so Rank(C) can be calculate by Gaussian elimination method, and its time complexity is $O(|P|^2)$. In step 2, augmented matrix $[C \mid (M - M_0)]$ of the equation $M = M_0 + CX$ is a $|P| \times (|T|+1)$ matrix, so the time complexity of

Rank($[C \mid (M - M_0)]$) calculated is also $O(|P|^2)$. In step 3, if Rank(C)≠Rank($[C \mid (M - M_0)]$) then state migrated to new model is not reachable, and it is not according with the correctness standard of migration, that is failure migration, and the time complexity of step 3 is constant level. The time complexity of step 4 is $O(|P|)$ and time complexity of step 5 is $O(|P|^2|T|^2)$ [8], and step 5 mainly validates condition② of Theorem 3. To sum up the above arguments the time complexity of this algorithm is $O(|P|^2|T|^2)$.

5 Conclusion

This paper discusses the workflow process changes, and puts forward a new workflow instance migration algorithm for improving time complexity, which is described by free choice nets theory and WF-net model based on Petri net, and analysis and verifies the state reachability of workflow model for the standard, and realizes the workflow instance migrated to changed model timely and accurately, and helps the workflow system running smoothly after the change to improve the adaptability of workflow system. However many problems have encountered in the process of the workflow dynamic change, such as the improvement of modifying algorithm, the redistribution of role, and the changes of system resources, etc., all of these are the direction in future research.

References

1. Smith, T.F., Waterman, M.S.: Identification of Common Molecular Subsequences. J. Mol. Biol. 147, 195–197 (1981)
2. ShenTu, X., Yao, M., Tang, X.: The research and application of flexible technology about workflow management system. Computer Technology and Development 20(1), 120–122 (2010)
3. Zhou, J., Shi, M., Ye, X.: The current situation and trend of flexible workflow technology research. Computer Integrated Manufacturing System 11(11), 1501–1510 (2005)
4. Aalst, W., Basten, T.: Inheritance of workflows:An approach to tackling problems related to change. Theoretical Computer Science 270(1-2), 125–203 (2002)
5. Aalst, W.: Exterminating the dynamic change bug:A concrete approach to support workflow change. Eindhoven University of Technology, Eindhoven (2000)
6. Wang, J., Wen, L.: Workflow management-model, method and system. Tsinghua university press, Beijing (2004)
7. Lin, C.: Stochastic Petri nets and system performance evaluation. Tsinghua university press, Beijing (2005)
8. Aalst, W.: The Application of Petri Nets to Workflow Management. Journal of Circuits, Systems and Computers 8(1), 22–66 (1998)
9. Best, E., Desel, J., Esparza, J.: Traps characterize home states in free choice systems. Theoretical Computer Science 101, 161–171 (1992)

Enterprise E-Business Information Systems Services Integration Architecture

Qing Chen

School of Management, Hubei University of Technology, Wuhan, 430068, P.R. China
cq29cn@126.com

Abstract. Enterprise e-business information systems utilize the technical methods to exchange the information between heterogeneous systems and share the resource. This paper focuses on the services integration architecture of enterprise e-business information systems. This paper first explores some issues about enterprise e-business information systems, including platform structure, data integration and interface integration. Then this paper analyses the front office architecture and advances a three-tier architecture comprising conceptual tier, user interface tier and operational tier. At last, this paper describes the back office architecture where the elementary services reside. In reality, back office and front office are not entirely separate.

Keywords: E-business, Information systems, Services integration, Enterprise.

1 Introduction

We can see a number of changes in market and society, enabled by advanced information and communication technology that strongly influence the way the world turns. These changes take place at a speed that cannot be compared to earlier changes in markets and society, i.e., they are more of a revolution than an evolution.

An enterprise creates value by processing information, particularly in the case of service enterprises. So, information has a much greater value because it contributes to achieving the enterprise's objectives. An information system represents all the elements involved in the management, processing, transport and distribution of information within the organization.

Traditionally, enterprise information systems were limited in their support for intra-organizational business processes. At the moment we see a growing importance of inter-organizational applications of enterprise information systems in particular in e-business contexts. More and more, this includes dynamical aspects in external links, e.g. with respect to offered functionality and/or with respect to collaborating parties. Emergence of electronic markets for business functions facilities this form of dynamism.

E-Business refers to the integration, within the enterprise, of tools based on information and communication technologies improve their functioning in order to create value for the enterprise, its clients, and its partners.

G. Shen and X. Huang (Eds.): CSIE 2011, Part II, CCIS 153, pp. 321–326, 2011.
© Springer-Verlag Berlin Heidelberg 2011

2 Enterprise E-Business Information Systems

Enterprise e-business information systems utilize the technical methods to exchange the information between heterogeneous systems and share the resource. Enterprise information systems are composed of the enterprise resource planning (ERP), customer relationship management (CRM), supply chain management (SCM) and other heterogeneous systems. These applications use different platforms and different programs and create the heterogeneous application integration. They are independent of each other, and the data and information can not be transferred and shared among the systems. Enterprise e-business information systems contact across the entire heterogeneous enterprise systems, applications, and data sources through establishing the underlying structure, completed in the enterprise ERP, CRM, SCM, databases, data warehouses, and other important internal systems to seamlessly process the need for data exchange and sharing. With the enterprise e-business information systems, enterprises can combine the core business applications with new solutions of Internet. Enterprise Information Systems will process integration, software, standards and hardware together to achieve seamless integration between the systems.

Enterprise e-business information systems platform takes the overall supervision on all information achievement, and is responsible for the registration of different enterprises resources, as well as releasing information, checking the data pooled in the database, to fulfill the information sharing and data exchange.

2.1 Platform Structure

Enterprise e-business information systems platform provides a unified entrance of information system to the users and it issues to the UDDI (Universal Description Discovery and Integration) registry queries by using WSDL (Web Services Description Language) to describe the required service.

Information systems users issue query request to Web service registry by using SOAP (Simple Object Access Protocol) message after receiving the services request described in WSDL. UDDI backs to the serviced WSDL the information system description their system through the analysis of Web services from the information center for the registration.

UDDI service is used for the management of the interface service information described by the WSDL form released by information systems. When the two systems the need for data exchange, it can find the related information that provides services from UDDI, and provides services to the request system and binding it.

When the information systems use SOAP, they should provide the exchange of data with XML (Extensible Markup Language) format, and the integration application is responsible of the work of the system conversion between XML with different data format.

Now enterprises are using the database such as SQL Server, My SQL, Access, etc., that exist the problem of database non-uniformed, rights management non-uniformed, platform non-uniformed, discrete distribution of hard access. In order to make their own enterprises to join the information integration platform, to allow other enterprises to take advantage of the shared information, we need to extract sharing data from the internal data, generate XML documents, and put them on to the XML server. And through monitoring the XML documents, put the obtained XML data on to the Internet and understand data changes. Then reflect to the other systems in a timely manner in order to ensure the consistency of data. This will enable enterprises to separate the internal data from the sharing data, and let them contact, thereby reducing the risk of the internal secret resources exposed to Internet.

2.2 Data Integration

XML can be used to exchange the data between heterogeneous systems. XML can be used as standards of the information transmission between heterogeneous platforms. We can formulate the rules of data exchange, and fulfill cross-platform heterogeneous data exchange in the enterprise information systems as the following steps:

XML standard data refers to exchange information on the needs of the organizational structure, content and the relationship between them through a mechanism. We propose that use the XML Schema data for exchanging the heterogeneous systems and sharing information.

There are differences between enterprise systems to realize XML format conversion, and it is also difficult to exchange data with other systems according to their own XML documents. However, XSLT (Extensible Stylesheet Language Transformations) can convert a corresponding XML format into a corresponding XML documents, and share information.

2.3 Interface Integration

Enterprise e-business information systems provide services that follow the SOAP protocol call Standard interface, and publish enterprise unified directory service through UDDI. The information system should support the SOAP protocol standard interface call way to call the other information systems interface services. Web Service provides a standard interface, so we can easily integrate through it. Then it is able to access the network integrate data through a shared database form. In order to achieve interoperability between systems, enterprise information system integrates data interface tier by using the adapter technology to package component of database systems, applications and network services. In order to solve the problem of the systems connection, adapter is created as a reusable and unified interface, and through these interfaces, each application requires can only connected with the enterprise systems integrated platform and there is no need for interacting with each of the applications. The development of system integration is an important part of integrated enterprise information interface.

3 Front Office Architecture

The front office refers to the front part of the enterprise, visible for the clients and in direct contact with them, such as the marketing, user support, or after-sales service teams.The front office architecture of enterprise e-business information system refers to the integrated interface. It can be depicted in the form of a three-tier architecture comprising conceptual tier, user interface tier and operational tier.

3.1 Conceptual Tier

On a conceptual tier, the integrated information system services need to be compiled into some sort of service bundles around single real-world situations where they apply. This tier includes all the information which is displayed by a web application such as information or data and instructions regarding the information system. It further contains information about e.g. the forms, procedures and descriptions about legal background. The content of a hypermedia application is organized by the structure.

3.2 User Interface Tier

Those service bundles must be logically presented on the user interface tier as responses to single real-world problems. This tier describes the visualization of services to the user. It includes the individual granules of information and dynamic features such as navigation. Here, the process flow and content for a specific service are integrated and visualized to the user through the interface.

3.3 Operational Tier

Those service bundles must be actually enacted and delivered on the operational tier as if they were individual (in contrast to bundled), atomic services. The following services have to be provided:

Forms Service. In order to invoke a service in a traditional way, an applicant has generally to fill in and hand in a form, where the requested data and documents have to be provided. Online forms basically have the same functionality, except that they can facilitate and guide the applicant in completing the data and that, with modern communication means, the user can be supported in pre-filling fields. In this way, the task of data-entry is shifted to the user at the front office side, while the information system, with the appropriate standardized interfaces to back office systems, can directly integrate the data into the electronic workflow and database systems. Despite of this feature, a good layout design of forms guides the user step-by-step in the provision of the right data and document resources.

Routing Service. In the one-stop concept, the offers and information towards the user are provided according to services. The user does not need to know the respective service at the back office side in charge of the service completion and delivery. So, a routing mechanism is required that directs the application of the user from the interface to the service in charge of the user service the user has applied for.

Information Service. It contains all information on the online request, the interface functionality and the description of the online offer. It includes details on the offered services such as the needed documents, the process structure, legal grounding of the process, fees, preconditions, etc.

Authentification. Since online service applications require a clear, unique and trusted identification of the applicant, identification and authentification mechanisms like login, digital identity and functionality for intermediaries are necessary.

Encryption, Security and Authenticity of Data. E-business processes deal with rather sensible and personal data and documents, which are transmitted via an insecure Internet. Security and encryption mechanisms have to be provided between the client at the user side, the interface and the back office to secure data and documents and to ensure that these are not manipulated, wiretapped and object to fraud.

Process Workflow on the Interface Tier. The front office needs to properly support the tasks to be performed by the user. A process workflow at the front office has to guide this interaction and task performance of the user within a running service from the invocation of the service until it's completion.

Interfaces to the Back Office. Despite of the workflow at the front office, appropriate standardized interfaces are required to ensure interoperability and direct integration to the back office.

4   Back Office Architecture

The Back Office refers to all parts of the information system to which the final user does not have access. The term therefore covers all internal processes within the enterprise (production, logistics, warehousing, sales, accounting, human resources management, etc.).The back office architecture of enterprise e-business information system is where the elementary services reside.

The current trend calls for integrated services that are effective, simple to use, shaped around and responding to the needs of the user and are not merely arranged for the provider's convenience. In this way, the user need have no knowledge of or direct interaction with the involved structures of system in order to conduct their business. Back office interoperability becomes a key enabler of services integration. System entities need to be interoperable, in order to allow for data and information to be exchanged and processed seamlessly.

In order for a front office integration of information system to be able to respond to the needs of the user, much more than the simple indexing of the user offerings is required. The need for services calls for solutions that will facilitate the creation of integrated services by joining together the service offerings based on the use that the user make of them.

Smart service-oriented information system should be focused on one goal: helping the user solve problems, not merely delivering same old services through a new medium.

In the light of the above, the development of integrated services by completely re-designing business processes from a customer's point of view, is considered to be a non-viable approach, since this would translate into a massive process reengineering wave and calling for the radical reorganization of online service (the reassigning of responsibilities, the elimination of redundant processes, the modification of organizational structures etc).

A more viable solution would be to allocate the integrated services to the enterprise information portal, maintaining the consolidated configuration of enterprise and the existing assignment of responsibilities and optimizing services on an elementary service level (intra-enterprise business process reengineering). This means that the internal business processes associated with each elementary service have to be modeled and redesigned, in order to transform traditional processes to enterprise e-business processes.

5 Conclusions

Nowadays, because of the different platforms of enterprise information system, development languages and database systems, enterprise information resources can not be shared, that caused the application division of enterprise information systems. Enterprise e-business information systems services integration architecture utilizes the technical methods to make the information between heterogeneous systems exchanging the information and sharing the resources.

References

1. Pahl, C., Hasselbring, W., Voss, M.: Service-Centric Integration Architecture for Enterprise Software Systems. Journal of Information Science and Engineering 25, 1321–1336 (2009)
2. Liu, Y.W., Fan, L.L.: System of Enterprise Application Integration Based on Web Services. Southwest Jiaotong University (2007) (in chinese)
3. Conrad, S., Hasselbring, W., Koschel, A., Tritsch, R.: Enterprise Application Integration. Elsevier, Spektrum (2006)
4. Olsson, A., Karlsson, S.: The Integration of Customer Needs in the Establishment of an E-Business System for Internal Service. International Journal of Logistics: Research & Applications 4, 305–317 (2003)
5. Boulianne, E.: A Contingency Framework for Effective Information Systems Design and E-Business Applications. International Journal of Information Technology & Management 1, 50–68 (2009)
6. Web Services Architecture Requirements, http://www.w3.org

Saliency-Based Automatic Target Detection in Remote Sensing Images*

Wei Li and Chunhong Pan

NLPR, Institute of Automation, Chinese Academy of Sciences
{wli,chpan}@nlpr.ia.ac.cn

Abstract. Automatic target detection in satellite images remains a challenging problem. Previous methods mainly focus on independent detection of multiple targets. In this paper, we propose a simultaneous multi-class target detection approach by using saliency computation. The advantages are twofold. First, saliency map is computed only once for all target types. This saves a large amount of computational time but does not miss any targets. Second, we use small regions, obtained from over-segmentation, to be the elementary unit of detection. This provides shape information to remove most false candidates for the final detection. Experiments show that the targets can be quickly detected and the detection rate is as high as the independent detecting methods.

1 Introduction

Automatic target recognition (ATR) in high resolution satellite images is a fundamental yet challenging task in computer vision. In general, an ATR system consists of several components such as detection, segmentation and classification. Our work focuses on the detection of man-made targets in satellite images of ground areas, typically the airplanes and oil tanks in complex airport scene.

A generic detection algorithm has two steps: candidate generation and object detection. Two kinds of methods for candidate generation have been proposed in literature: exhaustive search method [1] which regards all the windows in an image as candidates and segmentation based method [2] that extracts region of interest (ROI) to be candidates. The methods used in object detection are usually based on supervised learning [2] or shape matching [3]. Although these approaches have good performances in many situations, they exist a lot of problems in the case of detecting multiclass objects simultaneously. Exhaustive search method is time-consuming, when considering the variations of target type, orientation and size. Segmentation based method is more efficient, but heavily depends on the segmentation performance. It is often difficult to obtain ROIs of different targets by the same segmentation algorithm in complicated satellite images.

In spite of various sizes and appearances, salient object can attract human's attention at first glance. Inspired by this characteristic, different computational models [4] [5] have been proposed to detect salient object. A probabilistic mixture mode is

---

* This work was supported by the National Natural Science Foundation of China (Grant No. 61075016, Grant No. 60873161, and Grant No. 60975037).

G. Shen and X. Huang (Eds.): CSIE 2011, Part II, CCIS 153, pp. 327–333, 2011.
© Springer-Verlag Berlin Heidelberg 2011

proposed in [4] for detecting salient objects. This method is task-specific and requires many training samples to learn its parameters beforehand. By contrast, a learning-free model is proposed in [5], which computes saliency in a bottom-up way by using phase spectrum of the Fourier Transform. In this context, we propose a saliency-based multi-class target detection algorithm. Our algorithm differs from the previous methods in two aspects.

First, by using a task-independent saliency algorithm, we simultaneously detect two types of targets via the same three-stage procedure. In this way, the computation complexity will not increase linearly as the number of classes grows. In detail the three stages are hierarchically applied in an efficient way. For a satellite image, we first run a low-cost bottom-up saliency computing and a quick segmentation algorithm to yield initial ROIs, then use a ROI classification to remove most false ROIs, and finally perform accurate object matching to localize our targets.

Second, rather than using the pixel level, we use small regions, which are obtained from over-segmentation, to be the elementary unit. These regions can capture shape and size information of our objects, thus providing better contexts for the further detection. Moreover, the regions preserve the boundaries of salient target, which are often smoothed by saliency computation. Experiments show the efficiency and effectiveness of our proposed method.

2 Proposed Method

As illustrated in Fig. 1, our algorithm can be mainly divided into three stages, i.e. the Saliency Based ROI Extraction, the ROI Type Generation, and the Targets Detection. The input high resolution satellite image is first analyzed by extracting ROIs (in Sub-section. 2.1). These ROIs are then classified into three types, i.e. the oil tank ROI, the aircraft ROI, and others, based on the prior models (in Sub-section.2.2). Finally, the oil tanks and aircrafts are detected from the corresponding ROIs (in Sub-section.2.3).

2.1 Saliency Based ROI Extraction

Given an image I, we construct its saliency map SM by using phase spectrum of Fourier transform [5]

$$SM = \left\| F^{-1}(e^{i \cdot P(F(I))}) \right\| \otimes g \qquad (1)$$

where g is the two dimensional Gaussian kernel, $F(\cdot)$, $F^{-1}(\cdot)$, and $P(\cdot)$ are the Fourier transform, inverse Fourier transform, and image phase spectrum, respectively. The smoothing operation g weakens boundaries of salient object. If we apply a threshold operator on the saliency map (see Fig. 2(b)) directly, the resulted foreground mask may contain some background information, and adjacent target regions may be merged together. Thus, it is hard to extract accurate ROIs (see Fig. 2(d)). In order to solve this problem, we combine the saliency computation and over-segmentation together. In the application of airport scene target detection, it is well observed that typical target, e.g. aircraft or oil tank, is surrounded by a relatively homogeneous background region. If the image is over-segmented into small regions, the

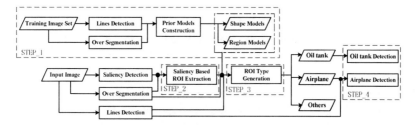

Fig. 1. The flowchart of the proposed approach. The dashed red rectangles show the four core steps of our algorithm.

boundaries of salient object are well kept. Accordingly, instead of raw pixel saliency value, we choose the average saliency value in each region. We can get the salient region, in which the average saliency value is higher than a threshold, and the foreground mask is obtained by combing all these salient regions.

Fig. 2. An example of the Saliency Based ROI Extraction stage. Sub-figures (b) and (c) give the saliency map and over-segmentation results respectively. Sub-figure (d) shows ROIs extracted from directly thresholding the saliency map. Comparatively, Sub-figure(e) illustrates the ROIs extracted with the proposed method.

Given an input image, we run the mean shift [6] algorithm to segment it into a set of small regions, denoted as $I = \bigcup_{i=1}^{N} R_i$, where N is the number of region (see Fig.2(c)). For each R_i, we compute its average saliency value sm_i, and regard it as a salient region if sm_i is higher than a threshold (0.1 times the maximum saliency value in the saliency map). Otherwise, we discard it as a background region. We use R_i^f to denote a salient region. Finally, with all the kept R_i^f s, we check their connectivities and merge all the connected ones into a large region unit. We use ROI to name such a unit, on which the postprocessing will be performed. Fig. 2(e) shows a ROI example. As can be seen, some adjacent target regions, such as the two airplanes at the left-bottom domain, are merged together (see Fig.2(d)). By contrast, our algorithm can correctly separate them from each other (see Fig. 2(e)).

2.2 ROI Type Generation

In this section, we generate target candidates from the above given ROIs. The goal is to reduce the number of false positives. To this end, we first need to generate a type hypothesis for each salient region. From a R_i^f, we first extract a feature vector f_i, and then classify it into one of the three types: oil tank, airplane and background, with a simple linear classifier. In the following, we will first present how to define the feature f_i.

In an airport scene, false alarms come mainly from the noisy manmade objects that have similar intensity and texture characteristics. However, these objects, such as small buildings, vehicles and embarkation ramps, have quite different shapes from our two targets. One can clearly see this phenomenon in Fig. 3. The shape of oil tank is approximate to a circle. A typical airplane is a group of such components: two wings, possibly two or more engines, a fuselage and two rear wings. Since they are linearly shaped, we can extract their skeleton lines. f_i is actually defined in terms of the regional and line properties of R_i^f. The former comes from the over-segmentation results while the latter from skeleton line detections [7]. In particular, we specify the regional property by its eccentricity f_i^e and its solidity f_i^s, which have been widely used for measuring regions. As for the line property, two new measures are proposed. We first compute the width of each point in the extracted skeleton line. Then we compute the average width f_i^w and filling ratio f_i^r of the skeleton line by

$$f_i^w = \frac{\sum_{j=1}^{N^p} w_j}{N^p}, \quad f_i^r = \frac{\sum_{j=1}^{N^p} w_j}{S(R_i^f)} \tag{2}$$

where w_j is the width of jth point, N^p is the number of points inside R_i^f and $S(\cdot)$ is the area function. Correspondingly, f_i is a concatenation of $\{f_i^e, f_i^s, f_i^r, f_i^w\}$.

The four measurements constitute a discriminative feature. As illustrated in Fig. 3, the oil tank ROI has a low eccentricity and a high solidity value while the inverse situation happens to the airplane ROI. Plus the two line features, it suffices to distinguish oil tank, airplane and clutters.

2.3 Targets Detection

This subsection focuses on detecting targets on the labeled ROIs. The oil tank and airplane are detected by different approaches illustrated as follows.

Oil Tank Detection. We first locate oil tank candidates by circle detection. Following it, we use the entropies of their color distributions to remove the false candidates. So far, many methods have been developed for the circle detection. Among them, Randomized Hough Transform [8] is one of the most widely used methods. In this work, Randomized Hough Transform algorithm is first utilized to obtain the candidate circles, $\{c_i\}_{i=1}^N$

$$\{c_i\}_{i=1}^N = RHT(r_{min}, r_{max}, \tau_{ratio}) \tag{3}$$

where r_{min}, r_{max} are the minimal and maximal radius, and τ_{ratio} is the minimal ratio of the number of detected edge pixels. Due to the effects of optical sensor devices and lighting conditions, there may be shape distortions or shadow for circle detection. Therefore, the false circles should be further removed. Our insight is that the color of an oil tank is evenly distributed. We measure the confidence each circle by calculating the entropy $h(c_i)$ of color distribution inside of the circle. If the entropy of circle $h(c_i)$ is larger than a threshold $\tau_{entropy}$, this circle is removed.

ROI	Salient Region	Skeleton Lines	Feature Values			
			$\mathbf{f}^e$	$\mathbf{f}^s$	$\mathbf{f}^r$	$\mathbf{f}^w$
			0.852	0.390	1.335	8.256
			$\mathbf{f}^e$	$\mathbf{f}^s$	$\mathbf{f}^r$	$\mathbf{f}^w$
			0.993	0.594	2.829	10.43
			$\mathbf{f}^e$	$\mathbf{f}^s$	$\mathbf{f}^r$	$\mathbf{f}^w$
			0.210	0.982	0.0	0.0

Fig. 3. The feature values of three salient regions. The bright regions in the second column are the salient regions. The red lines are skeleton lines (in column three), while the blues are the width. There is no skeleton line detected in the third salient region (oil tank) because its shape is approximate to a circle.

Airplane Detection. For each candidate region, we first extract its edge, then airplane can be distinguished by shape matching using the Shape Context algorithm [9]. To perform this, model shape is acquired and we use two templates as model. Each candidate region is matched with the two templates, and if the matching distance is below a threshold th_S, the region is declared as an airplane. Specifically, the distance metric D between the candidate M and a template T is defined as

$$D = \alpha D_{be} + \beta D_{sc} + \gamma D_{ac} \qquad (4)$$

where α, β, γ denote weighted parameters. D_{be} measures the bending energy between M and T ; D_{sc} accounts for the shape context distance, which captures the discrepancy between a set of boundary point correspondences; and D_{ac} represents the binary appearance difference between T and the transformation normalized M.

The above detections yield a set of more confident target candidates, most of which contain true airplanes and oil tanks. In practice, we can build on the topological relationship between airplane and oil tanks to further filter out some false candidates.

3   Experimental Result

Both qualitative and quantitative experiments were conducted to evaluate the proposed approach. The test data set consists of 40 satellite images of complex airport scenes. The image size varies from 600×600 to 2000×2000. In our implementation, the parameters are set as $r_{min} = 4$, $r_{max} = 24$, $\tau_{entropy} = 0.2$, D = 0.4 . Both the ROI extraction and object detection were extensively evaluated. The goal of ROI extraction is to detect all the targets of interest. To evaluate the extraction performance, two quantitative terms are used for this measurement. The first is the detection rate r, which is defined as the ratio of number of extracted airplane and oil tank ROIs to the ground-truthed number of targets in the image. We use it to measure the accuracy of ROI extraction in covering detected targets. In our experiments, the ROI detection rate of our method reaches 100%. The second term measures the ROI's location accuracy. We specify it by η, which is defined as the average intersection ratio of all the detected ROIs to the corresponding ground truths (GTs), given by $\eta = \sum_{i=1}^{N} \frac{ROI_i \cap GT_i}{ROI_i \cup GT_i}$, where N is the number of ROI. The location accuracy η is 0.91. Thus, our method obtains ROIs that are accurate enough for further detection stage.

To evaluate the final detection results, we compared our approach with two exhaustive search methods. We utilize the classical detection rate (DT) and false alarm rate (FA) as the measure metric. Tab. 1 shows the results. For oil tank detection, we compared the direct Randomized Hough Transform (RHT) circle detection method with our approach. And for airplane we compared our approach with the method proposed in [3] (OCM). The detection rate of oil tanks is 100% and false alarm rate is 0. The overall performance of airplane detection is worse than that of the oil tanks. The errors come mainly from the shape matching step. We only use two templates and shape matching by Shape Context and Thin Plate Spline algorithm often fail when confusing manmade objects such as small vehicles and embarkation ramps are scattered around the airplanes. However, saliency based ROI greatly reduces the image search space, so our method is smaller in time cost. In addition, by fusioning the saliency and region properties, the false alarm rate is largely reduced.

Table 1. Oil tank and airplane detection performance comparison

oil tank	DT	FA	Time
RHT	1.0	0.11	6.34min
our	1.0	0.0	31.2s
airplane	DT	FA	Time
OCM	0.95	0.3	4.31min
our	0.93	0.05	52.7s

Fig. 4 gives a representative result of our approach. Due to the saliency computation, our method is insensitive to target type, orientation and scale changes. As depicted in the figure, the airplane types, orientations and sizes are all having large variations. The sizes of the airplanes vary from 40 to 100 pixels. The airplanes have no favored orientation. Moreover, oil tank and airplane have totally different shapes. In spite of these difficulties, our approach performs well in detecting targets.

Fig. 4. The final detection result

4 Conclusion

In this paper, a new saliency-based multi-target detection algorithm is proposed. We combine a low-cost bottom-up saliency computing and a quick segmentation algorithm to yield initial ROIs. Following it, we use a simple classification to remove most false ROIs, and finally detect the airplane and oiltank targets via shape matching. Experimental results show that this approach is a fast and accurate way to detect multi-class targets. In future, we intend to improve the detection ratio by using more robust shape matching techniques. We believe that the proposed framework can also be a promising way to other tasks, such as fusion detection.

References

1. Viola, P., Jones, M.: Rapid object detection using a boosted cascade of simple features. In: Proceedings of IEEE Conference on Computer Vision and Pattern Recognition, pp. 511–518 (2001)
2. Yao, J., Zhang, Z.F.: Object detection in aerial imagery based on enhanced semi-supervised learning. In: Proceedings of IEEE International Conference on Computer Vision, pp. 1012–1017 (2005)
3. Olson, C.F., Huttenlocher, D.P.: Automatic target recognition by matching oriented edge pixels. IEEE Transactions Image Processing 6(1), 103–113 (1997)
4. Chalmond, B., Francesconi, B., Herbin, S.: Using hidden scale for salient object detection. IEEE Transactions Image Processing 15, 2644–2656 (2006)
5. Guo, C.L., Ma, Q., Zhang, L.M.: Spatio-temporal saliency detection using phase spectrum of quaternion fourier transform. In: Proceedings of IEEE Conference on Computer Vision and Pattern Recognition, pp. 1–8 (2008)
6. Comaniciu, D., Meer, P., Member, S.: Mean shift: A robust approach toward feature space analysis. IEEE Transactions on Pattern Analysis and Machine Intelligence 24, 603–619 (2002)
7. Steger, C.: An unbiased detector of curvilinear structures. IEEE Transactions on Pattern Analysis and Machine Intelligence 20, 113–125 (1998)
8. Xu, L., Oja, E., Kultanen, P.: A new curve detection method: Randomized hough transform. Pattern Recognition Letter 11(5), 331–338 (1990)
9. Belongie, S., Malik, J., Puzicha, J.: Shape matching and object recognition using shape context. IEEE Transactions on Pattern Analysis and Machine Intelligence 24(24), 509–522 (2002)

The Recursive Algorithm of Converting the Forest into the Corresponding Binary Tree

Min Wang

Computer Science Department, Weinan Teachers University, Weinan, Shanxi, China
wntcwm@126.com

Abstract. Through analyzing the storage structures of tree, forest and binary tree, the recursive algorithm design ideas of converting the forest into the corresponding binary tree are introduced, and the recursive conversion algorithm description in C was given in this paper. Finally, the algorithm was evaluated from the two aspects of time complexity and space complexity.

Keywords: Tree; Forest; Binary tree; Recursion; Time complexity; Space complexity.

1 Introduction

Trees or Forests can take many forms of storage structures in a large number of applications, but many "Data Structure" materials introduced their storage structures mainly about the parents representation, the children representation and the child and brother representation. Binary tree is another tree structure, and its characteristic is that each node of it has at most two subtrees which are ordered [1]. Binary tree is convenient for computer processing [2], thus the tree or forest can be converted into the corresponding binary tree, and then execute the relevant oprations. This paper will analyze and design the recursive algorithm of converting the forest into the corresponding binary tree, give the algorithm description in C, and analyze and evaluate the algorithm from the two aspects of time complexity and space complexity, so as to play a guiding role in teaching the relevant chapters in "Data Structure" curriculum.

2 The Child and Brother Representation of Tree

The child and brother representation of tree is also known as the binary tree representation or the binary linked list representation. That is the storage structure of the tree is the binary linked list. The two pointer fields, named *Firstchild* and *Nextsibling*, in each node of the linked list indicate respectively the first child and the next sibling of the node [1].

The storage structure of the linked node is shown as Fig.1.

Firstchild	*data*	*Nextsibling*

Fig. 1. The node structure of the binary linked list of tree

G. Shen and X. Huang (Eds.): CSIE 2011, Part II, CCIS 153, pp. 334–337, 2011.
© Springer-Verlag Berlin Heidelberg 2011

The node type can be defined in C as follows:

```
typedef struct node{
  DataType data;
  struct node *Firstchild,*Nextsibling;
} CSNode, *CSTree; [1,2]
```

3   The Storage Structure of the Binary Tree

For any binary tree, each node of it has only two children and one parent (root node without parent), and each node can be designed to include at least three fields: *data*, which is used to store the value of the node, *Lchild*, which points to the left child of the node, and *Rchild*, which points to the right child of the node. Its storage structure is shown as Fig.2.

Lchild	data	Rchild

Fig. 2. The node structure of the binary linked list of the binary tree

The node type can be defined in C as follows:

```
typedef struct node{
  DataType data;
  struct node *Lchild,*Rchild;
} Node, *BTree; [2]
```

4   Convert the Forest into the Corresponding Binary Tree

As the tree and the binary tree have the same binary linked storage structure, the binary linked list can be used as their relation medium. That is, given a tree, you can find one and only corresponding binary tree, and their storage structure are the same but only different in interpretation [1].

4.1   The Formalized Definition of the Converting Algorithm

Forest is a collection of some trees. As the tree can correspond to a unique binary tree, the forest can also correspond to a unique binary tree [2].

If $F=\{T_1,T_2,\ldots,T_n\}$ is a forest, according the following rules to convert F into a binary tree $B=\{root,LB,RB\}$:

(1) If F is empty, that is $n=0$, B will be an empty tree;
(2) Otherwise, follow these steps to convert:
   ① The root of B (named *root*) is the root of the first tree of the forest ($ROOT(T_1)$);
   ② The left subtree of B (named LB) is a binary tree converted from $F_1=\{T_{11},T_{12},\ldots,T_{1m}\}$, which is the subtree forest of the root of T_1;

③ The right subtree of B (named RB) is a binary tree converted from forest $F'=\{T_2,T_3,...,T_n\}$ [1].

4.2 Algorithm Description in C

According to the aforementioned steps of this algorithm, we can regard firstly the forest F as an ordered set of $T_1,T_2,...,T_n$, store all the trees in the forest with the child and brother binary linked structure type *CSTree* mention before, and then use the pointer array in C to store the forest. The converted binary tree adopts the binary linked type *BTree*. To obtain the subtree forest of the root of the first tree T_1, we can start from the node pointed by the *Firstchild* field of the root node of T_1, and then along with the *Nextsibling* fields of the nodes until the lower right node.

The conversion procedure can adopt the recursive design idea, and the algorithm description in C is as follows:

```
void TransForest(CSTree F[], int n, BTree *B)
{  CSTree TF[M],p;   int i;
//Macro name M is the maximum node amount of the forest.
   if(!n)
      *B=NULL;
   else{
      (*B)->data=F[0]->data;
      i=0;
      while(p){
         TF[i]=p;
         p=p->Nextsibling;
         i++;   }//End_while
      TransForest(TF,i,(*B)->Lchild);
      TransForest(&F[1],n-1,(*B)->Rchild);
   }//End_if
}//End
```

4.3 Algorithm Analysis and Evaluation

The returned result of each recursive calling does not be saved, so it must be computed once more whenever needed, this leads to the time complexity of recursive functions actually depend on the times of recursive calling [3,4].

Function *TransForest()* converts forest F into its corresponding binary tree B, and the first function call starts from F. If F is not empty, the root of B will be the root of the first tree T_1 of F. After the subtree forest of the root node of the first tree has been located (through the loop statement *while*), the recursive calling that get the left subtree of B can be executed, and then the right subtree of B can be get from another recursive calling. Since this function includes two recursive call statements, the times of recursive calling is actually the sum of the number of nodes in the forest and the number of null pointers. An n nodes binary linked list has $n+1$ null pointers, and then the total number of recursive calling is $2n+1$ times [4]. In addition, during each recursive calling execution, the loop statement is likely to be executed to get the subtree forest of the root of the first tree in the forest, thus, by considering the worst case, that is, only one tree in the forest, the subtree forest of the root node of the first tree will include all the remaining nodes except the root. Therefore, the maximum times of loop is subtracting 1 from the number of nodes in the forest. The number (n) of nodes in the forest is regarded as the scale of the problem. With the gradually increase of problem scale, the algorithm time complexity is nearly $T(n)=O(n(2n+1))$。

In addition to the storage space used by the function itself, function *TransForest()* introduced an assistant vector *TM[M]*, which is used to store the subtree nodes of the root node of T_1. According to the analysis aforementioned, and considering the worst case, the subtree forest of the root node of T_1 might be all the remaining nodes except the root, thus the macro name M is at most the number of nodes in the forest minus 1. Thus the algorithm space complexity is linear order, that is $S(n)=O(n)$.

5 Conclusion

This paper analyzed in detail the procedure of converting the forest into the corresponding binary tree, introduced the recursive analyze ideas and the concrete design process, and thus played a guiding role in teaching the relevant chapters in "Data Structure" curriculum.

Acknowledgments. This work is supported by Research Fund of Weinan Teachers University (No. 11YKS014).

References

1. Yan, W., Wu, W.: Data Structures(C language edition). Tsinghua University Press, Beijing (2002)
2. Geng, G.: Data Structure—C Language description. Xi'an Electronic Science and Technology University Press, Xi'an (2005)
3. Wang, M., Li, J.: Analysis of Time Efficiency in Recursion Algorithm. Journal of Weinan Teachers University 18(5), 61–62 (2003)
4. Wang, M.: Non-Recursive Simulation of the Recursive Algorithm for Searching the Longest Path in Binary Tree. Science Technology and Engineering 10(6), 1535–1539 (2010)

Igneous Rocks Recognition Based on Improved Fuzzy Neural Network

Xiaoyan Tang and Zhidi Liu

College of Geology and Environment, Xi'an University of Science and Technology, China
lzdtxy2004@sina.com

Abstract. The lithology recognition of igneous rock is the foundation of the lithofacies division, the reservoir synthetic evaluation, the well pattern deployment, and the development plan establishment. This paper selected the statistical model of logging-lithology, and established the model of recognizing igneous rock using improved fuzzy neural network method. This model recognized the igneous rock lithology in the research work area. The recognition result show that this method can accurately carry on the lithology recognition in this work area. It is compared with microscope analysis lithology. Results show that it is reliable. Recognition precision is high, and practicability is better.

Keywords: Igneous Rocks; Fuzzy; Improved Neural Network; Recognition.

1 Introduction

The igneous reservoir has become a new area of the world's oil and gas exploration. During the logging comprehensive evaluation of the igneous rock, the lithology or lithofacies interpretations play an important role in formation evaluation and reservoir description [1]. Therefore, the logging data, which have vast rock characterization information, is taken full advantage of, and the mathematical method with higher recognition accuracy is optimized to the recognition of igneous rocks.

The fuzzy neural network has powerful knowledge expression and powerful learning ability [2, 3]. Not only it expands the application scope of fuzzy technology, but also it is better than the conventional neural network in learning time, training steps and precision[4,5]. Because of its advantages, fuzzy neural network technologies are widely applied in petroleum exploration and development. During interpreting the complex rocks by using conventional logging data, there are some characteristics of uncertainty, ambiguity and highly nonlinear problem between the logging parameters and the lithology. Thus, the improved fuzzy neural network is applied to recognize the igneous rocks in this paper.

2 Improved Fuzzy Neural Network

The improved fuzzy neural network shows in Fig.1. There are four layers, namely, the input layer, the fuzzy layer, the fuzzy inference layer and the anti-fuzzy layer.

G. Shen and X. Huang (Eds.): CSIE 2011, Part II, CCIS 153, pp. 338–342, 2011.
© Springer-Verlag Berlin Heidelberg 2011

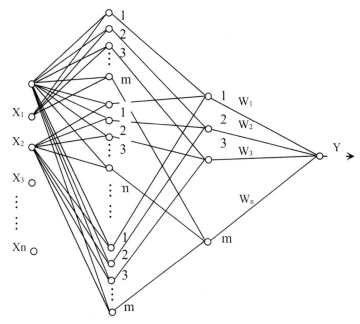

Input Layer   Fuzzy Layer   Fuzzy Inference Layer   Anti-fuzzy Layer

Fig. 1. The improved four layers fuzzy neural network structure

In the first layer, each neuron node is connected directly to each input component. Input variable x is an n-dimensional feature vector, n is determined by the specific problems.

In the second layer, each neuron node represents a fuzzy linguistic variable, which is to calculate the memberships of each component of the input vector belongs to the language variable corresponding to the fuzzy sets. The number of nodes of the fuzzy layer is $m \times n$ (m is the number of clusters). The input variables are x_i , the output is the degree of membership that each variable belongs to cluster.

The membership function is the following formula as follows,

$$u_{ij} = \exp(-(x_i - m_{ij})^2 / \sigma_{ij}^2) \quad 1 \le i \le n \;;\; 1 \le j \le m \tag{1}$$

Where, x_i is input variable, m_{ij} , σ_{ij}^2 corresponds to each node of the fuzzy layer.

In the third layer, each neuron node represents a fuzzy rule, which is to match the fuzzy rules and calculate the practical degree of each rule. The node output π_j is the multiply of membership. The number of nodes m is obtained by sample cluster analysis based on K-means method, which can also adjust the value of this function according to actual needs.

$$\pi_j = u_{1j} \bullet u_{2j} \bullet \cdots u_{nj} = \prod_{i=1}^{n} u_{ij} \qquad 1 \le j \le m \qquad (2)$$

In the fourth layer, each neuron node is carried on anti-fuzzy calculation, and the exact value of network output is obtained. The node output is respectively all input algebraic multiply. y is the ultimate anti-fuzzy output as follows,

$$y = \omega_1 \pi_1 + \omega_2 \pi_2 + \cdots + \omega_m \pi_m \qquad (3)$$

Where, ω_i is the weight between the fuzzy inference layer and the anti-fuzzy layer.

But the routine output based on fuzzy neural network as,

$$y = \sum_{i=1}^{m} \omega_i \pi_i / \sum_{i=1}^{m} \pi_i \qquad (4)$$

When training the samples, the denominator $\sum_{i=1}^{m} \omega_i \pi_i$ easily tend to zero, which leads into an infinite loop operation; the desired effects are not obtained. And the samples data have to make the appropriate changes. The credibility of the result is reduced. But the output of the improved network pattern is $\sum_{i=1}^{m} \omega_i \pi_i$, which corrects the shortcomings of conventional network pattern. It is obvious from figure 1 that this model is a new and improved fuzzy neural network, and it has the advantages of simple computation. The inference of each network has obvious physical meaning. Compared with existing network model, its physical meaning is more apparent.

During establishing rock recognition model, firstly, the rock information of key wells' continuous formation is obtained from the microscope data. Secondly, the characteristics of logging variable are extracted from logging curves and the corresponding correctly classifications are input to the neural network model by compared with the logging response data. Then the weights and thresholds are obtained after neural networks' learning, and the learning outcomes are saved in the model. Lastly the characteristic data of needing recognition rocks are input to the network, the rocks are correctly recognized and classified.

3   Igneous Rocks Recognition

During recognizing igneous rocks based on the method, the establishing center statistical pattern of logging-lithicfacies is necessary, then the rocks recognition are carried out according to the method of improved fuzzy neural network.

3.1   The Center Statistical Pattern Establishment of the Logging-Lithicfacies

The continuous formation rock information of key wells is obtained from core data. Comparing with the amplitude of logging curve and homing to the depth of formation lithology, and then the characteristics of formation section data is counted and picked up. The logging response characteristics of each layer are obtained, and it are given to the corresponding core lithology, then the correspondence of the logging-lithicfacies are established.

Considered the resolution ability and information of logging data and the logging quality, these five conventional logging curves, namely GR, Rt, AC, CNL, DEN, are involved in the logging facies analysis. And the well logging-lithicfacies statistical sub-pattern is established for these wells with thin section(shown Table 1). In the Tab.1 the LITH is the lithology, these values of GR, RT, AC, CNL and DEN represent the amplitude of the logging curve. The logging-lithicfacies categories can be recognized by this pattern.

Table 1. The well logging-lithicfacies statistics pattern of carboniferous formation in 69 areas

NO	WELL	GR (API)	RT (Ω.m)	AC (us/ft)	DEN (g/cm³)	CNL (pu.)	LITH
1	Bai2	58.7	186.6	62.4	2.6	18	Tuff
2	801	15.1	1165.1	63.2	2.59	16	Amygdaloidal Basalt
4	Bai17	19.4	34.7	68.4	2.59	22.2	Baslt
5	Bai17	17.1	34.4	68.5	2.59	22.1	Baslt
6	Ke94	17.3	57.1	64.4	2.56	30	Fragmentation Diabase
7	801	26.4	78	66.4	2.64	10	Sandy Conglomerate
8	Gul13	57.4	55.3	71.4	2.51	22.5	Sandy Conglomerate
...	...	...	...	...	...	...	...
49	801	20.7	1213	65.2	2.47	18.5	Amygdaloidal Basalt
50	801	28.3	100.3	66.6	2.62	9	Conglomerate

3.2 The Rock Recognition

The method is recognized the lithology of adjacent wells, the part recognition results are shown in Table 2. It is not difficult to learn from this table, the interpretation

Table 2. The rock recognition results

WELL	GR (API)	RT (Ω.m)	AC (us/ft)	DEN (g/cm³)	CNL (pu.)	Recognition Results	Microscope Naming
Bai2	58.7	186.6	62.4	2.60	18.0	Tuff	Tuff
801	16.5	1234.4	62.1	2.63	12.7	Amygdaloidal Basalt	Amygdaloidal Basalt
Bai17	16.4	31.2	67.1	2.60	21.4	Basalt	Basalt
Bai17	16.4	31.2	67.1	2.60	21.4	Basalt	Basalt Broken
Gu60	28.4	176.9	58.1	2.62	15.3	Basaltic Volcanic Breccia	Basaltic Volcanic Breccia
Gu107	26.3	336.8	52.9	2.62	21.5	Andesitic Tuff	Andesitic Bithic Tuff
Bai001	52.7	58.6	64.2	2.46	22.0	Vitric Tuff	Vitric Tuff
...	...	...	...	...	...	...	...
Bai001	48.8	62.4	62.8	2.46	25.0	Vitric Tuff	Vitric Tuff
Bai002	70.4	134.8	58.3	2.64	12.6	Ash Tuff	Altered Volcanic Ash Tuff
Bai4	26.3	319.3	57.4	2.78	18.4	Pyroxene Diorite	Pyroxene Diorite
Bai002	13.3	140.3	58.2	2.73	20.5	Pyroxene Diorite	Pyroxene Diorite
801	26.5	107.8	64.2	2.60	10.1	Sandy Conglomerate	Sandy Conglomerate
Bai001	49.1	22.0	67.1	2.55	20.0	Conglomerate	Conglomerate

lithology and the microscopic analysis lithology are very similar. The recognition rate is more than 85%. This fully shows that the method is more accurately identifying lithology, the interpretation rock section is more reasonable.

4   Conclusion

The establishment of the logging-lithicfacies center statistical pattern is the key problem in the model. The existing geological experience and the logging information must be full use. According to the sensitivity differences of the different logging curve which respond to the samples weights, the prediction result is more objective reality.

The igneous rock interpretation is carried out by using the improved fuzzy neural network method. The results show that is consistent with the logging interpretation lithology, and the compliance rate is higher.

References

1. Tang, X., Liu, Z., Zou, Z.-y., et al.: The Identification Method of Igneous Rock Lithology in 69 Area of Junggar Basin. Journal of Southwest Petroleum University 39(1), 29–32 (2009)
2. Xu, S., Liang, J.: Study on Pattern Selection and Generalization Ability for Neural Networks. Computer Science 28(6), 94–96 (2001)
3. Liu, Y., Geng, X., Xiao, C., et al.: Fuzzy Mathematics of Petroleum Engineering. Chengdu University of Science and Technology, Chengdu (1994)
4. Wang, L.: Fuzzy Systems and Fuzzy Control Tutorial. Tsinghua University Press, Beijing (2003)
5. Wang, S.: Fuzzy Neural System, Fuzzy Neural Network and Application Design. Shanghai Science and Technology Literature Publishing House, Shanghai (1998)

Recognizing Water-Flooded Zones Using the Maximum Subordinate Degree Method

Xiaoyan Tang and Zhidi Liu

College of Geology and Environment, Xi'an University of Science and Technology, China
lzdtxy2004@sina.com

Abstract. In the later periods of oilfield development, the effective recognition of water-flooded zones is especially important to research the remained oil distribution and the adjustment development plan. After the basic principle of the maximum subordinate degree method is in detail introduced, the recognition parameters are selected according to the logging characteristic of water-flooded zones in the research work area, and then the model of recognizing water-flooded zones is established. Based on this model, the water-flooded zones in the work area are distinguished. The recognition results show that this method can accurately distinguish water-flooded zones. The recognition rate can satisfy the precision request of water-flooded zones in oilfield development.

Keywords: Maximum Subordinate Degree; Water-flooded Zones; Recognition.

1 Introduction

The internal reservoir heterogeneity is serious in research work area, and the reservoir is affected by the injected water[1,3,4], the original logging interpretation standards of oil zones can't adapt to the current interpretation requirements of production well. A recognition model of water-flooded zones is very necessary to establish at later stages of reservoir development. In this paper, the maximum subordinate degree method is used to establish the recognition model of water-flooded zones, as the water-flooded degree and residual oil distribute are researched in the work area. The aim is that the perforation section is provided for oilfield development.

2 Theory of Maximum Subordinate Degree [2]

Generally, the domain of fuzzy set is called universe. Supposed universe U exists a model space that is called F, F respectively expressed as oil zones(O), oil-water zones(OW), water zones(W), high water-flooded zones(H), moderate water-flooded zones(M), weak water-flooded zones(WW), and dry zones(D), there are 7 kinds of fluid types fuzzy subspace altogether. The known sample models, which constitute logging response combination, are m in model space (F). Every sample is constituted

G. Shen and X. Huang (Eds.): CSIE 2011, Part II, CCIS 153, pp. 343–346, 2011.

by n logging parameters that reflect the fluid characteristics. The sample models are expressed as,

$$(S_{i1}^F, S_{i2}^F, \cdots, S_{in}^F), (i = 1, 2, \cdots, m) \tag{1}$$

In order to depict the changing characteristic of logging curves, it need to calculate the mathematical expectation and variance of logging parameter corresponding to curve segment of one fluid type. The logging parameter sets is that constituted by some period of reservoir corresponding to log value. If this set is represented with W, the logging parameter set can be expressed as,

$$W = \{VSH, AC, RLLD, RLLS, Fw\} \tag{2}$$

Where, $VSH = \{VSH_1, VSH_2, \ldots, VSH_n\}$. Other logging parameter is similar to VSH.

The mathematical expectation of logging parameter set express as,

$$U_F = (\overline{S_1^F}, \overline{S_2^F}, \cdots, \overline{S_n^F}) \tag{3}$$

And the sample variance of each component can get,

$$\sigma_{Fi}^2 (i = 1, 2, \cdots, n) \tag{4}$$

For an arbitrary unknown samples $S_i = (S_1, S_2, \ldots, S_n) \in U$, if U_F represent approximate center of F type fluid, the fuzzy relationship of components between the unknown sample S_i and standard sample U_F are respectively established. Firstly, the subordinate functions are established, this is the key to fuzzy discrimination. There are many methods to establish subordinate functions. The method of geometric center to approximate the relationship is used at here. The subordinate function of fuzzy relationship is constructed as follows.

$$\mu_{ij}^F = \begin{cases} \dfrac{1}{2}\exp\left[-\dfrac{(S_{ij} - \overline{S_j}(F))^2}{\sigma_j^2(F)}\right] & S_{ij} \geq \overline{S_j}(F) \\ 1 - \dfrac{1}{2}\exp\left[-\dfrac{(S_{ij} - \overline{S_j}(F))^2}{\sigma_j^2(F)}\right] & S_{ij} < \overline{S_j}(F) \end{cases} \tag{5}$$

The total subordinate of a sample is defined as for a fluid type.

$$\mu_i^F = \prod_{j=1}^{n} \mu_{ij}^F \tag{6}$$

For a given sample, it can calculate the 7 subordinate degrees μ_i^F (F is O, OW, W, H, M, WW and D respectively) that the principle of maximum subordinate degree is applied. Then there, $\mu_i^F = \mathrm{MAX}(\mu_i^O, \mu_i^{OW}, \mu_i^W, \mu_i^H, \mu_i^M, \mu_i^{WW}, \mu_i^D)$, it considers that the sample belongs to F-type fluid.

3 Establishing Recognition Model

3.1 Extracting Recognition Parameters

Firstly, the various logging parameters to determine the contribution of fluid type are studied. Secondly, lateral resistivity response to water-flooded zones is characterized by zones resistivity increases, and the magnitude difference also increases, it is similar to microelectrode curve. Acoustic curve is insensitive to water-flooded zones, but it is used to calculate the porosity of the important parameters. In addition, water production rate(FW) is the most direct parameters to determine flood levels. Therefore, the establishment of sample sets, which determine the fuzzy discrimination, can use these parameters. Those are VSH, AC, $RLLD$, $RLLS$, POR, SW, and FW.

3.2 Determining Fluid Types

From the view of mathematics aspect, the discriminating reservoir fluid belongs to the category of fuzzy pattern recognition. Because oil-water is usually coexistence, the distinction of reservoir water-flooded degree is also not exact. Usually, water-flooded zones is divided into three levels which those are high water-flooded, moderate water-flooded zones and weak water-flooded zones according to FW. The range of logging parameters and reservoir parameters that is used to divide oil zones, water zones, and the level of water-flooded zones. However, it is difficult to have clear boundaries.

According to oilfield production data, there are oil zones (O), oil-water zones(OW), water zones(W), high water-flooded zones(H), moderate water-flooded zones(M), weak water-flooded zones(WW), and dry zones(D). It can get 7 different subordinate degrees for a sample, which can determine the fluid types of this sample in accordance with the principle of maximum subordinate degree.

3.3 Determining Identification Standard

According to the regional geological characteristics and the logging data, we can chose 7 characteristic parameters which are shale content(VSH), interval transit time(AC), deep lateral resistivity($RLLD$) and shallow lateral resistivity($RLLS$), porosity(POR), water saturation(SW) and water production rate(FW). Six oil zones samples are selected from actual data, three oil-water zones samples, five water zones samples, twelve

Table 1. The part standard samples of identification fluid

RLLD	RLLS	AC	VSH	POR	SW	FW	Type
19.4	12.9	297.2	31.7	10.9	69.0	76.6	High water-flooded zones (*H*)
23.4	15.1	306.8	41.7	12.9	62.5	53.9	Moderate water-flooded zones (*M*)
35.8	23.1	286.0	22.7	13.6	67.3	40.3	Weak water-flooded zones (*WW*)
22.1	13.1	280.9	28.2	11.5	73.2	75.0	Water zones(*W*)
20.9	16.8	259.6	27.1	12.7	31.6	0.0	Oil zones (O)
12.7	11.1	293.3	52.3	12.2	31.3	40.6	Oil-water zones(*OW*)
29.2	20.2	278.8	42.2	1.6	7.7	0.0	Dry zones(*D*)

moderate water-flooded zones samples, six weak water-flooded zones samples, eleven high water-flooded zones samples and eight dry zones samples, and the sample database of identification fluid types are constructed (Table 1).

4 Application Analysis

The maximum subordinate degree fuzzy method is used to recognize more than 200 zones in the work area, the part of the recognition results are shown in Table 2.It is easy to know that recognition rate of this method is higher from this table. From all recognition results in work area, we can know that recognition rate of this method can reach 85%, more than 76% on water zones and high water-flooded zones, and 81% for weak water-flooded zones and moderate water-flooded zones. The recognition precision is high.

Table 2. Comparison table between part logging interpretation results and fuzzy identification

RLLD	RLLS	AC	VSH	POR	SW	FW	Fuzzy Identification result
16.09	12.20	277.15	25.42	10.70	30.0	34.0	Weak water-flooded zones(WW)
19.39	15.08	274.03	16.83	12.35	40.0	42.0	Moderate water-flooded zones(M)
28.11	21.42	262.36	20.79	9.29	26.0	24.0	Weak water-flooded zones(WW)
15.07	11.23	263.43	29.21	5.87	32.0	51.0	Moderate water-flooded zones(M)
29.50	22.50	279.66	32.95	12.16	41.0	31.8	Weak water-flooded zones(WW)
29.85	22.77	254.20	18.22	12.14	44.9	40.1	Moderate water-flooded zones(M)
39.98	30.25	247.16	17.98	13.14	63.6	62.5	High water-flooded zones(H)
32.20	32.20	303.20	38.27	13.69	43.0	38.0	Weak water-flooded zones(WW)
26.40	26.40	273.10	20.59	10.79	64.7	69.3	High water-flooded zones(H)
16.26	11.87	225.45	36.52	0.72	5.7	0.0	Dry zones(D)
14.93	10.98	242.92	46.91	0.27	18.4	0.0	Dry zones(D)

5 Conclusions

This paper analyzed the logging response characteristics of water-flooded zones in work area. The recognition model of maximum subordinate degree is established using logging parameters which have geophysics information of water-flooded zones. This model can more effectively recognize water-flooded zones. The recognition precision can satisfy the requirements of logging interpretation in water-flooded zones.

References

1. Wu, X.: The principles of Production logging. Petroleum industry press, Beijing (1996)
2. Liu, Y., Geng, X., Xiao, C., et al.: Petroleum Engineering Fuzzy Mathematics. Chengdu University of Science and Technology Press, Chengdu (1994)
3. Yong, S., Zhang, C.: Logging data processing and comprehensive explanation. Petroleum University press, Dongying (1996)
4. Zeng, X., Geng, X., Huang, X.: Based on reservoir water saturation prediction of fuzzy neural network. System Simulation Journal 15(5), 735–737 (2003)

Fouling Detection Based on Analysis of Ultrasonic Time-Domain Reflectometry Using Wavelet Transform

Lingfang Sun, Guoliang Feng, and Wenxuan Lu

School of Automation Engineering, Northeast Dianli University, Jilin Province, China
dr_sunlf@163.com

Abstract. Fouling testing based on the principle of UTDR (Ultrasonic Time-Domain Reflectometry) was studied with the pulse transmitting & receiving device and immersion transducer. The fouling on the panel was generated artificially with Sodium carbonate and Calcium chloride, the speed of sound in both of the fouling and water was calibrated by UTDR, then testing waves was recorded by the oscilloscope and deal with and analyze the ultrasonic signals in time-frequency domain with the theory of wavelet transform. The thickness of fouling on the panel was measured quantitatively.

Keywords: UTDR, fouling testing, wavelet transform, calibrating the speed of sound.

1 Introduction

Fouling refers to the layer of materials solid or oozy, which exists in the form of mixtures, accumulated gradually due to the deposits of organic and inorganic substance on the solid surface that contacting with fluids[1,2]. Fouling testing has been studied in many researches which testing fouling by using ultrasonic technology membrane [3-5]. While the research that using ultrasonic technology for fouling in pipelines has rarely been reported, in this paper, fouling testing will be studied by using UTDR. The ultrasonic echo signals have heavy noise. Thus, the analyzing and processing in the application of UTDR have equal importance [6]. In this paper, the echo signals will be de-noised by using the method of wavelet transform [7-9].

2 The Principle of Ultrasonic Time-Domain Reflectometry for Fouling Detection

The schematic in Fig. 1 shows a cross-section of fouling detection between two cast iron plates. Fig. 1(a) shows an ultrasonic transducer is externally placed in contact with the top plate, the transducer emits and receives ultrasonic signal. Each layer's acoustic impedance is different, so that the reflection echoes A and B are generated from the various interfaces within the multilayer structures [10]. The corresponding time domain response is shown in Fig. 1(b). The top plate/fouling interface is represented by echo A, and the fouling/ water solution interface by B. The difference

G. Shen and X. Huang (Eds.): CSIE 2011, Part II, CCIS 153, pp. 347–352, 2011.

in arrival times between echoes A and B (ΔT) is measured; the ΔT reflected the change of fouling layer.

The thickness of the fouling layer (ΔS) can be determined by the following equation:

$$\Delta S = 0.5c\Delta T \tag{1}$$

Here, c is the velocity of the ultrasonic wave in the fouling. If c is known, ΔS can be determined, or the thickness of fouling layer can only be qualitative analysis by using UTDR method.

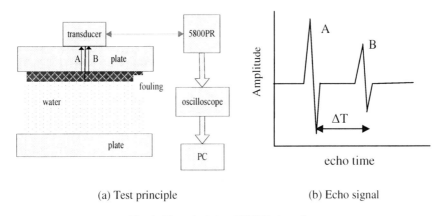

(a) Test principle   (b) Echo signal

Fig. 1. The principle of UTDR detection

3 Design of Experiments

3.1 Test Object and Fouling Forming

The panel used in the experiment is 190×100×8mm panel made of cast iron. The fouling is made by calcium carbonate generated from the chemical reaction as follow:

$$Na_2CO_3 + CaCl = CaCO_3\downarrow + 2NaCl \tag{2}$$

The fouling in water transferring pipelines or storage vessels, the main ingredients is calcium carbonate. Therefore, it is representative that using these reacting production sticking to the panel as fouling.

3.2 Test Object and Fouling Forming

The equipments for experiment as shown in Fig. 1, The pulse transmitting & receiving device is used for stimulating ultrasonic probe and receiving signals, model 5800PR(Olympus, USA). The ultrasonic probe is water-immersion transducer, frequency 10MHz. The three-dimensional precision testing frame is used for fixing probe and adjusting location. The echo signals of ultrasonic waves are collected by digital oscilloscope which is 100MSa/s per sampling.

3.3 The Calibration of Sound Velocity in Aqueous Solution

In the experiment, the sodium chloride and micro scale of calcium carbonate are dissolving in the water; the calibration of sound velocity is shown as follow:

(1) At room temperature, put certain water into a container, and then add 106g sodium chloride and 110g calcium carbonate into the water, the quantity of each substance is 1 mole. And let the chemical reaction is carried out completely.

(2) Pour the clarified water into another container, and then put the panel under the container. The distance between probe and panel is h (Fig. 2). The distance chosen is 19.4mm, and the echo wave measured is shown in Fig. 3.

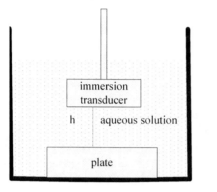

Fig. 2. The calibration of sound velocity

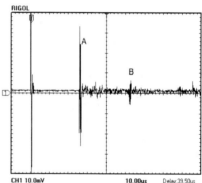

Fig. 3. echo wave

In Fig.3, A is first echo wave on the panel surface; B is a second echo wave. The sound velocity can be calculated by UTDR as:

$$c = 2h/t_{AB} \tag{3}$$

The date of echo waves that collected is 25.9μs, and the longitudinal wave of sound velocity C in the aqueous solution is 1.50mm/μs.

4 Fouling Detection of Plate

4.1 The Calibration Acoustic Velocity in the Fouling

The order of the sample for experiment is water/fouling/panel in Fig. 4. The echo wave measured is shown in Fig. 5. The curve in the Fig. 5, the start pulse is represented by first echo, the water/fouling interface is represented by second echo, the fouling/plate interface is represented by third echo. Because the surface of the fouling with structure loose is unsmooth, the second echo is tumble but also gather together.

Although the pulse transmitting & receiving device can realize low pass and high pass filter when receiving echo signal, there still has a lot of noises in the signal. Based on the time-frequency characteristics of wavelet transform, the echo signals are

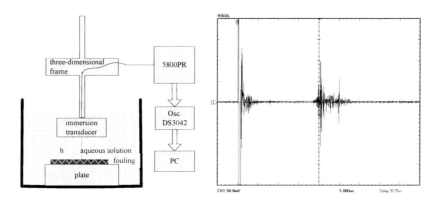

Fig. 4. Fouling detection on plate   **Fig. 5.** Echo wave of fouling detection on plate

decomposed in six layers by adopting db6 wavelet, de-noise and reconstruction. In order to filter, soft threshold method was used in wavelet filter to reconstitute wavelet coefficient in every level after gave them threshold, the waveform as shown in Fig. 6 is gained by filtering noise. The de-noise signal is clearer. The start pulse is shown as O. Wave is overlapped, because the unsmooth surface of the fouling. The echo of fouling is represented by echo A. The echo of plate is shown as echo B, the waveform is laconic.

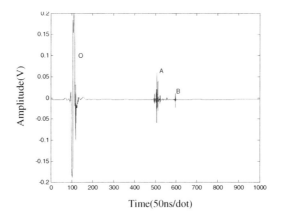

Fig. 6. The echo wave of fouling detection by filtering

Under the corresponding conditions, we can get the thickness of $CaCO_3$ on the plate and acoustic velocity in the fouling, these steps as follow:

(1) The filtered data-signal in Fig. 6 can calculate the time difference between O and A $t_{OA}=20.5\mu s$, and the time difference between A and B $t_{AB}=4.4\mu s$.

(2) The experiment of test plate fouling is shown in Fig. 4, the distance between bottom of the probe and plate surface is h=17.9mm.

(3) The sound velocity in aqueous solution, c=1.50mm/μs, we can calculate the distance Δh between probe and fouling surface is 15.4mm by using Equation (1). The thickness h_1 of fouling is 2.5mm, we can calculate sound velocity c_f in the fouling is 1.14 mm/μs from the Equation (3).

Multipoint fouling detection uses the same method, the speed of sound and thickness of fouling detected by multi-point can see in table 1.

Table 1. Test result

Test point	1	2	3	4	5	Average
Thickness of fouling(mm)	2.5	1.8	1.6	2	2	1.98
Sound velocity in fouling(mm/μs)	1.14	0.95	1.07	1.14	1.05	1.07

4.2 The Thickness of Fouling Detection

Using the method can get the thickness of fouling in the same situation. Turn the panel upside down, as shown in Fig. 7(a). The echo waveform tested in Fig. 7(b), the O point is the echo of interface between the panel and the fouling, the B point is the echo between fouling and water interface. The acoustic velocity in the fouling is 1.07mm/μs, the time t_{AB}=0.2ns, and the thickness of fouling is 0.21mm from the Equation (1).The fouling made by precipitated calcium carbonate is soft fouling and adhesion is weak. The thickness of fouling accumulated is several millimeters when plate is located on a lower, but there is rare fouling adhered to plate, precipitated calcium carbonate shed off when plate is reversed. The fouling thickness measured in the experiment is very thin, and it is better consistent with the fact.

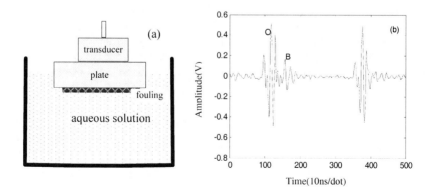

Fig. 7. Fouling detection of plate

5   Conclusions

Due to the variation of physical properties of fouling and the differences of forming conditions and external conditions, it is hard to provide the physical properties. Thus, the speed of sound and thickness of fouling under the same operation conditions are calibrated, then the fouling can be tested by the calibrated data. The working environment of a specific condition is relatively stable, so the calibration experiment can be used for the quantitative or qualitative analysis of fouling.

Acknowledgments. Supported by National Basic Research Program of China (2007CB206904).

References

1. Yang, S., Xu, Z., Sun, L.: Heat Exchanger Fouling and Its Countermeasure, vol. 2. Science Press, Beijing (2004) (in Chinese)
2. Rose, J.L.: Recent Advances in Guided Wave NDE. In: Proc. IEEE Ultrasonic Symposium, Seattle, USA, vol. 1, pp. 761–770 (1995)
3. Kujundzic, E., Cobryl, K., Greenberg, A.R., et al.: Use of ultrasonic sensors for characterization of membrane fouling and cleaning. Journal of Engineered Fibers and Fabrics, 35–44 (2008)
4. Li, J., Chai, G.Y., Sanderson, R.D.: A Focused Ultrasonic Sensor for Detection of Protein Fouling on Tubular UF Membranes. Sensor & Actuator B 114, 182–191 (2006)
5. Chakrabarty, B., Ghoshal, A.K., Purkait, M.K.: Ultrafiltration of Stable Oil-in-water Emulsion by Polysulfone Membrane. J. Membr. Sci. 325, 427–437 (2008)
6. Li, J.: Detection of Membrane Fouling Using Non-destructive Ultrasonic Technique. Membrane Science and Technology 27, 96–101 (2007) (in Chinese)
7. Sanderson, R.D., Li, J., Hallbauer, D.K., et al.: Fourier Wavelets from Ultrasonic Spectra: A New Approach for Detecting the Onset of Fouling during Micro-filtration of Paper Mill Effluent. Environ. Sci. Technol. 39, 7299–7305 (2005)
8. Xua, X., Li, J., Xu, N., et al.: Visualization of Fouling and Diffusion Behaviors During Hollow Fiber Microfiltration of Oily Wastewater by Ultrasonic Reflectometry and Wavelet Analysis. Journal of Membrane Science 341, 195–202 (2009)
9. Silva, J.J., Silva, K.M., Lima, A.M.N., et al.: Fouling Detection Based on Analysis of Ultrasonic Guided Waves Using Wavelet Transform. In: IEEE International Symposium on Industrial Electronics, Cambridge, pp. 1187–1191 (2008)
10. Ultrasonic Inspection. The Press of Electric Power, Beijing (1980) (in Chinese)

Design of Circuits for Transmitting and Receiving in Ultrasonic Transducers

Guoliang Feng and Lingfang Sun

School of Automation Engineering, Northeast Dianli University, Jilin Province, China
122750960@qq.com

Abstract. This paper introduces the design process of ultrasonic transmitting and receiving device. The designed circuit of DC/DC high voltage power supply's control chip is TL494, provide a voltage 260V DC. The transmitting and receiving circuits are based on the control of single chip computer, and generate high voltage pulsed by the theory of capacitor discharge. The wide-range dynamic echo signal is amplified by the circuit of logarithmic amplifier, and processed by the software resources on the PC. The experimental results show that the circuit completed works well and stable.

Keywords: RC circuits; DC/DC high voltage power circuits; pulse drive circuit; logarithmic amplifier.

1 Introduction

As one of the modern detection technologies, ultrasonic technology has the advantages of rapidity, harmless and nondestructive testing which is also on-line and detecting abundant information. As a simply and convenient testing method, UTDR (Ultrasonic Time-domain Reflectometry) especially, has been used widely in the field of nondestructive detection and material thickness detection. There is different acoustic impedance in different medium. Each layer corresponds to one echo, when the UTDR method is adopted to study multilayer structures [1, 2]. The circuits designed in this paper were used to measurement of multilayered media.

2 The Circuit Structure of Ultrasonic Transmitting and Receiving Device

The analog front end circuit of the ultrasonic testing system mainly includes high voltage power supply, transmitting circuit, receiving circuit [3]. The transceiver circuit's block diagram of the ultrasonic is shown in Fig. 1, the high voltage narrow pulse is transmitted by the designed circuit based on the principle of RC pulse discharging. The transmitted pulse width and the transmitted pulse repeated frequency are controlled by the MCU; after being amplified, the echo signals are collected by the oscilloscope, and the dates can be analyzed by rich software resources in the PC.

Only excitation frequency of the circuit and self-oscillation frequency of the transducer are the same, the probe may output the maximum power and reduce the

G. Shen and X. Huang (Eds.): CSIE 2011, Part II, CCIS 153, pp. 353–358, 2011.

harmonics, the ultrasonic probe has the optimum performance. In this design, the probes to different nominal frequency changed the pulse frequency of transmission circuit by regulating the driving pulse width which was transmitted from MCU.

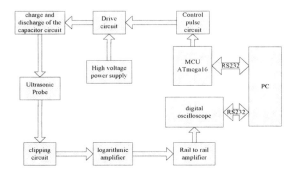

Fig. 1. The transceiver circuit's block diagram of the ultrasonic

3 The Design of High Voltage Power Supply Circuit

The ultrasonic technology in this project is designed to test multilayer medium. The driving circuit and the transmitting probe were demanded to transmit ultrasonic with a high energy, and the voltage of excitation pulse worked on the probe is ordinary above 100V [4]. The power supply was designed input DC12V, output DC260V, and its power was 20W.

The control chip of the power converting circuit is TL494 of TI Company, it incorporates all the functions required in the construction of a pulse-width-modulation (PWM) control, and it contains all the functions what a soft-switch power control system needs.

The internal structure of the TL494 can see the reference [5]. The on-chip oscillator, terminating R_T and C_T provide a sawtooth wave to the reference with external control voltage and feedback amplifier voltage, we can get controlled pulse with a certain duty ratio. The output frequency can be determined by the following equation:

$$f=1.1/R_T C_T \tag{1}$$

The design of DC/DC high voltage power supply is shown in Fig. 2, TL494's pins 9and 10 output inverse pulses, the pulse frequency can be calculated from Equation (1), capacitance of pin 5 and resistance pin 6, its oscillation frequency is 71kHz. Output voltage was transformed into DC voltage with rectifier filter. Pressure formed from the resistance R_{10} and R_{11} feedback to pin 1.

The high-frequency transformer design is essential in the design of power supply. The model of magnetic core in this design is E128.

When choose the transformer winding's cross-sectional area, the skin effect of wire need to consider. Δ—penetration depth, the radial depth when current density down to 0.368 times of the wire surface density.

$$\Delta = \sqrt{\frac{2}{wur}} \qquad (2)$$

Here, w ($w = 2\pi f$) is radian frequency, μ($u = 4\pi \times 10^{-7} H / m$) is cupreous magnetic permeability, r ($r = 58 \times 10^{6} / \Omega m$) is cupreous electric conductivity. The
diameter of wire R, $R \leq 2\Delta$. The maximum current limitation of copper conductor is
4~6A/mm^{2} . The secondary coil is wreathed with the original coil by transformer
winding to perform better coupling. The original coil chosen the enameled wire of
1mm in diameter to wind 7 times parallel, leaves a tap in the middle, the secondary
coil used enameled wire of 0.5mm winding 190 times in the direction of dotted
terminals.

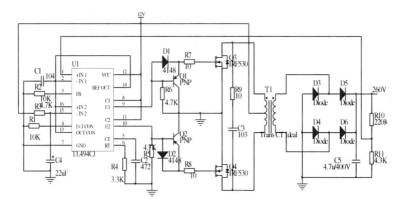

Fig. 2. DC/DC boost circuit

4   The Circuit Design of Ultrasonic Transmitter

By the theory of ultrasonic pulse, the principle of capacitor spark discharge emits the
high voltage pulse, as illustrated in Fig. 3. The AVR microprocessor ATmega16 output switch pulse with width of 800ns, amplitude of 5V. When the voltage level of
switch control pulse is greater than 10V, MOSFET turn on completely. The high
speed optocoupler 6N137 realizes the conversion of 5V level to 12V level and isolates
from the drive control circuit.

When the control pulse is low level, Q1 (IRF830) turns off; the supply voltage
through resistor R4 charge the capacitance C3 and with the diode D1 constitution
return route. When the control pulse is high, Q1 turns on. Charge storage capacitor C3
discharge through the circuit which is made up of resistor R3, Q1, and probe P1. Element parameter is shown in Fig. 3.

The TPS28xx series of high-speed MOSFET drivers are capable of delivering peak
currents of 2A into highly capacitive loads. MOSFET are voltage-driven devices that
require very little steady-state drive current. However, the large input capacitance
(200pF to 3000pF or greater) of these devices requires large current surges to reduce
the turn-on and turn-off times. The TPS2813 shaped the spike pulse pulsed by the
optocoupler. The control pulse was greater than 10V in Fig. 4.

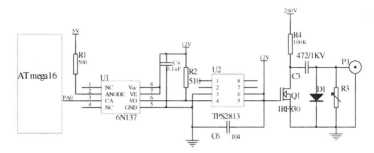

Fig. 3. The circuit of ultrasonic transmitting

Fig. 5 is the no-load pulse waveform of the ultrasonic transmitter circuit. The transmit power is a very important indicator of the transmitter circuit. Transmit power can be determined by the following equation:

$$P=V^2C/t \qquad\qquad (3)$$

Here, V is the real-time voltage of the capacitor discharge time; C is the capacity; t is the time of discharge.

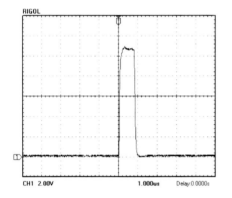

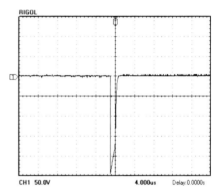

Fig. 4. The control pulse of MOS

Fig. 5. The no-load pulse waveform of the ultrasonic transmitter circuit

In Fig. 5, the MCU transmit pulse width of 800ns, and the transmit pulse of the ultrasonic transmitter circuit is also about 800ns.When we excitation different frequencies probe, it is only need to change the output pulse width of the MCU, the designed ultrasonic transmitter circuit can excitation frequency below 5MHz.

Another issue requiring attention of the ultrasonic transmitter circuit is the selection of the pulse transmission frequency of repetition (the pulse transmission frequency of the ultrasonic transmitter circuit per second). If the transmission frequency of the repetition is too high, it will lead to the insufficient attenuation of the transmitted signal into the next cycle, but if it is too low, it will reduce the detection efficiency, frequency of 50Hz is the most important interference in the field Testing. Generally speaking, the pulse transmission frequency of repetition is 100 Hz to several thousands; the designed Circuit is 300Hz.

5 The Design of Ultrasonic Receiving Circuit

Ultrasonic TR probe was adopted in this design. Because the high sensitive receiver circuit connect to the powerful ultrasonic transmitting circuit, an isolating circuit must be added to the echo signal receiving end of ultrasonic device in order to avoider the receiver circuit being destroyed by high voltage pulse. It forbad wide-range transmitting pulses passing or limited it to a small range; but the echo signal with small amplitude value could pass without attenuation; the separation circuit had no perceptible effect on sensitivity of the device. As shown in Fig. 2, the existence of diode D_1 and D_2 made the voltage between -0.7V to 0.7V can pass through. Ultrasonic echo signal is generally smaller, when large impulsive signal comes, D_1 or D_2 conducts, in the series loop of R and D, high voltages are almost on the resistance R_5, when echo signal comes, because the signal is usually less than 100mV, diode is in the blocking state, and the signal voltage enters the next unit.

The range of received signals is large; it contains the signals from microvolt to volt. It is usually necessary to know the echo time only, and lower the requirement of measured amplitude for detecting. The signal is nonlinear amplified by logarithmic amplifier. The AD8307 is a complete 500 MHz monolithic demodulating logarithmic amplifier, providing a dynamic range of 92 dB to ±3 dB law-conformance. Its output slope is a voltage scaled 25 mV/dB, intercept of −84 dBm, 20uV at input impedance 50Ω. The output signal is further amplified by rail to rail amplifier. Then, data acquisition uses the digital oscilloscope.

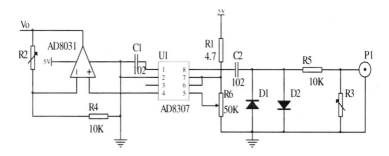

Fig. 6. The circuit of ultrasonic receiving

There is some measure of noise in the ultrasonic receipt signal. The software simulation is proposed to separate noise from the signal. So band pass filter circuit didn't be added to the receiver circuit, the hardware circuit has been simplified. By using a digital oscilloscope, the signal at the pulse output that is connected to the ultrasonic transducer transmitter (with load) was observed, as illustrated in Fig. 7.

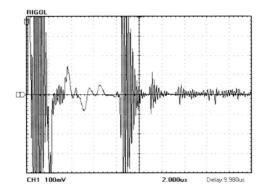

Fig. 7. The output waveform of ultrasonic receiving circuit

6 Conclusions

Being used for stimulating and receiving piezoelectric ultrasonic probe, the ultrasonic impulse transmitter circuit, which is designed in this paper, has been successfully applied to the experiment for testing multi-layer substance. The designed ultrasonic impulse transmitter circuit can be used for probes of different frequency for experiments by changing the width of transmitted pulse of the controller, adjusting the gain and voltage intercept of signal receiving circuit amplifier, calculating the signals processing of the software. The experiment results manifests that the function of the working circuit is stable and reliable.

Acknowledgments. Supported by National Basic Research Program of China (2007CB206904).

References

1. De Sousa, A.V.G., De Albuquerque Pereira, W.C., Carlos Machado, J.: An Ultrasonic Theoretical and Experimental Approach to Determine Thickness and Wave Speed in Layered Media. IEEE Transactions on Ultrasonics, Ferroelectrics, and Frequency Control 54, 386–393 (2007)
2. Renaldas, R., Rymantas, K., Liudas, M.: Ultrasonic Thickness Measurement of Multi-layered Aluminum Foam Precursor Material. IEEE Transactions on Instrumentation and Measurement 57, 2846–2855 (2008)
3. He, S., Liao, Q., Li, Y.: Design and Implementation of Front Circuit in Virtual Ultrasonic Nondestructive Flaw Detection System. Modem Electronic Technology 228, 116–119 (2009)
4. Zheng, H., Lin, S.: Ultrasonic Test. Press of China Social Security Publishing, Beijing (2008) (in Chinese)
5. Texas Instruments. TL494 Pulse-Width-Modulation Control Circuits (2005)

Research on Biomimetic Robot-Crocodile Used for Cleaning Industrial Pipes

Zhixiang Li, Jing Zheng, and Xin Lin

Institute of Mechanical and Electronic Engineering,
Wuhan University of Technology, China
{lzx1370,zhengjing19870718}@yahoo.com.cn,
lx6120@163.com

Abstract. Industry pipeworks has already seen a wide use, but cleaning piping is a problem needed to be solved urgently at present. Based on the types of cleaning piping, this paper presents a biomimetic robot in the shape of crocodile, and makes related research with the crocodile's physiological features, movement patterns, digestive mechanism and so on.The research correlates biological characteristics with the achieving function in actual system, at last forming a new industrial pipeline cleaning way by the method of combining physics and chemistry.

Keywords: Pipeline cleaning; Biomimetic robot-crocodile; Movement; Digestive.

1 Introduction

China is known for her massive land, industry pipeworks involves in more and more fields and there are various ventilation ducts, oil/gas pipeline, sewers and all that, which plays a major role in people's livelihood. Currently, the industrial pipeworks has been widely used in metallurgy, chemical industry, city water heating supply facilities and long distance transport devices using natural gas, petroleum, etc.Pipeline transport have many significant advantages in petroleum industry of the long distance transportation operations, such as low cost, easy operation, production process running continuously, and even performing preprocessing in transit. Because of pipelines stretching across the land and ocean, its normal operation is of critical importance.In the event of the failure, the loss may be incalculable. In addition, pipeline cleaning is implicated in improving the comprehensive efficiency.

2 The Existing Pipeline Cleaning Types

2.1 The Methods of Physical Cleaning

At present, the physical cleaning has around a 30% share of the cleaning products market.High pressure water washing has complete dominance over the whole market,

G. Shen and X. Huang (Eds.): CSIE 2011, Part II, CCIS 153, pp. 359–365, 2011.

accounting for 20%, other methods including PIG cleaning, ultrasonic cleaning (USC) and dry ice cleaning, etc.

High pressure water jet cleaning technology makes water pressure up to 147MPa through special equipment to form strong water jet, which can cut, crush, extrude, and wash the blockage and dirt in the pipeline. The technology is non-aggressive to metals and not leads to pollution, but this kind needs cutting pipeline section and not suitable for long distance pipeline cleaning.

PIG cleaning technology introduced from abroad is an advanced method of pipeline maintaining and cleaning. PIG material made of the polyurethane like bullet has very good elasticity and toughness. The cleaning with long distance but must run when free. Of course, this will affect transportation efficiency and reduce economic benefit.

2.2 The Methods of Chemical Cleaning

At present, chemical cleaning accounted for about industrial cleaning over 70% of the whole market share, its cleaning agents have experienced three stages of simple type, combination and special convenient type.

For more long pipeline cleaning, we usually have the following ways: (1) Pumpback cleaning is an intermittent cycle cleaning using pipeline cavity(regarding the lumen as containers) with lower cost and a little bit waste characteristics. (2) Soaking guide drench cleaning should pay attention that the pipe must be filled with cleaning fluid and guide and drink liquids regularly. (3) Convection cleaning is that the pipes respectively set up two washing grooves and establish workstation to realize two-way convection. (4) Open-circuit cleaning is that cleaning fluid was pumped through the pipeline by establishing cleaning station at one end, and then directly discharged into the trench. (5) Spray cleaning is only works with partitioned pipe, which requires a flange connection with very large limitations and attached devices. To sum up, they all have their own limitation and not too applicable to clean the oil pipeline.In addition, these cleaning types run only when stopping work, not in working hours, so the work efficiency is low, which is not only affecting the conveying efficiency but also increasing pipeline cleaning cost.

2.3 Oil Pipeline Grease Traps

The main sediments in oil transport pipeline are wax which was crystallized from the crude oil and deposited with other constituents in the pipe wall. That reduces the pipeline flow area and increases the oil pipeline flow resistance to lower pipeline transmission capacity. When observing our country long-distance pipeline cut mouth, it shows that sediments in the wall have obvious dividing line, in which clingy is dark brown hair, a similar sand thin layer. Its constitution is wax with certain shear strength.

For this kind of crude oil pipeline, putting the pig into the pipe to clean is a good choise. The pig in oil station or pigging standing was driven by oil flow with specific procedures and equipment, and at last scratched off the sediments.

The pig was push through line pipe by the fluid pressure to clean, measure, detecte and achieve other purposes. It was originally a leather dise-type piston and can strike off wax, which can improve pipeline transport ability in the circumstances of not increasing power and be used for cleaning up the water and other sundries inside.

3   The International Development and Dynamic Analysis

Currently, some foreign industry pipeworks (such as the ventilating duct of central air-conditioning) can use robot to clean, and other transporting liquid pipes (such as oil pipeline) clean only by physical and chemical way. Such as Japan wheeled spiral propulsion in-pipe robot, wheeled straight in-inner-pipe X-ray detection robot Beagle200, unique style structure of scissors MO GRER robot, American Gas Mouse and ROVV ER tube detecting robot, the tube homework robot from Britain and Germany. These robots generally only apply to clean solid in the central air conditioning ventilation pipe and its cost higher and clean effect not ideal, which was not suitable in liquid pipeline

According to the features of existing pipe robot at home and abroad, we found that most cleaning device with single function and cannot applicable for various of pipes.They can be for oil pipeline but not for discharging dust pipe, work unstably, fling the tail easily, move inflexibly and clean not thoroughly.In addition, with no dirt gathering unit it can not sweep down the big block from the pipeline. More important is that market pipe cleaning devices must require pipe transport assignment stop, so that reducing the mill's production efficiency and bring great economic losses.

4   The Clean Way Research about Biomimetic Robot-Crocodile

After the systematic investigation and study, we found that for common cleaning robots cannot meet such complicated environment of transportation in oil pipe, including dynamic liquid and empty pipeline environment when not conveying oil. This expects us to seek a compound type robot that includes two movement environments. The crocodile is by far the most primitive amphibians reptiles, So that it provides a good biological prototypes t for an amphibious robot that can meet the intricate oil transport environment. Based on the crocodile' living habits, its physical characteristics and movement patterns, we think out a robot-crocodile of cleaning oil pipeline combining with the principle of bionics.

On the basis of amphibious walking style of robot-crocodile, this study will be proposed to accomplish its physiological principles (such as mouth moving up and down, digesting food) of crocodile by mechanical methods.The research will connect the physiological structure and crocodile movement way with our achieved function, for example using chemical cleaning way in the oil transport pipes and ponds, lakes, etc. Based on the crocodile's walking style to design motion mechanism of amphibious bionic robot-crocodile, we make the machine move freely in water or land and the shallow area. Based on the crocodile's digestion way to design grinding digestive device in the pipe and carry out both chemical and biological cleaning methods to apply the foundation research. At the same time it can provide appropriate power-driven source for bionic robot-crocodile cleaning device, which may solve the long-distance oil pipeline transportation and deep water area cleaning.

4.1 Design Research Programs

Movement Pattern Research of Amphibian. When crocodile moves in the water, it uses its own as propeller to have wavelike swing movement. Its long tail is the rudder. Its body distorts transversely and reciprocates, it transmits from front to back as the transverse wave, and it uses the counterforce come from the fluid to acquire the propulsion of forward. We intend to use two propulsion modules which are head propulsion module and body propulsion module to drive the movement of the machine crocodile, it lets machine crocodile not only free-swimming in the water can also walks on land. Besides, for the four limbs of the machine crocodile, we intend to choose paddle-leg structure (As shown in figure 1).

Drive system generally includes motor drive, hydraulic drive and pneumatic drive and so on, motor drive uses the motor generates force or torque to drive the machine crocodile's joints directly or through reducing mechanism, it doesn't pollute environment, easy controlled and has high precision, but it requires the servo motor has a very high precision. The features of hydraulic drive are large output force to weight ratio, fast response, good load bearing capacity, but it pollutes environment. For the pneumatic drive, because of the compressibility of air, it has poor precision and controllability, so it isn't suitable for high-precision situation. After analysis and comparison of several experiments and all kind of factors considered, we choose hydraulic drive.

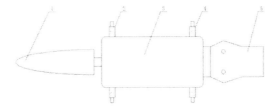

Fig. 1. Diagrammatic Sketch of the Machine Crocodile Structure (1-Tail, 2-Posterior Limb, 3-Body, 4-Forelimb, 5-Head)

Main waterproof methods currently used include mechanism seal and package seal. Package seal is very simple; however, the inclusion will be impacted by the change of the water's depth and has distortion, which will influence the movement performance. So, we choose the method of mechanism seal and design mechanical seal kit for all power output mechanism. Mechanical seal kit includes flange, bearing and O-ring. The two step holes of the flange interference fit with two bearings respectively and form a cavity in the middle, it filled with sealing medium-butter, when the output axle which through the bearing and the cavity is rotating, the cavity will keep sealed.

The Design of the Mouth On-Off Mechanism. We research the big mouth of the crocodile with the bionic method, the machine crocodile's mouth can open or close by the control mechanism, moreover, we design the on-off mechanism has the dentate edge, which are the crocodile's sharp teeth.

Our studies intend to choose the umbrella on-off mechanism as the filter device, mechanism model as shown in figure 2. We want to connect the open end of the umbrella mechanism with the mouth cavity of the machine crocodile to control the mouth's open and close by studying this mechanism. When the intermediate link pulled left machine crocodile's mouth closes and open when it pushed right. Soft steel wire will be fitted on the gaps between the supporting bars of the umbrella on-off mechanism's bottom, which is used to filter and has reasonable granularity. The debris will be filtered and left in the mouth of the machine crocodile. This structure is similar to the part of air-condition cleaning robot's which was studied before. Experiment results support that the structure can achieve the required movement.

Working in the water, machine crocodile's mouth will be impacted by the liquid when it opens, so we should have an analysis and test of the supporting bars' force and strength to ensure their reliability. We can find the optimal granularity of the soft steel wire mesh by investigating the practical environment and doing some relevant experiments.

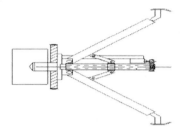

Fig. 2. Umbrella on-off Mechanism

The Research of the Head Movement Mechanism. Machine crocodile's head movement mechanism is to enable the head to move up and down and makes the mouth on-off mechanism move at the same time. It can adjust the on-off mechanism's position to ensure it in the center when the machine crocodile works in the oil pipeline and so on, in another word, it's aligning.

The elevator mechanism is shown as the figure 3, DC motor drives the rotation of the screw, so the nut achieves the relative movement of the vertical direction to spur the vertical direction of the working table, it can ensure the center of the on-off mechanism located in the pipe's center. The mechanism of this part is very simple and relatively easy to implement.

The Research of Crushed Digestive Device
Based on the way of crocodile's stomach to digest food, then crocodiles often swallow some stones, gastric peristalsis helps the stones to grind foods, foods will easier to digested with gastric acid. So, we choose a crushed digestive device to make the bulk of the impurities smaller.

We use a vertical grinding digestive device whose structure is a vertical cylinder (shown as figure 4), inside the cylinder equipped with a upper supported suspended spiral agitator, transmission in the upper, motor drives the spiral agitator to rotate, this make the grinding media in the cylinder rise along the central axis of the helix and down along the gap between the cylinder and the helix, again and again, it can grind the material. Sand pump ensure the slurry cycle between the cylinder and the classifier.

Grinded material overflow into the classifier finally, and the bigger ones will return to the cylinder through the sand pump. The energy needed in the vertical device to overcome gravity is much less than in the horizontal device, so the vertical device has the higher efficiency. The cylinder of the vertical device has small diameter, large height, it increases the pressure between the grinding media and the force on the grinding materials.

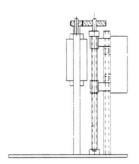

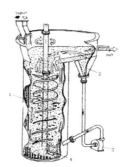

Fig. 3. Diagrammatic Sketch of the Elevator Structure   **Fig. 4.** Grinder

The particles crossed the filter in the mouth on-off mechanism reach the digestive mechanism are very small, and the device grinds the materials by the ball media mainly, the ball diameter of the grinding media is generally 10-25mm, maximum feed particle size is 5mm. If the particle is too large, it will make the grinding efficiency down. Our solution is setting a chemical release device in the bottom to speed up the grinding. Experiments show that using a combination of physical and chemical grinding method can achieve the desired objective.

5   The Application of the Machine Crocodile in the Oil Pipeline

Based on the research of the crocodile's motion and digestion mechanism, we can use the crocodile to clean the sediment on the wall of the oil pipeline. The increase of the sediment will reduce oil transport efficiency and slow the transport speed down thereby influence industrial transportation and manufacturing. So, the pipe should be cleaned up regularly. In the condition of normal transportation, the sediment in the pipeline can keep the oil warm and slow the formation of the impurities. When cleaning up oil pipeline, do not have to clean out sediment completely, and the thickness should be reserved for the corresponding.

In the oil pipeline, the machine crocodile walking in the bottom and adjust the head elevator's center to make it superpose with the center of the pipeline, then make the on-off mechanism rotating rapidly to remove the excess sediment by the sharp tooth-blade. The machine crocodile should move forward along the flow direction of oil when it working in the pipeline.

6 The Features and Innovations

1) We research the bionic machine crocodile based on the biological model of crocodile, it has original innovativeness. In its motion device we used paddle-leg structure, it has the feature of amphibious and moves smoothly and has a certain ability to cross barriers.

2) We intend to use the mouth on-off mechanism and head movement mechanism designed ourselves. We use the simple mechanical principle to solve the complex bionic movement, it is innovative completely.

3) We intend to use the combination of biological and chemical cleaning method and equipped machine crocodile with crushed digestive device based on the crocodile's digestive mechanism.

4) We try to set cleaning, filtering, crushing function as one in the machine crocodile, at same time, it can test the pipe. It is a bold vision and innovation based on summarizing our own works.

7 Summarise

Nowaday, there are many industrial pipe cleaning methods, but they have limitations in the application. Based on the researching the existing pipe cleaning robot home and abroad in detail, after investigation, our team designs a compound robot and crocodile is its prototype. Because of its amphibious feature, it has a strong ability to adapt to the environment and it can work in diverse terrain such as land or offshore. If it can use in cleaning oil pipelines, it will improve the efficiency of the entire industry and has good prospect.

References

1. Zhang, J.: Pig Cleaning Technology and Application, pp. 124–135. Petroleum Industry Press, Beijing (2005)
2. Liu, C.: Pro-test of chemical cleaning methods of long-distance pipeline. Cleaning World 22(5), 39–41 (2006)
3. Zhang, C.: Oil and natural gas pipeline cleaner and application. Journal of Shengli Oil Field Staff University 23(3), 70–72 (2009)
4. Ma, H., Bai, S., Run, R.: The Research of the Pipeline Robot System. Instrumentation Journal 26(8), 286–287 (2005)

Research on Test System of Automobile Clutch Comprehensive Performance Based on Virtual Instrument

JingXuan Jin and RongYi Cui

Intelligent Information Processing Lab, Dept. of Computer Science and Technology,
Yanbian University, Yanji, Jilin, 133002
{jinjx,cuirongyi}@ybu.edu.cn

Abstract. In order to obtain the clutch's operating performance and related characteristic accurately and completely, the automobile clutch comprehensive performance detection platform was designed. The working condition of the different models of clutch could be simulated and a variety of specifications clutch comprehensive performance could be tested by using the single device. According to the big disturbance torque and high requirement of control accuracy, a fuzzy-PID control algorithm was proposed for the rotational speed control. Based on the virtual instrument technology of National Instruments Corporation, the interface and data acquisition programs are developed. The results of simulation and experiment show that the accuracy and efficiency have been improved and the test system works stable and credible.

Keywords: Automobile clutch; Comprehensive performance; Industrial personal computer; Virtual instrument.

1 Introduction

Since the automobile clutch is a critical safety component of automobile transmission system, its performance index must be tested in order to ensure the security [1]. Using the comprehensive performance test system which is a platform system to test the clutch's performance, the clutch's operating performance and related characteristic can be obtained accurately and completely. Therefore, development of such machine is very significant to improve the quality of clutch and promote national automobile industry. The key of the test system of automobile clutch comprehensive performance is the control and detection systems which affect the accuracy of control, the accuracy of test data and the efficiency of test directly. The speed control accuracy of test system is directly related to the accuracy and reliability of test results, speed control subsystem is the key of the test system control. According to the high requirement of control accuracy, a fuzzy-PID control algorithm was proposed for the rotational speed control. Based on the virtual instrument technology of NI company, the interface and data acquisition programs are developed. The experiment and actual application results show that the accuracy and efficiency have been improved and the design test system of automobile clutch comprehensive performance works stably and reliably.

G. Shen and X. Huang (Eds.): CSIE 2011, Part II, CCIS 153, pp. 366–370, 2011.

2 Test System of the Overall and Operation Principle

The test system of automobile clutch comprehensive performance is composed of mechanical platform, control and test system. Mechanical platform is the foundation of clutch plate test, and the control system and test system perform the test action control and performance test separately. Structure of the mechanical platform is shown in Figure 1.

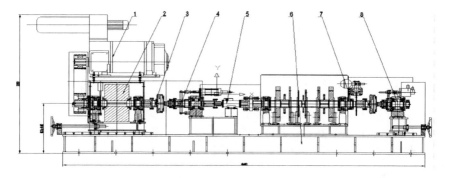

Fig. 1. Structural diagram of the mechanical platform. The label in the figure is referred to as the component as following:1.110KW DC motor; 2.Flywheel energy storage; 3.Specimen installation bodies; 4.The bonding and separation components; 5. Measurable bodies of torque speed; 6. The welding Chassis; 7.The brake; 8.The imposition of road resistance torque agencies.

3 The Design of Fuzzy PID Controller

3.1 Structure Design of Test System Speed Control System

The structure of speed control system of test system is shown in Figure 2, in which I_d^* is current settings; I_d is current feedback value; u_c is control signal; w is controlling the interference noise signal; v is measurement noise signal; y_n is speed signal of detected platform; y is the practical rotation speed output signal; y_c is rotation speed

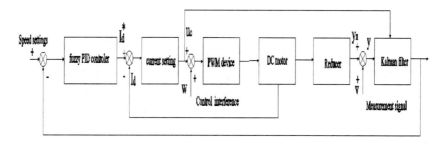

Fig. 2. Structure chart of detected system speed control system

output signal modified by Kalman filter. Speed control system of test system uses PWM DC speed system which is composed of the fuzzy PID controller, current controller, PWM devices, DC motors, reducer, Kalman filter and so on, its steady speed precision is high and speed range is wide [2].

3.2 Fuzzy PID Controller Design

3.2.1 The Structure of Fuzzy PID Controller Design

The PID controller is by far the most commonly used controller in process control application. The basic equation of a PID controller in discrete domain is given by document[3]:

$$u(k)=u(k-1)+K_p\left[e(k)-e(k-1)\right]+K_iT_{sam}e(k)+\frac{K_d}{T_{sam}}\left[e(k)-2e(k-1)+e(k-2)\right] \quad (1)$$

Because the parameters of conventional PID controller can not be tuned online, conventional PID controller can not satisfy the self-tuning requirements of system parameters under different conditions, so its control effect is affected. Using the theory of fuzzy PID to modify parameters online, the parameter self-setting fuzzy PID controller is constituted.

3.2.2 Fuzzy Linguistic Variables, Membership Function and Fuzzy Rules

Due to the large range of motor speed deviation and high precision, speed error (e) and change in error (e_c) are adopt as input linguistic variables, and seven fuzzy values is the linguistic variables values {NB, NM, NS, ZO, PS, PM, PB}. PID controller correct value ΔK_p, ΔK_i, ΔK_d of proportional coefficient, integral coefficient, differential coefficient are regarded as the output linguistic variables, and seven fuzzy values are the linguistic variables values {NB, NM, NS, ZO, PS, PM, PB}. The membership functions of input linguistic variables and output of linguistic variables are triangle membership function. Fuzzy rules are the core of the fuzzy controller. In accordance with the parameters self-tuning law of fuzzy PID, the fuzzy rules of ΔK_p, ΔK_i, ΔK_d are built which are shown in Figure 3.The fuzzy inference engine is Mamdani-type inference system and the defuzzification is the center of gravity model method [4].

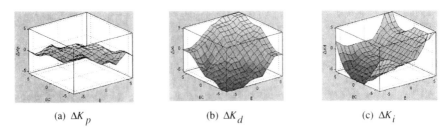

(a) ΔK_p (b) ΔK_d (c) ΔK_i

Fig. 3. Fuzzy rules

3.3 Simulation

The simulation result is shown in Figure 4. The quality control system is also enhanced.

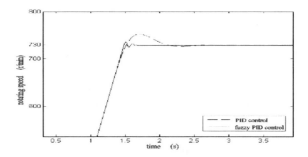

Fig. 4. The step response curve of PID control and fuzzy PID control

4 System Software Design and Experimental Results

4.1 System Software Design

The test system of automobile clutch comprehensive performance adopted LabVIEW software as a development platform. LabVIEW is an Image-based programming language applied in the Windows platform which is widely used in the development of measurement and control system[5]. LabVIEW programs are built on universal operating systems such as Windows and Linux and so on. The main function of human machine interface (HMI) is to provide the appropriate communication channels between users and the machinery equipment, which can simplify the operation of machinery to achieve the purpose of mechanical normal use. The human machine interface of automobile clutch comprehensive performance test system is developed. At this interface of LabVIEW software panel, users can intuitively observe the test curve and the real-time value of each measured parameters, and easily control the system.

4.2   Test Results

According to the requirements of QC/T 25-2004 "Technical requirements of the automobile friction clutch" and QC/T 27-2004 "test methods of the automobile friction clutch bench", performance tests of the comprehensive performance test system are performed. The performance indexes of the comprehensive performance test system are as follows: Maximum torque is 1000N·m; Temperature range is Room temperature to 450℃; the test Maximum rotate speed is 1500r/min; Maximum road resistance torque is 650 N·m; Relative error of indication torque and temperature is ±0.5%(F.S); Clutch measurable specifications is Φ160mm to Φ430mm.

5 Conclusion

The automobile clutch comprehensive performance test system adopts inertia disc to simulate the inertial moving mass which bring about inertia torque of the whole vehicle. The corresponding spline shaft is designed and the adjustment device in the installation is designed. In this way, the comprehensive performance test of automobile clutch in the specification Φ160-430mm range can be carried out conveniently, which includes heat load, static friction torque, sliding friction torque, friction wear linings, brake performance, etc. According to the high requirement of control accuracy, a fuzzy-PID control algorithm was proposed for the rotational speed control. Based on the virtual instrument technology of National Instruments Corporation, the interface and data acquisition programs are developed, which implement a series of functions of the system, such as data collection, data processing, data analysis, database management and test control. The results of simulation and experiments show that the accuracy and efficiency have been improved and the test system works stably and credibly.

Acknowledgments. Our work was supported by the Scientific Research Foundation of Yanbian University of China under Grant No.2010-009. We would like to thank Pro. BangCheng Zhang for his excellent technical assistance.

References

1. Xu, S.: Automobile clutch. Tsinghua University Press, Beijing (2005)
2. Chen, B.: Electric Traction Automatic Control Systems: Motion Control System. Mechanical Industry Press, Beijing (2003)
3. Bandyopadhyay, R., Chakraborty, U.K., Patranabis, D.: Autotuning a PID Controller: A Fuzzy-Genetic Approach. Journal of Systems Architecture 47, 663–673 (2001)
4. Liu, J., Chen, W.: Study on EPS Using Fuzzy and PID Multi-Mode Control with Kalman Filter. Transactions of the Chinese Society for Agricultural Machinery 38, 1–5 (2007)
5. Yang, S., Chen, K., Yang, Y., et al.: Numerical Control System for Pipe Connecting Trace Processing Based on Virtual Instrument. Transactions of the Chinese Society for Agricultural Machinery 38, 157–160 (2007)

An Enhanced System Level to Link Level Mapping Method for 3GPP LTE System Level Simulation

Yuan Gao[1] and HongYi Yu[2]

[1] Wireless and Mobile Communication Technology R&D Center,
Research Institute of Information Technology(RIIT), Tsinghua University, Beijing,China
[2] Information Science and Technology Institute, Zhengzhou, China
yuangao08@mails.tsinghua.edu.cn

Abstract. In this paper, we studied the mapping method between system level (SL) to link level (LL) in 3GPP LTE system level simulation using effective exponential SNR mapping (EESM) and mutual-information effective SNR mapping (MI-ESM). We present our faster way to find out the effective SINR in EESM based on statistical information of spatial channel model in LTE-A. A compare of computational complexity and accuracy between SL and LL using EESM, MI-ESM is performed to prove our idea.

Keywords: EESM; MI-ESM; system level; link level.

1 Introduction

The 3rd Generation Partnership Project (3GPP) has finished the standardization of Long Term Evolution (LTE) release 10. LTE and its related standards are called 3.9^{th} generation mobile cellular networks and will lead the further deployment of 4th mobile cellular networks all over the world. The system level simulation is an effective way to study and evaluate LTE system structure, new algorithms and other related works.

In this paper, we introduce two basic SL to LL mapping method and give some evaluation results about computation and accuracy as defined in LTE. Then, we present a new statistical-based algorithm in calculating effective SINR under widely used channel model: Spatial Channel Model (SCM) [1] and its enhanced version SCM enhanced (SCME) [2], which is widely used in LTE SL simulations. We also give an iteration-based way to calculate β instead of traversing the whole channel which will make the work faster and distortion controlled.

The paper is organized as follows. In part 2, we introduce the EESM and MI-ESM in SL to LL mapping. Part 3 presents our statistical-based effective SINR calculation and iteration –based β calculation method and some simulation results, including basic concepts of system level simulation. Conclusions are given in Part 4.

G. Shen and X. Huang (Eds.): CSIE 2011, Part II, CCIS 153, pp. 371–377, 2011.
© Springer-Verlag Berlin Heidelberg 2011

2   EESM and MI-ESM in SL Simulation

In LL simulation, people focus on a point-to-point link and its detailed algorithms. Different in SL simulation, people focus on the whole links in the simulation system and evaluate system features such as capacity, throughput, etc., which will cause large amount of calculations if full link activity is performed.

In order to solve the problem, LTE standardization proposed an effective mapping method between SL and LL. In given wireless multipath fading channels, the key point of the mapping method is to figure out the effective signal to noise-and-interference ratio (SINR) value $SINR_{eff}$ from subcarrier SINRs, and then search the basic LL SINR-BLER (Block Error Rate) table to find the estimate SINR value. The link level SINR-BLER table is got from the link level simulation result under Additive White Gaussian Noise (AWGN) channel and this mapping is unique [3] [4].

The mapping method can be described as follows:

$$BLER(SINR_k) = BLER_{AWGN}(SINR_{eff}) \quad (1)$$

The left side of the equation1 means the real BLER in channel model (e.g. SCME), and the right side is the simulated BLER value in AWGN channel. The effective SINR value is defined in equation (2).

$$SINR_{eff} = I^{-1}\left(\frac{1}{N}\sum_{n=1}^{N}I\left(SINR_n\right)\right) \quad (2)$$

Where $I(x)$ is the subcarrier SINR combining function, and n denotes the n th subcarrier. Figure 1shows the mapping process between SL to LL.

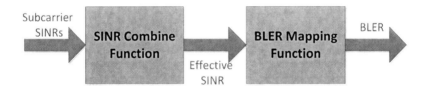

Fig. 1. Effective SINR mapping method in common system level simulations

2.1   Effective Exponential SNR Mapping

In EESM mapping method, the SINR combine function $I(x)$ is exponential. $I(x)$ is defined as follows:

$$I(x) = \exp\left(-\frac{x}{\beta}\right) \quad (3)$$

β is a correction factor that can solve mismatching between real SINRs and predicted SINRs and this value is only related with modulation and coding scheme (MCS) [5]. So the required SINR value is calculated using equation (4):

$$SINR_{eff} = -\beta \ln[\frac{1}{n}\sum_{n=1}^{N}\exp(-\frac{SINR_n}{\beta})] \tag{4}$$

Where n denotes the nth subcarrier and N is the total subcarriers. It is obvious that all subcarriers must have the same β value, so the EESM method requires the same modulation and coding scheme in all subcarriers which will limit the use of this mapping method.

2.2 Mutual-Information Effective SNR Mapping

In MI-ESM mapping method, the combine function $I(x)$ based on mutual information of transmitted data symbols [6] [7]. With same character meaning of EESM equation, the effective SINR is:

$$SINR_{eff} = I^{-1}(\frac{1}{N}\sum_{n=1}^{N}I(SINR_n)) \tag{5}$$

Where $I(SINR_n)$ is the capacity function when the nth data symbol using 2^n modulation symbols. The mutual information $I(x)$ is defined as follows [8]:

$$I(x) = m_p - E_Y\{\frac{1}{2^{m_p}}\sum_{i=1}^{m_p}\sum_{b=0}^{1}\sum_{z\in X_b^i}\log\frac{\sum_{x\in X}\exp(-|Y-\sqrt{x/\beta}(\hat{x}-z)|^2)}{\sum_{x\in X_b^i}\exp(-|Y-\sqrt{x/\beta}(\hat{x}-z)|^2)}\} \tag{6}$$

m_p is the bit number of per modulated symbol, X is the ensemble of the 2^{m_p} data symbols; X_b^i is the ensemble when i equals b; Y is the Gaussian random vector with zero mean.

Compared with EESM, MI-ESM do not need same MCS in all subcarriers, but need more calculations for the mutual information calculation of every subcarrier. In LTE simulator, common scheduler such as round robin (RR) and proportional fair (PF) [9] do not specify the condition that different subcarriers have different MCS, so EESM is in case enough under certain conditions. In system level, the simulation environment always contains multi cells and users, for each timeslot and each user, a mapping should be performed, which will cost most of the time. If we do not use different MCS in subcarriers, it is proved that EESM with correction factor is precisely enough. The specific prove will be talked in PART 3.

3   Enhanced Algorithm of Calculating Effective SINR

The common method of getting β is to traverse different channel samples. Note that this value is only depending on the combination of modulation scheme and code rate.

Assume there are N types of channels with different subcarrier SINR values, for X different noise powers, we can get the average BLERs. β can be trained using equation (7), where $f_n(\beta)$ is the required SINRs under the n th channel sample and f_{AWGN} is the required SINR value which can satisfy the target BLER in AWGN channel [10].

$$\hat{\beta} = \arg \min_{\beta} \max_{n \in N} | f_n(\beta) - f_{AWGN} | \qquad (7)$$

3.1 Statistical Features of SCM/SCME Channel Model

In order to get the proper value of β faster, the study on statistical features of multi-path fading channels is needed. In this paper, we take SCM channel an example, which is corrected by Winner Project and widely used in SL simulation [11].

The link between the u th receive and s th transmit antenna in given time sample t can be described as follows, where n denotes the n th path of overall 6 multi-path, M is the total number of subpath, P_n is the power of the nth path, σ_{SF} is the lognormal shadow fading, $\theta_{n,m,AoD}$ is the AoD for the m th subpath of the nth path, $\theta_{n,m,AoA}$ is the AoA for the m th subpath of the nth path, $G_{BS}(\theta_{n,m,AoD})$ is the BS antenna gain of each array element, $G_{MS}(\theta_{n,m,AoA})$ is the MS antenna gain of each array element.

$$h_{u,s,n}(t) = \sqrt{\frac{P_n \sigma_{SF}}{M}} \sum_{m=1}^{M} \begin{pmatrix} \sqrt{G_{BS}(\theta_{n,m,AoD})} \exp\left(j[kd_s \sin(\theta_{n,m,AoD}) + \Phi_{n,m}]\right) \times \\ \sqrt{G_{MS}(\theta_{n,m,AoA})} \exp\left(jkd_u \sin(\theta_{n,m,AoA})\right) \times \\ \exp\left(jk\|v\|\cos(\theta_{n,m,AoA} - \theta_v)t\right) \end{pmatrix} \qquad (8)$$

In the given channel model, the effective SINR is:

$$SINR_{eff} = -\beta \ln(\frac{1}{N} \sum_{k=1}^{N} e^{-\frac{r_k}{\beta}}) \qquad (9)$$

Where r_k is the k th subcarrier SNR. According to central-limit theorem, the mean value of sample is the unbiased estimation of expectation and β is get using algorithm in part 3.2. The effective SINR in equation (9) can be approximated as:

$$SINR_{eff} \approx -\beta \ln(E(e^{-\frac{|h_k|^2}{N_0\beta}})) \qquad (10)$$

The mean energy of the k th subcarrier is approximated as non-centrally χ^2 distribution with two degree of freedom [12], and after integral, the effective SINR is:

$$SINR_{eff} \approx -\beta \ln(\frac{\beta}{\beta + SINR}) \qquad (11)$$

3.2 Algorithm of Getting β

It is wise to make the distortion between real SINR and the effective SINR, under Minimum Mean Square Error (MMSE) criterion, the error function of β is:

$$f(\beta) = \frac{1}{M}\sum_{m=1}^{M} |[s(SINR_{eff}(m,\beta)) - f_{AWGN}(m)]|^2 \tag{11}$$

Define the minimum and maximum of β using empirical value of LL simulation and in the given intervals, $f(\beta)$ is concave [13]. The algorithm of finding β is to make the upper and lower bound tight and finally get perfect value through iteration, it is described as follows:

a) Define min and max value of β, increment x, iteration number N and simulation point M;

b) Let k=(min+max)/2, calculate M BLER value $BLER(SINR_{eff}(1),k),\dots$ and the mean square error $f(k)$, the effective SINR is calculated using LL simulator;

c) Calculate M BLER value $BLER(SINR_{eff}(1),k+x)\dots$, and then the mean square error $f(k+x)$

d) If iteration number is larger than N ,finish; else turn to step c)

e) If $f(k) > f(k+x)$, let min=k and turn to step a); if $f(k) < f(k+x)$, let max=k and turn to step a); if $f(k) = f(k+x)$,finish and β with minimum mean square error is selected.

3.3 Simulation Result

To testify the accuracy of our algorithm in finding β and the mapping method, we implement the tests in our LTE SL simulator based on Matlab. The simulation condition is shown in Table 1. Other parameters not listed in the table, we set it the same as in reference 5.

Table 1. LTE System Level Simulation Parameters

Name	Value
Channel Model	3GPP SCM
BS Number	19
Cells Per BS	3
Users	10/cell,570 total
Bandwidth	10MHz
SL to LL Mapping	EESM/MI-ESM
TxD	1*1

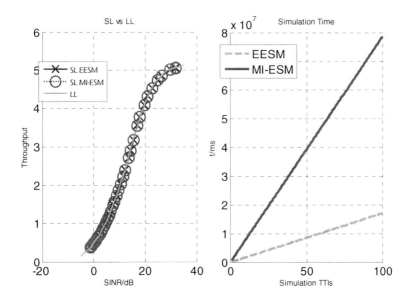

Fig. 2. Performance and time costs comparison of SL and LL simulation

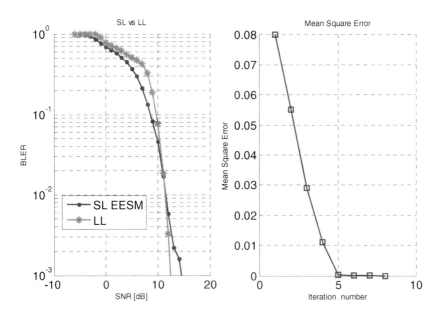

Fig. 3. EESM distortion and Mean Square Error of our algorithm in calculating β

Figure 2 shows the comparison between SL and LL simulation. In SL simulation, EESM and MI-ESM is performed. Compared with LL simulation, the SL simulation using EESM with our new algorithm of finding β and calculating effective SINR is trustiness. The SL to LL mapping table is calculated using LL simulator, and the real SL mapping is using both EESM and MI-ESM. It is obvious that both EESM and MI-ESM have nearly the same performance, compared with real LL simulation. But the calculation amount of EESM is much less than MI-ESM. The right figure of Fig. 2 shows the time cost between our modified EESM and MI-ESM, it is obvious that when simulation time increases, the time costs of MI-ESM is more than EESM but get nearly the same performance.

The left picture of Figure 3 shows the difference between SL EESM and LL. In SL EESM, we use statistical based EESM and iteration based β calculation. We can infer that the SL mapping method has a little different compared with real link level simulation, but the distortion is acceptable in large scale SL simulations. The right picture shows the relation between iteration number and the MSE defined in equation (11). It is obvious that with the increase of iteration number, the MSE will approach zero.

4 Conclusion

We presented simulation result between SL and LL and prove that: our new idea of the statistical-based effective SINR mapping in 3GPP LTE SCM/SCME channel model is faster and distortion-acceptable, and the iteration-based β calculation can help increase accuracy of EESM in SL simulation.

References

1. 3GPP TR25.996 V8.0.0 (2008-12), Spatial channel model for multiple input multiple output (MIMO) simulations, Release 8
2. Baum, D.S., Salo, J., Del Galdo, G., Milojevic, M., Kyösti, P., Hansen, J.: An interim channel model for beyond-3G systems. In: Proc. IEEE VTC 2005, Stockholm, Sweden (May 2005)
3. Wan, L., Tsai, S., Almgren, M.: A Fading-Insensitive Performance Metric for a Unified Link Quality Model, pp. 2110–2114. WCNC (2006)
4. R1-030999, RAN WG1 #34, Considerations on system performance evaluation of HSDP using OFDM modulations [S]
5. 3GPP TSG-RAN-1 Meeting #37,OFDM-HSDPA System level simulator calibration (R1-040500)
6. 3GPP2-C30-20030429-010,Effective-SNR Mapping for Modeling Frame Error Rates in Multiple-state channels
7. Ikuno, J.C., Wrulich, M., Rupp, M.: System level simulation of LTE networks. In: IEEE VTC 2010 (2010)
8. Caire, G., Taricco, G., Biglieri, E.: Electronics Letters, vol. (12) (1996)
9. Beh, K.C., Armour, S., Doufexi, A.: Joint Time-Frequency Domain Proportional Fair Scheduler with HARQ for 3GPP LTE Systems. In: IEEE 68th VTC 2008 (Fall, 2008)
10. 3GPP TSG RAN WG1 #36,New results on realistic OFDM interference (R1-040189)
11. 3GPP TR 25.996 v8.0.0 (2008-12), Spatial Channel Model for MIMO simulations
12. IEEE c802.16e 141r3, CINR measurement using EESM method, IEEE 802.16e Contribution (2005)
13. Mumtaz, S., Gamerio, A., Rodriguez, J., et al.: EESM for IEEE 802.16e: WiMaX. In: 7th IEEE/ACIS International Conference on Computer and Information Science, Portland, pp. 361–366 (2008)

Improved Sparsing of Extended Information Filter for Vision-SLAM

Xiaohua Wang[1] and Daixian Zhu[2]

[1] College of Electronic and Information, Xi'an Polytechnic University, Xi'an, China
[2] Communication and Information Engineering College, Xi'an Univ. of Science and Technology, Xi'an, China
w_xiaohua@126.com, zh_daixian@163.com

Abstract. There are a number of algorithms used on Simultaneous Localization and Mapping(SLAM). The sparse extended information filter (SEIF) algorithm is deduced by the sparsification treatment to EIF algorithm, which is the information form of EKF. SEIF has been successfully implemented with a variety of challenging real-world data sets and has lead to new insights into scalable SLAM. However, the computational burden related to information matrix balloons with respect to the increase of the mapped landmarks, the most computational cost is in recovery information matrix (inverse matrix).In this paper, by analyzing the every steps of information matrix update in SEIF process, A sparsification rule is put forward, which enforce the elements into zero according to setting a threshold and computer inverse information matrix with the method of tri-diagonal matrix splitting according to observation information of sparsification time. the computational complexity is much lower by using new sparsification rule. The algorithm used in vision-SLAM shows that the computational complexity of the SEIF algorithm is a constant, which is independent of environment features. That means SEIF has a high value of application in large-scale environment with a large number of features.

Keywords: component, SLAM, extended information filter, information matrix, sparsification.

1 Introduction

The simultaneous localization and map building (SLAM) is the key research of mobile robot navigation area[1]. The EKF based estimation algorithm is the basic solution to the SLAM problem. It can provide the optimal solution to the SLAM problem, but has the problem of large computational complexity, which is a quadratic relation with environment features. In the past few years, Explicit Sparse Information Filter (EIF)SLAM attracts more and more researchers recently for rigorous mathematics and accurate estimation, The initial work done by Thrun of "Victoria Park" is really classic research in EIF-SLAM field [2]. By using Markov blanket, sparsification is done by not considering the indirect influence on the robot pose or landmark.

Most SLAM approaches are feature-based which assumes that the robot can extract an abstract representation of features in the environment from its sensor data and then

G. Shen and X. Huang (Eds.): CSIE 2011, Part II, CCIS 153, pp. 378–383, 2011.

use re-observation of these features for localization[3]. In EIF-SLAM approach a landmark map is explicitly built and maintained, The process of concurrently performing localization and feature map building are inherently coupled. The robot must then represent a joint distribution over landmarks and current pose. Updating the joint correlations over map and robot leads to complexity per update, with N being the number of landmarks in the map.

In vision-SLAM natural landmarks are obtained by SIFT algorithm[4]. This feature scale of the image changes, image scaling, rotation or affine transformation is not only an invariable, but also has strong adaptability to changes in illumination and image distortion.

The analysis results indicate that most computation burden of SEIF is in recovery information matrix (inverse matrix). Because the information matrix of landmark based SLAM exhibits a natural sparseness where many of the off-diagonal elements are relatively weak. According to this characteristic, This paper deals with an explicit sparse of information matrix in EIF based on SLAM. a fast algorithm based on tri-diagonal matrix splitting for the inverse matrix is put forward according to observation information of sparsification time. As the new processing does not need direct matrix inversion, the computational complexity is much lower. Lastly, the experiment is shown to produce comparable to the full-covariance EKF and SEIF.

2 Information Filter SLAM

The information form is often called the canonical or natural representation of the Gaussian distribution. Most SLAM approaches are feature-based which assumes that the robot can extract an abstract representation of features in the environment from its sensor data and then use observation of these features for localization. In these approaches, a landmark map is explicitly built and maintained. The process of concurrently performing localization and feature map building are inherently coupled, therefore, the robot must then represent a joint-distribution over landmarks M and current robot pose X_k. Assume for the moment that our estimate at time is described by the following distribution expressed in both covariance and information form[5].

$$p\left(X_k, M \mid Z^k, u^k\right) = N\left(\begin{bmatrix} \mu_{x_k} \\ \mu_M \end{bmatrix}, \begin{bmatrix} \Sigma x_k x_k & \Sigma_{x_k M} \\ \Sigma_{M x_k} & \Sigma_{MM} \end{bmatrix}\right) = N^{-1}\left(\begin{bmatrix} \eta_{x_k} \\ \eta_M \end{bmatrix}, \begin{bmatrix} \Lambda x_k x_k & \Lambda_{x_k M} \\ \Lambda_{M x_k} & \Lambda_{MM} \end{bmatrix}\right) \quad (1)$$

where μ_k and Σ_k are mean vector and covariance matrix respectively. η_k and Λ_k show the information vector and information matrix respectively.

$$\Lambda_k = \Sigma^{-1}, \quad \eta_k = \Lambda_k \mu_k \quad (2)$$

Equation(2) shows how the two forms are mathematically related. The normalized information matrix exhibits natural sparseness with a majority of the elements being orders of magnitude smaller than the few dominant entries in Fig.1.

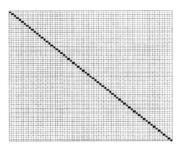

Fig. 1. Information matrix

2.1 Motion Updates

We augment the representation to include the time-propagated robot state X_{k+1} ,and obtaining the distribution $p(X_{k+1}, X_k, M | Z^k, u^{k+1})$, so $p(X_{k+1}, M | Z^k, u^{k+1})$ can be factored as

$$p\left(X_{k+1}, M | Z^k, u^{k+1}\right) = \int p\left(X_{k+1}, X_k, M | Z^k, u^{k+1}\right) dX_k \tag{3}$$
$$= N^{-1}(\overline{\eta}_{k+1}, \overline{\Lambda}_{k+1})$$

Where: $\overline{\eta}_{k+1} = \begin{bmatrix} Q^{-1}F(\Lambda x_k x_k + F^TQ^{-1}F)^{-1}\eta_{x_k} + (Q + F\Lambda_{x_k x_k}^{-1}F^T)^{-1}(f(\mu_{x_k}, u_{k+1}) - F\mu_{x_k}) \\ \eta_M - \Lambda_{Mx_k}(\Lambda x_k x_k + F^TQ^{-1}F)^{-1}(\eta_{x_k} - F^TQ^{-1}(f(\mu_{x_k}, u_{k+1}) - F\mu_{x_k})) \end{bmatrix}$

$\overline{\Lambda}_{+1} = \begin{bmatrix} (Q + F\Lambda_{x_k x_k}^{-1}F^T)^{-1} & Q^{-1}F(\Lambda x_k x_k + F^TQ^{-1}F)^{-1}\Lambda_{x_k M} \\ \Lambda_{Mx_k}(\Lambda x_k x_k + F^TQ^{-1}F)^{-1}F^TQ^{-1} & \Lambda_{MM} - \Lambda_{Mx_k}(\Lambda x_k x_k + F^TQ^{-1}F)^{-1}\Lambda_{x_k M} \end{bmatrix}$

2.2 Measurement Updates

Assume the general nonlinear measurement and its first-order linearized form (4):

$$Z_k = h(\xi_k) + V_k \approx h(\overline{\mu}_k) + H(\xi_k - \overline{\mu}_k) + V_k \tag{4}$$

The corresponding EIF update is given by (5):

$$\Lambda_k = \overline{\Lambda}_k + H^T R^{-1} H \tag{5}$$
$$\eta_k = \overline{\eta}_k + H^T R^{-1}(Z_k - h(\overline{\mu}_k) + H\overline{\mu}_k)$$

3 Improved Sparsing Method

The most computational complexity is in computing inverse information matrix. But the information matrix is the super sparse matrix. No zero elements exist in mostly main diagonal and auxiliary diagonal . in another words, other elements are approximately zero expect the main diagonal and auxiliary diagonal. In this paper, a new method is put forward. After the new measurement updates, expect the feature observed again, enforce other approximately zero elements turn into zero. so the information matrix is sparse matrix with many zero elements, so the computational complexity is low. As is shown in figure 2(a), are observed at moment K, in which the old method is used ;in figure 2 (b), the feature 4 is not observed again at moment K+1, so the corresponding element become zero. But the feature 7 is observed again at moment K+1, so the corresponding element is not zero.

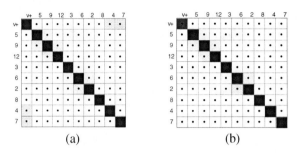

(a)   (b)

Fig. 2. Graphical information matrix

4 Visual Landmarks

The SIFT features was originally developed for image feature extraction in the context of object recognition applications. Landmarks are extracted which correspond to points in the 3-dimensional space using SIFT. Each point is accompanied by its SIFT descriptor and then matched across the images. The matching procedure is constrained by the epipolar geometry of the stereo rig. Fig.3 shows an example of a matching between the features of two stereo images.

Fig. 3. Vision Landmarks extraction

5 Experimental Results

5.1 Experimental Model

The odometer information is a representation for a two-wheeled movement of mobile robot, therefore odometer information can be used to build a mobile robot's motion model[6,7]. $X_r(k) \in R^n$ is the state of the kth step, $\theta_r(k)$ is time for kth azimuth of the robots, $\omega_r(k)$ denotes a zero-mean additive white Gaussian noise, which covariance matrix is $Q(k)$. When ΔD_k denotes arc length traversed for the robot in one step time and $\Delta \theta_k$ is the deflection angle of body's direction, in the global coordinate system, the robot motion model can be expressed as

$$X_r(k+1) = \begin{bmatrix} x_r(k+1) \\ y_r(k+1) \\ \theta_r(k+1) \end{bmatrix} = \begin{bmatrix} x_r(k) + \dfrac{\Delta D(k)}{\Delta \theta(k)}(\cos(\theta_r(k) + \Delta\theta(k)) - \cos\theta_r(k)) \\ y_r(k) + \dfrac{\Delta D(k)}{\Delta \theta(k)}(\sin(\theta_r(k) + \Delta\theta(k)) - \sin\theta_r(k)) \\ \theta_r(k) + \Delta\theta(k) \end{bmatrix} + \begin{bmatrix} \omega_{x_r}(k) \\ \omega_{y_r}(k) \\ \omega_{\theta_r}(k) \end{bmatrix} \quad (9)$$

In the global coordinate system, the sensor observation data specifically is expressed as

$$Z(k) = H(k) \begin{bmatrix} x_r + x_L^r \cos\theta_r - y_L^r \sin\theta_r \\ y_r + x_L^r \sin\theta_r + y_L^r \cos\theta_r \end{bmatrix} + \varepsilon(k). \quad (10)$$

Where, (x_L^r, y_L^r) is the location of environmental landmarks in the robot coordinate system, θ_r is the robot's azimuth.

5.2 SLAM Experimental Results and Analysis

In experiment, we compared both old method and new method. The required time for SLAM by using old method and new method are showed in Fig.4, as can be seen in Fig.4, new method can save time. —indicate new method, --- indicate old method. For both approaches, we tracked time and calculated the absolute error of the position of the robot with respect to the position. As can be seen in Fig.5, we obtained better localization results in both methods, —indicate new method, --- indicate old method.

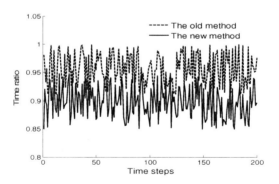

Fig. 4. The required time for SLAM

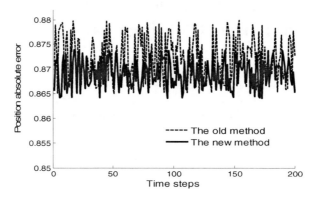

Fig. 5. Position absolute error

6 Conclusions

The robot runs along the track in Room. There are about 3000 landmarks in a squared region and the landmarks are randomly detected by vision senor. A new method summarized by this paper for the Sparse of the information filter. With the sparse information, the computational complexity is much lower. The Computer simulation results show that EIF process is faster and localization precision is no influence.

References

1. Reynolds, J., Highsmith, R., Konar, B.: Fisheries and Fisheries Habitat Investigations Using Undersea Technology. In: MTS/IEEE OCEANS 2001, Honolulu, HI, USA, pp. 812–820 (2001)
2. Thrun, S., Liu, Y., Koller, D., Durrant-Whyte, H.: Simultaneous Localization and Mapping with Sparse Extended Information Filters. International Journal of Robotics Research (accepted, to appear)
3. Singh, H., Armstrong, R., Gilbes, F., Eustice, R.: Imaging coral I:Imaging coral habitats with the Sea BED UV. Subsurface Sensing Tech. Appls. 5(1), 25–42 (2004)
4. Lowe, D.: Distinctive Image Features from Scale - Invariant Key-points. International Journal of Computer Vision 60, 91–110 (2004)
5. Frese, U., Hirzinger, G.: Simultaneous Localization and Mapping a Discussion. In: Proceedings of the IJCAI Workshop Reasoning with Uncertainty in Robotics, Seattle, WA, pp. 17–26 (2001)
6. Frese, U.: Tree map: An O(Log N)Algorithm for Simultaneous Localization and Mapping. In: Freksa, C. (ed.) Spatial Cognition IV. Springer, Heidelberg (2004)
7. Russell, S., Norvig, P.: Artifical Intelligence: A Modern Approach. Prentice Hall, Upper Saddle River (2003)

MPVS: A Method for the Repeats Masking-Off and Pre-merging in DNA Fragment Assembly

Kui Cai[1] and Jincai Yang[2]

[1] Department of Economy and Management, Wuhan University of Technology Huaxia College,
430223 Wuhan, China
kuicai@tom.com
[2] Department of Computer Science, Huazhong Normal University, 430079 Wuhan, China
jcyang@ccnu.edu.cn

Abstract. A method named MPVS (masking and pre-merging repeats based on variable-length substring) is proposed in this paper. The method records information of all variable-length substrings in shotgun set with a statistical table. It can recognize repeats in different shotgun fragments and merge them with the same variable-length substring by the statistical table. The computer simulations show that the rate of repeats recognition with MPVS is higher than with fixed-length substrings method, and the CPU time of DNA fragment assembly will be reduced too.

Keywords: fragment assembly; repeats; masking-off; pre-merging; variable-length substrings.

1 Introduction

Many genome assembly programs locate shotgun fragments that share one substring and compute an overlap between the fragments. A substring is highly repetitive if the number of its occurrences in the fragments is greater than a cut-off and is unique otherwise[1]. The substring length is a constant number, for example, it is 24 for the ARACHNE[2], and 20 for the RePS[3]. The reference [4] and [5] also proposed their masking methods based on substring of constant length k, and the value of k is computed by the number of fragments in the shotgun set. The PMMR[6] put forward the pre-merging method based on fixed-length substring. These methods are not good at masking repeats that is much longer than fixed-length substring. In these methods, the information got from scanning fixed-length substring in shotgun set is not very efficient in masking and pre-merging repeats. In reference [7], the "superword array" concept was presented in fragment assembly. The information of any length substrings could be found in superword array, but the information was not utilized to pre-merge repeats.

This paper proposes a new method that mask and pre-merge repeats by taking advantage of the variable-length substring statistical table (VSST) based on superword array. Because the information of any length substrings could be found in the VSST, the beginning and end position of repeats in every fragment can be identified efficiently. Similarly, these fragments with a same substring can be pre-merged more quickly.

G. Shen and X. Huang (Eds.): CSIE 2011, Part II, CCIS 153, pp. 384–390, 2011.

2   Methods

A word of length w is a string of w characters from the alphabet {A, C, G, T}. There are 4^w words according to length w in all, and each of them has a unique serial number (SN) from 1 to 4^w. Table 1 is a sample of the 4^w words SN with w=2.

Table 1. A sample of 4^2 words SN

words	SN	words	SN
AA	1	GA	9
AC	2	GC	10
AG	3	GG	11
AT	4	GT	12
CA	5	TA	13
CC	6	TC	14
CG	7	TG	15
CT	8	TT	16

Let long string F denote the concatenation of all fragments in the shotgun set with a special boundary character '#' added at the end of every fragment. Let m be the length of F, where the positions of F are numbered 1, 2, 3, ... , m. Let i be the position of one character in the F, and Code(i) denote the SN of a word from position i to i+w-1. If there is a character '#' in the word, Code(i)=-1. An example of F and its Code is shown in Figure 1 with w=2.

F: CGCTTCGTAATC#GCGTATCCC#CGTAATCGTGC#

i: 1 2 3 4 5 6 7 8 9 10 11 12 13 14 15 16 17 18 19 20 21 22 23 24 25 26 27 28 29 30 31 32 33 34 35

Code(i): 7 10 8 16 14 7 12 13 1 4 14 -1 -1 10 7 12 13 4 14 6 6 -1 -1 7 12 13 1 4 14 7 12 15 10 -1 -1

Fig. 1. An example of F and its Code

The repetitive regions including h words (length w) can be located in the fragments by the Code of F, where h and w is variable. Let n be the number of fragments in the shotgun set, in order to identify repeats, a constraint condition of h, w and n can be deduced that $h*w \geq \log_4 n$[4].

2.1   Constructing VSST

Let FM[n] store all fragments. The variable-length substring statistical table VSST={Pos, Fn, Loc, CArr}, Pos denotes the position of current character in the long string F; Fn denotes NO.Fn fragment in FM[n]; Loc denotes the position of current character in FM[Fn]; CArr=(Code(Pos),Code(Pos+w),...,Code(Pos+(h-1)*w)), it stores Codes of h consecutive words of length w. The VSST is sorted by the CArr in alphabet order. Table 2 is a sample part of VSST according to figure 1. Delete all records whose CArr is not the same as any other in VSST, and insert a new column named 'Fre' that denotes the number of same CArr. Table 3 is a sample of optimized VSST.

Table 2. A sample part of VSST

Pos	Fn	Loc	CArr
10	1	10	4,-1,10
11	1	11	14,-1,7
12	1	12	-1,10,12
13	0	0	-1,7,13
14	2	1	10,12,4
15	2	2	7,13,14

Table 3. A sample of optimized VSST

Pos	Fn	Loc	CArr	Fre
6	1	6	7,13,4	2
24	3	1	7,13,4	2
7	1	7	12,1,14	2
25	3	2	12,1,14	2

2.2 Pre-merging Unique VS

Let C be the clone number of the DNA target sequence, let T be the threshold and set T=C. According to Pos, Fn and Loc in optimized VSST, pre-merge directly fragments whose CArr is same and Fre<=T into a new larger fragment in shotgun set. Let LN[n] store the length of all fragments.

```
i =1; T=C;
while (NO.i record is not end of optimized VSST) {
    Si = the NO.i record of optimized VSST;
    LfFg = RtFg = Si.Fn; Fleft = Si.Loc; Fright = LN[Si.Fn]–Si.Loc; Time = Si.Fre;
    if (Time<=T) {
    for (j=i+1; j<i+Time; j++) {
      Sj = the NO.j record of optimized VSST;
        if (Sj.Loc > Fleft) {Fleft = Sj.Loc; LfFg = Sj.Fn;}
        if ((LN[Sj.Fn]–Sj.Loc) > Fright) {Fright = LN[Sj.Fn]–Sj.Loc; RtFg =
Sj.Fn;}}
    UnFgL=NO.1 to NO.Fleft character of FM[LfFg];
    UnFgR=NO.(LN[RtFg]-Fright+1) to last character of FM[RtFg];
    FM[LfFg] = UnFgL + UnFgR;
    for (j=i; j<i+Time; j++) {
    Sj = the NO.j record of optimized VSST;
        if(Sj.Fn != LfFg)  FM[Sj.Fn] = NULL;}}
i = i+Time;}
Review optimized VSST, delete all records whose Fre<=T.
```

2.3 Pre-merging Repetitive VS

After the above process, the remaining records in optimized VSST are all related to the repetitive substrings. According to Pos, Fn and Loc in optimized VSST, pre-merge fragments whose CArr is same forward and backward. The value of h and w has been assigned, and $h*w \geq \log_4 n$[4].

```
i = 1;
while (NO.i record is not end of optimized VSST) {
    Si = the NO.i record of optimized VSST; Time = Si.Fre;
    Set array FgL and FgR be NULL; Set array RpL and RpR be NULL;
    Let NO.t record be the record whose Loc is max from NO.i to i +Time-1 record;
    Swap position of NO.i and NO.t record in optimized VSST;
    Si = the new NO.i record of optimized VSST; Store Si.Fn into array FgL;
    for (j=i+1; j<i+Time; j++) {
      Sj = the NO.j record of optimized VSST;
      Pi = Si.Pos; Pj = Sj.Pos; Li = Si.Loc; Lj = Sj.Loc;
      while(Code(Pi)==Code(Pj)) {Pi = Pi-1; Pj = Pj-1; Li = Li-1; Lj = Lj-1;}
      if(Code(Pj)>0) {
        Append Sj.Fn into array FgL; RpFgL = NO.1 to NO.Li character of FM[Si.Fn];
        Store RpFgL into array RpL; RpFgL = NO.1 to NO.Lj character of FM[Sj.Fn];
        Store RpFgL into array RpL;
        ReptL = NO.(Li+1) to NO.(Si.Loc+h*w-1) character of FM[Si.Fn];}}
    Let NO.t record be the record whose LN[Fn]-Loc is max from NO.i to i +Time-1
record;
    Swap position of NO.i and NO.t record in optimized VSST;
    Si = the new NO.i record of optimized VSST; Store Si.Fn into array FgR;
    for (j=i+1; j<i+Time; j++) {
      Sj = the NO.j record of optimized VSST;
      Pi = Si.Pos+h*w; Pj = Sj.Pos+h*w; Li = Si.Loc+h*w; Lj = Sj.Loc+h*w;
      while(Code(Pi)==Code(Pj)) {Pi = Pi+1; Pj = Pj+1; Li = Li+1; Lj = Lj+1;}
      if(Code(Pj)>0) {
        Append Sj.Fn into array FgR; RpFgR = NO.Li to last character of FM[Si.Fn];
        Store RpFgR into array RpR; RpFgR = NO.Lj to last character of FM[Sj.Fn];
        Store RpFgR into array RpR;
        ReptR = NO.(Si.Loc+h*w) to NO.(Li-1) character of FM[Si.Fn];}}
    repeats = ReptL + ReptR;
    for(every Fn in FgL)
    Refresh the left part of FM[Fn] with the corresponding RpFgL in RpL by aligning
with repeats;
    for(every Fn in FgR)
    Refresh the right part of FM[Fn] with the corresponding RpFgR in RpR by aligning
with repeats;
    i = i+Time;}
```

2.4   Analysis of Computational Complexity

The complexity of scanning the long string F and obtaining VSST is $O(l \bullet n \bullet h \bullet 4^w)$, n is the number of fragments in the shotgun set, l is the average length of fragments, w is the length of word, h is the number of consecutive words. By the optimization of VSST, the number of records in optimized VSST has been decreased to the level of $[T \bullet 4^{(h \bullet w)}]$, T is the threshold. The pre-merging and refreshing work of every record is limited in $O(l \bullet n \bullet T)$, so that the complexity of pre-merging is $O(l \bullet n \bullet T^2 \bullet 4^{(h \bullet w)})$.

Accordingly, the whole complexity of MPVS is $O(l \bullet n \bullet T^2 \bullet 4^{(h \bullet w)})$, and it is slightly larger than $O(l \bullet n \bullet 4^k)$ of reference [4][5] and smaller than $O(l \bullet n \bullet 4^{2k})$ of reference [6], with the value of $h \bullet w$ is almost equal with k. Because the upper bound of l, T, h and w does exist, the final form of complexity will be $O(n)$.

Furthermore, MPVS can identify repeats more precisely and efficiently by the Code of long string F. By pre-merging fragments in the shotgun set more strongly, it can reduce the next computational complexity of DNA fragment assembly.

3   Results

The MPVS is programmed by VC6.0, the DNA sequence and fragments are stored in SQL Server 2000 database. All tests are executed in a lenovo PC, Intel Core2 E4300 CPU(1.8GHz) and 2G RAM(667MHz). Pick out five DNA sequences which are the same as reference [6]. According to the number of clones C and the number of fragments n, let T=C, $k=[\log_4 n]+2$, w=3, $h=[k/w]+1$.

Deal with these five shotgun sets by the RECON[8], PMMR[6] and MPVS respectively, the results are shown in table 4. The compare of running time is depicted in Figure 2: the horizontal axis denotes the length of DNA sequences-million bp (Mbp); the vertical axis denotes the running time-second(S).

In table 4, it is can be seen that the capability of MPVS exceeds the PMMR and RECON in recognizing repeats. It is shown in Figure 2 that the computation time of MPVS is less than the PMMR and RECON.

Table 4. The results of RECON, PMMR and MPVS

Sequence NO.	k	w	h	Repeats recognition			Recognition rate/%		
				RECON	PMMR	MPVS	RECON	PMMR	MPVS
3492857	7	3	3	33	159	210	5.6	26.9	35.6
160914588	7	3	3	68	352	473	6.3	32.6	43.8
154147533	8	3	3	89	605	711	6.9	46.9	55.1
160904213	8	3	3	101	787	861	7.1	55.3	60.5
12539724	8	3	3	150	1253	1397	7.3	61.0	68.0

After these five shotgun sets have been treated by PMMR, RECON and MPVS, they are assembled by the popular tool Phrap[9]. The compare of running time is shown in Figure 3: the horizontal axis denotes the length of DNA sequences-million bp(Mbp); the vertical axis denotes the running time-minute(M).

In Figure 3, it is known that the computation time of Phrap after MPVS process is less than that after RECON and PMMR process.

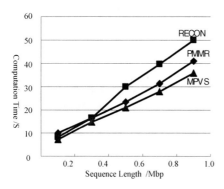 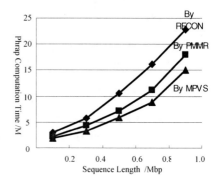

Fig. 2. The running time of RECON, PMMR and MPVS

Fig. 3. The running time of Phrap after RECON, PMMR and MPVS process

4 Discussion

The MPVS method in this paper takes full advantage of the Code of long string F, identifies the boundary of repeats precisely by scanning variable-length substring. It pre-merges fragments according to the information of variable-length substring also. The rate of repeats recognition is enhanced in this method, and the computation time of DNA fragment assembly will be reduced.

The MPVS method requires exact information of variable-length substring, and it is not good at dealing with error sequences. The next work is enhancing the capacity of processing error substring.

References

[1] Myers, E.W., Sutton, G.G., Delcher, A.L., et al.: A Whole Genome Assembly of Droso-phila. Science 287(5461), 2196–2204 (2000)

[2] Batzoglou, S., Jaffe, D.B., Stanley, K., et al.: ARACHNE: A Whole-Genome Shotgun Assembler. Genome Research 12(5), 177–189 (2002)

[3] Wang, J., Wong, G.K.-S., et al.: RePS: A Sequence Assembler That Masks Exact Repeats Identified from the Shotgun Data. Genome Research 12(5), 824–831 (2002)

[4] Zhang, B., Wang, Z.: Definite-sized Characteristic Substrings Based Method for the Masking-off of Repeats in DNA Fragment Assembly. Journal of National University of Defense Technology 24(6), 67–70 (2002)

[5] Wang, L., Zhang, Z., Chen, J.: Algorithms of Repeats in DNA Fragment Assembly. Computer Science 33(7), 164–170 (2006)

[6] Cai, K., Yang, J.: PMMR: A Method for Masking Repeats in DNA Fragment Assembly. In: Proceedings of 2009 Asia-Pacific Conference on Information Processing (APCIP 2009), Shenzhen, China, July 18-19 (2009)

[7] Huang, X., Yang, S.-P., et al.: Application of A Superword Array in Genome Assembly. Nucleic Acids Research 34(1), 201–205 (2006)

[8] Bao, Z., Eddy, S.R.: RECON documentation (2010),
     http://selab.janelia.org/recon.html

[9] Green, P.: Phrap documentation (2010),
     http://www.phrap.org/phredphrap/phrap.html

[10] International Human Genome Sequencing Consortium. Initial Sequencing and Analysis of the Human Genome. Nature 409(6822), 860–921 (2001)

[11] Pevzner, P.A., Tang, H., Waterman, M.S.: An Eulerian Path Approach to DNA Fragment Assembly. Proceedings of National Academy of Sciences 98(17), 9748–9753 (2001)

[12] Craig Venter, J., Adams, M.D., et al.: The Sequence of the Human Genome. Science 291(5507), 1304–1351 (2001)

[13] Myers, E.W., Sutton, G.G., Delcher, A.L., et al.: A Whole Genome Assembly of Drosophila. Science 287(5461), 2196–2204 (2000)

Local Fractional Laplace's Transform Based on the Local Fractional Calculus

Xiaojun Yang

Shanghai EAGTOP Electronic Technology Co., Ltd, Tangming Road 158, Songjiang District,
Shanghai, 201611, China
dyangxiaojun@163.com

Abstract. In this paper, a new modeling for the local fractional Laplace's transform based on the local fractional calculus is proposed in fractional space. The properties of the local fractional Laplace's transform are obtained and an illustrative example for the local fractional system is investigated in detail.

Keywords: local fractional Laplace's transform; local fractional calculus; fractional space; local fractional system.

Introduction

The local fractional calculus, introduced by Kolwankar and Gangal [1] in the 1990's, is revealed as a useful tool in areas ranging from fundamental science to engineering. The subject of the local fractional calculus has gained importance and popularity during the past more than ten years, due to dealing with the fractal and continuously non-differentiable functions in the real world. For example, Hölder exponents of irregular signals [2] and measuring functions smoothness with the local fractional derivative [3] were discussed. The numerical schemes for detecting fractional dimensional edges in signal processing were designed based on the local fractional derivative [4]. Leibniz's rule and chain rule for the local fractional derivative had been proved and the multivariable fractional Taylor's series of higher orders [5] had been presented. Local fractional Fokker–Planck equation [6] and the principle of virtual work in the mechanics of fractal media [7,8] had been discussed. Based on the Jumarie's fractional calculus [9,10], the local fractional calculus to deal with the continuously non-differentiable functions was re-proposed [11]. The fundamentals of the local fractional derivative of the one-variable non-differentiable functions were investigated [12]. Some results on the local fractional definite integral of the one-variable non-differentiable functions were discussed [13]. Based on the local fractional calculus, the main aim of this paper is to obtain the local fractional Laplace's transform based on the local fractional calculus and an illustrative example for the local fractional Laplace's transform applied in the local fractional system on a fractional space.

The organization of this paper is as follows. In section 2, the fractional-order complex number is proposed and the preliminary results on the local fractional calculus are discussed. The local fractional Laplace's transform is investigated in section 3. An example of local fractional system is described in section 4. Conclusions are presented in section 5.

G. Shen and X. Huang (Eds.): CSIE 2011, Part II, CCIS 153, pp. 391–397, 2011.

1 Preliminary

1.1 Results on the Mittag-Leffler Functions and Fractional-Order Complex Numbers

Definition 1. Let $E_\alpha : \Re \to \Re$, $x \to E_\alpha(x)$, denote a continuously function, which is so-called Mittag-Leffler function [9,10]

$$E_\alpha(x) := \sum_{k=0}^{\infty} \frac{x^k}{\Gamma(1+\alpha k)}, 0 < \alpha \le 1.$$

As further result of the above formula, one has a continuously non-differentiable function[15]

$$E_\alpha(x^\alpha) := \sum_{k=0}^{\infty} \frac{x^{\alpha k}}{\Gamma(1+k\alpha)}, 0 < \alpha \le 1, \tag{1}$$

and there is $E_\alpha(i^\alpha x^\alpha) E_\alpha(i^\alpha y^\alpha) = E_\alpha(i^\alpha (x+y)^\alpha)$. $\tag{2}$

Therefore, we conclude that the function $E_\alpha(i^\alpha x^\alpha)$ is periodic with the period P_α defined as the solution of the equation $E_\alpha(i^\alpha (P_\alpha)^\alpha) = 1$.

Analogously with the trigonometric function, we can read

$$E_\alpha(i^\alpha x^\alpha) := \cos_\alpha x^\alpha + i^\alpha \sin_\alpha x^\alpha \tag{3}$$

with $\cos_\alpha x^\alpha := \sum_{k=0}^{\infty} (-1)^k \dfrac{x^{2\alpha k}}{\Gamma(1+2\alpha k)}$ and $\sin_\alpha x^\alpha := \sum_{k=0}^{\infty} (-1)^k \dfrac{x^{\alpha(2k+1)}}{\Gamma[1+\alpha(2k+1)]}$, the properties of which are referred [15].

Remark 1. Analogously with a fractional-order complex number
$z = x^\alpha + i^\alpha y^\alpha$, $z \in C$, $x, y \in \Re$, $0 < \alpha \le 1$, whose conjugate of complex number
denotes $\overline{z} = x^\alpha - i^\alpha y^\alpha$, $\overline{z} \in C$, $x, y \in \Re$, $0 < \alpha \le 1$, one has the fractional modulus
defined by the expression[15] $|\overline{z}| = |z| = \sqrt{x^{2\alpha} + y^{2\alpha}} = \sqrt{\overline{z} \cdot z}$.

Remark 2. Analogously with a fractional-order number
$z = x^\alpha + i^\alpha y^\alpha$, $z \in C$, $x, y \in \Re$, $0 < \alpha \le 1$, one has the equivalent formula in
the form of the trigonometric function defined by the expression [15]

$$z = x^\alpha + i^\alpha y^\alpha = \sqrt{x^{2\alpha} + y^{2\alpha}} \left(\cos_\alpha \theta^\alpha + i^\alpha \sin_\alpha \theta^\alpha \right),$$

where $\cos_\alpha \theta^\alpha = \dfrac{x^\alpha}{\sqrt{x^{2\alpha} + y^{2\alpha}}}$ and $\sin_\alpha \theta^\alpha = \dfrac{y^\alpha}{\sqrt{x^{2\alpha} + y^{2\alpha}}}$.

Remark 3. Analogously with a fractional-order circle defined by the equality $x^{2\alpha} + y^{2\alpha} = R^{2\alpha}$, $x, y, R \in \Re$, $R > 0, 0 < \alpha \le 1$, one has a fractional-order trigonometric transform

$$\begin{cases} x^{\alpha} = R^{\alpha} \cos_{\alpha} \theta^{\alpha} \\ y^{\alpha} = R^{\alpha} \sin_{\alpha} \theta^{\alpha} \end{cases}, \text{ where } 0 \le \theta \le (2\pi)^{\frac{1}{\alpha}} \text{ and } P_{\alpha} = 2\pi.$$

Remark 4. As a further result, we can recall for convenience[15]

$$E_{\alpha}\left(i^{\alpha}\left(P_{\alpha}\right)^{\alpha}\right) := \cos_{\alpha} x^{\alpha} + i^{\alpha} \sin_{\alpha} x^{\alpha}, \tag{4}$$

whose period is also $P_{\alpha} = 2\pi$. Here, we revise the results.

1.2 Results on the Local Fractional Calculus

Definition 2. A non-differentiable function $f : \Re \to \Re$, $x \to f(x)$ is called to be continuous of order α, $0 < \alpha \le 1$, or shortly $\alpha - continuous$, when one has[15]

$$f(x) - f(x_0) = o\left((x - x_0)^{\alpha}\right). \tag{5}$$

Definition 3. Let $f(x)$ satisfy the condition of the definition (5). The local fractional derivative of function of $f(x)$ of order α at $x = x_0$ is defined by the expression [12, 13]

$$f^{(\alpha)}(x_0) = \frac{d^{\alpha} f(x)}{dx^{\alpha}}\bigg|_{x=x_0} = \lim_{x \to x_0} \frac{\Delta^{\alpha}\left(f(x) - f(x_0)\right)}{(x - x_0)^{\alpha}}, \tag{6}$$

where $\Delta^{\alpha}\left(f(x) - f(x_0)\right) \cong \Gamma(1+\alpha)\Delta\left(f(x) - f(x_0)\right)$.

Definition 4. Let $f(x)$ satisfy the condition of the definition (5). Local fractional integral of $f(x)$ in the interval $[a, b]$ is defined by the expression [12, 14]

$$_aI_b^{(\alpha)} f(x) = \frac{1}{\Gamma(1+\alpha)} \int_a^b f(t)(dt)^{\alpha} = \frac{1}{\Gamma(1+\alpha)} \lim_{\Delta t \to 0} \sum_{j=0}^{j=N} f(t_j)(\Delta t_j)^{\alpha} \tag{7}$$

where $\Delta t_j = t_{j+1} - t_j$, $\Delta t = \max\{\Delta t_1, \Delta t_2, \Delta t_j, ...\}$ and $[t_j, t_{j+1}]$, $j = 0, ..., N-1$, $t_0 = a, t_N = b$, is a partition of the interval $[a, b]$. For convenience, we assume that $_aI_a^{(\alpha)} f(x) = 0$ if $a = b$ and $_aI_b^{(\alpha)} f(x) = -_bI_a^{(\alpha)} f(x)$ if $a < b$.

Definition 5. The Dirac's distribution, or a generalized function, $\delta_\alpha(x)$ of fractional order α, $0 < \alpha \le 1$, is defined by the equality

$$\frac{1}{\Gamma(1+\alpha)} \int_{-\infty}^{+\infty} \delta_\alpha(x) f(x)(dx)^\alpha = f(0) \tag{8}$$

As a direct result, one has

$$\frac{1}{\Gamma(1+\alpha)} \int_{-\infty}^{+\infty} \delta_\alpha(x-a) f(x)(dx)^\alpha = f(a) \tag{9}$$

The following orthogonal conditions hold

$$\frac{1}{\Gamma(1+\alpha)} \int_{-\pi}^{\pi} \sin_\alpha x^\alpha (dt)^\alpha = 0, \qquad \frac{1}{\Gamma(1+\alpha)} \int_{-\pi}^{\pi} \cos_\alpha x^\alpha (dt)^\alpha = 0,$$

$$\frac{1}{\Gamma(1+\alpha)} \int_{-\pi}^{\pi} \sin^2_\alpha x^\alpha (dt)^\alpha = \frac{\pi}{\Gamma(1+\alpha)}, \qquad \frac{1}{\Gamma(1+\alpha)} \int_{-\pi}^{\pi} \cos^2_\alpha x^\alpha (dt)^\alpha = \frac{\pi}{\Gamma(1+\alpha)},$$

$$\frac{1}{\Gamma(1+\alpha)} \int_{-\pi}^{\pi} \sin_\alpha (nx)^\alpha (dt)^\alpha = 0, \qquad \frac{1}{\Gamma(1+\alpha)} \int_{-\pi}^{\pi} \cos_\alpha (nx)^\alpha (dt)^\alpha = 0,$$

$$\frac{1}{\Gamma(1+\alpha)} \int_{-\pi^\alpha}^{\pi^\alpha} \sin_\alpha (mx)^\alpha \sin_\alpha (nx)^\alpha (dt)^\alpha = \begin{cases} 0, & \text{if } m \ne n \\ \dfrac{\pi}{\Gamma(1+\alpha)}, & \text{if } m = n \end{cases}$$

$$\frac{1}{\Gamma(1+\alpha)} \int_{-\pi}^{\pi} \cos_\alpha (mx)^\alpha \cos_\alpha (nx)^\alpha (dt)^\alpha = \begin{cases} 0, & \text{if } m \ne n \\ \dfrac{\pi}{\Gamma(1+\alpha)}, & \text{if } m = n \end{cases}$$

where m and n are positive integers.

Remark 6. The functions 1, $\sin_\alpha x^\alpha$, $\cos_\alpha x^\alpha$, $\sin_\alpha (2x)^\alpha$, $\cos_\alpha (2x)^\alpha$, $\cdots$, $\sin_\alpha (mx)^\alpha$, $\cos_\alpha (mx)^\alpha$, $\cdots$ are orthogonal on the interval $-\pi \le x \le \pi$.

Proposition 1. Define the function

$$\delta_\alpha(x,\varepsilon) = \begin{cases} 0, & x \notin [0,\varepsilon], \\ \dfrac{\Gamma(1+\alpha)}{\varepsilon^\alpha}, & 0 < x \le \varepsilon, 0 < \alpha \le 1, \end{cases}$$

then one has the limit $\lim\limits_{\varepsilon \to 0} \delta_\alpha(x,\varepsilon) = \delta_\alpha(x)$. \hfill (10)

Proof. Using the definition (8), one has

$$\lim_{\varepsilon \to 0} \frac{1}{\Gamma(1+\alpha)} \int_{0}^{+\infty} \delta_\alpha(x,\varepsilon) f(x)(dx)^\alpha = \lim_{\varepsilon \to 0} \frac{1}{\Gamma(1+\alpha)} \int_{0}^{\varepsilon} \frac{\Gamma(1+\alpha)}{\varepsilon^\alpha} f(x)(dx)^\alpha \text{ and hence}$$

$$\lim_{\varepsilon \to 0} \frac{1}{\Gamma(1+\alpha)} \int_0^\varepsilon \frac{\Gamma(1+\alpha)}{\varepsilon^\alpha} f(x)(dx)^\alpha = \frac{1}{\Gamma(1+\alpha)} \int_0^{+\infty} \delta_\alpha(x) f(x)(dx)^\alpha.$$

Therefore $\lim_{\varepsilon \to 0} \delta_\alpha(x, \varepsilon) = \delta_\alpha(x)$.

2 Local Fractional Laplace's Transform of the Non-differentiable Functions

Based on the local fractional calculus, the local fractional Laplace's transform is derived as follows.

2.1 Local Fractional Laplace's transforms and Its Inverse formula

Definition 6. (Local Fractional Laplace's Transform)

The Laplace's transform $L_\alpha\{f(x)\} \equiv f_s^{L,\alpha}(s)$ of order α of the continuously non-differentiable function $f : \Re \to C$, $x \to f(x)$, which vanishes for negative values of x, is defined by the integration

$$f_s^{L,\alpha}(s) := \frac{1}{\Gamma(1+\alpha)} \int_0^{+\infty} E_\alpha(-s^\alpha x^\alpha) f(x)(dx)^\alpha, 0 < \alpha \le 1 \tag{11}$$

where the latter converges and $s^\alpha \in C$.

And of course, a sufficient condition for convergence is

$$\frac{1}{\Gamma(1+\alpha)} \int_0^{+\infty} |f(x)|(dx)^\alpha < K < \infty.$$

Then, the properties of the Matter-Leffler function and the integration by part yield

$$L_\alpha\{f^{(\alpha)}(x)\} = s^\alpha L_\alpha\{f(x)\} - f(0) \text{ and } L_\alpha\{{}_0 I_x^{(\alpha)} f(x)\} = \frac{1}{s^\alpha} L_\alpha\{f(x)\}.$$

Proposition 2. Suppose that a function $f(x)$, satisfies the condition of the definition (5), which has a local fractional derivative of order $k\alpha$, for any positive integer k and α, $0 < \alpha \le 1$, then the following equality holds, which is

$$L_\alpha\{f^{(k\alpha)}(x)\} = s^{k\alpha} L_\alpha\{f(x)\} - s^{(k-1)\alpha} f(0) - s^{(k-2)\alpha} f^{(\alpha)}(0) - \cdots - f^{((k-1)\alpha)}(0). \tag{12}$$

Definition 7. (Inversion formula of local fractional Laplace's transform)

Given the local fractional Laplace's transform (11) that we can recall here for convenience

$$L_\alpha\{f(x)\} = f_s^{L,\alpha}(s), 0 < \alpha \le 1$$

one has the inversion formula

$$f(t) = L_\alpha^{-1}\left(f_s^{L,\alpha}(s)\right) = \frac{1}{(2\pi)^\alpha}\int_{\beta-i^\alpha\infty}^{\beta+i^\alpha\infty} E_\alpha\left(s^\alpha x^\alpha\right) f_s^{L,\alpha}(s)(ds)^\alpha, \ (x > 0) \tag{13}$$

where $E_\alpha\left((2\pi)^\alpha i^\alpha\right) = 1$ and $\mathrm{Re}(s) = \beta > 0$.

Therefore, we obtain the result.

2.2 Some Basic Properties of Local Fractional Laplace's Transform

In the same manner, the following formulae are easily obtained,

$$L_\alpha\{af(x) + bg(x)\} = aL_\alpha\{f(x)\} + bL_\alpha\{g(x)\}, \ a, b \in C ;$$

$$L_\alpha\{E_\alpha(i^\alpha c^\alpha x^\alpha) f(x)\} = f_s^{L,\alpha}(s+c), \ \mathrm{Re}(s+a) > c, \ c > 0 ;$$

$$L_\alpha\{f(ax-b)\} = \frac{1}{a^\alpha} E_\alpha\left(\frac{-s^\alpha b^\alpha}{a^\alpha}\right) f_s^{L,\alpha}\left(\frac{s}{a}\right), \ a, b > 0 ;$$

$$L_\alpha\left\{\frac{f(x)}{x^\alpha}\right\} = \frac{1}{\Gamma(1+\alpha)}\int_s^{+\infty} f(s)(ds)^\alpha ;$$

$$L_\alpha^{-1}\{af_s^{L,\alpha}(s) + bg_s^{L,\alpha}(s)\} = aL_\alpha^{-1}\{f_s^{L,\alpha}(s)\} + bL_\alpha^{-1}\{g_s^{L,\alpha}(s)\} ;$$

$$L_\alpha^{-1}\{f_s^{L,\alpha}(s+c)\} = f(x)E_\alpha(-c^\alpha x^\alpha), \ c \in C .$$

3   An Illustrative Example of Initialization in Local Fractional Systems

$$f^{(\alpha)}(x) + f(x) = 0, \ 0 < \alpha \leq 1, \ f(x)|_{x=0} = 1.$$

The notation above is a local fractional-order system and by obtaining Laplace's transform the following formula is given

$$f_s^{L,\alpha}(s) = \frac{1}{\Gamma(1+\alpha)} \cdot \frac{1}{1+s^\alpha}.$$

The inverse local fractional Laplace's transform gives

$$f(x) = E_\alpha(-x^\alpha).$$

Therefore, we obtain the solution of the form as $f(x) = E_\alpha(-x^\alpha)$.

4 Conclusions

In present work the local fractional Laplace's transform based on the local fractional calculus and local fractional system are investigated and some of properties of local fractional Laplace's transform in a fractional space are obtained. The classical Fourier's transform is obtained for $\alpha \to 1$. The analytical solution of a local fractional system was discussed. The results can be applied to deal with the dynamical system based on the local fractional calculus. Moreover, some results on fractional-order complex number, the trigonometric functions and an orthogonal system of fractional-order trigonometric functions are discussed.

References

1. Kolwankar, K.M., Gangal, A.D.: Fractional differentiability of nowhere differentiable functions and dimensions. Chaos 6, 505–513 (1996)
2. Kolwankar, K.M., Gangal, A.D.: Hölder exponents of irregular signals and local fractional derivatives. Pramana J. Phys. 48, 49–68 (1997)
3. Kolwankar, K.M., Vehel, J.L.: Measuring Functions Smoothness with Local Fractional Derivatives. Fract. Calculus Appl. Anal. 4, 285–301 (2001)
4. Chen, Y., Yan, Y., Zhang, K.: On the local fractional derivative. Journal of Mathematical Analysis and Applications 362, 17–33 (2010)
5. Babakhani, A., Daftardar-Gejji, V.: On Calculus of Local Fractional Derivatives. Journal of Mathematical Analysis and Applications 270, 66–79 (2002)
6. Kolwankar, K.M., Gangal, A.D.: Local Fractional Fokker–Planck Equation. Phys. Rev. Lett. 80, 214–217 (1998)
7. Carpinteri, A., Chiaia, B., Cornetti, P.: Static-kinematic Duality and the Principle of Virtual Work in the Mechanics of Fractal Media. Comput. Methods Appl. Mech. Engrg. 191, 3–19 (2001)
8. Carpinteri, A., Chiaia, B., Cornetti, P.: A Fractal Theory for the Mechanics of Elastic Materials. Materials Science and Engineering A 365, 235–240 (2004)
9. Jumarie, G.: Fractional Master Equation: Non-standard Analysis and Liouville-Riemann Derivative. Chaos, Solitons and Fractals 12, 2577–2587 (2001)
10. Jumarie, G.: On the Representation of Fractional Brownian Motion as an Integral with Respect to $(dt)^a$. Appl. Math. Lett. 18, 739–748 (2005)
11. Jumarie, G.: Probability calculus of fractional order and fractional Taylor's series application to Fokker–Planck equation and information of non-random functions. Chaos, Solitons and Fractals 40, 1428–1448 (2009)
12. Gao, F., Yang, X., Kang, Z.: Local Fractional Newton's Method Derived from Modified Local Fractional Calculus. In: The 2th Scientific and Engineering Computing Symposium on Computational Sciences and Optimization, pp. 228–232. IEEE Computer Society, Los Alamitos (2009)
13. Yang, X., Gao, F.: The fundamentals of local fractional derivative of the one-variable non-differentiable functions. World SCI-TECH R&D 31, 920–921 (2009) (in Chinese)
14. Yang, X., Li, L., Yang, R.: Problems of local fractional definite integral of the one-variable non-differentiable function. World SCI-TECH R&D 31, 722–724 (2009) (in Chinese)
15. Yang, X., Kang, Z., Liu, C.: Local fractional Fourier's transform based on the local fractional calculus. In: The 2010 International Conference on Electrical and Control Engineering, pp. 1242–1245. IEEE Computer Society, Los Alamitos (2010)

Fundamentals of Local Fractional Iteration of the Continuously Nondifferentiable Functions Derived from Local Fractional Calculus

Xiaojun Yang[1] and Feng Gao[2]

[1] Shanghai EAGTOP Electronic Technology Co., Ltd, Tangming Road 158, Songjiang District, Shanghai, 201611, China
[2] College of Science, China University of Mining and Technology, Xuzhou, Jiangsu, 221008, China
dyangxiaojun@163.com

Abstract. A new possible modeling for the local fractional iteration process is proposed in this paper. Based on the local fractional Taylor's series, the fundamentals of local fractional iteration of the continuously non-differentiable functions are derived from local fractional calculus in fractional space.

Keywords: local fractional Taylor's series, local fractional iteration, continuously non-differentiable function, local fractional calculus, fractional space.

1 Introduction

Since the by-now classical textbook of Mandelbrot [1], fractals have been revealed a useful tool in several areas ranging from fundamental science to engineering, from microphysics to macrophysics, from chaotic dynamics to non-random phenomena. A fractal phenomenon is characterized by striking irregularities, and as a result, it is described by non-differentiable functions.

An idea is to generalize the notions of derivative and integral in order to take into account non-differentiable functions. In the 1990's, Kolwankar and Gangal [2-3] proposed local fractional derivative operator through renormalization of Riemann–Liouville definition. The local fractional derivative followed as a natural generalization of the usual derivatives to fractional order conserving the local nature of the derivatives in contrast to traditional definitions of fractional derivatives and integrals and was used further to explore local scaling properties of highly irregular and nowhere differentiable Weierstrass functions [2]. Recently, Jumarie had proposed modified fractional derivative [4-8] and integral [5], which could be deal with the non-differentiable function. More recently, the local fractional Newton's method derived from local fractional calculus was investigated [9] and the fundamentals of the local fractional derivatives and integrals of the one-variable non-differentiable functions were proved [10-11]. Based on the local fractional calculus, the definitions, properties and theorems of the local fractional Fourier transform [12] were also proposed.

As a pursuit of these we herein suggest that the fractional calculus to deal with the non-differentiable function is thought of as the local fractional calculus. In the present

G. Shen and X. Huang (Eds.): CSIE 2011, Part II, CCIS 153, pp. 398–404, 2011.

work, it is proposed that the fundamentals of local fractional iteration of the continuously non-differentiable functions are derived from the local fractional Taylor's
series based on the local fractional calculus.

This paper is organized as follows. In section 2, the preliminary results on the local
fractional calculus are introduced and the local fractional Taylor's series for the non-
differentiable functions are investigated. The fundamentals of local fractional iteration
of the continuously non-differentiable functions are derived from local fractional
calculus in section 3. The conclusions are described in section 4.

2 Preliminary Results

Definition 1. The function $f : \Re \rightarrow \Re, x \rightarrow f(x)$, is non-differentiable, which is
called to be continuous of order $\alpha, 0 < \alpha \leq 1$, or shortly αth continuous, when one
has[8,13]

$$f(x) - f(x_0) = O\left((x - x_0)^\alpha\right)$$
(1)

Definition 2. Let $f(x)$ satisfy the condition of the definition (1). Local fractional
derivative of function of $f(x)$ of αth is defined by the expression [9-11]

$$\frac{d^\alpha f(x)}{dx^\alpha}\bigg|_{x=x_0} = f^{(\alpha)}(x_0) = \lim_{x \rightarrow x_0} \frac{\Delta^\alpha f(x)}{(x - x_0)^\alpha}, 0 < \alpha \leq 1$$
(2)

where $\Delta^\alpha F(x) \cong \Gamma(1+\alpha)\left[F(x) - F(x_0)\right], 0 < \alpha \leq 1$, and with the notation
$\Gamma(1+\alpha) =: (\alpha)!$, where $\Gamma(\cdot)$ denotes the Euler gamma function.

Definition 3. Let $f(x)$ satisfy the condition of the definition (1). Local fractional
integral of function of $f(x)$ of αth in the interval $[a, b]$ is defined as [9,11,12]

$$_aI_b^\alpha f(t) = \frac{1}{\Gamma(1+\alpha)} \int_a^b f(t)(dt)^\alpha$$
(3)

Proposition 1. Suppose that $f(x)$ satisfy the condition of Equ.(1), which has a local
fractional derivative of $k\alpha$, for any positive integer k and $\alpha, 0 < \alpha \leq 1$, then the
following equality holds, which is

$$f(x) = \sum_{k=0}^{\infty} \frac{f^{(k\alpha)}(x_0)}{\Gamma(1+k\alpha)} (x - x_0)^{k\alpha}, 0 < \alpha \leq 1$$
(4)

which provides the local fractional Mc-Laurin's series

$$f(x) = \sum_{k=0}^{\infty} \frac{f^{(k\alpha)}(0)}{\Gamma(1+k\alpha)} x^{k\alpha}, 0 < \alpha \le 1 \tag{5}$$

,

where $f^{(k\alpha)}(x_0)$ is the local fractional derivatives of $k\alpha th$ of $f(x)$.

Remark 1. As a direct result, $E_\alpha(x^\alpha)$ is the Mittag–Leffler function in fractional space defined by the expression

$$E_\alpha(x^\alpha) = \sum_{k=0}^{\infty} \frac{x^{k\alpha}}{\Gamma(1+k\alpha)}, 0 < \alpha \le 1$$

.

Remark 2. In the case of formulas (4) and (5), taking into account the remainder of the integer order m of the local fractional Taylor's series for the non-differentiable

functions defined as $R_{m\alpha}(x-x_0) = \sum_{k=m}^{\infty} \frac{f^{(m\alpha)}(x_0)}{\Gamma(1+m\alpha)}(x-x_0)^{m\alpha}$, the following equal-

ity holds, which is $R_{m\alpha}(x-x_0) = O\left((x-x_0)^{m\alpha}\right)$. It is obtained when $f(x)$ satisfies the condition of a $m\alpha$ continuous function. Moreover, by using the local fractional Taylor's series, the remainder form of the local fractional Taylor's series for the non-differentiable functions is obtained, which is

$$f(x) = \sum_{k=0}^{m} \frac{f^{(m\alpha)}(x_0)}{\Gamma(1+m\alpha)}(x-x_0)^{m\alpha} + R_{m\alpha}(x-x_0), 0 < \alpha \le 1 \tag{6}$$

.

In the case of the remainder forms of them, its simplest form can be written as [3]

$$f(x) = f(x_0) + \frac{f^{(\alpha)}(x_0)}{\Gamma(1+\alpha)}(x-x_0)^\alpha + R_\alpha(x-x_0), 0 < \alpha \le 1$$

,

where $R_\alpha(x-x_0) = \left((x-x_0)^\alpha\right)$.   If $\dfrac{R_\alpha(x-x_0)}{(x-x_0)^\alpha} \to 0$,   for $x \to x_0$ and

$0 < \alpha \le 1$, then a following inequality holds, which is $f(x) \approx f(x_0) + \dfrac{f^{(\alpha)}(x_0)}{\Gamma(1+\alpha)}(x-x_0)^\alpha$.

Hence there is some ξ with $x_0 \le \xi \le x$ such that [9-10]

$$f(x) = f(x_0) + f^{(\alpha)}(\xi) \frac{(x-x_0)^\alpha}{\Gamma(\alpha+1)}, 0 < \alpha \le 1$$

.

Remark 3. Refer to Definition 1. A αth differentiable form for a αth continuously non-differentiable function

$$\Delta^\alpha f(x) = \Gamma(1+\alpha)\left[f(x)-f(x_0)\right]+O\left((x-x_0)^\alpha\right)$$ holds. As a direct result, the following

formula $\lim\limits_{x\to x_0} \Delta^\alpha f(x) = 0, 0 < \alpha \le 1$ holds.

Remark 4. The local fractional Taylor's series are different from the fractional Taylor's series for the non-differentiable functions [4-7]. In this case, there is a computing

formula for fractional space such that $(b\pm a)^\alpha = b^\alpha \pm a^\alpha$ holds [9], where α is fractal

dimension.

3 The Fundamentals of Local Fractional Iteration of the Continuously Non-differentiable Functions

3.1 The Fundamentals of Local Fractional Iteration of the Continuously Non-differentiable Functions

Assume that a function $g : \Re \to \Re, x \to g(x)$, satisfy the condition of the defini-

tion(1). For a given equation $g(x) = 0$, whose root is x^*, one has

$$x^\alpha = \varphi_\alpha(x)$$

(7)

For a point x_0 close to x^*, on substituting x_0 into (7), we can find that $x_1^\alpha = \varphi_\alpha(x_0)$.

In general, the two cases are taken into consideration as follows. (i) if $x_1 = x_0$,

then $x_1 = x^*$;(ii) if $x_1 \ne x_0$, as a new value x_1, which is substituting into (7), then

we can find that $x_2^\alpha = \varphi_\alpha(x_1)$. When this process continues, one has $x_{k+1}^\alpha = \varphi_\alpha(x_k)$,

$(k=0,1,2,\cdots)$, which is called a local fractional iteration function, which is a αth con-

tinuously non-differentiable function. Namely, there is an iteration series $x_0, x_1, \cdots, x_k$,

which converges $x^{*\alpha} = \lim\limits_{k\to\infty} x_k^\alpha$. If there is no limit, then the series is divergent.

3.2 The Convergence of Local Fractional Iteration Process

Theorem 1. Suppose that the local fractional iteration function $\varphi_\alpha : \Re \to \Re$,

$x^\alpha \to \varphi_\alpha(x)$, is a αth continuously non-differentiable function, $0 < \alpha \le 1$, which

satisfies the two constraint conditions:

i) for $0 < \alpha \leq 1$ and any $x \in [a,b]$, one has $\varphi_\alpha(x) \in [a,b]$;

ii) there exists a positive constant $L < 1$ such that for $x \in [a,b]$ holds

$$\left| \frac{\varphi_\alpha^{(\alpha)}(x)}{\Gamma(1+\alpha)} \right| \leq L < 1.$$

Then there exists a process $x_{k+1}^\alpha = \varphi_\alpha(x_k)$ converges the root of $g(x) = 0$ and its estimate value is that $\left| x^{*\alpha} - x_k^\alpha \right| \leq \dfrac{1}{1-L} < \left| x_{k+1}^\alpha - x_k^\alpha \right|$.

Proof. According to Equ.(5), there exist $0 < \alpha \leq 1$ and $\xi \in \left[x^*, x_{k-1} \right]$ such that

$$\left| x^{*\alpha} - x_k^\alpha \right| = \left| \varphi_\alpha(x^*) - \varphi_\alpha(x_{k-1}) \right| = \left| \frac{\varphi^{(\alpha)}(\xi)}{\Gamma(1+\alpha)} \right| \left| (x^* - x_{k-1})^\alpha \right| \leq L \left| x^{*\alpha} - x_{k-1}^\alpha \right|, \quad (8)$$

which provides the following formula,

$$\left| x^{*\alpha} - x_k^\alpha \right| \leq L \left| x^* - x_{k-1} \right|^\alpha \leq L^2 \left| x^* - x_{k-2} \right|^\alpha \leq \cdots \leq L^k \left| x^* - x_0 \right|^\alpha = L^k \left| x^{*\alpha} - x_0^\alpha \right|.$$

Therefore $x_k^\alpha \to x^{*\alpha}$ as $k \to \infty$.

For any positive integer p, we can find that

$$\left| x_{k+p}^\alpha - x_k^\alpha \right| \leq \left| x_{k+p}^\alpha - x_{k+p-1}^\alpha \right| + \left| x_{k+p-1}^\alpha - x_{k+p-2}^\alpha \right| + \cdots + \left| x_{k+1}^\alpha - x_k^\alpha \right|$$

$$\leq L^{p-1} \left| x_{k+1}^\alpha - x_k^\alpha \right| + L^{p-2} \left| x_{k+1}^\alpha - x_k^\alpha \right| + \cdots + \left| x_{k+1}^\alpha - x_k^\alpha \right| = \left(L^{p-1} + L^{p-2} + \cdots + 1 \right) \left| x_{k+1}^\alpha - x_k^\alpha \right|,$$

which provides $\left| x^{*\alpha} - x_k^\alpha \right| \leq \dfrac{1}{1-L} < \left| x_{k+1}^\alpha - x_k^\alpha \right|$ as $p \to \infty$.

Therefore, we have the result.

Definition 4. Assume that there exists a neighborhood

$$\Delta = \left\{ \left| x - x^* \right| \leq \delta, \delta > 0 \right\} \text{ such that } x_{k+1}^\alpha = \varphi_\alpha(x_k)$$

converges at any $x_0 \in \Delta$, this iteration process is called the local convergence of the local fractional iteration.

3.3 The Local Fractional Iteration of the Convergence Rate

Definition 5. Let $e_k = \left| x^* - x_k \right|^\alpha$ denote iterative error. There exists a con-

stant C such that $\dfrac{\left| e_{k+1} \right|}{\left| e_k \right|^p} \to C$ as $k \to \infty$, whose local fractional iteration processes

are called the convergence of order p.

Corollary 1. Let the local fractional iteration function $\varphi_\alpha : \Re \to \Re$, $x^\alpha \to \varphi_\alpha(x)$,

be a αth continuously non-differentiable function, which has a local fractional deriv-

ative of order $k\alpha$, for any positive integer k and α, $0 < \alpha \le 1$. Then this

process $x_{k+1}^\alpha = \varphi_\alpha(x_k)$ is the convergence of order $k\alpha$ if

$$\varphi_\alpha^{(\alpha)}(x) = \varphi_\alpha^{(2\alpha)}(x) = \cdots = \varphi_\alpha^{((k-1)\alpha)}(x) = 0 \text{ and } \varphi_\alpha^{(k\alpha)}(x) \neq 0.$$

Proof. According to Definition 3, then this iteration process $x_{k+1}^\alpha = \varphi_\alpha(x_k)$ has the

local convergence of the local fractional iteration. According to (4), we can find that

$$\varphi_\alpha(x_k) = \varphi_\alpha(x^*) + \frac{f^{(k\alpha)}(x^*)}{\Gamma(1+\alpha k)}(x-x_0)^\alpha + \frac{f^{(2\alpha)}(x^*)}{\Gamma(1+2k)}(x-x_0)^{2\alpha} + \cdots + \frac{f^{(k\alpha)}(x^*)}{\Gamma(1+\alpha k)}(x-x_0)^{k\alpha} = \varphi_\alpha(x^*) + \frac{f^{(k\alpha)}(\xi)}{\Gamma(1+\alpha k)}(x-x_0)^{k\alpha},$$

which provides

$$\varphi_\alpha(x_k) - \varphi_\alpha(x^*) = \frac{f^{(k\alpha)}(\xi)}{\Gamma(1+\alpha k)}(x_k - x^*)^{\alpha k}, \text{ where } \xi \in \left[x^*, x_{k-1} \right].$$

Since $\varphi_\alpha(x_k) = x_{k+1}^\alpha$ and $\varphi_\alpha(x^*) = x^{*\alpha}$, we can find that

$$\left| x_{k+1} - x^* \right|^\alpha = \left| \frac{f^{(k\alpha)}(\xi)}{\Gamma(1+\alpha k)} \right| \left| (x_k - x^*)^{\alpha k} \right|,$$

which provides $\dfrac{\left| e_{k+1} \right|}{\left| e_k \right|^{k\alpha}} = \left| \dfrac{f^{(k\alpha)}(\xi)}{\Gamma(1+\alpha k)} \right| \to \left| \dfrac{f^{(k\alpha)}(x^*)}{\Gamma(1+\alpha k)} \right| \neq 0$ as $k \to \infty$,

Therefore, we have the result.

4 Conclusions

In the present paper, we have proposed the elements of the local fractional iteration
process. The local fractional Taylor's series is proposed and some results are discussed. The convergence of the local fractional iteration process and the local fractional iteration of the convergence rate are taken into account. An illustrative example of

the local fractional iteration of the continuously non-differentiable functions had been investigated [9].

References

1. Mandelbrot, B.B.: The Fractal Geometry of Nature. W.H. Freeman, New York (1982)
2. Kolwankar, K.M., Gangal, A.D.: Fractional differentiability of nowhere differentiable functions and dimensions. Chaos 6(4), 505–513 (1996)
3. Kolwankar, K.M., Gangal, A.D.: Hölder exponents of irregular signals and local fractional derivatives. Pramana J. Phys. 48, 49–68 (1997)
4. Jumarie, G.: On the Representation of Fractional Brownian Motion as an Integral with Respect to $(dt)^a$. Appl. Math. Lett. 18, 739–748 (2005)
5. Jumarie, G.: Lagrange characteristic method for solving a class of nonlinear partial differential equations of fractional order. Appl. Math. Lett. 19, 873–880 (2006)
6. Jumarie, G.: Modeling fractional stochastic systems as non-random fractional dynamics driven by Brownian motions. Appl. Math. Mod. 32, 836–859 (2008)
7. Jumarie, G.: Table of some basic fractional calculus formulae derived from a modified Riemann–Liouville derivative for non-differentiable functions. Appl. Math. Lett. 22(3), 378–385 (2009)
8. Jumarie, G.: Fractional Master Equation: Non-standard Analysis and Liouville-Riemann Derivative. Chaos, Solitons and Fractals 12, 2577–2587 (2001)
9. Gao, F., Yang, X., Kang, Z.: Local Fractional Newton's Method Derived from Modified Local Fractional Calculus. In: The 2nd Scientific and Engineering Computing Symposium on Computational Sciences and Optimization, pp. 228–232. IEEE Computer Society, Los Alamitos (2009)
10. Yang, X., Gao, F.: The fundamentals of local fractional derivative of the one-variable non-differentiable functions. World SCI-TECH R&D 31(5), 920–921 (2009) (in Chinese)
11. Yang, X., Li, L., Yang, R.: Problems of local fractional definite integral of the one-variable non-differentiable function. World SCI-TECH R&D 31(4), 722–724 (2009) (in Chinese)
12. Yang, X., Kang, Z., Liu, C.: Local fractional Fourier's transform based on the local fractional calculus. In: The 2010 International Conference on Electrical and Control Engineering, pp. 1242–1245. IEEE Computer Society, Los Alamitos (2010)

Industrial Enterprises Development and Utilization of Information Resource

Jianmin Xie and Qin Qin

School of Economic and Management, Southwest University of Science and Technology,
621001, Mianyang, China

Abstract. The Information resource is an industrial enterprise after materials, energy of the important resource. Information resource development and will further promote the social progress and development, Will become the key of business survival and development. Present, a few enterprises are not enough to information resource development, Information resource values is not widespread. Development and use of information resource, should attach great importance of the enterprise. This paper out of information resource, Industrial Information Resource Utilization, Advanced enterprise information resource development and utilization of industrial experience in industrial enterprises in terms of development and utilization of information resource.

Keywords: Industrial enterprises; Information resource; Develop; Utilize.

1   Introduction

In the modern social, information is changing people's lives, but also affecting the entire economy. Information has become another important economic, strategic resource beside the material and energy. The development and use of Information resource significantly reduce the production of material consumption and energy consumption.At the same time, the information resource changes management coordination modes, and that becomes the key factor of enterprise competition. Therefore, the development and use of information resource on the development of enterprises has a far-reaching impact. Information resource is involved in the process to all documents, data, charts and data information in general; it involves the production and management activities in the production, acquisition, processing, storage, transmission and use of all information resources throughout the entire process of business management. Industrial enterprises Information resources refer to industrial enterprises in information resources management activities, through the orderly processing and accumulated a collection of useful information, such as internal information, competitor information, market demand and management of environmental information. This article is based on the study of industrial enterprise information resource management and the current status and role of industrial enterprises in China. Information Resource Development proposed on the basis of information resources to improve the development of industrial enterprises utilized.

G. Shen and X. Huang (Eds.): CSIE 2011, Part II, CCIS 153, pp. 405–409, 2011.

2 Industrial Enterprise Information Resources Management Role

Industrial enterprises Information resources refer to industrial enterprises in information resources management activities. Industrial enterprise information resource management will be enterprise-based information organization, systematic, digital, network, to serve the enterprise's management and development strategies, improve enterprise competitive ability. Enterprise information resources management is the important part of the management, and it is the key to enterprise information. In the global Information economy, it has a very important role to strength information resources management for enterprise development.

Industrial enterprise information resources are the foundation and tools to enhance the competitiveness of industrial enterprises; it is the same as material, energy for promoting enterprise development. Enterprise information resources management on the one hand to make quick business decisions, on the other hand so that enterprises in the fierce market competition can pinpoint the direction of their own development, the first to develop new markets, market share, timely and effective development of competition measures, thereby enhancing the competitiveness of enterprises.

Industrial enterprise information resource management is a key to industrial enterprise information. With the global economic integration and the market economy system and the rapid development of modern information technology, business survival and competitiveness of the internal and external environment has undergone fundamental changes in enterprise information technology and information management should and international practice. Enterprise information is comprehensive, not just an extension of information technology, more important is the extension of business management and organization. The enterprise informationization's essence is under the information technology support, the superintendent uses the information resource promptly, grasps the market opportunity, carries on the decision-making promptly. Therefore, enterprises should not only attach importance to information technology, greater emphasis should be the integration and management of information resources. The enterprise information management's development and the use are the enterprise information construction cores, which is also the enterprise information starting point and destination.

Industrial enterprise information resource management is to improve the economic efficiency of industrial enterprises and to protect the fundamental measures, and it also can improve the economic efficiency of production and operation purposes. Between enterprises besides in producer goods, production technology, product price competition, more importantly to information competition. Who forestalls to hold the information, who can grasp the market trend, first holds the market, raises the business economic efficiency. Therefore, possession and use of information become the ability to measure whether a company has become a key indicator of market power. The Apple is one of the enterprises who make market sales, product research and development, production and information networks linked together. The company under the same day around 10 million worldwide sales of vendors to aggregate, analyze, amend the second day of production and sales plan, then plan to send more than 150 manufacturers. Manufacturers according to plan production and sales of commercial time throughout the required receipt by volume purchasing, this management model brings to the company profitable. Thus, information resources management to enterprise management has a crucial role.

3 China's Industrial Enterprises Development and Utilization of Information Resources

3.1 Enterprises Lack of Knowledge of Information Resources Management

Information resources are strategic resources in industrial enterprises, which are the magic weapon to enhance competition of industrial enterprises in the fierce market at home and abroad. At present, many people in charge of the enterprise value of information resources and enhance the importance of information resource management lack understanding. In dealing with practical issues, information can still have decision-making, no information or insufficient information can still decision-making. Some business executives also believe that corporate responsibility, enterprise development, efficiency improvement is through the expansion of property rights reform and the extension made for information management considerations and the lack of long-term financial, material, human, cooperation and support, thus resulting in frequent mistakes in decision making. Many businesses tend to believe that information resources and material resources, energy resources, as in the role of the process of economic development the same as for general merchandise share information resources. In fact, the information resource with material resources, energy resources are essential differences. Information resources "reserves" unlimited and material resources and energy resources in a particular space and time deposits is limited. Information resources can be reused, development, and continuously generate new, higher-value information. Large amount of data shows that in a market economy, enterprises increasingly urgent demands for information, the scope of the demand is also growing.

3.2 Lack of Talent Building

Information on the quality of personnel is not high, hindered the development of industrial enterprise information resources, management and use. Information industry is the high-tech industry, the officers who engaged in the corporate information should both master information resources management expertise and technology, but also the knowledge to understand their production and operation order to adjust to market competitive needs. However, most industrial enterprises in China in the quality of information resources management not reach this requirement. Information management of cultural and professional qualities generally not high, many workers narrower range of knowledge, not been systematic professional training, do not have the information management expertise.In addition, the process of industrial production and operation activities, a lack of understanding, not control the collection, management, reflecting the business activities of all the information so as to impede the development of industrial enterprise information resources, management and use.

4   To Improve the Way of Information Resources Development and Utilization

The core of enterprise information technology strategy is the development and use of information resource, and both sharing it. The former Ministry of Information Advancement Department Xiao-Fan Zhao, deputy director of the "2000 Enterprise IT applications in China Forum" in his speech to the state information is defined as "planning and organization of national unity under the agriculture, industry, science and technology, defense and all aspects of social life the application of modern information technology, in-depth development and extensive use of information resources, speed up the process of modernization." From this definition, "in-depth development and extensive use of information resources", has clearly confirmed the development and use of information resources in the central position. Industrial enterprises in the development and use of information resources should have the following aspects.

4.1 Government Participation in Macro-control

Government should strengthen macro-control, develop or promote the World Trade Organization to develop the relevant laws, regulations and standards as soon as possible. Overseas development of domestic industrial enterprises continue to be blocked, one of the reasons that have not formed a good overall macroeconomic environment. Enterprises go out and not just a business thing, also need the guidance of the State, the overall national macro-policy environment and legal protection of the environment. In recent years, the Chinese Government in promoting increased business going out side management, and introduced a number of policies and regulations. However, we found more deficiency in practice. China's foreign investment mainly macro-management system not meet the requirements, especially in the overseas investment, financing, management of foreign enterprises in investment, operation, is still a lack of relevant laws and regulations. Therefore, our government should establish foreign investment in line with international practice, the development of the legal system.

4.2 Talent Is the Key

Modern enterprise competition is actually a talent competition. Talent is the information resource development and utilization of the key, is the business relations. Information resources development is a knowledge-intensive high-tech, specialized industries culture, gather a group of information professionals.It is the basic conditions to improve the development of information resources. Information Resource for the development and use needs to a large number of people to join. Successful enterprise information needs information specialists IT experts technology experts and management experts together, the special needs of information specialists.Because "the development of information resources" is the core of enterprise information. It is a long-term process; no information management professionals, there is no information resource development and resource sharing; No information management personnel, particularly chief information officer (CIO), there is no information. Only specialized training to information specialists, IT experts, technology experts and management experts, it can create a really senior information technology specialist only.

4.3 Establish a Sense of Information, Updates the Concept of Information

As the popularity of information technology and the rapid growth of information, At present the development and utilization of information resources, there are many technical difficulties, but the impact of ideology and theory on the lack of knowledge is the most important. Compared with foreign countries, China still a big gap in this regard. First of all, information is an important strategic economic resources, this concept has not yet accepted by the people it directly affects the level of development and utilization of information resources in China. Secondly, the basic knowledge of information resources development and utilization of the lack of a serious impact on our information management. Information management can not just stay in the building of information systems, but also further access to information sources and information services. Our business should be under the guidance of correct theory, take effective measures in practice, can really push forward the process of enterprise information.

5   Conclusion

Information resource is the technology basis for economic development, the level of development and utilization of an enterprise's comprehensive strength will become an important symbol. Industrial enterprises to succeed in the fierce competition, it must be "effective development and use of information resources, the sharing of resources". This is the current industrial enterprise information technology strategic task. Advanced in information technology and information-rich era, with the industrial enterprises of building strategies to promote and establish information awareness, the concept of updating information, the use of information management principles and methods,continue to improve information resources development and utilization of the security system, Development and utilization of information resources on the development of enterprises will certainly play an important role in promoting.

References

1. Severance, D.G., Passino, J.: Making I T work—An executive's guide to implementing information technology systems. Jossey-Bass, Michigan (2001)
2. Trilett, J.E.: The Solow Productivity Paradox: What Do Computers Do to Productivity. Canadian Journal of Economics Revue Canadienned'Economique (1999)
3. Prahalad, C.: The dynamic synchronization of strategy and information technology. MIT Sloan Management Review (2002)
4. Calantone, R.J., Cavusgil, S.T.: Tacit. knowledge transfer and firm innovation capability. The Journal of Business & Industrial Marketing (2003)
5. Shin, N.: The impact of information technology on the financial performance of diversified firms. Decision Support Systems (2006)
6. Mahtab, A., Bokhari, M.U.: Information Security Policy Architecture. In: Conference on Computational Intelligence and Multimedia Applications (2007)

A Corpus-Based Study on Vocabulary of College English Coursebooks

Yanhong Liu[1] and Zequan Liu[2]

[1] Liren College Yanshan University, QHD 066004, China
Liuyanhong77@163.com
[2] International Cooperation Yanshan University, QHD 066004, China
zqliu@ysu.edu.cn

Abstract. This study bases on self-built "College English Coursebook Corpus", using Cunningsworth [1] theories, taking College English Curriculum Requirements (Requirements) [2] as criterion, with a combination of quantitative and qualitative approach to explore the vocabulary of four sets of coursebooks. The comparative study on vocabulary includes four aspects: vocabulary size, coverage, distribution and frequency. It is hoped that the statistics examined in this study would be of some help for English teachers to take above aspects of vocabulary into account in teaching practice and possibly for administrators to adjust curriculum design and for editors or publishers to revise existing coursebooks.

Keywords: college English coursebooks; vocabulary; corpus; evaluation.

1 Introduction

A number of studies relevant to coursebook evaluation have been conducted. Huang and Yu [3] analyzed 120 papers related to college English coursebook studies which published from 1990 to 2007 and found that articles about theories and principles, methods and specific issues of coursebook compilation account for 36.3%, most of them are introductory studies, studies concerning criteria of coursebook evaluation only account for 5.9%, and empirical researches on coursebook evaluation only account for 2.22%, corpus-based approach to college English coursebook evaluations are rarely touched. Although most macro-evaluations certainly provide a useful and practical help, most of them fail to reflect the nature of coursebooks [4].

2 Corpus Development

Present study aims to create a corpus of college English coursebooks used in universities in China for non-English major learners to form the basis of an analysis. The study adopts Twenty-first Century College English (TCCE), Experiencing English (EE), New Horizon College English (NHCE), College English (CE) to build corpus, each of them consists of 4 volumes which are integrated coursebooks exclusively. These

G. Shen and X. Huang (Eds.): CSIE 2011, Part II, CCIS 153, pp. 410–415, 2011.
© Springer-Verlag Berlin Heidelberg 2011

coursebooks selected and adopted are almost all produced in China. The design and model of textbooks reflect the local concepts of teaching and learning of a foreign language. After removing proper nouns, the resulting corpus contained in total 239, 405 tokens (running words).

3 The Proposed Evaluation Algorithm

3.1 Criteria of Evaluation

Requirements was published by China's Ministry of Education in 2007. It was developed based on the program design used by colleges and universities in China. It proposed some requirements for basic, intermediate and advanced levels, as well as four wordlists: basic level vocabulary (4795 types), intermediate level vocabulary (6395 types), advanced level vocabulary (7675 types), active vocabulary (2000 types) and collocation list (1870 items). By and large, these lexical items are presumed to be the minimum ones for corresponding levels, therefore, the wordlists can be used as criteria to diagnose whether coursebooks contain Requirements' vocabulary.

3.2 Concepts of Evaluation

The term lemma is used to represent a group of words whose meanings can be inferred when the meaning of the base form in the group is known to a learner[5]. For instance, the headword talk, and its complete family members are talk, talks, talked, talking, from the example lemma talk, it consists of a headword, its inflected forms. Other related terms word type and token, for example, go, go, goes, going, gone, gone constitute one lemma, but they are four word types and six word tokens. Standardised type/token ratio represents the type/token ratio in the every 1000 words of each texts. All the measures of lexical variation were calculated with the WordSmith package.

4 Data Analysis and Discussion

4.1 Vocabulary Size

Wordlist will show the basic statistics of four sets of coursebooks, see Table 1.

Table 1. Statistics of four sets of coursebooks

Books	Tokens	Types	Lemma	Standardized type/token ratio (STTR)	Mean word length	Mean sentence length	Mean text length
TCCE	58348	7236	4662	45.12	4.50	15.62	912
EE	43258	6416	4220	44.76	4.57	16.63	685
CE	71450	8636	5608	44.82	4.39	14.10	1116
NHCE	65782	7852	4901	46.30	4.59	16.87	822

The statistics of coursebook corpus illustrated in Table1, NHCE containing 65782 tokens, 7852 types and 4901 lemmas and CE containing 71450 tokens, 8636 types and5608 lemmas top the word coverage, TCCE containing 58348 tokens, 7236 types and 4662 lemmas in the third place, and EE containing 43825 tokens, 6416 types and 4220 lemmas, with minimum vocabulary in the fourth place. Concerning types only, two sets of coursebooks reach the Requirements' 7675 types, while the other two sets of coursebooks labeled at intermediate and advanced level respectively fail to meet the Requirements.

4.2 The Coverage of Vocabulary of Requirements in Coursebooks

The functions concordance and detailed consistence of WordSmith software can be used to compare a text against Requirements' wordlists.

Table 2. The coverage of vocabulary of Requirements in four sets of coursebooks

Books	Basic		Intermediate		Advanced		Active vocabulary	
	lemma	%	lemma	%	lemma	%	lemma	%
TCCE	3162	67.52	372	23.28	182	14.22	1889	80
EE	2884	61.58	292	18.27	142	11.09	1733	78.8
CE	3501	74.76	399	24.97	214	16.72	1969	98.5
NHCE	4148	88.58	138	8.64	48	3.75	2126	106.3

Table 2 demonstrates that none of the four sets of coursebooks in the corpus seemed to meet the figure in Requirements. Regarding basic level vocabulary, the coursebook of highest coverage rate is NHCE (4148 in lemma, 88.5%), CE (3501 in lemma, 74.76%) and TCCE (3162 in lemma, 67.52%) are inferior to NHCE, in the third place, EE (2884 in lemma, 61.58%) relatively covers the least vocabulary of Requirements. The coverage of basic level vocabulary in four sets of coursebooks all fail to meet the Requirements (4683 in lemma). Basic level words are expected to be taught within two academic years, if properly selected or managed, a set of coursebook can contribute to the goal of vocabulary learning for the objective of graduating from university.

When it comes to the intermediate level and advanced level vocabulary, the objectives of coursebooks which were labeled by the publisher should be made clear. Concerning the coverage of intermediate level vocabulary, CE (399 in lemma, 24.97%) and TCCE (372 in lemma, 23.28%) which bore a close resemblance to each other have maximum coverage. EE gains a lower percentage of covering (292 in lemma, 18.27%) and NHCE has the lowest coverage (138 in lemma, 8.64%). The percentages of coverage reflect that CE has a higher coverage of intermediate words though it is designed for basic level study. Relating to advanced level vocabulary, the coursebook of highest coverage is CE (214, 16.72%), the rest are TCCE (182, 14.22%), EE (142, 11.09%) and NHCE (48, 3.75%).

Finally, the investigation of active vocabulary, we still have to take coursebooks' objectives into consideration. The top two coursebooks of higher coverage one NHCE (2126, 106.3%) and CE (1969, 98.5%), TCCE (80%) and EE (78.8%) have a lower coverage. We are pleased to find that NHCE and CE almost meet the Requirements in coverage of active vocabulary.

4.3 The Distribution of Intermediate Level and Advanced Level Vocabulary

Requirement suggests that learners with a good command of the basic level words need to consider their intended use of English. Intermediate wordlist containing 1598 words could be used to set vocabulary learning goals for college English courses as a launch pad for further English, and then advanced level. Ideally, these two level vocabulary should distribute progressively.

Table 3. The distribution of intermediate level and advanced level vocabulary

	Vol.	tokens	Intermediate		Advanced	
			tokens /%	types /%	tokens /%	types /%
TCCE	1	12187	38 / 0.31	33 / 1.25	29 / 0.24	25 / 0.95
	2	13398	99 / 0.74	77 / 2.6	22 / 0.16	19 / 0.64
	3	15037	124 / 0.82	104 / 3.01	49 / 0.33	40 / 1.16
	4	17726	134 / 0.76	106 / 3.02	95 / 0.54	60 / 1.70
EE	1	8228	27 / 0.33	22 / 1.94	23 / 0.28	16 / 0.86
	2	11044	58 / 0.53	51 / 1.91	26 / 0.24	21 / 0.79
	3	11435	70 / 0.61	49 / 1.81	58 / 0.50	33 / 1.21
	4	13118	116 / 0.89	93 / 2.96	58 / 0.44	41 / 1.31
CE	1	15146	43 / 0.28	36 / 1.12	37 / 0.24	15 / 0.47
	2	17172	103 / 0.59	70 / 1.98	43 / 0.25	30 / 0.85
	3	19365	146 / 0.75	96 / 2.47	69 / 0.36	49 / 1.26
	4	19767	159 / 0.80	118 / 2.78	100 / 0.50	73 / 1.72
NHCE	1	13998	29 / 0.20	20 / 0.71	9 / 0.06	7 / 0.25
	2	15622	38 / 0.24	30 / 0.88	10 / 0.06	8 / 0.23
	3	18019	27 / 0.15	23 / 0.59	13 / 0.07	6 / 0.16
	4	18143	50 / 0.28	32 / 0.80	29 / 0.15	13 / 0.33

From Table 3, we can see that the tokens were almost distributed progressively in four volumes of four sets of coursebooks. After extending to word types, four sets of coursebooks bore a resemblance in distribution. Both intermediate level and advanced level vocabulary selected and arranged in a progressive order even though the percentage of coverage is fairly low, especially in EE and TCCE coursebooks.

4.4 The Frequency of Vocabulary

The results of some previous studies suggest that there is a strong correlation between the word frequency and acquisition. Learners' sensitivity to frequency in all these domains has implications for theories of implicit and explicit learning and their

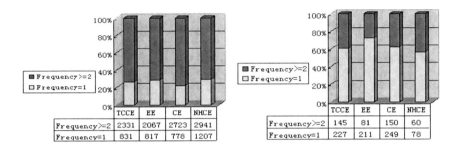

	TCCE	EE	CE	NHCE
Frequency>=2	2331	2067	2723	2941
Frequency=1	831	817	778	1207

Fig. 1. Basic level vocabulary

	TCCE	EE	CE	NHCE
Frequency>=2	145	81	150	60
Frequency=1	227	211	249	78

Fig. 2. Intermediate level vocabulary

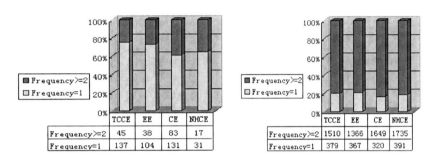

	TCCE	EE	CE	NHCE
Frequency>=2	45	38	83	17
Frequency=1	137	104	131	31

Fig. 3. Advanced level vocabulary

	TCCE	EE	CE	NHCE
Frequency>=2	1510	1366	1649	1735
Frequency=1	379	367	320	391

Fig. 4. Active level vocabulary

interactions. Figure 1 to Figure 4 will present the frequency of Requirement vocabulary in four sets of coursebooks.

As the Figures show that the basic level vocabulary contained in NHCE and appear once are 1207 lexical items, almost 30% of the total. In remaining three sets of coursebooks, this amount of vocabulary range from approximately 778-831 words. For the frequency of intermediate level vocabulary, four sets of coursebooks had the same tendency except for NHCE, 249 words in CE, 227 words in TCCE and 211 words in EE appeared once, more 60% words appeared once in coursebooks. As for the frequency of advanced level vocabulary, there were more words appeared once in four sets of coursebooks, the rate ranging from 62% to 80%. Active vocabulary was different from above three levels vocabulary, the situation have been improved. The figures indicate that the breadth of coverage and the depth of lexical items were not well balanced, some of which they would encounter only once or no more than a few times throughout the book.

5 Summary

The statistics of evaluation show that there is a gap between Requirements and coursebooks. Teachers may need to choose a coursebook containing more readings for this purposes or supplement them with different sources in this regard. Therefore, the lack of adequate learning material in coursebooks will jeopardize students' objective achievement, even their graduation. Apart from this awareness, it is hoped that the approach adopted in this study would provide English teachers an method to evaluate teaching materials.

Acknowledgement

The study was part of Corpus-based Study on College English Writing Teaching (201001A453), the authors would like to thank the support of Technology Bureau of QHD.

References

1. Cunningsworth, A.: Choosing your coursebook. Foreign Language Education Press, Shanghai (2002)
2. Higher Education Department of Ministry of Education: College English Curriculum Requirements. Shanghai Foreign Language Education Press, Shanghai (2007)
3. Huang, J., Yu, S.: The study on college English coursebooks since 90s, 20th century. J. Foreign Language World, 77–83 (2009)
4. Qian, Y.: An introduction of a checklist of coursebook evaluation. J. Foreign Language World, 45–48 (1995)
5. Kennedy, G.: An introduction to Corpus Linguistics. Foreign Language Teaching and Research Press, Beijing (2002)

A New Index for Maturity Measurement of On-Vine Tomato Fruits and Its Spectroscopic Finger-Print*

Haiqing Yang

College of Information Engineering, Zhejiang University of Technology,
Hangzhou 310032, P.R. China
yanghq@zjut.edu.cn

Abstract. This study aims to using visible and near infrared spectroscopy (VIS-NIRS) for *in situ* determination of tomato maturity. A new index (GS) defined as the ratio of current growing age (days) to on-vine duration before harvest (days) was proposed. A partial least squares regression (PLSR) with leave-one-out cross validation was used to build calibration models for each cultivar spectra and the combined spectra of all cultivars. Result shows that PLSR for GS is successful and robust in predicting tomato maturity with coefficient of determination (R^2) of 0.89-0.92, and residual prediction deviation (RPD) of 3.00-3.70 for the single cultivar model and the general one. The analysis of PLSR coefficient plot indicates the consistency of assigning important wavelength bands for tomato cultivars. It is concluded that the proposed GS index can be adopted with common-purpose for maturity determination of on-vine tomatoes, which allows for selective harvest of tomatoes by a picking robot.

Keywords: tomato; maturity; selective harvest; visible and near infrared spectroscopy.

1 Introduction

The influence of cultivar and ambient environment on the maturing of tomatoes is so significant that numerous labors are required for fruit harvesting, which is an important issue for cost-sensitive tomato plantations. Thus, tomato growers are increasingly interested in picking robots for selective harvest of fruits. The most widely used methods to predict tomato maturity are based on the physiological features of tomato fruits, such as pericarp color. The often-used laboratory measurements of tomato maturity include nuclear magnetic resonance (NMR) [1]. acoustic impulse-response technique [2]. electronic nose [3], quantitative magnetic resonance imaging (MRI) and NMR relaxometry [4]. These techniques are quite expensive and unsuitable for *in situ* measurement of on-vine tomatoes.

Recently, visible and near infrared (VIS-NIR) spectroscopy has become an excellent in-field technique for measuring the internal quality of tomatoes. It has been used to predict ripeness-related quality parameters in off-vine tomatoes [5-8]. VIS-NIRS

---

* Funded by the Natural Science Foundation of Zhejiang Province, P.R.China (No. Y1090885) and by the State Scholarship Fund of China (Grant No.[2009]3004).

G. Shen and X. Huang (Eds.): CSIE 2011, Part II, CCIS 153, pp. 416–421, 2011.

has been used for the quantitative determination of lycopene [9-10] and carotenoids [11] in tomatoes. Although these studies on the internal qualities of tomatoes using VIS-NIR spectroscopy may lead to fast determination of final harvest time, there is still lack of information about how to determine the maturity of pre-climacteric tomatoes, which is particularly important for a picking robot because tomato plants produce numerous fruits reaching fully-mature stage at various time. To our knowledge, no published studies have addressed the use of VIS-NIR spectroscopy for *in situ* determination of the maturity of on-vine tomatoes.

The objective of this study is to predict the maturity of on-vine tomatoes of three cultivars using the VIS-NIR spectroscopy. The paper also aims to evaluate the versatility of the developed models for different tomato cultivars.

2 Materials and Methods

2.1 Tomato Samples and Spectroscopic Measurement

Tomato plants of three cultivars were cultivated at the Silsoe Horticultural Centre, Bedfordshire, the United Kingdom, in the summer 2010. Cultivar 1 were growing outdoors while cultivars 2 and 3 were planted in two detached greenhouses. This caused different ambient temperatures among them, as the outdoor tomatoes were subjected to the climate. Selected fruits were marked with numbers. Spectroscopic measurement started on the 24th July with the interval of 2-3 days until the marked fruits turned red and picked (according to USDA colour classification of fresh tomatoes).

The reflectance spectra of tomatoes were measured with a mobile, fiber-type, AgroSpec VIS-NIR spectrophotometer (Tec5 Co., Germany) with spectral range of 350-2200nm. A USB cable was used for the data transmission between the spectrophotometer and a portable computer. The fiber probe was installed in a fiber holder which was used to touch the equator of a fruit at a 45° angle to eliminate light specular reflection. A 100% white reference was used before scanning. Measurement was made in three separate positions on the equator of a fruit. A total of ten scans were measured at each position and the spectra from the three positions were averaged as one sample.

2.2 Data Analysis and Spectral Pretreatment

The picking date for each tomato depends on cultivars and ambient environment. In order to build a general calibration model, a new index (GS) is defined as:

$$GS = \frac{\text{Current growing age (days)}}{\text{On-vine duration before harvest (days)}}$$

The current growing age of a tomato is defined as the duration from the date it was born to the date it is measured. The on-vine duration of a tomato before harvest refers to the duration from the date it was born to the date it is to be picked. The USDA Tomato Harvest Color Chart was used for the determination of whether a tomato is fully-mature or not. For a specific tomato, its GS value varies with a real number from

0 to 1. For example, GS values assigned as 0, 0.5 and 1 will be regarded as the first day, half of growing duration and fully mature (picking date), respectively. Values of GS>1 refer to over-ripe. The picking time will be determined by GS≥1.

The spectra were divided into a calibration set (70%) and an independent prediction set (30%). The calibration spectra were subjected to a partial least squares regression (PLSR) with leave-one-out cross validation. The PLSR relates the variations in one response variable (GS) to the variations of several predictors (wavelengths). The optimal number of latent variables (LVs) for PLSR was determined by minimizing the predicted residual error sum of squares (PRESS). In order to examine the effect of different tomato cultivars on the accuracy of the PLSR models, the PLSR analysis was applied separately on each cultivar spectra and the combined spectra of all cultivars.

Due to the low signal-to-noise ratio of both ends of each spectrum, only the region of 400-2100 nm was used to establish calibration models. Several spectral pretreatment algorithms, including Savitzky-Golay smoothing, multiplicative scatter correction (MSC), standard normal variate (SNV), baseline offset correction (BOC), 1st and 2nd order de-trending, and 1st and 2nd derivatives were investigated. The optimal selection of pretreatment algorithms was based on the performance of PLSR models in the cross validation and the independent prediction. The PLSR models were evaluated using coefficient of determination (R^2) and root-mean-square error (RMSE). Residual prediction deviation (RPD), which is the ratio of standard deviation of the reference data to RMSE of prediction, was recorded. Statistically, prediction with an RPD value between 2.5 and 3.0 and above 3.0 is classified as good and excellent, respectively.

3 Results and Discussion

3.1 Spectral Features

Reflectance spectra collected from tomato cultivar 1 at different maturity stages are shown in Fig. 1. In general, reflectance is stronger in less mature stages and reduces with tomato's growth. In the visible region, there is a noticeable reflectance valley at around 672 nm, corresponding to the absorption of chlorophyll a in immature fruit. This reflectance valley gradually decreases down to its minimum before 12 Aug. After this, reflectance tends to increase, with dramatic changes during the final harvest time. Another reflectance valley near 491 nm decreases with the increasing tomato maturity. This band might be linked with lycopene and β-carotene. In the NIR region, there are several noticeable water absorption bands at 763, 981, 1456 and 1928 nm. The band at 1202 nm can be attributed to sugar-linked absorption.

3.2 Accuracy of PLSR Models Developed for the GS Prediction

Table 2 reports the result of the PLSR models for single cultivar spectra and combined spectra that provide the best accuracy for GS prediction. In general, the performance of the calibration models for GS prediction is successful, although the accuracy of these PLSR models is a function of tomato cultivar. These models are evaluated to have good calibration performance with RPD≥2.5. The model for

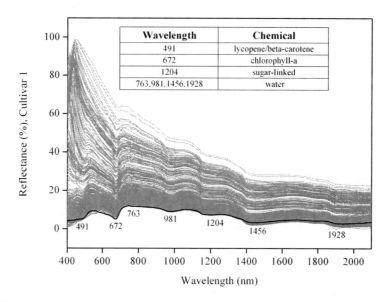

Wavelength	Chemical
491	lycopene/beta-carotene
672	chlorophyll-a
1204	sugar-linked
763,981,1456,1928	water

Fig. 1. Reflectance spectra of tomato fruits in cultivar 1 at different maturity stages

Table 2. Performance of PLS models developed for the prediction of GS index for individual cultivars 1, 2 and 3 spectra and for the mixed spectra of the three cultivars

Cultivar	LVs[a]	Cross-validation			Independent Validation		
		R^2	RMSE	RPD	R^2	RMSE	RPD
1	9	0.92	0.092	3.47	0.91	0.097	3.29
2	6	0.84	0.125	2.50	0.92	0.084	3.70
3	7	0.89	0.098	2.87	0.92	0.080	3.49
Combined[b]	9	0.88	0.105	2.88	0.89	0.101	3.00

[a] latent variables.
[b] the mixture of all cultivar spectra.

cultivar 1 produces excellent prediction with R^2 of 0.91and RPD of 3.29 for the independent validation set. The models for cultivar 2 and 3 produce more accurate predictions with R^2 and RPD of 091-0.92 and 3.70-3.49, respectively.

Although the general model developed for the combined spectra is less accurate than those for individual cultivar spectra, its prediction for the independent validation set still provides excellent performance with R^2 and RPD values of 0.89 and 3.00, respectively.

3.3   Effectiveness of GS Index for Tomatoes

Although the single cultivar models and the general one achieve high accuracy for GS prediction, it is still necessary to identify that GS index is effective for monitoring tomato maturity. To this end, we used PLSR coefficients to evaluate the quantitative impact of reflectance at each wavelength on these models. the evaluation was conducted based on the number of LVs from 1 to 10. Figure 2 illustrates one of the PLSR coefficients plots corresponding to 10 LVs. The comparison was also done among single cultivar and general one. The regression coefficients for each single cultivar appear to vary slightly in magnitude. However, important bands for GS prediction can be identified in the same spectral positions along the wavelength-axis. For example, the PLSR coefficients from 400nm to 600nm show that this range is significant for GS prediction. These identical spectral wavelengths constitute the spectroscopic figure-print of GS index for maturity measurement of on-vine tomatoes.

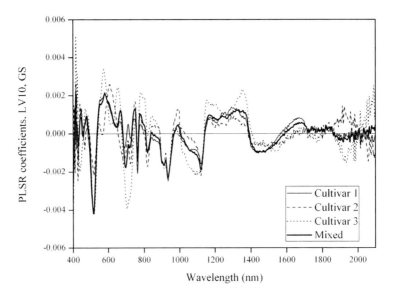

Fig. 2. PLSR coefficients plot with 10 LVs for tomato cultivars

4 Conclusions

The visible and near infrared (VIS-NIRS) spectroscopy was used to build calibration models for maturity determination of tomatoes of three cultivars. A new index of GS defined as the ratio of current growing age (days) to the on-vine duration before harvest (days) was proposed. Combined with relevant spectral pretreatment, the partial least squares regression (PLSR) enabled establishing successful and robust calibration models for GS prediction with R^2=0.89-0.92 and RPD≥3.0. Although the prediction accuracy of the PLSR models for single cultivars is relatively higher than a general model for combine spectra, the prediction using the general model is also satisfactory. The analysis of PLSR coefficient plots indicates that the proposed GS index is effective for all tomato cultivars and is worthy of further investigation for general application.

References

1. Saltveit Jr., M.E.: Determining tomato fruit maturity with nondestructive in vivo nuclear magnetic resonance imaging. Postharvest Biol. Technol. 1, 153–159 (1991)
2. Schotte, S., De Belie, N., De Baerdemaeker, J.: Acoustic impulse-response technique for evaluation and modelling of firmness of tomato fruit. Postharvest Biol. Technol. 17, 105–115 (1999)
3. Gómez, A.H., Hu, G., Wang, J., Pereira, A.G.: Evaluation of tomato maturity by electronic nose. Comput. Electron. Agric. 54, 44–52 (2006)
4. Musse, M., Quellec, S., Cambert, M., Devaux, M.F., Lahaye, M., Mariette, F.: Monitoring the postharvest ripening of tomato fruit using quantitative MRI and NMR relaxometry. Postharvest Biol. Technol. 53, 22–35 (2009)
5. Pedro, A.M.K., Ferreira, M.M.C.: Simultaneously calibrating solids, sugars and acidity of tomato products using PLS2 and NIR spectroscopy. Anal. Chim. Acta 595, 221–227 (2007)
6. Shao, Y., He, Y., Gómez, A.H., Pereir, A.G., Qiu, Z., Zhang, Y.: Visible/near infrared spectrometric technique for nondestructive assessment of tomato 'Heatwave' (*Lycopersicum esculentum*) quality characteristics. J. Food Eng. 81, 672–678 (2007)
7. Flores, K., Sánchez, M.T., Pérez-Marín, D., Guerrero, J.E., Garrido-Varo, A.: Feasibility in NIRS instruments for predicting internal quality in intact tomato. J. Food Eng. 91, 311–318 (2009)
8. Clément, A., Dorais, M., Vernon, M.: Multivariate Approach to the Measurement of Tomato Maturity and Gustatory Attributes and Their Rapid Assessment by Vis–NIR Spectroscopy. J. Agric. Food Chem. 56, 1538–1544 (2008)
9. Clément, A., Dorais, M., Vernon, M.: Multivariate Approach to the Measurement of Tomato Maturity and Gustatory Attributes and Their Rapid Assessment by Vis–NIR Spectroscopy. J. Agric. Food Chem. 56, 1538–1544 (2008)
10. Choudhary, R., Bowser, T.J., Weckler, P., Maness, N.O., McGlynn, W.: Rapid estimation of lycopene concentration in watermelon and tomato puree by fiber optic visible reflectance spectroscopy. Postharvest Biol. Technol. 52, 103–109 (2009)
11. Rubio-Diaz, D.E., De Nardo, T., Santos, A., de Jesus, S., Francis, D., Rodriguez-Saona, L.E.: Profiling of nutritionally important carotenoids from genetically-diverse tomatoes by infrared spectroscopy. Food Chem. 120, 282–289 (2010)

Modeling and Simulation of Rat Head Exposed to Mobile Phone Electromagnetic Field*

Lei Yang, Dongmei Hao**, Minglian Wang, Shuicai Wu, and Yi Zeng

College of Life Science and Bioengineering, Beijing University of Technology,
Beijing 100124, China

Abstract. Considering that electromagnetic radiation has a potential hazard to human body, rats is usually used to do long-time exposure experiments instead of human. It is necessary to investigate the distribution of electromagnetic field inside rats in order to guide experiment. The electromagnetic field simulation software HFSS was used in the paper to analyze the distribution of electromagnetic field and the specific absorption rate (SAR) inside rats' head. Results showed that most of the electric energy was absorbed by the skin and skull on the side near the antenna, a quarter of them penetrated into the brain. SAR distribution was similar to that of electromagnetic field, and decreased with the distance to antenna. The results suggest that rat model and simulation can help to understand the specific distribution of mobile phone electromagnetic fields inside the rat head.

Keywords: Electromagnetic fields; Modeling; Simulation; Rat.

1 Introduction

With the development of social economy and the advancement of science and technology, increasing number of people had their own mobile phone. According to the statistics in 2009, there are 4.1 billion mobile phone users in the world, among which 6.8 billion are in China. Electromagnetic radiation becomes an important environmental factor around us. People tend to take mobile phone close to their heads during conversation, thus brain tissue was exposed to electromagnetic radiation with high intensity, which may be harmful to the brain. Mobile phone users often have the symptoms of fatigue, headache, fever, burning sensation and aching. Some people even suspect that long-term use of mobile phone could induce brain tumor. United Nations Conference on the Human Environment has listed the electromagnetic radiation as a kind of pollution which must be controlled [1]. American senators suggested sticking carcinogenic warning on mobile phones. Therefore, the biological effect of

---

* This work was supported by the National Basic Research Program of China (973 Program, 2011CB503700/ 2011CB503702), the National Natural Science Foundation of China, No.81071231 and No. 30670543, Research Program of Beijing Municipal Education Commission (KM200910005016), and Fundamental Research Fund of the Beijing Municipal Education Commission Science and Technology Innovation Platform (JX015999201001).
** Corresponding author.

electromagnetic wave on the organism is one of the highest concerns to the public health and is becoming a major research topic in medical field.

The electromagnetic fields (EMF) radiation has delayed and cumulative effect. Human experiments are restricted because of the potential hazards. Animals are easy to be operated and managed, and have more advantages in the studying of long-term radiation effects and biological mechanism. Margaret Tzaphlidou et al [2] reported that after exposuring to 910 MHz, 2W radio frequency (RF) field for 30 days, 2 hours a day in vivo, the collagen fibril architecture was disturbed only in males while the fibril diameter decreased in both males and females. In most animal experiments, radiation parameters were determined according to mobile phone. It is difficult to measure the distribution of electromagnetic field inside the animal body.

Numerical simulation experiment can calculate all kinds of mobile phone radiation condition compared with the actual experiments. By theoretical analysis of Specific Absorption Rate (SAR) on the head of organism, the electromagnetic field distribution inside the brain can be revealed and quantitative results can be obtained, which can compensate the actual experimental limitation. Kong XiangMing et al [3] calculated and analyzed the electromagnetic field of a mobile phone antenna around a human head when the human was calling. Zhou XiaoMing et al [4] modeled a three-dimensional head and a mobile phone antenna. They discussed the radiation effect on human head in a vertical way and a three-dimensional rotation way. Sha Wei et al [5] studied electric field distribution inside the human head during mobile phone call and examined electromagnetic shielding effect of some material by using software Fidelity. Philippe Leveque et al [6] established a digital rat model and calculated the SAR value at rat intracranial, skin and meninges They also compared the results with those about human brain by using finite-difference time-domain (FDTD). Dirk Manteuffel and Winfried Simon [7] calculated the SAR value caused by mobile phone at human head in the same way. Ming Chen and David j. Mogul [8] established a digital human head model which included some details such as gyrus and brain ditch. They calculated and analyzed the distribution of electromagnetic field on human head particularly. Flyckt et al [9] calculated and analyzed SAR value and temperature changes at 900MHz, 1500MHz and 1800MHz electromagnetic field in the eyes.

At present, most of the numerical simulation experiments are based on human brain model, few are on rats. In order to design animal radiation experiments more effectively and understand the EMF distribution, this paper studied 900MHz EMF and SAR distribution and variation in rats head with numerical simulation method.

2 Modeling and Simulation

Firstly, a radiation antenna model was established. Secondly, two kinds of rat head model were established. One of them was based on anatomy atlas of rat and the other was based on sectional anatomy data of rat. Finally all of these models were imported into HFSS(High Frequency Structure Simulator, Ansoft Inc.) to start simulation analysis. HFSS is software based on the finite element method and can be used to analyze three-dimensional electromagnetic field [10-12].

2.1   Radiation Antenna Model

In this paper the double dipole antenna was used as a radiation antenna. The frequency of this antenna is 900MHz which is in the range of mobile phone frequency. Theory and practice have proven that the transmitting and receiving of antenna achieved the highest conversion efficiency when the antenna length is approximately 1/4 of the wavelength of radio signals. Therefore, the antenna length is set to 90mm in this study.

2.2   Rats Head Model

Two kinds of rat head models were established so as to compare the calculation complexity and accuracy. Model 1 was based on the book《 Rat Anatomy and Tissue》 [13] and the book《 The Anatomical Atlas of WISTAR Rats》 [14]. Model 2 was based on rats' sectional anatomy data set.

2.2.1   Rat Head Model 1

This model was based on the figures and data from the book《 Rat Anatomy and Organization》 and the book《 The Anatomical Atlas of WISTAR Rats》. Model 1 was composed of spheres and cylinders in HFSS. It consisted of six parts which were eyes, brain, muscle, fat, bone and skin. Electromagnetic parameters of each part were acquired from the document and showed in table 1 [15] .

Table 1. The electromagnetic parameters of rat under 900MHz EMF for the model

	eyes	brain	muscle	fat	bone	skin
The magnetic permeability (H/m)	1.97	1.23	1.21	0.6	0.105	0.6
Organization density (g/m3)	1.010	1.030	1.040	1.100	1.850	1.100
Volume conductivity (S/m)	0.7934	0.94227	0.94274	0.051043	0.34	0.88465
Dielectric loss Angle	0.34025	0.35694	0.32667	0.18665	0.32667	0.3661

2.2.2   Rat Head Model 2

A rat brain anatomy data set with the minimum slice space of 0.031mm was established with local tissue frozen section technique by Neuroimaging laboratories at University of California, Los Angeles [16]. 247 slices and Materiaise's interactive medical image control system (MIMICS) were utilized to reconstruct the model of rat head in this paper. The procedure consisted of image segmentation, image reconstruction and smooth.

First step: image segmentation

In computer vision, segmentation refers to the process of partitioning a digital image into multiple segments. The goal of segmentation is to simplify and/or change the representation of an image into something that is more meaningful and easier to analyze [17].There is two categories of Image segmentation methods: automatic segmentation and manual segmentation. Because the images in the rat sectional anatomy data set are black and white, automatic segmentation cannot divide them accurately. Because of the uneven surface of the brain, manual segmentation had to be used in order to select the the brain tissue from these images. The meaningful regions in each image were selected manually by the lasso tool in MIMICS according to the two books mentioned earlier.

The segmentation was according to the rats head three dimensional anatomical configuration, and the grayscale between the brain and surrounding tissue. The boundary could be determined by comparing sagittal, transverse, coronal images when it was difficult to select.

Second step: image reconstruction and smooth

After segmentation, a three-dimensional surface model was reconstructed automatically by MIMICS. Then the finite element analysis (FEA) module was used to mesh this model. Because the surface model edge was not smooth, there were a large number of grids. Therefore, the grid number must be decreased without model distortion. Then the model were smoothed, modified and saved.

This model was imported to HFSS and then bone tissue was added to bring the simulation closer to reality.

2.3 Simulation Calculation

2.3.1 Setting Boundary Conditions

An appropriate size of the electromagnetic space with certain boundary conditions was created to accommodate the radiation antenna model and rat head model. In real life electromagnetic wave propagates in free space without boundary, while simulation is only used in limited space. Therefore, boundary conditions were set in HFSS to simulate the unbounded free space. This system could absorb electromagnetic wave at the boundary and extend the boundary to infinity to simulate free space [18].

2.3.2 Analysis and Calculation

HFSS could automatically generate the finite element matrix equations according to Maxwell's equations and obtain their solution with the least time and the maximum accuracy by the adaptive iterative algorithm. This algorithm started with a rough finite element partition patterns to solve, equations, and then analyzed whether the solution accuracy met the requirements. If not, HFSS would refine the partition patterns until the solution reached a given precision. The distribution of electric field could be calculated by the above method. SAR values could be calculated with formula (1)

$$SAR = \frac{(\sigma |E|^2)}{\rho} \qquad (1)$$

Where σ represents tissue conductivity, E represents electric intensity, ρ represents tissue density. Rat tissue density was shown in table 1.

3 Model and Results

Fig. 2 shows the radiation antenna model, rat head model 1 and the electric field distribution. Fig. 3 shows the radiation antenna model, rat head model 2 and the electric field distribution. It can be seen from Fig. 2 and 3 that bone tissue absorbed most of the electric field energy. But there was still a lot of electric field energy penetrating into the brain. The hippocampal regions CA1, CA2 and CA3 related to learning and memory were indicated in Fig. 3. Electric field distribution in these regions could be observed intuitively. Magnetic field distribution was basically similar to the electric field; most of the magnetic field energy was absorbed by bone.

Fig. 4 shows SAR values distribution of rat head model 1. The ordinate represents SAR value, and the abscissa represents distance between the measuring point and the antenna. Rat head model 1 begins at 0mm and ends at 40mm in Fig. 4. In Fig. 5 rat head model 2 begins at 4mm and ends at 14.2mm. As indicated by these figures, the closer the brain to the antenna was, the higher the SAR was.

Please note that, if your email address is given in your paper, it will also be included in the meta data of the online version.

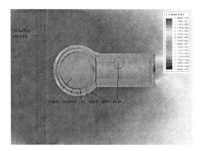

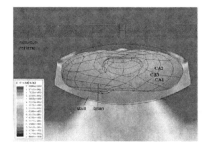

Fig. 1. The electric field distribution in the rat head model 1

Fig. 2. The electric field distribution in the rat head model 2

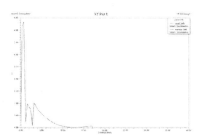

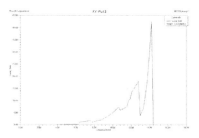

Fig. 3. The SAR distributions in the rat head model 1

Fig. 4. The SAR distributions in the rat head model 2

3 Analysis and Discussion

The distribution of electric field and SAR values at 900MHz were calculated by HFSS based on rat head model 1 and rat head model 2. Rat head model 1 consisted of six parts which were eyes, brain, muscle, fat, bone and skin. It could reflect the basic structure of the brain and was easy to model and calculate. However, there was obvious difference between the real rat head and model 1, because model 1 was composed of some simple three-dimensional units such as balls and cylinders. Rat head model 2 was based on rats' sectional anatomy data. It could represent real brain structure and reflect the distribution of the electric field and SAR in the main regions of rat head more accurately. The modeling and calculation were more complex for model 2. It can be seen from Fig. 2 and Fig. 3 that the electromagnetic energy was basically the same in the model 1 and model 2. It pointed out that skull play a major role in the absorption and resistance of the external electromagnetic wave. Although the two models have different structure, they have similar simulation results.

The results showed that most of the electric field energy was absorbed by scalp and skull on the side closer to antenna. The electric field energy decreased with the increasing distance from the antenna to rat head. A certain amount of electric energy penetrated into brain tissue. There was 50V/m of the electric field existed in hippocampus CA1, CA3 and CA2.

The electromagnetic energy in rat head could be reflected more accurately by SAR distribution. The shorter the distance between rat head and the antenna was, the higher the SAR value was. In Fig. 4 the first SAR peak ended at 1mm which was the boundary between skull and fat. It revealed that most electromagnetic energy was absorbed by skull. The minimum value appeared at the junction of tissue, because the tissue conductivity and density changed at this point. Inside each tissue SAR decreased with the increasing distance between rat head and the antenna.

The SAR value in the brain approached to one-fourth of SAR at skull. It pointed out that the external electromagnetic waves could penetrate into the brain and had harmful effects on brain. If the SAR value of external electromagnetic wave was more than four times of the national permission, the SAR in the brain will exceed the safety value and create health hazards.

References

1. Deng, Y.: Biologic effects of electromagnetic radiation and microwave. Foreign Medical Science. Radiomedicine and Nuclear Medicine 26, 191–193 (2002)
2. Margaret, T., Evangelos, F.: Collagen as a target for electromagnetic fields. In: International Symposium on Effects of 910-MHz, vol. 3, pp. 791–795 (2005)
3. Kong, X.M., Su, D.L., Wang, M.: Simulating Analysis of The Compatibility Between Cell Phone and Human Head. Electronic Measurement Technology 6, 45–46 (2003)
4. Zhou, X.M., Lai, S.L.: Numerical Simulation of the Interaction Between the Three-dimension Rotated Human Head Model and Handset monopole Antenna. Journal of South China University of Technology(Natural Science Edition) 32, 30–33 (2004)
5. Sha, W., Liu, Y., Bai, T.Y.: Shielding Effectiveness Modeling and Simulation of EM Radiation from Mobile Phones Based on FDTD Algorithm. Safety and Electro Magnetic Compatibility 3, 98–100, 102 (2005)
6. Philippe, L., Christian, D., Bernard, V., Joe, W.: Dosimetric Analysis of a 900-MHz Rat Head Exposure System. IEEE Transactions on Microwave Theory and Techniques 52, 2076–2083 (2004)

7. Manteuffel, D., Simon, W.: FDTD calculation of the SAR induced in the human head by mobile phones - New standards and procedures for the numerical assessment. In: 2005 IEEE International Workshop on Antenna Technology. Small Antennas and Novel Meta-materials, IWAT 2005, Singapore, United states, pp. 137–140 (2005)

8. Ming, C., David, J.M.: A Structurally-Detailed Finite Element Human Head Model for Brain-Electromagnetic Field Simulations. In: 2007 3rd International IEEE/EMBS Conference on Neural Engineering (IEEE Cat. No.07EX1609), USA, vol. 5, pp. 291–293, Koha-la Coast, HI (2007) ISBN 1-4244-0791-5

9. Flyckt, V.M.M., Raaymakers, B.W., Kroeze, H., WLagendijk, J.J.: Calculation of SAR and temperature rise in a high-resolution vascularized model of the human eye and orbit when exposed to a dipole antenna at 900, 1500 and 1800 MHz. Phys. Med. Biol. 52, 2691–2701 (2007)

10. Wu, Y.G., Xing, G.L., Chu, Y.: Design of Double-deck Broadband Microstrip Patch Antenna by Using HFSS. Electronic Technology 6, 65–67 (2009)

11. Zheng, S.J., Yao, M.: HFSS Simulation on the Microwave Sounding for Mammary Tumor. Chinese Journal of Scientific Instrument 26, 97–100 (2005)

12. Yang, Q., Li, Y.S., Yang, X.D., et al.: Design and analysis of wide wall slotted-waveguide array. Applied Science and Technology 37, 19–22 (2010)

13. Yang, A.F., Wang, P., et al.: The anatomy of the rats and organization, pp. 159–170. Economic Science Press (1985)

14. Wang, Z.T., Hao, L.W., Li, G.S., et al.: Anatomical map of WISTAR rat. Shandong Science and Technology Press

15. Gabriel, C., Gabriel, S., Corthout, E.: The dielectric properties of biological tissues: I. literature survey. J. Phys. Med. Biol. 41, 2231–2249 (1996)

16. Bai, X.L.: Research on SD Rat Digital Anatomy Atlas. [Doctoral dissertation]. Huazhong University of Science and Technology, (2006)

17. Linda, G.S., George, C.S.: Computer Vision, pp. 279–325. Prentice-Hall, New Jersey (2001) ISBN 0-13-030796-3

18. Cao, Y.S.: Ansoft HFSS Magnetic field analysis and application, pp. 284–304. China Water Power Press (2010)

Framework of an Expert System for Dust Explosion Risk Management Based on ASP.Net and Prolog

Qian Zhang, Shengjun Zhong, and Guanyu Jiang

School of Materials and Metallurgy Engineering, Northeastern University,
Liaoning Shenyang 10004

Abstract. Dust explosions always claim lives and cause huge financial loses. Dust explosion risk can be prevented by inherently safer design or mitigated by engineering protective system. Design of explosion prevention and protection need comprehensive knowledge and data on the process, workshop, equipment, and particulate combustible materials. The knowledge includes standards, expertise of experts, and practical experience. The databases include accidents, dust explosion characteristics, inherently safer design methods, and protective design methods. Integration of such a comprehensive knowledge system is very helpful. The developed system has the following functions: risk assessment, accident analysis, recommendation of prevention and protection solution, and computer aided design of explosion protection. The expert system is based on Browser/Server architecture. The software was developed using mixed programming of ASP.Net and Prolog. The developed expert system can be an assistant to explosion design engineers and safety engineers of combustible dust handling plant.

Keywords: dust explosion, expert system, explosion prevention, explosion protection, ASP.Net, Prolog.

1 Introduction

Dust explosions occur in a variety of industries and have a recorded history stretching back over 200 years. They almost always lead to serious financial losses in terms of damage to facilities and down time. They also often cause serious injuries to personnel, and fatalities. However, it is difficult for every equipment operator and technician to master the comprehensive professional knowledge and apply the knowledge to analyze and deal with the hazards because of the complexity of dust explosion affecting factors and the prevention and protection measures. Therefore, development of a dust explosion prevention and protection expert system using existed expert knowledge, experience and problem solving strategies instead of expertise of limited experts will reduce the hazard and losses dramatically.

The early attempts to develop expert systems (software) for dust-explosion vent design included Dust-Expert[1,2], ExTra[3]. Hesener and Kraus et al. have developed an expert system to be used to identify hazards due to the possible occurrence of various types of electrostatic discharges in various process situations. The system, using the CEN-ELEC report R044-001 as its technical basis, covers explosive gases/vapours/mists as well as explosible dusts[4].

G. Shen and X. Huang (Eds.): CSIE 2011, Part II, CCIS 153, pp. 429–435, 2011.
© Springer-Verlag Berlin Heidelberg 2011

Lorenz [5] has presented an expert system for the design of explosion venting arrangement based on the VDI 3673 venting code, which is very close to the new European Union code EN 14491[6]. The system accounts for the inertia of vent covers and doors and assesses forces acting on these covers and doors. The extent to which debris is ejected into the surroundings by destructive explosions is also accounted for.

Expert systems aimed to necessary auxiliary means of risk analysis of complex or disastrous fire hazard, such as risk assessment and risk management, were developed in the past 4 decades. In the 1970s, the U.S. National Bureau of Standards Center for Fire Research and Public Health Service Bureau developed a fire safety evaluation system that provided a unified approach to Fire Safety Assessment. Weng and Liao designed the basic fire risk assessment expert system based on semi-quantitative analysis[7]. Cai developed a fire and explosion risk assessment expert system using C[8]. The methods used included Dow Chemical Company (DOW) fire and explosion hazard index evaluation method, Richmond fire/explosion/toxicity evaluation indicators, Ammunition Enterprise quantitative assessment of major accident hazards et al. Qiu and Wang et al. designed a fire and explosion index safety assessment software using Visual Basic, which was mainly used in safety assessment of process plant in chemical companies[9].

The expert systems mentioned above are desktop applications. With the development and application of information technology, the traditional expert systems expose some problems and limitations[10]. Along with development of web technologies, it becomes a trend to build expert system on the internet, and it offers higher degree of sharing and expend the use widely that any internet user can log in the site running the expert system and consult through web browser. Because the program runs the server and no custom application is delivered, the management and maintenance are much easier.

An expert system for dust explosion risk management named "DustEx.Net" was developed based on Browser/Server architecture. The theoretical foundation, architecture and key technologies were introduced.

2   Framework of Dust Explosion Risk Management

The framework of dust explosion risk management is shown as Fig. 1. Before applying any method of explosion prevention and mitigation, risk assessment shall be carried out. Risk assessment includes risk analysis and risk evaluation. The most important parts of risk treatment are explosion prevention and explosion mitigation.

2.1   Methods of Dust Explosion Prevention and Mitigation

Methods of dust explosion prevention and mitigation are as follows:

(1) Inherent safe design of process and equipment to prevent occurrences of ignition sources and dust cloud.
(2) Apply inert atmosphere (inerting, or oxygen reduction).
(3) Additional engineering protective methods

(a) Explosion venting;
(b) Explosion suppression;
(c) Explosion isolation;
(d) Containment (explosion resistant design).

Different method has its own application conditions and limits, and the financial invests of different methods are various.

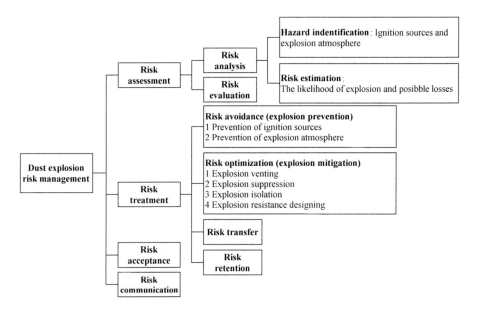

Fig. 1. Framework of dust explosion risk management

2.2 Dust Explosion Characteristics

Dust explosion characteristics (explosibility) are the input information of explosion risk assessment, and they are also used as supporting data in the designing of explosion prevention and mitigation[11]. The application of dust explosion characteristics is shown as Fig. 2.

The characteristics include:

(1) Minimum ignition energy (MIE);
(2) Minimum ignition temperature of dust layer (MIT-L);
(3) Minimum ignition temperature of dust cloud (MIT-C);
(4) Lower explosion limit (LEL), also called as minimum explosible concentration (MEC);
(5) Limiting oxygen concentration (LOC);
(6) Maximum explosion pressure p_{max};
(7) Normalized rate of explosion pressure rise (explosion index) K_{St};
(8) Dust volume resistivity (DR).

In risk assessment, MIE, MIT-L, MIT-C and LEL are characteristics to reflect the ignition likelihood, and p_{max} and K_{St} are characteristics to reflect the explosion severity (consequences). Likelihood has meanings of both probability and possibility.

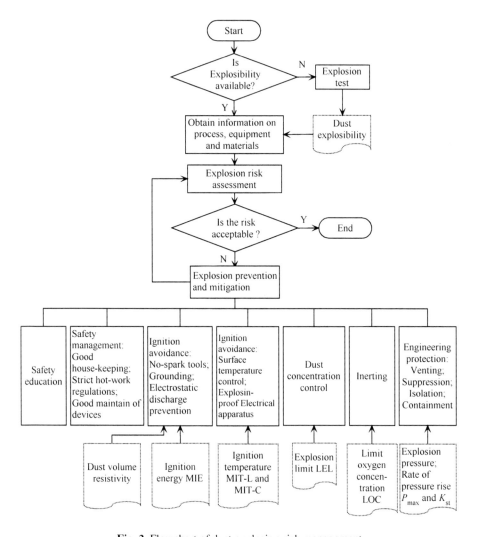

Fig. 2. Flowchart of dust explosion risk management

3   Architecture of the Expert System

The name of the expert system is DustEx.Net, which means the system is based on Microsoft .Net Framework, and B/S architecture. Currently DustEx.Net consists of five modules: accident analysis, risks assessment, prevention and mitigation decision making, explosion venting design and pressure-resistant design. Other modules might be added later.

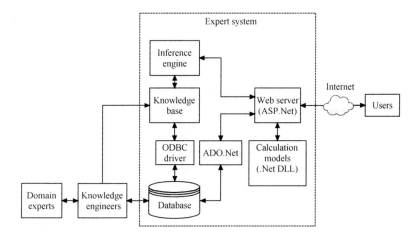

Fig. 3. Architecture of DustEx.Net

The architecture of the expert system is shown as Fig. 3. The expert system includes databases, knowledge bases, inference engine, calculation models and a web server interface.

The databases contains of historical accidents, dust explosion characteristics, typical processes, typical equipment, explosion prevention methods, explosion mitigation methods, protective devices, standards and references. The database platform is Microsoft SQL Server.

The knowledge bases contains: (a) the rules for decision making of explosion prevention and mitigation; (b) accident trees of typical processes and typical equipment. The knowledge bases are also called logic-bases, which are expressed as predicates in Prolog [12], and they can be compiled as dynamic link libraries (DLLs). Facts stored in databases can be loaded to the knowledge bases dynamically by ODBC driver.

The calculation models are based on related international standards. The venting calculation is based on NFPA 68[13] and EN 14491[6]. The pressure resistant design is based on EN 14460[14] and GB 150[15]. The risk assessment models are similar with the models used in reference [16] and [17]. The calculation models were written in C#, and were compiled to be .Net DLLs.

The inference engine is built in the Prolog software, and it can be redistributed together with user applications.

The web server was developed in ASP.Net platform using C#, javascript and HTML. It serves as the user interface and it calls: (a) the inference engine for logical inference; (b) ADO.Net for database management; and (c) calculation models for risk assessment, venting design and explosion resistant design.

4 Key Technologies

4.1 Knowledge Base Construction Using Prolog

Prolog is the most popular logic programming language used to develop expert systems. It is a *declarative* language, which is quite different with *procedural* languages such as C and Java. It is powerful in logical inference such as solution searching and reason tracing.

A prolog program is exactly a knowledge base consisting of *facts*, *rules* and *queries*. *Facts* describe the properties of objects, and *rules* define the relationship between objects. Prolog programming is all about constructing knowledge bases. A very simple example is given as follows, while the actual implementation is much complex.

A specific dust has a collection of characteristics, this can be defined as *functor* in *facts* section. The functor is similar to definition of a database record. The instances of different dusts are put into *clauses* section, which can be loaded from dust characteristics database dynamically. Note that the instances of dusts are actually *facts*. The rules are put into *predicates*. The following code demonstrates some rules: if MIE of a dust is less than 10 mJ, then ignition prevention doesn't work; if a dust is light metal or poisonous, then explosion venting can't be applied.

```
facts
  dust : (string ID, string Name, double MIE, integer
  IsLightMetal, integer Poisonous).
clauses
  dust("AluminumCompany1", "Aluminum", 2.0, 1, 0).
  dust("BifenthrinCompany2", "Bifenthrin", 8.9, 0, 1).
predicates
  canIgnitionPevention(dust(ID,Name,MIE,Is IsLightMetal,
  Poisonous)):- MIE>10.
  canVentingProtection(dust(ID,Name,MIE,Is IsLightMetal,
  Poisonous)):- Poisonous<>1, IsLightMetal<>1.
```

4.2 Mixing Programming of ASP.Net and Prolog

By using Prolog, the programmer only need to tell the computer facts and rules, and solution search is the business of Prolog's reference engine. However, Prolog is not suitable for mathematical calculation and user interface development.

Microsoft .Net Framework is a new generation of development platform for both desktop applications and web applications. ASP.Net is a web development environment for many different languages such as C#, VB.Net, F# and Delphi Prism. Traditional Javascript and HTML script can also be used in ASP.Net. So mixing programming of Prolog and ASP.Net can take the advantages of Prolog and ASP.Net and avoid the disadvantages. Many commercial Prolog compilers provide programming interface for C. C# can use the same interface by COM invoking.

5   Conclusions

A framework of expert system for dust explosion risk management was constructed. The functions include risk analysis, accident cause analysis, explosion prevention and mitigation decision making, venting design and explosion resistant design. The application is based on Brower/Server architecture, which enables users to access the developed system by Internet.

Prolog is good at solution searching and reason tracing, and it is a promising language for development of complex expert system. ASP.Net is a web development platform which provides powerful tools for development of user interface, database management, as well as mathematical calculation. Mixing language programming can take the advantages of both Prolog and ASP.Net.

The expert system is under construction, however, preliminary case tests proved that the finished modules worked very well.

References

1. Abbasi, T., Abbasi, S.A.: Dust Explosions–Cases, Causes, Consequences, and Control. Journal of Hazardous Materials 140, 7–44 (2007)
2. Vadera, S., Meziane, F., Huang, M.-L.L.: Experience with Mural in Formalizing Dust-Expert. Software Technol. 43, 231–240 (2001)
3. Hesener, U., Schecker, H.G.: ExTra—An Expert System for the Safety Analysis of Drying Plants. In: Mewis, J.J., Pasman, H.J., De Rademaeker, E.E. (eds.) Loss Prevention and Safety Promotion in the Process Industries, vol. 2, pp. 643–653. Elsevier, Amsterdam (1995)
4. Hesener, U., Kraus, A., Schecker, H.G.: Computer Based Assessment of Hazards Caused by Electrostatic Discharges. In: Proceedings of the Ninth International Symposium on Loss Prevention and Safety Promotion in the Process Industry, Barcelona, Spain, pp. 851–859 (1998)
5. Lorenz, D.: ExProtect: A Software Response to Important to Important Questions on Safety in Dust and Gas Explosion. In: Proceedings of the Third World Seminar on the Explosion Phenomenon and on the Application of Explosion Protection Techniques in Practice, Ghent, Belgium (1999)
6. EN 14491. Dust Explosion Venting Protective Systems (2006)
7. Weng, T., Liao, G.: Discussion on Systematic Construction of Expert Software for Assessment of Fire Risk Gradation. China Safety Science Journal 15, 37–40 (2005)
8. Cai, Z.: Evaluation of Fire and Explosion Hazard and Development of Expert System Software. Mining Safety and Environmental Protection, 1–3 (2004)
9. Qiu, K., Wang, Q.A.: A Primary Software Design in Fire Explosion Index Safety Evaluation. Chongqing Institute of Technology Journal 8, 102–105 (2006)
10. Duan, Y., Ewards, J.S., Xu, M.X.: Web-Based Expert Systems: Benefits and Challenges. Information and Management 42 (2005)
11. Eckhoff, R.K.: Dust Explosions in the Process Industries, 3rd edn. Gulf Professional Publishing/Elsevier, Boston (2003)
12. Bramer, M.: Logic Programming with Prolog. Springer, Heidelberg (2005)
13. NFPA 68. Standard on Explosion Protection by Deflagration Venting (2007)
14. EN 14460. Explosion Resistant Equipment (2007)
15. GB 150. Steel Pressure Vessels (1998)
16. Van der Voort, M.M., Klein, A.J.J.: A Quantitative Risk Assessment Tool for the External Safety of Industrial Plants with a Dust Explosion Hazard. Journal of Loss Prevention in the Process Industries 20, 375–386 (2007)
17. Markowski, A.S.: exLOPA for Explosion Risks Assessment. Journal of Hazardous Materials 142, 669–676 (2007)

Research on Recovery Training Techniques for Speed Skating Athletes

Yuezhi Wang

Sports Division, Northeast Agricultural University,
Harbin, 150030, China
yzwang.cn@gmail.com

Abstract. In this paper, a comprehensive literature review of speed skating is provided and a variety of recovery training techniques are discussed for speed skating athletes. First, speed skating is explained in details including its historical review, two kinds of skating and connection with Olympic Games, as well as a summary of Chinese athletes' performances on speed skating. Then, recovery training for speed skating is addressed at length considering its principles, physical and psychological speed skating recovery techniques.

Keywords: Speed skating, recovery training, physical recovery techniques, psychological recovery techniques.

1 Background Information

Speed skating is a competitive form of ice skating in which the competitors race each other in traveling a certain distance on skates [4]. Types of speed skating are long track speed skating, short track speed skating, and marathon speed skating. In the Olympic Games, long track speed skating is usually referred to as just "speed skating", while short track speed skating is known as "short track". There are two basic skills involved in speed skating, including curve track skating and straight track skating, respectively.

1.1 Historical Review

The roots of speed skating date back over a millennium to Scandinavia, Northern Europe and the Netherlands, where the natives added bones to their shoes and used them to travel on frozen rivers, canals and lakes. It was much later, in the 16th century, that people started seeing skating as fun and perhaps even a sporting activity. Later, in Norway, King Eystein Magnusson, later King Eystein I of Norway, boasts of his skills racing on ice legs [3].

By 1850, North America had discovered a love of the sport, and, indeed, North America went on to develop the all-steel blade, which was both lighter and sharper. The Netherlands came back to the fore in 1889 and organized the very first world championships, and, subsequently, the ISU (International Skating Union was born in 1892. Subsequently, by the start of the 20th century, skating and indeed speed skating had come into its own as a major popular sporting activity.

G. Shen and X. Huang (Eds.): CSIE 2011, Part II, CCIS 153, pp. 436–442, 2011.

1.1 Long Track Skating and Short Track Skating

The standard rink for long track is 400 meters long, but tracks of 200, 250 and 333 meters are used occasionally. It is one of two Olympic forms of the sport and the one with the longer history. An international federation was founded in 1892, the first for any winter sports. The sport enjoys large popularity in the Netherlands and Norway. There are top international rinks in a number of other countries, including Canada, the United States, Germany, Italy, Japan, South Korea, China and Russia. The sport is described as "long track" in North American usage, to distinguish it from 111 m oval on a hockey rink in short track skating. International Skating Union rules allow some leeway in the size and radius of curves [1, 4].

Short track skating takes place on a smaller rink, normally the size of an ice hockey rink [1, 2, 3]. Distances are shorter than in long track racing, with the longest Olympic race being 3000 meters. Races are usually held as knockouts, with the best two in heats of four or five qualifying for the final race, where medals are awarded. Disqualifications and falls are not uncommon. The sport originates from pack style events held in North America and was officially sanctioned in the 1970s, becoming an Olympic sport in 1992. Although this form of speed skating is newer, it is growing faster than long track speed skating, largely due to the fact that short track can be done on a regular ice rink rather than a long track oval.

1.2 Olympic Games and Speed Skating

At the 1914 Olympic Congress, the delegates agreed to include ice speed skating in the 1916 Olympics, after figure skating had featured in the 1908 Olympics. However, World War I put an end to the plans of Olympic competition, and it was not until the winter sports week in Chamonix in 1924-retroactively awarded Olympic status;[a]that ice speed skating reached the Olympic programme. Charles Jewtraw from Lake Placid, New York, won the first Olympic gold medal, though several Norwegians in attendance claimed Oskar Olsen had clocked a better time [2].

Timing issues on the 500 were a problem within the sport until electronic clocks arrived in the 1960s; during the 1936 Olympic 500-metre race, it was suggested that Ivar Ballangrud's 500-meter time was almost a second too good. Finland won the remaining four gold medals at the 1924 Games, with Clas Thunberg winning 1,500 meters, 5,000 meters, and allround. It was the first and only time an all-round Olympic gold medal has been awarded in speed skating.

There have significant developments of speed skating in China both in sport competition and mass sport activities. For example, Since 1980 China has participated in

Table 1. China's Speed Skating Performance in 2010 Vancouver Winter Olympics

Medal	Name	Event
Gold	Wang Meng	Women's 500 metres
Gold	Zhou Yang	Women's 1500 metres
Gold	Sun Linlin / Wang Meng/ Zhang Hui / Zhou Yang	Women's 3000 metres relay
Gold	Wang Meng	Women's 1000 metres
Bronze	Wang Beixing	Women's 500 metres

seven Olympic Winter Games. In 2010 Vancouver Winter Olympics, Chinese speed skating team obtained outstanding results: they swept the gold medals in all four events, winning four gold and one bronze metals, as shown in Table 1.

2   The Principles of Speed Skating Recovery Training

Speed skating recovery training is a general term used to describe the adaptations to workloads after a speed skating athlete has been exposed to training or competition. For a healthy and functioning athlete the term refers to a positive response to training stimuli leading to adaptation to those stressors. Such adaptation can be physical or psychological in nature and the recovery processes involved are often referred to as restoration and regeneration. Failure to recover from training and competition invariably leads to maladaptation. Failure to adapt to training stressors, either physical or psychological, can lead to detrimental conditions common to many speed skating athletes such as overtraining, overuse or burnout [5].

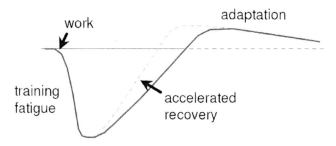

Fig. 1. Reducing residual fatigue from training by recovery techniques

Work alone is not enough to produce the best results; a speed skating athlete also needs time to adapt to training. The principle of recovery refers to that part of training where the benefits of the work undertaken are maximized through practices which reduce residual fatigue and enable the athlete to cope with workloads more effectively. This enhances the athlete's capacity to undertake more work, as well as their capacity to work more efficiently, which in turn encourages better adaptation to training. Fig. 1 demonstrates how appropriate recovery techniques can help speed skating athletes reduce residual fatigue from training, hence improve the speed skating athletes' performance.

3   Physical Speed Skating Recovery Techniques

There are many different physical activities and therapies that assist with recovery [6]. Some of those most commonly used include:

- Passive and active rest;
- Stretching;

- Sports massage;
- Acupressure and acupuncture

The detailed explanation is given below.

Passive Rest: Sleep is the most important form of passive rest. A good night's sleep of seven to nine hours provides invaluable adaptation time for athletes to adjust to the physical and emotional stressors they experience during the day. Other forms of passive rest involve techniques that help the mind to switch-off from all the surrounding stimuli. Getting to sleep can sometimes be difficult because of the excitement of the day's events so it is important that athletes develop habits to promote a good night's sleep.

Active Rest: The end of the training session is an ideal time to introduce active recovery activities, although active rest can also be incorporated throughout the session. Recovery activities are selected to fulfil a number of tasks. They can either help recover the physiological state of the athlete, for instance light walking or cycle to recover the lactate system, or they can focus on musculoskeletal recovery, for example stretching and exercises to promote a return to postural efficiency through musculoskeletal balancing programs.

Stretching: Stretching refers to tissue elongation, or extending a material or substance from its resting length [7]. This occurs as a continuum, so stretches can range from a minimal length to a maximum length. Stretching is an essential action for movement in skeletal muscles and it is often referred to as the way to improve flexibility. Post training or game, the most appropriate techniques are for short lightly held static stretches of about 6-10 seconds duration. Stretches should be performed in a warm environment and can be continued in the shower or bath. This type of stretching facilitates recovery of the athlete's normal resting muscle length.

Sports massage: Sports massage has two major physiological benefits [1]. First, some techniques can increase blood flow, and in doing so enhance the delivery of oxygen and nutrients to tired muscles and facilitate the removal of metabolic by-products such as lactic acid. Secondly, the warming and stretching of soft tissues provides temporary flexibility gains. There are also psychological benefits: as tired and tight muscles relax there is a corresponding improvement in mood states. Athletes feel less fatigued and more relaxed.

Acupuncture and acupressure: Acupuncture and acupressure are often performed as an adjunct to sports massage, but acupuncture requires more extensive qualifications and consequently it is less accessible and more expensive. Both techniques focus on balancing energy fields via specific points located on fourteen meridians that pass through the body. Acupuncture points have a lower electrical resistance than adjacent areas and these can be measured and evaluated.

4 Psychology Speed Skating Recovery Techniques

This aspect of sport psychology is sometimes referred to as mental toughness training or psychoregulatory training [8]. All athletes can benefit from learning to use a few simple psychological skills to control emotions and mood states. In particular, improving self-awareness and motivation and decreasing reactions to stress are essential life skills. Recognition of the complex interaction and strong relationship between physical and mental states is important for recovery training. This is evident when muscle relaxation is observed in conjunction with lowered heart rate and blood pressure, and improved mood states. Skills associated with developing mental toughness or emotional control involves a variety of relaxation strategies including: meditation, breathing exercises, music, relaxation massage and other techniques.

Meditation: Although passive rest is an important component of recovery practices, the time spent during passive rest can be used to include one of several relaxation and/or focusing techniques. Meditation trains the athlete to relax by controlling the parasympathetic (calming) nervous system through reducing noise or stimulation to the brain. By controlling this system the athlete can lower blood pressure, lower heart rate, slow down breathing rates, relax muscles and calm the sympathetic (excitatory) nervous system. This technique is useful for controlling stresses from training or competition particularly if the athlete is over-aroused. Meditation skills, like sport specific skills, take some time and practice to acquire and they are most readily learned by younger athletes who have fewer inhibitions and less noise to interfere with acquiring the skill.

Progressive Muscle Relaxation: Progressive muscle relaxation (PMR) can be done at the end of training or before going to bed. The technique involves tightening specific muscle groups, holding them firm for five seconds, and then relaxing. The regimen usually works by starting at either the feet or the head and neck, and working through muscle groups to the other end of the body. This process enables the athlete to identify the sensations of muscle tension and muscle relaxation in specific body parts. This increased awareness helps the athlete to recognize and then reduce muscle tension when it occurs. Like any sporting skill PMR needs to be practiced regularly for best effects to be gained.

Imagery and Visualization: All athletes have an imagination which can be developed to contribute to their training potential. Imagery relaxation, and visualization, involves using the imagination to create a vivid scene. Four senses are used to generate the image: sight, smell, sound and touch. The image created by the athlete should evoke feelings of comfort and relaxation. Escaping to a relaxing place at the end of each day just before going to bed is a useful way of practicing the technique and switching-off before going to sleep. Other images can be created and rehearsed to practice focusing on positives and game strategies.

Breathing Exercises: Breathing exercises are used frequently in the martial arts. Learning breathing techniques and focusing on relaxing tense muscles leads to a more efficient physical state. Applying static stretches also helps to produce a relaxation response in the body. Athletes need to be instructed carefully in the art of performing this technique. Breathing in through the nose and expanding the rib cage laterally (at the sides) rather than distending the abdomen in front is a more effective technique and helps the athlete to maintain good posture during this procedure. Breathing out should also be done through the nose.

Music: Music is enjoyed by almost all athletes but as an adjunct to training it is quite under-utilized. Although it is sometimes used in the weights gym to provide a motivational atmosphere conducive to sustaining repetitive workloads, it is equally as effective in evoking a relaxation response if the appropriate music is selected. Most athletes have access to a portable music system such as a mp3 player or small tape deck. Every athlete should be encouraged to create a bank of tapes they like which generate a range of moods and atmospheres, to produce either a stimulating or calming effect for them. These can be used in training and because they are quite portable they are also an excellent tool in competition or when an athlete is in an unfamiliar environment and is having difficulty relaxing. With practice, an athlete can learn to manipulate mood states to generate either optimal arousal or relaxation..

Emotional Recovery: At key times during the year, such as competitions and tournaments, school or university exams and Christmas, athletes are often excessively stressed. If they have lost a game or competition, or performed below their expectations they may benefit from some emotional recovery in their training program. Mood lifting activities can include watching an amusing video or comedy show on TV, reading an escapist or adventure novel, or going to a fun park, zoo or light entertainment center. A sense of humor or team support is invaluable in times of emotional stress. For teams or athletes in extended competitions away from home, and especially overseas, planning such activities as part of the tour is essential.

5 Conclusions

In this paper, we presented a detailed explanation of speed skating and explained several recovery training techniques. In all, selecting the best recovery techniques for speed skating depend on several factors. First, the athlete and coach will need to recognize what has been fatigued in training in order to recover any residual fatigue from the work done. Psychological fatigue can be addressed by relaxing mentally and physically or by choosing a light entertaining activity if emotional recovery is also required. Second, the use of recovery techniques depends on their availability and the cost and time involved in their delivery or use. Those techniques which can be self-administered and incur no cost are the ones most readily used and accessible to all athletes. Costs increase and techniques become less accessible if specialized equipment is needed or if skilled personnel are required to implement the technique.

References

1. Calder, A.: Sports Massage, State of the Art Review, technical report, No. 24, National Sports Research Centre, Australian Sports Commission, Canberra (1990)
2. Chapman, R.F., Stickford, J.L., Levine, B.D.: Altitude training considerations for the winter sport athlete. Expeimental Physiology 95, 411–421 (2010)

3. De Koning, J.J.: World Records: How Much Athlete? How Much Technology? International Journal of Sports Physiology and Performance 5, 262–267 (2010)
4. Holum, D.: The complete handbook of speed skating. Enslow Publication Inc., Berkeley Heights (1984)
5. Hooper, S.L.: Monitoring Overtraining in Athletes: Recommendations. Sports Medicine 20, 321–327 (1995)
6. Loehr, J.: The New Toughness Training for Sports. Dutton Books, New York (1992)
7. Mackinnon, L.T., Hooper, S.L.: Training Logs: an effective method of monitoring overtraining and tapering. Sports Coach 17(3), 10–12 (1994)
8. Schunk, D.H.: Self-efficacy, motivation, and performance. Journal of Applied Sport Psychology 7, 112–137 (1995)
9. Vesterinen, V., Mikkola, J., Nummela, A., Hynynen, E., Haekkinen, K.: Fatigue in a simulated cross-country skiing sprint competition. Journal of Sports Sciences 27, 1069–1077 (2009)

Efficient Service Discovery for Cloud Computing Environments

Fei Chen[*], Xiaoli Bai, and Bingbing Liu

Department of Computer and Information Management,
GuangXi University of Finance and Economics
Ming Xiu west road 100#, Nanning, Guang Xi, China, 530003
{gxchenfei,gxliubingbing}@gmail.com, gxbxl@yahoo.com.cn

Abstract. As cloud computing is getting popular, vast numbers of cloud services have been developed in the cloud computing environments. But it is a challenging task to find the relevant or similar cloud services. In this paper, one approach is to develop semantic cloud services where by the cloud services are annotated based on shared ontology, and use these annotations for semantics-based discovery of relevant cloud services. This approach can be efficiently used to retrieve similar or related cloud services in the cloud computing environment.

Keywords: cloud computing, semantic cloud services, ontology, WSDL, UDDI.

1 Introduction

Cloud Computing is the idea of abstracting computation. It allows users to make use of applications, services and software and increases productivity and efficiency by allowing resources to be used on expanding network function. It does not imply any particular system architecture. This environment is dynamic, reliable, and cost effective with a guaranteed quality of service. Many applications can be executed dynamically to meet user needs. Cloud Computing includes service oriented architecture (SOA) and virtual applications which is based on both hardware and software. Cloud Computing is broadly classified into three services: "Software", "Platform" and "Infrastructure" [1]. Each service serves a different purpose and offers different products for businesses and individual people around the world. In Cloud Computing, service is an organization's ability to supply the customer's needs. Service means an act of help or assistance to the user. Cloud services [2] are delivered by the specific service providers and are consumed by consumers in real time over the World Wide Web (WWW). In short, a cloud service is virtually any business or consumer service that is delivered and consumed over the Internet in real-time. Cloud computing, an important, but much narrower term, is the IT environment – encompassing all elements of the full "stack" of IT and network

---

[*] Corresponding author.

G. Shen and X. Huang (Eds.): CSIE 2011, Part II, CCIS 153, pp. 443–448, 2011.

products (and supporting services) – that enables the development, delivery and consumption of cloud services.

Cloud services rely on the on-demand provision of a set of resources. As cloud computing becomes more widely adopted, the size and scale of cloud computing systems will necessarily increase to meet a growing demand—both in terms of the number of individual requests as well as the amount of resources required per-request. In contrast to approaches used in Grid and high-performance computing, in which requests that cannot be immediately serviced are added to a queue for later service, requests for cloud computing resources must be immediately fulfilled, or denied due to a lack of available resources. The challenge facing cloud service providers is to provision and have available for immediate allocation sufficient resources ready to be deployed for service requests. Commercial cloud computing organizations seeking to operate a profitable cloud service face a serious dilemma. If there are not efficient approach of service discovery available during the busiest service times, requests that could generate revenue will need to be turned away.

In this section, we address this question. The rest of the paper is organized as follows. Section 2 outlines the related work. Our approach of adding semantics to WSDL and UDDI are discussed in Sections 3. Semantic cloud service discovery is discussed in Section 4. Finally in Section 5, we present conclusions and future work.

2   Related Works

Different cloud services are already classified by the researchers. Each of services serves distinct purpose. Service discovery essentially refers to the discovery of service description [3]. Although Web Service Description Language (WSDL) provides an XML-based general purpose description scheme, it is weak in supporting semantic information. There also have been many research literatures proposed to address the service discovery issues. However, most of them are designed just for local environments confined with fixed network conditions such as home and enterprise. A unified service discovery framework is presented in [10] by Jin et al. It, however, is a centralized architecture that is unsuitable for cloud computing environment. Different from previous work, we propose to store semantically annotated cloud service descriptions in UDDI, and use that semantic information for querying. Then, maps operations in cloud service descriptions to ontological concepts that represent functionalities and querying is based on templates.

3   Adding Semantics in WSDL and UDDI

Currently Web services are described using WSDL descriptions, which provide operational information. Although WSDL descriptions do not contain (or at least explicate) semantic description, they do specify the structure of message components using XML schema constructs. A cloud service is also described by WSDL file and is characterized by a name, description, and a set of operations that take input parameters and return output parameters. We used this WSDL information for computing similarity of cloud services. Specifically, we employed interface similarity assessment suggested by Wu &

Wu [4] in this work. Similarity between cloud services S1 with m operations and S2 with n operations is given by the following formula:

$$Sim_{Interfaces}(S_1, S_2) = Max \sum_{i=1}^{m} \sum_{j=1}^{n} Sim_{Operation}(O_{1i}, O_{2j}) \times X_{ij}$$

(1)

$$\sum_{j=1}^{n} X_{ij} = 1, i = 1, 2, ... m \quad \sum_{i=1}^{m} X_{ij} = 1, j = 1, 2, ... n$$

O_{1i} represents an operation from cloud service S1 and O_{2j} represents an operation from cloud service S2. X_{ij} indicates the weight and it is set to 1, while matching operation O_{1i} with operation O_{2j}. We suggest adding semantics to WSDL using extensibility in elements and attributes supported by WSDL specification version1.2. Using this extensibility we relate existing and extended WSDL constructs to DAML+OIL ontology. The use of ontology allows representing Web service descriptions in a machine-interpretable form like DAML-S. These extensions are similar to the extensions suggested for ServiceGrounding in DAML-S.

We provide semantic discovery using UDDI by doing the following two tasks. Firstly, we store the semantic annotation of cloud services in the existing structures of UDDI. Secondly, we provide an interface to construct queries that use that semantic annotation. This approach is similar to the one suggested by [5], which maps DAML-S to UDDI structures, but is consistent with the use of industry standard WSDL rather than requiring DAML-S.

4 Semantic Cloud Service Discovery

Semantic annotations added in WSDL and in UDDI are aimed at improving discovery and composition of services. In this section we briefly describe our mechanism for template based ontology enabled discovery. Figure 1 shows the conceptual process of mapping WSDL constructs, to the nodes in a domain specific ontology. This mapping is then stored in UDDI during cloud service publication. As shown in the figure 1, the operations buyTicket and cancelTicket are mapped to the nodes TicketBooking and TicketCancellation, respectively, the input concept TravelDetails and output concept Confirmation in WSDL file are mapped to the TicketInformation node and ConfirmationMessage in the TravelServices ontology, respectively.

We have developed an algorithm for semantic cloud service discovery that requires the users to enter service requirements as templates constructed using ontological concepts. In the first phase, the algorithm matches cloud services (operations in different WSDL files) based on the functionality they provide. In the second phase, the result set from the first phase is ranked on the basis of semantic similarity [6] between the input and output concepts of the selected operations and the input and output concepts of the template, respectively. The optional third phase involves ranking based on the semantic similarity between the precondition and effect concepts of the selected operations and preconditions and effect concepts of the template. Figure 1 shows the creation of a template using ontological nodes for semantic discovery of services. The template has the operation concept TicketBooking, the input concept TicketInformation and the output concept ConfirmationMessage. The template created by the user is converted to a UDDI query by our interface [7]. This template would map to an UDDI query which first searches for all cloud services categorized using a keyedReferenceGroup which has the TicketBooking mapped to the operation tModel. The result set is then ranked based on the semantic similarity [6] between the input concepts of the returned cloud services to the input concepts (TicketInformation) of the template and the output concepts of the returned cloud services to the output concepts (ConfirmationMessage) of the template.

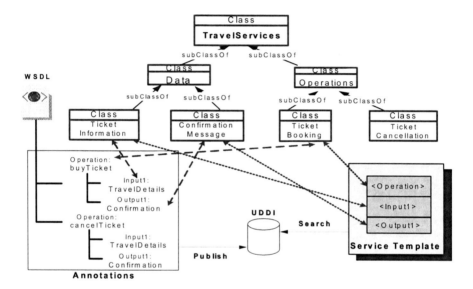

Fig. 1. Semantic Cloud service Discovery

5 Experiment

There is no publicly available cloud services dataset on the Internet. So, we downloaded a set of web services in 5 domains from xmethods.net website. WSDL data from these web services is then organized into 3 excel files, one for web service name and description, one for web service operation names and another for web service input and output parameter names. It was tedious to dig through WSDL files and organize data into three excel files. Similarly, we created another set of 3 files for representing the clusters. Then our program computed interface similarity between clusters and the test web services and found closest cluster to each test web service based on nearest neighbor approach. Actual cluster values are given based on semantic similarity of web service descriptions. All phases are represented in the following discovering algorithm.

```
discovering(R, S) {

 S' = query_Registry(Rt, S)
 S'' = query_Registry(Ro, S')
  forall s in S'' do {
          si = query_Inputs(s)
          if provided(si,Ri)  then {
            Precise.append(s)
             }
          else {
           if
query_ContextProviders(userID,missing_Inputs(si, Ri))
then
             {
               Precise.append(s)
             }
          else {
            Approximate.append(s)
             }
          }
     }
 P = order_with_ContextualAttributes(Precise)
 A = order_with_ContextualAttributes(Approximate)
 return result(P, A)

}
```

Our approach is embedded in the matchmaker component of the experimental platform. Service data are stored in MySql databases as persistent Jena models, and retrieved by executing RDQL statements. The approach is implemented modular by encapsulating it in web services. We evaluated the approach using the implemented prototype. Our approach yielded good results and accuracy is 74%.

6 Conclusions

In this paper, we have presented our approach of adding semantics to cloud services descriptions for improved cloud service discovery. The current approach involves using DAML-S for adding semantics to cloud services description. Since WSDL and UDDI are current industry standards, we believe that a pragmatic solution for adding semantics to cloud services would be to add semantics to both of them, instead of creating a new language. While DAML-S is a highly expressive language, in which the features are meant not only for discovery but also for composition, execution and monitoring. In this paper, we have concentrated on adding enough semantics to WSDL using DAML+OIL ontology, for it to have the same descriptive power as DAML-S for discovery. We have also discussed an algorithm for semantic discovery of cloud services which uses functionality of the service as the main criterion for search.

At present, there is no publicly available cloud services dataset. More work can be done in future with evaluating our approach, when such a dataset becomes available.

References

1. Zhang, L.J., Chang, C.K., Feig, E., Grossman, R.: Business Cloud: Bringing The Power of SOA and Cloud Computing. In: 2008 IEEE International Conference on Services Computing, pp. 120–126. IEEE Press, New York (2008)
2. Brandic, I.: Towards Selfmanageable Cloud Services. In: 33rd Annual IEEE International Computer Software and Applications Conference, pp. 128–133. IEEE Press, New York (2009)
3. Chinnici, R., Gudgin, M., Moreau, J., Weerawarana, S.: Web Services Description Language (WSDL) Version 1.2,
   http://www.w3.org/TR/2003/WD-wsdl12-20030124
4. Wu, J., Wu, Z.H.: Similarity-based Web service matchmaking. In: 2005 IEEE International Conference on Services Computing, pp. 287–294. IEEE Press, New York (2005)
5. Paolucci, M., Kawamura, T., Payne, T.R., Sycara, K.: Importing the Semantic Web in UDDI. In: Bussler, C.J., McIlraith, S.A., Orlowska, M.E., Pernici, B., Yang, J. (eds.) CAiSE 2002 and WES 2002. LNCS, vol. 2512, pp. 815–821. Springer, Heidelberg (2002)
6. Cardoso, J., Sheth, A.: Semantic e-Workflow Composition. Journal of Intelligent Information Systems 21(3), 191–225 (2003)
7. Verma, K., Sivashanmugam, K., Sheth, A., Patil, A., Oundhakar, S., Miller, J.: METEOR–S WSDI: A Scalable Infrastructure of Registries for Semantic Publication and Discovery of Web Services. Journal of Information Technology and Management 33(5), 88–109 (2005)
8. Ankolekar, A., Burstein, M., Hobbs, J., Lassila, O., Martin, D., McIlraith, S., Narayanan, S., Paolucci, M., Payne, T., Sycara, K., Zeng, H.: DAML-S:Semantic Markup for Web Services. In: The International Semantic Web Working Symposium, pp. 39–54. Stanford University, California (2001)
9. UDDI Technical White paper,
   http://www.uddi.org/pubs/Iru_UDDI_Technical_White_Paper.pdf
10. Jin, B.H., Zhang, L., Zang, Z.: A unified service discovery framework. In: The 6th International Conference on Grid and Cooperative Computing, pp. 203–209. IEEE Press, New York (2007)

Privacy Protection Based on Secure Electronic Transaction Protocol in E-Commerce

Huifang Cheng

School of Information and Electric Engineering
Hebei University of Engineering
Handan, China

Abstract. To strengthen privacy protection is not only the demand of respecting and maintenance of personality is but also an inherent requirement of e-commerce development. The security protocol mainly used Secure Sockets Layer Protocol and Secure Electronic Transaction. In this paper, after analysis two kinds of protocol and the security technology used in the protocol, put forward a small scale enterprise e-commerce transaction system design of network security protocols.

Keywords: Electronic Commerce, Privacy, SET, Network security, SSL.

1 Introduction

Enterprises participate in the e-commerce is the trend in order to have more room for development. However, the Internet covering a wide range, the data transferred easily intercepted or tampered by others if you did not take good security measures. Sometimes data transmit on the internet involving sensitive information of users and enterprises, so the security of privacy is particularly important. Since e-commerce related to the interests and other aspects of financial and corporate merchant, therefore, effective means must be used to ensure the safe operation of e-commerce systems.

2 The Security Status of e-Commerce

The main problem of e-commerce transaction security is to pay security, password management, network viruses, Trojan problem and fishing platforms. At present, various merchant and professional site commonly used by technical protection measures for the safety of e-commerce transactions, such as firewalls, long key communications, digital certificates, access control, authentication exchange, traffic padding, routing control, notarization and other encryption or authentication measures and intrusion detection systems etc, which have played a good role. There are good results of some anti-virus software and anti-hacking software using in the network. However, in fact there still is not a perfect solution, model or architecture to solve the security issues of e-commerce. For the security and reliable operation of network, besides to establish safety awareness, strengthen internal security management, also needs to process from the technology and facilities of the e-commerce systems.

G. Shen and X. Huang (Eds.): CSIE 2011, Part II, CCIS 153, pp. 449–453, 2011.
© Springer-Verlag Berlin Heidelberg 2011

Security threat and ensure security is the relationship between spear and shield. People have to focus on solving the security issues in the initial stage of e-commerce. People are fully aware of the importance of information security from the Internet without the lessons of development. At present, e-commerce security has been proven reliability and effective in mathematics, technology, gradually emerging international industry standards. The main technical of security mechanisms constituted is cryptography, message digest, digital signature technology and digital envelope technology, authentication (CA) technology, security audit technology etc.

At present, focusing mainly on e-commerce security has been introduced and used of e-merchant standards, can be divided into two categories, one is the online secure payment standards such as PKI, SSL, SET, X5.95 (Account Digital Signature Standard), X.509 (Certificate E-Commerce Payment standards), X500 (Electronic publication directory standard) the other is the safety certification standards such as ISO9594 (Key identification criteria), ISO10181 (Open Systems Interconnection standards in the security architecture) etc[1].

PKI technology is the infrastructure to provide security services established by the public key theories and techniques. PKI technology is the core of information security technology, also is the key and basic technology of e-commerce. As the e-commerce, e-government, e-transaction through the network lack of physical contact, therefore making the trust relationship with the electronic verification has become critical. The PKI technology happens to be a password technology suitable e-commerce, e-government and e-Services, which can solve the security issues such as confidentiality, authenticity, integrity, non-repudiation and access control applied in the e-business effectively [2]. A Practical PKI system should be safe, easy to use, flexible and economical. It must take full account of interoperability and scalability. It is the combination of functional modules such as certification authority (CA), Registry (RA), policy management, key and Certificate management, key backup and recovery, undo system etc.

3 E-Commerce and Privacy

The so-called e-commerce (Electronic Commerce) is the use of computer technology, network technology and telecommunication technology, the whole business (sale) process electronic, digital and network [2]. It is an open Internet environment, the transaction application, involving the transfer of funds and logistics information. Including not only directly related to buying and selling online advertising, online negotiation, ordering, receiving, payment, customer service, cargo to submit other activities, including online market research, financial accounting, production arrangements, the use of computer network development of commercial activities.

Privacy (Privacy) refers to private citizens to live in peace and private information are protected by law, unlawful interference by others, knows the collection, use and disclosure [3]. With the continuous development of computer technology, information (particularly in relation to personal information) of a large number of the collection, storage and use as possible. Internet privacy, privacy of the Internet age, as the product of a natural person's private information online is protected by law, unlawful infringement by others, aware of, collect, copy, use and disclosure; also refers to prohibit disclosure of certain individuals in the Internet-related sensitive information, including facts, images and opinions of defamation. American jurists Brandeis and Warren in the "Harvard Law Review" published "Privacy," a paper first proposed the concept of privacy, the privacy interpreted as "an individual under normal circumstances, the decision of his thoughts, opinions , Emotion in the extent to which the right to communicate with others. "

In e-commerce, if the consumer information gathered in somewhere, then the consumer's privacy is likely to get protection. For example: Bank control the user's personal information, if both users have been trading information, you can track, analyze a user's consumption preferences. If the information is sold to marketing companies as a marketing tool, would adversely affect consumers.

4   E-Commerce Security Protocol

In recent years, online payment security incidents continue to occur, such as: British bank has had to shut down consumer credit card information compromised their credit card Web site; Industrial and Commercial Bank of China credit card account online banking theft; Development Bank of Singapore hacking events, also makes consumer those of confidence in the credit card payment online. Studies show that nearly 60% of U.S. online consumers because of security risks and privacy issues do not choose to pay online. Thus, how to improve online payment security mechanism to protect cardholder privacy, the development of e-commerce to become an urgent problem.

Features for e-commerce business, the most influential security protocol is Secure Electronic Transaction protocol (Secure Electronic Transaction, SET) [4]. SET protocol by the two major credit cards VISA and MasterCard in May 1997 the company launched the joint specification. The core technology of the agreement are: public key encryption, digital signatures, electronic envelopes, electronic security certificate. SET link in electronic transactions provide greater trust, more complete transaction information, higher safety and less subject to the possibility of fraud. SET protocol to support the B to C (Business to Consumer) this type of e-business model, that consumers in online shopping and trading card mode.

SET protocol is mainly to address the users, merchants and banks to pay by credit card transaction security designed to ensure the confidentiality of payment information, complete the payment process, the legal status of merchants and cardholders, and interoperability. SET goal is to ensure the safety of the information flow between the various entities in the security flow. Include:

(1) to protect the confidentiality of information: the consumer's account number and payment information to the Internet through a secure means to transfer, and some information for business purposes should not be visible.

(2) to protect data integrity: the Internet on the transfer process, the consumer-to-business payment information can not be tampered with.

(3) authentication: mutual authentication of consumers and businesses to determine the identity of the legitimacy of each other.

SET transaction in three stages: in the purchase request phase, users and merchants to determine the details of payment methods used; in the payment confirmation stage, the business will be verified with the bank, with the progress of the transaction, they will receive payment; in the collection stage , business transactions to the bank to produce all the details, and bank transfer payments in an appropriate manner.

If not using a debit card, direct payment of cash, business after the completion of the second phase that can supply at any time. The third phase will cover the second phase followed the first phase of user transactions only with banks and the second and third stages, whereas the three phases of business and have a relationship. Each stage of the data related to RSA encryption, and RSA digital signatures.

SET workflow agreement are as follows:

(1) business users to send purchase orders and a signed, encrypted trust books. The book's credit card number is encrypted, the business is not known;

(2) business to trust the book sent to the acquiring banks, acquiring banks can decrypt the credit card number and signature verification by certification;

(3) The acquiring bank to the issuing bank for questioning to confirm the user card is true;

(4) and Visa card-issuing bank approved the transaction;

(5) The acquiring bank approved the transaction business and visas;

(6) business and the receipt of goods sent to the user;

(7) The transaction is successful, the merchant acquiring bank to demand payment;

(8) acquiring banks designated by the contract will be paid to the merchant;

(9) regularly sent to the user issuing bank credit card bill.

5 User Privacy Protection

Workflow from the SET protocol can be seen in, e-commerce activities need to consumers, merchants, acquiring banks, issuing banks and other entities involved, in which the issuing bank to save the consumer the relevant information to consumers, businesses closing single bank holds information on businesses, consumers and businesses in order there are consumers in the business of consumer information. If the transaction process, the merchant acquiring bank grasped the consumer's credit card information, or the consumer's issuing bank to learn the business in which consumers to spend, the consumer demand for privacy has not been met. In order to protect consumer privacy, according to Need-to-Know principle that participants in each transaction can only perform their own work that needed to know. That is, credit card information can only be known to the consumer and the issuing banks, merchants and acquiring banks do not need to know your credit card information to complete their work; order information can only be known to consumers and merchants, card issuing banks and acquiring Banks do not need to know the order information to complete their work; issuing bank where the consumer should know the cardholder, the card issuing bank only if authorized by the cardholder to confirm the deal on it.

The framework of the SET protocol, all information is encrypted transmissions. In particular the introduction of dual digital signature technology, not only meets the encrypted transmission of data, but also to ensure that only allow the main body should see a message that information. The purpose of the dual signature is to connect two different receiver of two pieces of information, including ordering information and to give businesses the payment of the letter sent to the bank. Among them, the merchant can not know the consumer's credit card information, bank customers do not need to know the details of ordering information.

Consumers with a digital signature to the signature of two news operations, implement a double signature. A double signature is by calculating the message digest of two messages generated, and together the two form a summary of the general summary, and with the user's private signature key cryptographic digest. Recipient of each message that they can see the message out, through the re-generated message digest to verify the information. Although the payment information that is passed through the merchant bank, but the merchants do not see payment information. Although the information passed to the order of the bank, but banks do not see the order information, only to see payment information.

6 Conclusions

The rapid development of e-commerce, the proliferation of online transactions, so network security is also growing concern, Internet privacy, security and ownership of the development and success of e-commerce is critical to this view has increasingly become the majority of manufacturers and consumer consensus. In network development environment, the whole society should work together, from a technical, legal and management aspects to improve and protect the privacy of users, and promote e-business.

References

1. Devaraj, S., Fan, M., Kohli, R.: Antecedents of B2C Channel Satisfaction and Preference: Validating e-Commerce Metrics. Information Systems Research 13(3), 316–333 (2002)
2. Berendt, B., Günther, O., Spiekermann, S.: Privacy in e-commerce: stated preferences vs. actual behavior. Communications of the ACM 48(4), 101–106 (2005)
3. Li, Z.: Current Situation and Existing Problems of Internet Content Filtering. Library and Information Service 2, 64, 91–92 (2004)
4. Rui, D.: Content Security Technology: the Swordsman among Assassins. China Computerworld 18, D3 (2004)
5. Rui, D.: Content Security Products: Mingled Hope and Fear. China Computerworld 18, D4 (2004)
6. Li, Z.: The Market Calls for Internet Content Filtering Technical Products. Science & Technology for China's Mass Media 4, 49, 53–53 (2003)
7. Hu, J.: Network Security and Privacy, pp. 192–212. Xidian University Press (2003)
8. PKI forum[EB/OL], http://www.pki.com.cn
9. SSL3.0 SPECIFICATION. NetscapeCommunications (1996), http://wp.nets-cape.com/eng/ssl3
10. Ding, X., Jiang, X., et al.: The study of e-commerce payment security based on SSL protocol and SET protocol. Science & Technology Information (28) (2010)

Virtual Reality of Tree Motion Based on Vega Prime

Wang Deyong

Department of Computer
Pingdingshan Industrial College of Technology
Pingdingshan, China

Abstract. Many visual simulation platforms and modeling tools are developed to simplify the process of simulation. In a variety of modeling tools, Creator is a simple and convenient modeling tool. It works with the visual simulation platform Vega Prime. They play an important role in the field of visualized simulation. Thus, a solution for simulating tree's motion in the environment of Creator and Vega Prime is proposed. Each of branches around the tree's 3D shape is built in Creator, and then is gradually merged together into a tree in Vega Prime. The simulation of tree's motion is accomplished faithfully. Experiment results show that the solution reduces the process of development and realizes the vivid simulation.

Keywords: Virtual Reality, 3D modeling, Vega Prime.

1   Introduction

Vega Prime, with its cross-platform, scalable environment, is the most productive COTS toolkit for real-time 3D application development and deployment.

Through features and functionality designed specifically for the requirements of visual simulation, Vega Prime provides developers and programmers with the means to rapidly and flexibly develop high performance applications with minimum effort and maximum productivity and flexibility. Based on the Vega Scene Graph (VSG) advanced cross platform scene graph API, Vega Prime includes.

An advanced abstraction API for ease of use and increased productivity,The LynX Prime GUI configuration tool for accelerating the creation and delivery of your real-time 3D applications for simulation, training, and general visualization.

Presagis also offers several powerful COTS application-specific modules that work with Vega Prime for solving the challenges of real-time 3D application development. The Vega Prime infrastructure allows you to create your own custom development modules and to scale the functionality based on the complexity of the application.

Vega Prime delivers the infrastructure needed for the optimal end-to-end solution. Its extendable architecture supports a high degree of customization, allowing you to tailor the application to fit your design rather than altering your software to fit within a product's constraints. In addition, its scalable architecture prevents unnecessary performance overhead because you are able to scale the functionality based on the complexity of the application.

G. Shen and X. Huang (Eds.): CSIE 2011, Part II, CCIS 153, pp. 454–459, 2011.
© Springer-Verlag Berlin Heidelberg 2011

Ideal for both high performance and low cost hardware platforms, Vega Prime's plug-in architecture facilitates the rapid design and prototyping of real-time 3D applications. With access to all of the functionality available in VSG while providing an enhanced level of functionality, ease-of-use, and productivity, Vega Prime allows you to spend more time on the application-specific functionality required by your project.

Vega Prime provides a development environment designed specifically to increase your ability to rapidly create and deploy advanced real-time 3D applications. In addition to the flexibility of VSG and the ease of use of a GUI configuration tool, Vega Prime delivers such functionality as environment effects, motion models, coordinate systems, virtual texture, and path/navigator tools.

By taking advantage of core capabilities, Vega Prime is designed to facilitate the development and deployment of applications that require very large or complex databases. High performance levels are guaranteed by optimizing the loading and organization of large datasets through the dynamic paging of "tiles" and user definable paging centers or Areas of Interest. Vega Prime offers optimized rendering that is fully customizable and scalable to take advantage of available resources.

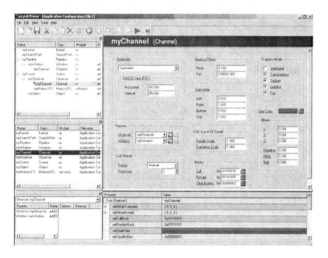

Fig. 1. Vega Prime

2   Creation

Modeling. The construction of non-foliaged tree has been accomplished in the paper. The skeleton (trunk and the major branches) of the tree is created in the environment of Creator and Vega Prime.

2.1   Branch Modeling

Small branches around the tree's 3D shape are presented by truncated cone. Each branch model is stored in the format of OpenFlight.

2.2 Tree Modeling

Small branches have been created in the Creator. They are merged together in to a tree according to the relationship between branches in the Vega Prime. The relative position and offset angle are set correctly.

2.3 Texture Mapping

Textures are bitmapped images. They are mapped onto polygons to render your model with a photo-realistic appearance without increasing the polygon count. The common texture tools are as follow: 4-Point Put Texture Tool is used to wrap a texture pattern around a corner; Surface Project Texture Tool is particularly useful for texturing walls and fences.; Spherical Project Texture is mainly used to wrap a texture around a sphere; Radial Project Texture Tool is typically used to wrap texture around a cone, cylinder, or cube using a user-defined center point (first vertex) and a direction vector (second vertex)[2]. The Radial Project Texture Tool is geared toward mapping the texture of branch models. To apply a texture pattern to the branch model, you must load the bark texture file into a Texture palette and select it as the current texture. Then you select faces to which the pattern will be applied, and apply the pattern using Radial Project Texture tool. The bark texture is used to render tree.

2.4 Tree Structure

The information on structure of tree is stored in the file named "branch.txt". The information is accessed by object of vector. Vector is similar to a dynamic array that can store various types of objects. It can increase and compress data. The type of vector is "TNode". It is defined as follow.

```
Typedef struct
{int ix;                                    // index of branch
   CString branch;                          // name of branch
   float d;                                 // radius of branch
   int subnum;                       // number of child branch
   float l;                                // length of branch
   double x;                        // offset angel in the x direction
   double y;                        // offset angel in the y direction
   double z;                        // offset angel in the z direction
   int parent;                          // index of parent branch
   }TNode;
```

3 Simulation of Tree Motion

3.1 Motion Analysis

The regulation of wind is quite complicated, so it is almost impossible to deter-mine with a realistic amount of calculating the behavior of a fluid flowing around or inside a tree that has a structure. Paper [3] proposed a wind model in connection with wind speed and wind force based on a stochastic method and aerodynamics analysis [5].

Tree motion is impacted by wind force, gravity and noise force. The gravity isn't considered because gravity is always existed. In fact, tree in the wind is not only influenced by the forces, but also influenced by restoring force. The branch is regard as a lever in the paper. The end of the lever is applied a load wind force F_1 and a load restoring force F_2. The restoring force F_2 is less than the wind force F_1 slightly and the directions of them are opposite. And the noise force is random force. The resultant force acting on the branch can be expressed by Eq.1. The offset angles are calculated on the basis of the forces on branches. SetRotate() is a Vega Prime API and the offset angle of branch can be realized by it [6].

$$F = F_1 + F_2 + F_{noise}.$$ (1)

The branch breaks when the force acting on the branch exceeds the force that the branch can bear. It is a process that the branch bends and it begins to break when it bends to some degree. The branch is subject to gravity and wind force after it has been broken. According to Newton's second law, the trajectory of falling branches can be calculated. The branch falling trajectory can be realized by Vega Prime API named setTranslate().

3.2 Collision Detection and Response

In the process of tree motion, collision happens in two situations. One is between branch and ground, and the other is between branch and branch. The first one can be realized by setting collision detection method in Vega Prime. There are some collision detection methods in Vega Prime such as vpIsectorHAT and vpIsectorTripod[4]. They are based on base class vpIsector. The vpIsectorHAT can be used to compute the Height Above Terrain (HAT). The vpIsectorTripod can be used to orient a moving platform on uneven terrain [7]. It is named tripod, because its construction looks somewhat like a three-footed camera stand. It uses three verticle line segments to compute intersection points with the terrain. In the beginning, vpIsectorHAT is selected to calculate the distance between falling branch and ground. Once the branch touched the ground, vpIsectorTripod is selected to calculate the rolling angle. At last, the collision detection is achieved in the situation. And the collision detection can't use the method above between branch and branch, because the method that realizes collision detection between object and object is not existed in Vega Prime. The relationship between branches must be removed, and then one of the branches is copied and added to the scene's child. In the end, the original branch is deleted and the detection is changed into the first one.

4 System and Results

4.1 Environment Framework

The tree motion method is visual simulation based on .net and Vega Prime. Vega Prime includes a complete C++ language application program interface and provides maximum control and flexibility to accelerate the pace of software development for developers of software. Vega Prime's API provides a window and event management functions, but a "window" system is also needed to complete the program design of

Vega Prime real-time simulation. Through the "window" in the dialog boxes and menus tree motion can be controlled.

Vega Prime is configured in vc.net development environment. The specific process is as follows.

```
vp::initialize(argc, argv);          // create a instance
vpApp *app = new vpApp;              // load acf file
app->define("simple.acf");           // configure my app
app->configure();                    // frame loop
app->run();                          // unref instance
app->unref();                        // shutdown
vp::shutdown();
```

4.2 Experiment Results

The results of the 3D non-foliaged tree in wind are shown in Figs. 2 and 3. There are three parameters in the wind field model: wind initial speed V_0, wind amplitude A and wind frequency f. In the nature, changes of the frequency and amplitude are large and the initial velocity is relative small. Its magnitude is equal to the imposed force of a unit deformation. The force is decided by unit length and unit area of the material. The greater the elastic modulus is, the less the branch easily deformed. The parameter values are as follows: for branches, the value of elastic modulus E is 18000, the noise parameter is 2 and the restoring force parameter is 0.9. For wind field, when V_0 is 2, A is 5 and f is 5, the branch is swaying in wind and is not broken, which is shown in Fig.2; when V_0 is 2, A is 16 and f is 16, the branch is broken, which is shown in Fig.3. The contrast results verify the faithful of the simulation.

Fig. 2. Swaying Tree

Fig. 3. Broken Tree

5   Conclusions

We have proposed a solution for simulating a faithful tree's motion in the environment of Creator and Vega Prime. 3D non-foliaged model has been created by the Creator. The process of tree's motion is simulated by the Vega Prime API. Different effects of tree's motion can be obtained by adjusting the parameters. Experiment results show that the solution is efficient and is geared toward real-time simulation of tree's motion.

References

1. Zheng, C., Tao: Virtual reality system of ancient architecture based on Vega Prime. Engineering Journal of Wuhan University (2001)
2. Shangyi, H.: Development Course of Moive Art. Journal of Beijing Film Academy (2), 4–12 (1994)
3. Li, Z.: Research on Real-time Animation of Trees Swaying in Wind. Journal of System Simulation (2008)
4. Chen, J., Liu, H.: Modeling 3D Tree Based on Growth. Journal of System Simulation (2006)
5. MultiGen Vega Prime User's Guide. MultiGen-Paradigm Inc., USA (2001)
6. Ohanian, T.A., et al.: Digital Filmmaking, vol. 73. China Film Press, Beijing (1998)
7. Wang, H., Fan, Z.: On Digitalized Film Art. Journal of Beijing Film Academy (5), 84–90 (2006)

An Interactive Design in Smart Classroom

Fan Yang, Xingjia Lu, Zhirong Chen, Junwei Cai, and Longzhang Liu

Ningbo University of Technology, Ningbo, Zhejiang China
yangfanon19@mail.dhu.edu.cn

Abstract. In order to enable participant-devices to become fully functional clients in the smart environment, there's a need for a program that accesses and makes available those services to the participant. The Smart Classroom program provides that access and monitoring in a smart classroom environment. The project also specifies a framework that contributors can use to program services for the smart classroom.

Keywords: PDAs, ubiquitous computing, Smart Classroom.

1 Introduction

Ubiquitous or pervasive computing seeks to create smart environments in rooms, buildings, houses, classrooms and other physical locations. The fundamental design behind such smart environments is computational devices that are embedded into the structure. These devices can range from simple desktop computers to cameras, microphones, motion detection sensors, large displays, wearable devices, and appliances for every day use. To use these devices, the embedded environments provide certain services to their users. For example, the BlueBoard system, a touch based large plasma display with badge reader, can identify individual users and allow access to their web-based content, and can let users collaborate via sketching, sharing, or exchanging notes and other contents [1].

Mark Weiser, at the Computer Science Lab at Xerox PARC, first described ubiquitous computing as "different from PDAs, Dynabooks, or information at your fingertips. The inspiration behind ubiquitous computing seeks to connect human and computers whenever they want, wherever they want [2]. Hypothetically speaking, this interaction can be realized by smart environments that allow users to interact with each other by using computing devices. It is invisible; everywhere computing that does not live on a personal device of any sort, but is in the woodwork everywhere. "[3]

Looking at a glance on the research being done in smart environments, most research focuses on either utilizing existing infrastructure that is part of a physical location, or providing added devices that should be configured to use specific services within that physical environment. Although this type of coupled infrastructure can be useful in many instances, it is inherently restrictive because the users must use only the pre-existing resources in that physical environment to participate.

The interesting fact is that most users, even students, now carry their own personal devices, which could be utilized, to take advantage of the smart environments.

G. Shen and X. Huang (Eds.): CSIE 2011, Part II, CCIS 153, pp. 460–465, 2011.

However, most research is not intended to support the addition of these devices dynamically to participate in such smart environments and therefore cannot collaborate with the services or other users. Moreover, in fixed environments, users are not able to port, share or discuss the information resulting from interaction with the collaborative services, elsewhere.

This project attempts to address the key problems of dynamically adding new participants with their own devices and dynamically adding new services in to the smart classroom, without requiring extensive configuration.

This project describes the design, implementation, and testing of a control and visualization structure for the smart classroom.

It keeps track of the classroom services and participants in real-time, allows users to launch available services that collaborate with each other, and maintains a visual representation of participants and services in the classroom [4].

The remainder of this paper is organized as follows. In section 2 we provide Design of Smart Classroom enter. In sections 3and 4 we describe Smart Classroom Requirements. Section 5 we describe implementing for the Smart Classroom. Finally, section 6 we make a conclusion of the paper.

2   Design of Smart Classroom Enter

The advent of newer and better technologies in computing world has resulted in most people possessing affordable personal devices that are not only portable, but also powerful enough to process complex computations. This is evident by the common sightings of laptop computers, handheld PDAs, and tablet PCs etc., in the hands of general public. Even in academic world, most teachers use their own laptops, and so do many students.

Surveys of the students showed that technology made the classroom experience more interesting, and capturing notes made students pay better attention to the class lecture. Students also appreciated the audio and video augmentation to the lecture notes. One interesting observation that surfaced was that availability of lecture notes made students less worried about missing classes.

However, many students were divided over the view that availability of the live lectures for later retrieval actually encouraged them to miss the class.

A common assumption is the existence of configured infrastructure that both students and teachers must use to benefit from applications in the smart classrooms.

Since everyone is all too familiar with the use of his or her own device, it is all the more desirable that teachers are able to use their preferred devices to give lecture notes while students be able to retrieve those notes on their devices without having to engage in the complex web of installations and configurations.

Most students would like to be able to retrieve live lecture notes on their devices and be able annotate them in real-time. The students can share these annotated notes with fellow students who missed the class, or simply compare and share each other's notes in group-study sessions to get a better understanding of the course material.

However, enabling dynamic participation of new devices in the room is not easy. We created a "boot-loader" application to be used by a client as an entry point to the environment. The boot loader launches the main application that controls the smart classroom services. Once installed, the boot-loader application would hardly need any modification because it's simply a mechanism of entering the services and would always be able to access the Smart Classroom environment. However, we even eliminated the need to preinstall this boot-loader application. Now, users can visit a web page and simply click on the application link to download and run the boot-loader application as fig1 show.

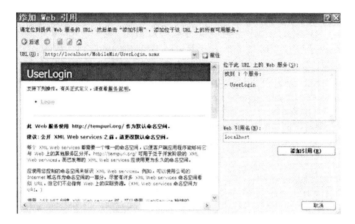

Fig. 1. Boot-loader application

We need to think of an application that not only accesses the available services in the room and allows a mechanism to launch them, but also tracks the participants dynamically.

3   Smart Classroom Requirements

We think that the program for a smart environment should enable its users to gain access to the services without needing to configure the client for every specific service in that environment. In most cases, the set of services are static and already known in an environment, however, in a serendipitous environment where even participating clients would want to introduce their own services, this static programming model doesn't work. To dynamically add or remove services and participants, the program should be aware of the services and participants that interact with the smart environment. To be able to do that, though, the controller must be aware of the interfaces that services must implement to become part of the smart environment.

Earlier, we noted that the two key components of the classroom are available services and the participants. Therefore our primary consideration when designing the Smart Classroom Controller was to bring both services and participants together, approachable and executable.

Obviously, since services and participants are two different entities, we need two sets of interfaces that any service must adhere to implement. Once the user selects his or her role in the class, either as a student or as a professor, he/she is presented with a subsequent dialogue box asking for the login information as fig2 show. This information includes required fields of user-name and email address, and optional fields of user's web page URL and picture. Note that this dialogue box is the same for both students and professor. In the case of a student, only the user's name is used for display with their picture. For a professor, Controller UI displays his/her email address and web URL along with the picture and name.

Fig. 2. Login box

4 Implementing a Program the Smart Classroom

The bulk of Smart Classroom Program implementation deals with behind the scenes communication with various services in the environment. Assuming a user has already installed Java runtime environment on her machine that is hooked up with the network, all she needs now is a visit to a web page to download and run the boot-loader application. The boot-loader application will access the web services and retrieve the application, which in turn, will facilitate all other interaction in the class environment.

Here are the components that comprise the service execution.

1. The client boot-loader application accesses and launches the Smart Classroom.

2 The Participant Service keeps track of the users in the classroom environment. It maintains the list of users in real-time by registering them upon entry, and removing them from its list when they exit the classroom.

3. Obtaining and launching services compose another portion of the large Controller application.

4. Controller's graphical user interface is the dynamic display of services and participants in real-time.

These "group" devices, or services, are important in our discussion as they differ from public devices, by allowing authorized groups to securely interact with each other without being exposed to the entire world as would be the case in the public devices. For example, in the case of a classroom, only authorized students would be able to join a particular class in which that student is enrolled. In other example, several note-sharing services could be running concurrently in a smart environment, but allowing only authorized members to join their corresponding groups who could be collaboratively working on a project. Fig 3 shows user interface.

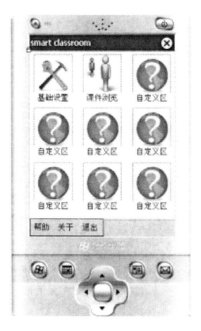

Fig. 3. User interface

5   Conclusion

In order to enable participant-devices to become fully functional clients in the smart environment we provides a program that access and monitoring in a smart classroom environment. This project describes the design, implementation, and visualization structure for the smart classroom. The project also specifies a framework to program services for the smart classroom. Our project resulted in most people carry their personal devices, which could be utilized, to take advantage of the smart classroom.

Acknowledgement. This research is supported in part by 2010 topic for Educational Technology Research plan of ZheJiang Province.Supported by National Natural Science Funds for Young Scholar（40901241）and Natural Science Foundation of Zhejiang Province, China(Y5090377).

References

1. Bardram, J.E., Kjær, R.E., Pedersen, M.Ø.: Context-aware user authentication – supporting proximity-based login in pervasive computing. In: Dey, A.K., Schmidt, A., McCarthy, J.F. (eds.) UbiComp 2003. LNCS, vol. 2864, pp. 107–123. Springer, Heidelberg (2003)
2. Domermuth, D.: Creating a Smart Classroom. Tech. Directions Academic Search Premier, Ipswich, MA (accessed April 17, 2007)
3. Rasicot, J.: Off to a Fresh Start With Fresh Tools. The Washington Post, pp. GZ08 (2007)
4. Hunleth, F., Cytron, R.K.: Footprint and feature management using aspect-oriented programming techniques. In: Joint Conference on Languages,Compilers and Tools for Embeded Systems. ACM Press, Berlin (2008)

A New Strategy for Disambiguation in Segmentation of Chinese Words

Yueqi Liao and Shaoxian Tang

Information Science and Technology School of Hunan Agricultural University
Changsha of China, Post Code: 410078

Abstract. Segmentation is the base of information processing in Chinese, the difficulty of lies in disambiguation. This paper puts forward a new method for disambiguation according to the frequency of single characters functioning as independent meaningful words, context and the frequency of word collocation as well. It has been proved by experiments to be able to greatly improve the accuracy and efficiency of segmentation.

Keywords: natural language processing, segmentation of Chinese words, one-character word entries, disambiguation.

1 Introduction

The dramatic increase of information resulted in the complexity of information processing. Knowledge search engine technology and information retrieval technology are both important strategies for information processing, the technical premise of which is successful Chinese information processing. After development of more than ten years, the Chinese Word Segmentation technology gradually move toward maturity [4]. There is no denying that the technology of Chinese information processing has greatly improved, however, it is still far behind the human intelligence level and thus far from satisfactory in practical use. After all, Chinese is quite different English, they should be segmented in different ways. There is no clear boundary between words in Chinese, whereas blank space is usually used as a hint of different words in English, for example, I like English means wo xi huan ying yu in Chinese. The computer can easily know that English is a word because of the blank space, but it is very difficult for it to know that ying and yu together is a fixed meaningful phrase in Chinese. Therefore, whether there is a boundary between Chinese words is critical for the computer to process Chinese information. Different means of the boundary between Words is also the key problem for word ambiguity, but also had many scholars to propose according to the context, the statistical probability and so on to be solved the problem of ambiguity string.This paper puts forward a new method for disambiguation according to the frequency of single characters functioning as independent meaningful words, context and the frequency of word collocation in hopes of effectively improving the accuracy and efficiency of segmentation.

G. Shen and X. Huang (Eds.): CSIE 2011, Part II, CCIS 153, pp. 466–472, 2011.

2   The Function of Single Characters Functioning as Independent Meaningful Words in Disambiguation

In Chinese, "word" is a string that can independently express meaning, unable to be further divided in terms of semantics. Eg.*sha fa, shu dan hong*. Words are made up of morphemes, which are the minimal grammatical unit. For instance, *ta│zuo│zai│sha fa│li│kan│shu*(which means *He is reading books on the sofa*)each part took apart is meaningful as morphemes and cannot be further segmented. On the contrary, non-morphemes refer to separated characters that cannot be used independently, such as "*bian, ting, zhe*" and so on.

Definition 1: One-character word entries in Chinese are monosyllable and contain only one character, which can express meaning independently, just like "*wo,hao,you*"and so on.

Suppose there is a character W which alone cannot act as meaningful word entry, then we use F(W)=0 to express its word frequency in Chinese. F(W)=0.9,1.0 means that the character are usually used as meaningful word entries; and F(W)=0.1—0.8 means that they are meaningful word entries under certain circumstances. Subsequently, we should use F(W)=0 to express the frequency of such Chinese character as *bian*, F(W)=1.0 for *wo*, and F(W)=0.5 for *kong*.

Definition 2: ambiguous segmentation strings (called ambiguity strings for short) refer to ones which can be segmented in more than two different ways.

Word entries in Chinese can classified as one- character word entries, two -character word entries, three-character word entries, and "n"- character word entry(n>3) due to different number of characters in each entry. In the most frequently used 9000 Chinese words collected in the Modern Chinese frequency vocabulary [11] (shown in table 1 below [3]), the one –character word entries take up 47.27%, word entries with two characters 44.99%, and entries with three characters 4.95%.

In other words, one- character word entries and two-character word entries are in vast majority of the most frequently used words in Chinese.

Therefore, the author gave priority to two-character word entries and three-character ones in segmentation. In the dictionary named Chinese Character Collections [7] mainly by Leng yulong, there are more than 8,500 characters (only 6,000 to 7,000 characters are used in practical application), among which one-character word entries are in the minority and the majority should be used together with another character or word entry to be meaningful in specific contexts. We can imagine that: if we have the frequency of all single characters when used as word entries, and we can single out the characters which cannot be used independently as a meaningful word entry $(F(W)=0)$, and then store them in the database. Consequently, the computer can be able to correctly segment sentences with the help of the database when meeting ambiguity word entries by leaving out single characters ($F(W)=0$).

Table 1. Distribution of the word entries containing different number of Chinese characters

category	number	percentage/%
One- character word entries （including punctuations)524,721		47.27
Two- character word entries	499,329	44.99
Three -character word entries	54,973	4.95

Given that there is an ambiguity string "S", $C(S)$ represents the number of characters "S", when "$W_1, W_2, ..., W_n \in S$", we can consider the following situations:

(1) When "$C(S)=3$", there are two methods for segmenting the string "S": "W_1/W_2W_3"and "W_1W_2/W_3".In that case, we first consider "$F(W_1)$" and "$F(W_2)$".If "$F(W_1)=0$", we chose the first method, but if "$F(W_2)=0$", we chose the second.

(2) When "$C(S)=4$", "S" can be segmented in four different ways: "$W_1/W_2W_3/W_4$", "$W_1W_2/W_3 W_4$", "$W_1W_2W_3/W_4$" and "$W_1/W_2W_3W_4$". Firstly taking account of "$F(W_1)$", if "$F(W_1)=0$" and "$F(W_4)=0$", then the second method is chosen; if "$F(W_1)=1.0$" and "$F(W_4)=1.0$", the first one is chosen; if "$F(W_1)=0$" and "$F(W_4)=1.0$", we chose the third one; and when "$F(W_1)=1.0$" and "$F(W_4)=0$", the fourth one is our choice..

(3) When "$C(S)=5$", six different segmentation methods are available: "$W_1/W_2W_3/W_4 W_5$", "$W_1W_2/W_3 W_4/W_5$", "$W_1W_2/W_3/W_4 W_5$", "$W_1W_2W_3/W_4 W_5$", "$W_1W_2/W_3 W_4 W_5$" and "$W_1/W_2W_3 W_4/W_5$".We firstly pay attention to "$F(W_1)$" and "$F(W_5)$".If "$F(W_1)=0$" and "$F(W_5)>0$",the first method is chosen; if "$F(W_1)>0$" and "$F(W_5)=0$", the second one is chosen; and if "$F(W_1)>0$" and "$F(W_5)>0$", the third one is chosen for segmentation.

3   Building the Database of One-Character Word Entries

3.1 Taking Statistics of One-Character Word Entries

The author chose the People's Daily annotated corpus for statistics of one-character word entries. Because the word entries in the corpus have already been segmented and marked for different part of speech, we can easily get a database of one-character word entries (with marked part of speech) including 6,764 entries just by collecting statistics of one-character word entries in the corpus. Please look at Table 2 showed blow:

Table 2. Statistics of one-character word entries

ID	words
1	Li
2	Qiao
3	Bian
4	Xin
5	Kui
6	Bo

3.2 Designing the Property of the Database

For a more correct segmentation, we designed the following properties to supply more references for disambiguation: "part of speech", "the frequency of being a word entry", "the frequency of being an independent meaningful word entry" and "the position of characters in different word entries" (showed in table 3).

Among the properties, "the frequency of being a word entry" is the most important one. Three bit will be used to show the position, to illustrate, "000"→and independent meaningful word entry, "100"→ located in the beginning of a word, "010"→ located in the middle, "001"→located in the end, and "111"→uncertain position.

Table 3. Properties of word entries

single word entry	word construction frequency	word independent frequency	part of speech	position in word entry
qian	.9	.1	n	101
ji	1	0		100
shu	1	0	ng	111
zhe	1	0	u	1

3.3 Collecting the Statistics of the Frequency of One–Character Word Entries

This author took statistics of single characters in "People's Daily annotated corpus", "Modern Chinese dictionary [8]", and "Modern Chinese frequency dictionary [11]" and analyzed the morpheme database in "Modern Chinese grammar information dictionary[5]" to calculate the total number of occurrences, the times of independent and dependent occurrences, the appearance in each word entry and the part of speech. After that the author added weight value to the single characters among the most frequently used 8000 words in "Modern Chinese frequency dictionary". At last, the author collected statistics of its application in specific fields-- the context. This paper focuses on the application of one-character word entries in agriculture.

Specifically, we firstly take statistics of the frequency of independent occurrence of each one-character word entry: $f_S(W_i) = n_S/(n_S + n_M)$, and that of co-occurrence with others: $f_M(W_i) = n_M/(n_S + n_M)$. In the latter, we get $f_{M-head}(W_i)$, $f_{M-body}(W_i)$ and

$f_{M-tail}(W_i)$ respectively (f is for frequency) according to different position of character in different word entries---in the beginning, middle or the end, and then we give the context to detect its construction ability. Take agriculture for example: $C(s)$, $f_M(x/W_i)$, $x \in rice$.

4 Realizing Disambiguation by Making Use of One-Character Word Entries

Firstly, we use the crossing ambiguity detection algorithm to extract the ambiguous word string "S" from sentences before disambiguation. The algorithm is as follows:

a) Drawing out the ambiguity string and then identify its structure (to calculate $C(s)$).

b) After listing all the possible segmentation methods, we exclude the method that regard characters whose "$F(W)=0$" as one-character entry words and the method that fail to identify one-character entry words whose "$F(W)=1.0$" by inquiring and analyzing the frequency of characters used in the initial position and final position of word entries.

c) For segmentation methods whose $C(S)$ value is difficult to be compared, we refer to the detailed frequency database of one-character word entries , for example, "the frequency when appearing in the beginning", "the frequency of being independent in context" to get the correct segmentation method.

The arithmetic is shown in Fig.1:

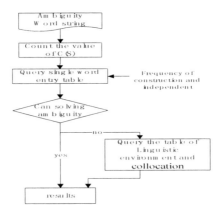

Fig. 1. Crossing ambiguity detection algorithm

5 Contrasting by Simulation Experiments

The arithmetic was tested in the platform of C# (shown in figure 2.) The author choose China agricultural information network as the linguistic material and then took out 1000 crossing ambiguity strings in it in order to eliminate ambiguity with the arithmetic put forward in this paper.

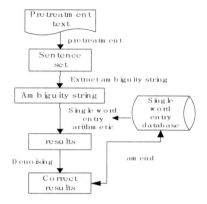

Fig. 2. Ambiguity Eliminating Processing Diagram

We can know from the test result (shown in Chart 6) that the arithmetic brought forward in this paper has a very high accuracy when dealing with crossing ambiguity strings, which demonstrates the importance of the database in disambiguation.

Table 4. Results of Disambiguation

number of literature	total number of ambiguity strings	number of crossing ambiguity strings
1000	800	798

Number of correct segmentation	accuracy
780	97%

6 Conclusions

The model of disambiguation proposed in this paper can be combined with other segmentation methods to be applied, together with agricultural thesaurus, in such agricultural information platform as Agricultural Search Engine, Agricultural Knowledge,Retrieval and Agricultural Data Mining and so on. In this paper, the author give priority to crossing ambiguity strings, which take up about 90% of all the ambiguous strings, leaving combinational ambiguity strings for future study. The accuracy of the arithmetic raised r has been proved by experiments to be as high as above 98% when handling four-character ambiguity strings. In the following research, the author will concentrate on further improving the accuracy and practicability of the arithmetic, especially on how to be interfaced with other word segmentation methods and applied in the Agricultural automatic abstract.

References

1. Liu, J., Zhang, W.: Fast crossing ambiguity detection method. Application Research of Computers 25(11) (2008)
2. Ma, Y., Song, H.: Research of Chinese Word Segmentation Based on the Web. Computer Applications 24(4) (2004)
3. Zhang, C., Zhao, L., Wu, C.: Method of Chinese word segmentation based on character-word classification. Computer Applications 30(8) (2010)
4. Huang, C., Zhao, H.: Chinese Word Segmentation: A Decade Review. Journal of Chinese Information Processing 21(3), 8–20 (2007)
5. Yu, S.: Modern Chinese grammar information dictionary. Tsinghua University Press, Beijing (2003)
6. Guo, H.: An Improved Maximum Matching Method for Chinese Word Segmentation. Mini Computer Application 18(1), 22–32 (2002)
7. Len, Y.: Chinese Character Collections. China friendship press, Beijing (2000)
8. Institute of Linguistics in Chinese Academy of Social Sciences. Modern Chinese dictionary. Commerce Press, Beijing (2005)
9. Tan, Q., Shi, Z.: Ambiguity Processing in Word Segmenting. Computer Engineering and Applications 11(25) (2002)
10. Yun, X., Maosong, S., Tsou, B.K.: Covering Ambiguity Resolution in Chinese Word egmentation Based on Contextual Information. Computer Engineering And Applications (19) (2001)
11. Wang, H.: Modern Chinese frequency vocabulary. Language (1986)
12. Wilks, S.M.Y.: Combining Weak Knowledge Sources for Sense Disambiguation (1999)
13. Stevenson, W.Y.M.: Combining Independent Knowledge Sources for Word Sense Disambiguation (1997)

A New Soil Erosion Model for Hilly Region Based on Information Technology

Yu Tian[1,2], Jihui Fan[1], Feipeng Xiao[3], and Genwei Cheng[1,*]

[1] Institute of Mountain Hazards and Environment, Chinese Academy of Sciences and Ministry of
Water Conservancy, Chengdu 610041, China
[2] Graduate University of Chinese Academy of Sciences, Beijing 100049, China
[3] Guangxi Technical College of Water Conservancy and Electric Power,
Nanning 530023, China
rain_cas@126.com, gwcheng@imde.ac.cn

Abstract. Research and development of watershed scale soil erosion model has
been the frontiers in the field of soil erosion in the past 50 years and has been
focused on by water and soil conservation workers around the world. However,
the present models cannot well simulate the actual conditions of soil erosion in
hilly areas. Soil erosion model for small-watershed of hilly areas (SEM-SHA) is
a new distributed hydrological model which is developed according to the
physical process of sediment yield in the hilly areas. This paper introduced
the development, characteristics, structure and function, and input and output of
the model. The model was also used in the Lizi River watershed in the hilly areas
of the Jialing River. The simulation results showed the SEM-SHA model was fit
for the hilly region.

Keywords: hilly area, hydrological model, Jialing River, SEM-SHA, water and
soil loss.

1 Introduction

Soil erosion and sediment yield in a watershed is a very complicated phenomenon
occurred on the surface of the earth. Dispersion and movement of land surface
substances under exterior forces (i.e. gravity, rain and water) is called soil erosion. The
eroded materials merge into the rivers and move downward along the river bed. Part of
them deposits downward and the rest accumulates in the outlets of the basin and yields
sediment [1, 2]. Soil erosion and deposition is not only a complex physical process [3],
but also a complicated system, which is controlled by a lot of natural factors that
interacts each other [1, 3]. Soil erosion is a global problem, leading to thinner soil layer,
soil nutrient loss, lower land productivity and water pollution [4]. Soil erosion model,

---

* Corresponding author.

G. Shen and X. Huang (Eds.): CSIE 2011, Part II, CCIS 153, pp. 473–483, 2011.
© Springer-Verlag Berlin Heidelberg 2011

as an effective tool for prediction of soil and water loss, optimization of water and soil resource utilization, and guidance for regulating water and soil conservation measures, has been concerned by domestic and foreign scholars for a long time [5, 6, 7]. The small basin, as a comprehensive system of runoff formation, soil erosion, sediment production and sediment transport, is the basic unit of comprehensive soil erosion. Research and development of watershed scale soil erosion forecast model has been the frontiers in the field of soil erosion in the past 50 years and focused on by water and soil conservation workers [8, 9, 10, 11].

In the hilly region, sediment from slope and gully flows into the channels with water and runs in rivers or reservoirs where the suspended matters in the water subsides. The deposits may stay in the basin for a long time, or re-move and flow out with a mountain torrent [1]. A practical erosion model should have a better performance for simulating the deposition and re-movement of the sediment. However, the present soil erosion models are almost incapable of that. To calculate the sediment yield, these models generally use sediment carrying capacity formulae or diffusion equation for suspended sediment, or simply add all deposits in each unit, which cannot reflect the process of soil erosion and sediment yield in the hill region [1].

Soil erosion model for small-watershed of hilly areas (SEM-SHA) is a new distributed hydrological model for small basin that is based on the physical process of sediment deposition, storage and re-transportation in reservoirs. The model is developed by Research Fellow Cheng GW and Doctor Fan JH in institute of mountain hazards and environment of Chinese Academy of Science (CAS), who studied the characteristics of hydrology and sediment movement in hilly regions for a long period. In this paper, the authors introduced development, characteristics, main structure and functions, and input and output of the SEM-SHA and used it in the hilly area of Jialing River basin, so as to investigate its simulation results.

2 The New Hydrological Model

2.1 Development

Fellow Cheng and Doctor Fan developed the SEM-SHA. In order to better simulate the runoff and sediment yield in the hilly area, the inventors investigated the actual conditions of major sediment yield area in upper reaches of the Yangtze River, analyzed the process of "rainfall - soil erosion - sediment deposition" and "sedimentation - sediment remotion - sediment yield" in hilly region of Middle Sichuan of China, investigated the soil erosion and sediment yield mechanism in Jialing River basin, and then developed the model [1].

SEM-SHA was developed under MS-Windows System with Borland-Delphi language, and Arc-GIS was also be used to deal with geographical information (i.e. DEM). When running, the hardware support for the SEM-SHA is given in table 1.

Table 1. Hardware support for the SEM-SHA

Hardware	Requirement
Operation systems	Microsoft Windows Server 2000/2003, Microsoft Windows 2000/XP
CPU	$\geq 1.5GHz$
Browser	$\geq IE5.0$
Memory	$\geq 256M$
Hard disk space	$\geq 2GB$

The main objective for the development of the model is to simulate and forecast the process of runoff formation and soil erosion, assess the effect of land use and agricultural management on soil erosion so as to formulate suitable land management issues. The detailed targets of the model can be listed as follows:

- to recreate a rainfall-runoff module to simulate the rainfall, so as to predict the effect of hydrological parameters on runoff
- to recreate slope erosion module to simulate water erosion, so as to calculate the total sediment yield in a basin
- to recreate a reservoir sedimentation-based watershed sediment yield module to simulate the process of sediment formation in hill region
- to recreate a display and statistics module to implements a graphical display and present the statistical results
- to recreate a parameter module to easily modify the model's parameters
- to integrate the above mentioned modules and develop a concise and friendly user interface by using windows and dialog boxes, so that the model is convenient to operate.

2.2 Characteristics

The model has the following features:

- It is a physically based model, and every parameter has definite physical meaning.
- Simple and luminous user interface provides convenience for operators.
- Parameters input and renewal is very easy. Various data in the model is stored in the same file folder, and new information, such as new runoff and precipitation data, can be added to the model timely and easily.

The physically based model generally requires extensive amount of data [12, 13], however, as a standalone model, the SEM-SHA has simple structure and convenient parameter input interface, so it runs faster and is best fit for the dynamic forecast of regional soil erosion and sediment yield.

2.3 Structure and Function

The model mainly consists of 3 functional modules (rainfall-runoff module, slope erosion module and watershed sediment yield module), input and output modules and user's visualization/interface modules (see Fig 1).

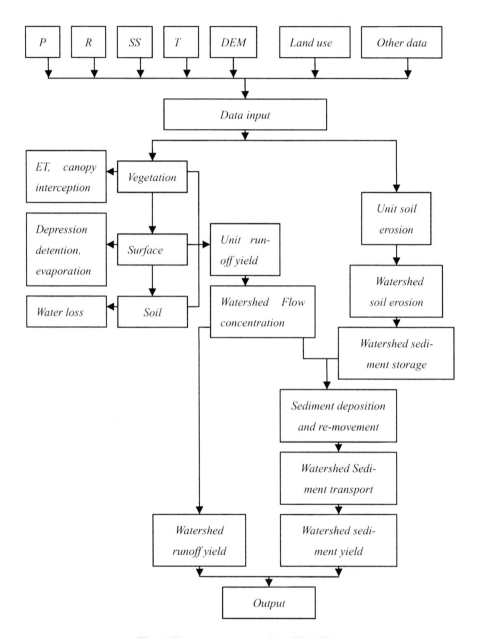

Fig. 1. The main structure of the SEM-SHA

- rainfall-runoff module

SEM-SHA is a distributed hydrological model. It can compute the canopy interception, water uptake and transpiration, respectively. The model divide a basin into many uniform cells horizontally and several layers (i.e. canopy layer, soil layer, underground layer) vertically to describe spatial distribution pattern of meteorology, soil and vegetation. The model can simulates infiltration, runoff yield, and evapotranspiration of each cell and it can also predict the effect of precipitation, air temperature, vegetation, soil and topography on hydrological process [1].

The module contains two sub-modules: runoff yield sub-module and runoff conflux sub-module. On the basis of the characteristics of hilly region of Jialing River basin, runoff yield sub-module is used to simulate the practical physical process of rainfall-runoff, including several components (i.e. canopy interception, snowmelt runoff calculation, water conservation capacity of soil calculation, evapotranspiration calculation and Dunne runoff calculation), and runoff concentration sub-module contains unit conflux and watershed conflux. Unit confluence and basin confluence are calculated by free-water sluice reservoir method and unit hydrograph method, respectively [14].

- slope erosion module

In the module, USLE (Universal Soil Loss Equation) is used to calculate slope erosion [8, 9]. This module first calculates unit soil erosion and then calculates the soil erosion of a watershed, and lastly calculates the total sediment storage (see Fig 1).

- watershed sediment yield module

During the physical process of "soil erosion - sediment yield - sediment deposition – sediment transport", sediment transport ratio is an important parameter to reveal the relationship between soil erosion, sediment and sand transport. If the total soil loss in the upper reaches of a river can be estimated, the sediment discharge in the lower

Table 2. Basic parameters for SEM-SHA

Parameter type	Components
DEM	DEM of a basin
	rainfall
Meteorological and	air temperature
hydrological elements	water flow
	sediment transport rate
	land use and land cover
	proportion of land type
Land use and land cover	area of land type
	surface coverage
	recession constant
Runoff confluence	initial groundwater level
Slope map	slope for each unit of a basin

Table 3. Main variable parameter for SEM-SHA

Parameter type	Components
Fundamental parameters	latitude of a basin
	cell numbers
	simulation time step
Evaporation	evaporation conversion coefficient
	evaporation weight for each soil layer
	evopotranspiration available factors
	soil water evaporation parameters
	free water surface evaporation coefficient
	evopotranspiration deficit factors
	soil water outflow coefficient
Soil parameters	distribution curve index for soil water storage capacity
	regulating coefficient of surface water and subsurface flow
	regulating coefficient of surface water
	daily snow-melting amount
	percolation coefficient from vadose zone to shallow aquifer
	daily sublimation amount
	voidage of soil preferential flow
	daily soil water freezing coefficient
	threshold temperature of rain and snow
	freezing point of soil water
	soil saturated water content
	field capacity
	wilting coefficients
	thickness of unsaturated zone
	drainage rate
Soil erodibility	soil erodibility in a homogeneous basin
	soil erodibility for different soil type in a heterogeneous basin
Sediment transport	initial sediment storage in a reservoir
	sediment-carrying capacity coefficient (k)
	sedimentation coefficient (w)

reaches can also be predicted when sediment transport ratio is given. In the model, the parameter of sediment transport ratio is used for calculate the amount of sediment. Furthermore, two physical parameters, sediment reservoir and sediment reservoir capacity are also be used in the mode, so as to calculate the sediment yield of watershed.

2.4 Input and Output

The inputted parameters consist of the basic data and the variable parameter. For a given basin, the basic data in SEM-SHA comprises topography, meteorological and hydrographic conditions, land cover and land use, runoff confluence, etc (see table 2). These parameters are pre-treated into a set format ("*.in" format) and inputted into the model.

Besides the above mentioned basic data, some variable parameters are also needed to be set (see Fig. 3). These parameters are stored in a file and can be modified through the interface dialog box. Through calibration of the variable parameter, a good simulation effect can be performed.

The output of the SEM-SHA includes the simulated daily runoff yield and sediment yield, and monthly and annual statistics results (see Table 4). All the data is displayed by figure and/or table. Hydrological processes and sediment yield process are showed through figures in which both the measured value and the simulation value are simultaneously displayed. Monthly and annual statistics results of measured and simulated runoff and sediment yield are showed through a table. The other data is saved in text files (Table 4).

Table 4. The output of SEM-SHA

Data type	Function	Format
Runoff yield	to show the results of daily watershed evapotranspiration, runoff in the outlet of the basin, shallow groundwater and canopy interception	figure or text file
Sediment yield	to show the results of daily soil erosion amount, sand storage in reservoir and total sediment yield	figure or text file
Statistics document	to show the statistics results of measured and simulated runoff and sediment yield	table

3 Application of the Model

3.1 Study Sites

In order to test the model, we simulated the soil erosion in Lizi River watershed. The watershed (E: 105°41'~106°06'; N: 30° 22'~30° 42') is located in hilly areas along the lower-middle reaches of the Jialing River, covering an area of 437 km^2 and with an elevation of 250~650 m. The climate is mainly wet-warm, and rainfall is abundant and mainly concentrates in summer in the area (see Table 5). However, this region has serious soil erosion and has been one of the regions for severe soil and water loss in upper Changjiang River [1].The detailed climate and hydrological conditions in the watershed are given as Table 5.

Table 5. The climate and hydrological conditions in the Lizi River watershed

	Parameter	Value
Climate	annual average temperature (°C)	17.4
	annual highest temperature (°C)	40.1
	annual lowest temperature (°C)	-2.5
	precipitation (mm)	1010.6
Hydrological	annual water flow (m^3)	1.304×10^8
	sediment discharge (t/a)	42.6×10^4
	the modulus of sediments (t/($km^2 \cdot a$))	971

The land types in the Lizi River watershed are mainly based on agricultural lands (Fig.2). The main crops of the area are *Oryza sativa, Triticum aestivum, Brassica campestris, Zea mays, Arachis hypogaea, Pyrus spp* and *Corchorus capsularis*. There are sparse natural vegetations in the region and the dominant species are *Biota orientalis, Pinus thunbergii, Robinia pseudoacacia,Vitex negundo, Coriaria nepalensis, Amorpha fruticosa, Citrus reticulata, Prunus persica, Prunus salicina, pyrus sorotina, Morus alba*. The main soil types are alluvial soil, yellow soil and purplish soil [1].

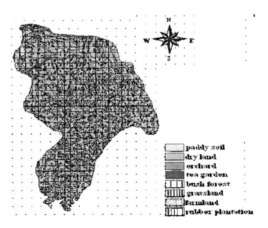

Fig. 2. Land types in Lizi River watershed

3.2 Modelling Set-Up and Calibration

The available time series for daily precipitation covered the period January 1981 to December 1987. Three precipitation stations were chosen for the simulation. Time series for daily water flow covering the period January 1981 to December 1987 were available at three gauging stations. A 1:4,000,000 pedological soil map was available from the Data Sharing Infrastructure of Earth System Science as well as a textural profile description for all major soils. A 1:100,000 land cover map was available from the Data Sharing Infrastructure of Earth System Science. A 30 m grid DEM was available for the discretization procedure, and a threshold area of 1000*1000 m^2 was selected to discretize the catchment into sub-catchments of homogeneous size.

The model was calibrated sequentially by optimizing the determination coefficient (DC), which (DC) is a figure indicating the match condition between the calculated and real time measured sediment amount. It is given by

$$DC = 1 - \frac{\sum_{i=1}^{n}[y_c(i) - y_0(i)]^2}{\sum_{i=1}^{n}[y_0(i) - \overline{y_0}]^2} \qquad (1)$$

Where, DC is determination coefficient, $y_0(i)$ is real observational value, $y_c(i)$ is the simulated value, $\overline{y_0}$ is the mean observational value, n is the days.

First, the hydrological component of the model was calibrated by adjusting the runoff-related parameters (see Table 3) to optimize water flow. The soil erosion component was then calibrated by adjusting the management factor (parameter used in the MUSLE equation) for the various land covers [15], sediment-carrying capacity coefficient (k) and sedimentation coefficient (w) (see Table 3) until predicted and observational sediment yield were in close agreement. The calibration was performed for the period from 1982 to 1987. The calibrated values were then used to the validation for the period of 1981, and the coefficient of determination (DC) was also reported for the validation period.

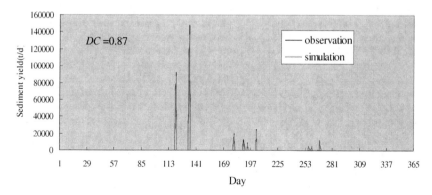

Fig. 3. The result comparison between the simulated sediment yield by DSWSEM and observational sediment yield in the Lizi River watershed in 1981

3.3 Modelling Results

The modeling results are given in Fig.3. It can be seen from the figure that the simulation agrees with the observational result perfectly. The DC reaches 0.87.

4 Conclusions

SEM-SHA is a small watershed scale soil erosion simulation model, which is developed based on a thorough study on the law of soil erosion in the hilly areas of the Jialing River watershed. As a distributed and physically based model, it adopts many advantages of present models, and also introduces several new parameters such as sediment transport ratio, basin sediment reservoir and sediment reservoir capacity. The SEM-SHA model is characterized by simple structure, less parameters, convenient operation, and better simulation results. So, the model is a practicable model.

Acknowledgements. We thank Data Sharing Infrastructure of Earth System Science (webpage: http://www.geodata.cn/) for providing the DEM, pedological soil maps and land cover maps.

References

1. Xiao, F.P.: Study on runoff and sediment models for small watershed in hilly areas of Jialing River. Institute of Mountain Hazards and Environment, CAS, Chengdu (2009) (in Chinese)
2. Tian, L., Dai, J., Yi, L.G.: Comment on Model of Erosion and Sediment Production in Watershed. Res. Soil Water Conserv. 9, 77–79 (2002) (in Chinese)
3. Chandramohan, T., Durbude, D.G.: Estimation of soil erosion potential using Universal Soil Loss Equation. J. Indian Soc. Remote Sens. 30, 181–190 (2002)
4. Maximina, A.L., Larry, C.G., Sadiqul, L.B.: Impacts of soil erosion in the upper Manupali watershed on irrigated lowlands in the Philippines. Paddy Water Environ. 1, 19–26 (2003)
5. Wang, G.Q., Yu, J.S., Shrestha, S., Ishidaira, H., Takeuchi, K.: Application of a distributed erosion model for the assessment of spatial erosion patterns in the Lushi catchment. China Environ. Earth Sci. 61, 787–797 (2010)
6. Dabral, P.P., Baithuri, N., Pandey, A.: Soil Erosion Assessment in a Hilly Catchment of North Eastern India Using USLE, GIS and Remote Sensing. Water Resour. Manage. 22, 1783–1798 (2008)
7. Chou, W.C.: Modelling Watershed Scale Soil Loss Prediction and Sediment Yield Estimation. Water Resour. Manage. 24, 2075–2090 (2010)
8. Chen, Y.N.: Study on the model for predicting soil erosion and its application in arid area. Chin. Geogr. Sci. 9, 373–376 (1999)
9. Boyle, J.F., Plater, A.J., Mayers, C., Turner, S.D., Stroud, R.W., Weber, J.E.: Land use, soil erosion, and sediment yield at Pinto Lake, California: comparison of a simplified USLE model with the lake sediment record. J. Paleolimnol. 45, 199–212 (2011)
10. Brazier, R.: Quantifying soil erosion by water in the UK: a review of monitoring and modelling approaches. Prog. Phys. Geogr. 28, 340–365 (2004)

11. Wang, W.W.: Managing soil erosion potential by integrating digital elevation models with the southern China's revised universal soil loss equation-A case study for the West Lake Scenic Spots area of Hangzhou, China. J. Mt. Sci. 4, 237–247 (2007)
12. Arnold, J.G., Srinivasan, R., Muttiah, R.S., Williams, J.R.: Large area hydrologic modeling and assessment part 1: model development. J. Am. Water Resour. Assoc. 34, 73–89 (1998)
13. Jetten, V., Govers, G., Hessel, R.: Erosion models: quality of spatial predictions. Hydrol. Process. 17, 887–900 (2003)
14. Xiao, S.S., Gu, Z.B., Zhou, Z.X.: Improving the Xin anjiang flow-producing model by free-water sluice. J. Water Resour. Water Eng. 17, 76–78 (2006)
15. Bouraoui, F., Benabdallah, S., Jrad, A., Bidoglio, G.: Application of the SWAT model on the Medjerda river basin (Tunisia). Phys. Chem. Earth. 30, 497–507 (2005)

A Unified Operational Semantics for UML
in Situation Calculus

Qiang Liu[*], Liang Dou, and Zongyuan Yang

School of Information Science and Technology, East China Normal University,
Shanghai, China
lqiangecnu@gmail.com, ldou@cs.ecnu.edu.cn, yzyuan@cs.ecnu.edu.cn

Abstract. An arising interest in the study of UML formal semantics is to
integrate UML Diagrams into a uniform semantic model. In this paper, we
propose a unified operational semantics for UML based on the Situation
Calculus (SC) which is a sophisticated action theory and capable of modeling
general dynamic systems. Specifically, UML models are treated as tailored
dynamic systems in SC, with vocabularies borrowed from the UML metamodel.
Structural diagrams, Class Diagrams and Object Diagrams, are modeled by
Eternals for consistency checking. Behavioral diagram, the State Machine
Diagram is modeled by Fluents and corresponding Axioms in SC. To analyze
and test these dynamic diagrams, we appeal to Golog, an executable high-level
programming language based on the SC. By executing Golog programs, UML
diagrams can be analyzed and tested under a single semantic model.

Keywords: Formal semantics, UML, Situation Calculus, Golog.

1   Introduction

The formalization of UML formal semantics has been an active research area in the
past decade. Both denotational and operational semantics are proposed for separate
UML diagrams, e.g. Sequence Diagram (SD), State Machine Diagram (SMD).
However, an arising interest is to unify the semantics of a core part of UML diagrams
into a single formal language. For example, System Model [1] offers a unified
denotational semantics, ASM [2] and Graph Transformations [3] proposed integrated
operational semantics for UML.

This paper gives a unified operational semantics for UML based on the Situation
Calculus (SC). SC is a theoretically well-studied action theory and capable of
modeling general dynamic systems. The main idea of our approach is to treat UML
[6] models as tailored dynamic systems in SC with vocabularies borrowed from the
UML metamodel. The structural foundations of a system are described in UML
structural diagrams, especially the Class Diagram (CD). The foundations for
specifying system behaviors are Primitive Actions in UML. UML specification

---

[*] This work is supported by National Natural Science Foundation of China(No.61070226),
Shanghai Key Science Project of Fundamental Researches(No.09JC1405000), and PhD
Program Scholarship Fund of ECNU(No.2010038).

G. Shen and X. Huang (Eds.): CSIE 2011, Part II, CCIS 153, pp. 484–490, 2011.
© Springer-Verlag Berlin Heidelberg 2011

defined 45 actions to deal with objects, structural features and variables, etc. Although the terminology 'Primitive Actions' in UML is exactly the same as that in SC, we argue this is not just a trivial syntactical coincident. In both UML and SC, actions are the only cause of changes of the world. Actions should take parameters, have a set of preconditions before being performed, and have effects after being performed. Both UML and SC take this intuitive philosophy of *Action*. Furthermore, a set of *Primitive Actions* are distinguished, from which, infinitely many *Composite Actions* can be constructed by common sense constructors (sequence, parallel, loop, etc). High-level behavioral diagrams in UML, the Composite Actions, are defined based on the low-level behavioral definition, the Primitive Actions. In SC, a high-level programming language Golog is also defined to serve the same purpose. The overview of our approach is described in Figure 1.

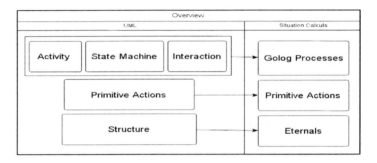

Fig. 1. Overview of the approach

Based on the above picture, we can come up with an approach to formalize the whole UML concepts in SC. Each primitive action defined in UML can be formalized by a primitive action in SC. The informal semantics of actions in UML can be captured by axioms in SC. High-level behaviors, the Activities, State Machines and Interactions can be modeled by processes in Golog (or its variants, e.g. ConGolog). However, in this paper, as a pilot towards this direction, we formalize UML in a slightly different way. For the CD, we use Eternals (ordinary first-order predicates, without situation term as last argument), which serve as the bases of the dynamic system in SC. Then, when modeling high-level system behaviors, a designer can capture state transitions of Objects using State Machine Diagrams (SMD). State transitions in a SMD can be mapped to Primitive Actions in SC system and the whole SMD can be built from constructors. The value of an execution of SMD is a sequence of primitive actions which can be used to generate corresponding Sequence Diagram.

This paper is organized as follows. Section 2 introduces the basic concepts in SC. Section 3 is the main part of this paper, which illustrates the process of unifying UML core diagrams into dynamic systems in SC. Section 4 demonstrates how to use SC for system analyzing and simulation. Section 5 is related work. Section 6 is conclusions and future works.

2   Situation Calculus

Situation Calculus is a second order language which can be used to model dynamical systems [5]. The core concepts in Situation Calculus are Actions, Fluents and Axioms.

This paper uses Golog, a high-level programming language defined as macros in Situation Calculus. It is used to define complex actions, based on primitive actions. Golog provide the following constructs:

- Primitive actions : a
- Test actions : ? Φ. Test whether Φ is true
- Sequence : δ1 ; δ2. Execute δ1 and then execute δ2
- Nondeterministic Action Choice : δ1 # δ2. Executeδ1 or δ2
- Nondeterministic Choice of Arguments : (π z)δ. Nondeterministic pick a value for z, then execute δ for the picked value
- Repetition : δ*. Execute δ zero or more times of δ
- Concurrency : δ1 | δ2. Concurrency of δ1 and δ2
- Procedures, proc ProcName(v) δ endProc. Define a procedure ProcName(v), with parameter v and body δ.

3   Unifying the Semantics

The static information in CD can be described by Eternals, which are determined by the number of concepts in the metamodel of CD. Figure2 shows our running example.

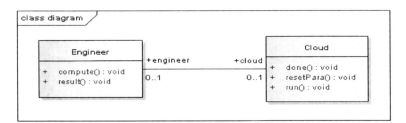

Fig. 2. Class Diagram of the example

The corresponding prolog code for the above class diagram is:

```
/*  Class Diagram */
class(engineer).  class(cloud).
/* Operations */
operation(engineer,compute,void). operation(engineer,result,void).
operation(cloud,run,void).  operation(cloud,done,void).
operation(cloud,resetPara,void).
/*  Associations */
association(engineer,cloud,cloud,0,1).
association(cloud,engineer,engineer,0,1).
```

To capture the structure of OD, we also need to define some new redicates. Here, we use Eternals for simplicity, though OD should be defined in Fluents. This is because some primitive actions in UML, like CreateObjectAction can change the number of objects in a system.

Fig. 3. Object Diagram of the example

The corresponding code for Figure 3 is:

```
object(sophia,engineer).  object(giantM,cloud).
link(sophia,giantM,1).    link(giantM,sophia,1).
```

Each transition in SMD is mapped as a primitive action in SC. The precondition axioms for each primitive action are automatically extracted from the SMD. For simplicity we define an abstract syntax of SMD:

$$\text{Transition} = \text{State} \times \text{State} \times \text{Guard} \times \text{Event} \times \text{Call},$$
$$\text{Call} = \text{Class} \times \text{Class} \times \text{Operation}$$

The main restriction here is on the effect of a transition. According to the UML specification, the effect can be any *behavior* element which can even be a behavioral diagram. However, the above syntax requires the effect can only be a method call, with the specified calling class, called class and operation. This seems slightly restrictive. However, in order to automatically extract axioms from SMD, we have to temporarily stick to the restriction. As a future work, we can extend the *behavior* element to allow composite Golog-like actions. By providing corresponding parser, axioms can also be extracted mechanically. We define an abstract syntax for SMD. For any t :Transition,

$$t \in \text{SMD};$$
$$s1, s2 \in \text{SMD} \Rightarrow s1 : s2 \in \text{SMD};$$
$$s \in \text{SMD} \Rightarrow s^* \in \text{SMD};$$
$$s1, s2 \in \text{SMD} \Rightarrow s1 \,\#\, s2 \in \text{SMD}$$

In order to simulate the execution of SMD, we define two Fluents named inState(X,Y,St,S) and eventQueue(E, X,Y,S). The fluent inState(X,Y,St,S) means in situation S, object X of class Y is in the state St(the names of variables do not matter, they are just placeholders). Similarly, eventQueue(E,X,Y,S) means in situation S, the event E is in the eventQueue of object X (of class Y). Note we assume the size of the event queue for each object is 1, though arbitrary size can be defined (as in [4]). For our simplified abstract syntax, the two fluents are enough to capture all the information we need in execution. More fluents can be defined for complex computation models. New it is ready define Successor State Axioms for fluents, consider the two fluents: inState(X,Y,St,S) and eventQueue(E,X,Y,S):

$$inState(Object,Class,State,do(A,S)) \equiv$$
$$\bigvee_{1\le i \le n} (A=trans_i(Object,To) \wedge State=tgtState_i) \vee$$
$$\bigvee_{1\le i \le n} (inState(Object,Class,State,S) \wedge A=trans_i(O1,O2) \wedge$$
$$\neg(A=trans_i(Object,To) \wedge State=srcState_i \wedge \neg(srcState_i=tgtState_i))).$$

$$eventQueue(Event,Object,Class,do(A,S)) \equiv$$
$$\bigvee_{1\le i \le n} (A=trans_i(SO,Object) \wedge Event=Op) \vee$$
$$\bigvee_{1\le i \le n} (A=trans_i(Object,TO) \wedge Event=null) \vee$$
$$\bigvee_{1\le i \le n} (eventQueue(Event,Object,Class,S) \wedge$$
$$A=transi(O1,O2) \wedge \neg(A=transi(Object,TO) \vee A=transi(SO,Object))).$$

A transition changes the state of the caller object to the target state. This is captured by the first part of the first axiom. The second part of the axiom says the state of objects can only be changed by corresponding transitions, otherwise they will remain in the state where they are. The second axiom says a transition will put Op into the caller object's event queue(the first part) and meanwhile consume the current event in the queue(the second part). The SMD example is described in Figure 4.

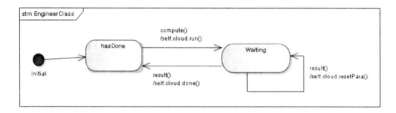

Fig. 4. State Machine Diagram of Engineer class

Based on our generating strategy, we can implement the diagram in Figure4.

```
/* Precondition Axioms */
poss(trans1(SO,TO),S):-
        inState(SO,engineer,done,S),eventQueue(compute,SO,engineer,S),
        testGuard,o_link(SO,TO,Multi),object(TO,cloud).
poss(trans2(SO,TO),S):-
        inState(SO,engineer,wait,S),eventQueue(result,SO,engineer,S),
        testGuard,o_link(SO,TO,Multi),object(TO,cloud).
poss(trans3(SO,TO),S):-
        inState(SO,engineer,wait,S),eventQueue(result,SO,engineer,S),
        testGuard,o_link(SO,TO,Multi),object(TO,cloud).
```

```
poss(trans4(SO,TO),S):-
        inState(SO,cloud,accepting,S),eventQueue(run,SO,cloud,S),
        testGuard,o_link(SO,TO,Multi),object(TO,engineer).
poss(trans5(SO,TO),S):-
        inState(SO,cloud,inUse,S),eventQueue(resetPara,SO,cloud,S),
        testGuard,o_link(SO,TO,Multi),object(TO,engineer).
poss(trans6(SO,TO),S):-
        inState(SO,cloud,inUse,S),eventQueue(done,SO,cloud,Multi),
        testGuard.
/* Successor State Axioms for inState */
inState(Object,Class,State,do(A,S)):-
        A=trans1(Object,TO),State=wait;
        A=trans2(Object,TO),State=wait;
        A=trans3(Object,TO),State=done;
        A=trans4(Object,TO),State=inUse;
        A=trans5(Object,TO),State=inUse;
        A=trans6(Object,TO),State=accepting;
        inState(Object,Class,State,S),A=trans1(O1,O2),
        not((A=trans1(Object,To),State=done,not(State=wait)));
        inState(Object,Class,State,S),A=trans2(O1,O2),
        not((A=trans2(Object,To),State=wait,not(State=wait)));
        inState(Object,Class,State,S),A=trans3(O1,O2),
        not((A=trans3(Object,To),State=wait,not(State=done)));
        inState(Object,Class,State,S),A=trans4(O1,O2),
        not((A=trans4(Object,To),State=accepting,not(State=inUse)));
        inState(Object,Class,State,S),A=trans5(O1,O2),
        not((A=trans5(Object,To),State=inUse,not(State=inUse)));
        inState(Object,Class,State,S),A=trans6(O1,O2),
        not((A=trans6(Object,To),State=inUse,not(State=accepting))).
```

4 Related Works

Much research has been done on various aspects of UML formal semantics. Among these, we want to highlight approaches based on logical frameworks. For structural diagrams, in [7], CD is captured by a set of predicates in prolog making static checkings possible for system structure. In [8], the whole UML metamodel is translated into first order logic to check the static consistency of the whole system structure. Another more general approach [9] captures all model elements using one single predicate, thus translating all model elements into prolog for static checking. Our treatment of static checking is rather open, since Eternals in SC can be any predicate used in the above approaches. For behavior diagrams, various formalisms are also proposed, the Process algebra, ASM [10], and Model Checking [11], to mention only a few. Process Algebra, especially the Pi Calculus is naturally suitable for the semantics of SD. However, the properties can be checked by Pi Calculus are limited to deadlock, bi-simulation, etc. This would be insufficient for a thorough analyzing and testing. ASM [10] is a powerful tool for model analyzing and testing. It really executes the model and the results are returned for analyzing and testing.

5 Conclusion and Future Works

This paper proposes SC as the logical framework for UML formal semantics. Instead of a thorough and detailed implementation of operational semantics for UML diagrams, we initiate an effort toward this direction. A particular point of this approach is to bring SC, a sophisticated action theory in AI into the field of model analyzing and testing. Where does this direction lead to remains to be seen, though insofar as we know, it opens opportunities to utilize the elegant solution of the frame problem and the planning service in SC.

In our future work, we will explore the how to use ConGolog programs to generate high quality test cases. Additionally, we will prove some properties of the automatically generated axioms. An obvious property we want to assure is every object can only be in one state after every execution of a primitive action. Furthermore, if we are to be mathematically sure about our operational semantics, a denotational semantic model for UML diagrams will be needed .Then we can prove the soundness and completeness of the operational semantics against the denotational model. Finally, prolog implementation of our approach should be developed and integrated into some UML tools for real-world model analyzing and testing.

References

1. Crane, M.L.: Slicing UML's Three-layer Architecture: A Semantic Foundation for Behavioural Specification. PhD thesis, Queen's University (January 2009)
2. Kohlmeyer, J., Guttmann, W.: Unifying the semantics of UML 2 state, activity and interaction diagrams. In: Pnueli, A., Virbitskaite, I., Voronkov, A. (eds.) PSI 2009. LNCS, vol. 5947, pp. 206–217. Springer, Heidelberg (2010)
3. Kuske, S., Gogolla, M., Kreowski, H.-J., Ziemann, P.: Towards an integrated graph-based semantics for UML. Softw. Syst. Model (2009)
4. Claßen, J., Lakemeyer, G.: A logic for non-terminating Golog programs. In: Proceedings of Principles of Knowledge Representation and Reasoning (KR), pp. 589–599 (2008)
5. Reiter, R.: Knowledge in Action: Logical Foundations for Specifying and Implementing Dynamical Systems. MIT Press, Cambridge (2001)
6. Object Management Group: UML2.1.2 Superstructure Specification (2007)
7. Jing, D., Paulo, A., Donald, C.: Ensuring structure and behavior correctness in design composition. In: Proceedings of the 7th Annual IEEE International Conference and Workshop on Engineering of Computer Based Systems (ECBS), Edinburgh UK, pp.279–287 (2000)
8. Shan, L., Zhu, H.: A formal descriptive semantics of UML. In: Liu, S., Araki, K. (eds.) ICFEM 2008. LNCS, vol. 5256, pp. 375–396. Springer, Heidelberg (2008)
9. Storrle, H.: A prolog-based approach to representing and querying software engineering models. In: Proceedings of the VLL workshop on Visual Languages and Logic (2007)
10. Börger, E., Cavarra, A., Riccobene, E.: On formalizing UML state machines using ASMs. Information and Software Technology 46(5), 287–292 (2004)
11. Lilius, J., Paltor, I.P.: Formalizing UML state machines for model checking. TUCS Technical Report No.273 (1999)
12. Dong, J., Alencar, P., Cowan, D.: A Formal Framework for Design Component Contracts. In: Proceedings of the IEEE International Conference on Information Reuse and Integration, Las Vegas, US, pp. 53–60 (2003)

The Design and Implementation
of Public Service Platform
# of Web-Based 3D Urban Geographical Names

Long-Bao Mei and Hao Zhang

Digital Media Institute of Jiujiang University,
Jiangxi, China
meilb@jju.edu.cn, zhanghao@jju.edu.cn

Abstract. Place-names digitization, networking and 3d visualization are the current major issues in place-names public service. Through the demand analysis and the function design, by using single perspective fast generation 3d simulation maps, j2EE, Richfaces technology etc., realize three-dimensional city digital place-name public service platform. Through test, it(the platform) realizes fuzzy query and 3d visualization browsing, connect to database time, 3d graphics control response time, data added or modified update time is less than or equal to 3S.

Keywords: digital Place-names, public service platform, 3d visualization, urban simulation, design, implementation.

1 Introduction

Geographical names are a social phenomenon. It exists in society as a tool for communication. It is the foundation of communication and media. It is a language sign which stands for places such as location; region etc., al. Geographical names is recognized all over the world. Geographical names, an important social Public resources, included society, economy, history, geography etc. It plays an important role in politics, military, foreign affairs and national economy development.

2 The Design of Public Service Platform of 3d City Geographical Names

Public Service Platform of 3D City Geographical Names, based on the web, using GIS and 3D simulation technology, can automatically manage place-names, addresses, components, making digital and visible. It can provide place-names information what we need accurately and quickly and innovate place-names management model.

G. Shen and X. Huang (Eds.): CSIE 2011, Part II, CCIS 153, pp. 491–496, 2011.
© Springer-Verlag Berlin Heidelberg 2011

2.1   Objective Design of Public Service Platform of 3D City Digital Names

Establish and Improve the Spatial Database of Geographical Names. Establish and improve the spatial database of geographical names which meet the planning and encoding service, sharing spatial data all over the city.

   Establish Geographic Names Information System. Geographic Names Information System provides a platform which is visual data management, query, statistics and results output, making data acquisition, management, analysis and leadership decision-making system graphical and visible.

   Establish Web GIS Public Information Platform of 3D City. It provide users visual interface. Users can intuitively understand name information in city, positioning geographical names, inquiring names, calculating data and so on.

2.2   Demand Analysis of Public Service Platform of 3D City

Public Service Platform of Geographical Names can be divided into geographical names management system, door management system, system management system, parts management system and 3D urban simulation system.

   The functional modules as shown below:

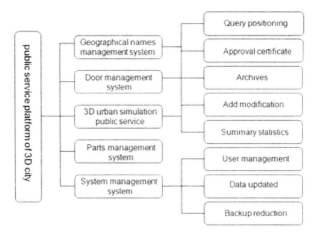

Fig. 1. Functional modules

3D Urban Simulation Public Service Platform. **Users can operate on 3D simulation map, finding a specific location by names or house numbers and showing real geographic environment.**

Door Management System. **Users may manage door information and related business process by inquiring, adding, changing and canceling.**

Geographical Names Management System. **Users manage door information and related business process by inquiring, adding, changing and canceling.**

Parts Management System. **Users can manage community cards, signs, buildings cards, unit cards, house and village licensing.**

System Management System. **Users can manage the internal doors, people and systems permissions.**

3 3D Urban Digital Realization of Names Service Platform

3.1 Architecture of Digital Names of Service Platform in 3D City System

System use Browser/Server structure. All data store in large relational database. Its characteristic is that users can inquire geographic names and related information according to user's permissions. System uses data service layer, application logic layer and presentation layer.

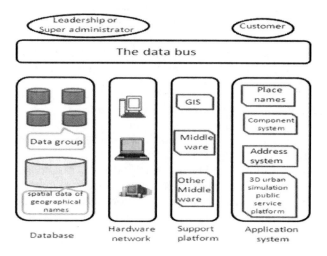

Fig. 2. System Development Construction

3.2 Implement of 3D Urban Simulation Service System

We found that 3D urban simulation has some problems as follows: The process of 3D scene modeling is quite complicated. Its computation load is very big. Users can't spend much time on virtual scene. The methods of feature-based 3D sense modeling have small computation load and Unlimited. But the virtual object in sense is 2D. Users can not be able to communicate with 2D objects. There are many problems on 3D data processing, the combination of 2D and 3D and data browsing speed although the way of modeling of virtual reality is real and Interaction.

Therefore, this paper is proposed to the way of rapid generation of 3D city modeling in a single perspective. This technology combines vector modeling with texture paste technology. We may map and render 3D modeling of urban environment construction by it, reducing the computation load of modeling, quickly generating city models, improving the WEB browsing speed. The principle is that building 3D models of Geometric by the way of 3D modeling, generating a big map according to the proportion. Putting unit building model on the 2D map after 3D modeling generating.

Mapping and rendering the map in the same view, system can generate a 3D city fast. The process and methods are as follows:

3D Modeling. Platform can collect data from city simulation architectural entities by digital photography and DV in multi-angles and model for unit architectural entities, non-building body and a special three-dimensional terrain and so on. In addition, platform can establish 3D vector model library with using 3DSMAX.

Generate 2D Vector Base Map. Adjusting original Satellite Map and original flat map to according to the proportion, mostly at the rate of 1024 pixels equaling to 300 miles. Base map is large-scale GTS 2D vector map by Photoshop/Cad/3dsmas.

Establish A Basic Framework for Urban Simulation. Cell building model such as the single building entities, scenic spots, roads and bridges, mountains, lakes, rivers, green, transport etc. is placed on 2D vector map by calling the model in 3D vector model library, rolling and moving it in order to correct the direction and position of model. At that moment, the model displays the outline of model without showing rendering results. Displaying fast and match can generate a system of infrastructure and framework of 3D simulation urban.

Focus of Configuration and Attribute. Focus of configuration and attribute of architectural entity are to obtain relevant information and community between users and architectural entities in city. Each unit in 3D modeling library has a unique ID which match the records of hotspot and operation attribute. The function of each building unit can be distinguished by selecting categories. The region of hotpots can be operating effectively. Regional hot spots can automatically match the four walls out of construction entities and manually adjust each side, increasing the number of nodes, forming polygons hot spots in order to meet the features of different architectural.

Single-view Rendering and Mapping. 3D simulation city sense can be rendered and mapped in the unique view (overlooking 45°) in order to be operated on web. Each architectural entity is match operating hotpots and attribute by adding transparent to pictures after rendering 3D simulation city.

Browse Fast. Platform can separate images which 3D sense generates in order to browse fast on web. City simulation sense can be separated the same size which can meet the needs of browsers, so that Script processing in browsers can generate and delete nodes, taking up less memory space. Computer algorithm is width or height equals to -N × 2n/size, N stands for Network bandwidth coefficient, N stands for bandwidth which is 128 bps. N is positive integer, size is the capacity of small map, units is Kbyte. Small maps which separated by height and width of 3D sense can enlarge and narrow 3D sense in multi-angles views.

3.3 Geographic Names Management Information Service System

Geographic Names management Information Service System use j2EE and Web. J2EE (Java 2 Platform Enterprise Edition) which is different from traditional technology and include many components can simplify and standardize the development and deploy of application system, improving portability, safe and reusable. The core of J2EE which include all kinds of components, service structure and technical layer which have the same standard and specifications is a technical specifications and guide. The system has good interaction among geographic names management, place-names addresses, geographic name service system and 3D city simulation system.

Hibernate which is an open-source framework for object / relational mapping can package JDBC object so that programmers can use the object-oriented programming to manipulate relational database. It is published in accordance with the open source LGPL license and used for persistence and query service of ultra-high performance object for Java / relational.

Richfaces is open-source framework which adds Ajax (Active JavaScript and Xml) to JSF page instead of writing JS code. The framework uses a component library to add Ajax technology to existed pages without writing any js code or new Ajax widgets. Richfaces use the page-wide Ajax instead of traditional component-wide. This means that events can be defined in the page to activate the Ajax request and synchronized page when the Ajax request changed the server's data according to the client of the events. Therefore, the interactive service connection and positioning of geographical names, numbers query and 3D urban simulation system, development and application of the results as below:

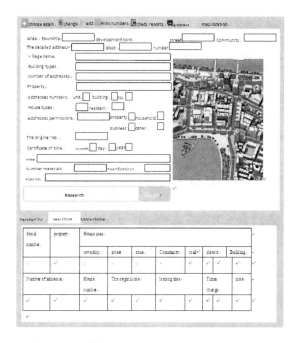

Fig. 3. 3D urban simulation system. This shows the interactive service connection and positioning of geographical names, numbers query and 3D urban simulation system, development and application of the results.

System is stable windows operating system, interface style uniform. Through the network on-line testing, query, object name or code for the entity does not require an exact match of input can be fuzzy query. Connect to the database time, three-dimensional graphics manipulation response time, data added or modified update time is less than or equal to 3S. Operates simply, the visualization degree is high, sees obtained.

The Fund Project. The science and technology key project of Educational Office of Jiangxi Province 【GJJ09348】.

References

1. Liu, Y.: Digital three-dimensional simulation of urban research and design. In: Full Text Database of China's Outstanding Master's Degree Thesis (2009)
2. Zhang, J.: Based on MultiGen and Vega's virtual city simulation technology. Computer (October 2009)
3. Wang, Y.: Digital names system development and application of modern mapping (January 2003)
4. Shi, X., Li, M., Li, A.: Data Query of Geographic Names Information System based on MapInfo. Nanjing Technology University, China (2008)

Recognition the Target Object
Based on More Image Information

Qinjun Du[1], Xueyi Zhang[2], and Leping Li[1]

[1] School of Electrical and Electronic Engineering,
Shandong University of Technology, Shandong Zibo, China
qinjundu@sohu.com
[2] Traffic and Vehicle Engineering School,
Shandong University of Technology, Shandong Zibo, China
zhangxueyi@sdut.edu.cn

Abstract. In robot visual perception system, the information for image segmentation is depth, color, shape, edge, motion and so on. Structured in an ideal environment, a single image feature can be separated from the target object and background, and, for example, in a single background condition, the target object color information can be extracted from the background. However, experiments in a complex environment, using single image information often can not complete the image segmentation; image information based on multi-object segmentation is the ideal way to solve the problem. This humanoid robot using stereo vision system, designed a fast image segmentation method gradually approaching the target areas that is to integrate depth, color and shape.

Keywords: Recognition, location, image information.

1 Introduction

The stability of object image segmentation system is an important performance and technical for robot visual perception system [1] [2] [3]. Image segmentation results will directly affect the robot's visual perception effects, In recent years many scholars have conducted research in this area, most of the target object image segmentation use a single image information, and some using color information [4], some using object contour information [5]. However, in the complex unstructured indoor, single image information can not guarantee stability to recognize the target object. The integration of a variety of image information is one way to track target object stability.

Image segmentation based on multi-image information selected image feature information should be complementary, color and shape is to achieve the ideal goal of segmentation information, for different objects, the color contrast is the maximum. However, when the background and objectives, including the same color of the object or the color of target is inconsistent, it is hard to recognize the target object only depend on color information, the combination of color and shape information to solve the problem is an effective method.

Using the depth of the discontinuity, can quickly find the outline of objects, but the results are sketchy. In the early stages of detection target to find the general area of

G. Shen and X. Huang (Eds.): CSIE 2011, Part II, CCIS 153, pp. 497–502, 2011.
© Springer-Verlag Berlin Heidelberg 2011

the target, this method is very effective. But when the target and its background is not obvious difference in the distance, the depth map of the method is not very applicable.

Correlation template matching method is more intuitive to object image segmentation, for segmentation of rich texture objects, it is a good image features, But when the target exists in the gray scale is inconsistent; this approach can not achieve good effects.

In the operation object of humanoid robot, the main purpose of image segmentation is to segment the object in a separate area. If the segmentation results are correct, then as long as they recognize this region is naturally able to obtain the target position in the image, according to the principle of stereoscopic vision, the target objects can be obtained on the location in space.

2   Depth Information

Using the depth of the discontinuity, you can segment the target from the background [6]. Figure.1 shows the scene depth map. Among them, the left image is the real scene; the right image is the scene depth map. Obviously, the more recent of the target object, the higher the brightness. Through the depth segmentation, the target object and its associated parts can be separated from the background, and easy to find a target divided into a smaller area. In this way, the foreground can be extracted from the background; the mess background would not have a huge impact for the segmentation.

Fig. 1. Real scene depth figures

SVS stereo vision system provides the depth image of each frame image, depth images in the scene graph reflects the distance from the imaging plane, the closer the object from the imaging plane, the greater the depth value, the brighter the image depth map. Fig.1 is the left upper right figure corresponds to the depth of the image can be seen from the figure, the closer from the camera, the greater the depth value, the brighter the image.

Depth image histogram for the typical multi-peak distribution, the number of the peaks depend the scene level of objects. This paper first successful use of depth segmentation segmented foreground from the background area, the candidate obtained the initial target area, the depth of image segmentation as follows:

(1) The use of morphological closing operation on the depth of image filtering to remove noise.

(2) The image segmentation threshold is calculated from the deep image histogram.

(3) The foreground area is made from the adaptive threshold the.

Can be seen from the depth images, depth information is discontinuity, in the segmentation process to maximize the system to get an approximate target candidates, and ensure that moving objects are included in the target candidate region

3 Color Information

Color is widely used in color image segmentation, color image segmentation has two aspects, first select the appropriate color space, and the second is to use the appropriate segmentation strategies and methods. Color space is a way to describe the color; they are often based on different applications and different purposes proposed.

Color images using RGB color model is usually model, YUV model, HSV model and so on. The system, after image acquisition card to obtain the RGB format, bmp image, that is expressed by the RGB model, each pixel colors red, green, and blue components constituted by a certain percentage of each component taken range of values, including, but RGB model is sensitive to changes in ambient light, usually not suitable for directly used for image segmentation, usually needs to be transformed into YUV or HSV space segmentation.

This paper selected HSV space model (color, saturation and brightness), it is not very sensitive to light changes. The literature [7] proposed an improved HSV model, which effectively solved the light change on the impact of machine vision. Fig.2 shows the improved HSV space model, the model is to describe the color of an elliptical distribution.

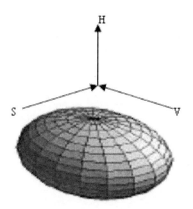

Fig. 2. Improved HSV space model

To take full advantage of the color that effective tracking information, we use the Cartesian equation of elliptical sphere. Under normal circumstances, oval ball will fall on the improved distribution of HSV model.

$$\frac{(x-k)^2}{a^2} + \frac{(y-l)^2}{b^2} + \frac{(z-m)^2}{c^2} \leq 1 \qquad (1)$$

where $0 \leq k \leq 360^0, 0 \leq l \leq 100, 0 \leq k \leq 100$

Formula (1) is a point in the HSV model; k is colors, l is saturation, m is brightness. (a, b, c) is the elliptical radius of the three axis. In the segmentation process, all color, brightness, saturation, oval ball falls within the pixel, are considered to be of interest to our target point.

Initialized process before the image segmentation, the system will identify the colors chosen a priori. Although the HSV model, changes in the environment is not very sensitive to light, but the brightness value of the HSV model, the changes will be minor. In order to achieve the effectiveness of segmentation, the system selected a 20 × 20 (or more) of the pixel region to calculate the brightness value of the HSV model, and as the prior value of next frame. Obviously, we need to make some limited for segmentation background to ensure the convergence of transcendental value.

Using HSV space model has the following obvious advantages than the RGB color model: calculation method is simple and calculate very small, and therefore suitable for real-time image segmentation system; In addition, the improved HSV model is not very sensitive to light changes. However, when the background contains the same color with the target object, the system will fail.

4 Shape Information

Based on RHT (Random Hough transform) algorithm the shape of the detector can detect a variety of geometric shapes, such as: oval, triangle and polygon [8]. Use of the object shape information, the system does not require prior knowledge of the shape of target objects. The system chose ball color as the target object, oval shape that is the right goal. Before the oval detection, it is need to extract the outline of the target object, the color filter is easy to segment the target object and get the regional profile. In [9] describes in detail the shape detection algorithm based on RHT.

5 Template Matching

Correlation template matching is a more intuitive object extraction method. The meaning of correlation is to find match the template region in the images. Correlation is one routine method for tracking target object. This approach can achieve better tracking performance only in the target object is basically the same in the collecting a series of tracking images.

6 Sports Information

Human use of motion information is important for the background of the object never related the details of the information extracted from the strong. Assumed the position of the camera constant and a constant light intensity, the images collected at different times, only the moving object position change occurs, then we can take to achieve target tracking motion information. Graphic mapping in two consecutive images and, if the coordinates (i, j) the gray value changes, and its value is greater than the predetermined change in a positive real number ε, then make that image (i , J) pixel is in motion.

$$d(i, j) = 1 \ (\left| f_1(i, j) - f_2(i, j) \right| \leq \varepsilon)$$
$$d(i, j) = 0 \ (\left| f_1(i, j) - f_2(i, j) \right| > \varepsilon)$$

For the extracted points $d(i, j) = 1$, the use of median filter, we can filter out some isolated (noise points) points, save a lot of focus point in a region, and its anti-light display. In the acquisition of images, only the target has been a change in position, the scene will be divided into two parts, rest and exercise area, and this approach to be effective.

7   Target Object Segmentation Based on More Information

Under laboratory conditions to complex image segmentation colored balls, color, shape and depth of information fusion is a viable approach. This method is also applicable human face segmentation in video sequences. Object color is the most significant features of the object for the target segmentation. When the background color is the same as the objects, based on the color separation will fail. Based on a rough outline of the depth information of the prospect of help system has been a rough area, which is the goal of moving objects including the candidate window, the other a rough segmentation based on depth profile obtained computation speed. Detection of the same color the shape of objects can be distinguished.

Perceptual system for robot vision, depth, color and shape is the ideal candidate information. This humanoid robot using stereo vision system, designed to integrate the depth, color, shape, gradually approaching the three target areas of information fast image segmentation. Utilization method of multi-image information can be divided into three modules, namely the depth of segmentation module, the color filter and shape detector. Firstly, the depth of information to the robot out of concern for the prospects of regional division, are ROF (Region of Foreground) region, that is, a rough target candidate region. The use of color filters in the ROF divided by ROIC (Region of Interest Color) area. Finally, the use of ROIC shape the target object detector. In the segmentation process, narrowing the candidate target region and approaching the target area. Gradually narrow the candidate target area to reduce the amount of computation and improve the processing speed.

8   Conclusion

Image segmentation is the image processing and machine vision the basic problem is that the robot visual perception of the important technical foundation. Image segmentation results will directly affect the robot's visual perception effects.

In this paper, the main purpose of image segmentation is to object image segmentation in a separate area. If the segmentation results are correct, then as long as they recognize this region is naturally able to obtain the target position in the image, according to the principle of stereoscopic vision, goals can be obtained on the location in space.

Acknowledgment

This research is supported by the Natural Science Foundation of Shandong Province, No: ZR2010FL001.

References

1. Jia, D.Y., Huang, Q., Tian, Y., et al.: Object Manipulation of a Humanoid Robot Based on Visual Feedforward and Visual Feedback. Transactions of Beijing Institute of Technology 29(11), 983–987 (2009)
2. Du, X.F., Xiong, R., Chu, J.: Fast recognition and precise localization of humanoid soccer robot vision system. Journal of Zhejiang University (Engineering Science) 43(11), 1975–1980 (2009)
3. Taylor, G., Kleeman, L.: Integration of robust visual perception and control for a domestic humanoid robot. In: IEEE International Conference on Robotics and Automation, Sendai, Japan, pp. 1010–1015 (September 2004)
4. Bentivegna, D.C., Ude, A., Atkeson, C.G., et al.: Humanoid Robot Learning and Game Playing Using PC-based Vision. In: Proceeding of the IEEE International Conference on Intelligent Robots and Systems, pp. 2449–2454 (2002)
5. Pardas, M., Sayrol, E.: A New Approach to Tracking With Active Contours. In: Proceedings of International Conference on Image Processing, pp. 259–262 (2000)
6. Nanda, H., Fujimura, K.: Visual Tracking Using Depth Data. In: Proceedings of IEEE Computer Society Conference on Computer Vision and Pattern Recognition Workshops, pp. 32–41 (2004)
7. Price, A., Taylor, G., Kleeman, L.: Fast robust colour vision for the Monash humanoid. In: Proceedings of the Australian Conference on Robotics and Automation, pp. 141–146 (2000)
8. Jong, H.J., Reuz, Y.W.: Adaptive Visual Tracking of Moving Objects Modeled with Unknown Parameterized Shape Contour. In: International Conference on Networking, Sensing and Control, pp. 76–81 (2004)
9. Westmore, D.B., Wilson, W.J.: Direct Dynamic Control of a Robot Using an End-point Mounted Camera and Kalman Filter Position Estimation. In: Proceedings of the IEEE International Conference on Robotics and Automation, pp. 2376–2384 (1991)

GPRS Based Embedded Wireless Physiological Monitor for Telemedicine Applications

Ying Liu[1], Xiao Min Xu[2], and Mamie Liu[3]

[1] Department of Electronic and Computer Engineering
University of Portsmouth, Portsmouth PO1 3DJ, United Kingdom
[2] Department of Medical Imaging Technology, Shandong Medical College,
5460 Er Huan Nan Road, Jinan, Shandong, China
[3] School of Medicine, King's College of London, London, United Kingdom

Abstract. The rapid development of information technologies and mobile communication has tempted researchers to explore wireless communication based tele medicine applications. The wireless technologies such as GSM, GPRS, UMTS and 3G opens up many prospects for radical changes in tele-health delivery at home and community. This paper presents our work in developing a GPRS based mobile tele homecare system, in particular, our development of a wireless multichannel physiological data monitor for teleme-dicine applications.

Keywords: Tele-medicine, Wireless communication, Physiological monitoring.

1 Introduction

Advances in medical science and technology have greatly improved the quality of the health care over the last 20 years. The availability of new treatments together with improved life-expectancy means that demand is rapidly exceeding the resources available. The task of providing quality patient care and managing scarce medical resources is a major economic and ethical challenge.

All industrialised countries are developing tele healthcare programs to help their health care services to cope with the increasing demands. Tele homecare has became a rapidly growing sector. Tele homecare delivers health and social care services to people in their own homes using telecommunication and information technologies [1], [2]. Applications of the telemedicine aimed at improving the efficiency of patient data management, information exchange between health professionals and patient education have been enormously successful (e.g. the multimedia based medical image transmission and management system and the Internet based virtual medical library.

Generally, a tele homecare systems should include three fundamental components:

i)   Sensors such as digital and video cameras, integrated intelligent sensors, and physiologic monitors (e.g. ECGs, oxygen saturation monitors).
ii) telecommunication network.

G. Shen and X. Huang (Eds.): CSIE 2011, Part II, CCIS 153, pp. 503–506, 2011.

iii)   Intelligent diagnosis and data management software, electronic data storage facilities (e.g. disk arrays to store patient records and/or digital images)

One of the early development of the tele homecare system was reported by Dansky et al. [3] which used a personal computer and video equipment to transfer data and information over the telephone line for home healthcare providers. This system provided an efficient and low-cost monitoring for patients at home with landline connection.

The rapid development of the mobile communication, in particular 3G network, has tempted researchers to explore wireless communication in the tele homecare work. It is believed that the wireless technologies such as GSM, GPRS, UMTS and 3G will open up many prospects for radical changes in tele-health delivery at home [4], [5], [6].

As a part of our endeavor in developing an integrated interactive tele homecare solution: smart home, we have developed a wireless physiological monitoring system that allows the condition of the patients to be continuously monitored at their own home and enable information exchange between the monitor and the medical center. This paper presents the design and implementation of the system.

2 System Design and Implementation

The monitoring system developed was multi-channel intended for general purpose application. The physiological data collected were body temperature, blood pressure (BP), blood sugar level, continuous ECG and activities. The data were stored in the flash memories of the embedded processor. A GSM/GPRS modem was integrated to the system via a serial interface. The patient group in the initial application was elderly patients with cardiologic disorders living in their own home. All the data captured has very low bitrate except ECG signal. The single channel ECG was sampled at 400 samples/second. The data is buffered before being stored in the flash memories. Algorithms were developed to process the data in the buffer and identify the abnormal activities. If the one segment data is classified as normal, the data is then dumped, otherwise the data is compressed and stored in the flash memories. Optionally, this data can be transmitted to the medical center via GPRS link or GMS SMS for analysis.

SMS is an integral part of the original 2G GSM system and its evolution. SMS can be selected as a transmission means, for the ECG data, and dedicated application software is required at the receiving device. The experimental setup can be operated for monitoring from anywhere in the globe covered by a cellular network that offers data services.

The development work in this project provides a low cost method of transmitting ECG data to a remote location preferably a healthcare center, wirelessly. By processing the data locally on a microcontroller unit, an ECG data session is initiated and transmitted in the form of packets using short messaging service (SMS) to healthcare center. A pair of GSM modem is used as a communication source between sender (Microcontroller side) and receiver (PC side). While PC side software which is developed using VisualBasic6.0 is used extract ECG data from received messages, decompress the data. This reduces the workload of medical staff, communication costs and motivates the patient's self-care. The system optionally enable the real time

ECG data acquisition and use of GPRS to upload the data to internet directly. The ECG data transmission using GSM SMS is illustrated in Figure 1 and the schematic of the mobile monitor control unit is shown in Figure 2.

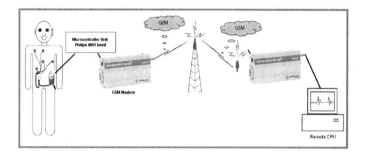

Fig. 1.

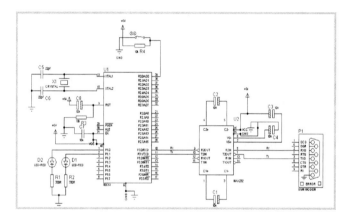

Fig. 2.

The 'D' connector in Figure 2 is the interface to the mobile modem. The GSM modems used for this project are WAVCOME's dual-band E-GSM 900/1800 modem. The GSM modem interfaces to the host (Microcontroller or PC) via a serial communication which is interfaced by host using RS232 line driver chip. This interface is used to transfer the AT commands as standard ASCII character strings from host to GSM modem. The GSM modems are controlled by this industry standard AT commands which are defined by ETSI in GSM 07.07, GSM 07.05, V.25 and T.32. For each AT command GSM modem sends a response to the host.

3 Data Compression

In order to reduce the amount of the data to be transmitted, a modified Amplitude Zone Time Epoch Coding (AZTEC) algorithm is used to compress the data. The

AZTEC was originally developed to pre-process ECGs for rhythm analysis; it has a data reduction algorithm that decomposes raw ECG sample points into plateaus and slopes. AZTEC provides a sequence of line segments that form a piecewise-linear approximation to the ECG [Willis Tompkins, 1993, p.p 193-215][Vinod Kumaar, S.C Saxena, V.K Giri and Dilbag Sigh, June-July 2005, p.p 334-344]. The threshold value recalculation is used for the signal adaptation of the parameters. Information content and data reduction of the signal was traded off between to optimize the adaptive algorithm.

The compression algorithm is evaluated using MIT-BIH arrhythmia database. A compression ratio of 3.3:1 can be achieved without introducing significant distortion.

References

1. Woolham, J., Frisby, B., Quinn, S., Smart, W., Moore, A.: The Safe at Home Project: Using Technology to Support the Care of People with Dementia in Their Own Homes. Hawker Publication, London (2002)
2. Brownsell, S., Bradley, D.: Assistive Technology and Telecare-Forging Solutions for Independent Living. Policy Press, Bristol (2003)
3. Dansky, K.H., Palmer, L., Shea, D., Bowles, K.H.: Cost analysis of telehomecare. Telemedicine Journal & E-Health 7(3), 14–17 (2001)
4. Norris, A.C.: Essentials of Telemedicine and Telecare. John Wiley & Sons, Ltd., England (2002) ISBN: 0-471-53151-0
5. Ferrer, R.O., Cardenas, A., Diaz, C.A., Pulido, P.: Mobile phone text messaging in the management of diabetes. Journal of Telemedicine and Telecare 10(5), 282–285 (2004)
6. Reponen, J.: Radiology as a part of a comprehensive telemedicine and ehealth network in northern Finland. International J. Circumpolar Health 63(4), 429–435 (2004)

Author Index